DHMorris.
Aleck Manns
Liverpool

The Financial Services Act 1986

A Guide to the New Law

The Financial Services Act 1986

A Guide to the New Law

Andrew Whittaker

MA(Oxon), Solicitor
Assistant Legal Director
The Securities and Investments Board Ltd

Geoffrey Morse

LLB, Barrister
Reader in Law and Head of Department
Faculty of Law, University of Liverpool

London
BUTTERWORTHS
1987

United Kingdom	Butterworth & Co (Publishers) Ltd, 88 Kingsway, LONDON WC2B 6AB and 61A North Castle Street, EDINBURGH EH2 3LJ
Australia	Butterworths Pty Ltd, SYDNEY, MELBOURNE, BRISBANE, ADELAIDE, PERTH, CANBERRA and HOBART
Canada	Butterworths, A division of Reed Inc., TORONTO and VANCOUVER
New Zealand	Butterworths of New Zealand Ltd, WELLINGTON and AUCKLAND
Singapore	Butterworth & Co (Asia) Pte Ltd, SINGAPORE
South Africa	Butterworth Publishers (Pty) Ltd, DURBAN and PRETORIA
USA	Butterworths Legal Publishers, ST PAUL, Minnesota, SEATTLE, Washington, BOSTON, Massachusetts, AUSTIN, Texas and D & S Publishers, CLEARWATER, Florida

© Andrew Whittaker, Geoffrey Morse 1987

ISBN 0 406 54842 0

Typeset by Kerrypress Ltd, Luton
Printed by Billings, Worcester

Preface

On the 27th October 1986 the City of London underwent a great upheaval ("the Big Bang") which on one day ended single capacity, minimum commissions and an antiquated method of dealing. At the same time the London markets became open to more competition from overseas conglomerates, which in turn has resulted in a large number of multi-service, UK based, financial conglomerates. None of this was foreseen when Professor L C B Gower was first invited by the Government to draw up a report on and to make proposals for the reform of the law of investor protection, and it is from that report that the Financial Services Act can claim direct descent. It has, however, inevitably acquired a mixed parentage. The agreement between the Stock Exchange and the Government which averted a reference to the Restrictive Practices Court and which in turn led to Big Bang, can undoubtedly be used to explain the growth in the Act during its Parliamentary journey; the inevitable City scandals, even the much maligned EEC can also claim their influence. It is not surprising therefore that the Act has been generally regarded as a concomitant of Big Bang and that there has been misguided criticism of the failure to synchronise the timing of the two.

Much of the debate has inevitably been technical but certain issues were, and remain, contentious. The position of the City Panel on Take-overs and Mergers and of Lloyd's, both currently outside the Act, must be uncertain. The central concept of the Secretary of State transferring his supervisory and regulatory functions to a private limited company will, together with the whole concept of self-regulation, inevitably remain open to scrutiny. Each successive City scandal will raise these, and doubtless other, issues. Self-regulation will have to be seen to be working if the pressures for a full statutory system of control are to be averted.

The Act does not just deal with regulation of the City. It also replaces the Stock Exchange (Listing) Regulations 1984 and the Companies Act 1985 prospectus provisions, amends the 1985 Act with regard to take-overs and both that Act and the Company Securities (Insider Dealing) Act 1985 in other ways. Its scope is very wide and far reaching and much needs to be done to implement it in full. The stone has been thrown into the lake and time will tell where and when the ripples will end.

The book has been written on the basis that the Act is fully in force. The book was jointly planned but separately written. Andrew Whittaker wrote chapters 1 to 14 and 19. Geoffrey Morse wrote chapters 15 to 18 and 20. Parts of chapter 21 were written by both of us. It should be emphasised that Andrew Whittaker is writing as a private individual and must in no way be taken as expressing the views of The Securities and Investments Board Ltd. We must thank the staff of Butterworths for their prompt and efficient assistance and our magnificent secretaries Herrica Willis in London and Edith Jones in Liverpool.

Speaking on the 27th October 1986 in the House of Lords the Earl of Limerick in completing the debate on third reading said: "The future for the financial services sector in so far as it has changed is uncertain. We can be certain only that nothing will be the same again and that nobody knows what the changes are going to be. but we now have a framework within which to work ... This Bill has a good chance. We must wish it well and look to the future." Perhaps we too may end by saying Amen to that.

Andrew Whittaker
Geoffrey Morse   November, 1986

Contents

Chapter 1

Regulation of investment business: background and outline

Background

1.01 Before outlining the new system of regulation of investment business itself, it will be useful to understand its background.

1.02 The City's financial markets, and the investment community generally, are undergoing rapid and far-reaching changes, triggered by the liberalisation of The Stock Exchange's rulebook, (culminating in the 'Big Bang' on 27 October 1986), and by increasing internationalisation in financial markets. In parallel with these changes, there has been a growing appreciation of the need for a new structure to regulate investment business in the interests of reinforced investor protection and confidence.

1.03 In 1981, following the collapse of two investment businesses, the then Secretary of State commissioned Professor L C B Gower to undertake a review of investor protection and advise on the need for new legislation. Part 1 of Professor Gower's Report, published in January 1984 (Cmnd 9125), recommended a new system of statute-backed self-regulation, subject to supervision by a government regulator. This received substantial and widespread support, but two issues remained to be settled. These were the number and kind of self-regulatory bodies and the nature of the government regulator. Accordingly, in May 1984, advisory groups were set up under Mr (now Sir) Martin Jacomb and Mr Marshall Field. Following their reports, the government set out its proposals in January 1985 in a White Paper entitled 'Financial Services in the United Kingdom: A new framework for investor protection' (Cmnd 9432). These were to a large extent based on the recommendations of Pt 1 of Professor Gower's report, but they adopted a rather different institutional structure. They form the basis of the new system to be established under Pt 1 of the Act and are outlined in the remainder of this chapter.

Outline of system

1.04 The new system for the regulation of investment business covers all those 'carrying on investment business in the United Kingdom' and also extends to certain managers of occupational pension schemes, even though their activities may not involve carrying on investment business. Everyone who is covered by the new system will be required to be 'authorised' unless he is within one of the exempted categories. A breach of this requirement will attract both criminal and civil sanctions.

1.05   Authorisation is to be available by a variety of routes. In order to lay stress on the importance of self-regulation, the Act begins by providing for authorisation by membership of a recognised self-regulating organisation or by certification by a recognised professional body. The powers to recognise self-regulating organisations and professional bodies are given to the Secretary of State, but like many other functions under the Act, are capable of transfer by him to a 'designated agency', of which more later. The Act provides, too, automatic authorisation for certain authorised insurers and friendly societies and for the operators and trustees of (EEC) collective investment schemes recognised under s 86. The next route of general significance, though, is the procedure for direct authorisation by the Secretary of State, or, again, a designated agency. This direct authorisation regime is essentially a statutory system of regulation, which can also be expected to set the standards to be met by recognised self-regulating organisations and professional bodies. The Act provides for thorough procedures before direct authorisation is obtained. Finally, the Act provides automatic authorisation for those carrying on investment business in the United Kingdom on a services basis and who are authorised under an equivalent or harmonised regime in another member state of the EEC.

1.06   The alternative to authorisation is exemption, although this is much more restricted. Among those exempted are recognised investment exchanges and the recognised clearing houses which provide clearing services to them. The recognition of bodies of this kind enables the markets on which business is done to be brought within the scope of the regulatory regime. Also exempted are Lloyd's itself, and underwriting agents at Lloyd's. An enquiry was commissioned under Sir Patrick Neill to examine the protection offered to names under the Lloyd's Act 1982 and to compare it with the protection to be offered to investors under the Financial Services Bill. 'Listed money-market institutions' are exempted too, so long as they limit themselves to certain activities in the wholesale money markets. And an 'appointed representative' of an authorised person receives a limited exemption, for marketing activities for which the authorised person has accepted responsibility, enabling the representative to be treated essentially as an employee for regulatory purposes. Finally, there are exemptions for the Bank of England and various miscellaneous exemptions.

1.07   The main difference between authorisation and exemption concerns regulation. Some of the Act's regulatory provisions—like the false statements and markets offences and the ban on unsolicited calls—apply both to authorised persons and to exempted persons and those not carrying on investment business at all. But most of these provisions—like the various powers to make rules and regulations—can apply only to authorised persons. Regulation under these powers would only cover an exempted person who actually obtained authorisation to carry on some activity not covered by his exemption.

1.08 By including powers to make rules and regulations, the Act makes it possible for the detailed requirements on the conduct of investment business to be filled in subsequently. This also makes them more readily adaptable to changing circumstances than primary legislation. Powers of this kind enable requirements to be introduced on the conduct of investment business itself, on the financial resources an investment business needs, on the cancellation of investment agreements, to make possible 'cooling-off', on the information to be provided to regulators, on indemnity against claims and compensation for investors, and on the treatment of clients' money. Rules or regulations under these powers are not mere codes of practice, only of use for guidance; they are part of the law of the land, backed by disciplinary powers enabling individuals to be banned from involvement in investment business and, in general, enabling a firm's authorisation to be withdrawn, as well as giving new rights to investors. Powers to make regulations also enable the Act's provisions on unsolicited calls and advertising to be modified, so providing added flexibility there.

1.09 Even where there is a strong framework for investment businesses to work within, the need may arise for a regulator to intervene in the running of a business in the interests of investors. The Act provides a range of intervention powers for this purpose, enabling the regulator to restrict a firm's business or its dealings with assets or to require assets to be vested in a trustee, or maintained in the United Kingdom. There are also powers for the regulator to apply for winding up or the appointment of an administrator—all powers exercisable essentially against authorised persons and their appointed representatives. In order to enable them to act without fear of ruinous litigation, the main regulators are given an exemption from liability in damages.

1.10 The Act's disciplinary and intervention powers can, of course, affect people's livelihoods so a special safeguard is provided in cases of these kinds for the final decision to be taken by a Financial Services Tribunal, independent of the regulator, whose task is to look at the issues afresh.

1.11 There are new provisions too for keeping the public informed about who is entitled to carry on investment business, in the form of a requirement for a central register to be kept and a power for the Secretary of State (or designated agency) to publish or give information and advice. Confidentiality is, though, to be maintained, with a criminal penalty for unlawful disclosures. There are also investigation powers backed by effective powers of entry, so that evidence can be obtained, and provisions to promote the role of auditors as watchdogs against wrongdoing. The subject-access provisions of the Data Protection Act can be disapplied to promote the provision and recording of information necessary to minimise fraud.

DESIGNATED AGENCIES: THE SECURITIES AND INVESTMENTS BOARD

1.12 It will have been seen that at the apex of the system will be an authority exercising statutory powers. Under the Financial Services Act, powers to regulate investment business (including supervising self-regulators and investment markets, and prosecution powers) are given initially to the Secretary of State for Trade and Industry. But many of these powers are capable of transfer by him to an independent regulatory body, or 'designated agency', so long as it meets certain requirements. The Securities and Investments Board Limited was formed to act as a designated agency and the Act itself provides that, so long as it satisfies the requirements, it will be the first body to which such powers are transferred. Indeed, it is generally expected that most, if not all, the transferable powers under the Act will be transferred, in whole or in part, to the Board. (Transferable powers are indicators in this commentary either expressly or by a parenthetical reference to the possibility of a designated agency role.)

1.13 This does not mean, though, that the Board, or any designated agency, will itself be a statutory body. Indeed, the Act expressly provides that a designated agency is not to be regarded as acting on behalf of the Crown, and that its members, officers and staff are not to be regarded as Crown servants. A designated agency can be a private sector body, exercising statutory powers only under an order transferring them from the Secretary of State. Although virtually unique, this arrangement is considered to have two particular advantages. First, it enables the agency to be closer to the financial services industry than a government department. Second, it frees it from the financial constraints applied to bodies within the public sector.

1.14 In addition to its role in regulating investment business, the Board may also receive powers under the Financial Services Act for the authorisation and recognition of collective investment schemes like unit trusts and may be appointed as 'administrative authority' to administer the EEC directive on misleading advertising (Council Directive on the approximation of the laws, regulations and administrative provisions of the member states concerning misleading advertising, Dir 84/450/EEC) in the financial services sector.

1.15   Regulation inevitably involves restrictions on competition, so the Act provides a special mechanism for any anti-competitive effects to be assessed to see whether they are necessary for the protection of investors. This mechanism substitutes prior and continuing assessment of the merits for the provisions for subsequent and often ad hoc evaluation under mainstream competition law.

Chapter 2

'Investment business'

Introduction

IMPORTANCE OF CONCEPT

2.01   The most important concept of the new system of regulation is that of 'investment business'. It is central to the need for authorisation (see para **3.02**) and to a large extent determines the ambit of the regulatory system. It also circumscribes the kinds of liability which can be covered by compensation arrangements (see para **4.49**). Finally, its elements delimit exemptions from the Gaming (para **4.107**) and Banking (para **21.29**) Acts.

'CARRYING ON INVESTMENT BUSINESS'

2.02   'Investment business' means the business of engaging in one or more of the activities which fall within the paragraphs in Pt II of Sch 1 and are not excluded by Pt III of that Schedule (s 1(2)). A person carries on investment business in the United Kingdom if he:

(a) carries on investment business from a permanent place of business maintained by him in the United Kingdom, or

(b) engages in the United Kingdom in one or more of the activities which fall within the paragraphs of Pt II of that Schedule and are not excluded by Pt III or IV of that Schedule and his doing so constitutes the carrying on by him of a business in the United Kingdom (s 1(3)).

The requirement in (b) for engaging in the activities to constitute the carrying on by the person concerned of a business in the United Kingdom is designed to avoid engaging in an isolated transaction in the United Kingdom amounting to carrying on investment business there because it forms part of an investment business carried on elsewhere. While Pts II and III of the Schedule are to be interpreted in accordance with Pt V ('Interpretation') (s 1(4)) it should be noted that Pt IV ('Additional exclusions for persons without permanent place of business in the United Kingdom') does not qualify Pt II. That Part of the Schedule affects who needs authorisation, but not the concept of investment business. For convenience, however, it will be examined in this chapter.

2.03 The status of the 'notes' included in some of the paragraphs of Sch 1 is interesting. It is clear from their content that their status can be explanatory, providing for the exclusion of some matters which would in any event not be covered. It is also clear that they can be substantive, including or excluding matters where that would otherwise not be the case.

'Investments'

2.04 Before looking in detail at what activities with 'investments' amount to 'investment business', we need to consider what are 'investments'. These are 'any asset, right or interest falling within any paragraph in Part 1 of Schedule 1' (s 1(1)). It should be noted that, in general, the paragraphs in Sch 1 are not mutually exclusive, so that a particular investment may fall within several different paragraphs. It should also be appreciated that the usual name in the market of a particular kind of investment may not always be reflected in the paragraph headings in the Schedule, so that, for example, an investment commonly known as an option may fall within para 8 (headed 'Futures') rather than para 7 (headed 'options'). Let us examine all these paragraphs in turn.

'SHARES'

2.05 The best known investments are probably shares (or stock) in a company, brought in by para 1 of the Schedule. For these purposes 'company' covers not merely companies registered under the Companies Act but other bodies corporate constituted in the UK, such as chartered companies, and, in the case of bodies constituted outside the UK, extends to unincorporated bodies. It does not, though, cover open-ended investment companies, which are treated as collective investment schemes (see para **6.20**). Nor does it cover building societies, industrial and provident societies, or credit unions.

'DEBENTURES'

2.06 Paragraph 2 of the Schedule is headed 'debentures'. Although expressly excluding instruments covered by para 3 ('Government and public securities'), this extends beyond debentures and debenture stock to 'bonds, certificates of deposit and other instruments creating or acknowledging indebtedness'. The notes exclude from the definition instruments where the indebtedness relates to the consideration payable under a contract for the supply of goods or services, together with cheques, bills of exchange, bankers' drafts and letters of credit. It also excludes banknotes, statements of the balance in a current, deposit or savings account, leases and other dispositions of property, heritable securities and insurance policies. All these could come within the definition of 'debentures' but are not appropriately to be regulated as debentures, although some, such as some insurance contracts may be covered by the other paragraphs.

'GOVERNMENT AND PUBLIC SECURITIES'

2.07 Paragraph 3 of Sch 1 identifies as a separate kind of investment 'loan stock, bonds and other instruments creating or acknowledging indebtedness' which are 'issued by or on behalf of a government, local authority or public authority'. These authorities include, by note (1)(c), 'any international organisation the members of which include the United Kingdom or another member state'.

'INSTRUMENTS ENTITLING TO SHARES OR SECURITIES'

2.08 Paragraph 4 of Sch 1 covers 'warrants or other instruments entitling the holder to subscribe for' those investments described as 'shares', 'debentures' and 'government and public securities'. The note to the paragraph tells us that it is immaterial whether the investments are for the time being in existence or identifiable. It would appear that this paragraph, in referring to a holder, is to be taken as going beyond pure bearer instruments. An investment within this paragraph is not to be regarded as falling within the paragraphs relating to 'Options', 'Futures' and 'Contracts for differences'.

'CERTIFICATES REPRESENTING SECURITIES'

2.09 Paragraph 5 covers certificates and other instruments conferring various rights of property or acquisition in relation to investments covered by the paragraphs relating to 'shares', 'debentures', 'government and public securities' and 'instruments entitling to shares or securities'. It is designed to reflect the EEC concept, to be found in the Listing Directives (see para **15.02**) of 'certificates representing shares', as is clear from the application to these instruments of the sections of the Act on listing. It would also appear to cover depository receipts, including American Depository Receipts (ADRs). The paragraph does not cover rights in respect of two or more investments, issued by different persons or, in the case of government and public securities, in respect of two or more different investments issued by the same person. These may, though, amount to units in a collective investment scheme.

'UNITS IN A COLLECTIVE INVESTMENT SCHEME'

2.10 Paragraph 6 ensures that units in a collective investment scheme, including shares in or securities of an open-ended investment company, are treated as investments. For collective investment schemes, see Ch 6, and, for 'units' para **6.22**.

'OPTIONS'

2.11   The options covered by para 7 are options to acquire or dispose (see para **2.56**) of:

(a) other investments;

(b) currency of the United Kingdom or of any other country or territory;

(c) gold or silver; or

(d) options covered by (a) to (c).

It would appear, for example, that LIFFE contracts in sterling and dollars would fall within this paragraph by virtue of (b). It should be noted that 'options' on platinum and other commodities do not fall within this paragraph, although some may fall within others, for example, para 8.

'FUTURES'

2.12   Paragraph 8 of the Schedule attempts to identify from a wide group of contracts commonly known as futures or forward contracts those which ought to be treated as investments under this paragraph. These it entitles 'futures'. The basic concept, to be found in para 8 itself, is that the investments to be covered are 'rights under a contract for the sale of a commodity or property of any other description under which delivery is to be made at a future date and at a price agreed upon when the contract is made'. (For futures on indices, see para **2.14**).

2.13   The basic concept cannot, however, stand alone, since otherwise it would include purely commercial contracts for forward delivery—even ordering goods from a department store! It is accordingly qualified by the notes, which exclude a contract 'made for commercial and not investment purposes'. It will be noted that the distinction is not one between hedging and speculating. It is suggested that it should be seen as essentially an objective rather than a subjective test. It is the purpose of the contract, rather than the motives of the parties, which is at issue. The notes elaborate a number of different aspects of whether a contract is made for commercial and not investment purposes. Note (2) has the effect that certain recognised investment exchange contracts are to be regarded as made for investment purposes. Note (3) takes out spot contracts not covered by Note (2). Note (4) gives two 'indications', applying *both* ways, as to whether a contract is made for commercial or investment purposes. Note (5) provides for it to be an indication that a contract *is* made for commercial purposes that particular terms are determined by the parties for the purposes of the particular contract. Note (6) identifies certain indications again applying only one way, to indicate that a contract *is* made for investment purposes. While 'indications' are clearly not intended to be more than that, it is suggested that a court would accord them considerable force, weighing one against another, together with other relevant factors, to determine whether the note (1) exclusion applies. Note (7) expands on the reference in paragraph 8 itself to prices agreed upon when the contract is made.

'CONTRACTS FOR DIFFERENCES'

2.14 Paragraph 9 includes as investments 'rights under a contract for differences or any other contract the purpose or pretended purpose of which is to secure a profit or avoid a loss by reference to fluctuations in the value or price of property of any description or in an index or other factor designated for that purpose in the contract'. The note excludes contracts where the parties intend that the profit is to be taken or loss avoided by taking delivery of any property to which the contract relates. (These may fall within the paragraphs on 'futures' or 'options'.) Accordingly, this paragraph appears apt to cover a range of purely contractual investments, such as futures on indices, forward rate agreements and interest rate swaps, as well as betting on prices or indices.

2.15 It should be observed that, by note (4) to para 10, long term insurance contracts under that paragraph are not to be regarded as covered by this paragraph as contracts for differences. This, together with the exemption of contracts of insurance from the definition of 'collective investment scheme' (see para **6.16**) broadly continues the effect of the former s 79 of the Insurance Companies Act 1982, which is accordingly repealed. Insurance contracts may now be investments in their own right, however, as explained in the next paragraph.

'LONG TERM INSURANCE CONTRACTS'

2.16 Long term insurance contracts are treated as investments by para 10 of Sch 1. That paragraph covers 'rights under a contract the effecting and carrying out of which constitutes long term business within the meaning of the Insurance Companies Act 1982' (see s 1 of and Sch 1 to that Act for definition of long-term business). But the words of the paragraph itself are again qualified by the notes, so as to exclude contracts purely for protection against risk as distinct from investment purposes. Rights under a reinsurance contract are also excluded.

'RIGHTS AND INTERESTS IN INVESTMENTS'

2.17 Paragraph 11 covers rights to and interests in anything which is itself an investment. Note (1) excludes 'interests under the trusts of an occupational pension scheme'. These interests are already outside the definition of 'units in a collective investment scheme' because of the exclusion in s 75(6)(k). This note is designed to ensure that they are not investments, so that promotion of interests in schemes (for example, by employers to their staff) does not require authorisation. (For management of occupational pension schemes, see para **21.16**.)

21.17

'Activities constituting investment business'

2.18 Part II of Sch 1 to the Act sets out the activities which, subject to the exclusions in Pt III (see paras **2.25–2.47**), and as interpreted by Pt V (see paras **2.55–2.62**), are to constitute 'investment business'. It will be recalled that the position of Pt IV was discussed at para **2.02**.

'DEALING IN INVESTMENTS'

2.19 Paragraph 12 introduces the first kind of investment business activity, 'buying, selling, subscribing for or underwriting investments, or offering or agreeing to do so, either as principal or as an agent'. References to 'buying and selling' are defined (see para **2.56**). Otherwise, this paragraph is self-explanatory.

'ARRANGING DEALS IN INVESTMENTS'

2.20 Another investment business activity is 'making, or offering or agreeing to make, arrangements with a view to another person buying, selling, subscribing for or underwriting a particular investment or with a view to a person who participates in the arrangements buying, selling, subscribing for or underwriting investments'. It thus covers arrangements with two different aims in view. The first are those with a view to another dealing in a *particular* investment. The second are those with a view to a person *who participates in the arrangements* dealing in *investments* (not 'a particular investment'). The latter covers arrangements under which participants in the arrangements deal under them in any of a range of investments, for example a computerised deal-matching service. It is suggested that the reference to participating in arrangements imports the flavour of a continuing relationship. A mere 'introducer', who does no more than introducing a potential investor to an investment business (even though for reward), may not to be caught, since he may not be arranging a deal in a particular investment or acting for a person who could be said to participate in arrangements. But of course this will depend on exactly what is done. By note (1), this paragraph and para 12 are essentially made mutually exclusive, with the intention that activities covered by para 12 will not also fall within this paragraph. Note (2) excludes from the first limb arrangements which neither do nor would bring about the transaction in question, assisting 'introducers'.

'MANAGING INVESTMENTS'

2.21 The third activity constituting investment business is 'managing, or offering or agreeing to manage, assets belonging to another person if those assets consist of or include investments'. Managing assets belonging to another person can also be covered even where they do not consist of or include investments if the arrangements for their management are such that they could do so at the discretion of the manager. This will only be the case, though, where they have actually done so at any time after the coming into force of s 3 of the Act or where (whether before or after that date) the arrangements have been *held out* as arrangements under which they would do so. It is important to note that the assets under management must be assets 'belonging to' another person. Cash may be an asset 'belonging to' another person but it may simply be *owed* to another person. Managing cash is not caught if it is held under a simple debt relationship. The activity of management covered by this paragraph is given an extended application where the assets are held for the purposes of an occupational pension scheme, so that the activity may be authorisable even if not done by way of business.

'ADVISING ON INVESTMENTS'

2.22 Under this heading para 15 deals with 'giving or offering or agreeing to give, to persons in their capacity as investors or potential investors advice on the merits of their purchasing, selling, subscribing for or underwriting an investment or excercising any right conferred by an investment to acquire, dispose of, underwrite or convert an investment'. It should be noted that the paragraph does not cover advice about investment businesses, so that, for example, a firm which merely advised on where to obtain advice about investments, acting perhaps as an 'introducer' (see also para **2.20**) would appear not to fall within this paragraph unless its activities include advising on investments (or rights covered by the paragraph) themselves.

2.23 The references to advising persons 'in their capacity as investors or potential investors' appear to exclude, for example, corporate finance advice given to companies seeking finance by the issue of shares. The words 'on the merits' also provide a narrowing element.

'ESTABLISHING ETC COLLECTIVE INVESTMENT SCHEMES'

2.24 Paragraph 16 includes as investment activities 'establishing, operating or winding up a collective investment scheme, including acting as trustee of an authorised unit trust scheme'. Collective investment schemes are considered in Ch 6.

'Excluded activities'

2.25 As noted in para **2.02**, the activities in Pt III of Sch 1 are excluded from being considered as 'investment business'.

'DEALINGS AS PRINCIPAL'

2.26 The two exclusions for own account dealings contained in para 17 are of considerable complexity, but their broad intention is simple enough. This is to take out of 'investment business' activities which would otherwise fall within para 12 but which are done by the person concerned for his own account, rather than, in the broadest sense, for clients or customers.

2.27 The first, in para 17(1), applies only to investments falling within paras 1–6 of Sch 1, together with rights to or interests in them which are themselves investments, so sub-para (3) provides. It excludes from para 12 things done by a person as principal unless:

(a) he holds himself out as willing to enter into transactions of that kind at prices determined by him generally and continuously rather than in respect of each particular transaction;

(b) he holds himself out as engaging in the business of buying investments with a view to selling them and those investments are or include investments of the kind to which the transaction relates; or

(c) he regularly solicits members of the public for the purpose of inducing them to enter into transactions to which that paragraph applies and the transaction is or is to be entered into as a result of his having solicited members of the public in that manner.

'Buying' and 'selling' here mean buying and selling by transactions to which para 12 applies. This enables other disapplications of para 12 to apply for the purpose of deciding whether a person holds himself out as engaging in the business of buying with a view to selling. 'Members of the public' is defined for the purpose of the regular solicitation test as any person (other than the person soliciting) except authorised persons, exempted persons, permitted persons (under para 23 of the Schedule), members of the same group as the person doing the soliciting, persons who are or propose to become participators with him in a joint enterprise, persons solicited in certain circumstances involving strategic shareholdings, and certain overseas professionals solicited outside the United Kingdom.

2.28 The second 'own account' exclusion is to be found in para 17(2). It applies to the investments to which the first does not apply, that is, those described as 'options', 'futures', 'contracts for differences' and 'long term insurance contracts', together with any rights to or interests in them which are themselves investments. The form of the exclusion is to provide that para 12 does not apply to a transaction which 'is or is to be entered into by a person as principal if he is not an authorised person and the transaction is or is to be entered into by him' *either* with or through an authorised person, an exempted person or a permitted person under para 23 *or* through an office outside the United Kingdom, maintained by a party to the transaction, and with or through certain overseas professionals. Two particular points should be noted on this exclusion. First, it applies only when the person concerned is not himself authorised. Where, for some reason, the person concerned is authorised, it will not apply and, unless excluded for some other reason, the activity will fall to be considered as investment business. Second, it is not sufficient for the transaction to be undertaken as principal, it must be undertaken with or through one of a limited range of counterparties.

'GROUPS AND JOINT ENTERPRISES'

2.29 Paragraph 18 creates a series of exclusions for activities engaged in by a person with or for a body corporate in the same group (see para **2.59**) or who is a participator with him in a joint enterprise (see para **2.60**).

2.30 The first exclusion qualifies the activities described as 'dealing in investments'. Here, the exclusion takes out transactions entered into or to be entered into *as principal* between bodies corporate in the same group or, where the transaction is for the purposes of a joint enterprise, between participants in that enterprise. The effect of sub-paras (1) and (2) together is then essentially that transactions undertaken by a person *as agent* for members of the extended group but which would otherwise have qualified for the exclusion will still do so if they fulfil the conditions for exclusion of own account transactions. In other words, although there are some minimal variations, these transactions are treated broadly as undertaken by the agent for his own account.

2.31 The next exclusion for groups and joint enterprises tackles the issue of 'arranging deals in investments' (para 18(3)). The exclusion takes out arrangements which a person makes or offers to make with another person if:

(a) that person is a body corporate and the arrangements are with another body corporate in the same group 'dealing'; or

(b) that person is or purposes to be a participator in a joint enterpise (see para **2.60**) and the arrangements are with a view to another person who is or purposes to become a participator in the enterprise entering into such transaction for the purposes of or in connection with that enterprise.

2.32 Managing and advising on investments are also taken out if they are done for bodies corporate in the same group or both for the purposes of a joint enterprise and for participators or persons proposing to become participators in that enterprise (Sch 1, paras 18(4) and (5)).

2.33 The definitions applying for 'dealings as principal' are applied with one adaptation (para 18(6)).

SALE OF GOODS AND SUPPLY OF SERVICES

2.34 Paragraph 19 provides an exclusion where a supplier sells (or offers or agrees to sell) goods to a customer or supplies (or offers or agrees to supply) him with services *and* the supplier's main business is to supply goods or services and not to engage in activities falling within Pt II of the Schedule. The exclusion—which applies to all the relevant heads of investment activity—essentially takes out transactions for the purposes of or in connection with the sale or supply or a related sale or supply. (A related sale or supply is one for or in connection with the same purpose as the main sale or supply but by a different person.) The exclusion accordingly covers various activities concerned with financing the sale of goods or supply of services. As far as the 'dealing' exclusion is concerned, it is subject to essentially similar qualifications as the 'dealings as principal' and 'groups and joint enterprises' exclusions. Members of a group can be treated as a single person for these purposes (para 19(7)) and the definitions in the 'dealings as principal' exclusion are applied (para 19(8)).

'EMPLOYEES' SHARE SCHEMES'

2.35 Paragraph 20 provides an exclusion from the activities of 'dealing in investments' and 'arranging deals in investments' for activities undertaken by a body corporate, a body corporate connected with it, or a trustee in an employee share scheme, for particular purposes. These purposes are enabling or facilitating transactions in shares or debentures of the body corporate between or for the benefit of employees or former employees of bodies corporate within the group or certain members of their families or the holding of such shares or debentures by them or for their benefit. For this purpose, 'shares' and 'debentures' are given an extended meaning and the usual definition of 'group' is extended to cover certain other connected bodies corporate. It should be noted that this exclusion does not cover activities falling within para 15, so that if the body corporate gives advice, the exclusion will not be adequate to cover it.

'SALE OF PRIVATE COMPANY'

2.36 Paragraph 21 provides an exclusion for the acquisition or disposal of, and anything done for the purposes of the acquisition or disposal of, shares in a private company. The exclusion covers activities which would otherwise fall to be treated as 'dealing in investments', 'arranging deals in investments' and 'advising on investments'. The exclusion only applies, however, if:

(a) the shares carry 75% or more of the share capital voting rights exercisable in all circumstances at any general meeting of the company; or

(b) the shares, together with any already held by the person acquiring them, carry not less than that percentage of those voting rights; and

(c) in either case the acquisition and disposal is, or is to be, between parties each of whom is a body corporate, a partnership, a single individual or a group of connected individuals.

In the case of the person disposing of the shares, the expression 'group of connected individuals' means directors and managers of the company and their close relatives. In the case of the person acquiring the shares it means the prospective directors and managers and their close relatives. The exclusion thus takes out, for example, the sale by an estate agent of shop premises where the sale is put into effect by a transfer of the shares in the company owning the shop. Similarly, it should take out most activities of company transfer agents.

'TRUSTEES AND PERSONAL REPRESENTATIVES'

2.37 Paragraph 22 contains a number of exclusions for the activities of trustees and personal representatives. Of course (except in the case of the trustees of an occupational pension scheme), a trustee or personal representative will only need authorisation if he not merely engages in these activities, but does so by way of business carried on in the UK. (For trustees of occupational pension schemes, see para **21.16**.) Accordingly, these special exclusions will not need to apply to those trustees or personal representatives who carry on what would otherwise be investment activities but without doing so by way of business. It will be seen too that the paragraph contains only a limited exclusion from the activity of 'dealing in investments', covering solely bare trustees. It may be, however, that a trustee or personal representative will be able to avail himself of the exemption for 'dealings on own account' to cover other dealing activities. It will also be noted that these provisions do not qualify para 16 of Sch 1, the provision which brings in the activities of the trustee of an authorised unit trust.

2.38 The first exclusion for trustees and personal representatives disapplies the paragraph on 'dealing' activities where the person concerned buys, sells or subscribes for an investment (or offers or agrees to do so) if the investment is, or, as the case may be, is to be, held by him as bare trustee (or in Scotland, as nominee for another person), he is acting on that person's instructions and he does not hold himself out as providing a service of buying and selling investments. As noted above, a trustee or personal representative may be able to use the 'dealings as principal' exclusion for other dealing activities. He will not, though, be able to do so where he acts as a bare trustee on the beneficiary's instructions, by para 22(5).

2.39 The second special exclusion, for 'arranging deals in investments', relates to anything done by a person as trustee or personal representative with a view to:

(a) a fellow trustee or personal representative and himself engaging in dealing activities in their capacity as such; or

(b) a beneficiary under the trust, will or intestacy engaging in any such activity.

2.40 Anything done by a person as trustee or personal representative is also excluded from the activity of 'managing investments' unless the person concerned holds himself out as offering investment management services.

2.41 The exclusion for 'advising on investments' covers advice given by a trustee or personal representative to:

(a) a fellow trustee or personal representative, for the purposes of the trust or estate; or

(b) a beneficiary under the trust, will or intestacy, concerning his interest in the trust fund or estate.

2.42 None of the special exclusions for trustees and personal representatives (except the first) apply if the person concerned is remunerated for the activity in addition to any remuneration he receives for discharging his duties as trustee or personal representative.

'DEALINGS IN COURSE OF NON-INVESTMENT BUSINESS'

2.43 Paragraph 23 of the Schedule enables the paragraph on 'dealing' activities to be partially disapplied by the grant of permissions to particular persons. This procedure is designed to enable the exclusion of certain 'corporate treasury' functions of non-investment businesses. These functions may involve activities, which, if engaged in elsewhere, would need to be covered but which it is inappropriate to cover in the context of a corporate treasury. For the transitional provision applying, see para 15 of Sch 15.

2.44 The exclusion takes the form of a provision that the paragraph on 'dealing' activities does not apply to anything done by a person as principal, as agent for another company in the same group, or as agent for a person who is or proposes to become a participator with him in a joint enterprise (where done for the purposes of the enterprise,) *if* it is done in accordance with the terms and conditions of a permission granted to the person by the Secretary of State (or, on transfer, agency) under the paragraph. A permission of this kind may be granted if it appears:

(a) that the applicant's *main* business, or, if he is a member of a group, the main business of the group, does not consist of activities requiring authorisation;

(b) that the applicant's business is likely to involve authorisable 'dealing' activities; and

(c) that having regard to the nature of the applicant's main business and, if he is a member of a group, the main business of the group taken as a whole, the manner in which, the persons with whom and the purposes for which the applicant purposes to engage in activities requiring him to be authorised, and to any other relevant matters it is inappropriate to require him to be subject to regulation as an authorised person.

2.45 A permission of this kind is to be granted by written notice and can be withdrawn by a further notice if for any reason it appears that it is not appropriate for it to continue in force. Notification regulations can be made for the purpose of enabling the Secretary of State (or agency) to determine whether permissions should remain in force. Where permissions are granted subject to conditions, injunctions and restitution orders are to be available in support of the conditions (para 23(6)). In addition, of course, the exclusion will cease to apply where conditions are broken, so that a breach of section 3 may result. The provisions of the Act on 'powers to call for information', 'investigation powers' and 'exercise of investigation powers by officers' are also applied (para 23(7)).

'ADVICE GIVEN IN COURSE OF PROFESSION OR NON-INVESTMENT BUSINESS'

2.46 The next exclusion is a narrowly drawn one for advice:

(a) which is given in the course of the carrying on of any profession or of a business not otherwise constituting investment business; *and*

(b) the giving of which is a necessary part of other advice or services given in the course of carrying on that profession or business.

2.47 The narrowness of the exclusion stems from the requirement for the advice to be a 'necessary part of other advice or services'. Advice which is merely 'incidental to' other advice will not fall within the exclusion. For example, if a professional adviser advises that investments need to be sold in order to meet tax liabilities, the exclusion applies. If, however, he also advises on which investments should be sold, that advice would not be necessary, but merely incidental, and would not be covered by the exclusion. Advice is not to be regarded as a necessary part of other advice or services if it is remunerated separately from them.

'NEWSPAPERS'

2.48 Paragraph 25 provides a special exclusion for 'advice given in a newspaper, journal, magazine or other periodical publication'. In order for the exclusion not to apply to investment circulars adopting the format of newspapers or journals, it is also necessary for the principal purpose of the publication, taken as a whole and including any advertisements contained in it, not to be to lead persons to invest in any particular investment. There is a procedure for conclusive certification that a publication is entitled to the benefit of the exclusion, delegable to a designated agency.

'Additional exclusions for persons without permanent place of business in the United Kingdom'

2.49   As noted (see para **2.02**, ante) these exclusions do not affect the meaning of 'investment business' but are merely exclusions from the requirement for authorisation or exemption for persons, known as 'overseas persons' who do not carry on investment business from a permanent place of business maintained by them in the UK. In other words, they apply to business carried on on a 'services' basis from overseas.

'TRANSACTIONS WITH OR THROUGH AUTHORISED OR EXEMPTED PERSONS'

2.50   Paragraph 26(1) contains the exclusion applying to the activity of 'dealing in investments'. The exclusion applies to transactions with or through:

(a) an authorised person; or

(b) an exempted person acting in the course of business in respect of which he is exempt.

So, for example, an overseas person can deal in shares with a stockbroker without requiring authorisation. Similarly, an overseas person could deal through a recognised investment exchange, as an exempted person, so long as the exchange was acting in the course of the business for which it was exempt. This would not, of course, apply to deals through an unrecognised investment exchange.

2.51   There is a parallel exclusion for the activity of 'arranging deals in investments'. This applies if the arrangements are made by the overseas person with an authorised person or with an exempted person with a view to his entering into a transaction in respect of which he is exempt. It also applies to offers to make and agreements to make arrangements of this kind. A second limb to the exclusion covers arrangements where the transactions with a view to which the arrangements were made are confined to transactions by authorised persons and transactions by exempted persons in respect of which they are exempt.

'UNSOLICITED OR LEGITIMATELY SOLICITED TRANSACTIONS ETC WITH OR FOR OTHER PERSONS'

2.52   In addition to the exclusion for transactions with or through authorised or exempted persons, overseas persons will not need authorisation for certain unsolicited or legitimately solicited transactions. The same exclusion also deals with 'advising on investments'.

2.53   The exclusion applies essentially to activities between an overseas person and a person in the UK. The first situation in which it applies is where the activities result from an approach by the person in the UK which was not itself solicited by the overseas person or which he solicited legimately, that is, without breaking the sections of the Act relating to 'unsolicited calls' or 'restrictions on advertising'. The exclusion also applies to activities which do result from an approach by the overseas person so long as the approach did not breach either of those sections.

2.54 In the case of transactions entered into by the overseas person as agent for a person in the UK, the exclusion only applies if the other party is outside the UK or, where the other party is in the UK, the transaction is the result of an unsolicited or legitimately solicited approach by the counterparty or of his legitimate solicitation by the overseas person.

Interpretation

2.55 The interpretation provisions in Pt V of the Schedule apply for the interpretation only of the Schedule, and not for the interpretation of the Act as a whole. However, except where otherwise stated, they apply according to their terms to the interpretation of all Parts of the Schedule.

BUYING AND SELLING

2.56 Paragraph 28 contains definitions of 'property', 'instrument', and 'offer', but of particular interest are the provisions explaining 'references to buying and selling'. By para 28(1)(d) these 'include references to any acquisition or disposal for valuable consideration' and, by virtue of the next sub-paragraph, the word 'disposal' is given an extended meaning. At first sight this definition appears an unusual one. The schedule contains no references to 'buying and selling', only to one or the other. It appears, however, that this formulation ensures that the extended meaning given to 'disposal' applies both to references to 'selling' and, in the case of references to 'buying', to the disposal made by the other party to the transaction. It should be noted, however, that the word 'acquire' is not defined so that where this is used in the Schedule, rather than 'buy', the extended meaning will not apply.

ISSUE OF OWN SHARES, SHARE WARRANTS OR DEBENTURES

2.57 Paragraph 28(3) provides that a company is not, by issuing its own shares or share warrants, and a person is not, by issuing his own debentures, to be regarded for the purposes of the Schedule as disposing of them. Equally, such a company or person is not, because of anything done for the purposes of issuing investments of that kind, to be regarded as making arrangements with a view to a person subscribing for or otherwise acquiring or underwriting them. It should, however, be noted that this interpretation does not apply to the activity of 'advising on investments'.

TRANSACTIONS THROUGH OTHER PERSONS

2.58 By para 29, a transaction is entered into *through* a person if he enters into it as agent or arranges for it to be entered into by another person as principal or agent.

2.59 The expression 'group' is given, for the purposes of the Schedule, a wider meaning than s 207(1) gives for the purposes of the Act as a whole. In the Schedule, the expression is to be treated as including any body corporate 'which is a related company (within the meaning of para 92 of Sch 4 to the Companies Act 1985) of any member of the group or would be such a related company if the member of the group were a company within the meaning of that Act (para 30 of Sch 1).

JOINT ENTERPRISE

2.60 Paragraph 31 defines the expressions 'joint enterprise' and 'the participators'. A joint enterprise is one into which two or more persons enter for commercial reasons related to a business or businesses (other than investment business) carried on by them. In other words, a joint enterprise is the kind of non-investment enterprise which may be carried on by a joint venture company or under a joint venture agreement. The participators in a joint enterprise are those who have entered into it and, where a participator is a body corporate, any other member of the same group.

EXEMPTED PERSONS

2.61 By para 32, where a person is an exempted person as respects only part of the investment business carried on by him, anything done by him in carrying on that part is to be disregarded in determining whether any paragraph of Pt III or IV of the Schedule applies to anything done by him in the course of business in respect of which he is not exempt. For example, in deciding whether a person holds himself out as engaging in the business of buying investments with a view to selling them, for the purposes of the exclusion for 'dealings as principal' in para 17, no account would be taken of activities covered by the exemption for listed institutions.

GAMING

2.62 Paragraph 33 makes it irrelevant in deciding whether a contract counts as an investment or an activity constitutes carrying on investment business that a particular contract may be legally unenforceable as a gaming or wagering contract. This could otherwise have been an issue, particularly in relation to some contracts potentially falling to be treated as contracts for differences.

Changing Scope of Act

POWER TO EXTEND OR RESTRICT SCOPE OF ACT

2.63   The scope of the Act may be changed under a procedure in s 2. This gives a power to the Secretary of State (not transferable to a designated agency):

'(a) to extend or restrict the meaning of investment for the purposes of all or any of the provisions of [the Act], or

(b) to extend or restrict for the purposes of all or any of those provisions the activities that are to constitute the carrying on of investment business or the carrying on of such business in the United Kingdom.'

2.64   It will thus be noted that the power effectively enables the Secretary of State to amend Sch 1. He can, though, limit such changes to apply only for particular purposes. For example, it would be possible to amend the Schedule for the purposes of the authorisation requirement, but leave it unchanged for the purpose of, say, the section on 'unsolicited calls'. The powers even cover (by s 2(2)) conferring powers on the Secretary of State in the way presently done in para 23 of the Schedule. For further powers where an order under this power amends references to a collective investment scheme, see para **6.23**.

2.65   Where the power is used to extend the scope of the Act it needs to be approved by resolution of both Houses of Parliament. Where the scope of the Act is to be restricted, it is subject to annulment on a resolution by either House (s 2(5)). Provision can be made for transitional arrangements.

Chapter 3
Authorisation and exemption

Introductory

3.01 This chapter considers the requirement to be authorised or exempted, the criminal and civil consequences of failing to comply with the requirement, and the different routes by which authorisation may be obtained and situations in which exemptions will apply. It also covers the recognition of self-regulating organisations, professional bodies, investment exchanges and clearing houses.

NEED FOR AUTHORISATION OR EXEMPTION

3.02 Any person who carries on or purports to carry on investment business in the United Kingdom must be either authorised or exempted (s 3).

CRIMINAL SANCTION

3.03 Any person who carries on, or purports to carry on investment business in contravention of section 3 is guilty of a criminal offence. The penalties provided are:

(a) on conviction on indictment, imprisonment for up to two years or a fine or both;

(b) on summary conviction, imprisonment for up to six months or a fine up to the statutory maximum or both.

There is a 'due diligence' defence provided, but it is clear from its formulation that error of law will be no excuse.

AGREEMENTS MADE BY OR THROUGH UNAUTHORISED PERSONS

3.04 Section 5 provides for certain agreements to be unenforceable where they are made by or through a person carrying on investment business in contravention of s 3. This applies to any agreement the making or performance of which by the person seeking to enforce it (or from whom money or property is recoverable under the section) constitutes an activity which falls within any paragraph of Pt II of Sch 1 and is not excluded by Pt III or IV of that Schedule. An agreement of this kind which is entered into by a person in the course of carrying on investment business in contravention of section 3, or which is entered into by an authorised or exempted person but in consequence of anything said or done by a person in the course of carrying on investment business in contravention of that section.

3.05 This provision can only make the agreement unenforceable. The agreement is not void and can still be enforced by an investor or other counterparty whose acts are not tainted by the illegality.

3.06 In the absence, though, of special provision, unenforceability of this kind could operate unduly harshly and a court may therefore allow such an agreement to be enforced (or money and property paid or transferred under it to be retained) so long as it is satisfied of one of two particular matters (s 5(3)). The first applies in the case of an agreement entered into by a person in the course of carrying on investment business in contravention of s 3, where the court must be satisfied that the person reasonably believed that his entering into the agreement did not constitute a contravention of s 3. The second is that in the case of an agreement entered into *through* an unauthorised person, the authorised or exempted person who entered into it neither knew nor ought to have known that the agreement was entered into through an unauthorised person. In addition, in both cases the court must also be satisfied that it is 'just and equitable' for the agreement to be upheld (s 5(3)).

INJUNCTIONS AND RESTITUTION ORDERS

3.07 The Act contains special provisions for the grant of injunctions and restitution orders in support of the restriction on carrying on investment business in the United Kingdom without authorisation. These are dealt with separately in the following paragraphs, although they are contained in a single section in the Act (s 6). Nothing in that section, though, affects the right of any person other than the Secretary of State (or, on transfer, designated agency) to bring proceedings in respect of the matters to which it applies. For the similar provisions applying in support of provisions of the Act on the conduct of investment business, see paras **4.88**ff.

INJUNCTIONS

3.08 The first civil remedy which the Act provides for carrying on investment business in breach of s 3 is for the granting of an injunction (or, in Scotland, an interdict). This can be granted

' . . . if, on the application of the Secretary of State, the court is satisfied:

(a) that there is a reasonable likelihood that a person will contravene section 3; or

(b) that any person has contravened that section and that there is a reasonable likelihood that the contravention will continue or be repeated.'

3.09 The function of applying for such orders is capable of transfer to a designated agency. In addition, if, on the application of the Secretary of State (again the power is transferable) the court is satisfied that a person has entered into any transaction in contravention of s 3, it may order that person *and any other person who appears to the court to have been knowingly concerned in the contravention (for example a director)* to take such steps as the court may direct for restoring the parties to the position in which they were before the transaction was entered into.

3.10 It may seem surprising that this provision enables the court to grant injunctions to enforce a provision which itself creates a criminal offence. It is suggested that the explanation is that injunctions granted will restrain the performance of an act, rather than the commission of an offence. They accordingly enable the court, on a civil burden of proof, to be satisfied that a particular act or course of conduct will constitute a contravention, and to grant an injunction accordingly. Performing that act or engaging in that course of conduct then becomes an offence as a contempt of court and is punishable as such, without it being necessary to establish the commission of the substantive offence on the stricter burden of proof applying in criminal cases. For a similar argument, see para **4.92**.

RESTITUTION ORDERS

3.11 Again, on the application of the Secretary of State (and with the function again being transferable to a designated agency) the court can make restitution orders, as has been the practice in this field in the US and Canada. The procedure varies slightly as between England, where the sums concerned are paid into court, and Scotland, where they are paid to the applicant. In either case the court can make an order if satisfied that a person has been carrying on investment business in contravention of s 3, and:

(a) that profits have accrued to that person as a result of carrying on that business; or

(b) that one or more investors has suffered loss or been otherwise adversely affected as a result of his contravention of the sections of the Act relating to unsolicited calls or restrictions on advertising or failure to act substantially in accordance with any rules or regulations made under Ch V of Pt I of the Act.

3.12 The amount the investment business may be ordered to pay is the sum which appears to the court to be just having regard:

(a) to any profits appearing to the court to have accrued;

(b) to the extent of any loss or other adverse effect; or

(c) both to any profits and to the extent of any loss or other adverse effect.

3.13   Accordingly, the court can order both compensation for the loss or other adverse effect which has occurred and disgorgement of the profits resulting. The sums concerned are to be paid out to or distributed among such persons as the court may direct. These are to be persons appearing to the court to have entered into transactions as a result of which the profits have accrued or the loss or other adverse effect has been suffered. (The requirement for transactions to have been entered into with the person concerned is noteworthy. The remedy does not appear to be available to benefit those who have suffered loss or other adverse effect on the basis of advice alone.) There is a provision for the court to require accounts or other information to be provided to enable it to decide on the profits which have accrued and on how any amounts are to be paid or distributed. These accounts and other information can be required to be verified in such manner as the court may direct, for example, by requiring them to be audited.

Authorised persons

MEMBERS OF RECOGNISED SELF-REGULATING ORGANISATIONS

3.14   Members of recognised self-regulating organisations are authorised persons by virtue of their membership unless they are already authorised by virtue of the provisions applying to regulated insurance companies or friendly societies or are insurance companies authorised by the provisions applying to Europersons (s 7). For the transitional provision applying, see para 1 of Sch 15.

SELF-REGULATING ORGANISATIONS: CONCEPTS EXPLAINED

3.15   Section 8(1) of the Act defines a self-regulating organisation essentially by reference to its function. It is a body (including a body corporate as defined by s 207(1)) which 'regulates the carrying on of investment business of any kind by enforcing rules which are binding on persons carrying on business of that kind either because they are members of that body or because they are otherwise subject to its control'. The words 'otherwise subject to its control' are apt to cover a body which has statutory powers over non-members, and might have been expected to have been of greater relevance in the parallel provisions applying to recognition of professional bodies. The word 'members' is given an extended meaning, to include all those who are subject to its rules in carrying on the business in question (s 8(2)). In addition, the 'rules' of a self-regulating organisation include both rules it can enforce in relation to the carrying on of the business in question, and rules relating to the admission and expulsion of members or otherwise as to its constitution (s 8(3)). 'Guidance' issued by a self-regulating organisation is also defined to mean guidance (including recommendations) which would, if it were a rule, come within sub-s (3) (s 8(4)). So guidance is clearly distinguished from rules, the difference being, of course, that rules are binding on those to whom they are addressed.

SELF-REGULATING ORGANISATIONS: APPLICATIONS FOR RECOGNITION

3.16   Section 9(1) provides that a self-regulating organisation may apply to the Secretary of State for an order declaring it to be a recognised self-regulating organisation. The function of recognising a self-regulating organisation is transferable to a designated agency (see Ch 11). In view of the definition of a self-regulating organisation as a 'body . . . which regulates', an application cannot be made by a body which merely *proposes* to regulate. Subsections (2)–(6) deal with the procedure for an application for recognition. For self-regulating organisations for friendly societies, see paras 2–12 of Sch 11.

SELF-REGULATING ORGANISATIONS: BASIS OF RECOGNITION

3.17   Section 10 contains the power to make an order declaring an applicant to be a recognised self-regulating organisation. Subsection (2) of that section requires the Secretary of State to make a recognition order if it appears to him that the requirements of sub-s (3) and of Sch 2 are satisfied. The importance of this public law right to be recognised should not, however, be exaggerated. The test itself contains a substantial subjective element and is in any event subject to a discretion, in sub-s (4), for the Secretary of State (or agency) to refuse to make a recognition order if he considers that recognition of the organisation is unnecessary 'having regard to the existence of one or more other organisations which are concerned with investment business of a kind with which the applicant is concerned and which have been or are likely to be recognised' (the 'need' criterion). Unlike, though, the other criteria for recognition, it is to be noted that this is not mandatory. A self-regulating organisation may be recognised—so far as the legislation is concerned—even though the recognising authority considers that its recognition is not necessary. This is the reason why s 10(4) is discretionary in form.

SELF-REGULATING ORGANISATIONS: STATUTORY REQUIREMENTS FOR RECOGNITION

3.18   As mentioned above, s 10(2) ties the making of a recognition order to it appearing to the recognising authority that the requirements of sub-s (3) and of Sch 2 are satisfied. Subsection (3) requires an organisation which is not concerned with every kind of investment business to have a scope rule, precluding a member from straying outside it without separate authorisation or exemption. This enables some of the requirements in Sch 2 to apply only to investment business of the kind with which the organisation is concerned. For provisions applying to a self-regulating organisation with insurance company members, see para 3 of Sch 10.

SELF-REGULATING ORGANISATIONS: STATUTORY REQUIREMENTS FOR RECOGNITION: MEMBERS TO BE 'FIT AND PROPER' PERSONS

3.19   Paragraph 1 of Sch 2 contains the 'fit and proper' test for membership of a self-regulating organisation. Although there is no general requirement for equivalence of technique with the fit and proper test for direct authorisation, broadly the same result is to be achieved. The only aspect involving equivalence of technique is contained in para 1(3), which allows to be imported into the test the matters which the Secretary of State (or agency) may take into account. By para 1(4), a self-regulating organisation's fit and proper test does not apply to a person who is not an authorised person by virtue of being a member of the organisation: This excludes the insurance companies and friendly societies authorised by s 22 or 23 respectively and EEC insurance companies authorised as Europersons by s 31 (see s 7(2)).

SELF-REGULATING ORGANISATIONS: STATUTORY REQUIREMENTS FOR RECOGNITION: ADMISSION, EXPULSION AND DISCIPLINE

3.20   By para 2 of the Schedule, the rules and practices of the organisation relating to:

(a) the admission and the expulsion of members; and

(b) the discipline it exercises over its members;

must be fair and reasonable and include adequate provisions for appeals.

SELF-REGULATING ORGANISATIONS: STATUTORY REQUIREMENTS FOR RECOGNITION: SAFEGUARDS FOR INVESTORS

3.21   Paragraph 3(1) of the Schedule establishes an 'equivalence test' for an SRO's rules. This is that its rules 'governing the carrying on of investment businesses of any kind by its members must afford investors protection at least equivalent to that afforded in respect of investment business of that kind by the rules and regulations for the time being in force under Chapter V of Part I' of the Act. By paragraph 3(2) the equivalence test also covers financial resources rules, indemnity rules and compensation fund rules.

3.22   It should be noted that this does not mean that the SRO's rules must be identical to the statutory rules applying. Unless, though, an SRO wishes its rules to be more stringent than the statutory ones, there would seem no reason in principle why a new SRO (as distinct from one with existing rules in place) should not adopt the statutory rules *en bloc* or even incorporate them by reference. This would avoid disputes over differences between the rules, but will no doubt depend to some degree on perceptions of the statutory rules themselves. It is, though, doubtful to what extent it will be possible to claim that a general principle is 'at least equivalent' to a specific rule so that it should not be thought that relying on 'equivalence' rather than identity will enable the requirements to be any looser.

3.23 In addition, the organisation must, so far as practicable, have powers for purposes corresponding to those of the intervention powers provided for by Ch VI of Pt I of the Act. The rules must also enable the organisation to prevent a member resigning if the organisation considers that any matter affecting him should be investigated as a preliminary to a decision on whether he should be expelled, disciplined or be or continue to be intervened against. This parallels a similar requirement for direct authorisation (see para **3.81**).

SELF-REGULATING ORGANISATIONS: STATUTORY REQUIREMENTS FOR RECOGNITION: MONITORING AND ENFORCEMENT

3.24 It must also appear to the recognising authority that the SRO has adequate arrangements and resources for the effective monitoring and enforcement of compliance with its rules and with any rules or regulations to which its members are subject under Ch V of Pt I of the Act (statutory rules and regulations on the conduct of investment business) in respect of investment business of a kind regulated by the organisation (Sch 2, para 4(1)).

3.25 The arrangements for monitoring (but not enforcement) may make provision for that function to be performed on behalf of the organisation (and without affecting its responsibility) by any other body or person who is able and willing to perform it. This can include overseas regulatory authorities.

SELF-REGULATING ORGANISATIONS: STATUTORY REQUIREMENTS FOR RECOGNITION: GOVERNING BODY

3.26 The next requirement which must appear to the recognising authority to be satisfied is that the arrangements of the organisation with respect to the appointment, removal from office and functions of those responsible for making or enforcing its rules (not merely its formal governing body) must be such as to secure a proper balance (the word 'proper' introducing a subjective element):

(a) between the interests of the different members of the organisation; and

(b) between the interests of the organisation or its members and the interests of the public (Sch 2, para 5(1)).

It is expressly provided that those responsible must include a number of persons independent of the organisation and its members sufficient to secure such a balance.

SELF-REGULATING ORGANISATIONS: STATUTORY REQUIREMENTS FOR RECOGNITION: INVESTIGATION OF COMPLAINTS

3.27   Another requirement which must 'appear to' be fulfilled is that the organisation must have effective arrangements for the investigation of complaints against it or its members. These may allow the whole or part of that function to be performed by and be the responsibility of an independent body or person.

SELF-REGULATING ORGANISATIONS: STATUTORY REQUIREMENTS FOR RECOGNITION: PROMOTION AND MAINTENANCE OF STANDARDS

3.28   A self-regulating organisation must appear to fulfil a requirement relating to its ability and willingness:

'. . . to promote and maintain high standards of integrity and fair dealing in the carrying on of investment business and to co-operate, by the sharing of information and otherwise, with the Secretary of State and any other authority body or person having responsibility for the supervision or regulation of investment business or other financial services.'

Similar provisions apply to all other recognised organisations or bodies under the Act. The provision of information to the Secretary of State or designated agency can be enforced under s 104(2).

SELF-REGULATING ORGANISATIONS: REVOCATION OF RECOGNITION

3.29   An SRO's recognition may be revoked by the Secretary of State (transferable to agency) if at any time it appears that the requirements for recognition are not satisfied, that the organisation has failed to comply with any obligation to which it is subject by virtue of the Act, or that its continued recognition is undesirable (not merely unnecessary) having regard to the existence of one or more other organisations which have been or are to be recognised as self-regulating organisations (s 11). The Act contains a procedure for representations to be made to the authority concerned before the recognition order is revoked. This procedure may, however, be overridden if the Secretary of State (or agency) considers it essential to do so in the interest of investors and will not apply in any event where a recognition order is revoked at the request or with the consent of the recognised organisation.

SELF-REGULATING ORGANISATIONS: INTERMEDIATE CONTROLS: COMPLIANCE ORDERS

3.30   The Act also contains two further powers for control over recognised self-regulating organisations in the interests of investor protection. The first of these is contained in s 12. It applies where it appears to the Secretary of State (or, on transfer, agency) either that the requirements for recognition are not satisfied or that the organisation has failed to comply with any obligation to which it is subject by virtue of the

Act. In this case, instead of revoking the recognition order, the Secretary of State (or agency) can make an application to the court. The court is empowered, if it decides that a requirement for recognition is not satisfied or, as the case may be, that the organisation has failed to comply with the obligation in question, to order the organisation to take such steps as it directs for securing that the requirement is satisfied or the obligation complied with.

SELF-REGULATING ORGANISATIONS: INTERMEDIATE CONTROLS: ALTERATION OF RULES FOR PROTECTION OF INVESTORS

3.31 The second less Draconian power for which the Act provides is contained in s 13. This applies only where it appears that the *rules* of the organisation do not satisfy the equivalence test. In this case, instead of revoking the recognition order or applying to the court, the Secretary of State (or agency) can direct the organisation to alter or himself alter its rules in such manner as he considers necessary for securing that the rules satisfy the test. There is a similar power in relation to an SRO's 'scope rule', but this applies not merely to its rules fulfilling the equivalence test, but also to its 'rules and practices' satisfying the requirements of Sch 2. Before giving a direction or making any alteration under this section, the Secretary of State has to consult the organisation and undertake the same formal notice procedure as for a revocation of recognition.

3.32 Although the powers under this section can apply with immediate effect without the need to apply to the court, there is a procedure for the organisation concerned to apply to the court. If the court is satisfied either that the rules without the alterations satisfy the requirements, or that other alterations proposed by the organisation would result in them doing so, it may set aside the alteration and order the organisation to make any alteration which it proposed.

3.33 There are no equivalent direct powers over a recognised professional body, investment exchange or clearing house.

RECOGNISED SELF-REGULATING ORGANISATIONS: NOTIFICATION REQUIREMENTS

3.34 The Act contains a transferable power to make regulations imposing notification requirements on a recognised self-regulating organisation (s 14). These may either require notice of specified *events* relating to the organisation or its members or require information at specified *times* or in respect of specified *periods*. The notice or information required must be reasonably needed by the Secretary of State for the exercise of his functions under the Act. The regulations may require the information to be given in a specified form or to be verified in a specified manner. Verificiation may take the form of an auditor's or an accountant's report or confirmation by some other third party or, for example, a statutory declaration by the person giving the notice or supplying the information. Section 14(5) enables the Secretary of State (or agency) to approve direct computer links for the serving of notices or provision of information under the regulations.

3.35 In addition to the notification requirements which can be imposed by regulations, the Act itself imposes a requirement on recognised organisations which amend, revoke or add to their rules or, where it is intended to have continuing effect and is issued in writing or other legible form, their guidance, to give to the Secretary of State a written notice (s 14(6)).

3.36 Contravention of notification requirements is expressly provided not to be an offence (s 14(7)). Although the section is silent on any civil liability, it is considered unlikely that this would arise without express words, in view of the express words creating it to be found elsewhere in the Act. The practical importance of this is in any event small in view of the exemption from liability in damages provided.

PERSONS AUTHORISED BY RECOGNISED PROFESSIONAL BODIES

3.37 The Act provides that a person holding a certificate issued for the purpose by a recognised professional body is to be an authorised person (s 15). Such a certificate may be issued to an individual, a body corporate, a partnership or an incorporated association. For the transitional provision applying, see para 5 of Sch 15.

PROFESSIONAL BODIES: CONCEPTS EXPLAINED

3.38 The concepts involved in the procedure for recognition of a professional body are essentially similar to those applying on recognition of a self-regulating organisation. A professional body is one which regulates the practice of a profession, but 'references to the practice of a profession do not include references to carrying on a business consisting wholly or mainly of investment business'. So, for example, it could not be suggested that stockbroking or insurance broking was a profession for these purposes.

3.39 Section 16(2) gives an extended definition to the word 'members' in relation to a professional body. These are individuals who, whether or not members of the body, are entitled to practise the profession in question and, in practising it, are subject to its rules. An example of a professional body which regulates non-members is The Law Society, which does so under statutory powers provided in the Solicitors Act 1974. It should be noted that the expression 'members' is limited to individuals. It is therefore not necessarily appropriate to cover all persons certificated to carry on investment business. 'Rules' and 'guidance' are given meanings similar to those applying in the case of self-regulating organisations (s 16(3)–(4)).

PROFESSIONAL BODIES: PROCEDURE ON APPLICATION FOR RECOGNITION

3.40   The procedure for applying for recognition as a professional body is the same as that for applying to be a recognised self-regulating organisation (s 17(2)).

PROFESSIONAL BODIES: BASIS OF GRANT OF RECOGNITION

3.41   The basis of grant of recognition is also similar. There is, however, no 'need criterion' for recognition of a professional body and the requirements established by the Act for recognition are signficantly less onerous. By s 18(2), however, it appears that the Secretary of State (or agency) has an open discretion on making a recognition order and could therefore impose other requirements for recognition which are within the purposes of the Act. For the transitional provision applying in recognitions, see para 4 of Sch 15.

PROFESSIONAL BODIES: STATUTORY REQUIREMENTS FOR RECOGNITION: SCOPE RULE

3.42   The first of the Act's requirements for recognition of a professional body is for it to have a scope rule (s 18(3)). This is a more stringent requirement than that applying to an SRO, which only applies where there is a kind of investment business with which the organisation is not concerned. In the case of a professional body, the scope rule must 'impose acceptable limits' on the kinds of investment business which may be carried on and the circumstances in which it may be carried on. The requirement as to 'circumstances' may be used to require a connection between the practice of the profession concerned and the investment business.

PROFESSIONAL BODIES: STATUTORY REQUIREMENTS FOR RECOGNITION: STATUTORY STATUS

3.43   The first requirement of the Schedule is that the body must have a statutory status. There are some twelve bodies at present thought to fall within the criteria specified, including the Law Societies, the four recognised accountancy bodies, the Institute and Faculty of Actuaries and the Royal Institution of Chartered Surveyors. The statutory status of the body is substituted for an express requirement for a 'fit and proper' test to apply to its members.

PROFESSIONAL BODIES: STATUTORY REQUIREMENTS FOR RECOGNITION: CERTIFICATION

3.44   The body must have rules, practices and arrangements for securing that certified persons fulfil specified requirements (para 2 of Sch 3). The first of these is that the certified person must be either an individual who is a member of the body or a person (including bodies corporate, partnerships and unincorporated associations) managed and controlled by one or more individuals each of whom is a member of a recognised professional body (not necessarily the certifying body) and at least one of whom is a member of the certifying body. In addition, an *individual* can be certified only if his main business is the practice of the profession regulated by the certifying body and he is a sole practitioner. Where an individual is practising the profession in partnership, it will therefore be the partnership which needs to apply for certification. Where the certified person is not an individual, that person's main business must be the practice of the profession or professions regulated by the recognised professional body or, in the case of a 'mixed practice' by professional bodies of which the individual managers or controllers are members.

PROFESSIONAL BODIES: STATUTORY REQUIREMENTS FOR RECOGNITION: SAFEGUARDS FOR INVESTORS

3.45   There is an equivalence test for a professional body's rules similar to that for a recognised self-regulating organisation. (For the powers conferred to assist in fulfilling this requirement among owners, see para 6 of Sch 15.) There is no express requirement for a professional body to have powers for purposes corresponding to those of the Act's intervention powers or for its rules to enable it to prevent members resigning to avoid investigation, discipline or intervention.

PROFESSIONAL BODIES: STATUTORY REQUIREMENTS FOR RECOGNITION: MONITORING AND ENFORCEMENT

3.46   The body must have adequate arrangements and resources for monitoring compliance with the conditions for certification. It must also have rules, practices and arrangements for the withdrawal or suspension of certification in the event of any of those conditions ceasing to be satisfied.

3.47   The requirements for its arrangements and resources for monitoring and enforcement of investment business rules are essentially similar to those applying to a recognising self-regulating organisation. In addition, it is expressly provided that the arrangements for enforcement are to include provision for the withdrawal or suspension of certification and may include provision for disciplining members of the body who manage or control a certified person.

3.48   Arrangements for *enforcement* may enable the whole or part of that function to be performed by and be the responsibility of an independent body or person. They must be such as to secure a proper balance between the interests of persons certified by the body and the interests of the public. Arrangements are not to be regarded as satisfying that requirement unless the persons responsible for enforcement include a sufficient number of persons who are independent of the body and its members or of persons certified by it. However, there is no 'proper balance' requirement for rule making, as there is for a self-regulating organisation.

3.49 As with a self-regulating organisation, the arrangements for monitoring (but not enforcement) may make provision for delegation of this task (see para **3.25**).

PROFESSIONAL BODIES: STATUTORY REQUIREMENTS FOR RECOGNITION: INVESTIGATION OF COMPLAINTS

3.50 The body must have effective arrangements for the investigation of complaints relating to:

(a) the carrying on by persons certified by it of investment business in respect of which they are subject to its rules; and

(b) its regulation of investment business.

Again, an independent body or person may be used.

There is no complaints requirement extending to the non-investment business of the body's members.

PROFESSIONAL BODIES: STATUTORY REQUIREMENTS FOR RECOGNITION: PROMOTION AND MAINTENANCE OF STANDARDS

3.51 The standard requirement applies to a professional body (see para **3.28**).

PROFESSIONAL BODIES: REVOCATION OF RECOGNITION

3.52 The recognition of a professional body can be revoked on corresponding grounds to those for the revocation of recognition of a self-regulating organisation, except that, because there is no 'need criterion' for professional bodies, there is no provision for revocation where this criterion is no longer satisfied. The procedure on revocation of recognition of a professional body is the same as that for revocation of recognition of a self-regulating organisation (s 19(2), and see para **3.29**).

PROFESSIONAL BODIES: INTERMEDIATE POWERS: COMPLIANCE ORDERS

3.53 The powers to apply to the court for a compliance order against a recognised professional body correspond to those for compliance orders against recognised self-regulating organisations (s 20 and para **3.30**).

PROFESSIONAL BODIES: INTERMEDIATE POWERS: ABSENCE OF DIRECT POWERS

3.54 Although, as explained above, there are powers to revoke the recognition of a professional body or to seek compliance orders, it should be noted that there is no direct power to change the rules of such a body (even its 'scope rule') which would correspond to the power available in respect of a recognised self-regulating organisation. The reason for the distinction is that the nature of the investment business activities regulated by a professional body may be expected to be such that the primary advantage of a direct power, that is, its speed, will be of less significance than in the case of those in the mainstream of the investment world.

RECOGNISED PROFESSIONAL BODIES: NOTIFICATION REQUIREMENTS

3.55 The regulation-making powers which enable notification requirements to be imposed on a recognised professional body are essentially similar to those applying in the case of a recognised self-regulating organisation, except that, because of the distinction between the individuals who are 'members' of the body for the purposes of the Act and the persons certified by it to do investment business, each of these is mentioned specifically in the powers. However, the notice requirement imposed by the section itself, for amendment, revocation or addition to rules or guidance, is slightly different. The difference is that it contains a dispensing power, enabling the Secretary of State (or agency) to waive compliance for particular rules or guidance or descriptions of rules or guidance. This would enable the Secretary of State (or agency) to waive the requirement to notify changes etc in rules or guidance which were only relevant to the practice of the profession regulated by the body.

AUTHORISED INSURERS

3.56 The Act confers automatic exemption on 'a body which is authorised under section 3 or 4 of the Insurance Companies Act 1982 to carry on insurance business which is investment business and carries on such insurance business in the United Kingdom' (s 22). The authorisation is limited to:

'(a) any insurance business which is investment business; and
(b) any other investment business which that body may carry on without contravening section 16 of that Act.'

3.57 This applies, accordingly, only to UK-authorised insurance companies. Section 3 of the 1982 Act contains the procedure for authorisation by the Secretary of State which is established by that Act. Section 4 continues the authorisation of existing insurance companies. It will be observed that the structure of the automatic authorisation for which this section provides is that if a body is authorised to carry on *any* insurance business which is investment business and actually does so in the UK, it has Financial Services Act authorisation not merely for that insurance business but for any insurance business which is investment business. (This does not provide authorisation to do insurance business under the 1982 Act: see Sch 10, para 2(4).) Accordingly, if such an insurance company undertakes a class of insurance business which is investment business which is not one of the classes for which it is authorised under the Insurance Companies Act 1982, it does not thereby also exceed its authorisation under the Financial Services Act.

3.58 Section 16 of the Insurance Companies Act 1982 prohibits certain insurance companies (apparently including all those to which section 22 applies) from carrying on 'any activities, in the United Kingdom or elsewhere, otherwise than in connection with or for the purposes of its insurance business'. For these purposes pension fund management is treated as carried on in connection with insurance business (see s 16(2) of the 1982 Act). An insurance company authorised by s 22 cannot be *authorised* by any other route (para 2(1) of Sch 10) although it may join an SRO for its *regulation*. See also para 2(2) of Sch 10.

FRIENDLY SOCIETIES

3.59 Section 23 confers automatic authorisation on registered friendly societies other than those which are merely registered as branches. This is limited to investment business carried on for or in connection with any of [their statutory purposes]. For substantive provisions on friendly societies, see Ch 14, commenting on ss 140–141. The Act provides special transitional provisions for friendly societies in para 14 of Sch 15.

COLLECTIVE INVESTMENT SCHEMES

3.60 The operator or trustee of a scheme recognised under s 86 of the Act is an authorised person as respects:

(a) investment business which consists in operating or acting as trustee in relation to that scheme; and

(b) any investment business which is carried on by him in connection with or for the purposes of that scheme.

3.61 It should be noted that this automatic authorisation applies only in the case of a scheme recognised under s 86. It does not apply to the other classes of recognised collective investment scheme for which the Act provides. In those cases, any operator or trustee who needs authorisation must obtain it by one of the other routes. It should also be noted that the automatic authorisation for which this section provides cannot be terminated by action of the UK authorities, but must depend on action taken in the home member state of the scheme. The reason for this is that the government concluded that, although art 52(2) of the UCITS directive permits action by a host state in support of marketing rules, termination of authorisation would not be proportionate to the end to be achieved and would accordingly be inconsistent with Community law. The authorisation is, however, limited to activities in relation to the scheme itself.

PERSONS AUTHORISED BY THE SECRETARY OF STATE

3.62 Section 25 provides for a person holding an authorisation granted by the Secretary of State to be an authorised person. The functions of the Secretary of State under this direct authorisation regime are capable of transfer to a designated agency. Applications for authorisation are dealt with by s 26. For the transitional provision applying, see para 1 of Sch 15.

GRANT AND REFUSAL OF DIRECT AUTHORISATION

3.63 By s 27(2), the Secretary of State (or, on transfer, agency) must grant an application for direct authorisation made in accordance with the required procedure if it appears to him from the information provided by the applicant and having regard to any other information in his possession that the applicant is a 'fit and proper' person to carry on the investment business and provide the services described in the application.

3.64 The expression 'fit and proper' is one of the fundamental concepts of the legislation. It applies not only for the direct authorisation regime, but also to those authorised as members of a recognised self-regulating organisation. But it is not a concept with any clearly defined content. Instead, it requires a judgment to be made. Nor does that judgment require all applicants to meet the same standards. What is needed to be 'fit and proper' will vary according to the investment business to be carried on and services to be held out as capable of being provided. It is clear, though, that the concept includes considerations of honesty, competence and solvency.

3.65 While it will be noted that the subsection creates a presumptive right to authorisation, this only arises if 'it appears' that the applicant satisfies the 'fit and proper' test. Where the Secretary of State (or agency) is unable to form the view that the applicant appears to satisfy the fit and proper test, he has a discretion whether or not to grant authorisation, under s 27(1). It is considered, however, that the Secretary of State may in these circumstances be reluctant to exercise the discretion by granting authorisation, in view of the fact that the provisions on grant, refusal, withdrawal and suspension of direct authorisation involve an investigatory Tribunal (see para **7.01**). Where there is any reasonable doubt whether a person is fit and proper to be authorised, the Act provides for the Tribunal to be the body which investigates the case.

3.66 In deciding whether to grant or refuse an application, the Secretary of State (or agency) may take into account any matter relating to any person who is or will be employed by or associated with the applicant for the purposes of the business in question, to any person who is or will be acting as an appointed representative in relation to that business, and:

(a) if the applicant is a body corporate, to any director or controller of the body, to any other body corporate in the same group or to any director or controller of any such body corporate;

(b) if the applicant is a partnership, to any of the partners;

(c) if the applicant is an unincorporated association, to any member of the governing body of the association or any officer or controller of the association (s 27(3)) (but see para 39 of Sch 11 as to regulated friendly societies).

The Secretary of State (or agency) may also have regard to any business which the applicant proposes to carry on in connection with his investment business (s 27(4)).

3.67 On an initial application (but not on a subsequent withdrawal or suspension or authorisation) the Secretary of State (or agency) has to have regard to any authorisation of the applicant to carry on investment business in a member state of the EEC other than the United Kingdom (s 27(5)).

3.68 Section 27(6)–(8) contains special provisions applying to authorisations granted to partnerships and unincorporated associations and as to notice of the grant of authorisation.

WITHDRAWAL AND SUSPENSION OF DIRECT AUTHORISATION

3.69 The Secretary of State (or agency) may withdraw or suspend any authorisation granted by him if it appears:

(a) that the holder of the authorisation is not a fit and proper person to carry on the investment business which he is carrying on or proposing to carry on; or

(b) without prejudice to para (a) above, that the holder of the authorisation has committed certain regulatory infringements (s 28(1)).

3.70 It may appear surprising that ground (b) has been included in addition to ground (a). It is suggested that the reason is that, even where there are not sufficient grounds for it to appear to the Secretary of State (or agency) that the holder of the authorisation does not satisfy the fit and proper test, he should be able to withdraw or suspend the authorisation pending an investigation by the Tribunal.

3.71 In deciding whether to withdraw or suspend authorisation on 'fit and proper' grounds, the same factors can be taken into account as on grant of authorisation, except, as noted above, that authorisation in other EEC Member States will not be relevant (s 28(2)). The regulatory infringements whose commission can trigger withdrawal or suspension of authorisation are:

(a) contravening any provision of the Act or any rules or regulations made under it;

(b) furnishing false, inaccurate or misleading information in purported compliance with any such provisions; and

(c) contravening any prohibition or requirement imposed under the Act (s 28(1)(b)).

In addition, these rules, prohibitions and requirements are taken to include, where they apply, the rules of a recognised self-regulating organisation, the investment business rules of a recognised professional body and prohibitions or requirements imposed by virtue of any of them (s 28(3)).

3.72 When authorisation is suspended the holder is not an authorised person (s 28(4)). Notwithstanding this, intervention powers and powers to obtain winding-up and administration orders are exercisable against authorised persons whose authorisation has been suspended.

3.73 The procedure for refusal of applications (including applications to vary the terms of a suspension of authorisation) and for withdrawal or suspension of authorisation includes a notice of the intention to act. This must state the reasons for which the action is proposed, where the case concerns a proposed withdrawal or suspension, the date on which it is proposed to take effect and, in the case of a suspension, its proposed duration (s 29).

3.74 The notice is to be given to the applicant or authorised person, but in addition may need to be given to other persons. This arises where the reasons stated in the notice:

'relate specifically to matters which:

(a) refer to a person identified in the notice other than the applicant or the holder of the authorisation; and
(b) are in the opinion of the Secretary of State (or, on transfer, agency) prejudicial to that person in any office or employment.' (s 29(3))

An example would be where one of the reasons given was that a particular director of the applicant or authorised person had acted improperly. No notice need be given where the Secretary of State considers it impracticable to do so. This is likely to arise, for example, where the whereabouts of the person concerned are not known.

3.75 A notice given under this procedure must give 'particulars of the right to require the case to be referred to the Tribunal'. This right arises not merely for the person on whom the notice is served but also for those on whom copies are served on the basis of matters prejudicial to them in an office or employment. The particulars given will clearly need to include the period within which the person concerned can require the case to be referred to the Tribunal.

3.76 Where a case is not required to be referred to the Tribunal within that period by a person on whom a notice (not a copy notice) is served, the Secretary of State (or, on transfer, agency) must:

(a) give that person written notice of the refusal, withdrawal or suspension; or

(b) give that person written notice of the grant of the application or, as the case may be, written notice that the authorisation is not to be withdrawn or suspended (s 29(5)).

3.77 The fact that this subsection contemplates the Secretary (or agency) changing his mind after service of the notice but without a reference to the Tribunal would appear to contemplate informal explanations or representations being given or made by the person concerned during the period.

3.78 The Secretary of State (or agency) is expressly empowered to give public notice of final decisions of this kind, with reasons, except that, for notices that the application is to be granted or authorisation is not to be withdrawn or suspended, he cannot do so unless the person concerned consents. There is no express power to give public notice of service of a notice of intention. Public notice may however be given of the exercise of intervention powers, including a statement of reasons, at any time (s 70(6)).

3.79 The provisions of s 29(5) on notice to the person concerned and public notice also apply where the person concerned withdraws the case from the Tribunal (s 100(5)).

DIRECT AUTHORISATION: WITHDRAWAL OF APPLICATIONS AND AUTHORISATIONS BY CONSENT

3.80 An application for direct authorisation may be withdrawn before it is granted or refused (s 30(1)). The Secretary of State (or agency) therefore has no power to prevent the withdrawal of an application, although he may refuse it before it is withdrawn.

3.81 An authorisation can itself be withdrawn by the Secretary of State (or agency) at the request or with the consent of the authorised person, except that there is a special entitlement to refuse where it is considered 'that the public interest requires any matter affecting the authorised person to be investigated as a preliminary to a decision on the question whether the Secretary of State should in respect of that person exercise his powers' to withdraw or suspend authorisation under any other provision of Pt I of the Act. Withdrawal of authorisation can also be refused where in the opinion of the Secretary of State (or, on transfer, agency) it is desirable that the intervention powers should be exercised or continue in force.

3.82 There is an express provision for public notice to be given of withdrawal of authorisation at the request or with the consent of the authorised person (s 30(4)). There is no such provision for withdrawal of applications.

'PERSONS AUTHORISED IN OTHER MEMBER STATES'

3.83 The Act provides automatic authorisation for 'Europersons', that is, those carrying on investment business here on a 'services' basis from another EEC member state who hold an authorisation there granted under an equivalent or harmonised regime (s 31). The details of this authorisation route will be considered in the following paragraphs. For its effect in relation to insurance companies, see para 2(3) of Sch 10.

3.84 A person carrying on investment business in the UK is authorised by this route if:

'(a) he is established in a member state other than the United Kingdom (see para **3.86** below),

(b) the law of that state recognises him as a national of that or another member state; *and*

(c) he is for the time being authorised under that law to carry on investment business or investment business of any particular kind.'

3.85 It will also be appreciated that the category of those authorised by this route will be reduced by the 'Additional exclusions for persons without permanent place of business in the United Kingdom' in Pt IV of Sch 1. This is because the authorisation only applies to persons 'carrying on investment business *in the United Kingdom*'. Once authorised, however, these activities will be subject to regulation, as explained in para **2.02**.

3.86 The expression 'established in a member state other than the United Kingdom' is given a special meaning. A person so established must not merely have his head office situated in the member state concerned. In addition, he must not transact investment business from a permanent place of business maintained by him in the UK (s 31(2)). It is this which limits the scope of the authorisation to business done on a 'services' basis.

3.87 This authorisation applies to a person only if particular requirements are satisfied by the provisions of 'the law under which he is authorised to carry on the investment business in question'. It is considered that, from its role within the Act as a whole, the reference to 'the law under which he is *authorised* to carry on the investment business in question' must be regarded as referring only to the law as to authorisation (including suspension and withdrawal of authorisation). In particular, it is considered that there is no requirement for equivalence of rules or monitoring and enforcement. These are the responsibility of the Secretary of State (or, on transfer, agency).

3.88   The first of the two alternative requirements to be satisfied is that the provisions of the law under which the person is authorised must:

'. . . afford to investors in the United Kingdom protection, in relation to his carrying on of that business, which is at least equivalent to that provided for them by the provisions of (Ch 3 of Pt I of the Act) relating to members of recognised self-regulating organisations or to persons authorised by the Secretary of State' (s 31(3)(a))

It will be noted that, consistently with the test applying only to authorisation, suspension and withdrawal of authorisation, equivalence is only to be with the provisions of Ch 3 relating to members of a recognised self-regulating organisation or to direct authorisation. The provisions of Ch 3 concerning *members* of recognised self-regulating organisations are for them to be authorised by virtue of their membership, and, they are to authorised only for so long as they meet the organisation's 'fit and proper' test. Similarly, the provisions of Ch 3 concerning persons with direct authorisation relate only to the grant of authorisation and its suspension or withdrawal. The provisions of the law under which persons are authorised can be equivalent either to the 'fit and proper' test for direct authorisation or to that for members of recognised self-regulating organisations. It may be authorisation under a public system or a private one, so long as it is an authorisation in the sense of authority to carry on business which may not otherwise lawfully be carried on.

3.89   The second of the two alternatives looks essentially to the future rather than the present and requires the law under which the person concerned is authorised to satisfy the provisions of a Community 'harmonisation' instrument relating to the carrying on of investment business or investment business of a particular kind (s 31(3)(b)). This alternative would appear to apply even to the case of a 'minimum standards' directive not specifically directed to establishing the necessary standards for freedom to provide services within the Community.

3.90   There are procedures for the Secretary of State (or, on transfer, agency) to certify equivalence and for the home member state to certify compliance with a Community instrument (s 31(4) and (5)).

3.91   It will be seen that, even if the conditions for authorisation are only satisfied for one kind of investment business, the scope of the authorisation is not itself limited to that kind of investment business. The business which may be carried on under the authorisation may, however, be limited, as explained in paragraphs below.

EUROPERSON'S NOTICE OF COMMENCEMENT OF BUSINESS

3.92   A Europerson will be guilty of an offence 'unless, not less than seven days before beginning to carry on investment business in the United

Kingdom, he has given notice of his intention to do so to the Secretary of State (or, on transfer, agency)' (and see also para 7 of Sch 15). The notice must be in writing unless another method, for example, a direct computer link, has been approved.

3.93   The notice must contain particular items of information required by the Act and comply with any requirements as to form and verification which are prescribed. Among the items of information required by the Act is a 'business plan' for the firm's UK activities, that is 'information as to the investment business which that person proposes to carry on in the United Kingdom and the services which he will hold himself out as able to provide in the carrying on of that business'. By s 48(2)(a)(ii), conduct of business rules can prohibit a Europerson from 'carrying on, or holding himself out as carrying on, investment business of a kind or on a scale other than that notified' in this notice or, to enable the business plan to be varied, in accordance with the rules themselves.

3.94   In addition, the notice must contain information about a Europerson's authorisation in his home member state. If the Europerson's UK business plan goes beyond the business covered by his home state authorisation, exercise of the intervention powers, particularly the 'restriction of business' power, may be appropriate.

3.95   Failure to give the required notice is an offence, punishable by fine, but subject to a 'due diligence' defence. Since giving the notice is not a condition for the applicability of authorisation as a Europerson, however, the validity of the authorisation is not affected.

TERMINATION AND SUSPENSION OF EUROPERSON'S AUTHORISATION

3.96   The Act provides for the termination or suspension of a Europerson's authorisation (s 33). (The expression 'termination' appears to have been chosen, rather than 'withdrawal', because the authorisation is not *granted*, but is an automatic one for which the Act provides.) The grounds are essentially similar to those for withdrawal and suspension of direct authorisation, discussed at para **3.69** ff, ante, except that they do not include failure to satisfy a 'fit and proper' test, again, presumably, on the basis that the 'fit and proper' test is a matter for the authorities of the home member state. In addition, however, there is a procedure for consulting those authorities (s 33(4)) and the Secretary of State (or agency) must revoke a direction terminating or suspending a Europerson's authorisation if he is satisfied, after consulting them, that they will secure the Europerson's compliance with those requirements here whose breach can give rise to termination or suspension under the procedure (s 33(5)). For limitations on mere powers in the case of insurance companies, see para 8 of Sch 10.

NOTICE OF PROPOSED TERMINATION OR SUSPENSION OF EUROPERSON'S AUTHORISATION

3.97 The procedure for notice of proposed termination or suspension of a Europerson's authorisation is essentially the same in effect as that for withdrawal or suspension of direct authorisation. The provisions on references to the Tribunal and public notice of decisions are also materially unchanged. The latter are again applied on withdrawal of a reference by the person concerned (s 100(5)).

Exempted persons

BANK OF ENGLAND

3.98 The Bank of England is an exempted person (s 35).

INVESTMENT EXCHANGES

3.99 A recognised investment exchange is an exempted person 'as repects anything done in its capacity as such which constitutes investment business' (s 36).

INVESTMENT EXCHANGES: CONCEPTS EXPLAINED

3.100 The Act makes no attempt to define 'investment exchange', but allows for applications for recognition to be made by 'any body corporate or unincorporated association' (s 37(1)). Rules and guidance of an investment exchange are, however, defined and distinguished (s 36(2)–(3)).

INVESTMENT EXCHANGES: PROCEDURE ON APPLICATION FOR RECOGNITION

3.101 The procedure on application to be recognised as an investment exchange is the same as that for recognition as a self-regulating organisation, although different information is required to be given by s 37(2).

INVESTMENT EXCHANGES: BASIS OF GRANT OF RECOGNITION

3.102 There is a discretion whether or not to recognise an investment exchange which fulfils the specified minimum requirements for recognition. In other words, in contradistinction to the position on recognition of a self-regulating organisation, there is no 'presumptive right' to recognition, even of the limited kind which applies there (see para **3.17**). This reflects the absence of an express 'need criterion' of the kind provided for recognition of SROs. It does, however, within the overall purposes of the Act, provide greater scope for other requirements, additional to those specified in the Act, to be imposed as conditions for recognition.

3.103   Recognition is, of course, subject to the competition scrutiny procedure discussed post (Ch 12). Otherwise the Act allows for recognition if 'it appears' that the requirements of Sch 4 are satisfied. Reasons are to be given in writing on a refusal.

INVESTMENT EXCHANGES: STATUTORY REQUIREMENTS FOR RECOGNITION: FINANCIAL RESOURCES

3.104   The first of the Sch 4 requirements is that the exchange must have 'financial resources sufficient for the proper performance of its functions'. An express general requirement of this kind is needed for an investment exchange, but not for a self-regulating organisation, because of an investment exchange's potential role in ensuring performance of transactions done on it (see para **3.106**). A self-regulating organisation's financial resources, in the absence of such a function, are addressed by the other requirements applicable, particularly that for an SRO to have adequate arrangements and resources for effective monitoring and enforcement.

INVESTMENT EXCHANGES: STATUTORY REQUIREMENTS FOR RECOGNITION: SAFEGUARDS FOR INVESTORS

3.105   By para 2 of the Schedule the rules and practices of the exchange must 'ensure that business transacted by means of its facilities is conducted in an orderly manner and so as to afford proper protection to investors'. In particular, it must:

'(a) limit dealings on the exchange to investments in which there is a proper market; and

(b) where relevant, require issuers of investments dealt in on the exchange to comply with such obligations as will, so far as possible, afford to persons dealing in the investments proper information for determining their current value.'

For listed securities, compliance by The Stock Exchange with the Act's provisions on listing are to be taken as satisfying this requirement.

3.106   In addition, as contemplated by the comments made about the 'financial resources' requirement, the exchange 'must either have its own arrangements for ensuring the performance of transactions effected on [it], or ensure their performance by means of services provided under clearing arrangements made by it with a recognised clearing house'. The exchange must also 'either itself have, or secure the provision on its behalf, of satisfactory arrangements for recording' transactions effected on it (Sch 4 para 2(5)).

INVESTMENT EXCHANGES: OTHER STATUTORY REQUIREMENTS

3.107 An investment exchange must also, to be recognised, comply with essentially standard requirements as to 'monitoring and enforcement', 'investigation of complaints' and 'promotion and maintenance of standards'.

INVESTMENT EXCHANGES: REVOCATION OF RECOGNITION

3.108 The recognition of an investment exchange can be revoked if at any time it appears that any requirement of Sch 4 is not satisfied, or that the exchange has failed to comply with any obligation to which it is subject by virtue of the Act (s 37(7)) (for example, to supply information). The notice and representations procedure on revocation of the recognition of a self-regulating organisation also applies here.

INVESTMENT EXCHANGES: INTERMEDIATE CONTROLS

3.109 In addition to revocation of recognition, the compliance order procedure is also available, both for the requirements of the Schedule and the other obligations mentioned (s 37(8)).

CLEARING HOUSES

3.110 A recognised clearing house is an exempted person 'as respects anything done by it in its capacity as a person providing clearing services for the transaction of investment business'. The Act eschews a definition of 'clearing house', but provides ones for the rules of a clearing house and guidance issued by one, again distinguishing rules from guidance (s 38(2)–(3)).

CLEARING HOUSES: PROCEDURE ON APPLICATION FOR RECOGNITION

3.111 The application procedure is also the same as that for recognition as a self-regulating organisation, but of course, different information is to be provided to assess the fulfilment of different requirements (s 39(2)).

CLEARING HOUSES: BASIS OF GRANT OF RECOGNITION

3.112 As with recognition of an investment exchange, there is a discretion whether or not to recognise a clearing house, for similar reasons and with similar effects. Recognition is, too, subject to the competition scrutiny discussed in Ch 12.

CLEARING HOUSES: STATUTORY REQUIREMENTS FOR RECOGNITION

3.113 The prescribed requirements for recognition, though, are that the clearing house:

(a) has sufficient financial resources for the proper performance of its functions;

(b) fulfils the standard requrement for adequacy of monitoring and enforcement arrangements;

(c) provides or is able to provide clearing services which would enable a recognised investment exchange to make arrangements with it that satisfy the requirements of Sch 4; and

(d) fulfils the standard requirement for promotion and maintenance of standards (s 39(4)).

3.114 The role of a recognised clearing house is thus one which is performed in conjunction with a recognised investment exchange, by it providing clearing services to the exchange. This does not, though, mean that the status of being a recognised clearing house is a dependent one, which cannot be held by a body which does not have arrangements with a recognised investment exchange. The requirements linking clearing houses to exchanges are hypothetical in form, and, so long as a body is 'able to provide' clearing services fulfilling the necessary requirements, it is not necessary that such services should actually be provided. However, it is difficult to see that satisfaction of the requirements could be assessed other than in relation to a particular investment exchange.

CONTROLS OVER RECOGNISED CLEARING HOUSE

3.115 A recognised clearing house is subject to the same statutory controls as a recognised investment exchange, that is, the revocation of its recognition, and the compliance order procedure. These may be invoked in corresponding circumstances (having regard to the different requirements) and are subject to the same safeguards. For the notification requirements applicable, see para **3.119**.

OVERSEAS INVESTMENT EXCHANGES AND CLEARING HOUSES

3.116 Some overseas investment exchanges and clearing houses might, it could be thought, have difficulty fulfilling the usual requirements, but nevertheless be suitable candidates for a form of recognition. Accordingly, special provisions apply where a body or association applying for recognition as an investment exchange or clearing house has its head office situated in a country (including any territory or part of a country or territory) outside the UK. The applicant must provide a UK address for service and different recognition requirements apply. Instead of the requirements of the relevant schedule needing to be satisfied:

(a) the applicant must be subject to supervision in its home country, which, together with its own rules and practices, provides UK investors with equivalent protection to that provided by the Act for domestic exchanges and clearing houses;

(b) the applicant must be able and willing to co-operate, by the sharing of information and otherwise, with relevant UK regulators; and

(c) there must be adequate arrangements for such co-operation between the home country supervisors and relevant UK regulators.

3.117 It should be noted that deciding on recognitions of this kind, perhaps because of the possibility of implications for international relations, is not capable of transfer to a designated agency (s 114(6)). The Secretary of State is also empowered to refuse recognition under this route on grounds of reciprocity (s 40(3)).

3.118 A recognised investment exchange or clearing house which is recognised under this route is described as an 'overseas investment exchange' or 'overseas clearing house' (s 40(6)). The usual revocation and compliance order procedures apply, on corresponding grounds and revocation is also possible on the basis that it appears desirable in the interest of investors or potential investors in the United Kingdom (s 40(4)). There appears to be no procedure to revoke recognition on the basis that adequate arrangements do not exist for co-operation between the home supervisors and the UK authorities or on grounds of reciprocity.

RECOGNISED INVESTMENT EXCHANGES AND CLEARING HOUSES: NOTIFICATION REQUIREMENTS

3.119 Recognised investment exchanges and recognised clearing houses (including overseas investment exchanges and clearing houses) may be subject to notice and information requirements under regulation-making powers for this purpose in standard form (s 41). They are also subject to the standard requirement to give seven days' notice of changes to rules or to guidance 'intended to have continuing effect and issued in writing or other legible form'. In addition, they are required to give seven days' notice of certain changes in clearing relationships (s 41(5)–(6)).

LLOYD'S

3.120 There is an exemption for 'the Society of Lloyd's and persons permitted by the Council of Lloyd's to act as *underwriting agents* at Lloyd's'. The exemption covers 'investment business carried on in connection with or for the purpose of insurance business at Lloyd's'. It will be appreciated that the exemption does not extend to 'names' at Lloyd's or to Lloyd's brokers.

3.121 A Lloyd's syndicate may be a collective investment scheme under the Act (unless it falls within s 76(6)(b)). If it is a collective investment scheme, its establishment, operation or winding up will be investment business as well as any investment management. Accordingly, these activities would be authorisable if undertaken by persons not covered by the exemption, although this must be very rare. In addition, the rights of 'names' would be investments, as units in a collective investment scheme (Sch 1, para 6). Advice on, or promotion of, participation in syndicates would thus be authorisable if those concerned are not exempt, but, by an authorised person, would be subject to the restriction on authorised persons promoting collective investment schemes which are not authorised unit trusts or recognised schemes. Again, no doubt, examples would be rare. Promotion by a person who is not authorised, for example, a person acting within the exemption provided by this section, is however not restricted.

LISTED MONEY MARKET INSTITUTIONS

3.122   The Act provides an exemption procedure for listed money market institutions (s 43). A 'listed institution' is 'a person for the time being included in a list maintained by the Bank of England' for the purpose (s 43(1)). The conditions for admission and removal require the approval of the Treasury (s 43(2)). There are provisions for publication of the list and the provision of certified copies, which are to be evidence of their contents (s 43(3)–(4)). The exemption is designed to enable the Bank of England to act as regulator of the wholesale money markets.

3.123   A listed institution is to be an exempt person 'in respect of, and of anything done for the purposes of, any transaction to which Part I or Part II of Schedule 5' applies. The words 'anything done for the purposes of' will presumably cover giving advice as to such transactions. In addition, the exemption covers any arrangements made by the institution with a view to other persons entering into a transaction to which Pt III of that Schedule applies. Since this is an exemption, rather than an exclusion from the activities constituting investment, activities covered by the exemption remain investment business. If done by a person who is authorised, they could accordingly be regulated as investment business.

3.124   The kinds of investments these transactions may involve are, broadly, of three kinds. The first kind, which are essentially debt instruments, are set out in para 2(2)(a) to (e) of the Schedule. Transactions in these investments are capable of falling within the exemption only if they are not 'regulated by the rules of a recognised investment exchange'. Any debt instruments which are admitted to listing on a recognised investment exchange but not subject to rules are therefore capable of falling within the exemption.

3.125   The second kind of investments to which the exemption can apply may be described as contractual investments. Those involved are, broadly, options and futures on debt instruments, on currency, and on gold or silver, together with corresponding 'contracts for differences' and options on any of them (paras 2(2)(f)–(i). In this case, the exemption will not be available where the transaction is not made on a recognised investment exchange or 'expressed to be as so made'. The reference to transactions 'expressed to be' as made on a recognised investment exchange would appear to cover 'back to back' transactions with an exchange member, so keeping these within the Financial Services Act regime.

3.126 The third kind of transaction which may be covered by the exemption is a repurchase agreement (known as a 'repo') involving 'debentures' or 'government and public securities' (Sch 5, para 3). No investment exchange qualification applies in this case.

3.127 Part I of the Schedule covers transactions entered into by a listed institution *as principal* (or as agent for another listed institution). In this case, no minimum size criterion or 'monetary limit' applies. Part II of the Schedule covers transactions involving outsiders ('unlisted persons') for which monetary limits are prescribed. In the case of the kinds of investment described above as 'debt instruments' and 'contractual investments', the size criterion is satisfied if the transaction is of the prescribed size or if a transaction fulfilling particular conditions has been entered into in the prescribed size with the same person in the previous eighteen months (para 6). In the case of a 'repo', a size is also prescribed, but this applies for every transaction (para 7). Part III of the Schedule covers transactions *arranged by* listed institutions (para 9). In this case any monetary limit applying to the transaction arranged will apply and monetary limits are also applied to arranging transactions between unlisted persons (paras 9–11).

APPOINTED REPRESENTATIVES

3.128 An 'appointed representative' is an exempted person 'as respects investment business carried on by him *as such a representative*' (s 44). This provision enables certain activities by firms to be regulated essentially as if they had been engaged in by employees, rather than a firm carrying on a business. It may be expected to be of particular use to self-employed 'agents' of life assurance and unit trust companies, although it is not limited to firms of this kind.

3.129 An appointed representative is a person who is employed by an authorised person ('his principal') under a contract for services complying with particular requirements and for whose activities in carrying on particular investment business his principal has accepted responsibility in writing. This is the investment business carried on by the representative in his capacity as such to which the exemption applies (s 44(2)). It should be noted that the investment business activities to which the exemption can apply are limited to particular activities in procuring and advising on entering into investment agreements with the principal or, if not prohibited by the contract, with other authorised persons (s 44(3)).

3.130 Essentially, then, an appointed representative is brought within the scope of his principal's authorisation. He is, though, limited in the activities which he can carry on under the exemption. In particular, it does not enable him to enter into investment agreements himself, so he cannot deal in investments, undertake investment management, or even be retained by his customers as an adviser.

3.131 The exemption could permit a person to be the appointed representative of more than one principal (see references in s 64(4)(b)). An appointed representative's activities in marketing and advising can be limited, though, in view of the references to 'investment agreements entered into with his principal, or (*if not prohibited by his contract*), with other persons'. The Act enables conduct of business rules to include provision 'requiring the principals of appointed representatives to impose restrictions on the investment business carried on by them' (s 48(2)(f)). This can accordingly be used to restrict the activities which may be carried on by an appointed representative 'as such a representative'. The contract of services under which an appointed representative is employed must also make provision for such restrictions to be imposed, so that the exercise of the conduct of business rule power need not involve requiring the principal to break existing contracts (s 44(4) and (5)).

3.132 In order to give effect to the principal's acceptance of responsibility the Act itself provides for a principal to be 'responsible to the same extent as if he had expressly authorised it, for anything said or done or omitted by the representative in carrying on the investment business for which (the principal) has accepted responsibility' (s 44(6)). This gives third parties clear recourse directly against the principal so it avoids the difficulties which could otherwise result from the fact that they were not parties to the contract accepting responsibility, and also avoids any need to fulfil the usual conditions for making a principal liable for his agent's actions.

3.133 Further, in determining whether an authorised person has complied with any provision contained in or made under the Act or any rules of a recognised self-regulating organisation or professional body, anything which an appointed representative of his has said, done or omitted 'as respects investment business for which the authorised person has accepted responsibility' is to be treated as having been said, done or omitted by the authorised person (s 44(7)). In this case special provision is made to limit the effect in attributing the representative's knowledge or intentions to the principal for the purposes of deciding whether the principal has committed a criminal offence. These are to be attributed only where, in all the circumstances, this is reasonable. The effect of this subsection should be particularly noted in connection with s 83. Their combined effect would appear to be to preclude a manager of an authorised unit trust from accepting responsibility for the activities of an appointed representative in, for example, marketing the products of a life office in the same group. The reason for this is that the representative's activities in selling life assurance would be attributed to the unit trust manager and cause him to contravene s 83. It is suggested, though, that s 44(7) cannot result in a contravention of s 16 of the Insurance Companies Act 1982. The inclusion of a reference to that section in section 22 of the Financial Services Act is not considered to make it a 'provision contained in' the Act.

MISCELLANEOUS EXEMPTIONS

3.134   Section 45(1) provides a series of miscellaneous exemptions which are self-explanatory. Section 45(2) provides a special exemption for the trustee in bankruptcy or liquidator of an authorised person (or a person whose direct authorisation or authorisation as a European is suspended). This applies where a bankruptcy order is made or a winding up order is made in respect of a partnership. Provisions on conduct of investment business (ss 48 to 63) and intervention powers applying to firms (ss 64 to 71) are applied together with, where relevant to any of those provisions, the Chapter of the Act on references to the Tribunal. The investigation powers in ss 104, 105 and 106 are also applied in each case, the provisions concerned are applied to the same extent as they applied to the firm. In addition, if the bankrupt or partnership was subject to the rules of a recognised self-regulating organisation or professional body, the trustee or liquidator will also be subject to them. Similar provision is made for Scotland and Northern Ireland (s 45(3) and (4)).

POWER TO EXTEND OR RESTRICT EXEMPTIONS

3.135   A power is given to the Secretary of State, which is not capable of transfer to a designated agency, to provide by order for additional exemptions (s 46(1)(a)). The power can also be used to remove or restrict some of the existing exemptions. Those which can be removed or restricted are those for Lloyd's and listed money market institutions and the miscellaneous exemptions (s 46(1)(b)).

3.136   Where the order creates additional exemptions it is subject to annulment on a resolution by either House of Parliament. Where it removes or restricts one of the specified existing exemptions, a draft must be laid before and approved by each House (s 46(2)).

Chapter 4

Conduct of investment business

4.01 This chapter deals with the provisions of the Act dealt with under the heading of 'conduct of investment business'. It should be noted, though, that some of these provisions apply even to those who are not carrying on investment business or may extend to other business carried on. Even for authorised persons the coverage varies, in particular according to the extent to which use is made of self-regulation. The Securities and Investments Board Limited, as prospective designated agency, is publishing drafts of the rules and regulations it would propose to make in the exercise of transferable powers under these provisions. Subscription to regular releases may be obtained by forwarding a cheque for £25 per copy to the Board at 3 Royal Exchange Buildings, London EC3V 3NL.

Misleading statements and practices

MISLEADING STATEMENTS

4.02 Section 47(1) creates an offence applying to a person who:

'(a) makes a statement, promise or forecast which he knows to be misleading, false or deceptive or dishonestly conceals any material facts; or

(b) recklessly makes (dishonestly or otherwise) a statement, promise or forecast which is misleading false or deceptive.'

4.03 The offence only applies, however, where the person makes the statement, promise or forecast or conceals the facts for the purpose of inducing, or is reckless as to whether it may induce 'another person' to enter or offer to enter into, or to refrain from entering or offering to enter into, an investment agreement (see s 44(9)) or to exercise or refrain from exercising any rights conferred by an investment. It does not matter whether or not the person who is or may be induced is the person to whom the statement, promise or forecast is made or from whom the facts are concealed.

4.04 This provision is substantially similar to s 13(1) of the Prevention of Fraud (Investments) Act 1958, which is, of course, repealed. Together with s 133, which contains a similar provision applying to contracts of insurance which are not investment agreements, it also replaces s 73 of the Insurance Companies Act 1982.

4.05   Conduct of business rules concerning 'Chinese Walls' can have the effect of providing an exemption from this offence (see s 48(6) and para **4.31**).

MISLEADING PRACTICES

4.06   Supplementing the provision on misleading statements is a new prohibition applying to misleading acts and courses of conduct, similar in intention, if not in form, to 10b-5 of the American Securities and Exchange Commission, which prohibits manipulative or deceptive devices and contrivances.

4.07   The offence applies to a person 'who does any act or engages in any course of conduct which creates a false or misleading impression as to the market in or the price or value of any investments'. The necessary mental element is satisfied if the person does the act (or engages in the course of conduct) for the purpose of creating the false or misleading impression and 'of thereby inducing another person to acquire, dispose of, subscribe for or underwrite those investments or to refrain from doing so or to exercise, or refrain from exercising, any rights conferred by those investments' (s 47(2)). In this case, it is a defence for the person concerned to prove that he reasonably believed that his act or conduct would not create an impression that was false or misleading as to the market in or price or value of the investments (s 47(3)).

4.08   In addition, conduct of business rules about Chinese Walls (s 48(6) and see para **4.31**) or stabilisation of issues (s 48(7) and see para **4.32**) can provide exemption.

TERRITORIAL EXTENT OF OFFENCES

4.09   It was held in *Secretary of State for Trade* v *Markus* [1976] AC 35, [1975] 1 All ER 958, HL, that s 13(1) of the 1958 Act created a 'result' crime. Accordingly, it applied to acts abroad producing results in the United Kingdom, as well as to acts actually performed in the United Kingdom. This effect is preserved by a special provision on the territorial ambit of sub-s (1) (s 47(4)). Although this is negative in form, it is considered that its effect is to make clear that the offence will apply in the circumstances specified, by exhausting any other presumption of territorial limitation which would otherwise arise. There is also an extended territorial effect provided for sub-s (2) (s 47(5)).

4.10   Both the misleading statements and misleading practices offences carry penalties on indictment of up to seven years in prison, as did the provisions replaced by s 47(1).

Powers to make rules and regulations

CONDUCT OF BUSINESS RULES

4.11 Section 48 enables the Secretary of State to make rules 'regulating the conduct of investment business by authorised persons'. This power is capable of transfer to a designated agency. For general provisions as to rules regulations and orders, see para **21.70**. For provisions as to rules and regulations made by a designated agency, see Sch 9, paras 5–9.

4.12 Conduct of business rules are potentially the main way of regulating how business is actually done. The power is accordingly central to the direct regulation regime. In addition, of course, through the 'equivalence test' for the rules of a recognised self-regulating organisation (see paras **3.21–3.22**) or professional body (see para **3.45**), conduct of business rules (together with other statutory rules and regulations) will set the standards for self-regulation.

4.13 The power to make statutory conduct of business rules can be exercised to make rules which cover not just those who are directly authorised by the Secretary of State or designated agency, but also a wider category of those who are directly regulated. By sub-s (1), the rules can regulate the conduct of business *by authorised persons* 'but shall not apply to members of a recognised self-regulating organisation or recognised professional body in respect of investment business in the carrying on of which they are subject to the rules of the organisation or body'.

4.14 In addition to those directly authorised, the direct regulation regime extends—where they are not regulated by a recognised self-regulating organisation or recognised professional body—to those authorised by the provisions relating to authorised insurers, operators and trustees of recognised (EEC) collective investment schemes, and Europersons. In addition, under the transitional arrangements in para 1 of Sch 15, it will also cover those who have applied for membership of a recognised self-regulating organisation or for authorisation by the Secretary of State and who, until the application is determined, are treated as directly authorised. It is to be assumed that, on a transfer of the power to grant direct authorisations, this transitional arrangement would apply to those who had applied for authorisation by the designated agency. For the position of conduct of business rules applying to friendly societies, see the separate powers in para 14 of Sch 11, effectively extending the direct regulation regime.

4.15 On the detailed construction of the power, the expression 'investment business' may be taken to have the meaning conferred by s 1(2). But the concept of 'regulating the conduct' of investment business is extended by sub-s (2) to some matters which might not otherwise have been covered by that expression, some of which are discussed in the following paragraphs.

RESTRICTION OF BUSINESS

4.16 First, conduct of business rules may 'prohibit a person from carrying on, or holding himself out as carrying on, investment business of any kind specified in the rules' (s 48(2)(a)(i)). This could be used, for example, to prohibit an investment manager from carrying on corporate finance business, off-market dealers from dealing in shares whose listing has been suspended, or, as contemplated by s 78(4), particular persons from acting as the operator or trustee of a unit trust.

BUSINESS PLANS

4.17 Conduct of business rules may also 'prohibit a person from carrying on or holding himself out as carrying on investment business of a kind or on a scale other than that notified' (s 48(2)(a)(ii)). This enables an authorised person to be required to keep to a 'business plan'. The business plan may be one notified on the person's application for authorisation, in the case of a directly authorised person (see para **3.63**). Or it may be one notified by a Europerson under s 32(2)(a) (see para **3.93**). Or, indeed, it may be one notified under the rules themselves, in the case of other directly regulated firms and changes to business plans notified by holders of direct authorisation and Europersons.

CLASSES OF CUSTOMERS

4.18 Conduct of business rules may also prohibit a person from carrying on investment business in relation to persons other than those of a specified class or description (s 48(2)(b)). This power could be used to prohibit futures brokers from selling 'home-made' futures to non-professionals.

'MARKET MAKING'

4.19 Conduct of business rules can regulate the manner in which a person makes a market in any investments (s 48(2)(d)). It is suggested that this power could be used to impose a duty to deal.

HOLDING OUT

4.20 Conduct of business rules may regulate the manner in which a person may 'hold himself' out as carrying on investment business (s 48(2)(c)). This is potentially wider than the powers to make rules on the form and content of advertisements, since it may be doubted whether these could apply to simple oral communications. It could, perhaps, be used to regulate marketing of those transactions which ought properly not to be promoted, but may be used in response to particular situations, like the contangos and backwardations formerly restricted by r 16(2) of the Licensed Dealers (Conduct of Business) Rules 1983 (SI 1983 No 585).

ADVERTISEMENTS

4.21   Conduct of business rules may also make provision as to the form and content of advertisements in respect of investment business (s 48(2)(e)). 'Advertisements' is, of course, given its general meaning for the purposes of the legislation by s 207(2). For the purposes of this power, though, the expression does not include any advertisement which is subject to s 154 or 'which is required or permitted to be published by listing rules under Part IV of [the Act] and relates to securities which have been admitted to listing under that Part'. In addition, conduct of business rules on advertisements have effect subject to the provisions of Pt V of the Act (s 48(5)). The relationship of this power with the restrictions on advertising in ss 57–58 will also be noted. Section 57(1) restricts the issue of investment advertisements in the United Kingdom unless their contents have been approved by an authorised person. The ability to make conduct of business rules as to the form and contents of advertisements thus enables the safeguard this provides to be given concrete effect. For the particular effect of rules under this power on advertisements by nationals of other member states, see para **4.71**.

RESTRICTING THE INVESTMENT BUSINESS OF APPOINTED REPRESENTATIVES

4.22   Conduct of business rules 'can require the *principals* of appointed representatives to impose restrictions on the investment business carried on by them' (s 48(2)(f)). As explained in para **3.129**, this has the effect of restricting the scope of the appointed representative's exemption.

COMMISSIONS AND INDUCEMENTS

4.23   Conduct of business rules may require 'the disclosure of the amount or value of . . . commissions or other inducements'. They may also restrict 'the matters by reference to which or the manner in which the amount or value of commissions or inducements may be determined' (s 48(2)(g)). Accordingly, not merely may disclosure be required, but it is also possible to prohibit certain methods of calculation of commissions or inducements. This would accordingly enable conduct of business rules to prohibit, for example, calculation of commission or other inducements by reference to transaction volume or amount, the so-called 'overrider'. For a limit on the powers to control commissions and other inducements, see para **4.29**.

'CHINESE WALLS'

4.24 Conduct of business rules may make provision 'enabling or requiring information obtained by an authorised person in the course of carrying on one part of its business to be withheld by him from persons with whom he deals in the course of carrying on another part' (s 48(2)(h)). So the power is designed to assist or require the establishment of Chinese Walls across which information is not to be passed. As explained in para **4.31**, rules made under this paragraph create an exemption from the 'misleading statements' and misleading practices offences in s 47.

STABILISATION OF ISSUES

4.25 Conduct of business rules may also contain provisions as to the 'circumstances and manner in which and the time when and the period during which action may be taken for the purpose of stabilising the price of investments of any specified description' (s 48(2)(i)). Similarly, as explained in para **4.32**, post, rules under this paragraph can create an exemption from the 'misleading practices' offence in s 47(2). They can also provide an exemption from insider dealing legislation, by virtue of s 175.

SETTLEMENT OF DISPUTES

4.26 Conduct of business powers may make provision for 'arrangements for the settlement of disputes' (s 48(2)(j)). The Industrial Assurance Commissioner can delegate his functions to enable disputes to be settled under these rules (s 139(3)). Disputes under these rules can also be referred to him (s 139(4)). For a similar provision for friendly societies, see para 43 of Sch 11.

Conduct of business rules : general

RECORDS AND INSPECTION

4.27 Conduct of business rules can, too, make provision requiring the keeping of accounts and other records, as to their form and content, and for their inspection (s 48(2)(k)). The ability to provide for inspection enables 'spot-checks' to be performed.

4.28 It is expressly provided that the detailed powers for which sub-s (2) provides are 'without prejudice in the generality of subsection (1)' (s 48(3)). Accordingly, rules under the power can make provision for matters other than those mentioned in sub-s (2) or further provision as to the matters mentioned. By s 48(4), conduct of business rules 'may also regulate or prohibit the carrying on in connection with investment business of any other business' or (apparently whether or not to be carried on in connection with investment business) 'the carrying on of any other business which is held out as being for the purposes of investment'.

LIMITATIONS ON POWER TO MAKE CONDUCT OF BUSINESS RULES

4.29 While, as noted above, conduct of business rules can restrict the kinds of commission or other inducement which can be paid, they cannot impose limits on the *amount* or *value* of commissions or inducements paid or provided in connection with investment business (s 48(3)).

4.30 In addition, the scope of the power is limited in the case of 'regulated insurance companies' to marketing and pension fund management activities (Sch 10, para 4) and, in the case of the operator or trustee of a recognised (EEC) collective investment scheme, to marketing activities (s 86(7)). Although para 14 of Sch 11 prohibits rules under this section from applying to a regulated friendly society, conduct of business rules on marketing or pension fund management can be made by the Registrar. This function can also be transferred (see Sch 11, para 28).

EXEMPTION FROM CRIMINAL OFFENCES

4.31 Nothing done in conformity with rules made under the paragraph relating to Chinese Walls is to be regarded as a contravention of the misleading statements or practices offences (s 48(6)). This may be particularly relevant where the offence would otherwise be committed by a company by reason of knowledge attributed to its directors, but not in fact possessed by them. It appears that action which 'conforms' to the relevant statutory rules will be protected even if done by persons not subject to them. There is no equivalent effect for rules made by a recognised self-regulating organisation or professional body, which would appear to support this understanding.

4.32 Similarly, the misleading practices offence is not to be regarded as contravened by anything done for the purpose of stabilising the price of investments if it is done 'in conformity' with conduct of business rules made under the section (s 48(7)). For the time being, this is only to apply in respect of investments which fall within any of paras 1 to 5 of Sch 1 and are specified by the rules *and* during such period before or after the *issue* of those investments as is specified by the rules. However, the Secretary of State has power (not capable of transfer to a designated agency) to amend the provision (s 48(8)), for example, to cover stabilisation of investments already in issue. An order making such a change must be laid in draft and approved by resolution of each House (s 48(9)).

FINANCIAL RESOURCES RULES

4.33 Section 49 contains a power to make 'financial resources' rules. These are rules requiring persons authorised to carry on investment business by the direct authorisation route or as Europersons (except for insurers: para 4(4) of Sch 10) to 'have and maintain in respect of that business such financial resources as are required by the rules'. The power is exercisable by the Secretary of State, or, on transfer, a designated agency. For general provisions as to rules, regulations and orders, see para **21.70**. For provisions as to rules and regulations made by a designated agency, see Sch 9, paras 5–9. There is, though, no principle which expressly requires a designated agency to make financial resources rules.

4.34 Financial resources rules may impose requirements which are absolute or which are to vary from time to time by reference to such factors as are specified in or determined in accordance with the rules (s 49(2)(a)). It is considered that the reference to 'factors determined in accordance with the rules' would enable the rules to contain a formula, according to which the requirements could be determined. It is not, though, thought adequate to authorise sub-delegation by the Secretary of State or designated agency of the power to establish the requirements. Financial resources rules may also take account of non-investment business carried on by the person concerned, and contain provision for valuation of assets (s 49(2)(b) and (c)).

4.35 The role to be played by financial resources rules is an interesting one. On an application for direct authorisation, it will clearly be relevant to whether the applicant is fit and proper whether he would, on authorisation, find himself in breach of financial resources rules. In that sense, they can be seen as capable of establishing a minimum level of financial resources needed by an applicant for direct authorisation. A breach of financial resources rules would be a breach of a provision of rules made under the Act for the purposes of the powers to withdraw/terminate or suspend authorisation. It would clearly also be of relevance on a reference to the Tribunal (whether on a refusal or on withdrawal or suspension of authorisation) since it would seem effectively to establish that the firm does not have sufficient financial resources to carry on its business, rather than leaving the matter at large. In neither case, though, would it seem that the existence of rules would exhaust the ability to act on lack of resources under the 'fit and proper' test.

4.36 In the case of a Europerson, the existence of rules has a particular significance. It enables authorisation to be terminated by the UK authorities for lack of capital, where, if it were left to the 'fit and proper' test, this would be a matter for the home authorities (see para **3.96**).

4.37 As explained in para **4.104**, a breach of financial resources rules does not give rise to the action for damages provided for breaches of other rules.

MODIFICATION OF CONDUCT OF BUSINESS RULES AND FINANCIAL RESOURCES RULES FOR PARTICULAR CASES

4.38 The Secretary of State is given power, which is capable of transfer to a designated agency, to modify conduct of business rules and financial resources rules for particular cases (s 50). This enables him, on the application of any person to whom the rules apply, to 'alter the requirements of the rules so as to adapt them to the circumstances of that person or to any particular kind of business carried on or to be carried on by him'.

4.39 The power is not exercisable, unless it appears that:

(a) compliance with the requirements in question would be unduly burdensome for the applicant having regard to the benefit which compliance would confer on investors; and

(b) the exercise of those powers will not result in any undue risk to investors.

4.40 It should be noted that the power is not one to waive the requirements of the rules, but to alter their requirements in their application to a particular person. The altered rules need not, however, provide equivalent investor protection, so long as the no 'undue risk' requirement is fulfilled.

4.41 The powers may be exercised unconditionally or subject to conditions.

Similar power is provided for rules applying to regulated friendly societies (para 14(3) of Sch 11), although since they are not subject to financial resources rules has no application here.

CANCELLATION RULES

4.42 Power is also provided to make 'cancellation rules' (s 51). These are rules 'for enabling a person who has entered into or offered to enter into an investment agreement with an authorised person to rescind the agreement or withdraw the offer'. In other words, it is a power to allow for 'cooling off'. The power can apply to investment agreements with persons authorised by any route except regulated friendly societies, where a separate power is available (see para 15 of Sch 11). The powers are capable of transfer to a designated agency. For general provisions as to rules regulations and orders, see para **21.70**. For provisions as to rules and regulations made by a designated agency, see Sch 9, paras 5–9.

4.43 It will be seen that the power contains provision, inter alia, for the service of notices. For a principle applicable to rules under this power made by a designated agency, see para **11.10**.

NOTIFICATION REGULATIONS

4.44 Section 52 empowers the Secretary of State to make notification regulations. The power is capable of transfer to a designated agency. For general provisions as to rules regulations and orders, see para **21.70**. For provisions as to rules and regulations made by a designated agency, see Sch 9, paras 5–9. None of the 'principles applicable to designated agency's rules and regulations' is expressly relevant.

4.45   Notification regulations under this section can apply to almost all kinds of authorised persons. They cannot apply, though, to members of recognised self-regulating organisations or professional bodies unless they carry on investment business to which statutory conduct of business rules apply (s 52(3)) since it is for the organisation or body to monitor them. A separate power enables corresponding regulations to be made for regulated friendly societies (see para 16 of Sch 11).

4.46   As with notification regulations applying to recognised self-regulating organisations (see paras **3.34–3.36**) professional bodies (see para **3.55**), and investment exchanges and clearing houses (see para **3.119**), the basic provisions enable requirements to be imposed either to give notice of the occurrence of particular events (s 52(1)) or at specified times or for specified periods (s 52(2)). In addition, in this case a flavour is given of the possible content of the regulations by s 52(4).

4.47   Notification regulations can require information to be given in a specified form or be verified in a particular manner. There is also an option for the Secretary of State (or agency) to approve a 'manner' of giving notice other than in writing (s 52(5)–(6)).

INDEMNITY RULES

4.48   A power is provided to make 'rules concerning indemnity in respect of any description of civil liability incurred by an authorised person in connection with his investment business' (s 53). It will be seen that in some respects the wording here is similar to that of section 37 of the Solicitors Act 1974. These rules cannot apply to a member of a recognised self-regulating organisation or person certified by a recognised professional body in respect of business regulated by that organisation or body unless it has requested that they should do so. For the 'principle applicable to designated agencies rules and regulations' relevant to this power, see para 10 of Sch 8. (It is considered likely that the practical value of this power is likely to be eclipsed by the power, in the next section, to establish a compensation fund to which members of recognised self-regulation organisations can be compelled to subscribe.) The power cannot apply to loss arising as a result of a regulated insurance company being unable to meet its liabilities under a contract of insurance (see para 4(4) of Sch 10). For the provision applying to friendly societies, see para 17 of Sch 11.

COMPENSATION FUND

4.49   The Secretary of State is given a power, by making rules under s 54, to establish a scheme for compensating investors. The power is designed to cover 'cases where persons who are or have been authorised persons are unable, or likely to be unable, to satisfy claims in respect of any description of civil liability incurred by them in connection with their investment business' (but see para 4(4) of Sch 10). The most likely situation in which a firm will be unable to satisfy claims is where it is insolvent. It should be noted that the scheme is one for compensating investors, rather than for protecting firms. Detailed aspects of the power are dealt with in s 54(2).

4.50 A scheme made under this power is not to apply to members of a recognised self-regulating organisation except after consultation with that organisation (s 54(3)). Accordingly, as noted previously, a scheme can be made so as to apply to members of a recognised SRO even in the absence of a request by the SRO. A request is, though, needed to cover persons certified by a recognised professional body and subject to its rules in carrying on all their investment business. A scheme may not, however, apply to those in either category unless the Secretary of State (this function not being capable of transfer to a designated agency) is satisfied that the rules make sufficient provision for the administration of the scheme by a body on which their interests are adequately represented *and* for securing that the amounts they are likely to contribute reflect, so far as practicable, the amount of the claims made or likely to be made in respect of them. When a scheme applies to such persons the powers enable it to provide for the RSVO or RPB itself to administer it and to be responsible for contributions and also allow separate funds to be established within the one scheme—although with scope for payments and repayments between funds (s 54(4)). A request by a recognised professional body is not capable of being withdrawn after the rules giving effect to it have been made but the Secretary of State could still revoke (or, by implication, amend) the rules if he thought fit: s 54(5)). Rules may also be made for integrating certain procedures under these arrangements into the general procedure on a winding up, bankruptcy or sequestration (s 54(6)). For the equivalent power applying to regulated friendly societies, see para 18 of Sch 11.

CLIENTS' MONEY

4.51 The next power conferred is one to make 'clients' money' regulations (s 55). The power is capable of transfer to a designated agency. For general provisions as to rules and regulations and orders, see para **21.70**. For provisions as to rules and regulations made by a designated agency, see Sch 9, paras 5–9. Of the 'principles applicable to designated agency's rules and regulations', the principle specifically addressing these regulations is discussed in para **11.10** below, commenting on Sch 8, para 10. For the provision applying to regulated friendly societies, see para 19 of Sch 11.

4.52 Clients' money regulations under this section can apply to all authorised persons except regulated friendly societies (for their position, see para 19 of Sch 11). The power is thus unusual in enabling regulations under the Act to apply directly to members of recognised self-regulating organisations and persons certified by recognised professional bodies. This may be to avoid difficulties arising for firms with more than one regulator, who might otherwise find themselves having to operate several different client accounts, perhaps according to different rules. An even more important reason is that it is considered that the rules in a recognised self-regulating organisation could not have the effect described in para **4.54** below of providing that clients' money is held on trust.

4.53 The regulations can apply to money 'which authorised persons . . . hold in such circumstances as are specified in the regulations'. They are not limited to money which is held for clients of a firm, but can also extend to money held for counterparties or, it is considered, the firm's own account. Money to which the regulations apply is then labelled 'clients' money' in the section.

4.54 The central part of the power enables regulations under the section to 'provide that clients' money held by an authorised person is held on trust'. Money held on trust does not fall to be treated as a firm's asset on its insolvency, so protecting the beneficiaries. It is to be noted that the power actually enables the regulations to create the trust—it does not merely enable them to require firms to do so. This distinction is important, of course, because if it had been left to the firm, the sanctions for breach of the requirement would not have provided any alternative protection to 'clients'.

4.55 Clients' money regulations can also require clients' money to be paid into a client account with an institution (such as a recognised bank or licensed deposit-taker) of a kind specified in the regulations. Where the firm concerned is a member of a recognised self-regulating organisation or is a person certified by a recognised professional body, the rules of the organisation or body can determine the kind of institution where a client account can be held (s 55(2)(b)). Such an institution will not be liable as constructive trustee where money is wrongfully paid from the account unless the institution permits the payment with knowledge that it is wrongful or having deliberately failed to make enquiries in circumstances in which a reasonable and honest person would have done so (s 55(4)).

4.56 Clients' money regulations can be used to regulate payments to and from a client account (s 55(2)(c)). They can also require the keeping of accounts and records in respect of clients' money and require them to be examined and reported on by an accountant (s 55(2)(d)–(e)). The accountant must have 'such qualifications as are specified in the regulations', for example, as a member of one of the four recognised accountancy bodies. There is no scope for a recognised self-regulating organisation or professional body to substitute alternative qualifications to those specified. Where the authorised person is required to have an auditor, the regulations can require the examination and report to be performed by that auditor (s 55(3)). The requirement to have an auditor may be a statutory one or may be imposed by the rules of a recognised self-regulating organisation or professional body.

4.57 Clients' money regulations may also 'authorise the retention, to such extent and in such cases as may be specified in the regulations, of so much of clients' money as represents interest' (s 55(2)(f)). This wording reflects the principle that interest on money held on trust belongs to the beneficiary of the trust. It may, though, be desirable to obtain the benefit of the trust to protect clients' money on an insolvency even where it is legitimate for the firm to be able to retain the interest. This provision enables this to be done.

Unsolicited calls and advertising

UNSOLICITED CALLS

4.58 The Act deals with the practice of 'cold-calling' by a provision that:

' . . . except so far as permitted by regulations made by the Secretary of State, no person shall, in the course of or on consequence of an unsolicited call:

(a) made on a person in the United Kingdom; or

(b) made from the United Kingdom on a person elsewhere,

by way of business enter into an investment agreement with the person on whom the call is made or procure or endeavour to procure that person to enter into such an agreement' (s 56(1)).

'Unsolicited call' means a personal visit or oral communication made without express invitation (s 56(8)). 'Investment agreement' has the meaning given by s 44(9).

4.59 The ban is not limited to those who are authorised or even to those carrying on investment business, or doing so in the United Kingdom. It prohibits entering into investment agreements (or procuring or endeavouring to procure people to do so) 'in the course of or in consequence of an unsolicited call', so it is not a direct ban on making unsolicited calls. This reflects the fact that the provision is not directed to protection of privacy, but against undue pressure to enter into investment agreements. It also enables it to apply not merely to callers, but also to those who take the benefit of what they do.

4.60 There is an extended territorial extent, so that the prohibition can apply for calls made from overseas on persons here, as well as for calls made here on persons overseas. For the relation of this provision with the exclusion from the authorisation requirement for overseas persons, see paras **2.53–2.54**.

4.61 The prohibition only applies 'except so far as permitted by regulations made by the Secretary of State'. The power to make excepting regulations of this kind is capable of transfer to a designated agency. For general provisions as to rules, regulations and orders, see para **21.70**. For provisions as to rules and regulations made by a designated agency, see Sch 9, paras 5–9. None of the 'principles applicable to designated agency's rules and regulations' expressly deals with these regulations. The rules of a recognised self regulating organisation or recognised professional body can have a similar permissive effect (s 56(7)). For the similar provision applying to regulated friendly societies, see Sch 11, para 20.

4.62 A person is not guilty of a criminal offence by contravening the unsolicited calls prohibition (s 56(2)). He has, though, contravened a provision of the Act. This is relevant, inter alia, to provisions on withdrawal or suspension of authorisation and exercise of intervention powers.

4.63 In addition, the Act contains provisions for investment agreements entered into in the course of or in consequence of an unsolicited call to be unenforceable against the person on whom the call was made (s 56(2)). The provisions on unenforceability of such agreements are similar to—but not the same as—those on 'agreements made by or through unauthorised persons' discussed at para **3.04–3.06**. These include provisions for a court to allow such an agreement to be enforced or money and property paid or transferred under it to be retained if it is satisfied that one of three conditions applies. The first of these relates to absence of material influence on the person called (s 56(4)(a)). The second, which is without prejudice to the first, deals with the situation where the agreement can fairly be regarded as a consequence of other discussions between the parties, rather than the call, and where the person called was aware of the nature of the agreement and any risks involved in entering into it (s 56(4)(b)). The third concerns calls made by third parties satisfying particular requirements (s 56(4)(c)).

RESTRICTIONS ON ADVERTISING

4.64 Subject to a series of exceptions, 'no person other than an authorised person shall issue or cause to be issued an investment advertisement in the United Kingdom' unless its contents have been approved by an authorised person (s 57(1)). As noted previously (para **4.21**), the ability to make conduct of business rules as to the form and content of advertisements enables this safeguard to be given concrete effect. For the transitional provision applying, see Sch 15, para 8.

4.65   The expression 'investment advertisement' means 'any advertisement inviting persons to enter or offer to enter into an investment agreement or to exercise any rights conferred by an investment to acquire, dispose of, underwrite or convert an investment or containing information calculated to lead directly or indirectly to persons doing so'. 'Advertisement' is also widely defined (see s 207(2)). Finally, investment advertisements actually issued outside the United Kingdom are to be treated as issued in the United Kingdom if they are directed to persons there or made available to them 'otherwise than in a newspaper, journal, magazine or other periodical publication published or circulating principally outside the United Kingdom or in a sound or television broadcast transmitted principally for reception outside the United Kingdom' (s 207(3)).

4.66   This prohibition is treated similarly, for purposes of sanctions, to carrying on business in the United Kingdom without authorisation. The same criminal penalties apply (s 57(3)) and there is a parallel to the due diligence defence, although more limited in scope (s 57(4)). Further, similar provisions apply on unenforceability of agreements and recovery of money or other property paid or transferred. These are extended in the case of advertisements inviting people to exercise rights or containing information calculated to lead to them doing so.

4.67   The court may allow an agreement or obligation to be enforced (or money or other property paid under it to be retained) if it is satisfied that either of two conditions is fulfilled. The first relates to absence of material influence (s 57(8)(a)). The second requires the advertisement not to be misleading about particular matters and fairly to state the risks involved in them (s 57(8)(b)). There are consequential provisions similar to those for agreements made with or through unauthorised persons (s 57(9)–(10)).

EXCEPTIONS FROM RESTRICTIONS ON ADVERTISING

4.68   The restriction on advertising in s 57 is subject to a number of exceptions.

4.69   The first is for any advertisement issued or caused to be issued by, and relating only to investments issued by, certain specified kinds of public bodies (s 58(1)(a)).

4.70   The second is for any advertisement issued or caused to be issued by a person who is exempt under the provisions applying to recognised investment exchanges, recognised clearing houses, Lloyd's, listed money market institutions, appointed representatives or under the 'miscellaneous exemptions'. In this case, the advertisement must relate to a matter in respect of which the person is exempt (s 58(1)(b)).

4.71   The third is for an advertisement which is issued or caused to be issued by a national of a member state other than the United Kingdom in the course of investment business lawfully carried on by him in such a state. The advertisement must conform to any conduct of business rules 'as to the form and content of advertisements in respect of investment business' (s 58(2)(c)). As noted in the contexts of rules on stabilisation of issues and Chinese Walls, it is not necessary to be subject to rules to act in conformity with them. This exception does not apply, however, to advertisements relating to the investments described as 'certificates representing securities' (s 58(6)).

4.72   The fourth exemption covers any advertisement which is subject to the section of the Act on 'advertisements etc in connection with listing applications' or consists of or any part of listing particulars or any other document required or permitted to be published by listing rules under Pt IV of the Act or by an approved exchange under Pt V of the Act (s 58(1)(d)).

4.73   There is an exception, too, for an advertisement inviting persons to subscribe in cash for any investments to which Pt V applies (s 58(2)). This exception does not apply to any advertisement relating to 'certificates representing securities' (s 58(6)). It only applies to other investments if it is issued or caused to be issued by the person by whom the investments are to be issued and the limitation to subscription in cash excludes takeover offers. In addition, the advertisement must either be a prospectus registered in accordance with Pt V, or must be a 'mini-prospectus' containing specified matters 'and no others which would make it an investment advertisement'. The matters to be contained are:

(a) the name of the person by whom the investments are to be issued and his address or particulars of other means of communicating with him;

(b) the nature of the investments, the number offered for subscription and their nominal value and price;

(c) a statement that a prospectus for the purposes of Pt V is or will be available and, if it is not yet available, when it will be; and

(d) instructions for obtaining a copy of the prospectus.

4.74   There is also a power for the Secretary of State to disapply the restriction for investment advertisements issued in particular circumstances. This is not capable of transfer to a designated agency. For general provisions as to rules, regulations and orders, see para **21.70**. The power is to be exercised for the purpose of exempting:

(a) advertisements appearing to have a private character, whether by reason of a connection between the person issuing them and those to whom they are addressed, or otherwise;

(b) advertisements appearing to deal with investments only incidentally;

(c) advertisements issued to persons appearing to be sufficiently expert to understand any risks involved; or

(d) such other classes of advertisements as thought fit (s 58(3)).

4.75 This power may be expected to fulfil a similar role in relation to the restriction on advertisements as was fulfilled by the power to issue general consents under s 14 of the Prevention of Fraud (Investments) Act 1958. In particular, the 'private character' criterion will recall the 'domestic concern' general permission, General Permission No 4. The second criterion, for advertisements appearing to deal with investments only incidentally, would, for example, enable the exemption of advertisements for flats which also offer a share in the company managing the block. The third, 'sufficiently expert', criterion, would appear, for example to enable the exemption of screen and telex advertisements in international securities markets. The similar provision in s 160(6) should be noted.

4.76 Exempting orders of this kind may require a person who, by virtue of the order, is authorised to issue an advertisement, to comply with such requirements as are specified in the order. Exempting orders are subject to negative resolution procedure.

EMPLOYMENT OF PROHIBITED PERSONS

4.77 Most controls under the Act apply to persons who are actually carrying on investment business or, in the case of certain managers of occupational pension schemes, are treated as doing so. A power is also provided, however, over individuals employed in connection with investment business.

4.78 By s 59(1):

'. . . if it appears to the Secretary of State that any individual is not a fit and proper person to be employed in connection with investment business, or investment business of a particular kind, he may direct that he shall not, without the written consent of the Secretary of State, be employed in connection with investment business, or, as the case may be, investment business of that kind:

(a) by authorised persons or exempted persons; or

(b) by any specified authorised or exempted person or persons, or by authorised or exempted persons of any specified description.'

The references to 'employment' include references to employment 'otherwise than under a contract of service' (s 59(8)). The power is capable of transfer to a designated agency.

4.79 A direction under this section is referred to as a disqualification direction (s 59(2)). A disqualification direction must specify the date on which it is to take effect and a copy is to be served on the person to whom it relates.

4.80   It will be noted that the power does not extend to directing that an individual is not to be employed in connection with investment business at all, but only that he may not be so employed without the consent of the Secretary of State (or, on transfer, agency). Any consent to the employment of a person who is subject to a disqualification may relate to employment generally or to employment of a particular kind, may be given subject to conditions and restrictions and may also be varied from time to time (s 59(3)). A disqualification direction may be revoked (s 59(7)). The power is limited for employees of regulated insurance companies by para 4(5) of Sch 10.

4.81   Where it is proposed to make a disqualification direction in respect of a person, or to refuse an application for consent or for the variation of consent, written notice must be given to that person, or to the applicant, stating the reasons and giving particulars of the right to require the case to be referred to the Tribunal (s 59(4)). The reference to 'the applicant' here indicates that an application for consent or variation of consent may be made by a person other than the person to whom the direction relates, such as an employer or prospective employer. In this case it would appear to be the applicant, and not the person to whom the direction relates, who is invited to refer the matter to the Tribunal (s 97(1)(a), and see para **7.06**).

4.82   A person who accepts or continues in any employment in contravention of a disqualification direction is guilty of an offence and liable on summary conviction to a fine not exceeding the fifth level on the standard scale (s 59(5)).

4.83   By s 59(6), it is the duty of authorised persons and appointed representatives to take reasonable care not to employ or continue to employ a person in contravention of a disqualification direction. A breach of this duty is actionable under s 62(1)(d). For availability of information as to disqualified persons, see para **8.06**.

PUBLIC STATEMENT AS TO PERSON'S MISCONDUCT

4.84   If it appears to the Secretary of State (or, on transfer, agency) that a person who is or was an authorised person by virtue of particular sections of the Act has contravened:

(a) any provision of the statutory rules or regulations made under Ch V of Pt I or of the sections of the Act relating to unsolicited calls, restrictions on advertising or employment of prohibited persons; or

(b) any condition imposed under the section relating to modification of conduct of business rules and financial resources rules for particular cases, he may publish a statement to that effect (s 60(1)).

4.85   The persons concerned are those who are or were authorised by the sections of the Act relating to authorised insurers, operators and trustees of recognised EEC collective investment schemes, direct authorisation and authorisation of Europersons. The equivalent provision for friendly societies (Sch 11, para 21) means that the entire direct regulation regime is covered. The provision does not, though, cover public statements about individuals employed in connection with investment business. While it may be doubted whether an express power is needed in order to make a public statement of the kinds which this provision covers, its inclusion has a number of potential advantages. In particular, where the function is transferred to a designated agency, it brings it clearly within the agency's exemption from liability in damages (see para **21.05**).

4.86   Before publishing a public statement as to misconduct, the Secretary of State (or agency) must give the person concerned written notice of the proposed statement and of the reasons (s 60(2)). Where the reasons relate specifically to matters which:

(a) refer to a person identified in the notice other than the person who is or was the authorised person; and

(b) are in the opinion of the Secretary of State (or agency) prejudicial to that person in any office or employment,

the Secretary of State (or agency) must, unless he considers impracticable to do so, serve a copy of the notice on the other person (s 60(3)). For commentary on the similar provision applying to notices of refusal, suspension or withdrawal of direct authorisation, see para **3.74**. A notice under this procedure must give particulars of the right to require the case to be referred to the Tribunal (s 60(4)). This right extends to those on whom a copy of the notice is served on the basis of matters prejudicial in an office or employment (s 97(1)(b)). Where the case is not required to be referred to the Tribunal within the prescribed period by a person on whom a notice (not a copy of a notice) is served, the Secretary of State (or, on transfer, agency) must give that person notice that the statement is or is not to be published (s 60(5)). If it is to be published then, after publication, a copy must be sent to the person concerned and to any person on whom a copy of the notice was served on the basis of 'matters prejudicial'. The provisions on notice where the case is not referred to the Tribunal also apply where the person concerned withdraws it (s 100).

4.87   For the application of this provision to exercise of intervention powers against firms, see s 71. For its application to the exercise of intervention powers against authorised unit trusts, see s 91(4).

INJUNCTIONS

4.88 The Act enables the court to grant injunctions (or, in Scotland, interdicts) on the application of the Secretary of State or, on transfer, a designated agency (s 61(1)–(2)). The similar procedure applying to contraventions of the restrictions on persons entitled to carry on investment business is discussed at paras **3.07–3.10**. The provisions on interdicts are the same as those for injunctions and are not discussed separately. The court may grant such orders if it is satisfied:

(a) that there is a reasonable likelihood that any person will contravene particular provisions or conditions;

(b) that any person has contravened any such provision or condition and that there is a reasonable likelihood that the contravention will continue or be repeated; or

(c) that any person has contravened any such provision or condition and that there are steps that could be taken for remedying the contravention (s 61(1)).

A similar provision for regulated friendly societies is to be found in para 22 of Sch 11.

4.89 The provisions and conditions which are specified in s 60 as able to be enforced in this way (and which may also be enforced by the restitution order procedure described at para **4.94** ff) are:

(a) statutory rules or regulations made under Ch V of Pt 1 of the Act;

(b) the sections of the Act relating to misleading statements and practices, unsolicited calls, restrictions on advertising and employment of prohibited persons;

(c) any requirements imposed by an order making exceptions from the section on restrictions on advertising;

(d) the rules of a recognised self-regulating organisation, recognised professional body, recognised investment exchange or recognised clearing house to which the person concerned is subject and which regulate the carrying on by him of investment business (but see para **4.91**); and

(e) any conditions imposed under the section relating to modification of conduct of business rules and financial resources rules for particular cases.

4.90 Where the powers are available the court may grant an injunction restraining the contravention (or, in Scotland, an interdict prohibiting the contravention) or, as the case may be, make an order requiring that person, and any other person who appears to the court to have been knowingly concerned in the contravention, to take such steps as the court may direct to remedy it.

4.91   An application cannot be made to enforce rules of a recognised self-regulating organisation, professional body, investment exchange or clearing house unless it appears that it is itself unable or unwilling to act (s 61(2)).

4.92   It may seem surprising that this provision enables the court to grant injunctions to enforce provisions, such as those relating to misleading statements and practices, which create criminal offences. This cannot be solely in order to enable orders to be made requiring remedial steps to be taken (although this is an important practical addition) since the provision clearly enables injunctions to be granted too. It is suggested that the explanation is that injunctions granted will restrain the performance of an act, rather than the commission of an offence. They accordingly enable the court to be satisfied that a particular act or course of conduct will constitute a contravention, and to grant an injunction accordingly. Committing that act or engaging in that course of conduct then becomes an offence as a contempt of court and punishable as such, without it being necessary to establish the commission of the substantive offence. For a similar argument, see para **3.10**.

4.93   For the application of this provision to exercise of intervention powers against firms, see s 71. For its application to the exercise of intervention powers against authorised unit trusts, see s 91(4).

RESTITUTION ORDERS

4.94   The provisions and conditions which can be enforced by the injunction procedure may also be enforced by means of a restitution order granted under the same section (s 61(3)). Again, the procedure is similar to that in the section applying to contraventions of the section on persons entitled to carry on investment business (see paras **3.11–3.13**). An application for a restitution order may be made by the Secretary of State, or, on transfer, a designated agency.

4.95   The procedure varies slightly as between England, where the sums concerned are paid into court, and Scotland, where they paid to the applicant. In either case the court can make an order if satisfied:

(a) that profits have accrued to any person as a result of his contravention of any of the provisions or conditions to which the procedure applies (see para **4.89** above); or

(b) that one or more investors have suffered loss or been otherwise adversely affected as a result of that contravention (s 61(3)). Again, a similar provision for regulated friendly societies is to be found in para 22 of Sch 11.

4.96   The amount which the person concerned may be ordered to pay is the sum which appears to the court to be just having regard:

(a) to any profits appearing to the court to have accrued;

(b) to the extent of any loss or other adverse effect; or

(c) both to any profits and to the extent of any loss or other adverse effect (s 61(4)).

4.97   Accordingly, the court can order both compensation for the loss or other adverse effect which has occurred and disgorgement of the profits resulting. The sums concerned are to be paid out to or distributed among such persons as the court may direct. These are to be persons appearing to the court to have entered into transactions with the person concerned as a result of which the profits have accrued or the loss or other adverse effect has been suffered. The requirement for transactions to have been entered into with the person concerned is noteworthy. The remedy may not be available to benefit those who have suffered loss or other adverse effect on the basis of advice alone, at any rate if 'transaction' is narrowly construed. There is a provision for the court to require accounts or other information to be provided to enable it to decide on the profits which have accrued and on how any amounts are to be paid or distributed. These accounts and other information can be required to be verified in such manner as the court may direct, for example, by requiring them to be audited.

4.98   For the application of this provision to exercise of intervention powers against firms, see s 71. For its application to the exercise of intervention powers against authorised unit trusts, see s 91(4).

ACTIONS FOR DAMAGES

4.99   One of the Act's more notable features is its deployment of actions for damages as a sanction against misconduct. This has the advantages:

(a) that it provides compensation for those who have suffered loss;

(b) that the sums involved may be expected to act as a more powerful financial disincentive than a fine of the usual level;

(c) that only the civil burden of proof need be discharged.

4.100   By section 62(1), a contravention of particular provisions is to be 'actionable at the suit of a person who suffers loss as a result of the contravention subject to the defences and other incidents applying to actions for breach of statutory duty'. The provision potentially creates a strict liability, so that an action will be available even for an unavoidable contravention. This effect can, of course, be avoided or reduced where appropriate by introducing appropriate qualifications in the rules themselves, so that, for example, the rule is not contravened where the person concerned took all reasonable care to avoid doing so. Similarly, where a rule applies to misstatements, it would not appear necessary for the person who sues to have relied on the statement, so long as he has suffered loss or been adversely affected. Finally, it should be noted that the provision is not limited to compensation for investors or clients or the firm concerned, but extends to counterparties and, it appears, competitors. However, the reference to the 'defences and other incidents' applying to actions for breach of statutory duty may be expected to enable the courts to avoid the section operating unduly harshly. The right is without prejudice to the section providing for injunctions and restitution orders.

4.101   The provisions for which this right of action applies are:

(a) statutory rules or regulations made under Ch V of Pt 1 of the Act (but see also coverage of the rules of self-regulating organisations and professional bodies, dealt with at para **4.102**, and ss 95 and 171, requiring certain other contraventions to be treated as contraventions of statutory rules and regulations);

(b) any conditions imposed under the section relating to modification of conduct of business rules and financial resources rules for particular cases;

(c) any requirements imposed by an order making exceptions from the section on restrictions on advertising;

(d) the duty of an authorised person or appointed representative to take reasonable care not to employ or continue to employ a person in contravention of a disqualification direction.

4.102   This special right of action also applies to

'. . . a contravention by a member of a recognised self-regulating organisation or person certified by a recognised professional body of any rules of the organisation or body relating to a matter in respect of which rules or regulations have been or could be made under Chapter V of Part I of [the Act] in relation to an authorised person who is not such a member' (s 62(2)).

It will be observed that this applies not just to rules which parallel statutory rules or regulations which have been made, but also which could be made. This is particularly important for the equivalence test for rules of self-regulating organisations and professional bodies. The reason is that the equivalence test contemplates the equivalence of the rules of a self-regulating organisation or professional body governing the conduct of investment business being assessed as a whole. If any of those rules were not backed by a right of action for damages, it might need to be given correspondingly less weight for the purposes of the equivalence test.

4.103   It should also be noted that there is no provision for actions for damages for breach of the rules of a recognised investment exchange or clearing house. This contrasts with the availability of the 'injunctions and restitution orders' provisions in their support.

4.104   Nor does the right to an action for damages apply in connection with financial resources rules (s 62(3)). By their nature, financial resources rules are capable of unintentional contravention, as the scale of business done, and value of resources held, fluctuate. An action for damages might also be expected to be of less importance in this area; where the loss or adverse affect suffered is likely to be the inability to pay a particular sum, conferring an additional right to receive the same sum would be of little benefit.

4.105   It is expressly stated that a person is not guilty of an offence by reason of any contravention for which the right to an action for damages is conferred (s 62(4)) or of financial resources rules or conditions imposed in connection with an alteration of the requirements of those rules, so that it cannot be argued that they give rise to a contempt of statute. Similarly, no such contravention will invalidate any transaction.

4.106   For the application of this provision to exercise of intervention powers against firms, see s 71. For its application to the exercise of intervention powers against authorised unit trusts, see s 91(4). For the similar provision applying in regulated friendly societies, see para 22(3)–(5) of Sch 11.

GAMING CONTRACTS

4.107   Particular contracts are not to be void or unenforceable by reason of:

(a) s 18 of the Gaming Act 1845, s 1 of the Gaming Act 1892 or any corresponding provisions in force in Northern Ireland; or

(b) any rule of the law of Scotland whereby a contract by way of gaming or wagering is not legally enforceable (s 63). The contracts covered are contracts which are entered into by either or each party by way of business and the making or performance of which by either party constitutes an activity which falls within para 12 of Sch 1 to the Act or would do apart from Pts III and IV of that Schedule (s 63(2)).

4.108   This provision puts beyond doubt the enforceability of a number of contracts where this might otherwise have been called into question on the basis that they amounted to gaming or wagering. It is likely to be particularly relevant to the contracts described as 'contracts for differences'.

Chapter 5

Intervention powers applying to firms

INTRODUCTION

5.01 This chapter deals with statutory intervention powers applying to firms. It describes when they are exercisable, the powers themselves, the right to refer their exercise to the Tribunal, and their enforcement. Some similarities will be noted between these provisions and those contained in ss 37 to 48 of the Insurance Companies Act 1982.

5.02 For the right to require the exercise of intervention powers to be referred to the Tribunal, see para **7.06**. For the enforcement of intervention powers, see para **5.25** ff. For corresponding powers exercisable by recognised self-regulating organisations, see para **3.23**. For the absence of a requirement for such powers for recognised professional bodies, see para **3.45**. For intervention powers applying to collective investment schemes, see para **6.85** ff. For limitations on the application of the powers for regulated insurance companies, see para 6 of Sch 10. For intervention powers for regulated friendly societies, see para 23 of Sch 11.

SCOPE OF POWERS

5.03 Intervention powers are exercisable by the Secretary of State, or, on transfer, a designated agency. Exercise is possible if it appears:

(a) that it is desirable for the protection of investors;

(b) that the authorised person concerned (for appointed representatives, see para **5.07**) is not fit to carry on investment business of a particular kind or to the extent to which he is carrying it on or proposing to carry it on (see para **5.06**); or

(c) that the authorised person concerned (for appointed representatives, again see para **5.07**) has committed certain regulatory infringements (s 64(1)).

5.04 It may appear surprising that grounds (b) and (c) have been included in addition to ground (a) in para **5.03**, ante. It is suggested that they enable intervention powers to be exercised even where, perhaps because they could involve adverse effects on investors, it is open to question whether exercise is in their interests. These grounds also appear to enable the powers to be exercised to protect counterparties and, it is suggested, the integrity of the system.

5.05 The regulatory infringements whose commission can trigger the exercise of these powers are:

(a) contravening any provision of the Act or of any rules or regulations made under it;

(b) furnishing false, inaccurate or misleading information in purported compliance with any such provision;

(c) contravening any prohibition or requirement imposed under the Act.

5.06 For the purpose of deciding whether it appears that an authorised person is fit to carry on investment business of a particular kind or to the extent to which he is carrying it on or proposing to carry it on, the Secretary of State (or agency) can take into account any matters that could be taken into account in deciding whether to withdraw or suspend an authorisation under Ch III of Pt I of the Act (s 64(2)).

5.07 Intervention powers are exercisable over authorised persons, including those whose direct authorisation or authorisation as Europersons has been suspended (s 64(3)). Except for the restriction of business power (on which, see paras **5.10–5.12**), intervention powers are also exercisable over the appointed representative of an authorised person, including the appointed representative of a person whose authorisation has been so suspended. In the case of exercise over an appointed representative, the effect of s 44(7) in treating acts of a representative as those of his principal will be relevant, particularly to the exercise of powers on grounds (b) and (c), which are expressed by reference to authorised persons.

5.08 Except as explained in the next paragraph intervention powers are not exercisable in relation to:

(a) an *authorised person* who is a member of a recognised self-regulating organisation or a person certified by a recognised professional body and is subject to the rules of such an organisation or body in carrying on all the investment business carried on by him; or

(b) an *appointed representative* whose principal (or each of whose principals) is a member of such an organisation or body and is subject to the rules of such an organisation or body in carrying on the investment business in respect of which the principal (or each of the principals) has accepted responsibility (s 64(4)).

5.09 The exception is that the power to require investors' assets to be transferred to and held by a trustee is exercisable in relation to such a person at the request of any recognised self-regulating organisation of which he (or any of his principals) is a member or at the request of any recognised professional body by which he (or any of his principals) is certified.

RESTRICTION OF BUSINESS

5.10   The first intervention power is to prohibit an authorised person from:

(a) entering into transactions of any specified kind or entering into them except in specified circumstances or to a specified extent;

(b) soliciting business from persons of a specified kind or in a specified country or territory outside the United Kingdom;

(c) carrying on business in a specified manner or otherwise than in a specified manner (s 65(1)).

5.11   A prohibition under this 'restriction of business' power may relate 'to transactions entered into in connection with or for the purposes of investment business or to other business which is carried on in connection with or for the purposes of investment business' (s 65(2)).

5.12   As noted earlier, the restriction of business power is not exercisable directly over an appointed representative.

5.13   For the application of this power to the manager of an authorised unit trust scheme, see para **6.50**.

RESTRICTION ON DEALING WITH ASSETS

5.14   The Secretary of State (or, on transfer, agency) may also 'prohibit an authorised person or appointed representative from disposing of or otherwise dealing with any assets, or any specified assets, of that person or, as the case may be, representative in any specified manner or otherwise than in a specified manner' (s 66(1)). It is expressly stated that a prohibition of this kind may relate to assets outside the United Kingdom (s 66(2)). It is not, though, considered that this limits exercise of the power to assets outside the United Kingdom. Rather it is suggested that the express statement disapplies any presumption of territorial limitation which would otherwise arise.

VESTING OF ASSETS IN TRUSTEE

5.15   The Secretary of State (or, on transfer, agency) may also impose a requirement that

'. . . all assets, or all assets of any specified class or description, which at any time while the requirement is in force:

(a) belong to an authorised person or appointed representative; or

(b) belong to investors and are held by or to the order of an authorised person or appointed representative;'

are to be transferred to and held by a trustee approved by the Secretary of State (or agency) (s 67(1)).

5.16   This provision is directed at safeguarding assets, for example, on an impending insolvency. It is not apt to changing the beneficial ownership of assets. It should be noted, too, that the power is to impose a requirement, not to impose a requirement on an authorised person or appointed representative. This appears to be intentional. The power can be exercised over assets which 'belong to investors and are held by or to the order of an authorised person or appointed representative'. In order for the power to apply to assets of this kind, it must be capable of affecting not merely the rights of the authorised person or appointed representative, but also those of investors. This would also appear to account for the fact that provision is made for this aspect of the power to be exercisable even over those whose investment business is entirely subject to self-regulation. The essentially contractual nature of self-regulatory systems means that they are unlikely to be able to affect the rights of third parties in this way.

5.17   Where a requirement is imposed under this power, it is the duty of the authorised person or, as the case may be, appointed representative, to transfer the assets to the trustee and to give him all such other assistance as may be required to enable him to discharge his functions in accordance with the requirement (s 67(2)). Assets held by a trustee in accordance with a requirement under this power are 'not to be released or dealt with except in accordance with directions given by the Secretary of State or in such circumstances as may be specified by him' (s 67(3)). A requirement under this power may relate to assets outside the United Kingdom (s 67(4), and see para **5.14**).

MAINTENANCE OF ASSETS IN UNITED KINGDOM

5.18   The Secretary of State, or, on transfer, agency, may

' . . . require an authorised person or appointed representative to maintain in the United Kingdom assets of such value as appears . . . to be desirable . . . with a view to ensuring that the authorised person or, as the case may be, appointed representative, will be able to meet his liabilities in respect of investment business carried on by him in the United Kingdom.' (s 68(1)).

The Secretary of State (or agency) may also direct that, for the purposes of any requirement under this power, assets of any specified class or description are not to be taken into account (s 68(2)).

INTERVENTION POWERS: RESCISSION AND VARIATION

5.19 A power is provided to rescind or vary a prohibition or requirement imposed under the intervention powers (s 69). This is exercisable by the Secretary of State, either on his own initiative or on the application of the person on whom the prohibition or requirement is imposed. The power is capable of transfer to a designated agency. It is exercisable 'if it appears . . . that it is no longer necessary for the prohibition or requirement to take effect or continue in force or, as the case may be, that it should take effect or continue in force in a different form'.

INTERVENTION POWERS: NOTICES

5.20 The power to impose, rescind or vary a prohibition or requirement under the intervention powers is exercisable by written notice served on the person concerned, taking effect on such date as is specified in it (s 70(1)). If the Secretary of State (or, on transfer, agency) refuses to rescind or vary a prohibition or requirement on the application of the person to whom it applies he (or it) must serve that person with a written notice of the refusal (s 70(2)).

5.21 Reasons for the decision must be given in a notice:

(a) imposing a prohibition or requirement;

(b) varying a prohibition or requirement, except on the application of the person to whom it applies;

(c) refusing to rescind or vary a prohibition or requirement on the application of the person to whom it applies (s 70(3)).

5.22 Where the reasons stated in such a notice relate specifically to matters which:

(a) refer to a person identified in the notice other than the person to whom the prohibition or requirement applies; and

(b) are in the opinion of the Secretary of State (or, on transfer, agency) prejudicial to that person in any office or employment, the Secretary of State (or agency) shall, unless he considers it impractical to do so, serve a copy of the notice on that person (s 70(4)).

5.23 Any notice where reasons are to be given for the decision must give 'particulars of the right to have the case referred to the Tribunal' (s 70(5)). This right arises not merely for the person on whom the notice is served, but also for those on whom copies are served on the basis of matters prejudicial to them in an office or employment (s 97(1)(b)). The particulars given will clearly need to include the period within which the person concerned can require the case to be referred to the Tribunal. But in contrast to the position on withdrawal or suspension of authorisation, prohibitions and requirements imposed under the intervention powers can remain in force during a Tribunal investigation.

5.24 Public notice may be given of any prohibition or requirement imposed under these powers and of the rescission or variation of any such prohibition or requirement and such a notice may, if thought fit, include a statement of the reasons for which the prohibition or requirement was imposed, rescinded or varied (s 70(6)).

BREACH OF PROHIBITION OR REQUIREMENT

5.25 The sections of the Act relating to public statements as to misconduct, injunctions and restitution orders, and actions for damages apply to a contravention of a prohibition or requirement imposed under the statutory intervention powers applying to firms as they apply to the contraventions mentioned in those sections (s 71(1)). In addition, actions for damages are to be available in support of prohibitions and requirements imposed by a recognised self-regulating organisation or recognised professional body under powers for purposes corresponding to those of the provisions of the Act on statutory intervention powers for firms (s 71(2)). It would appear that it is necessary to make this special provision for actions for damages in order to confer rights on third parties, but that analogies to the other sanctions can be achieved without express statutory provision.

5.26 These express provisions on enforcement are without prejudice to any equitable remedy available in respect of property which is subject to a trust by virtue of a requirement under the section relating to vesting of assets in a trustee (s 71(3)).

5.27 Contravention of prohibitions and requirements imposed under these powers will also, of course, trigger various other provisions of the Act.

Winding up and administration orders

WINDING UP ORDERS

5.28 Section 72 gives the court (that is the court having jurisdiction under the Insolvency Act 1986) special powers to wind up certain authorised persons and appointed representatives. These powers are available on a petition presented by the Secretary of State, or, on transfer, a designated agency, if:

(a) the person to be wound up is unable to pay his debts within the meaning of s 123, or, as the case may be s 221 of that Act (and see para **5.30**); or

(b) the court is of the opinion that it is just and equitable that the person should be wound up (s 72(1)).

5.29   These special powers apply to any authorised person (including a person whose direct authorisation or authorisation as a Europerson has been suspended) or any appointed representative who is:

(a) a company within the meaning of s 735 of the Companies Act 1985;

(b) an unregistered company within the meaning of s 220 of the Insolvency Act 1986;

(c) an overseas company within the meaning of s 744 of the Companies Act 1985; or

(d) a partnership (see para **5.31**) (s 72(2)).

5.30   For the purposes of a petition made under these special powers for winding up, a person who defaults in an obligation to pay any sum due and payable under any investment agreement is deemed to be unable to pay his debts (s 72(3)). For the definition of 'investment agreement', see s 44(9).

5.31   Where, a petition is presented under these special powers for the winding up of a partnership on the just and equitable ground, 'the court shall have jurisdiction and the Insolvency Act 1986 shall have effect as if the partnership were an unregistered company within the meaning of section 220 of that Act' (s 72(4)).

5.32   A petition is not to be presented under these special powers for the winding up of any person who is an authorised person by virtue of membership of a recognised self-regulating organisation or certification by a recognised professional body and is subject to the rules of the organisation or body in the carrying on of all investment business carried on by him, unless the organisation or body has consented (s 72(5)).

WINDING UP ORDERS: NORTHERN IRELAND

5.33   Section 73 contains similar provisions to section 72 for Northern Ireland.

ADMINISTRATION ORDERS

5.34   The appointment of an administrator is an alternative procedure for use where a company is in financial difficulty. It is directed, broadly, at the survival of the company as a going concern or 'a more advantageous realisation of the company's assets than would be effected on a winding up' (see s 8(3) of the Insolvency Act 1986). Section 74 of the Financial Services Act accordingly provides that a petition may be presented under s 9 of the Insolvency Act 1986 'in relation to a company to which s 8 of that Act applies which is an authorised person' (including a person whose direct authorisation or authorisation as a Europerson has been suspended) or an appointed representative. The petition may be presented:

(a) in the case of an authorised person who is an authorised person by virtue of membership of a recognised self-regulating organisation or certification by a recognised professional body, by that organisation or body; and

(b) in the case of:

  (i) an appointed representative; or

  (ii) an authorised person who is not authorised by virtue of membership of a recognised self-regulating organisation or certification by a recognised professional body; or

  (iii) an authorised person who is so authorised but is not subject to the rules of the organisation or body in question in the carrying on of all investment business carried on by him;

by the Secretary of State, or, on transfer, a designated agency.

5.35 It will be noted that the essential feature of this provision is to extend the categories of person who may petition to include an appropriate regulator. The categories of firm covered and the grounds for making an order are unaffected.

Chapter 6

Collective investment schemes

INTRODUCTION

6.01 This chapter deals with the Act's provisions on collective investment schemes. In addition to unit trusts and open-ended investment companies, collective investment schemes could include commodity pools, Lloyd's syndicates, container leasing schemes, forestry schemes, partnerships (including oil and farming partnerships), racing syndicates, certain timesharing schemes, and schemes for the financing of theatrical productions by 'angels'.

6.02 In considering these provisions, it needs to be remembered that they not only update the provisions of the Prevention of Fraud (Investments) Act 1958, but also take advantage of concepts from the UCITS Directive (Council Directive 85/611/EEC on the co-ordination of laws, regulations and administrative provisions relating to undertakings for collective investment in transferable securities), whose provisions they are designed to implement.

Collective investment schemes: preliminary

INTERPRETATION

6.03 'Collective investment scheme' means (subject to the exceptions discussed in paras **6.04** to **6.18**)

> ' . . . any arrangements with respect to property of any description including money, the purpose or effect of which is to enable persons taking part in the arrangements (whether by becoming owners of the property or any part of it or otherwise) to participate in or receive profits or income arising from the acquisition, holding, management or disposal of the property or sums paid out of such profits or income.' (s 75(1))

This wording is based on s 13(1)(b) of the Prevention of Fraud (Investments) Act, as amended, and the similar definition of 'unit trust scheme' in s 26 of that Act.

6.04 Not all arrangements of this kind will be collective investment schemes. They must be such that the participants do not have day to day control over the management of the property in question, whether or not they have the right to be consulted or to give directions. In addition, either:

(a) the contributions of the participants and the profits or income out of which payments are to be made to them must be pooled ('pooling'); or

(b) the property in question must be managed as a whole by or on behalf of the operator of the scheme ('common management') (s 75(2)).

6.05 Where any arrangements provide for pooling in relation to separate parts of the property in question, the arrangements are not to be regarded as constituting a single collective investment scheme unless the participants are entitled to exchange rights in one part for rights in another (s 75(4)).

6.06 Arrangements are not a collective investment scheme if:

(a) the property to which the arrangements relate (other than cash awaiting investment) consists of investments falling within particular paragraphs of the Schedule, broadly covering certain securities together with long term life assurance contracts;

(b) each participant is the owner of a particular part of that property and entitled to withdraw it at any time; and

(c) there is no pooling and there is common management only because the parts of the property belonging to different participants are not bought and sold separately except where a person becomes or ceases to be a participant (s 75(5)).

This exception will thus be likely to exclude most investment management arrangements where there is common management, including personal equity plans ('PEPs') and Business Expansion Schemes.

6.07 Arrangements operated by a person otherwise than by way of business are not a collective investment scheme (s 75(6)(a)). This would appear to exclude many investment clubs.

6.08 Arrangements where each of the participants carries on a business other than investment business and enters into the arrangements for commercial purposes related to that business are not collective investment schemes (s 75(6)(b)). This would appear apt to exclude many partnerships and joint-ventures, including arrangements entered into by share fishermen, as well as certain activities by corporate treasurers.

6.09 Arrangements where each of the participants is a body corporate in the same group as the operator are not collective investment schemes (s 75(6)(c)). This should exclude the management of a group's assets as a whole.

6.10 Employee share schemes (as defined) are not collective investment schemes (s 75(6)(d)).

6.11. Arrangements 'where the receipt of the participants' contributions constitutes the acceptance of deposits in the course of a business which is a deposit-taking business for the purposes of the Banking Act 1979 and does not constitute a transaction prescribed for the purposes of section 2 of that Act by regulations made by the Treasury' are not collective investment schemes (s 75(6)(e)). This appears apt to exclude those money funds where a sum of money is paid on terms providing for the repayment of that sum, that is, essentially under a debt relationship (see Banking Act 1979, s 1(4)). Where money is not so paid, a money fund would appear to be a collective investment scheme.

6.12 Franchise arrangements where 'a person earns profits or income by exploiting a right conferred by the arrangements to use a trade name or design or other intellectual property or the goodwill attached to it' are not a collective investment scheme (s 75(6)(f)). It should be noted that this only applies to arrangements where the profits or income are *earned*. Mere receipt of profits or income, without involvement in a business, would appear not to be excluded.

6.13 Certain timesharing arrangements are not collective investment schemes (s 75(6)(g)). These are timesharing arrangements whose predominant purpose is to 'enable persons participating in them to share in the use or enjoyment of a particular property or to make its use or enjoyment available gratuitously to other persons.' It will be noted that this is a strict test. If timesharing arrangements have multiple purposes, no one of which is predominant, they will not be excluded. The inclusion of the words 'make its use or enjoyment available *gratitiously*' should particularly be noted. Timesharing arrangements involving arrangements for letting on behalf of timeshare owners may have difficulty fulfilling this requirement.

6.14 Arrangements under which the rights or interests of participants (not the underlying assets) are 'certificates representing securities' are not collective investment schemes (s 75(6)(h)). This exclusion extends the effect of the former general permission under the Prevention of Fraud (Investments) Act for 'heavy shares'.

6.15 Certain clearing arrangements are not collective investment schemes. These are arrangements the purpose of which is the provision of clearing services and which are operated by an authorised person, a recognised clearing house or a recognised investment exchange (s 75(6)(i)).

6.16 Contracts of insurance are not collective investment schemes (s 75(6)(j)). This exclusion continues, with note (4) to para 10 Sch 1, the effect of s 79 of the Insurance Companies Act 1982, which is repealed. This provision implemented a recommendation of the Scott Committee's Report on Property Bonds and Equity Linked Life Assurance (Cmnd 5281, see paras 69-74).

6.17 Occupational pension schemes are not collective investment schemes (s 75(6)(k)). With note (1) to para 11 of Sch 1, this means that rights under an occupational pension scheme are not investments. Accordingly promotion of rights under such schemes, for example by an employer, is not investment business. For managing occupational pension schemes, see para **21.17** ff.

6.18 Building societies, industrial and provident societies and friendly societies are not collective investment schemes and nor is any other body corporate other than an open-ended investment company (s 75(7), and see para **6.20**).

COLLECTIVE INVESTMENT SCHEMES: OTHER CONCEPTS EXPLAINED

6.19 A 'unit trust scheme' is 'a collective investment scheme under which the property in question is held on trust for the participants' (s 75(8)). For authorisation of unit trusts, see paras **6.30** ff.

6.20 An 'open-ended investment company' is a collective investment scheme under which:

(a) the property in question belongs beneficially to, and is managed by or on behalf of, a body corporate having as its purpose the investment of its funds with the aim of spreading investment risk and giving its members the benefit of the results of the management of those funds by or on behalf of that body; and

(b) the rights of the participants are represented by shares in or securities of that body which:

    (i) the participants are entitled to have redeemed or repurchased or which (other than under the Companies Act 1985 provisions on 'redeemable shares', and 'purchase by a company of its own shares' or the corresponding Northern Ireland provisions) are redeemed or repurchased from them by, or out of funds provided by, that body; or

    (ii) the body ensure can be sold by the participants on an investment exchange at a price related to the value of the property to which they relate (s 75(8)).

This appears apt to cover overseas mutual funds in corporate form.

6.21 'Trustee', in relation to a unit trust scheme, means 'the person holding the property in question on trust for the participants'. In relation to a collective investment scheme constituted under the law of a country or territory outside the United Kingdom, 'trustee' means any person who (whether or not under a trust) is entrusted with the custody of the property in question (s 75(8)).

6.22 'Units' means the rights or interests (however described) of the participants in a collective investment scheme. The 'operator', in relation to a collective investment scheme with a separate trustee, means the manager. In relation to an open-ended investment company, 'the operator' is that company (s 75(8)).

6.23 If an order under the power to extend or restrict the scope of the Act amends the references to a collective investment scheme in Sch 1, it may also amend the provisions of the interpretation section relating to collective investment schemes (s 75(9)).

PROMOTION OF COLLECTIVE INVESTMENT SCHEMES

6.24 Subject to certain exceptions, an authorised person shall not:

(a) issue or cause to be issued in the United Kingdom any advertisement inviting persons to become or offer to become participants in a collective investment scheme, or containing information, calculated to lead directly or indirectly to persons doing so, or

(b) advise or procure any person in the United Kingdom to become or offer to become a participant in such a scheme,

unless the scheme is an authorised unit trust scheme or a recognised scheme (s 76(1)).

6.25 It will be noted that this provision applies only to authorised persons, although it applies irrespective of authorisation route. For restrictions on advertising by unauthorised persons, see para **4.64** ff, commenting on s 57. The combined effect of that section and this is similar in intention to the effect of the former s 14 of the Prevention of Fraud (Investments) Act 1958 in its application to arrangements of the kind described in s 13(1)(b) of that Act. This is to restrict the promotion of collective investment schemes to those with some seal of approval. Under the 1958 Act, this was essentially authorisation as a unit trust. It is now extended to cover the new categories of recognised collective investment schemes. In addition, the new provision adds a prohibition on advising and procuring, not found in the 1958 Act.

6.26 The restriction on promotion of collective investment schemes does not apply, though, if the person to whom the advertisement is issued, or who is advised or procured, is:

(a) an authorised person; or

(b) a person whose ordinary business involves the acquisition and disposal of property of the same kind as the property, or a substantial part of the property, to which the scheme relates (s 76(2)).

The exemption in (a) is similar in role to the former s 14(5) of the 1958 Act. That in (b) would appear to allow, for example, promotion of 'units' in a commodity pool to dealers in the underlying commodity.

6.27 In addition, there is an exempting power. The restriction on promotion of collective investment schemes by authorised persons does not apply to 'anything done in accordance with regulations made by the Secretary of State for the purpose of exempting ... the promotion otherwise than to the general public of schemes of such descriptions as are specified in the regulations' (s 76(3)). This appears to be inspired by similar sentiments to those behind the power to exempt from the general restriction on advertisements appearing to have a 'private character'. It is capable of transfer to a designated agency.

6.28 The Secretary of State is also given power to make regulations exempting 'single property schemes' from the restriction on promotion (s 76(4)). For this purpose, a single property scheme is defined in s 76(5), (6), so as to require listing of the units to have been sought or obtained. This is important to provide an alternative to repurchase of units, which could prove difficult with a single property scheme. Exempting regulations may, inter alia, encompass requirements for corresponding purposes to scheme particulars under s 85.

Authorised unit trust schemes

INTRODUCTORY

6.29 The Department of Trade and Industry issued in 1986 a document entitled 'The Regulation of Authorised Unit Trust Schemes: a consultative document on the proposed regulations for unit trust schemes authorised under the Financial Services Bill' (HMSO, £9.85), whose contents are relevant to the exercise of the powers described in the following paragraphs.

APPLICATIONS FOR AUTHORISATION

6.30 An application for an order declaring a unit trust scheme to be an authorised unit trust scheme is to be made by the manager and trustee or proposed manager and trustee of the scheme, who must be different persons (s 77(1), based on art 10.1 of the UCITS Directive). The procedure for applications in s 77(2)–(5) is essentially self-explanatory.

AUTHORISATION ORDERS

6.31   The Secretary of State (or, on transfer, a designated agency) may, on an application duly made, and after being furnished with all such information as he may require, make an order declaring a unit trust scheme to be an authorised unit trust scheme. (For the transitional provision applying, see para 9 of Sch 15.) A scheme may only be authorised, though, if:

(a) it appears that it complies with the requirements of constitution and management regulations made under s 81 and that the additional requirements described in the following paragraphs are satisfied; and

(b) a copy of the trust deed is furnished together with a certificate signed by a solicitor to the effect that it (the deed) complies with requirements of constitution and management regulations relating to its contents (s 78(1)).

6.32   The first of the additional requirements to be satisfied is that the manager and trustee, in addition to being separate persons (see para **6.30**), are 'independent of each other' (s 78(2) extending art 10.2 of the UCITS Directive, which merely requires them to act independently). It appears that this may be determined by the recognising authority on a case by case basis.

6.33   The second additional requirement is that the manager and trustee must each:

(a) be a body corporate incorporated in the United Kingdom or another member state;

(b) have its affairs administered in the country in which it is incorporated;

(c) have a place of business in the United Kingdom; and

(d) if the manager is incorporated in another member state, not be a scheme which satisfies the requirements (see para **6.56** ff) for automatic recognition as an EEC scheme (s 78(3)).

6.34   The manager and trustee must also each be an authorised person (s 78(4)). Neither must be prohibited from acting as manager or trustee, as the case may be:

(a) by or under conduct of business rules made under s 48, ante, or

(b) by or under the rules of any recognised self-regulating organisation of which the manager or trustee is a member; or

(c) by a prohibition imposed under the 'restriction of business' intervention power in s 65 (s 78(4)).

6.35 The name of the scheme must not be undesirable or misleading and its purposes must be reasonably capable of being successfully carried into effect (s 78(5)).

6.36 The participants in the scheme must be entitled to have their units redeemed in accordance with the scheme, at a price related to the net value of the property to which the units related, and determined in accordance with the scheme. But a scheme will be treated as complying with this requirement if it *requires* the manager to ensure that a participant is able to sell his units on an investment exchange at a price not significantly different from that price (s 78(6), reflecting art 1(2) of the UCITS Directive).

6.37 The applicants must be informed of the decision on authorisation not later than six months after the application is received (s 78(7)). On making an order for authorisation of a unit trust, the Secretary of State (or agency) may 'issue a certificate to the effect that it complies with the conditions necessary for it to enjoy the rights conferred by any relevant Community instrument' (s 78(8)). The only relevant Community instrument at present is the UCITS Directive.

AUTHORISED UNIT TRUST SCHEMES: REVOCATION OF AUTHORISATION

6.38 The Secretary of State (or, on transfer, agency) may revoke an order declaring a scheme to be an authorised unit trust scheme if it appears:

(a) that any of the requirements for the making of the order are no longer satisfied;

(b) that it is undesirable in the interests of the participants or potential participants that the scheme should continue to be authorised; or

(c) without prejudice to (b) above, that the manager or trustee of the scheme has committed certain regulatory infringements (s 79(1)).

6.39 For the purposes of deciding whether it is undesirable in the interests of participants or potential participants that a scheme should continue to be authorised, the Secretary of State (or agency) may take into account any matter relating to:

(a) the scheme;

(b) the manager or trustee;

(c) a director or controller of the manager or trustee; or

(d) any person employed by or associated with the manager or trustee in connection with the scheme (s 79(2)).

6.40 The regulatory infringements whose commission can trigger the exercise of these powers are:

(a) contravening any provision of the Act or of any rules or regulations made under it;

(b) furnishing false, inaccurate or misleading information in purported compliance with any such provision;

(c) contravening any prohibition or requirement imposed under the Act.

In addition, these rules, prohibitions and requirements are taken to include the rules of a recognised self-regulating organisation and prohibitions and requirements imposed by virtue of them (s 79(3)).

6.41 The Secretary of State (or agency) may also revoke an order declaring a unit trust scheme to be an authorised unit trust scheme at the request of the manager or trustee of the scheme, but may refuse to do so if he considers that any matter concerning the scheme should be investigated as a preliminary to a decision on the question whether the order should be revoked (s 79(4)). Revocation may also be refused if it is considered that it would not be in the interest of the participants or would be incompatible with a Community obligation.

REPRESENTATIONS AGAINST REFUSAL OR REVOCATION

6.42 There is a procedure for representations to be made against particular decisions concerning the authorisation of unit trusts. (There is no right in these cases to require the case to be referred to the Tribunal.) Where the Secretary of State (or agency) proposes:

(a) to refuse an application for an order declaring a unit trust scheme to be an authorised unit trust scheme; or

(b) to revoke such an order otherwise than at the request of the manager or trustee;

written notice of the intention to do so is to be given to the manager and trustee, stating the reasons and giving particulars of the rights to make representations (s 80(1)). A person (whether manager or trustee) served with a notice of intention to refuse or revoke authorisation may, within twenty-one days, make written representations to the Secretary of State (or, on transfer, agency), and, if desired, make oral representations to a person appointed to hear them (s 80(2)). It would appear that oral representations may only be made in addition to written ones, and not on their own. The Secretary of State (or agency) must 'have regard' to any representations made in accordance with the procedure (s 80(3)). There is no express provision for public notice of refusal or revocation of recognition.

AUTHORISED UNIT TRUSTS: CONSTITUTION AND MANAGEMENT REGULATIONS

6.43   The Secretary of State (or, on transfer, a designated agency) may make regulations as to the constitution and management of authorised unit trust schemes. These may also deal with the powers and duties of the manager and trustee of an authorised unit trust and the rights and obligations of the participants. Unlike regulations on publication of scheme particulars (see para **6.55**) these are not applied to other kinds of collective investment scheme. For their relevance to 'other overseas schemes', see para **6.73**. None of the 'provisions applicable to designated agency's rules and regulations' is expressly relevant, although various provisions of the UCITS Directive may be expected to be.

6.44   Without prejudice to the general scope of constitution and management regulations, described in the previous paragraph, they may make provision:

(a) as to the issue and redemption of the units under the scheme;

(b) as to the expenses of the scheme and the means of meeting them;

(c) for the appointment, removal, powers and duties of an auditor for the scheme;

(d) for restricting or regulating the investment and borrowing powers exercisable in relation to the scheme;

(e) requiring the keeping of records with respect to the transactions and financial position of the scheme;

(f) requiring the preparation of periodical reports with respect to the scheme and the furnishing of those reports to the participants and to the Secretary of State (or agency); and

(g) with respect to the amendment of the scheme (s 81(2)).

6.45   Constitution and management regulations may make provision as to the contents of the trust deed, and require the matters described in the previous paragraph to be dealt with in it (s 81(3)). (For the requirement for a certificate signed by a solicitor as to the contents of a deed, see para **6.31**.) Constitution and management regulations are, though, binding on the manager and trustee and indeed the participants, independently of the contents of the deed (ibid). Accordingly, subjection to overriding constitution and management regulations is substituted for the requirement in s 17(1)(c) of the Prevention of Fraud (Investments) Act 1958 for a unit trust deed to provide for particular matters 'to the satisfaction of' the Secretary of State. Constitution and management regulations may not impose limits on the remuneration payable to the manager of a scheme (s 81(4)), but the requirements of art 43 of the UCITS Directive would appear to mean that the deed will need to contain some provision on remuneration. The regulations may also 'contain such incidental and transitional provisions' as the Secretary of State (or agency) thinks necessary or expedient (s 81(5)).

AUTHORISED UNITS TRUSTS: ALTERATION OF SCHEMES AND CHANGES OF MANAGER OR TRUSTEE

6.46 The manager of an authorised unit trust scheme must give written notice to the Secretary of State (or, on transfer, agency) of any proposed alteration to the scheme and of any proposal to replace the trustee of the scheme (s 82(1)). A notice of a proposed alteration which involves a change in the trust deed must be accompanied by a certificate signed by a solicitor that the change will not effect the compliance of the deed with constitution and management regulations. The trustee of an authorised unit trust scheme must also give written notice to the Secretary of State (or, on transfer, agency) of any proposal to replace the manager of the scheme (s 82(2)).

6.47 Effect is not to be given to a proposal to alter an authorised unit trust scheme or to replace the trustee or manager unless the Secretary of State (or agency) has given his or its approval or one month has elapsed since the date on which notice was given without the Secretary of State (or agency) having notified the manager or trustee that the proposal is not approved (s 82(3), based on art 4.4 of the UCITS Directive). Neither the manager or trustee can be replaced by a person who does not satisfy the necessary requirements (s 82(4)).

6.48 The provisions on alteration of schemes and changes of manager or trustee are extended (with variations) to 'other overseas schemes' (s 88(9)).

RESTRICTIONS ON ACTIVITIES OF MANAGER

6.49 The activities of the manager of an authorised unit trust scheme are limited to acting as manager of various kinds of collective investment scheme and investment company, together with activities 'for the purposes of or in connection with' doing so (s 83(1), (2)). This provision accordingly imposes on unit trust managers a limitation similar to that imposed on authorised insurers by s 16 of the Insurance Companies Act 1982. It reflects art 6 of the UCITS Directive. For the operation of s 44(7) in this connection, see para **3.133**.

6.50 A prohibition under the 'restriction of business' intervention power applying to firms (s 65) may 'prohibit the manager of an authorised unit trust scheme from inviting persons in any specified country or territory outside the United Kingdom to become participants in the scheme' (s 83(3)) This provision appears to reflect a view that under the UCITS Directive the authorities of the home member state of a UCITS may intervene at the request of a state where its units are marketed.

AVOIDANCE OF EXCLUSION CLAUSES

6.51 Any provision of the trust deed of an authorised unit trust is to be void in so far as it would have the effect of exempting the manager or trustee from liability for any failure to exercise due care and diligence in the discharge of his functions in respect of the scheme (s 84). Articles 7.2 and 9 of the UCITS Directive contain requirements to which this provision may be relevant. The provision would not appear to affect ss 23 and 31 of the Trustee Act 1925.

PUBLICATION OF SCHEME PARTICULARS

6.52 The Act enables the Secretary of State to make regulations requiring the manager of an authorised unit trust scheme to submit to him and publish or make available to the public on request 'scheme particulars' containing information about the scheme and complying with such requirements as are specified in the regulations (s 85(1)). The power is capable of transfer to a designated agency, but none of the 'principles applicable to designated agency rules and regulations' is expressly relevant. Publication of scheme particulars is, though, required by arts 27-29 of the UCITS Directive and it may accordingly be expected that regulations will be made to implement this requirement.

6.53 Regulations on scheme particulars may require revised or further scheme particulars if there is a significant change affecting any matter contained in such particulars previously published or made available whose inclusion was required by the regulations or if a significant new matter arises about which information would have been required in previous particulars if it had arisen when those particulars were prepared (s 85(2)). (Provisions of this kind are required by art 30 of the UCITS Directive. The similarity of the provision to s 147, which implements a similar provision in the Listing Particulars Directive, will be noted).

6.54 Scheme particulars regulations may

'. . . provide for the payment, by the person or persons who in accordance with the regulations are treated as responsible for any scheme particulars, of compensation to any person who has become or agreed to become a participant in the scheme and suffered loss as a result of any untrue or misleading statement in the particulars or the omission from them of any matter which the regulations required to be included.' (s 85(3))

This would appear to contemplate a provision similar to s 150 of the Act

As in s 150(4), this is not to affect any of the liability which any person may incur apart from the regulations (s 85(4)).

6.55 For the extension of the power to require scheme particulars to schemes recognised under s 87 ('schemes authorised in designated countries or territories') see para **6.71**. For its extension to schemes authorised under s 88 ('other overseas schemes') see para **6.76**. The Act makes no equivalent provision for schemes recognised under s 86 ('schemes constituted in other member states').

Recognition of overseas schemes

SCHEMES CONSTITUTED IN OTHER MEMBER STATES

6.56 A collective investment scheme constituted in a member state other than the United Kingdom is a recognised scheme if it satisfies any requirements prescribed (s 86(1)). The Act does not amplify the kind of requirements which may be prescribed. It may be expected, though, that they will be designed to implement the UCITS Directive. The power to prescribe requirements of this kind is not capable of transfer to a designated agency. For the transitional provision applying, see para 10 of Sch 15.

6.57 It will thus be seen that the section provides for automatic 'recognition' for schemes from other member states. It will also be recalled that the operators and trustees of such schemes receive automatic authorisation by virtue of s 24. These provisions are designed to reflect principles of community law, and in particular the UCITS directive.

6.58 Not less than two months before inviting persons to the United Kingdom to become participants in a scheme, the operator must give written notice to the Secretary of State (or, on transfer, agency) of his intention to do so, specifying the manner in which the invitation is to be made (s 86(2), reflecting art 46 of the UCITS Directive). Automatic authorisation will not arise:

' . . . if within two months of receiving the notice the Secretary of State (or agency) notifies:

(a) the operator of the scheme; and

(b) the authorities of the State in question who are responsible for the authorisation of collective investment schemes,

that the manner in which the invitation is to be made does not comply with the law in force in the United Kingdom.' (s 86(2) again reflecting art 46 of the UCITS Directive.)

6.59 It will be noted that the power of the UK authorities over the automatic recognition of schemes of this kind arises only as a veto exercisable before recognition takes effect. There is no power for the UK authorities subsequently to terminate such recognition or the corresponding authorisation of the operator and trustee, except on the operator's request (see para **6.65**). Even the power of veto is exercisable only on the very limited ground that the manner in which the invitation is to be made does not comply with the law in force in the UK.

6.60 The notice of intention to invite persons in the UK to become participants must:

(a) be accompanied by a certificate from the authorities of the State in question who are responsible for the authorisation of collective investment schemes to the effect that the scheme 'complies with the conditions necessary for it to enjoy the rights conferred by any relevant Community instrument';

(b) 'contain the address of a place in the United Kingdom for the service on the operator of notices or other documents required or authorised to be served on him' under the Act; and

(c) contain or be accompanied by such other information and documents as may be prescribed (s 86(3) based on art 46 of the UCITS Directive).

6.61 The UCITS Directive itself appears at present to be the only relevant Community instrument. The Treaty itself is not a Community instrument since it is not 'an instrument issued by a Community institution' (see s 1(2) of and Sch 1 to the European Communities Act 1972). The power to require additional contents or accompanying documents is capable of transfer to a designated agency.

6.62 A veto notice given by the Secretary of State (or agency) must give the reasons for which it is considered that the law in force in the United Kingdom will not be complied with, and give particulars of the rights to make representations conferred (s 86(4)). These are that a person served with a veto notice may, within twenty-one days of the date of service, make written representations to the Secretary of State (or agency) and, if desired, oral representations to a person appointed for the purpose (s 86(5)). It would appear that oral representations can only be made in addition to written representations, not alone. The Secretary of State (or agency) may in the light of any representations so made withdraw the veto notice and in that event the scheme is to be a 'recognised' scheme from the date on which the notice is withdrawn (s 86(6)).

6.63 The power in s 48 to make statutory conduct of business rules is limited in the case of operators and trustees of schemes recognised under this section. The limit applies to investment business consisting acting as operator or trustee of the schemes and any investment business carried on by them in connection with or for the purposes of the schemes (ss 86(7) and

24). The rules cannot apply to this business 'except so far as they make provision as respects procuring persons to become participants in the scheme and advising persons on the scheme and the exercise of the rights conferred by it' and as respects incidental matters. In other words, the limit is essentially to 'marketing' activities. This limitation is believed to be regarded as necessary to comply with Community obligations (see art 1.6 of the UCITS Directive). For the similar but slightly wider provision applying to regulated insurance companies, see para **4.30**. For that applying to regulated friendly societies, see also para **4.30**.

6.64 For the purposes of s 86, a collective investment scheme is constituted in a member state if:

(a) it is constituted under the law of that member state by a contract or under a trust and is managed by a body corporate incorporated under that law; or

(b) it takes the form of an open-ended investment company incorporated under that law (s 86(8), based on art 3 of the UCITS directive).

6.65 If the operator of the scheme gives written notice to the Secretary of State (or agency) stating that he desires the scheme no longer to be automatically recognised under s 86, it ceases to be so recognised when the notice is given (s 86(9)).

SCHEMES AUTHORISED IN DESIGNATED COUNTRIES OR TERRITORIES

6.66 There is a similar automatic recognition provision for collective investment schemes in designated overseas countries or territories. This does not, though, confer automatic authorisation on the operator and trustee. They must seek authorisation by one of the other routes if they carry on investment business in the United Kingdom. Automatic recognition under this provision applies to 'a collective investment scheme which is not a recognised scheme by virtue of s 86' (schemes constituted in other member states) 'but is managed in and authorised under the law of a country or territory outside the United Kingdom' (s 87(1)). It only arises, though, if:

(a) that country or territory is designated for the purpose by an order made by the Secretary of State; and

(b) the scheme is of a class specified by the order.

6.67 It will be seen that, as well as covering schemes from outside the Community, recognition of this kind could cover schemes from other member states which do not have automatic recognition as such. This could be of value, for example, where the member state's authorisation and supervision of the scheme satisfies the 'equivalent protection' test for designation, even though, perhaps, the scheme is not covered by a 'Community instrument'.

6.68 The Secretary of State's power to designate a country or territory for the purposes of this section is not capable of transfer to a designated agency. (For supplementary provisions on the power, see para **6.72**). The Secretary of State may not make an order designating any country or territory for the purposes of this provision unless he is satisfied that 'the law under which collective investment schemes are authorised and supervised in that territory affords to investors in the United Kingdom protection at least equivalent to that provided for them by Ch VIII of Pt I of the Act in the case of an authorised unit trust scheme' (s 87(2)). It will be observed that this requirement applies to the *law* of the country or territory. Adequate practice alone cannot be sufficient. In addition, in contrast to the equivalence test for authorisation as a Europerson, this applies not merely to authorisation, but also to supervision. This gives a greater significance to the requirement applying for 'investors in the United Kingdom'. In order to fulfil this requirement, it would appear that the home authorities may need to supervise activities in relation to investors in the United Kingdom.

6.69 A scheme is not automatically recognised by s 87(3) unless the operator gives written notice to the Secretary of State (or agency) that he wishes it to be recognised and nor will it be if, within such period from receiving the notice as may be prescribed, the Secretary of State notifies the operator that it is not to be (s 87(3)).

6.70 The notice to be given by the operator must contain the address of a place in the United Kingdom for the service on the operator of notices or other documents required or authorised to be served on him under the Act and contain or be accompanied by such information and documents as may be prescribed (s 87(4)). It will be noted that there is no provision for a certificate of compliance in this case.

6.71 The power to make scheme particulars regulations is available for schemes recognised under this section, applying mutatis mutandis as it does in relation to authorised unit trusts (s 87(5)). It is expressly provided that scheme particulars regulations applying to schemes authorised in designated overseas countries or territories 'may make provision whereby compliance with any requirements imposed by or under the law of [a designated country or territory] is treated as compliance with any requirement of the regulations' (s 87(5)). The inclusion of this express provision would appear to cast doubt on the ability to make similar provision in the case of other schemes.

6.72 An order designating a country or territory may contain such transitional provisions as the Secretary of State thinks necessary or expedient and such an order is subject to annulment in pursuance of a resolution of either House of Parliament (s 87(6)).

OTHER OVERSEAS SCHEMES

6.73 The Act also provides a procedure for the grant of individual recognitions to overseas collective investment schemes. The schemes which are eligible for such recognition are those which are managed in a country or territory outside the United Kingdom but which do not satisfy the requirements for automatic recognition as schemes constituted in other member states or in designated countries or territories (s 88(1)). The Secretary of State (or, on transfer, a designated agency) may, on the application of the operator of a scheme of this kind, make an order declaring it to be a recognised scheme. In order to do so, it must appear to him that the scheme affords adequate protection to the participants, makes adequate provision for the matters dealt with by constitution and management regulations (see para **6.43**) and satisfies the requirements described in the next paragraph.

6.74 The operator must be a body corporate or the scheme must take the form of an open-ended investment company (s 88(2)). The operator and trustee, if any, must also be fit and proper persons to act as operator, or, as the case may be, trustee (s 88(3)). For that purpose, the Secretary of State (or agency) may take into account any matter relating to any person who is or will be employed by or associated with the operator or trustee for the purposes of the scheme, any director or controller of the operator or trustee and any other body corporate in the same group as the operator or trustee and any director or controller of any such other body (ibid). The fit and proper requirement does not apply, though, to an operator or trustee who is an authorised person, so long as he is not prohibited from acting as operator or trustee 'by or under' statutory conduct of business rules under s 48, by or under the rules of any recognised self-regulating organisation of which he is a member, or by any prohibition imposed under the restriction of business intervention powers (s 88(4)). It will be noted that prohibitions imposed in the exercise of the powers of a recognised self-regulating organisation corresponding to the statutory intervention powers under the Act are included by the means of the words '*or under* the rules of any recognised self-regulating organisation'. (The extension of the restriction of business intervention power by s 81(3) will not be relevant for this purpose since it only applies to inviting persons to become participants in an authorised unit trust scheme.) If the operator is not an authorised person he must have a representative in the United Kingdom who is an authorised person and has power to act generally for the operator and to accept service of notices and other documents on his behalf (s 88(5)). The exception where the operator is an authorised person may be thought to suggest that conduct of business rules can require authorised persons to have a representative of this kind. The name of the scheme must not be undesirable or misleading and its purposes must be reasonably capable of being successfully carried into effect (s 88(6)). Finally, the participants must be entitled to have their units redeemed in accordance with the scheme at a price related to the net value of the property to which the units relate, and determined in accordance with the scheme, but a scheme is to be treated as complying with this requirement if it requires the operator to ensure that a participant is able to sell his units on an investment exchange at a price which is not significantly different (s 88(7)—but see the transitional provision in para 11 of Sch 15).

6.75 The procedure for applying for individual recognition is the same as that for applying for authorisation as a unit trust (s 88(8), and see s 77(2)–(5)). In addition, the requirement of s 82 of giving written notice of proposed alterations applies to individually recognised schemes, mutatis mutandis, as it applies to authorised unit trusts. Different provisions apply if the operator or trustee is to be replaced. In this case, the operator or, as the case may be, the trustee, or in either case the person who is to replace him, must give at least one month's notice to the Secretary of State or agency (s 88(9)).

6.76 The power to make scheme particulars regulations in s 85 applies to individually recognised schemes, mutatis mutandis, as it applies to authorised unit trusts (s 88(10). It should be noted that in this case there is no power for the regulations to treat compliance with the law of the overseas country or territory as compliance with their requirements (contrast para **6.71**).

REFUSAL AND REVOCATION OF RECOGNITION

6.77 Section 89(1) confers powers to to give directions ending the recognition of schemes recognised by virtue of s 87 ('Schemes authorised in designated countries or territories') and to revoke orders recognising schemes under s 88 ('Other overseas schemes'). There is no equivalent UK power applying to schemes recognised under s 86 ('Schemes constituted in other member states'). The powers are capable of transfer to a designated agency and arise where it appears:

(a) that it is undesirable in the interest of the participants or potential participants in the United Kingdom that the scheme should continue to be recognised;

(b) without prejudice to para (a), that the operator or trustee of the scheme has committed certain regulatory infringements; or

(c) in the case of an order granting individual recognition, that any of the requirements for the making of the order are no longer satisfied (s 89(1)).

6.78 For the purposes of ground (a) the Secretary of State or agency may take into account any matter relating to the scheme, the operator or trustee, a director or controller of the operator or trustee or any person employed by or associated with the operator or trustee in connection with the scheme (s 89(2)).

6.79   The regulatory infringements whose commission can trigger the exercise of the power are:

(a) contravening any provision of the Act or any rules or regulations made under it;

(b) furnishing false, inaccurate or misleading information in purported compliance with any such provision; and

(c) contravening any prohibition or requirement imposed under the Act (s 89(1)(b)).

These rules, prohibitions and requirements are taken to include the rules of a recognised self-regulating organisation and prohibitions and requirements imposed by virtue of those rules (s 89(3)). It appears to be assumed that a manager, operator or trustee will not be a member of a recognised professional body.

6.80   The Secretary of State (or agency) may give a direction or revoke an order at the request of the operator or trustee of the scheme (s 89(4)). He may, though, refuse to do so if he considers that any matter concerning the scheme should be investigated as a preliminary to a decision on the question whether the direction should be given or the order revoked or that the direction or revocation would not be in the interest of the participants (s 89(4)). This provision is similar to that in s 79(4) except that it does not enable the Secretary of State to revoke on the ground of incompatibility with a Community obligation. It is arguable that this could nevertheless be done under the coda to s 2(2) of the European Communities Act 1972.

6.81   Section 89(5)–(7) sets out the written representation procedure which applies where the Secretary of State (or agency) proposes:

(a) to veto the recognition of a scheme authorised in a designated country or territory;

(b) to give such a direction, or to refuse to make, or to revoke an order granting individual recognition to an overseas scheme (s 89(5)).

Under this procedure, the Secretary of State must give the operator a written notice of his intention to act, stating the reasons and giving particulars of the right to make representations (s 89(5)). This right enables a person on whom a notice is served under the procedure, within 21 days of the date of service, to make written representations to the Secretary of State (or agency) and if desired, oral representations to a person appointed for that purpose by the Secretary of State (or agency) (s 89(6)). It would appear that oral representations may be made only in addition to and not in place of written representations. The Secretary of State (or agency) is under a duty to have regard to any representations made in accordance with this procedure in determining whether to act (s 89(7)).

FACILITIES AND INFORMATION IN THE UNITED KINGDOM

6.82   The Act confers a power to make regulations requiring operators of recognised schemes of all kinds to maintain facilities in the United Kingdom (s 90). The power is exercisable by the Secretary of State and is capable of transfer to a designated agency but none of the 'principles applicable to designated agency's rules and regulations' expressly relates to it. The regulations may extend to requiring the facilities to be kept in such part or parts of the United Kingdom as may be specified in the regulations. The facilities are to be 'such facilities as he thinks desirable in the interests of participants and as are specified in the regulations'. They may be expected to cover payments to unit holders, repurchases and redemptions of units and making information available, as required by art 45 of the UCITS Directive.

6.83   There is also a power (s 90(2)) to require an operator of any recognised scheme to include explanatory information in investment advertisements issued or caused to be issued by him in the United Kingdom. This is exercisable by the Secretary of State (or agency) by notice in writing. The notice must specify the explanatory information to be given. The power only applies to investment advertisements in which the scheme is named. For the sanction, see para **6.112**, commenting on s 95(2).

Collective investment schemes: powers of intervention

6.84   The powers of intervention which are available in relation to collective investment schemes are less wide-ranging than those applying against firms under Ch 5 of Pt I. It should be noted, though, that they are exercisable irrespective of the authorisation, or authorisation route, of the operator or trustee of the scheme.

POWERS OF INTERVENTION OVER AUTHORISED UNIT TRUST

6.85   The first of the intervention powers provided applies in relation to authorsised unit trusts. It is exercisable if it appears to the Secretary of State (or, on transfer, agency):

(a) that any of the requirements for the making of an order declaring a scheme to be an authorised unit trust scheme are no longer satisfied;

(b) that the exercise of the power is desirable in the interest of participants or potential participants in the scheme;

(c) without prejudice to (b), that the manager or trustee has committed certain regulatory infringements (s 91(1)).

6.86   For the purposes of deciding whether the exercise of the power is desirable in the interests of participants or potential participants in the scheme, the Secretary of State (or agency) may take into account any matter relating to the scheme, the manager, operator or trustee, a director or controller of the manager or operator or trustee or any person employed by or associated with the manager, operator or trustee in connection with the scheme (s 91(6)).

6.87   The regulatory infringements whose commission can trigger the exercise of the power are:

(a) contravening any provision of the Act or any rules or regulations made under it;

(b) furnishing false, inaccurate or misleading information in purported compliance with any such provision; and

(c) contravening any prohibition or requirement imposed under the Act (s 91(1)(c)).

These rules, prohibitions and requirements are taken to include the rules of a recognised self-regulating organisation and prohibitions and requirements imposed by virtue of those rules (s 91(7)). It appears to be assumed that a manager, operator or trustee will not be a member of a recognised professional body.

6.88   There is a power for the Secretary of State (or agency) to withdraw or vary a direction given under this power. He may do so either on his own initiative or on the application of the manager or trustee. He may only do so, though, if it appears that it is no longer necessary for the direction to take effect or continue in force or, as the case may be, that it should take effect or continue in force in a different form (s 91(8)).

6.89   The powers of intervention are exercised by the Secretary of State giving directions. A direction in relation to an authorised unit trust scheme may:

(a) require the manager of the scheme to cease the issue or redemption, or both the issue and redemption, of units under the scheme on a date specified in the direction until such further date as is specified in that or another direction;

(b) require the manager and trustee of the scheme to wind it up by such date as is specified in the direction or, if no date is specified, as soon as practicable (s 91(2)).

6.90   It will be recalled that the main effect of authorisation of a unit trust for regulatory purposes is that the restriction on promotion will not apply.

Accordingly, mere withdrawal of authorisation may be inadequate as a protection for participants. These powers accordingly enable the manager to be required to cease the issue or redemption of units and also provide for it to be wound up.

6.91   The revocation of an order authorising a unit trust will not affect the operation of any direction given under these powers which is in force (s 91(3)). A direction may be given where the authorisation of a unit trust has been revoked if a direction was already in force under these powers at the time of revocation (s 91(3)). The provisions of the Act relating to public statements as to misconduct, injunctions and restitution orders and actions for damages apply also to a contravention of a direction under the intervention powers applying to authorised unit trusts (s 91(4)).

OTHER COLLECTIVE INVESTMENT SCHEMES: INTERVENTION POWERS

6.92   The Act also provides for certain intervention powers to be exercisable in relation to schemes recognised on the basis of authorisation in designated countries or territories and schemes with individual recognition. The powers are exercisable in this case where it appears to the Secretary of State (or agency):

(a) that the exercise of the power is desirable in the interests of participants or potential participants who are in the United Kingdom;

(b) without prejudice to (a), that the operator has committed certain regulatory infringement; or

(c) that any of the requirements for individual recognition are no longer satisfied (s 91(5)).

6.93   For the purpose of deciding whether it appears that the exercise of the power is desirable in the interests of participants or potential participants in the United Kingdom, the Secretary of State (or agency) may again take into account any matter relating to the scheme, the manager, operator or trustee, a director or controller of the manager, operator or trustee or any person employed by or associated with the manager, operator or trustee in connection with the scheme (s 91(6)).

6.94   The regulatory infringements whose commission can trigger the exercise of the power are again:

(a) contravening any provision of the Act or any rules or regulations made under it;

(b) furnishing false, inaccurate or misleading information in purported compliance with any such provision; and

(c) contravening any prohibition or requirement imposed under the Act (s 91(5)(b)).

In addition, these rules, prohibitions and requirements are taken to include the rules of a recognised self regulating organisation and any prohibition or requirement imposed by virtue of those rules (s 91(7)).

6.95   There is a power for the Secretary of State (or agency) to withdraw or vary directions given under this power. He may do so either on his own initiative or on the application of the manager, trustee or operator. He may only do so, though, if it appears that it is no longer necessary for the direction to take effect or continue in force or, as the case may be, that it should take effect or continue in force in a different form (s 91(8)).

6.96   The directions which may be given in relation to a scheme of this kind are that the scheme is not to be a recognised scheme for a specified period or until the occurrence of a specified event or until specified conditions are complied with. In this case, accordingly, there is no power to impede issue and redemption of units or to require the winding up of a scheme. The power is only to suspend its recognition. For this reason, there is no provision applying the sections of the Act relating to public statements as to misconduct, injunctions and restitution orders or actions for damages comparable to s 91(4).

COLLECTIVE INVESTMENT SCHEME INTERVENTION POWERS: NOTICE OF DIRECTIONS

6.97   Intervention powers against authorised unit trusts and, where available, collective investment schemes, are to be exercised by written notice. The notice is to be served by the Secretary of State (or agency) on the manager and trustee, or, as the case may be, on the operator of the scheme. A notice of this kind takes effect on the date specified in the notice (s 92(1)).

6.98   If the Secretary of State (or agency) refuses to withdraw or vary a direction on the application of the manager, trustee or operator of the scheme concerned, he is to serve him with a written notice of refusal (s 92(2)). A notice giving a direction, or varying it otherwise than on the application of the manager, trustee or operator concerned, or refusing to withdraw or vary a direction on the application of such a person, is to state the reasons (s 92(3)). There is, though, no express right to make representations.

6.99   The Secretary of State (or agency) may give public notice of a direction given under the intervention powers applying to collective investment schemes and of any withdrawal or variation of such a direction. The notice may, if thought fit, include a statement of the reasons (s 92(4)).

APPLICATIONS TO THE COURT: UNIT TRUSTS

6.100   There is an additional power applying in relation to authorised unit trust schemes and to formerly authorised schemes where a direction was in force at the time of the revocation of the authorisation. This power applies where the Secretary of State (or agency) has power to give a direction in relation to the scheme. It enables him (or it) to apply to the court:

(a) for an order removing the manager or trustee, or both, and replacing either or both of them with a nominated person appearing to satisfy the requirements of s 78; or

(b) if it appears that no, or no suitable, person satisfying those requirements is available, for an order removing the manager or trustee, or both the manager and trustee and appointing an authorised person to wind up the scheme (s 93(1)).

6.101 On an application of this kind the court make such order as it thinks fit. In particular, on the application of the Secretary of State (or agency) it can replace a person appointed under para (b) above with a person appointed under para (a) above (s 93(2)).

6.102 The Secretary of State (or agency) must give written notice of the making of an application to the court under this power to the manager and trustee of the scheme concerned. He must also take such steps as he considers appropriate for bringing the application to the attention of the participants (s 93(3)).

6.103 The courts to which applications of this kind can be made are the High Court and the Court of Session (s 93(4)).

6.104 The usual restrictions on the activities of a manager of an authorised unit trust contained in s 83 do not apply to a manager appointed under para (b) above to wind up the scheme.

COLLECTIVE INVESTMENT SCHEMES: INVESTIGATIONS

6.105 Section 94 provides a power for the Secretary of State to appoint inspectors in relation to collective investment schemes. This replaces s 12 of the Prevention of Fraud (Investments) Act 1958. The power is capable of transfer to a designated agency but the transfer must be subject to a reservation that it is exercisable concurrently by the Secretary of State. For the similar power applying to certain investment businesses, see para **8.08**.

6.106 Inspectors appointed under this power may investigate and report on:

(a) the affairs of, or of the manager or trustee of, any authorised unit trust scheme;

(b) the affairs of, or of the operator or trustee of, any recognised scheme *so far as relating to activities carried on in the United Kingdom*; or

(c) the affairs of, or of the operators or trustee of, any other collective investment scheme (s 94(1)).

The power is exercisable if it appears to the Secretary of State (or agency) that its exercise is in the interest of the participants or that the matter is of public concern.

6.107   An inspector appointed under these powers may also, if he thinks it necessary for the purposes of his investigation, investigate the affairs of any other collective investment scheme with the same manager, trustee or operator. In addition, he may also, again if he thinks it necessary for the purposes of the initial investigation, investigate the affairs of other managers, trustees or operators of those other schemes (s 94(2)).

6.108   Certain provisions of the Companies Act 1985 are applied, with variations, to investigations of this kind (s 94(3)). These relate to the production of documents and evidence to inspectors, an inspector's power to call for directors' bank accounts and the destruction of records being treated as contempt of court. Modifications made are essentially consequential, the only modification of substance qualifying the ability to call for directors' bank accounts, which cannot apply on the usual grounds relating to investigation of undisclosed emoluments or undisclosed transactions, arrangements or agreements.

6.109   Legal professional privilege is maintained except that a lawyer may be required to furnish the name and address of his client (s 94(5)). Where a person claims a lien on a document its production is to be without prejudice to the lien (s 94(6)).

6.110   These investigation powers do not 'require a person carrying on the business of banking to disclose any information or produce any document relating to the affairs of a customer unless the customer is a person whom the inspector has reason to believe may be able to give information relevant to the investigation and the Secretary of State (or, on transfer, agency) is satisfied that the disclosure or production is necessary for the purposes of the investigation' (s 94(7)). It is considered that this position supersedes any common law privilege of non-disclosure and that accordingly disclosure can be required in the exceptional situation mentioned.

6.111   An inspector appointed under this power may and, if so directed by the Secretary of State (or agency) shall make an interim report to the Secretary of State and on the conclusion of his investigation shall make a final report to him (s 94(8)). Any such report is to be written or printed as the Secretary of State (or agency) may direct. The Secretary of State (or agency) may, if thought fit:

(a) furnish a copy, on request and on payment of the prescribed fee, to the manager, trustee or operator or any participants in a scheme under investigation or any other person whose conduct is referred to in the report; and

(b) cause the report to be published (s 94(9)).

CONTRAVENTIONS

6.112   A person who contravenes any provision of Ch VIII of Pt I of the Act or any regulations made under it is to be treated as having contravened rules made under Ch V of Pt I. In the case of a person who is an authorised person by virtue of membership of a recognised self-regulating organisation or certification by a recognised professional body, any such contravention is to be treated as a contravention of the rules of that organisation or body (s 95(1)). It will be noted that a person who contravenes directions has not contravened any provision of the Chapter or any regulations made under it. Accordingly, this provision does not apply to directions. It does, though, apply to requirements imposed on operators of recognised schemes to include explanatory information in investment advertisements (s 95(2)).

Chapter 7

The Tribunal

7.01 The Act establishes a Tribunal, known as the Financial Services Tribunal, to fulfil certain functions. Its status is analogous to that of the former tribunal of inquiry under s 6 of the Prevention of Fraud (Investments) Act 1958 and to that of the Insolvency Practitioners Tribunal (see s 396 of the Insolvency Act 1986). That is, it is an investigative body, whose role is to investigate and report (see s 98(1)). It is not an appeal body. Accordingly it is considered that the initial decision which gives rise to the right to refer the matter to the Tribunal can be taken without having sufficient evidence to satisfy the Tribunal. It is a decision that there is a case for it to investigate. For the adaptation of these provisions for regulated friendly societies, see para 25 of Sch 11.

THE FINANCIAL SERVICES TRIBUNAL

7.02 Section 96(1) establishes the Tribunal. It is not to have a constant membership. Instead, there is to be a panel of not less than ten persons standing ready to serve as its members when nominated to do so (s 96(2)). The panel from which nominees are to be drawn is to consist of:

(a) persons with legal qualifications (appointed by the Lord Chancellor after consultation with the Lord Advocate) including at least one person qualified in Scots law; and

(b) persons appointed by the Secretary of State who appear to be qualified, by experience or otherwise, to deal with the cases that may be referred.

Powers relating to the Tribunal's composition are not capable of transfer to a designated agency. It is an independent body not subject to the agency and paid for out of public funds.

7.03 Where a case is referred to the Tribunal, the Secretary of State nominates three members of the panel to serve as members of the Tribunal for that case (s 96(3)). The chairman is also nominated by the Secretary of State and must be legally qualified (s 96(4)). In addition, so far as practicable, at least one of the other members is to be a person with recent practical experience in business relevant to the case.

7.04   If during a case one of the three Tribunal members dealing with it becomes unable to act, then, with the consent of the Secretary of State *and* of the person at whose request the case was referred, the case may be dealt with by the other two members (s 96(5)).

7.05   Schedule 6 'has effect with respect to the Tribunal and its proceedings' (s 96(6)). It deals with the term of office of Tribunal members and their expenses, the Tribunal's staff, procedure, evidence before it, appeals and supervision by the Council on Tribunals, and parliamentary disqualification of paid members. It is to be noted that the Secretary of State may make rules on the Tribunal's procedure, 'including provisions for the holding of any proceedings in private, for the award of costs ... and for the payment of expenses to persons required to attend.' The Insolvency Practitioners Tribunal (Conduct of Investigations) Rules 1986 (SI 1986 No 952) may form a model for these rules. The Tribunal also has wide-ranging powers to require evidence (Sch 6, para 5).

REFERENCES TO THE TRIBUNAL

7.06   The Secretary of State (or, on transfer, agency) can be required to refer a matter to the Tribunal by a person served with a notice relating to refusal, withdrawal or suspension of direct authorisation, termination or suspension of a Europerson's authorisation, disqualification directions, public statements about misconduct or exercise of intervention powers against firms (s 97(1)(a)). A reference may also be required by a person served with a copy notice under any of those provisions on the basis of matters prejudicial to him in an office or employment, or who the Secretary of State (or agency) considers would have been served with a copy notice if it had been practical to do so (s 97(1)(b)). (There is no provision for the service of copy notices in relation to disqualification directions.) The time limit for requiring a matter to be referred to the Tribunal is twenty-eight days from the date of service of the notice (not any copy notice), although this may be extended where a substituted notice is served (see para **7.08**).

7.07   The Secretary of State (or agency) does not need to refer a matter to the Tribunal where it has already been resolved in some other way. In the case of notices (not copy notices) other than those relating to the exercise of intervention powers, a matter need not be referred if, within the time limit, the Secretary of State (or agency) decides to grant the application, or, as the case may be, that he will not take the other action proposed, and gives written notice of his decision to the person concerned (s 97(2)). Similarly, where the notice relates to an application to rescind or vary a prohibition or requirement under the intervention powers, no reference needs to be made if, within the time limit, a decision is taken to grant the application, and the applicant is given written notice (s 97(3)(a)). The same applies to a change of mind on the imposition of a prohibition or requirement, except where it has already taken effect (s 97(3)(b)). For withdrawal of references, see para **7.17** ff.

7.08   There is also a power to serve a substituted notice, in place of the original one, but only in the case of a proposed withdrawal or suspension of direct authorisation or a proposed termination or suspension of authorisation as a Europerson (s 97(4)). The substituted notice must be served within the time limit. Where it is in substitution for a notice proposing withdrawal or termination of authorisation, it may propose instead either suspension or a public statement as to misconduct (s 97(5)). Where it is in substitution for a notice proposing suspension, it may propose instead a less severe suspension or, again, a public statement as to misconduct (ibid). A substituted notice replaces the original notice. The twenty-eight day limit will be replaced by a period ending fourteen days after service of the substituted notice, if this results in an extension. It is suggested that a further substituted notice may be served at any time during the time limit applying to a previous substituted notice.

7.09   The view is also taken that the power not to refer in these circumstances contemplates informal representations being made after a request is made for a reference to the Tribunal but during the time limit. It should be noted, though, that a decision must be taken before the end of that period. There is no power subsequently to decide not to refer, so there can be no question of representations continuing beyond that period with the reference unmade.

7.10   Referring an exercise of the intervention powers to the Tribunal does not affect the date on which the action taken comes into effect (s 97(6)). Other references, of course, relate to *proposed* decisions. These decisions may be taken on the expiry of the requisite period without a reference being required, or following the Tribunal's investigation and report.

DECISIONS ON REFERENCES BY APPLICANT OR AUTHORISED PERSON ETC

7.11   The Act deals differently with the decisions taken following a reference according to whether it was made at the request of a person served with a *notice* or, on the 'matters prejudicial' ground, a copy notice.

7.12   Where a case is referred to the Tribunal at the request of a person served with a *notice*, the Tribunal is to 'investigate the case and make a report stating what would in its opinion be the appropriate decision in the matter, and the reasons for that opinion' (s 98(1)). It is then the duty of the Secretary of State or agency forthwith to decide the matter in accordance with the Tribunal's report.

7.13   Where the matter referred is the refusal of an *application*, the Tribunal may report that the appropriate decision would be to grant or refuse it (s 98(2)). It need not do so, though, in the case of an *application to vary* a suspension, direction, consent, prohibition or requirement, where it can recommend any appropriate variation (s 98(2)(a)). Where the application is to rescind a prohibition or requirement, it can similarly recommend a variation instead (s 98(2)(b)).

7.14   On a reference of any action other than the refusal of an application, the Tribunal may report that the appropriate decision would be to take or not to take the action taken or proposed to be taken or to take any other action which the Secretary of State (or agency) can take under the provision in question (s 98(3)). Alternatively, it may report that the appropriate decision would be to take instead or in addition any action that the Secretary of State (or agency) can take 'in the case of the person concerned' under certain other provisions of the Act. These are the provisions relating to withdrawal or suspension of direct authorisation, termination or suspension of authorisation as a Europerson and public statements as to misconduct (s 98(4)). For adaptation of these powers for regulated insurance companies, see para 9 of Sch 10. The procedures for notice and requiring the matter to be referred to the Tribunal do not, of course, apply to action taken in accordance with the Tribunal's report (ibid).

7.15   In the case of a reference made at the request of a person served with a notice, the Tribunal must send that person a copy of its report (s 98(5)).

DECISIONS ON REFERENCES BY THIRD PARTIES

7.16   Where a case is referred to the Tribunal at the request of a person served with a copy notice on the basis of 'matters prejudicial in an office or employment', the Tribunal's task is to report 'whether the reasons stated in the notice in question which relate to that person are substantiated' (s 99). The Tribunal must send a copy of the report to the person concerned and to the person served with the notice itself.

WITHDRAWAL OF REFERENCES

7.17   A person who has required a case to be referred to the Tribunal may withdraw the reference at any time before the conclusion of the proceedings (s 100). For 'reports to date' in this situation, see para **7.19**.

7.18   The Secretary of State (or, on transfer, agency) may withdraw a reference made at the request of a person served with a notice (s 100(2)). (It should be noted that this provision does not enable him to withdraw references made at the request of a person served with a copy notice on the basis of 'matters prejudicial in an office or employment'.) The grounds on which he (or the agency) may withdraw a reference are essentially the same as those where a reference need not, after all, be made (see s 97(2), (3)). The difference is, of course, that the decision not to take the action originally proposed does not need to be taken within a specified time limit. A reference on the imposition or variation of a prohibition or requirement may not be withdrawn after it has taken effect.

7.19 Where a case is withdrawn from the Tribunal under s 100, the Tribunal is not to investigate the case further (s 100(3)). Where the reference is withdrawn by a person other than the Secretary of State (or, on transfer, agency) the Tribunal may be required to make a report on the result of its investigations up to the time the investigation was withdrawn.

7.20 The Act provides that where two or more persons have required a case to be referred to the Tribunal, the withdrawal of the reference *by* one or more of them does not affect the functions of the Tribunal as respects the case so far as relating to a person *who* has not withdrawn the reference (s 100(4).) Where a person on whom a notice was served under s 29, 34, or 59 withdraws a case from the Tribunal, the appropriate provision for notice to be given applies as if he had not required the case to be referred (s 100(5)). Neither of these provisions applies where the case is withdrawn by the Secretary of State.

TRIBUNAL REPORTS

7.21 In preparing its report on any case the Tribunal is to:

'. . . have regard to the need to exclude, so far as practicable, any matter which relates to the affairs of a particular person (not being a person who required or could have required the case to be referred to the Tribunal) where the publication of that matter would or might, in the opinion of the Tribunal, seriously and prejudicially affect the interests of that person.' (s 101(1))

7.22 This provision is in common form, being similar in its terms to, for example, s 82(1) of the Fair Trading Act 1973. It may be noted, though, that there is no express provision similar to that in s 82(2) of that Act for these reports to be protected by absolute privilege in the law of defamation. The privilege applicable will accordingly fall to be determined under general principles.

7.23 The Secretary of State (or agency) may, in such cases as he thinks fit, publish the Tribunal's report and offer copies for sale (s 101(2)). The Secretary of State (or agency) also has power, on request and on payment of the prescribed fee, to supply a copy of a Tribunal report to any person whose conduct is referred to in the report or whose interests as a client or creditor are affected by the conduct of a person to whom the proceedings before the Tribunal related (s 101(3)). This power may be expected to be of value where the report has not been published.

7.24 If the Secretary of State (or, on transfer, agency) is of the opinion that there is good reason for not disclosing any part of a report he may cause that part to be omitted from the report as published or from copies supplied (s 101(4)). Where matters are excluded from reports under the parallel provision in the Fair Trading Act (s 83(3), which is dependent on a 'public interest' test), the practice is for the fact of the omission to be made clear on the face of the report.

7.25   A copy of a report of the Tribunal endorsed with a certificate signed by or on behalf of the Secretary of State (or, on transfer, agency) stating that it is a true copy is to be evidence of the opinion of the Tribunal as to any matter referred to in the report (s 101(5)). A certificate purporting to be so signed is to be treated as having been duly signed unless the contrary is shown.

Chapter 8

Information

THE REGISTER

8.01   The Secretary of State (or, on transfer, agency) must keep a register containing entries in respect of:

(a) each directly authorised person;

(b) each other person who appears to be an authorised person by virtue of any provision of Pt I of the Act;

(c) each recognised self-regulating organisation, professional body, investment exchange and clearing house;

(d) each authorised unit trust scheme and recognised scheme;

(e) each person against whom a disqualification direction is in force (s 102(1)).

8.02   It is considered that those with interim authorisation under para 1 of Sch 15 need not be included. Paragraph 1(4) of Sch 15 disapplies s 102(1)(a), and s 102(1)(b) will not be relevant since those concerned are not authorised by virtue of a provision of Pt I.

8.03   In the case of an authorised person, the entry is to consist of:

(a) a statement of the provision by which he is an authorised person;

(b) the name and address of any authorising self-regulating organisation or professional body;

(c) for a person who is directly authorised, or authorised as a Europerson, information as to 'the services which that person holds himself out as able to provide';

(d) for a person authorised as a Europerson, the address for service notified;

(e) for a person authorised by any provision other than section 31 (Europersons), the date on which he became an authorised person by virtue of that provision; and

(f) such other information as the Secretary of State or, on transfer, agency, may determine (s 102(2)).

8.04 The entry for a recognised self-regulating organisation, professional body, investment exchange or clearing house is to consist of its name and address and such other information as the Secretary of State (or agency) may determine (s 102(3)). The entry for an authorised unit trust scheme or recognised scheme is to contain its name and, in the case of an authorised unit trust scheme, the name and address of the manager and trustee. In the case of a recognised scheme, in addition to its name there must be included the name and address of the operator and of any UK representative of the operator. In either case the entry must also contain such other information as the Secretary of State (or agency) may determine (s 102(4)). The entry for a person who is subject to a disqualification direction must contain particulars of any consent to his employment (s 102(5)).

8.05 Where it appears to the Secretary of State (or, on transfer, agency) that any person for whom there is a register entry as an authorised person has ceased to be authorised (for whatever reason), the Secretary of State (or agency) is to make a note to that effect in the entry together with the reason (s 102(6)). A note is similarly to be made to the register entry where:

(a) a recognised self-regulating organisation, professional body, investment exchange or clearing house has ceased to be recognised or to exist;

(b) an authorised unit trust scheme or recognised scheme has ceased to be authorised or recognised;

(c) a disqualification direction has ceased to have effect (s 102(7)).

Entries with notes of these kinds may be removed from the register at the end of such period as the Secretary of State (or agency) thinks appropriate (s 102(8)).

INSPECTION OF REGISTER

8.06 The information contained in entries included in the register (except entries for persons who are subject to disqualification directions) is to be open to inspection. The Secretary of State (or, on transfer, agency) may also publish the information contained in those entries in any form he thinks appropriate and may offer copies for sale (s 103(1)). Any person is entitled to ascertain whether there is a disqualification direction entry (other than one which is noted as having ceased to have effect) in respect of a *particular* person specified by him, and, if there is such an entry, to inspect it (s 103(2)). Apart from that, the information in disqualification direction entries is not to be open to inspection by any person unless he satisfies the

Secretary of State (or, on transfer, agency) that he has a good reason for seeking it (s 103(3)). A person to whom information is made available by the Secretary of State (or agency) on the basis of a 'good reason' must not, without the consent of the Secretary of State (or agency) or of the person to whom the information relates, make use of it except for the purpose for which it was made available (s 103(4)). Information which this section makes open to inspection is to be open to inspection free of charge but only at such times and places as the Secretary of State (or agency) may appoint (s 103(5)). A person entitled to inspect any information may obtain a certified copy of it from the Secretary of State on payment of the prescribed fee (s 103(5)). The register may be kept in such form as is thought appropriate with a view to facilitating inspection of the information which it contains (s 103(6)).

POWER TO CALL FOR INFORMATION

8.07 The Secretary of State (or, on transfer, agency) may by notice in writing require a person who is authorised to carry on investment business by the sections of the Act relating to authorised insurers, operators and trustees of recognised (EEC) collective investment schemes, direct authorisation or authorisation of Europersons, to furnish such information as he (or it) may reasonably require for the exercise of his (or its) functions under the Act (s 104(1)). This power, together with the parallel power for regulated friendly societies (Sch 11, para 24), accordingly covers the entire direct regulation regime. The Secretary of State (or agency) may similarly, by notice in writing, require a recognised self-regulating organisation, professional body, investment exchange or clearing house to furnish him (or it) with such information (s 104(2) and Sch 11, para 24). The Secretary of State (or agency) may also require any information required under this power to be furnished within such reasonable time and verified in such manner as he may specify (s 104(3)). The provisions of the Act on public statements as to misconduct, injunctions and restitution orders and actions for damages apply to a contravention of a requirement under this power as they apply to a contravention of the provisions to which those sections apply (s 104(4)).

INVESTIGATION POWERS

8.08 Section 105 confers on the Secretary of State (or, on transfer, agency) investigation powers which are exercisable in any case in which it appears that there is good reason to do so for the purpose of investigating the affairs, or any aspect of the affairs, of any person so far as relevant to any investment business which he is or was carrying on or appears to be or to have been carrying on (s 105(1)). They are not, though, exercisable for the purpose of investigating the affairs of any exempted person unless he is an appointed representative or the investigation is in respect of investment business in respect of which he is not an exempted person (s 105(2)). Nor are they exercisable for the purpose of investigating the affairs of a member of a recognised self-regulating organisation or a person certified by a recognised professional body in respect of investment business subject to its rules, unless the organisation or body has requested the investigation of those affairs or it appears that the organisation or body is unable or unwilling to investigate them in a satisfactory manner (s 105(2)).

8.09   Where the powers are exercisable, the Secretary of State (or agency) may require the person under investigation or any connected person to attend before the Secretary of State (or agency) at a specified time and place and answer questions or otherwise furnish information with respect to any matter relevant to the investigation (s 105(3)). The Secretary of State (or agency) may also require the person under investigation or any other person (whether or not a 'connected person') to produce at a specified time and place any specified documents which appear to relate to any matter relevant to the investigation (s 105(4)). If any such documents are produced, the Secretary of State (or agency) may take copies or extracts from them or require the person producing them or any connected person to provide an explanation of any of them. If any such documents are not produced the Secretary of State (or agency) may require the person who was required to produce them to state, to the best of his knowledge and belief, where they are (ibid).

8.10   Significantly, a statement by a person in compliance with a requirement imposed under these investigation powers may be used in evidence against him (s 105(5)). A person is not, though, to be required under these powers to disclose any information or produce any document which he would be entitled to refuse to disclose or produce on grounds of legal professional privilege in proceedings in the High Court or on grounds of confidentiality as between client and professional legal adviser in proceedings in the Court of Session, except that a lawyer may be required to furnish the name of his client (s 105(6)). Nor is a recognised bank or licensed deposit-taker to be required to disclose any information or produce any document relating to the affairs of a customer unless the Secretary of State (or agency) considers it necessary to require it for the purpose of investigating any investment business carried on, or appearing to be carried on or to have been carried on, by the bank, institution or customer or, if the customer is a related company of the person under investigation, by that person (s 105(7)). Where a person claims a lien on a document its production under these investigation powers does not prejudice the lien (s 105(8)). The expressions 'connected person', 'documents' and 'related company' are widely defined (s 105(9)).

8.11   A person who without reasonable excuse fails to comply with a requirement imposed on him under the investigation powers is guilty of an offence and liable on summary conviction to imprisonment for a term not exceeding six months or to a fine not exceeding the fifth level on the standard scale, or to both (s 105(10)). For the power of entry available in support of these investigation powers, see para **8.12**.

EXERCISE OF INVESTIGATION POWERS BY OFFICER ETC

8.12   The Secretary of State (or, on transfer, agency) may authorise any officer of his or any other competent person to exercise on his behalf all or any of the investigation powers discussed in the immediately preceding paragraphs, but only for the purpose of investigating the affairs of a person specified in the authority (s 106(1)). Accordingly, a standing authority is not possible. A person is not bound to comply with a requirement imposed by a person exercising powers under an authority of this kind unless the person exercising the powers has, if required, produced evidence of his authority. Where the Secretary of State (or agency) authorises a person who is not one of his (or its) own officers, the person concerned must report to the Secretary of State (or agency) on the exercise of the powers and the results of exercising them (s 106(3)).

Chapter 9

Auditors

APPOINTMENT OF AUDITORS

9.01   The Secretary of State (or, on transfer, agency) may make rules requiring a person who is directly authorised or authorised as a Europerson and who, apart from the rules, is not required by or under any enactment to appoint an auditor, to appoint as an auditor a person satisfying such conditions as to qualifications and otherwise as may be specified in or imposed under the rules (s 107(1)). Rules under this power may make provision:

(a) specifying the manner in which and the time within which an auditor is to be appointed;

(b) requiring the Secretary of State (or, on transfer, agency) to be notified of any such appointment and enabling the Secretary of State (or agency) to make an appointment if no appointment is made or notified as required by the rules;

(c) with respect to the remuneration of an auditor appointed under the rules;

(d) with respect to the term of office, removal and resignation of any such auditor;

(e) requiring any such auditor who is removed, resigns or is not reappointed to notify the Secretary of State (or agency) whether there are any circumstances connected with his ceasing to hold office which he considers should be brought to the attention of the Secretary of State (or agency) (s 107(2)).

9.02   The task of an auditor appointed under the rules is to examine and report in accordance with the rules on the accounts of the authorised person, and, for that purpose, he is to have such powers and duties as are specified in the rules (s 107(3)).

9.03   This provision accordingly makes it possible to require some of those within the direct regulation regime to appoint an auditor. The requirement does not extend to those with automatic authorisation by virtue of their authorisation as insurers, who may in any event be subjected to a requirement to appoint an auditor under s 21 of the Insurance Companies Act 1982. Nor does it extend to those who are automatically authorised as the operators or trustees of a recognised (EEC) collective investment scheme, where the general approach appears to be that only marketing activities are to be regulated under the Act (see s 86(7)). As far as concerns members of a recognised self-regulating organisation and persons certified by a recognised professional body, rules about auditors would appear to fall to be treated under the requirements for monitoring and enforcement, since they do not appear to be 'rules governing the carrying on of investment business'. The ability to require a firm to have an auditor should be distinguished from any requirement for particular information to be verified by a person qualified to act as an auditor. The essential feature of this provision is that it can be used to require a firm to appoint a person to hold the office of auditor on a continuing basis. This is not, of course, necessary where the firm is already required to appoint an auditor 'by or under any enactment'.

POWER TO REQUIRE SECOND AUDIT

9.04　If in any case it appears to the Secretary of State (or, on transfer, agency) that there is good reason to do so he (or it) may direct any person who is directly authorised or authorised as a Europerson to submit for further examination by a person approved by the Secretary of State (or agency):

(a) any accounts on which that person's auditor has reported or any information verified by him and given by the authorised person under notification regulations or the power to call for information; or

(b) such matters contained in any such accounts or information as are specified in the direction,

and the person making the further examination shall report his conclusions to the Secretary of State (or agency) (s 108(1)).

9.05　Any further examination and report required under this power is to be at the expense of the authorised person concerned and is to take place within a time specified in the direction or within such further time as the Secretary of State (or agency) may allow (s 108(2)). The person carrying out an examination under this power is given all the powers and duties that were available to the auditor and the auditor is under a duty to give him all the assistance he requires (s 108(3)). For enforcement of this duty, see para **9.12**.

Where a report is made of the conclusions of a further examination under this power which relates to accounts which under any enactment are required to be sent to or made available for inspection by any person or to be delivered for registration, the report, or any part of it (or a note that such a report has been made) may be similarly sent, made available or delivered by the Secretary of State (or agency) (s 108(4)).

COMMUNICATION BY AUDITOR WITH SUPERVISORY AUTHORITIES

9.06   By s 109(1) an auditor of an investment business is not prevented by his duties from communicating in good faith with the Secretary of State (or agency) any relevant information or opinion. In the absence of a provision of this kind it might have been suggested that an auditor who communicated with a supervisor could break a duty to act in the best interests of his client, or, perhaps, a duty of confidence. The provision prevents any duty being broken and applies whether or not the communication is in response to a request.

9.07   It may be expected that in due course the main accountancy bodies will formulate rules or guidance on when communications of this kind are to be made. If, though, it appears that any auditor or class of auditor of an authorised person is not subject to satisfactory rules or guidance, the Secretary of State may himself make rules for the purpose with which the auditors concerned will be duty bound to comply (s 109(2)). These can extend to information or opinions about third parties (s 109(3)). Both the freedom to communicate and the power to make rules can also apply to communication with a recognised self-regulating organisation or recognised professional body of 'matters relevant to its function of determining whether a person is a fit and proper person to carry on investment business' (s 109(5)(a)) even though, as noted in para **3.43**, there is no express requirement for a recognised professional body to operate a 'fit and proper' test. They can both apply too to communications to such an organisation or body, or to any authority or person, of 'matters relevant to its or his function of determining whether a person is complying with the rules applicable to his conduct of investment business' (s 109(5)(b)).

OVERSEAS BUSINESS

9.08   Section 110 contains special provisions for the auditors of firms who are directly authorised or authorised as Europersons and which are incorporated or have their head office outside the United Kingdom, enabling them to appoint an auditor - to whom all these provisions apply - solely for investment business carried on in the United Kingdom. It is expressly provided that rules requiring the appointment of an auditor may treat equivalent overseas qualifications as satisfying their requirements (s 110(2)).

9.09   Where a person incorporated or with his head office outside the United Kingdom applies for direct authorisation, he is not to be regarded as fit and proper unless either he has appointed an auditor in accordance with rules made under s 107 in respect of the investment business carried on by him in the United Kingdom; or he has an auditor having qualifications, powers and duties which appear to the Secretary of State (or agency) to be equivalent to those of an auditor appointed in accordance with those rules (s 110(3)). In addition, the auditor must be able and willing to communicate with the supervisory authorities in accordance with s 109.

9.10 It should be noted that this provision appears to contemplate that rules will be made under s 107, at any rate for those with direct authorisation, even though none of the 'principles applicable to designated agency's rules and regulations' expressly requires it. The provision's status in the absence of such rules is unclear. Where such rules exist the aim is, of course, to ensure that the auditor is in place before authorisation is granted. If the matter were purely left to rules applying after authorisation, the usual remedies for breach of rules would not make up for the absence of the reporting route the auditor can provide.

OFFENCES AND ENFORCEMENT

9.11 Any authorised person and any officer, controller or manager of an authorised person, who knowingly or recklessly furnishes an auditor appointed under the rules made under s 107 or a person carrying out an examination under s 108 with information which the auditor or 'second auditor' requires or is entitled to require and which is false or misleading in a material particular is to be guilty of an offence and liable:

(a) on conviction on indictment, to imprisonment for a term not exceeding two years or to a fine or to both;

(b) on summary conviction, to imprisonment for a term not exceeding six months or to a fine not exceeding the statutory maximum or to both (s 111(1)).

9.12 The duty of an auditor to assist on a second audit is enforceable by mandamus or, in Scotland, by an order for specific performance under s 91 of the Court of Session Act 1868 (s 111(2)). If it appears to the Secretary of State (not transferable to a designated agency) that an auditor has failed, in breach of his duty, to communicate with a supervisory authority, the Secretary of State may disqualify him from being the auditor of an authorised person or any class of authorised person. But he can lift a disqualification of this kind if satisfied that the person in question will do so in future (s 111(3)). An authorised person is not to appoint a disqualified person as auditor and, if he is authorised by membership of a recognised self-regulating organisation or certification by a recognised professional body, doing so is to be treated as a breach of the rules of the organisation or body (s 111(4)).

Chapter 10

Fees

10.01 This chapter deals with the sections of the Act on fees payable in relation to the regulation of investment business. It should be noted that these are statutory fees payable in relation to statutory functions. They are not charges made for services supplied. For provisions affecting the role of a designated agency in relation to fees, see para **11.18**, commenting on para 10 of Sch 9.

APPLICATION FEES

10.02 An applicant to be a recognised self-regulating organisation, professional body, investment exchange (including an overseas exchange) or clearing house is to pay fees in accordance with a scheme made and published by the Secretary of State (or, on transfer, agency). An application is not to be regarded as duly made unless this requirement is satisfied (s 112(1)). A scheme made for these purposes must specify the time when the fees are to be paid and may provide for them to be determined in accordance with a specified scale or other specified factors (s 112(2)) although it is not considered that this would enable a scheme to provide for fees to be determined in accordance with factors within the control of the recognising authority, such as the time spent on the application. Since the fees are payable in respect of the application, they are not automatically returnable if an application is refused or withdrawn, although a scheme may 'provide for the return or abatement of any fees' in these circumstances (s 112(2)(b)). A scheme may also make different provision for different cases (s 112(2)(c)) and be varied or revoked (s 112(4)). Schemes cannot be made to apply retrospectively (s 112(3)).

10.03 Applications for direct authorisation, or to be an authorised unit trust or an individually recognised collective investment scheme, must all be accompanied by the prescribed fee (s 112(5)). For these purposes, 'prescribed' means prescribed by regulations. The same applies to notices given by Europersons under s 32 and by operators of collective investment schemes constituted in other member states under s 86 or schemes authorised in designated countries or territories under s 87(3). In the absence of the fee, an application or notice of this kind is similarly not to be regarded as duly made.

PERIODICAL FEES

10.04 Every recognised self-regulating organisation, recognised professional body, investment exchange (including overseas investment exchanges) and clearing house is to pay the prescribed periodical fee to the Secretary of State (or, where relevant, agency) (s 113(1)). So long as a body has the automatic authorisation applying to authorised insurers, it must also pay such periodical fees as may be prescribed (s 113(2)) and there is a similar provision for automatically authorised friendly societies (s 113(3)). Finally, a person who is directly authorised or authorised as a Europerson must pay the periodical fee prescribed (s 113(4)), failing which the Secretary of State (or agency) may serve a written notice requiring payment within 28 days. The authorisation will cease unless the fee is paid within that period or the Secretary of State (or agency) otherwise directs (s 113(5)). A direction of this kind may be retrospective and may also be only temporary (s 113(6)). These special provisions are without prejudice to the recovery of any fee as a debt due to the Crown (s 113(7)). Managers of authorised unit trusts and operators of recognised collective investment schemes must similarly pay the prescribed periodical fee (s 113(8)) although in this case there is no automatic termination of authorisation or recognition.

Chapter 11

Transfer of functions to designated agency

INTRODUCTION: NATURE OF TRANSFER

11.01 This work has, in referring to functions under the Act, noted whether or not they are capable of transfer to a designated agency. The ability to transfer functions to 'a designated agency' (or to the 'transferee body' which fulfils the same role in relation to regulated friendly societies), enables the functions of the statutory regulator under the Act to be performed by an outside body, rather than the Secretary of State. (For the provisions applying in relation to friendly societies see paras 28 to 37 of Sch 11).

11.02 It should be noted that the provision is for transfer, not delegation of functions. Transfers of functions of this kind are common on machinery of government changes when one government department transfers functions to another, but this is believed to be the only example of a provision for such a transfer to a non-governmental body. Once transferred, the functions become those of the designated agency. Notwithstanding the names 'designated agency' and 'delegation order', given by s 114(3), it is considered that a designated agency exercises transferred functions in its own right, not as the agent or delegate of the Secretary of State. A delegation order may transfer a function even though it has not come into force but the function will not be exercisable until the provision is in force (Sch 15, para 12).

POWER TO TRANSFER FUNCTIONS TO DESIGNATED AGENCY

TRANSFER OF FUNCTIONS: REQUIREMENTS AS TO AGENCY

11.03 The Secretary of State can make an order transferring functions to a designated agency, subject to the competition vetting procedure discussed in the next Chapter and to certain requirements discussed below, if it appears to him that 'a body corporate' has been established which is able and willing to discharge all or any of the functions which are transferable and that the body itself satisfies particular requirements (s 114(1)).

11.04   The qualifications which a designated agency needs to appear to satisfy are dealt with in Schedule 7. Its constitution must provide for it to have a chairman and a governing body of the chairman and other members, who must all be appointed and liable to removal by the Secretary of State and the Governor of the Bank of England acting jointly (Sch 7, para 1(1), (2)). The members of the governing body must include both persons with experience of investment business of a kind relevant to the functions or proposed functions of the agency and other persons, including regular users on their own account or on behalf of others of services provided by persons carrying on investment business of any such kind (para 1(3)). The constitution of the body must be designed to secure a proper balance between the interests of persons carrying on investment business and the interests of the public. The requirements or arrangements for the discharge of the agency's functions are essentially directed to the internal distribution of its decision making functions (see para 2 of the Schedule). As far as concerns monitoring and enforcement (para 3 of the Schedule) the requirements are also similar to those for a recognised self-regulating organisation, the differences reflecting the difference in the nature of the agency's powers as a body exercising statutory functions. The requirement on investigation of complaints (para 4) is essentially similar too, although also covering complaints against recognised self-regulating organisations, professional bodies, investment exchanges and clearing houses. The 'promotion and maintenance of standards' requirement (para 5) is the standard one. A designated agency must also have satisfactory arrangements for recording decisions made in the exercise of its functions and for the safekeeping of those records which ought to be preserved (para 6).

11.05   By s 114(2), the body to which functions are transferred by the first 'delegation order' is to be the body known as The Securities and Investments Board Limited, at any rate so long as it appears to the Secretary of State that the Board fulfils the conditions for transfer. The Board was established for the purpose of acting as designated agency under the Act. Special provisions enable a designated agency to drop the word 'Limited' from its name (see Sch 9, para 2).

TRANSFER OF FUNCTIONS: FUNCTIONS TRANSFERABLE

11.06   The functions which are capable of transfer to a designated agency are essentially those for the regulation of investment business given to the Secretary of State by Ch II to XII of Pt I of the Act (s 114(4)). They also include his functions of certifying periodical publications and his functions in relation to 'permitted persons', as well as functions concerned with the interim recognition of professional bodies, all dealt with in the Schedules rather than in the body of the Act itself. For transfer of investigation and prosecution functions, see ss 178(10), 199(7), 201(4). For transfer of information and advice functions, see s 206(4).

11.07   The Secretary of State is not, though, given power to transfer his functions under:

(a) section 31(4) (certifying equivalence of investor protection in other member states);

(b) section 46 (power to extend or restrict exemptions);

(c) section 48(8) (amendment to stabilisation exemption);

(d) section 58(3) (orders exempting from restrictions of advertising);

(e) section 86(1) or 87(1) (requirements for automatic recognition of EEC collective investment schemes; designation of territories for other automatic recognitions);

(f) section 96 (membership of Tribunal);

(g) section 109(2) (rules specifying circumstances in which auditors are to communicate) (s 114(5)).

Nor may the Secretary of State transfer certain functions relating to overseas investment exchanges and clearing houses. The functions concerned are the making or revocation of a recognition order and applying to the court for a compliance order (s 114(6)).

It will be noted that the functions not capable of transfer are essentially those affecting the scope of the regulatory system itself, the Tribunal (to enable it clearly to be independent of the agency) persons who are not carrying on investment business (auditors), or those functions which may have possible international implications.

11.08   Any function may be transferred by a delegation order either in whole or in part (s 114(7)). Some functions can be transferred subject to a reservation that they are exercisable by the Secretary of State concurrently with the designated agency. These are the functions under s 6 (injunctions and restitution orders for contravening the restriction on persons entitled to carry on investment business), and s 72 (winding up orders) together with the functions of applying for injunctions and restitution orders under s 61 on the ground of breach of provisions of the Act itself or of an order providing an exemption from the Act's restrictions on advertising (s 114(8)). The investigation powers under ss 94, 105 and 106 can *only* be transferred subject to a reservation that they are capable of concurrent exercise by the Secretary of State.

TRANSFER OF FUNCTIONS: PRINCIPLES APPLICABLE TO DESIGNATED AGENCY'S RULES AND REGULATIONS

11.09   In addition to being satisfied as to the qualifications of the agency itself, by s 114(9), the Secretary of State must not transfer a function of making rules or regulations (that is, a legislative as distinct from an administrative function), unless:

(a) the agency has furnished him with a copy of the rules and regulations which it proposes to make in the exercise of those functions; and

(b) he is satisfied that those rules and regulations afford investors an adequate level of protection and, in the case of the rules and regulations mentioned in Sch 8 (principles applicable to designated agency's rules and regulations) comply with the principles set out in that Schedule.

11.10   The first principle that a designated agency's rules and regulations must satisfy is a general one, both in its terms and in its application. This is that conduct of business rules, and the other rules and regulations made under Part I of the Act, must 'promote high standards of integrity and fair dealing in the conduct of investment business' (Sch 8, para 1). The next five principles relate only to conduct of business rules. These must make 'proper provision' on the exercise of skill, care and diligence (Sch 8, para 2), on subordination of interests and fair dealing (Sch 8, para 3) and for due regard to be had to a customer's circumstances (Sch 8, para 4). They must also make 'proper provision' for disclosure of material interests and facts (Sch 8, para 5) and of capacity (Sch 8, para 6). In substance, if not in form, para 7 elaborates on the material facts principle by a further principle to promote disclosure of 'such information as to the nature of the investment and the financial implications of the transaction as will enable [the customer] to make an informed decision'. This principle was included to address concerns in the marketing of life assurance products, which may be of considerable complexity. It applies to conduct of business rules and cancellation rules taken together. A disclosure requirement also exists for stabilisation rules (Sch 8, para 8). Conduct of business rules and clients' money regulations must together make proper provision for the protection of other persons' property (Sch 8, para 9), and indemnity rules and rules establishing a compensation fund must make the best provision that can reasonably be made under the relevant sections (Sch 8, para 10)—so allowing the availability or otherwise of insurance facilities to be taken into account. Proper records must be required and provision made for their inspection in appropriate cases (Sch 8, para 11). Finally, the different protection appropriate for different classes of investors is to be taken into account (Sch 8, para 12).

References to 'proper provision' clearly permit an element of subjectivity in the Secretary of State's assessment of proposals for rules before transferring the powers to make them.

11.11   In addition, before making an order transferring functions to a designated agency, the Secretary of State must require it to furnish him with a copy of any guidance intended to have continuing effect which it proposes to issue in writing or other legible form (s 114(10)). The Secretary of State may take any such guidance into account in determining whether he is satisfied about the agency's rules and regulations. 'Guidance' issued by a designated agency is defined in s 114(12), the definition being of particular significance for the exemptions from competition legislation (see para **12.15** ff).

RESUMPTION OF TRANSFERRED FUNCTIONS

11.12 The provisions of the Act on resumption of transferred functions by the Secretary of State attempt to achieve the twofold objectives of ultimate accountability to Parliament and reasonable independence on operational matters for the designated agency.

11.13 Firstly, the Secretary of State may make an order resuming all or any transferred functions 'at the request or with the consent of the designated agency', so providing for agreed redistribution of functions (s 115(1)).

11.14 Secondly, in certain circumstances, an order may be made resuming:

(a) all the functions transferred to a designated agency by a delegation order; or

(b) all legislative or all administrative functions transferred by a delegation order so far as relating to investments or investment business of any class (s 115(2)). Accordingly, for example, it would not be possible to resume the power to make conduct of business rules for futures business without also resuming the power to make client money regulations for that business.

11.15 The circumstances in which an order resuming transferred powers may only be made other than at the request or with the consent of the agency are:

(a) if at any time it appears to the Secretary of State that the agency does not satisfy the requirements of Sch 7 to the Act (Qualifications of designated agency) (s 115(3));

(b) as respects functions relating to any class of investment or investment business, if at any time it appears to the Secretary of State that the agency is unable or unwilling to discharge all or any of the transferred functions for all or any investments or investment business falling within that class (s 115(4)) and

(c) where the transferred functions consist of or include any functions of making rules or regulations, if it appears to the Secretary of State that the rules or regulations made by the agency do not afford investors an adequate level of protection or do not comply with any of the applicable 'principles' (s 115(5)).

11.16 An order resuming transferred functions at the request or with the consent of the designated agency is to be subject to annulment on a resolution by either House of Parliament. Any other order resuming transferred functions must be laid before and approved by resolution of each House of Parliament (s 115(6)).

11.17 It will be recalled that the provisions for partial resumption of powers distinguish expressly between 'legislative' and 'administrative' functions, following a distinction implicit in the procedure on transfer. 'Legislative functions' are defined as functions of making rules or regulations, and 'administrative functions' means functions which are not legislative functions. Although prescribing fees and requiring information to be furnished are both legislative functions, the Act does enable these functions to be retained or resumed with any administrative functions to which they relate (s 115(7)).

STATUS OF DESIGNATED AGENCY AND EXERCISE OF TRANSFERRED FUNCTIONS

11.18 By s 116, Sch 9 to the Act 'has effect as respects the status of a designated agency and the exercise of the functions transferred to it by a delegation order.' The Schedule begins by providing that a designated agency is not to be regarded as acting on behalf of the Crown, and its members, officers and servants are not to be regarded as Crown servants (para 1(1)). A paid chairman of a designated agency may not be a member of the House of Commons or of the Northern Ireland Assembly (para 1(2)–(3)). Paragraph 2 of the Schedule enables a designated agency not to include the word 'limited' as part of its name. The Schedule next addresses the relationship with the Tribunal, requiring the Tribunal to copy to the Secretary of State any report made to an agency and enabling it, where disciplinary powers are shared between the Secretary of State and one or more agencies, to require any of them to exercise powers held (para 3). A designated agency must send the Secretary of State a copy of any rules or regulations made under functions transferred by a delegation order (a corresponding provision applying for functions relating to friendly societies) and give him written notice of any amendment, revocation or addition affecting such rules or regulations (para 4(1)). Similar provisions apply to guidance (para 4(2)). The procedure where a designated agency makes rules or regulations is also set out (paras 5–9): it will be noted that this does not involve a Parliamentary procedure. There is also a provision for rules or regulations to be made available to the public (para 8(1)) and one derived from the Statutory Instruments Act 1946 to cover contraventions where a rule or regulation has not been duly made available (para 8(2)). The admission as evidence of printed copies of rules and regulations is also provided for (para 9). A designated agency is entitled to keep any fees payable to it by virtue of a designation order, apply them for meeting its expenses in discharging its functions under the order and set them at a level which enables it to defray expenses incurred in making preparations for the agency becoming a designated agency (paras 10, 11).

There is also a consultation procedure for a designated agency's rules and regulations, although this does not apply to the agency where the delay involved would be prejudicial to the interests of investors or where the rules or regulations are in the same or substantially the same terms as those furnished on the application for designation (para 12). The Secretary of State is authorised to communicate to a designated agency information he could himself have used for the purpose of any function transferred to it and it can itself communicate the information in the exercise of its transferred powers if he could have done so. A communication by the Secretary of State to the agency will not amount to a 'publication' for the purposes of the law of defamation (para 13), although it appears that a communication by the agency may do so. There is, of course, an exemption from liability for damages in s 187.

DESIGNATED AGENCIES: REPORTS AND ACCOUNTS

11.19   A designated agency must make an annual report to the Secretary of State on the discharge of its transferred functions which must be laid before Parliament (s 117(1), (2)). Where the designated agency is not subject to the accounting requirements of s 227 of the Companies Act 1985 (or the corresponding Northern Ireland provisions) the Secretary of State may give it directions with respect to its accounts and the audit of its accounts, and it is to be its duty to comply with them (s 117(3), (4)). The Secretary of State may, irrespective of whether those requirements apply, require a designated agency to 'comply with any provisions of that Act which would not otherwise apply to it or direct that any provision of that Act shall apply to the agency with such modifications as are specified in the direction.' Again, the agency will be under a duty to comply (s 117(4)).

DESIGNATED AGENCIES: TRANSITIONAL AND SUPPLEMENTARY PROVISIONS

11.20   Section 118 contains transitional and supplementary provisions on orders transferring or resuming functions under the Act.

Chapter 12

Prevention of restrictive practices

12.01 Chapter XIV of Part I of the Act establishes a special competition regime for much of the financial services sector. It accordingly extends the effect of the Restrictive Trade Practices (Stock Exchange) Act 1984 in providing exemption from mainstream United Kingdom competition legislation. That Act, which it supersedes, is repealed. For the provisions applying to regulated friendly societies, see Sch 11.

Examination of Rules and Practices

RECOGNISED SELF-REGULATING ORGANISATIONS, INVESTMENT EXCHANGES AND CLEARING HOUSES

12.02 It will be recalled that the various provisions of the Act on recognition of self-regulating organisations, investment exchanges and clearing houses were all expressed to be subject to the provisions of the Act on prevention of restrictive practices. Section 119(1) establishes the competition test applying on a recognition by the Secretary of State. This is that he may not make a recognition order unless he is satisfied that the rules and any guidance supplied on the application and, in the case of an investment exchange, any clearing arrangements of which particulars were supplied:

'. . . do not have, and are not intended or likely to have, to any significant extent, the effect of restricting, distorting or preventing competition or, if they have or are intended or likely to have that effect to any significant extent, that the effect is not greater than is necessary for the protection of investors.'

It will be noted that the first part of this test is derived from s 2(1) of the Competition Act 1980. Comparison between the two brings out in particular that, under the Financial Services Act, the effect is not limited to an effect in the United Kingdom.

12.03 The special competition regime for recognised self-regulating organisations, investment exchanges and clearing houses does not apply only in the initial recognition process. In order to parallel mainstream competition legislation, it must also apply subsequently. Accordingly, the Secretary of State is given a continuing role over certain of their rules, guidance, arrangements and practices, and over particular practices of their members (see s 119(2) and (5)). If at any time it appears to the Secretary of State that any such rules, guidance, arrangements or practices 'have or are intended or likely to have, to a significant extent, the effect of restricting, distorting or preventing competition and that that effect is greater than is necessary for the protection of investors', he has powers to act accordingly (s 119(2)). These are:

(a) to revoke the recognition under the usual procedure;

(b) to direct that specified steps are taken for the purpose of securing that they do not have that effect;

(c) to make alterations in the rules (except, by s 119(4), the rules of an overseas investment exchange or clearing house) for that purpose (s 119(3)).

MODIFICATION OF SECTION 117 WHERE RECOGNITION FUNCTION IS TRANSFERRED

12.04 A modified procedure applies where the recognition function has been transferred to a designated agency, in order to enable the Secretary of State himself to retain the decision on whether any anti-competitive effect is greater than necessary for the protection of investors. Under this modified procedure, the designated agency sends the Secretary of State copies of the rules, guidance or arrangements (together with any other information supplied) and is not to grant the recognition without the leave of the Secretary of State, who may not grant leave if he would himself have been unable to grant the recognition on competition grounds (s 120(1), (2)).

12.05 The provisions for subsequent action on competition grounds are also adapted. First, in order to keep the Secretary of State informed, a designated agency must send him copies of notices received under notification regulations of any amendment, revocation or addition to the rules or guidance of a recognised organisation or investment exchange and, in the case of an investment exchange, of the making, termination or variation of any clearing arrangements (s 120(3)). If it then, at any time, appears to the Secretary of State that, apart from the delegation order, he could himself have taken action on competition grounds under the powers in s 119(3) (described at para **12.03**, ante) he can himself revoke the recognition order or as an alternative, can direct the designated agency either to direct that specified steps are taken or to make appropriate alterations to the rules itself (s 120(4)).

DESIGNATED AGENCIES

12.06 A similar competition test is to be met on the transfer of functions to a designated agency (although there is no such test where powers to make rules or regulations are exercised by the Secretary of State himself). The imposition of a competition test should avoid the rules and regulations of an agency themselves being more anti-competitive than is necessary for the protection of investors. It will be recalled that the rules of a self-regulating organisation or professional body must be at least equivalent in terms of the protection of investors to those of the Secretary of State or agency. Since, where the rules are made by an agency, they will accordingly already have satisfied a competition test, this provides a further reason why such organisations and bodies may wish to replicate or incorporate these rules.

12.07 The basis of the test applying on the transfer of functions to a designated agency is that the Secretary of State cannot make a delegation order transferring any function to a designated agency unless he is satisfied that the rules, regulations and guidance supplied to him under the transfer of functions procedure:

'. . . do not have, and are not intended or likely to have, to any significant extent the effect of restricting, distorting or preventing competition or, if they have or are intended or likely to have that effect, that the effect is not greater than is necessary for the protection of investors.' (s 121(1))

12.08 The Secretary of State has a continuing competition role here too, with powers similar to these applying following the recognition of a self-regulating organisation, investment exchange or clearing house (s 121(2)–(4)). These permit withdrawal of the transferred powers and directions to take specified steps. (This and the power to make directions in support of international obligations are the only direct controls by the Secretary of State over the activities of an agency once designated.) It will be noted that, in contrast to the position for recognised self-regulating organisations, investment exchanges and clearing houses, there is no power for an external authority to make alterations in the rules of a designated agency. This should assist in promoting its independence.

Consultation with Director General of Fair Trading

REPORTS BY DIRECTOR GENERAL OF FAIR TRADING

12.09 In order to assist the Secretary of State in exercising his competition functions on a designation or recognition there are provisions for the Director General of Fair Trading to report his opinion on whether rules, regulations, guidance or arrangements 'have or are intended or likely to have, to any significant extent, the effect of restricting, distorting or preventing competition and, if so, what that effect is likely to be.' The Secretary of State is to 'have regard to' the Director's report in these circumstances (s 122 (1), (2)). It will be noted that the Director General has no role in advising on the protection of investors or on whether any anti-competitive effect is greater than is necessary for the protection of investors: these are matters for the Secretary of State.

12.10   The Director General is also to keep under review various rules, guidance, arrangements and regulations of designated agencies and recognised self-regulating organisations, investment exchanges and clearing houses, together with changes in them. If at any time he is of the opinion that any such rules, guidance, arrangements or regulations, in their current form, 'have, or are intended or likely to have, to any significant extent, the effect of restricting, distorting or preventing competition', he is to make a report to the Secretary of State stating his opinion and what that effect is or is likely to be (s 122(4)). Again, the Director General's role is limited to competition, and it will be noted that he does not report on the effect of the changes but rather on the effect of the provisions as amended. While the Director General is under a duty to report if in his opinion there is a significant anti-competitive effect, he may also report on a change itself if it does not in his opinion have, and is not intended or likely to have, any significant anti-competitive effect (s 122(5)). Accordingly, a clearance procedure may be operated.

12.11   In addition to his roles on initial designation or recognition and on the continuing effect of rules, guidance, arrangements and regulations, the Director General has a roving brief on the anti-competitive effects of *practices*, again resulting in a report to the Secretary of State (s 122(6)).

12.12   It will have been observed that the Act does not impose a duty on the Secretary of State to 'have regard to' reports made by the Director General either under his continuing review of rules etc, or under his roving brief on practices. It would appear that imposing such a duty is inappropriate outside the context of a specific decision. The Secretary of State cannot, though, exercise the powers to act on competition grounds except after receiving and considering a report from the Director General (s 122(7)).

12.13   The Director may, if he thinks fit, publish any report made by him under these powers but must exclude from a published report, so far as practicable, any matter which relates to the affairs of a particular person (other than the self-regulatory organisation, investment exchange, clearing house or designated agency concerned) whose publication would or might in his opinion seriously and prejudicially affect the interests of that person (s 122(8)).

INVESTIGATIONS BY DIRECTOR GENERAL OF FAIR TRADING

12.14   The Director General of Fair Trading is given powers 'for the purpose of investigating any matter with a view to its consideration under s 122.' These enable him, by notice in writing, to require the production of documents relating to any matter relevant to the investigation or to require any person carrying on a business to provide any information specified or described in the notice (s 123(1)). They do not, however, enable him to require information from a person who would be entitled to refuse to produce it on grounds of legal professional privilege in proceedings in the High Court or on grounds of confidentiality between client and professional legal adviser in proceedings in the Court of Session (s 123(2)). Notices under this power are enforceable in the same way as notices under s 85 of the Fair Trading Act 1973 (s 123(3)).

Consequential exemptions from competition law

THE FAIR TRADING ACT 1973

12.15 Section 7 (1)(c) of the Fair Trading Act 1973 provides for a 'monopoly situation' to exist when one quarter of the services of a particular description supplied in the United Kingdom are supplied by (or for) members of a group of persons (although not a group of 'interconnected bodies corporate') who 'so conduct their affairs as to prevent, restrict or distort competition' in connection with the supply of services of that description. An apparent monopoly situation can, of course, be referred to the Monopolies and Mergers Commission. Under s 124 of the Financial Services Act, though, for the purpose of deciding whether such a monopoly situation exists no account is to be taken of:

(a) rules, regulations or guidance of a designated agency, recognised self-regulating organisation, recognised investment exchange or recognised clearing house;

(b) any clearing arrangements or any conduct required or contemplated by them; or

(c) any conduct constituting a practice covered by the special competition regime (s 124(1)).

12.16 This effect is preserved after the revocation of a recognition order for conduct while the order was in force (s 124(2)).

12.17 There is also a provision applying on a monopoly reference (whether by the Director General of Fair Trading or by ministers) which is not limited to the facts, that is, one where a finding on the public interest is sought. This applies where, on such a reference, the Monopolies and Mergers Commission find that a monopoly situation exists (even though taking no account of the matters mentioned above), and:

(a) that the person (or, if more than one, any of the persons) in whose favour it exists is subject to rules or regulations within the special competition regime; or

(b) that any such person's conduct in carrying on any business to which those rules or regulations relate is the subject of guidance issued by a recognised organisation, exchange, or clearing house or by a designated agency; or

(c) that any such person is a party to clearing arrangements; or

(d) that the person (if more than one, any of the persons) in whose favour the monopoly exists is itself a recognised organisation, exchange or clearing house, or a designated agency. In that case the Commission, in making its report on the reference, must exclude from consideration the question whether the rules, regulations, guidance or clearing arrangements, or indeed the acts or omissions, of the authority concerned in its capacity as such, operate or may be expected to operate against the public interest (s 124(3)).

THE RESTRICTIVE TRADE PRACTICES ACT 1976

12.18 The Restrictive Trade Practices Act 1976 provides for agreements containing certain restrictions to be furnished to the Director General of Fair Trading for registration and possible reference to the Restrictive Practices Court.

12.19 These agreements could potentially include agreements for the constitution of a recognised self-regulating organisation, investment exchange or clearing house and the Act is accordingly generally disapplied from these agreements including any recommendations deemed to be included in them by the provisions of the 1976 Act applying to trade associations and 'services supply associations' (s 125(1)).

12.20 In addition to the constitutions of these authorities themselves, it is also provided that the Act will not apply to any agreement whose parties consist of or include any such authority or a person who is subject to its rules, or rules or regulations made by a designated agency in the exercise of its transferred powers, by reason of any term whose inclusion in the agreement is required or contemplated by the rules, regulations or guidance of that organisation, exchange, clearing house or agency (s 125(2)). So, for example, if a principal of an appointed representative is required by such rules to impose restrictions on the business done by the representative the restrictions imposed will not bring the agreement within the scope of the 1976 Act.

12.21 Nor will the 1976 Act apply to any clearing arrangements or to any agreement involving a recognised clearing house by reason of any term (perhaps for the provision of information) whose inclusion is required or contemplated by any clearing arrangements (s 125(3)).

12.22 Where the exemptions provided mean that an existing agreement ceases to be subject to registration under the 1976 Act, the Director General is to remove particulars of it from the register and any proceedings pending before the Restrictive Practices Court are to be discontinued (s 125(5)). Where the recognition order in respect of a self-regulating organisation, investment exchange or clearing house is revoked, the exemptions from the 1976 Act are to have effect as if the organisation, exchange or clearing house had continued to be recognised until the end of the period of six months beginning with the day on which the revocation takes effect (s 125(4)). This would appear to be designed to provide a period during which the agreement may be varied or terminated. Where an agreement which has been exempt from registration under these provisions ceases to be exempt following the revocation of a recognition order, one month is allowed for furnishing particulars of the agreement (s 125(6)). Effectively the same applies where an agreement has been registered and a term ceases to be exempt following the revocation of a recognition: particulars must be furnished within one month (s 125(7)). This is the usual period applying under the 1976 Act following the revocation of an exemption.

12.23   As noted in the introductory paragraph to this chapter, the Restrictive Trade Practices (Stock Exchange) Act 1984 is repealed (s 125(8)).

THE COMPETITION ACT 1980

12.24   This Act provides for the investigation and control of anti-competitive practices (see ss 2-10). Section 126 of the Financial Services Act provides an exemption from it by providing that 'no course of conduct constituting any such practice as is mentioned in section 119(2) or 121(2),' is to constitute an anti-competitive practice for the purposes of the 1980 Act. It will be recalled that these are those practices of recognised self-regulating organisations, investment exchanges, and clearing houses, of designated agencies, and of those who are subject to the rules and regulations of any of them, which fall within the special competition regime. Where a recognition order or delegation order is revoked the exemption continues to apply to courses of conduct which occurred while the order was in force (s 126(2)).

Recognised professional bodies

MODIFICATION OF RESTRICTIVE PRACTICES ACT 1976 IN RELATION TO RECOGNISED PROFESSIONAL BODIES

12.25   Special provision on competition matters is also made for recognised professional bodies, although this is rather different from that made for designated agencies and the other recognised authorities. This reflects the fact that recognised professional bodies will be regulating investment business only incidentally, so making the special regime applying elsewhere difficult to apply. It also rests, though, on the principle that where they are regulating investment business it should be the special competition test, weighing restrictions on competition against the needs of investor protection, which applies. Since the provisions of the Fair Trading Act and Competition Act involve discretion (for example, in making references to the Monopolies and Mergers Commission), no modification is strictly necessary there. In view of the difficulties in application of special provisions for professional bodies a minimalist approach has been adopted, with modifications only to the 1976 Act.

12.26 The recognised professional bodies exemption applies to:

(a) any agreement for the constitution of a recognised professional body (including any recommendation deemed to be a term of such an agreement by the provisions applying to services supply associations); and

(b) any other agreement whose parties consist of or include such a body, a person certified by such a body or a member of such a body, and which is an agreement to which the 1976 Act applies by virtue of any term whose inclusion in the agreement is required or contemplated by rules or guidance of that body relating to the carrying on of investment business by persons certified by it (s 127(1)).

12.27 If it appears to the Secretary of State that the restrictions (that is, all the restrictions) in an agreement to which these provisions apply:

(a) do not have and are not intended or likely to have, to any significant extent, the effect of restricting, distorting or preventing competition; or

(b) if all or any of them have, or likely to have, or are intended to have that effect, that the effect is not greater than is necessary for the protection of investors;

he may give a direction to the Director General of Fair Trading requiring him not to make an application to the Restrictive Practices Court in respect of the agreement (s 127(2)).

It will be noted that this procedure is similar to that in section 21(2) of the Restrictive Trade Practices Act 1976. Under that procedure, where it appears to the Secretary of State, on the Director General of Fair Trading's representation, that the restrictions accepted or information provisions made under an agreement are not of such significance as to call for investigation by the court, the Secretary of State may give directions discharging the Director from taking proceedings in the Restrictive Practices Court. The professional bodies procedure adapts the general financial services test for this purpose, and removes the Director General's power, not merely his duty.

12.28 It may sometimes be the case that not all the restrictions in an agreement are insignificant or necessary for the protection of investors, but that some are. Where this appears to the Secretary of State to be the position he can make a declaration accordingly and give notice of it to the Director General of Fair Trading and to the Restrictive Practices Court (s 127(3)). If proceedings in the court are begun by an application made after notice is given to it of a declaration of this kind, it may not make any finding or exercise any power under Pt I of the 1976 Act (for example, the power to order the parties not to give effect to the agreement) in relation to the restriction (s 127(4)). Accordingly, the declaration may be said to bind the court in subsequent proceedings.

12.29   The Director General cannot apply to the court in respect of an agreement to which the special provision applies unless he has notified the Secretary of State of his intention to do so. Where he is proposing to apply to the court, he must supply to the Secretary of State information to enable him to decide whether to give a direction or make a declaration (s 127(5)). He may not then apply until the Secretary of State has either notified him that he does not intend to make a direction or declaration, or has actually given notice of the declaration (s 127(5)). Of course, the Director cannot apply where a direction is given in any event.

12.30   The Secretary of State is given a limited power to revoke a direction or declaration of this kind, to vary a declaration, or to give a direction or make a declaration even though he has previously notified the Director that he did not intend to do so. In order to do so, though, he must be satisfied that there has been a material change of circumstances, so that the grounds for the declaration have ceased to exist, that there are grounds for a different declaration, or that there are, after all, grounds for giving a direction or making a declaration, as the case may be (s 127(6)). The 'material changes of circumstances' test is again to be found in the procedure in section 21 of the 1976 Act.

12.31   Notice is to be given of a revocation of a direction to the Director. Both the Director and the court are to be notified of the revocation or variation of a declaration but a variation of a declaration cannot restrict the powers of the court (although it could apparently increase them) in any proceedings begun by an application already made by the Director (s 127(7)). This is consistent with the limit on the effect of a declaration itself to proceedings on subsequent applications. A direction or declaration ceases to have effect if the agreement ceases to be one to which the section applies (s 127(8)).

12.32   The 1976 Act applies to agreements containing 'information provisions' as well as to agreements containing restrictions. Information provisions are, broadly, provisions for sharing information on matters such as charges made. The special competition regime for professional bodies applies to information provisions as it applies to restrictions (s 127(9)).

Supplemental

SUPPLEMENTARY PROVISIONS

12.33   The Act contains a special notice and representations procedure applying to particular powers of the Secretary of State under the provisions on prevention of restrictive practices. These are essentially his powers over recognised self-regulating organisations, investment exchanges, clearing houses and designated agencies, relating to directing steps to be taken, altering rules, refusing leave for recognition, and, where the function of revoking recognition is transferred, revoking it on competition grounds. Before the Secretary of State exercises one of these powers he must give written notice of his intention to the authority concerned and take such steps (whether by publication or otherwise) as he thinks appropriate for bringing the notice to the attention of any other person who in his opinion is likely to be affected by the exercise of the power. He must then have regard to any representation made (within such time as he considers reasonable) by the authority concerned or by any other such person (s 128(1)). A notice of this kind must give particulars of the manner in which the Secretary of State proposes to exercise the power and state the reasons for which he proposes to act. The statement of reasons may include any matters contained in a report of the Director General of Fair Trading under s 122 (s 128(2)).

12.34   Any direction given under the provisions on prevention of restrictive practices is to be enforceable, on the application of the person by whom it was made, by mandamus or, in Scotland, by an order for specific performance under s 91 of the Court of Session Act 1868 (s 128(3)).

12.35   The fact that any rules or regulations have been altered by or pursuant to a direction given by the Secretary of State under these provisions is not to preclude their subsequent alteration or revocation by the organisation, exchange, clearing house or agency (s 128(4)). This is a standard provision to avoid such alterations having a stultifying effect, found also in the section on alteration of a self-regulating organisation's rules for the protection of investors. It is also provided that in determining whether any guidance has, or is likely to have, any particular effect, the Secretary of State and the Director may assume that the persons to whom it is addressed will act in conformity with it (s 128(5)).

Chapter 13

Insurance business

Application of investment business provisions to regulated insurance companies

13.01   The investment business provisions of Part I of the Act are adapted for 'regulated insurance companies' by Sch 10 (s 129). A regulated insurance company is one to which Part II of the Insurance Companies Act 1982 applies or which is authorised as a Europerson. The insurance companies to which Part II of the 1982 Act applies are, subject to certain exceptions, 'all insurance companies, whether established within or outside the United Kingdom, which carry on insurance business within the United Kingdom' (s 15 of 1982 Act). The exceptions include registered friendly societies and certain members of Lloyd's. The adaptations made are referred to in conjunction with the provisions adapted and no detailed discussion is appropriate here. Their purpose is to take account of the prudential supervision of insurance companies and to retain ultimate control over them in the hands of those responsible for that supervision. The Schedule also amends, by para 7, the grounds on which insurance business authorisation can be withdrawn under the 1982 Act and, in para 10, provides for consultation between the Secretary of State and designated agencies.

Restrictions on promotion of contracts of insurance

13.02   Subject to certain exceptions, 'no person shall:

(a) issue or cause to be issued in the United Kingdom' (whether or not in the course of a business) 'an advertisement:

  (i)   inviting any person to enter into or offer to enter into a contract of insurance rights under which constitute an investment for the purposes of (the Act), or
  (ii) containing information calculated to lead directly or indirectly to persons doing so; or

146

(b) in the course of a business, advise or procure any person in the United Kingdom to enter into such a contract' (s 130(1)).

13.03   This restriction does not apply, though, where the contract is to be with:

(a) a UK-authorised insurer;

(b) a registered friendly society;

(c) an insurance company whose head office is in a member state other than the United Kingdom and which is entitled to carry on there insurance business of the relevant class;

(d) an insurance company which has a branch or agency in such a member state and is entitled to carry on there insurance business of the relevant class (s 130(2)).

13.04   Nor does the restriction apply where the contract is to be with an insurance company authorised to effect or carry out such contracts of insurance in a designated country or territory so long as any conditions imposed by the designation order have been satisfied (s 130(3)). Before the Secretary of State makes such an order (the function is not capable of transfer to a designated agency) he must be satisfied that the *law* under which insurance companies are authorised and supervised in that country or territory affords adequate (not 'equivalent') protection to policyholders and potential policyholders against the risk that the companies may be unable to meet their liabilities. The order (which is subject to annulment by resolution of either House of Parliament) may be revoked where it appears that this is no longer the case (s 130(4), (5)).

13.05   It will be seen that this restriction, designed to meet concerns over promotion of insurance contracts by inadequately regulated insurers, fulfils a similar role to the restriction on promotion of collective investment schemes contained in s 76, although, of course, it does not apply only to authorised persons. It also goes beyond the parallel provision in s 57, which only requires advertisements to be approved by an authorised person. Contravening the restriction is an offence (s 130(6)) subject to two defences. The first is for a person—perhaps a newspaper company—who in the ordinary course of a business other than investment business issues an advertisement to the order of another person. He does not commit the offence if he proves that the matters contained in the advertisement were not (wholly or in part) devised or selected by him or by any person under his direction or control and that he believed on reasonable grounds after due inquiry that the person to whose order the advertisement was issued was an authorised person (s 130(7)). The second is that a person other than the insurance company with which the contract is to be made is not guilty of an offence if he proves that he believed on reasonable grounds after due enquiry that one of the two exceptions to the offence (paras **13.03** and **13.04**) applied (s 130(8)).

Contracts made after contravention of s 130

13.06 Section 131 provides for contracts of insurance made after contravention of s 130 to be unenforceable by the insurance company and for the other party to be able to recover any money or other property paid or transferred by him, together with compensation for loss, broadly on the pattern of s 5. There are also provisions for the court to allow the contract to be enforced and money or property to be retained, also similar in approach to those in s 5 (see s 131(3), (4)) and consequential provisions (see s 131(5), (6)). A contravention by an authorised person is actionable at the suit of any person who suffers loss as a result (s 131(7) and the injunction and restitution order powers apply (s 131(8)).

Insurance contracts effected in contravention of s 2 of the Insurance Companies Act 1982

13.07 Section 132 of the Financial Services Act arises from three cases dealing with the effect of contravention of s 2 of the Insurance Companies Act 1982 on the validity of contracts of insurance effected in breach of that section. In *Bedford Insurance Co v Instituto de Resseaguros do Brazil* ([1984] 3 All ER 766, [1984] 3 WLR 726) the court expressed the view that contracts made in breach of s 2 were void *ab initio*. *Stewart v Oriental Fire and Marine Insurance Co* ([1984] 3 All ER 777, [1984] 3 WLR 741) decided that such contracts were not invalidated, but were enforceable, at least by the insured. *Phoenix Insurance v Halvanon Insurance*, in this respect, followed the approach of *Stewart* at first instance ([1986] 1 All ER 908) but the *Bedford* view was preferred, although *obiter*, by the Court of Appeal (Financial Times, 15 October 1986).

13.08 The new provision applies only to insurance contracts whose validity does not fall to be treated under s 5. Where such a contract is entered into by a person in the course of carrying on insurance business in contravention of s 2, it is unenforceable against the other party, who is also entitled to recover any money or other property paid or transferred by him under the contract, together with compensation for loss (s 132(1)). There are provisions for the court to uphold the agreement where particular conditions are satisfied (s 132(3)) and there are also the usual consequential provisions (s 132(4)–(6)). It is expressly provided that a contravention in respect of a contract of insurance is not to affect the validity of a reinsurance contract in respect of it (s 132(6)).

Misleading statements as to insurance contracts

13.09   Section 133 contains an analogue to s 47(1) (discussed at para **4.02** ff) for inducements to enter into or offer to enter into, (or to refrain from entering into or offering to enter into) a contract of insurance *with* an insurance company. Inducements to the insurance company itself (such as misleading statements in proposal forms) are not therefore covered. This provision does not apply, of course, where section 47(1) applies, this result being achieved by the words in brackets in the section itself. The territorial extent is the same as for section 47(1) (s 133(2)) as are the penalties (s 133(3)).

Controllers of insurance companies

13.10   The expression 'controller' is defined in s 7(4) of the Insurance Companies Act 1982. This definition includes, by s 7(4)(c)(ii), a person who, either alone or with any associate or associates is entitled to exercise, or control the exercise, of a particular proportion of voting power at general meetings. By s 134, the proportion concerned is reduced from 'one-third or more' to '15 per cent', so bringing the definition into line with the Financial Services Act definition in s 207(5), and also with that in the Banking Act 1979. This change also reflects the level at which material influence may be taken to arise under s 65 of the Fair Trading Act 1973, triggering the power to refer mergers to the Monopolies and Mergers Commission.

Communication by auditor with Secretary of State

13.11   Section 135 inserts a new section in the Insurance Companies Act 1982 to facilitate direct communication with the Secretary of State by the auditor of an insurance company within Part II of the 1982 Act. This is in similar terms to s 109, discussed at para **9.06** ff ante.

Arrangements to avoid unfairness between separate insurance funds

13.12   A new section is also inserted in the 1982 Act to provide for arrangements to avoid unfairness between separate insurance funds (s 136(1)). This applies to insurance companies to which Part II of the 1982 Act applies which carry on long term business in the United Kingdom. It requires them to 'secure that adequate arrangements are in force for securing that transactions affecting assets of the company (other than transactions outside its control) do not operate unfairly between the section 28 fund or funds and the other assets of the company or, in a case where the company has more than one identified fund, between those funds'. The funds mentioned are defined (s 136(1)).

13.13 The purpose of the new provision is to avoid companies unfairly favouring particular funds, for example, in order to promote them as particularly successful. Fairness between funds can be achieved for unit trusts by conduct of business rules since their fund management is investment business. This will not be so for insurance companies managing their own assets.

Regulations in respect of linked long term policies

13.14 Section 78(2)(a) of the 1982 Act enables regulations on linked long term policies to restrict the descriptions of property (or the indices of the value of property) by reference to which benefits can be determined. The amendment made by s 137 also enables them to restrict the *proportion* of those benefits which may be determined by reference to property of a specified description or a specified index. This provides greater flexibility in the regulation-making power, enabling a similar effect to be achieved to a restriction on the investment powers of an authorised unit trust under s 81(2)(d).

Insurance brokers

13.15 Section 138 deals with insurance brokers. The Insurance Brokers (Registration) Act 1977 provides for the regulation of registered insurance brokers and enrolled insurance broking firms. It is based on control not of the activity of insurance broking, but of the use of the description 'insurance broker'. The 1977 Act continues in force as a method of regulating those who use this description, even though many of those doing so will also be subject to regulation under the Financial Services Act. Section 138(1)–(5) accordingly integrates the two systems of regulation.

13.16 Section 8 of the 1977 Act enables the Insurance Brokers' Registration Council to make rules on, *inter alia*, the making of applications for registration or enrolment. It is now expressly provided that these rules may require an applicant (for either registration or enrolment) to state whether he is an authorised or exempted person and, if so, to give particulars of the authorisation or exemption (s 138(1)). An individual is to be treated as having satisfied the Council as to his character and suitability to be a registered insurance broker if he is an authorised person or a member of a partnershp or unincorporated association which is an authorised person. There is no such provision for exempted persons. In addition, in drawing up a code of conduct, making requirements for carrying on business as insurance brokers or making indemnity rules, after the coming into force of section 138, the Council is to take proper account of any provisions (such as conduct of business rules) applicable and powers (such as intervention powers) exercisable under the Financial Services Act (s 138(2)).

13.17   Section 12 of the 1977 Act, which concerns indemnity rules, is also modified. Previously, it *required* indemnity rules to be made covering any description of civil liability incurred. This is no longer appropriate in view of changes in the availability of insurance and of the powers in ss 53 and 54 of the Financial Services Act. Accordingly, the Council's duty is replaced with a power (s 138(3)).

13.18   An amendment is also made to the disciplinary procedures under the 1977 Act (s 138(4)). This enables the Disciplinary Committee under the 1977 Act to erase the name of a broker from the register (or of an enrolled firm from the list) if it appears to the Committee that the relevant regulator under the Financial Services Act has concluded that the broker (or a related person) or the body corporate has contravened or failed to comply with particular requirements. This special procedure relieves the Council from the need to undertake a further investigation. It covers requirements of provisions of the Act, of rules and regulations made under it, and of rules of a recognised self-regulating organisation or recognised professional body, but only where the requirements relate to life assurance investments. Action on other contraventions or failures to comply is to be dealt with as before.

13.19   The Insurance Brokers' Registration Council is subjected to a duty to cooperate with other regulators in similar terms to the requirement applying on recognitions (s 138(5)).

13.20   The expression 'authorised insurers' in the 1977 Act is extended to include insurers in other member States. The definition is relevant for the purposes of indemnity rules under s 12 of the 1977 Act. Its extension enables insurance under those rules to be taken out and maintained with EEC insurers, so promoting freedom to provide insurance services within the Community and making similar provision to s 53(3).

Industrial assurance

13.21   Industrial assurance is essentially life assurance where the premiums are 'received by means of collectors'. Section 139 amends the Industrial Assurance Act 1923 in the light of the Financial Services Act.

13.22   The first change made is to s 5 of the 1923 Act, which, *inter alia*, provides for the owner of a policy which has been unlawfully issued to be paid its surrender value or, for policies issued after the commencement of the 1923 Act, a sum equal to the amount of premiums paid. This is not needed for policies issued in contravention of s 3 of the Financial Services Act, where s 5 of that Act will apply. Nor is it needed for policies issued in contravention of s 2 of the Insurance Companies Act 1982, where s 132 of the Financial Services Act will apply. Section 139(1) disapplies s 5 of the 1923 Act accordingly.

13.23   A change is also made to s 20(4) of the 1923 Act. That provision limits the insurer's entitlement to question the validity of an industrial assurance policy on the basis of a misstatement in a proposal form filled in wholly or partly by its own employee. The change made extends this to forms filled in by appointed representatives (s 139(2)).

13.24   The position of appointed representatives is also addressed in a change to s 34 of the 1923 Act. Formerly, promotion of industrial assurance was limited to those in the regular employment of a collecting society or industrial insurance company. By s 139(2) their appointed representatives also become entitled to do so, but only where investment agreements are concerned.

13.25   The functions of the Industrial Assurance Commissioner in settling disputes can also be integrated with arrangements established by conduct of business rules under s 48(2), (3) or corresponding SRO rules (s 139(3), (4)).

13.26   These amendments also apply to industrial assurance in Northern Ireland (s 139(5)).

Chapter 14

Friendly societies

Friendly societies

14.01 The investment business provisions of Part I of the Act are mirrored for friendly societies in Sch 11 (s 140). The purpose is essentially that regulated friendly societies should be treated in the same way, for investment business purposes, as regulated insurance companies. However, existing powers over friendly societies are vested in the various Registrars rather than in the Secretary of State. For this reason, Sch 11 gives the new Financial Services Act powers to the appropriate Registrar. He may then make a separate transfer of functions to a 'transferee body'— fulfilling the same role as a designated agency and again with The Securities and Investments Board Limited as prospectively the first recipient.

14.02 It will be recalled that para 14 of Sch 15 provides an exemption for friendly societies which undertake no new investment business after s 3 of the Act comes into force. It may be that this route, rather than authorisation, will be chosen by a number of the smaller societies for whom the costs of authorisation could be prohibitive.

Indemnity schemes

14.03 The Act also provides for any two or more registered friendly societies 'to enter into arrangements for the purpose of making funds available to meet losses incurred by any society which is a party to the arrangements' (s 141(1)). These can also cover losses incurred by members of a society by virtue of their membership and can be made notwithstanding any provision to the contrary in the societies' rules. No such arrangements can come into force unless approved by the relevant Registrar (s 141(2)). The existence of such schemes may reduce the need for friendly societies to be covered by rules under paras 17 and 18 of Sch 11, which parallel the sections of the Act on indemnity rules (s 53) and compensation (s 54).

Chapter 15

Official listing of securities

Introduction – listed and unlisted securities

15.01 Part IV of the Act applies to the official listing of securities on the Official List of the Stock Exchange. It replaces the Stock Exchange (Listing) Regulations 1984 as the means of implementing three European Community directives which apply legal criteria to the listing process. Prior to the directives, listing was a private matter between the Stock Exchange and the listed issuer. The Stock Exchange (Listing) Regulations 1984 ('the 1984 Regulations') are repealed by Pt II of Sch 17 to the Act. Part IV of the Act is the subject of this chapter.

Part V of the Act applies to offers of unlisted securities, ie those not listed or the subject of an application for listing under Pt IV. It applies both to offers on admission to dealings on an approved exchange and to other primary and secondary offers. The European Community directives have no application in such cases. Part V replaces the prospectus provisions in Pt III of the Companies Act 1985, which are repealed by Pt I of Sch 17 to the Act, and is the subject of the following chapter. The important point to note is that the two Parts are mutually exclusive and that two distinct legal regimes apply to offers of listed and unlisted securities.

Background – the EEC directives and the 1984 Listing Regulations

15.02 The 1984 Listing Regulations implemented three EEC directives on official listing. These were: Directive 79/279/EEC, co-ordinating the conditions for the admission of securities to official stock exchange listing (the Admissions Directive); Directive 80/390/EEC, co-ordinating the requirements for the drawing up, scrutiny and distribution of the listing particulars to be published for the admission of securities to official stock exchange listing (the Listing Particulars Directive); and Directive 82/121/EEC, on information to be published on a regular basis by companies the shares of which have been admitted to official stock exchange listing (the Interim Reports Directive). The original method of implementation by the 1984 Regulations under s 2 of the European Communities Act 1972 involved the unusual step of adopting the text of the three directives directly into UK law by incorporating them as Schedules to the Regulations. At the same time the Stock Exchange issued a new edition of its manual, Admission of Securities to Listing (the Yellow Book), which repeated the directives together with additional requirements permitted by the directives.

The 1984 Regulations were, however, suspect in at least two areas. First, they created areas of doubt as to liability for breach of the Regulations, and second, it was debatable as to how far the Regulations, deriving their validity from s 2 of the European Communities Act 1972, provided a secure legal foundation for the Yellow Book insofar as it went beyond the directives.

The implementation of the directives is therefore now to be found in Pt IV of the Act. In general the Act provides the framework under which The Stock Exchange itself can implement the detailed requirements of the directives, with a secure statutory foundation going beyond the actual requirements of the directives. The Act also provides for both civil and criminal liability for those in breach of the requirements.

Official listing – the scope of the provisions

15.03 Section 142(1) provides that no investments covered by that section are to be admitted to the Official List of The Stock Exchange except in accordance with Pt IV (ss 142–157). In effect this means that no application for listing or admissions to listing can be made or granted unless the 'competent authority's' requirements are complied with (ss 143, 144). These requirements are those set out in the listing rules to be made by that competent authority in compliance with s 156.

THE COMPETENT AUTHORITY

15.04 All three directives require member states to designate a national authority competent to give effect to the directives which is to be given all the necessary powers for that purpose. Section 142(6) designates the Council of The Stock Exchange as the competent authority and gives it the power to make rules for the purposes of Pt IV, ie the listing rules. Section 142(8) allows the Council to delegate its functions to any committee, sub-committee, officer or servant of the Council although the making of listing rules can only be delegated to a committee, or sub-committee and if so made must be ratified by the Council within 28 days. Failure to ratify will render the rules invalid from that date onwards (without prejudice to anything done under them). Under similar provisions in the 1984 Regulations, the Council arranged for the Committee on Quotations, advised by the Quotations Department, to discharge all its functions under the directives (see the Yellow Book, s 1, ch 1, para 2).

Section 157(1) allows the Secretary of State to transfer the functions of the competent authority from the Council of The Stock Exchange to another body if the Council requests it, or if it appears to him, either that the Council is exercising its functions in a manner which is unnecessary for the protection of investors and fails to take into account the proper interests of issuers and proposed issuers of securities, or that it is necessary to do so for the protection of investors.

Such a transfer must be made by an order subject to a negative resolution if it is made at the request of the Council, or subject to positive resolutions in other cases (s 157(3)). Subsequent orders can be made for all or any of the functions to be transferred to other bodies (s 157(2)).

It is interesting to note that the initial power of transfer away from the Council relates only to its functions and not to 'all or any of those functions', as in the power to effect a subsequent transfer. However, it is clear from s 157(5) that a partial transfer of functions from the Council is envisaged since, by virtue of that subsection, where the functions of admission to or discontinuance or suspension of listing are exercised by a body other than the Council, the Act is to apply to the giving of directions as to admissions etc by that transferee body to the Council, which must comply with such directions.

If the functions of the competent authority are so transferred the transfer order is not to affect anything previously done and may make transitional provisions as detailed in s 157(4).

INVESTMENTS TO WHICH PT IV APPLIES

15.05 Section 142(2)–(5) lays down the scope of Pt IV in relation to the investments concerned. Section 142(9) makes it clear that Pt IV has no application to other investments, which remain solely within the province of the Council of The Stock Exchange.

The investments subject to Pt IV are those in paras 1 (company shares and stock), 2 (debentures), 4 (instruments entitling to shares or securities) and 5 (certificates representing securities) of Sch 1 to the Act. However, rights to subscribe for shares and certificates representing securities (ie within paras 4 and 5) are only included if they relate to company shares or stock within para 1. On the other hand, for the purposes of official listing, para 1 includes shares and stock of building societies, industrial and provident societies and credit unions which would otherwise be excluded by that para. Again, for the purpose of official listing, debentures in para 2 include loan stock and bonds etc issued by a non–EEC government or local authority or by an international organisation involving at least one EEC member state, as defined in para 3 of Sch 1. Sch 1 is dealt with in Chapter 2 ante.

Units in a collective investment scheme or shares in an open-ended investment company may be included later by order subject to a negative resolution. This is an option available under art 2 of the Admissions Directive.

Listing rules
15.06 Section 142(6) enables the competent authority, ie the Council of The Stock Exchange, to make listing rules for the purposes of Pt IV. Section 156 governs the general content and form of these rules in addition to the specific requirements of other sections. The rules may make different provisions for different cases and may authorise the Council (in practice its Quotations Committee) to modify or ignore the rules in particular cases or circumstances (see Admissions Directive, art 7).

The rules must be made in writing and then printed and made available to the public. If it can be shown that any particular rule is not so available it is a defence to any charge of contravention of the rule (s 156(5)).

Production of a printed copy of an instrument purporting to be made by the Council, endorsed by a certificate signed by an officer of the Council authorised by it for that purpose, stating that the instrument was made by the Council, that the copy is a true copy and was on a specified date available to the public, is to be prima facie evidence of those statements. The signature on such a certificate is deemed to have been an authorised signature unless the contrary is shown. The Council must certify such a copy if required to do so for the purposes of legal proceedings. Presumably authority for this purpose includes implied and apparent authority (cf Companies Act 1985, s 184).

Section 155 provides that the listing rules may require the payment of fees to the Council of The Stock Exchange in respect of an application for listing and the retention of securities on the Official List.

Applications and admissions to listing

15.07 Applications for listing must be made in accordance with the listing rules (s 143(1)). No application can be made without the consent of the issuer of the securities: (s 143(2)). This is the person by whom they have been or are to be issued. In the case of certificates representing securities, the issuer is the person who has or is to issue the securities (ie shares) to which the certificates relate (s 142(7)). The reason for this requirement is that the issuer of the securities becomes subject to certain obligations and liabilities in respect of the listing, eg for misleading statements, whether or not he obtained the listing in the first place.

No private company (as defined in s 1(3) of the Companies Act 1985), or old public company (as defined in s 1 of the Companies Consolidation (Consequential Provisions) Act 1985) securities can be the subject of an application for listing (s 143(3)). This partially replaces s 81 of the Companies Act 1985 which prohibited private companies from making public offers of their shares. Section 81 is repealed by Pt I of Sch 17 to this Act. Part V contains a corresponding provision for unlisted securities of such companies.

15.08 In a similar vein, s 144(1) provides that no securities shall be admitted to the Official List except on a proper application under s 143 and only if the competent authority (ie, in practice, The Stock Exchange) is satisfied both that the listing rules current at the date of application and any other requirements imposed in relation to that application have been complied with.

The competent authority may refuse an application for listing if it considers that it would be detrimental to the interests of investors having regard to the issuer of those securities (as defined in s 142(7) – see above), or alternatively, if the securities are already listed in another member state, if the issuer has failed to comply with its obligations in respect of that listing. A decision on an application must be made within six months from the date of application (or production of requested additional information, if later), although if no decision is notified to the applicant within that time the application is deemed to have been refused (s 144(3)–(5)).

Once listing has been achieved the admission of the securities to listing cannot be challenged on the grounds of non-compliance with the listing requirements (s 144(6)).

DISCONTINUANCE AND SUSPENSION OF LISTING

15.09   The listing rules may allow the competent authority to discontinue the listing if normal regular dealings in those securities are precluded by special circumstances. Alternatively the listing rules can allow for a suspension of listing (although in such cases the securities are deemed to be listed for the purposes of ss 153-155 (continuing obligations, restrictions on advertisements and payment of fees)). Such powers of discontinuance and suspension apply to shares already listed prior to the Act (s 145).

Listing particulars

15.10   One of the most important aspects of the listing rules is the requirement for the submission, approval and publication of listing particulars relating to the securities to be listed. In some cases the publication of a document other than listing particulars can be required (s 144(2)). Listing particulars were required by the 1984 Regulations and the form and content must comply with the Listing Particulars Directive. Listing particulars are in fact the prospectus of old.

GENERAL DUTY OF DISCLOSURE

15.11   Whilst the detailed requirements relating to the content of the listing particulars will be found in the listing rules or other requirements of The Stock Exchange, s 146 provides an additional general duty of disclosure in listing particulars. Failure to comply may lead to civil liability under s 145 (see para **15.17**, post). This general duty arises from art 4 of the Listing Particulars Directive

The duty is to disclose:

'. . . all such information as investors and their professional advisers would reasonably require and reasonably expect to find there, for the purpose of making an informed assessment of – (a) the assets and liabilities, financial position, profits and losses, and prospects of the issuer of the securities; and (b) the rights attaching to those securities.'

15.12 Section 146(2) imposes a limit on this general duty to such information as is within the knowledge of any person responsible for the listing particulars or which it would be reasonable for him to obtain by making enquiries. This raises the question as to the extent of constructive knowledge which will be imputed to such a person. Similar questions have arisen in the area of constructive trusts and the duty to account. The most recent analysis of the possibilities is given by Peter Gibson J in *Baden Delvaux and Lecuit* v *Societe General etc* [1983] BCLC 325. Since an omission can give rise to liability, this an important issue. 'Persons responsible for the listing particulars' are defined in s 152 – see para **15.27**, post. Note that it is the knowledge of any such person which is relevant.

15.13 Section 146(3) provides guidelines to decide the information required by this duty. These are: the nature of the securities and the issuer, the nature of persons likely to consider their acquisition, the fact that certain matters will be known to professional advisers whom those persons may reasonably be expected to consult, and any information already available to investors or their professional advisers either under s 153 (continuing obligations – ie interim reports on listed securities) or any other statutory provision, or by virtue of information available from a recognised investment exchange (as defined in s 207) giving the current value of investments dealt with on that exchange (Sch 4, para 2(2)(b) – see para **3.106**, ante). The intention of this subsection is to avoid the obligation to disclose matters which are already available to investors and their advisers as a mattter of course, in particular in regard to specialised issues, eg the Eurobond market.

EXEMPTIONS FROM DISCLOSURE

15.14 Section 148 allows the competent authority, without prejudice to any of its powers under the listing rules, to exempt specific information from disclosure under the general duty in s 146 on any of three grounds. These are:

(a) that disclosure would be contrary to the public interest. This can be certified as such by the Secretary of State or the Treasury, including particulars for which they themselves are responsible;

(b) that disclosure would be seriously detrimental to the issuer of the securities (as defined in s 142(7)). However, this cannot apply, or be taken to apply, to information which if not disclosed would be likely to mislead a potential acquiror as to any facts which would be essential for him to make an informed assessment;

(c) if the securities are debentures within the meaning of para 2 of Sch 1 as modified by s 142 (see para **15.05**, ante), of a class specified in the listing rules, that such disclosure is unnecessary bearing in mind the potential buyers and dealers in such securities (eg Eurobonds). This applies to both domestic and international debt securities traded in by experts.

REGISTRATION OF LISTING PARTICULARS

15.15   Section 149 requires registration of the listing particulars with the registrar of companies on or before the date of publication. A statement that a copy has been delivered to him must appear in the particulars. If the company issuing the securities is incorporated in Great Britain, the appropriate registrar depends upon the location of its registered office. For those incorporated in Northern Ireland it is the registrar there, but for overseas companies there is a complete choice of registrar.

Failure to deliver a copy for registration prior to publication of the listing particulars is an offence and anyone knowingly a party to the publication is liable to a fine. This is one of only two criminal offences in this Part of the Act – it is not an offence to register misleading particulars, whereas it is to register accurate particulars late. For the liability of those involved with a company charged with this offence see s 202, para **21.65**, post.

Supplementary listing particulars

15.16   In two circumstances the issuer of securities is to be required by the listing rules to submit supplementary listing particulars to the competent authority for approval and publication. By virtue of s 147 these are either where there is a significant change or where a significant new matter has arisen between the preparation of the listing particulars and the commencement of dealings relating to a matter disclosed (or which ought to be disclosed) under the listing rules, the competent authority's specific requirements or the general duty of disclosure under s 146(1) (see para **15.11**, ante). Significant in this context is the making of an informed assessment of the items specified in s 146(1) (see para **15.11**, ante).

Whilst the obligation to prepare supplementary listing particulars is on the issuer of the securities (defined in s 142(7)), this only applies if he is aware of the change or new matter in question. However, if he is notified of it by any person responsible for the listing particulars (as defined in s 152 – see para **15.28**, post) he is liable to do so and it is the duty of any such person to notify him of any such matters of which that person is aware.

Sections 148 (exemptions from disclosure – see para **15.14**, ante) and 149 (registration – para **15.15**, ante) apply equally to supplementary listing particulars as they apply to listing particulars.

Compensation for false or misleading particulars

15.17 Sections 150–152 provide a statutory remedy for misrepresentations and omissions in listing particulars or supplementary listing particulars. Sections 166–168 provide a parallel remedy in relation to unlisted securities. They replace ss 67–69 of the Companies Act 1985, repealed by Pt I of Sch 17.

This remedy is in addition to other common law and statutory remedies eg rescission, damages for negligent mistatement etc (s 150(4)).

There are two basic heads of liability contained in s 150. Section 151 sets out the various defences available and s 152 details those who may be liable under s 150.

HEADS OF LIABILITY

15.18 (a) Under s 150(1) any person responsible for listing particulars (or supplementary listing particulars) *shall be liable* to compensate anyone who has acquired or contracted to acquire an interest in relevant securities and has suffered loss in respect of them as the result of any untrue or misleading statement in the particulars, or the omission of anything required to be included by virtue of the general duty of disclosure under s 146(1) (para **15.11**, ante) or the duty to publish particulars of any significant new matter or change under s 147 (para **15.16**, ante). It has long been established that an omission may in fact make what is stated misleading: see *R v Lord Kylsant* [1932] 1 KB 442.

Where the listing rules require either a statement as to any particular matter or an affirmation that there is no such matter, its omission from the particulars is to be regarded as a statement that there is no such matter for this purpose (s 150(2)).

As with s 67 of the Companies Act 1985 proof of an untrue or misleading statement or an omission together with acquisition and loss consequent on that misstatement or omission will suffice to ground liability – there is no need to prove fraud or negligence. It is for those so liable to establish one of the defences under s 151. There must be a causal connection, however, between the misstatement/omission and the loss. The wording of s 67 required the securities to be acquired 'on the faith of the prospectus'. The causal connection in s 150 is simply that the loss is a result of the misstatement or omission and this can include subsequent purchasers on the market within some reasonable time span from the issue of the particulars, which was not the case under s 67. (See *Pennington's Company Law* (5th edn) p 317). Sections 151(1)(d) and 151(2)(d) lend additional support to this conclusion since the defences there set out would otherwise be irrelevant.

(b) Under s 150(3) anyone who fails to issue supplementary listing particulars as required by s 147 (para **15.16**, ante) or who fails to notify the issuer of the securities as required by that section, is liable to compensate anyone who has acquired or contracted to acquire an interest in the securities in question and suffered loss as a result of that failure. The defences under s 151 are available.

15.19 There is no liability for anyone, whether acting as a company promoter or otherwise, for failing to disclose any information which he would not be required to disclose in listing particulars or has been exempted from so disclosing if he was responsible for them (s 150(6)). However, by virtue of s 150(4) this cannot affect any liability incurred apart from s 150, ie under the general law of negligence or misrepresentation. It does, however, ensure that any non-inclusion by virtue of an exemption under s 148 (eg on grounds of public interest), will not make a promoter or other person liable if that non-disclosure makes the information given misleading.

EXEMPTIONS FROM LIABILITY

15.20 There are six possible defences for anyone who is sued for compensation under s 150 above. Four are applicable only to liability under heading (a) in para **15.18**, ante, ie the general liability for misstatements or omissions, one is only applicable to liability under heading (b) in para **15.18**, ante, ie failure to issue supplementary listing particulars, or notify the issuer of a significant change or new matter, whilst one is applicable to either. Some of these defences are updated versions of those available under s 68 of the Companies Act 1985. The four defences applicable only to the general liability are as follows.

(A) REASONABLE BELIEF – s 151(1)

15.21 If the defendant can show that having made reasonable enquiries he reasonably believed at the time when the particulars were submitted, either that the statement was true or not misleading or that any omission was properly omitted, then he is not liable under s 150(1) provided he can also show one of four additional factors relating to a later time: (i) that he still held that belief when the securities or any interest in them were acquired; (ii) that they were so acquired before he could bring the matter to the attention of persons likely to acquire the securities; (iii) that he took all reasonable steps to bring a correction to the notice of such persons before they acquired the securities (cf para **15.23**, post); or (iv) that he held that belief until dealings commenced after listing and that the securities were so acquired after such a lapse of time that he ought fairly to be excused.

This defence is a modern version of that found in s 68(2)(a) of the Companies Act 1985, although it differs in detail. Situation (iv) above demonstrates that liability under s 150 is intended to run after listing for some considerable time, since lapse of time on its own is not a defence, although it might at some stage break the chain of causation.

(B) EXPERTS' STATEMENTS – s 151(2)

15.22 The second defence available applies where the offending statement (ie the cause of the investor's loss) purports to be made by or on the authority of an expert and which is, and is stated to be, with that expert's consent. In such a case it is a defence to show a belief on reasonable grounds that the expert was competent to make or authorise the statement and consented to its inclusion in the form and context in which it was included. This belief must exist both at the time when the particulars were submitted and also when the securities or any interest in them were acquired, unless either: (i) they were acquired before it was reasonably practicable to bring the incompetence or lack of consent of the expert to the investors' attention; (ii) he took reasonable steps to bring that fact to the notice of such investors before the securities were acquired; or (iii) he held that belief until dealings commenced after listing and the securities were so acquired after such a lapse of time that he ought fairly to be excused. It is not clear from the wording whether this defence applies to a pure omission in an expert's statement.

This defence is based on that formerly available under s 68(2)(b) of the Companies Act 1985. An expert for this purpose is defined in s 151(7) to include any engineer, valuer, accountant or other person whose profession, qualifications or experience gives authority to a statement made by him. This is the same as the former definition in s 62 of the Companies Act 1985.

(C) REASONABLE STEPS TO CORRECT DEFECT – s 151(3)

15.23 If the defendant can show either that a correction or the fact that an expert was not competent or had not consented to publication was published 'in a manner calculated' to bring that fact to the notice of potential investors, or that he took reasonable steps to secure such publication before the time where the securities were acquired, he will not be liable under s 150.

This defence, based on the former s 68(1)(c) of the Companies Act 1985, is in addition to defences (A) and (B), ante. Unlike those defences it requires no proof of reasonable belief but of prompt and efficient action.

(D) OFFICIAL STATEMENTS AND DOCUMENTS – s 151(4)

15.24 There is no liability for any loss resulting from the accurate and fair reproduction of a statement by an official person or contained in a public official document. There is no definition of an 'official person' or an 'official document'. This defence is based on that formerly contained in s 68(2)(c) of the Companies Act 1985.

The defence applicable both to liability under the general head and in relation to supplementary listing particulars is set out below.

(E) PLAINTIFF'S KNOWLEDGE – s 151(5)

15.25 If the defendant can prove that the person suffering the loss acquired the securities 'with knowledge' that the statement was false or misleading, or of the omitted matter, or of the change or new matter, as appropriate, he will not be liable.

This defence was not available under s 68 of the Companies Act 1985 and it is doubtful if it adds anything, since the plaintiff, to establish prima facie liability under s 150, must prove that he suffered the loss as a result of the misrepresentation or omission. If he knew of the matter then the loss is not incurred as a result of the misrepresentation or omission but by his decision to acquire the securities with that knowledge. The wording of s 151(5) does not make it clear whether constructive or imputed knowledge will suffice – see the comments in para **15.12**, ante.

The defence available solely against liability in relation to supplementary listing particulars is as follows.

(F) REASONABLE BELIEF AND SUPPLEMENTARY LISTING PARTICULARS – s 151(6)

15.26   Reasonable belief that the change or new matter was not such as to call for supplementary listing particulars under s 147 is a defence to liability under s 150(3) for not producing them (see paras **15.16** and **15.18**, ante).

PERSONS RESPONSIBLE FOR PARTICULARS

15.27   Section 152(1) details five groups of persons who are deemed to be responsible for the listing or supplementary listing particulars and so liable for any misrepresentations or omissions under s 150.

These groups are:

(a) the issuer of the securities to which the particulars relate (ie the person by whom they have been or are to be issued);

(b) the directors of the issuer at the date of submission of the particulars;

(c) anyone who has authorised himself to be named, and is named in the particulars as a director of the issuer or as having agreed to become a director at some future time;

(d) those who accept and are stated as having accepted responsibility for all or any part of the particulars; and

(e) anyone else who has authorised the contents of all or any part of the particulars (even if not stated to have done so).

NB   para (e) requires a finding of fact that the person concerned *authorised* the particulars. It is not enough that he took part in their preparation.

15.28   If anyone in categories (d) or (e) (eg an expert) is responsible or has authorised part only of the particulars their liability extends only to that part, and then only if that part is included in substantially the form and content to which he has agreed (s 152(3)). No one is to be regarded as being responsible for listing particulars if he has simply given professional advice as to its contents (s 152(8)).

If the issuer of the securities is liable to pay compensation, no account is to be taken of that payment or liability in determining the different question of the amount paid on subscription for those shares or the amount paid up or deemed to be paid up on them. That comes under the different principle of capital maintenance (s 152(9)).

SECURITIES OFFERED IN CONNECTION WITH OFFER FOR OTHERS – s 152(4)

15.29   Section 152(4) applies where the particulars relate to securities to be issued by X in connection with:

(i) an offer by X or its wholly owned subsidiary for securities issued by Y;

(ii) an agreement by X or its wholly owned subsidiary for the acquisition of securities issued to Y; or

(iii) any agreement whereby the whole of Y's undertaking is to become the undertaking of X, or its wholly owned subsidiary, or of a company which will become X's wholly owned subsidairy as a result of the arrangement, and Y (and its directors, actual or named with their authority as such in the particulars) have accepted responsibility for that part of the particulars relating to the relevant securities or undertaking of Y under para **15.27** (d), ante. If X is not a company, a wholly owned subsidiary for this purpose means any company which would be his wholly owned subsidiary if he were a company (s 152(7)).

In such cases X and its directors (actual or stated, with authority, as being or going to be directors) are not liable as such for that part of the particulars under para **15.27** (a)–(c), ante, although they may still be liable under para **15.27** (d) as accepting responsibility.

DIRECTORS OF THE ISSUER – s 152(2)(5)(6)

15.30   The basic principle is that all directors of the issuer are responsible for the particulars and liable as such under para **15.27** (b), ante. This liability extends to those who have authorised themselves to be described as a director or on having agreed to become a director in the particulars under para **15.27** (c), ante. These directors may, of course, rely on the defences under s 151 but s 152(2) provides an exemption from liability for those in category (b) and s 152(4) provides two further exemptions for those in categories (b) and (c).

Section 152(2) provides that no director under category (b) is to be regarded as being responsible if the particulars were issued without his knowledge or consent provided that when he became aware of their publication he gave reasonable public notice of that fact. Such notice must be given 'forthwith'. This continues the exemption formerly available under s 68(1)(b) of the Companies Act 1985.

Section 152(5) applies first to directors (under para **15.27** (b) or (c)) of an issuer of international securities of a class as specified in the listing rules for the purposes of s 148(1)(c) (exemptions from need to disclose information on specialist issues to professional investors – see para **15.14**, ante). International securities for this purpose are 'debentures' as defined in para 2 of Sch 1, as modified by s 142(3)(b) (see para **15.05**, ante), ie private debt securities which are likely to be dealt in by bodies incorporated or persons resident outside the United Kingdom, are denominated otherwise than in sterling or are otherwise connected with an overseas country (s 152(6)). If the securities are international and of the class specified in the listing rules, the directors of the issuer cannot be liable under para **15.27** (b) or (c), ante. Liability under para **15.27** (d), (e), however, is not excluded.

15.31   Of more general importance is the second exemption. The aim is to provide an advance exemption from liability in certain circumstances, eg where it would be inappropriate for a director to disclose certain matters, eg because it would infringe the confidentiality rules arising from single capacity. To this end liability under para **15.27** (b) or (c), ante (or under s 152(4)(b) for directors of the offeree company: see para **15.29**, ante) is excluded for any director certified by the competent authority as exempted from the appropriate paragraph by reason of his having an interest, or any other circumstance which make it inappropriate for him to be responsible for the particulars. Directors must claim this exemption.

Obligations of issuers of listed securities

15.32   Section 153 authorises the listing rules to specify requirements to be complied with by issuers of listed securities (including those already listed at the time of this Act coming into force). 'Issuer' is defined in s 142(7).

The section also allows the rules to provide for non-compliance, including publication by The Stock Exchange of the fact of non-compliance and of any information which the issuer, although required to do so, fails to publish.

This section provides the authority to implement the Interim Reports Directive.

Advertisements in connection with listing applications

15.33   Section 57 (see para **4.61**, ante) provides restrictions on investment advertisements, but by virtue of s 58 that does not apply to advertisements which are connected with the publication of listing particulars. Instead they are subject to control by the competent authority under s 154.

Section 154 applies to any advertisement or other information specified in the listing rules at a time when listing particulars are or are to be issued. Issue of the advertisement etc is prohibited unless the competent authority has either approved its contents or authorised issue without approval. This ban applies to advertisements issued in the United Kingdom but by virtue of s 207(7) it extends to those issued overseas if they are directed to or made available to persons in the United Kingdom otherwise than in a literary or broadcasting form aimed principally outside the United Kingdom.

If approval has been obtained or its issue has been authorised, neither the issuer nor the persons responsible for it are to be liable in damages for any misstatement or omission in it if, taken together with the listing particulars, it would not be likely to mislead potential investors in the type of securities in question (s 154(5)).

There are both civil and criminal consequences of a breach of s 154(5). If the offender is a member of an SRO or of a recognised professional body he will be deemed to have acted in breach of its rules, and in other cases to have breached the conduct of business rules to be made under Ch V of Pt I of the Act. In all such cases s 62 will apply and an action for damages will be available to anyone who suffers loss as a result (s 154(2)).

Contravention is also a criminal offence under s 154(3) which can lead to imprisonment for up to two years. There is a defence to this charge (but not to civil liability) for anyone who issues the advertisment etc in the course of a non-investment business and who proves that he believed on reasonable grounds after due enquiry that it had been approved or authorised by the competent authority.

For the liability of those involved in a company charged with this offence, see s 202 (para **21.65**, post).

Chapter 16

Offers of unlisted securities

Introduction and background

16.01   The Stock Exchange (Listing) Regulations 1984 and its three parent European Community directives applied only to applications for listing on the Official List of the Stock Exchange (see para **15.01**, ante). Part IV of the Financial Services Act 1986 which replaced the 1984 Regulations is similarly limited in its scope. All other offers were governed by Pt III of the Companies Act 1985, the prospectus provisions. Part III has been repealed by Pt I of Sch 17 to the Financial Services Act 1986 and the provisions relating to offers of unlisted securities are now contained in Part V of the Act, which is the subject of this chapter. Parts IV and V are mutually exclusive – see s 158(1)(a).

The theme of Pt V is to replace the Companies Act prospectus provisions, dating back to 1947, with a more flexible and modern approach. A prospectus is still required but its contents are to be modernised, and considerable flexibility will be allowed where the securities are to be traded on an 'approved recognised investment exchange' eg the Unlisted Securities Market. On the other hand the general duty of disclosure and liabilities for misrepresentation in such documents closely resemble those for listed securities in Pt IV. Part V also applies to the terms and implementation of any such offer, replacing ss 82 and 83 of the Companies Act 1985.

Scope of the provisions

16.02   Part V is concerned with the control of specified offers of certain non-listed securities by restricting advertisements for such offers unless a prospectus or its equivalent has been registered with the registrar of companies. The appropriate registrar for this purpose depends upon the place of incorporation of the company issuing the securities, overseas companies having a choice (s 158(5)), (see s 149, para **15.15**, ante).

In general an advertisement offers securities if it invites a person to enter into an agreement for, or with a view to subscribing for or otherwise acquiring or underwriting any securities, or it contains information calculated to lead directly or indirectly to a person entering into such an agreement (s 158(4)). Such advertisements connected with admission to dealings on an approved exchange (see para **16.04**, post) or with primary or secondary offers (see para **16.08**, post) are those which are controlled by Pt V, provided they are issued in the United Kingdom. This also includes advertisements issued overseas if they are directed to, or made available to, persons in the United Kingdom, otherwise than in a literary or broadcasting form which is aimed principally outside the United Kingdom (s 207(3)). There is also a new attempt to exclude purely private offers from such control.

INVESTMENTS TO WHICH PT V APPLIES

16.03   Part V applies to securities falling within paras 1 (company shares or stock), 2 (debentures), 4 (instruments entitling to shares or securities) and 5 (certificates representing securities) of Sch 1. Paragraphs 4 and 5 have effect without reference to securities within para 3 (government and public securities) and instruments within para 4 are included only if they are issued by the issuer of the investments to be subscribed for (s 158(1)(2)). In relation to certificates representing securities the issuer is the person who issued the securities to which the certificate relates (s 158(3)).

Thus Pt V applies to a more restricted category of investments than Pt IV (eg the exclusion of building society shares applies to Pt V); cf para **15.05**, ante.

APPROVED EXCHANGES

16.04   Part V applies in different ways to offers relating to securities which are to be admitted to dealings on an approved exchange than to other offers. Section 158(6) defines an approved exchange as a recognised investment exchange (ie one declared to be so by the Secretary of State – s 207(1)) which has been approved by the Secretary of State for Pt V, either generally or in relation to specific dealings. Such approval may be given by notice in an appropriate manner.

Approved recognised investment exchanges may be referred to, following government practice, as ARIES.

Offers of securities on admission to an approved exchange

PROSPECTUS REQUIREMENTS

16.05   Section 159(1) prohibits the issue of an advertisement offering securities (see paras **16.02**, **16.03**, ante) on the occasion of their admission to dealings on an approved exchange (see para **16.04**, ante), or on terms that they will be issued if admitted to such dealings, unless either a prospectus has been submitted to and approved by the exchange and delivered for registration with the appropriate registrar of companies (see para **16.02**, ante), or the advertisement is so worded that no agreement can be made as a result of it until such submission etc of a prospectus. The contents of such a prospectus are covered by s 162 and it may be that the exchange's own rules as to content will apply – see para **16.10**, post).

EXCEPTIONS TO THE NEED FOR A PROSPECTUS

16.06   Section 159(1) is however subject to five exceptions.

(i) PROSPECTUS REGISTERED WITHIN TWELVE MONTHS – s 159(2)

Where a prospectus in respect of the securities has been delivered within the previous twelve months and the exchange certifies that the potential investors will have sufficient information from that earlier prospectus and any other information published with respect to their admission to dealings, no further prospectus is required under s 159(1). This is a new exemption.

(ii) SECURITIES LISTED OR TO BE LISTED ON STOCK EXCHANGE – s 161(1)

Section 159 does not apply if the offer under the advertisement is conditional on the securities being listed under Pt IV of the Act or if they have been so listed in the previous twelve months and The Stock Exchange certifies that potential investors will have sufficient information to enable them to decide as to an acquisition. This further establishes the mutual exclusion of Pts IV and V.

(iii) WHERE THE ADVERTISEMENT CONSISTS OF A REGISTERED PROSPECTUS OR IS LIMITED IN CONTENT – s 161(2)

Section 159 does not apply to those advertisements mentioned in s 58(2) of the Act. These advertisements are those inviting subscriptions in cash and issued by the issuer of the investments in question and either: (a) the advertisement itself consists simply of a prospectus registered under s 159; or (b) contains only the following information as to the investments concerned: (i) the name and address of the issuer; (ii) the nature, number, nominal value and price of the investments; (iii) a statement that a prospectus is or will be available (and if so when) and (iv) instructions for obtaining a copy of the prospectus.

(iv) SECURITIES ALREADY DEALT WITH ON THE EXCHANGE – s 161(3)

Section 159 does not apply if other securities issued by the same person (whether or not of the same class) are already dealt with on the exchange, and it certifies that potential investors will have sufficient information for that purpose, having regard to the steps taken with respect to those other securities, to comply with the obligation of all recognised exchanges to compel issuers to provide information for determining their current value (see Sch 4, para 2(2)(b)), and to the nature of the securities, the circumstances of their issue, and the information already available about the issuer under any other statutory provision. This is a modified form of the former s 55(5)(b) of the **Companies Act 1985**.

(v) OVERSEAS SECURITIES – s 161(4)

The Secretary of State may by order exempt from s 159 securities dealt in on an exchange in a country outside the United Kingdom if he is satisfied that the local law provides United Kingdom investors with protection equivalent to that provided by Pt IV (see chapter 15, ante) or Pt V of this Act. Such an order would be subject to negative resolution – s 161(5).

Contravention of s 159 may give rise to both civil and criminal liability (see s 171, para **16.22**, post).

Other offers of securities

16.07 Where no dealings on an approved exchange are sought, s 160 applies. The difficulty here is to distinguish between public and private offers. Under the former prospectus provisions of the Companies Act the key criteria were that the document be issued to the public by a company, and ss 58(3), 59 and 60 of that Act involved complex definitions. There was also the decision in *Governments Stock and Other Securities Investment Co Ltd v Christopher* [1956] 1 All ER 490 that an offer of shares as consideration for a takeover was not an issue to the public since it involved non-renounceable letters of allotment. The solution in Pt V is to include all 'primary' and 'secondary' offers and allows the Secretary of State to exclude advertisements of a private character. In general private companies cannot make any offers under Pt V (s 170 – see para **16.21**, post).

PRIMARY AND SECONDARY OFFERS – PROSPECTUS REQUIREMENT

16.08 No advertisement offering securities (see paras **16.02** and **16.03**, ante) which amounts to a primary or secondary offer (as defined below) can be made unless a prospectus has been delivered to the appropriate registrar of companies in respect of the offer and no agreement can be entered into as a result of the advertisement until such delivery for registration (s 160(1)).

A *primary offer* is an advertisement (not connected with admission to an approved exchange) inviting persons to enter into an agreement for or with a view to subscribe for or to underwrite the securities involved or which contains information calculated to lead directly or indirectly to their doing so (s 160(2)).

A *secondary offer* arises where the advertisement (having no connection with an approved exchange application) invites agreements to acquire or with a view to acquire the securities to which it relates or which contains information calculated to lead directly or indirectly to such agreements. In such a case, however, the offeror must be either a person who acquired the securities from the issuer with a view to making such an offer; or a person who has acquired securities otherwise than from the issuer with a view to on-selling them, unless they have at any stage been admitted to dealings on an approved exchange or were held by a person who acquired them as an investment as opposed to on-selling them; or a controller of the issuer (now or within the previous twelve months) and who is acting with the consent of the issuer in making the offer (s 160(3)). A person is presumed to have acquired the securities with a view to making such an offer if he makes it within six months of the issue of the securities or before he has paid the issuer for those securities (s 160(4)).

The wording of s 160(4) is based on s 58(3) of the Companies Act 1985 and applies to offers for sale. The distinction between primary and secondary offers is clear – subscription and underwriting offers are primary offers, others are secondary offers.

The contents of the prospectus are covered by ss 162 and 163 (see paras **16.10** and **16.11**, post).

EXCEPTIONS TO THE NEED FOR A PROSPECTUS

16.09   There are six exceptions to s 160.

(1) PROSPECTUS ISSUED IN PREVIOUS SIX MONTHS – s 160(5)

A prospectus need not be issued in connection with a secondary offer if one has been delivered for registration relating to the same securities in the previous six months by a primary or secondary offeror.

(2) EXEMPTIONS BY ORDER OF SECRETARY OF STATE – s 160(6)–(9)

The Secretary of State may by an order (subject to negative resolution) exempt primary or secondary offerors from the need to register a prospectus, in specified circumstances, if they fall within one of five categories:

(a) advertisements of a private character, eg by reason of a connection between the issuer and the persons to whom it is addressed. This replaces the former 'issued to the public' criteria under the Companies Act 1985;

(b) advertisements dealing with investments only incidentally;

(c) advertisements issued only to experts (ie those who can understand any risks involved);

(d) any other classes of advertisement he thinks fit (ss 160 and 169); and

(e) without prejudice to (c) above, s 160(7) also allows the Secretary of State to exempt any advertisement 'issued in whatever circumstances' which relates to securities normally dealt in by experts who can understand the risks involved without the need of a prospectus, eg sterling commercial paper.

Any order of this nature may specify other requirements which must be complied with (s 160(8)). Any such order is to be subject to a negative resolution unless it is brought under (d) above in which case it must be approved by a resolution of each House (s 160(9)).

Clearly the types of offers exempt under this procedure will be of great significance.

(3) SECURITIES LISTED OR TO BE LISTED ON THE STOCK EXCHANGE – s161(1)

(4) ADVERTISEMENTS CONSISTING OF A REGISTERED PROSPECTUS OR LIMITED IN CONTENT – s 161(2)

(5) SECURITIES ALREADY DEALT WITH ON AN APPROVED EXCHANGE – s 161(3)

(6) OVERSEAS SECURITIES – s 161(4)

(for comment on (3)-(6) see para **16.06**, ante).

Breach of s 160 may lead to civil and criminal liability under s 171 (see para **16.22**, post).

Form and content of prospectus

16.10 Section 162(1) requires a prospectus issued in accordance with s 159 or 160 to contain such information and otherwise comply with rules to be made by the Secretary of State. These will replace Sch 3 to the Companies Act 1985 and are the equivalent of the listing rules in Pt IV. Compliance with overseas requirements may be treated by the rules as compliance with those rules (s 162(2)).

In accordance with the policy of allowing approved exchanges to govern their own investments, s 162(3) allows the Secretary of State to direct that a prospectus issued in connection with dealings on that exchange shall be governed by the rules of that exchange if they, together with the practices in relation to the exercise of any powers conferred thereby, provide investors with equivalent protection.

GENERAL DUTY OF DISCLOSURE

16.11 Section 163 imposes a general duty of disclosure in relation to a prospectus whether governed by the Secretary of State's rules or those of an exchange, which is in addition to the requirement of those rules. Section 163 is written in virtually identical terms to s 146 which imposes such a duty in relation to listing particulars based on art 4 of the Listing Particulars Directive. In the same way breach of the duty may give rise to liability.

Thus s 163(1) lays down the duty, s 163(2) imposes limits on that duty and s 163(3) provides guidelines to decide the information required. The only difference between s 163 and s 146 is that the former does not refer in its guidelines to information provided under the continuing obligation provisions in s 153 which are not applicable to unlisted securities. With that caveat the comments in paras **15.11**, **15.12** and **15.13**, ante, are equally applicable to s 163.

EXEMPTIONS FROM DISCLOSURES

16.12   Section 165 allows the Secretary of State to authorise an approved exchange to exempt specific information from disclosure in a prospectus or supplementary prospectus (see para **16.13**, post) under the general duty of disclosure in s 163 on any of three grounds:

(a) disclosure contrary to the public interest (as certified by the Secretary of State or the Treasury);

(b) disclosure seriously detrimental to the issuer (as defined in s 158(3)) unless it is essential for an informed assessment to be made; or

(c) specialised securities (eg Eurobonds).

These grounds are the same as those relating to listing particulars in s 148 and the detailed comments in para **15.14** are equally applicable to this section.

Supplementary prospectus

16.13   Section 164 requires the person who delivered the prospectus for registration to deliver a supplementary prospectus in those circumstances in which s 147 requires the issuer of securities to submit supplementary listing particulars in relation to an application for listing. Suitably modified, s 164 is substantially the same as s 147, eg the persons responsible for the listing particulars become the persons responsible for the prospectus. The comments in para **15.16**, ante, are applicable on that basis to s 164.

Compensation for false or misleading prospectus

16.14   Section 166 provides a statutory remedy of compensation for anyone who acquires securities to which a prospectus relates, and suffers loss as a result of an untrue or misleading statement or omission of anything required by s 163 or 164 in that prospectus.

Section 166 corresponds, with suitable wording, almost exactly with s 150 in Pt IV to provide a uniform basis of liability for listing particulars and prospectuses alike. The only difference of substance is that the general defence for promoters etc in s 150(6) has no counterpart in s 166. Subject to that, the comments in paras **15.17** and **15.18**, ante, are equally applicable to s 166.

EXEMPTIONS FROM LIABILITY

16.15   Section 167 provides six defences to those liable under s 166. These correspond to the six defences available under s 151 for liability under s 150. The comments in paras **15.21**, **15.22**, **15.23**, **15.24**, **15.25**, **15.26** and

15.27, ante, apply equally to s 167 with the prospectus, person responsible for the prospectus and supplementary prospectus being substituted for listing particulars etc, as appropriate. The only material difference is that in s 167(1)(d) the reference to the commencement of dealings applies only where an approved exchange is involved: cf s 151(1)(d).

PERSONS RESPONSIBLE FOR THE PROSPECTUS

16.16 Liability under s 166 attaches to those responsible for the prospectus in the same way as it does to persons responsible for the listing particulars under s 150. The persons responsible for the prospectus are set out in s 168, which in most respects corresponds to the provisions of s 152, setting out those responsible for the listing particulars. With three exceptions the sections are substantially the same.

Section 168(1) details five groups of persons who are deemed to be responsible for the prospectus or supplementary prospectus, as appropriate:

(a) the issuer of the securities to which the prospectus relates;

(b) the directors of the issuer at the date of delivery for registration;

(c) anyone who has authorised himself to be named, and is named in the particulars as a director of the issuer or as having agreed to become a director at some future time;

(d) those who accept and are stated as having accepted responsibility for all or any part of the particulars; and

(e) anyone else who has authorised the contents of all or any part of the prospectus (even if not stated to have done so).

NB: para (e) requires that the person concerned has *authorised* the prospectus. It is not enough to show that he took part in its preparation.

If anyone in categories (d) and (e) is responsible or has authorised part only of the prospectus (eg an expert) their liability extends only to that part and then only if it is included substantially in the form and context to which he has agreed (s 168(3)). Similarly no one is to be regarded as being responsible for any prospectus if he has simply given professional advice on its contents (s 168(7)).

Unlike the equivalent provision in s 152, however, no one is to be liable under categories (a)–(c) unless the issuer has made or authorised the offer to which the prospectus relates. This is of particular relevance to secondary offers.

16.17 If the issuer is liable to pay compensation no account is to be taken of that payment or liability in determining the different questions as to the amount paid on subscription for those shares or as to the amount paid up or deemed to be paid up on them (s 168(8)). That comes under the different principle of capital maintenance.

PROSPECTUS ISSUED IN CONNECTION WITH OFFER FOR OTHER SECURITIES – s 168(6)

16.18 Section 168(6) is the equivalent of s 152(4) and the comments in para **15.29**, ante, are equally applicable to prospectuses as to listing particulars.

DIRECTORS OF THE ISSUER – s 168(5)

16.19 Although directors of the issuer are prima facie liable under s 168(1)(b) if they have authorised the offer in question they may, like their counterparts in listing applications, obtain advance exemption from liability under that head (or under s 168(4)(b) for directors of an offeree company) if an approved exchange is involved in the offer and its rules govern the content of the prospectus. In such cases the exchange may certify that he should be exempted from the appropriate paragraph by reason of his having an interest, or any other circumstances which make it inappropriate for him to be responsible for the prospectus.

Terms and implementation of the offer

16.20 Section 169 authorises the Secretary of State to make rules regulating both the terms of any offer governed by Pt V of the Act and the conduct of the offeror. In the latter case the rules are to ensure that the persons to whom the offer is addressed are treated equally and fairly.

Section 169(2) stresses that the rules may regulate the giving of priority between persons to whom the offer is made and and also with regard to commissions. The rules may also allow compliance with equivalent overseas rules as compliance with United Kingdom rules.

These rules will replace ss 82 and 83 of the Companies Act 1985.

Private companies

16.21 In general no private company (as defined as s 1(3) of the Companies Act 1985) may issue or cause to be issued any advertisement offering its securities as defined in s 158(4) (see para **16.02**, ante). This ban also extends to old public companies within s 1 of the Companies Consolidation (Consequential Provisions) Act 1985 (s 170(1)(5)).

However, a private company may be allowed to issue an advertisement if it falls within one of the categories of exempt advertisements under s 160(6), ie those primary or secondary offers which the Secretary of State may by order exempt on the grounds of their private character, incidental nature or specialist market (see para **16.09**, ante). In such cases the separate order exempting the advertisement from s 170(1) may specify additional requirements for private companies. Such an order is to be subject to negative resolution (s 170(2)–(4)).

Section 170 replaces s 81 of the Companies Act 1985. Breach of s 170 may lead to civil or criminal liability (see para **16.22**, post).

Civil and criminal liability

16.22   In addition to the liability for misstatements and omissions in a prospectus under s 166 (see para **16.13**, ante), s 171 provides additional liability for contravention of the various restrictions contained in Pt V.

AUTHORISED PERSONS – CIVIL LIABILITY

16.23   An authorised person (ie authorised under Pt I of the Act who contravenes s 159 or 160 (no offers without a prospectus), the implementation of offer rules under s 170, or the exempt offer rules under ss 160(7) and 170(2), or issues a prohibited advertisement on behalf of a private company, is to be regarded as having contravened the conduct of business rules or the rules of his SRO or recognised professional body, as appropriate: s 171(1).

The effect of this will be to invoke ss 60–62 of the Act, allowing, in particular, an action for damages (see para **4.81**, ante). Such an action may be brought by anyone who suffers loss as a result of the breach (s 166(6)).

For the purposes of s 171 (but not s 166 liability for misstatements etc) there is no breach of s 159 or 160 (prospectus requirement) if the only defect is that the prospectus did not fully comply with the form and content rules of Pt V. If a defective prospectus is issued, the investors' remedy is compensation for misstatements etc and not for breach of the prospectus obligation itself (s 171(5)).

PRIVATE COMPANY ISSUING PROHIBITED ADVERTISEMENT

16.24   If a private company acts in breach of s 170 (see para **16.21**, ante) it is to be treated as having acted in breach of s 57 (general restriction on investment advertisements). The effect of this is to produce criminal liability under s 57(4) and to render any agreement or obligation derived from the advertisement unenforceable and enable the investor to recover any money paid, subject to the court's discretion (s 161(2)). (For comments on s 57, see para **4.61**, ante.) If a company is criminally liable, the liability of its directors is governed by s 202 (see para **21.65**, post).

UNAUTHORISED PERSONS – CRIMINAL LIABILITY

16.25   It is a criminal offence for a non-authorised person (ie not authorised under Pt I of the Act) to contravene s 159 or 160 (prospectus requirement), the implementation of offer rules under s 169, or the exempt offer rules under s 160(7) or 170(2) (s 171(3)).

The standard defence is available for breaches of s 159 or 160, however, for advertisements issued in the course of a non-investment business to the order of another person, provided the publisher can prove that he reasonably believed after due enquiry either that the section in question did not apply or had been complied with (s 171(4)).

There is no breach of s 159 or 160 for this purpose simply because the prospectus did not fully comply with the requirements of Pt V as to the form and contents of a prospectus.

Chapter 17

Takeover offers

Replacement of ss 428–430 of the Companies Act 1985

17.01   Section 172 provides that Sch 12 to the Act will substitute new ss 428–430F into the Companies Act 1985. The former ss 428–430 are repealed by Sch 17, Pt I. Those provisions, the consolidated form of s 209 of the Companies Act 1948, allowed the purchaser under a scheme or contract, who had obtained 90 per cent of the shares of a company, compulsorily to acquire the remainder or, alternatively, to allow that minority to require that they be bought out. To prevent abuse there was a right to petition the court.

That basic framework remains intact. However, the procedures have been tightened and modernised and specifically linked to takeover offers. Some of the recommendations of the Jenkins Committee (1962, Cmnd 1749) have also been adopted. The stated aims of the changes are to protect the rights of dissentients to resist compulsory acquisition if they have reasonable cause to do so, and that they should be treated no less fairly than those shareholders who accepted the offer. The 90 per cent threshold has been tightened and there are new rules for shares already held by the offeror and his associates. Dissentients are to be informed of their rights earlier and those who petition the court may be protected as to costs.

Scope of the new ss 428–432F of the Companies Act 1985

NB References in this chapter are to the subsituted ss of the Companies Act 1985.

17.02   The new sections only apply if there is a 'takeover offer', ie an offer to acquire all the shares (or all of a class of shares) in a company on the same terms except for shares already owned by the offeror (s 428(1)). This contrasts with the wording of the former s 428 'a scheme or contract involving the transfer of shares' and adopts a recommendation of the Jenkins Committee (1962, Cmnd 1749, para 283).

There must of be necessity be an 'offeror', who is the person making the offer and a company whose shares are the subject of an offer (s 428(8)). The provisions apply to 'joint offerors' (see para **17.14**, post).

The offer must be for all the shares (or class of shares). By virtue of s 428(2) this means shares allotted on the date of the offer, but it may include shares allotted subsequently before a date specified by or determined in accordance with the offer. In certain circumstances it can include securities converted into shares during the offer period (see para **17.14**, post).

The offer must be 'on the same terms' for all the shares involved. By virtue of s 428(3) and (4) a variation which is necessary for the offeror to comply with overseas laws as to the consideration which may be offered (either because the normal consideration is prohibited or so circumscribed with conditions which cannot be complied with or which the offeror regards as unduly onerous), and which allows such overseas shareholders to receive a different but equally valuable form of consideration, is permitted and the offer will nevertheless be regarded as being on the same terms.

17.03   In deciding whether the offer applies to all the shares involved the following are discounted (and so do not form part of the calculation for the 90 per cent threshold):

(i)   shares already owned by the offeror or his associate at the date of the offer (ss 428(1), 430E(1));

(ii)   shares which the offeror or his associate has contracted to acquire at that date (excluding contracts without consideration and under seal or where the only consideration for the contract is the offeror's promise to make the offer) (ss 428(5), 430E(1)). In Scotland the requirement that the contract be under seal is omitted (s 428(6)).

NB shares acquired during the offer will count towards the threshold in appropriate circumstances. These rules replace the former requirement of 75 per cent in number of independent shares.

Offeror buying out the minority – compulsory purchase

THE POWER TO ISSUE AN ACQUISITION NOTICE

17.04   If the offer applies to a single class of shares and the offeror has 'by virtue of acceptances of the offer acquired or contracted to acquire not less than nine-tenths in value of the shares to which the offer relates' he can serve a notice on those who have not accepted the offer that he desires to acquire those shares (s 429(1)).

Section 429(2) applies a similar test where the offer relates to shares of different classes so that the necessary threshold must be met for each class before the notice can be served in relation to that class. This new departure enables converted shares to be dealt with properly (see para **17.19**, post).

This power only arises if the threshold is met with respect to acceptances in relation to shares to which the offer relates. Thus shares in categories (i) and (ii) in para **17.03**, ante, are excluded from the calculation. By virtue of s 429(8), however, acquisitions by the offeror otherwise than by acceptances during the offer period (ie as controlled by the City Code on Takeovers and Mergers – 60 days), may be counted towards the threshold provided that they were so acquired at no more than the offer price or, if the offer price is revised, upwards to the price paid (as would be required by the City Code on Takeovers and Mergers). Other purchases etc by the offeror cannot be counted in. Section 430E(2) applies similar rules to shares acquired by the offeror's associates (see para **17.16**, post).

PROCEDURAL REQUIREMENTS

17.05   No notice may be issued under s 429 (1) or (2) unless the threshold has been acquired within four mouths of the offer being made and the notice must then be served within two months of notifying that requirement.

Any notice must be in the prescribed manner and when it is first given a copy must be sent by the offeror to the offeree company together with a statutory declaration (by any one of joint offerors) that the conditions for its use have been complied with, signed by a director if appropriate. Failure to send a copy and/or a declaration, or making a false declaration without having reasonable grounds for believing it to be true, is a criminal offence. It is a defence to an allegation of failure to send a copy etc, for the person to prove that he took reasonable steps for securing compliance with the obligations (s 429 (3)–(7)).

For the purposes of s 429, where the offer makes provisions for a revision of its terms and for acceptances on the previous terms to count as acceptances on the revised terms, such a revision does not count as a fresh offer, so that eg the four month period continues to run (s 428(7)).

EFFECT OF NOTICE TO ACQUIRE

17.06   If the acquisition notice is duly given, the offeror 'shall be entitled and bound' to acquire the dissentient's shares 'on the terms of the offer' (s 430(2)). Since the acquisition must be 'on the terms of the offer', if the offer included a choice of consideration (eg cash or shares) the notice must give the non-acceptors that same choice, within six weeks to indicate their choice in writing to the offeror (or any one of joint offerers). The notice must also indicate which consideration will be paid if no choice is made (s 430(3)). This choice must be made available to the non-acceptors irrespective of any time limits or other condition in the original offer. If the consideration so chosen is not cash and is no longer available (either because the offeror, or any of joint offerors is unable to provide it or a third party is no longer able or bound to provide it) the cash equivalent at the date of the notice must be paid (s 430 (4)). These sections follow the approach taken in *Re Carlton Holdings Ltd* [1971] 1 WLR 918.

MECHANICS OF THE ACQUISITION

17.07 After a period of six weeks from the date of the notice (ie the time within which any choice of consideration must be made) the offeror must send a copy of the notice to the offeror company and pay to it the consideration for the non-acceptors' shares (or allot to it shares in the offeror company as appropriate), together with an instrument of transfer executed on behalf of the shareholder by a person nominated by the offeror (or one of joint offerors). The offeror company must then register the offeror as holder of those shares (s 430(5), (6), (8)).

If the non-acceptors' shares are transferable by share warrants, the offeror must send the offeree company a statement to that effect. The offeree company must then issue new warrants to the offeror and those already in issue become void (s 430(7)).

Any consideration, or dividend or other sums accruing from that consideration, which is so received by the offeree company, must be kept in a separate bank account which pays interest and allows for withdrawal either by giving notice or on demand (s 430(10)). All such consideration is held by the offeree company on trust for the non-acceptors (s 430(9)). This will prevent such sums being available for the creditors of the offeree company.

If the non-acceptors cannot be found after reasonable enquiries have been made at reasonable intervals (no definitions given) and either twelve years have elapsed since the consideration was received or the offeree is wound up, the contents of the trust fund are to be paid into court (s 430(11)). The expenses of such enquiries can be met out of that trust fund (s 430(15)). Section 430(11) only applies to companies registered in England and Wales. Companies registered in Scotland are subject to similar rules by virtue of s 430(12)–(14).

NB This six week timetable etc will be halted if there is an application by the minority to the court to prevent the acquisition. Only when such an application has been disposed of will the procedure come into operation again (s 430C(2)) (see para **17.09**, post).

APPLICATION BY OFFEROR TO LOWER THRESHOLD

17.08 If the offeror has failed to achieve the necessary number of acceptances to give an acquisition notice under s 429 (see para **17.04**, ante), he may apply to the court to be allowed to give such notices if the reason for the shortfall is that some shareholders are untraceable (after reasonable enquiry by the offeror or one of joint offerors) and the total of acceptances plus untraceable shareholders amounts to 90 per cent of the total. The offeror must also show that the consideration is fair and reasonable.

The court will only make such an order if it would be just and equitable to do so having regard to the number of traced non-acceptors of the offer (s 430(5)).

MINORITY RIGHT TO APPLY TO PREVENT ACQUISITIONS

17.09   Within six weeks of receiving an acquisition notice under s 429 (see para **17.04**, ante) any shareholder may apply to the court for an order either (a) preventing the compulsory purchase or (b) specifying different terms of acquisition (s 430C(1)). Paragraph (b) is a new provision following a recommendation of the Jenkins Committee (1962 Cmnd 1749).

Another new provision is s 430C(4). This provides that no application for costs or expenses may be made against an applicant under s 430C(1) unless his application was unnecessary, improper or vexatious or he has been guilty of unreasonable delay or unreasonable conduct in conducting the proceedings.

However, nothing in s 430C suggests that there will be any alteration in the court's attitude to preventing a purchase going ahead. Thus the established case law may prevail in that the applicant must show that the section is unfair to the general body of shareholders in the offeree company: see eg *Re Grierson, Oldham & Adams Ltd* [1968] Ch 17; *Re Evertite Locknuts Ltd* [1945] Ch 220 and *Re Press Caps Ltd* [1949] Ch 434, CA. Whether the new power to order a revision of the terms of the purchase will have any effect on this attitude is open to doubt.

An application under s 430C(1) will halt any steps by the offeror to enforce the acquisition notice (s 430C(2)) (see para **17.07**, ante).

Right of minority shareholder to be bought out – reverse compulsory purchase

POWER TO ISSUE REVERSE ACQUISITION COMMUNICATION

17.10   If the offer applies to all the shares in the offeree company, and before the end of the offer period the offeror has acquired by virtue of acceptances of the offer sufficient of those shares which, when added with other such shares he has acquired or contracted to acquire, amounts to not less than nine-tenths in value of all the shares, any non-acceptor may require the offeror to acquire his shares by addressing a written communication to the offeror or one of joint offerors) (s 430A(1)).

Section 430A(2) applies a similar test where the offer relates to shares of different classes – again the principle being that each class is dealt with separately in relation to acquisitions (see para **17.04**, ante), and allows converted shares to be assimilated into the procedure (see para **17.19**, ante).

It is important to note that the nine-tenths threshold for the purposes of a reverse compulsory purchase by the offeror under s 430A is not identical to that for a compulsory purchase under s 429. For a reverse compulsory purchase, it includes all shares held by the offeror or his associates whether by acceptance or purchase. For a compulsory purchase, only certain shares acquired by purchase are counted (see s 429(8), para **17.04**, ante).

17.11   The importance of this distinction is increased because s 430A(3) imposes an obligation on the offeror to give any non-acceptor a notice of his rights to be bought out within one month of the threshold under s 430A(1) and (2) being achieved. If the notice is issued before the end of the offer period it must also state that the offer is still open for acceptances. It is incumbent on the offeror therefore to monitor both thresholds.

Any notices issued under s 430A(3) may restrict the time within which the non-acceptors can exercise their rights under that section, but this cannot be less than three months from the end of the offer period (s 430A(4)).

Failure to send such a notice is a criminal offence and this extends to every officer of the offeror, if it is a company, who is in default or to whose neglect the failure is attributable. If the offeror is an individual it is a defence to such a charge that he took all reasonable steps to comply with the requirements (s 430A(6)(7)).

No notice need be issued under s 430A(3) if the offeror has already given a compulsory purchase notice under s 429 (s 430A(5)).

EFFECT OF REVERSE ACQUISITION COMMUNICATION

17.12 If a minority shareholder exercises his rights under s 430A above by a written communication to the offeror, then s 430B(2) provides that the offeror shall be entitled and bound to acquire his shares 'on the terms of the offer or on such other terms as may be agreed' (subject to s 430C(3); see para **17.13**, post).

The requirement involves making provision for offers which give a choice of consideration, eg cash or shares in the offeror. The solution, in s 430B(3) and (4), is essentially the same as that provided by s 430(3) and (4) in relation to a compulsory purchase (see para **17.06**, ante). The notice issued under s 430(3) must indicate the choice available, the right of the non-acceptor to choose and which consideration will be paid if no choice is made.

Such a choice should be made in the written communication exercising the non-acceptor's rights (s 430B(3)). The choice must be made available to the non-acceptors irrespective of any time limits or other conditions in the original offer. If the consideration so chosen is not cash and is no longer available (either because the offeror, or any of joint offerors, is unable to provide it, or a third party is no longer able or bound to provide it) the cash equivalent at the date of the written communication must be paid (s 430B(4)).

APPLICATION TO COURT BY MINORITY SHAREHOLDER OR OFFEROR

17.13 Where a minority shareholder exercises his right of reverse compulsory purchase under s 430A either he or the offeror may apply to the court for an order that the terms of the purchase shall be such as the court thinks fit to impose (s 430C(3)).

The minority shareholder is protected as to costs and expenses under s 430C(4) in the same way as on an application under s 430C(1) to prevent or vary the terms of a compulsory purchase order under s 429 (see para **17.09**, ante).

Joint Offerors

17.14 Section 430D allows joint offerors to take advantage of or be subject to the rights of compulsory purchase and reverse compulsory purchase under ss 429 and 430A above.

To enable these rights to apply, the joint offerors must acquire the shares by virtue of acceptances of the offer jointly, and acquire shares in other ways, eg by purchase, either jointly or severally. The various rights, eg of compulsory purchase, are joint rights, and the various obligations, eg of reverse compulsory purchase, are joint and several obligations (s 430D(2)). The importance of this distinction is that they must act together to enforce a compulsory purchase (ie by one application etc) whereas a minority shareholder may enforce the reverse compulsory purchase against any one or all of them, in succession if necessary.

This section reverses the Privy Council decision in *Blue Metal Industries Ltd v Dilley* [1970] AC 827.

MODIFICATIONS IN THE CASE OF JOINT OFFEROR

17.15 (i) Any notice or other document will be deemed to have been given or sent by or to the joint offerors if it is given or sent by or to any of them, except for the statutory declaration under s 429(4) (that the condition for giving a compulsory purchase notice has been satisfied – see para **17.05**, ante) which must be signed by all of them (or a director of each company as appropriate) (s 430D(3)).

(ii) In general the definitions of a 'takeover offer' and 'offeror' include joint offerors. 'Shares acquired by an offeror' during the offer period other than by acceptances of the offer under s 429(8) (see para **17.04**, ante) apply to shares acquired by any joint offeror (s 430D(4)).

(iii) Associates of offerors (see para **17.16**, post) include associates of joint offerors (s 430D(4)).

(iv) The procedure for compulsory acquisitions, ie the transfer of shares by instrument or warrant under s 430(6) or (7) (see para **17.07**, ante), may be achieved by any one of the joint offerors as they may determine (s 430D(5)).

(v) The provisions applicable where one form of consideration under the offer is no longer available because the offeror cannot provide it, only apply where all the joint offerors are no longer able to provide it and ss 430(4)(a) and 430B(4)(a) apply accordingly (see paras **17.06** and **17.12**, ante) (s 430D(6)).

(vi) Applications to the court under s 430C apply as if offeror equalled joint offerors – except that an application for variation of the terms of a reverse compulsory purchase (s 430(3); see para **17.13**, ante) or for a lowering of the compulsory purchase threshold (s 430(5); see para **17.08**, ante) may be made by any of them. In an application for a lowering of the threshold they must show that none of the joint offerors has been able to trace the shareholders concerned (s 430D(7)).

Associates

17.16   Shares held, or acquired by purchase during the offer period, by an associate of the offeror are treated in the same way as shares so held or acquired by the offeror himself (s 430E(1) and (2)). Thus shares originally held are discounted and only shares purchased at the offer price or below, or where the offer price is revised upwards to that level, count towards the compulsory purchase threshold under s 429.

With regard to a reverse compulsory purchase, s 430E(3) provides that shares acquired by an associate are to be treated as shares acquired by the offeror in order to calculate the threshold for such purchases under s 430A.

DEFINITION OF AN ASSOCIATE

17.17   There are four categories of associates where the offeror is not an individual. These are:

(1) a nominee of the offeror (s 430E(4)(a));

(2) a holding company, subsidiary or fellow subsidiary of the offeror, or a nominee of any such company (s 430E(4)(b)). For this purpose a company is a fellow subsidiary of the offeror if both are subsidiaries of the same holding company but neither is a subsidiary of the other (s 430E(5));

(3) any company in which the offeror is substantially interested (s 430E(4)(c)). A substantial interest is defined as either where the company or its directors are accustomed to act in accordance with the offeror's direction or instruction, or where he can exercise or control one-third of the voting power of the company at a general meeting (s 430E(6)). For the latter, one-third voting rights in a company which in turn has one-third voting rights in another company will give the offeror voting control of the second company, and a right or obligation which would give him one-third control will also suffice (s 430E(7), applying s 203(3) and (4) as applied to s 203(b) of the Companies Act 1985);

(4) any person who has made an agreement with the offeror for the acquisition of the shares in question, or the nominee of such a person, provided the agreement includes provisions relating to the use, retention or disposal of the shares (s 430E(4)(d), importing s 204(2)(2) of the Companies Act 1985, relating to the obligation to disclose interests in shares). Section 430E(7) also applies s 204(5), (6) of the 1985 Act to such

agreements to include any agreement or arrangement and undertakings, expectation and understandings as to the terms of the agreement whether express or implied, and to exclude non-legally binding agreements with no mutuality in the arrangements or underwriting agreements.

17.18   Where the offeror is an individual, categories (1), (3) and (4) are equally applicable, and by virtue of s 430E(8), his 'associates' include his spouse and any minor child or step-child of his.

Convertible securities

17.19   The former sections presented problems for converted and convertible shares. In *Re Simo Securities Trust Ltd* [1971] 1 WLR 1455 the question arose, for the purpose of calculating the threshold for a compulsory purchase, as to the status of: (a) debentures converted into shares during the offer period and transferred to the offeror; (b) debentures converted into shares in the name of the offeror; and (c) debentures which could have been but were not so converted. The solution was to include (a) and (b) and to ignore (c).

The new solution is contained in s 430F. All securities which are convertible into shares or which entitle the holder to subscribe for shares are to be regarded as a separate class of shares (separate even from the class of shares to which they may be so converted). Since the structure of both the compulsory purchase rights under s 429 and reverse compulsory purchase rights under s 430A allows for each class of shares to be treated separately for calculating the relevant threshold, such securities, whether converted or not, cannot affect any other shares subject to the offer.

Chapter 18

Insider dealing

Introduction

18.01 Part VII of the Act contains six sections amending and supplementing the Company Securities (Insider Dealing) Act 1985. That Act, part of the 1985 Companies consolidation, re-enacted Pt V of the Companies Act 1980. In essence it provides that, subject to exemptions, any individual who seeks to make a profit or take an advantage through the sale or purchase of securities on The Stock Exchange or certain deals in advertised securities, involving the misuse of any confidential or inside information, commits a crime. Section 173 amends s 2 of the 1985 Act (abuse of information by public officials); s 174 amends ss 3 and 13 of the 1985 Act (actions exempt from the Act); s 175 replaces s 6 of the 1985 Act (exemption for international bonds); s 176 amends s 13 of the 1985 Act (definition of dealing); and ss 177 and 178 provide new sections allowing for investigation into insider dealing. Thus four of the six new sections will be absorbed into the 1985 Act.

Information obtained in an official capacity

18.02 Section 173 amends and supplements s 2 of the Company Securities (Insider Dealing) Act 1985. Section 2 provides restrictions on the use of inside information (unpublished price-sensitive information – see s 10 of the 1985 Act) by a Crown servant or former Crown servant. The effect of the s 173 amendments is to expand the restrictions from Crown servants to 'public servants'. Thus the word 'public' is to be substituted for the word 'Crown' in sub-ss (1) and (2) of s 2.

A new sub-s (4) is added to s 2 in order to categorise the new concept of a 'public' servant. A public servant for this purpose is:

(a) a Crown servant;

(b) a member, officer or servant of a designated agency (expected to be The Securities and Investments Board Ltd – s 114(3)); a competent authority (ie the Stock Exchange – s 142(6)); or transferee body (expected to be The Securities and Investments Board – Sch 11, para 27) – ie those private bodies involved in the statutory control of the investment industry under the Financial Services Act;

(c) an offeror or servant of a recognised self-regulating organisation (ie recognised under Pt I of this Act); a recognised investment exchange (ie a recognised clearing house recognised under Pt I);

(d) any person declared by an order under the new sub-s (5) to be a public servant for this purpose.

The new sub-s (5) allows the Secretary of State to make an order relating to the members, officers or employees or other persons connected with any body exercising a public function which may have access to unpublished price sensitive information relating to securities (see s 10 of the 1985 Act).

New sub-s (6) provides that an order under sub-s (5) is to be subject to a negative resolution.

Market makers and off-market dealers

BACKGROUND TO THE CHANGES

18.03 Section 174 provides amendments to ss 3, 4 and 13 of the Company Securities (Insider Dealing) Act 1985. These amendments are all designed to provide for the change in the Stock Exchange practices, which came into force on 27 October 1986, under which the old separation between broker and jobber no longer exists.

Section 3 of the 1985 Act exempts jobbers in certain circumstances from the insider dealing restrictions. Section 174 amends that section to allow a similar exemption for 'market makers' and defines them. Section 4 of the 1985 Act applies the prohibition and exemption on market deals to certain off-market deals. Section 174 thus adopts the new exemption for market makers in relation to off-market deals. Finally s 13 of the 1985 Act defines, inter alia, 'dealing in securities' and 'off-market deals'. These definitions are re-worded to take account of developments in the 1986 Act.

AMENDMENTS TO s 3 OF THE 1985 ACT

18.04 Section 174(1) adds a new para (d) to s 3(1) of the Company Securities (Insider Dealing) Act 1985. This provides a new exemption from ss 1 and 2 of that Act (restrictions on insider dealing on The Stock Exchange) for market makers. There is no restriction if the information in question was: (i) obtained in the course of business as a market maker in the relevant securities; (ii) was such as it would be reasonable to expect such a person to obtain in the ordinary course of that business; and (iii) the act involved was done in good faith in the course of that business.

This is identical in form to the existing exemption for jobbers, who are to be replaced by market makers (see above).

Section 174(2) adds at the end of s 3(1) of the 1985 Act a definition of a market maker for this purpose. He is someone recognised by The Stock Exchange as holding himself out at all normal times in compliance with its rules as willing to buy and sell securities at prices specified by him.

AMENDMENT TO s 4 OF THE 1985 ACT

18.05 Section 174(3) adds a new sub-s (2) to s 4 of the Company Securities (Insider Dealing) Act 1985. Section 4 applies the restrictions of ss 1 and 2 and the exemptions of s 3 of the 1985 Act to dealing in advertised securities using an off-market dealer to make a market in those securities. (An off-market dealer is defined in s 13 of the 1985 Act, as amended by s 174(4) of the Act – see para **18.06**, post.)

The exemption for a market maker acting bona fide in the course of his business in s 3(1)(d) of the 1985 Act (see para **18.04**, ante) applies to such off-market dealings, except that he must be recognised by and dealing on a recognised investment exchange rather than just on The Stock Exchange. A recognised investment exchange does not include an overseas investment exchange (see s 40 of the 1986 Act, para **3.118**, ante) for this purpose.

AMENDMENTS TO s 13 OF THE 1985 ACT

18.06 Section 174(4)(a) alters the wording of s 13(1) of the Company Securities (Insider Dealing) Act 1985 from dealings on a recognised stock exchange to dealings through an investment exchange. Thus ss 1–3 of the 1985 Act will not apply to investment exchanges – instead they will be covered by s 4 of that Act.

Section 174(4)(b) substitutes a new sub-s (3) in s 13 of the 1985 Act and re-defines an 'off-market dealer' for the 1985 Act as a person authorised under Pt I of the 1986 Act to carry on an investment business.

International bonds

18.07 Section 175 substitutes a new s 6 of the Company Securities (Insider Dealing) Act 1985 providing exemption from liability under that Act for those dealing in international bonds. Section 15 of the 1985 Act which supplemented s 6 is repealed by Pt I of Sch 17 to the 1986 Act.

The new section provides that there is to be no liability under ss 1, 2, 4 or 5 of the 1985 Act (ie the various offences of insider dealing) if what has been done was for the purpose of stabilising the price of securities and it complies with the Conduct of Business Rules made under s 48 of the 1986 Act.

Section 48(2)(i) allows these rules to lay down 'the circumstances and manner in which, and the time when or the period during which action may be taken for the purpose of stabilising the price of investments of any description.' In applying this to the 1985 Act, however, the substituted s 6 will only apply to those securities within paras 1 to 5 of Sch 1 to the 1986 Act as are actually specified by the rules, and to activities during the period before or after the issue of the securities as are specified by the rules.

Contracts for differences – dealing in securities

18.08   Section 176 adds a new sub-s (1A) to s 13 of the Company Securities (Insider Dealing) Act 1985. Section 13 contains various definitions for the purpose of that Act and the new subsection extends the concept of 'dealing in securities' (one of the main aspects of liability under the 1985 Act) to buying or selling contracts for differences as defined in para 9 of Sch 1 to the 1986 Act (see para **2.14**, ante).

Where a person buys or sells (or agrees to buy or sell) an investment within para 9 of Sch 2 and the purpose or pretended purpose of that transaction is to secure a profit or avoid a loss wholly or partly by reference to fluctuations in the value or price of securities, he is to be regarded for the purposes of the 1985 Act as dealing in those securities.

Investigations into insider dealing

18.09   Sections 177 and 178 introduce a new aspect to the legal control of insider dealing. Under the Company Securities (Insider Dealing) Act 1985 there are no provisions for the investigation of suspicious events. Since 1980 (when the criminal offences were first introduced) about 80 cases of possible insider dealing have been reported to the DTI but only eight have been prosecuted, with only four convictions. The main reason has been the difficulty of obtaining sufficient evidence to prove beyond reasonable doubt that the suspect dealt in the securities while he possessed information that he knew to be both unpublished and price-sensitive.

To remedy this, s 177 provides for investigations by inspectors with powers similar to those given to those investigating company affairs under s 432 of the Companies Act 1985. Section 178 provides various penalties for failure to co-operate with such an investigation. Sections 177 and 178 will not be absorbed into the 1985 Act at this stage.

APPOINTMENT AND POWERS OF INVESTIGATORS

18.10   Section 177(1) authorises the Secretary of State (but not a designated agency) to appoint inspectors if there are circumstances which suggest that there may have been a contravention of ss 1, 2, 4 or 5 of the

Company Securities (Insider Dealing) Act 1985 (ie the various restrictions on insider dealing). The function of the inspectors will be to carry out such investigations as are necessary to establish whether or not there has been such a contravention and to make a report to the Secretary of State. Such inspectors may be appointed for a limited time or for specific matters (s 177(2)).

Inspectors appointed under s 177 are to be given some of the powers of inspectors appointed to investigate company affairs under the Companies Act 1985. These are designed to enable them to obtain evidence. Unlike company inspectors, however, who may have to unravel very complex situations, an inspector under s 177 will start with a list of transactions and his job will not be to explain them but to discover any individuals behind any who are anonymous, and to form a view as to whether those involved should be proceeded against. For that reason the government rejected an opposition amendment protecting those subject to such an enquiry by reference to the rules of natural justice.

18.11   The powers given to inspectors are as follows:

(1) production of documents from any person who may be able to give information relating to the company whose securities are involved or those securities. These are documents which are in such a person's possession and control (s 177(3)(a)). This corresponds to s 434(1)(a) of the Companies Act 1985. A document for this purpose includes information recorded in any form – a legible copy being required if necessary (s 177(10));

(2) attendance before them of any such person (s 177(3)(b)). This corresponds to s 434(1)(b) of the Companies Act 1985;

(3) requiring such a person to give all reasonable assistance in connection with the investigation (s 177(3)(c)). This corresponds to s 434(1)(c) of the Companies Act 1985;

(4) examination on oath of such a person and power to administer the oath (s 177(4)). This corresponds to s 434(3) of the Companies Act 1985.

Any statement made by a person under these powers may be used in evidence against him (s 177(6)). This corresponds to s 434(5) of the Companies Act 1985.

18.12   The powers given to inspectors are subject to the following restrictions and limitations:

(1) refusal to give information or produce a document on the grounds of legal professional privilege (for High Court or Court of Session proceedings) (s 177(7)). This corresponds to s 452(1)(a) of the Companies Act 1985;

(2) refusal by a person carrying on the business of banking to give

information or produce any document relating to the affairs of a customer unless the customer is a person subject to the powers above and the Secretary of State is satisifed that the disclosure etc is necessary for the purposes of the investigations (s 177(8)). This is a narrower restriction than that in s 452(1)(b) of the Companies Act 1985.

Finally s 177(9) provides that nothing in this section is to affect a lien claimed on any document. This corresponds to s 447(4) of the Companies Act 1985.

The inspectors' report will then be given to the Secretary of State who must decide whether to bring a prosecution under the 1985 Act. Interim reports may also be made (s 177(5), which corresponds to s 437(1) of the Companies Act 1985).

PENALTIES FOR FAILURE TO CO-OPERATE WITH INVESTIGATIONS

18.13   Section 178 provides new penalties for anyone who fails to comply with a request to produce a document, attend before the inspectors or give them assistance under s 178(3) (above), or refuses to answer any questions put to him by the inspector which are relevant to establishing whether or not the suspected insider dealing has taken place. In such a case s 178(1) allows the inspector to certify that fact in writing to the court and the court may enquire into the case.

After hearing any witnesses and any statement offered in defence, if the court is satisfied that a person has refused a request or to answer any such question, the court has two alternative powers: (1) to treat the matter as a contempt of court; or (2) direct that the Secretary of State may exercise his powers under this section in respect of him (s 178(2)). A direction under (2) may be given against a person who is outside the jurisdiction if the court is satisfied that he was notified of his right to appear before the court and of its powers under this section.

If the suspected insider dealing relates to dealing by a person on behalf of another, it is not a defence to a charge of refusal to comply with a request or to answer a question, to say either that he did not know the identity of his principal or that he was subject to a foregin law which prohibits from disclosing information without his principal's consent if in the latter case he might have obtained such consent or exemption from that prohibition (s 178(6)).

ISSUE OF NOTICE WHEN AUTHORISED PERSON IN DEFAULT

18.14   If the court directs the Secretary of State to exercise his powers under this section against an authorised person, the Secretary of State may give him a notice under s 178(3). (An authorised person is a person authorised under Pt I of this Act.) The Secretary of State may transfer this function to the designated agency but only on terms that he may exercise it concurrently and subject to such conditions and restrictions as he may from time to time impose (s 178(10)). (For the definition of an authorised person see para **3.01**, ante).

A notice served on an authorised person may do any of the following:

(1) cancel his authority to carry on investment business after a specified period (ie a period which allows him to complete the performance of any contracts entered into before the notice was given and to terminate any continuing contracts (s 178(4), s 178(3)(a));

(2) disqualify him from being so authorised after a specified period (see (1) above) (s 178(3)(b));

(3) restrict such authority during the specified period (see (1) above) to the performance of contracts entered into before the notice was given (s 178(3)(c));

(4) prohibit him from entering into specified kinds of transactions or from entering into them except in specified circumstances and to a specified extent (s 178(3)(d));

(5) prohibit him from soliciting business from specified kinds of persons or otherwise than from such persons (s 178(3)(e));

(6) prohibit him from carrying on business in a specified manner or otherwise than in a specified manner (s 178(3)(f)).

18.15   Such a notice may be revoked if the Secretary of State (or agency) considers that the defaulter has agreed to comply with the request or to answer the question in issue. This is to be by a revocation notice (s 178(7)). However, this revocation does not automatically revive that person's authority unless he has that by virtue of being a member of an SRO or a recognised professional body in which case revocation of the notice re-establishes his authority. Those directly authorised must seek re-authorisation (s 178(8)).

When a notice is issued under s 178(3) or a revocation notice is served under s 178(7) a copy of that notice must be served on the agency (if the defaulter was at the time of serving the first notice directly authorised by it) or on the appropriate SRO or recognised professional body (if his authority derived from that body at the time of serving of the first notice) (s 178(9)).

ISSUE OF NOTICE WHEN UNAUTHORISED PERSON IN DEFAULT

18.16   If the court directs the Secretary of State to exercise his functions under this section in respect of an unauthorised person (ie one not authorised under the Act to carry on an investment business) then the Secretary of State (or agency – see s 178(10), para **18.14**, ante) may direct that any authorised person who knowingly transacts investment business of a specified kind or in specified circumstances or to a specified extent with or on behalf of that unauthorised person, is to be regarded as being in breach of the conduct of business rules, the rules of his SRO or those of his recognised professional body, as appropriate (s 178(5)).

This in effect 'blacks' the unauthorised person from access to the investment industry. The penalty for an authorised person in breach will be a possible public statement as to his misconduct, an injunction or restitution order or an action for damages, under ss 60 to 62 of the 1986 Act.

Chapter 19

Restrictions on disclosure of information

19.01 This Chapter deals with the restrictions on disclosure of information contained in Pt VIII of the Act.

Restrictions on disclosure of information

19.02 The main restriction on disclosure is contained in s 179(1). It is that, subject to certain exceptions (discussed at paras **19.06–19.10** infra), restricted information which 'relates to the business or other affairs of any person' is not to be disclosed either by the primary recipient, or by any person obtaining the information directly or indirectly from him, without the consent of the person from whom the primary recipient received the information *and*, if different, the person to whom the information relates.

19.03 The fundamental concept is that of 'restricted information'. This is information obtained by certain primary recipients for the purposes of, or in the discharge of functions under, the Act or any rules or regulations made under it. This is so whether or not the information was obtained by a requirement to supply it under those provisions (s 179(2)). The primary recipients concerned are specified in s 179(3), and exclude recognised self-regulating organisations, professional bodies, investment exchanges and clearing houses. These have no powers to obtain information under the Act, so the restrictions on disclosure applying can usually be determined on general principles and by their constitutions. These authorities may, of course, obtain restricted information directly or indirectly from one of the specified primary recipients, in which case the statutory restrictions of s 179(1) will apply. Information is not to be treated as restricted information for these purposes if it has been made available to the public by a disclosure which is not precluded by s 179 (s 179(4)).

19.04 A slightly different restriction applies to information obtained by the competent authority in the exercise of its functions under Part IV of the Act or received by it pursuant to a community obligation from any authority exercising coresponding functions in another member State. In this case, the information protected is not limited to information about the business or other affairs of any person. Subject to the same exceptions as the main restriction, information protected under this provision is not to be disclosed without the consent of the person from whom the authority obtained it and, again, if different, the person to whom it relates (s 179(5)).

19.05   A contravention of s 179 is an offence, punishable:

(a) on conviction on indictment, by imprisonment for a period not exceeding two years, a fine, or both; and

(b) on summary conviction, by imprisonment for a period not exceeding three months, a fine not exceeding the statutory maximum, or both (s 179(6)).

Exceptions from restrictions on disclosure

19.06   Section 180(1) contains a series of exceptions to the restrictions on disclosure in s 179. These cover disclosure:

(a) with a view to the institution of or otherwise for the purposes of criminal proceedings;

(b) with a view to the institution of, or otherwise for the purpose of, any civil proceedings arising under or by virtue of the Act or proceedings before the Tribunal;

(c)–(n) for the purpose of enabling or assisting various specified authorities to carry out particular functions;

(o) with a view to the institution of, or otherwise for the purpose of, any disciplinary proceedings relating to the exercise by a solicitor, auditor, accountant, valuer or actuary of his professional duties;

(p) for the purpose of enabling or assisting any person appointed or authorised to exercise investigatory powers under s 94, 106 or 177 to discharge his functions;

(q) for the purpose of enabling or assisting an auditor of an authorised person or a person approved under the power to require a second audit (s 108) to discharge his functions;

(r) if the information is or has been available to the public from other sources;

(s) in a summary or collection of information framed in such a way as not to enable the identity of any person to whom the information relates to be ascertained; or

(t) in pursuance of any Community obligation.

19.07 Nor does s 179 preclude the disclosure of information to the Secretary of State or to the Treasury if the disclosure is made in the interests of investors or in the public interest (s 180(2)). There is, too, a power by order to permit disclosures for the purpose of enabling or assisting other authorities to discharge functions specified in the order (s 180(3)–(4)).

19.08 Section 180(5) permits certain other legitimate disclosures. The first covers the situation where an unpublished Tribunal report has been made available to a person under the Act, and allows disclosure of information contained in the report by the person to whom it was made available or by anyone obtaining the information directly or indirectly from him. The second is a corresponding one for information contained in notices and copy notices served under the Act. The third is for information contained in the register of disqualified persons and permits disclosures by those who have inspected it or obtained the information directly or indirectly from them.

19.09 There are provisions permitting disclosure for the purpose of enabling or assisting certain overseas regulators to discharge their functions (s 180(6)). In determining whether their functions correspond to those of the Secretary of State under the Financial Services Act — one of the grounds stated — the Financial Services Act provisions are to be regarded as in force (Sch 15, para 13). There are also provisions enabling the Director General of Fair Trading to disclose information obtained for the purposes, or in the discharge, of his functions under the Financial Services Act for the purpose of enabling or assisting authorities under UK competition legislation to discharge their functions or for the purposes of civil proceedings under that legislation (s 180(7)). The information which may be disclosed includes both information of which the Director General was himself the 'primary recipient' and other restricted information, for example, information received under s 180(1)(m). The provision also applies to the Director General's staff and persons obtaining the information directly or indirectly from him. This provision does not enable restricted information to be disclosed *to* the Director. This is dealt with primarily by s 180(1)(m).

19.10 A power is taken to modify the section on permitted disclosures to prevent or restrict disclosures of information received by specified persons pursuant to a community obligation from persons exercising functions in relation to a collective investment scheme (s 180(8)). This will facilitate the restriction of disclosure of information obtained under the UCITS directive.

Directions restricting the disclosure of information overseas

19.11 Section 181(1) enables the Secretary of State, if it appears to him to be in the public interest, to give a direction prohibiting the disclosure of specified information to any person (or to named persons) in a named country or territory outside the UK. A direction of this kind may prohibit disclosure by all persons or only by specified persons or classes of person. It may be absolute, or apply only in specified cases or subject to specified conditions (for example, requiring consent to be obtained). A direction prohibiting disclosure by all persons is to be published by the Secretary of State 'in such manner as appears to him to be appropriate' (s 181(2)).

19.12 These powers only apply to information which relates to someone's business or other affairs and which was obtained (whether or not by virtue of any requirement to supply it) directly or indirectly by particular financial services authorities or investigators in the exercise of particular functions (s 181(3)). The powers cannot be used to prevent a person who is not an authority or investigator of this kind from disclosing information relating to his own affairs or information which he did not obtain directly or indirectly from such an authority or investigator (s 181(5)). A direction under this section is not to prohibit the disclosure of information in pursuance of a community obligation (s 181(6)).

19.13 The basis on which this power may be exercised is a general one, that it appears to the Secretary of State to be in the public interest. The most likely basis on which such a direction should be given would be that information was not effectively safeguarded in the country or territory concerned. Although s 181(8) disapplies any presumption of limited territorial effect which would otherwise apply, a close connection with the UK has been maintained for purposes of international law by the express limitations on the persons whose acts and omissions outside the UK are covered.

19.14 The penalties are criminal, with the same limits as for the other restrictions on disclosure (s 181(7)).

Disclosure of information under enactments relating to fair trading, banking, insurance and companies

19.15 Amendments are made by Sch 13 to facilitate disclosure of information among financial services regulators and others in cognate fields (s 182).

Chapter 20

Reciprocity

Introduction

20.01   Part IX of the Act contains four sections which are designed to give the United Kingdom leverage in seeking access for its financial services firms to foreign markets. Under the pre-existing law there were no powers to prevent foreign firms from becoming established in the United Kingdom investment industry provided they met the legal requirements. Part IX allows the Secretary of State (the power is transferable to a designated agency) to disqualify or restrict a foreign connected firm from carrying out investment or insurance business here if British firms do not enjoy access to that foreign market equivalent to that which foreign firms enjoy here. The Treasury has a similar power to disqualify in respect of banking business. The powers will apply to those seeking authorisation under the Act as well as to those already authorised to do business.

  The government has expressed its reluctance to use these powers but insisted that they were necessary as an aid in seeking access to foreign markets and would be used if necessary. Belgium, Denmark, France, Germany and Austria are among other countries which have such powers. The powers are discretionary and flexible.

General power to serve a notice

20.02   Where it appears to the Secretary of State (or the Treasury as appropriate) that by reason of the law of any overseas country (including any territory or part of a country or territory) or any action taken by or the practices of the government or any other body in that country, persons connected with the United Kingdom are unable to carry out investment, insurance or banking business in relation to that country (as defined above) on terms as favourable as those connected with that country may carry on such a business in relation to the United Kingdom, he may serve a notice under s 183 (ss 183(1), (5)).

  Such a notice may be served on any person connected with the overseas country who is carrying on or appears to intend to carry on any such business in or in relation to the United Kingdom.

20.03 A person is connected with a country if it appears to the Secretary of State (or the Treasury) that:

(a) if he is an individual, he is a national of or resident in that country or carries on an investment etc business with a principal place of business there;

(b) if it is a company, that it is incorporated or has a principal place of business in that country and is controlled by persons connected with that country;

(c) if it is a partnership, that its principal place of business is in that country, or that any partner is connected with that country; or

(d) if it is another form of unincorporated association, that it is formed in that country, has a principal place of business there, or is controlled by a person or persons connected with that country (s 183(4)).

20.04 The types of notice which may be issued are detailed in ss 184 and 185. Any such notice must state the grounds upon which it is given (including the country involved) and specify a day where it is to come into force (s 183(3)).

The power is discretionary and under s 183(2) the Secretary of State or Treasury must consider that it is in the national interest to serve a notice, and must consult (insofar as it seems expedient to do so) such body or bodies which represent the interests of persons likely to be affected. The latter category includes not only those subject to the notice but those who deal with eg overseas banks and insurance companies.

Notices with respect to investment and insurance business

20.05 If a notice is issued under s 183 (above) relating to an investment business (see Sch 1 to this Act) or an insurance business (see Schs 1 and 2 to the Insurance Companies Act 1982) it must be served by the Secretary of State. Such a notice may relate to one or both types of business. Three types of notice may be served: a disqualification notice, a restriction notice or a partial restriction notice (s 184(1)). These notices may be varied or revoked under s 186 (see para **20.15**, post).

DISQUALIFICATION NOTICES

20.06 Such a notice (for either class of business) has three consequences:

(1) cancelling that person's authority to carry on that business (either under Pt I of this Act or under ss 3 and 4 of the Insurance Companies Act 1982) after the expiry of a period specified in it. Such a period must be a reasonable one to enable the person concerned to complete the performance of contracts entered into prior to the notice coming into force and to terminate continuing contracts (s 184(2)(a));

(2) disqualifying him from carrying on that business after that specified period (s 184(2)(b)); and

(3) restricting his authority during the specified period to those contracts entered into prior to the notice coming into effect (s 184(2)(c)).

RESTRICTION NOTICES

20.07 Such a notice simply restricts the person's authority (in relation to either type of business to the performance of contracts entered into before the notice comes into force) (s 184(3)).

PARTIAL RESTRICTION NOTICES – INVESTMENT BUSINESS

20.08 Such a notice has three possible effects in relation to an investment business:

(1) it can prohibit the person from entering into transactions of any specified kind, or entering into them except in specified circumstances or to a specified extent;

(2) it can prohibit him from soliciting business from persons of a specified kind or otherwise than from such persons; or

(3) it can prohibit the carrying on of business in a specified manner or otherwise than in a specified manner (s 184(4)).

Such notices allow the authorities flexibility in exercising their powers under this Part of the Act. It must be remembered that none of these notices is issued because of the default of the persons involved (cf those notices issuable under s 179 (para **18.14**, ante)).

If a person contravenes a partial restriction notice and grounds for issuing a s 182 notice still obtain (see para **20.02**, ante), the Secretary of State may serve a disqualification or restriction notice instead (s 184(7)). In addition the following sections apply in that a breach of such a notice will be regarded as a breach within those sections: s 28 (withdrawal and suspension of authorisation to carry on investment business); s 33 (termination and suspension of authorisation); s 60 (public statements as to misconduct); s 61 (injunction and restitution orders for potential or actual contraventions); and s 62 (actions for damages) (s 184(8)).

PARTIAL RESTRICTION NOTICES – INSURANCE BUSINESS

20.09 Such a notice may have the following effect in relation to an insurance business. It may direct that the person concerned may cease to be authorised under either ss 3 or 4 of the Insurance Companies Act 1982 (authorisation by the Secretary of State to carry on insurance business within Schs 1 and 2 to that Act) in respect of those types of insurance contracts specified in the notice (s 184(5)).

Contravention may lead to a disqualification or restriction notice being served under s 184(7) (see para **20.08**, ante).

COPIES OF THE NOTICE WITH RESPECT TO INVESTMENT BUSINESS

20.10 If the person served with any of the notices detailed above is an authorised person to carry on an investment business, a copy of the notice must be sent to a designated agency (for those directly authorised) or to the relevant SRO or recognised professional body as appropriate (s 184(6)).

Notices with respect to banking business

20.11 Section 185(1) provides that if a notice under s 183 (see para **20.02**, ante) is served in respect of a banking business it must be served by the Treasury and may be either a disqualification or a partial restriction notice. Banking business for this purpose is the carrying on of a deposit-taking business as a recognised bank or licensed institution within the meaning of the Banking Act 1979 (ss 1 and 3). Such notices may be varied or revoked under s 186 (see para **20.15**, post).

DISQUALIFICATION NOTICES

20.12 Such a notice has two consequences by virtue of s 185(2):

(1) it cancels the recognition or licence granted to the person concerned under the Banking Act 1979, and

(2) it disqualifies him from becoming a recognised bank or licensed institution under that Act.

The effects of such an immediate disqualification are controlled not by this section but by s 8 of the Banking Act 1979, which enables the Bank of England to give directions to protect the interests of depositors when authority under that Act is terminated. Section 185(7) adds a new para (d) to s 8(1) of the 1979 Act to achieve this.

PARTIAL RESTRICTION NOTICES

20.13 A partial restriction notice may provide for all or any of the following restrictions by virtue of s 185(3):

(1) the prohibition of the dealing with or disposing of assets in any specified manner;

(2) the imposition of limitations on the acceptance of deposits;

(3) the prohibition of the soliciting of deposits either generally or from those who are not already depositors;

(4) the prohibition of the entering into any other transaction or type of transactions; and

(5) the requirement of the taking of certain steps, restricting the scope of

business in a particular way, or requiring the pursuing or not pursuing of a particular course of activies.

Contravention of a partial restriction notice is a criminal offence (no mens rea is needed) and is actionable at the suit of anyone who suffers loss as a result, subject to the usual defences etc applicable to actions for breach of statutory duty. The transaction, however, is not invalidated (s 185(5)(6)).

There is no express power to issue a disqualification notice for breach of a partial restriction notice equivalent to s 184(7) (see para **20.09**, ante). On the other hand if a s 183 notice could still be issued at that time there seems no reason why one should not be issued under s 185(1).

COPIES OF THE NOTICE

20.14 A copy of any notice served under s 185 must be served on the Bank of England – the effective monitoring agency (s 185(4)).

Variation and revocation of notices

VARIATION OF A PARTIAL RESTRICTION NOTICE

20.15 Any partial restriction notice issued by the Secretary of State in relation to investment or insurance business (under s 184, para **20.08**, ante) or by the Treasury in relation to a banking business (under s 185, para **20.13**, ante) may be varied by a subsequent written notice coming into effect on the date specified (s 186(1)). A copy of such variation notice must be served, if the notice relates to investment business, on the body granting the relevant person authority to conduct investment business (ie the designated agency, SRO or recognised professional body as appropriate, or on the Bank of England in respect of a banking business) (s 186(6),(7)).

This is only a power of variation. It does not empower the issuing of a different category of notice (see paras **20.08 20.09** and **20.13**, ante).

REVOCATION OF A DISQUALIFICATION NOTICE

20.16 Any disqualification notice issued under s 183, either by the Secretary of State or the Treasury, may be revoked if the grounds for issuing that notice no longer apply to the country concerned (see para **20.02**, ante). Revocation is to be achieved by the issue of a revocation notice (s 186(2)). A copy of such a revocation notice must be served, if the notice relates to investment business, on the body granting the relevant person authority to conduct investment business at the time when the original notice was served (ie the designated agency, SRO or recognised professional body as appropriate, or on the Bank of England in respect of a banking business) (s 186(6),(7)).

EFFECT OF REVOCATION

20.17   The revocation of a disqualification notice does not revive the authorisation of the person concerned vis à vis insurance business or the recognition or licence under the Banking Act 1979 for a banking business. If the disqualification notice related to investment business, revocation of that notice will revive the authority to carry on that business if the person concerned would have been so authorised at the time of the revocation apart from that disqualification either by membership of an SRO or a recognised professional body (but not directly by a designated agency) (s 186(3)(4)).

If the authority is not revived by the issue of a revocation notice a fresh application for authorisation or recognition etc as appropriate will have to be made under the 1986 Act, the Insurance Companies Act 1982 or the Banking Act 1979 as appropriate. In such a case nothing in s 186 is to prevent such re-authorisation etc (s 186(5)).

Chapter 21

Miscellaneous and supplementary provisions

EXEMPTION FROM LIABILITY IN DAMAGES

21.01 The Act contains three separate exemptions from liability in damages, applying in the cases of a recognised self-regulating organisation, a designated agency and 'the competent authority' (s 187). It will be noted that these concern only liability in damages. Other remedies, such as injunctions, are unaffected. The Act contains no similar exemptions for recognised professional bodies, investment exchanges, or clearing houses.

21.02 In the case of a recognised self-regulating organisation, the exemption applies both to the organisation and to 'any of its officers or servants or members of its governing body', extending to 'anything done or omitted in the discharge or purported discharge' of certain specified functions, unless the act or omission is shown to have been in bad faith (s 187(1)).

21.03 The specified functions broadly delineate what a recognised self-regulating organisation does in its capacity as such. They are its functions relating to, or to matters arising out of:

(a) the rules, practices, powers and arrangements to which the statutory requirements for recognition in Sch 2 (other than the requirement as to 'promotion and maintenance of standards') apply;

(b) the obligations with which the 'promotion and maintenance of standards' requirement requires it to comply;

(c) any guidance issued by it;

(d) its powers to make certain requests in relation to its members (for indemnity rules to apply, for investors' assets to be transferred to and held by a trustee, for a petition for winding up of a member, whether in Great Britain or Northern Ireland, or investigation of a member's affairs); or

(e) the obligations to which the organisation is subject by virtue of the Act (s 187(1)).

It will be noted that a distinction is drawn in dealing with different requirements of the Schedule. For all the requirements except the requirement on promotion and maintenance of standards, the exemption covers rules etc to which the requirements apply, even if they go further than the requirement entails. In the case of 'promotion and maintenance of standards' the exemption only covers the obligations with which the organisation is required to comply, perhaps reflecting a sensitivity in the provision for co-operation by sharing information. While the Act itself does not give a clear content to the obligations with which the organisation must comply, such a content may be expected to be given during the recognition process and this may well be relevant to the scope of the exemption. For the extension of the exemption to certain delegated monitoring functions, see para **21.05**.

21.04 In the case of a designated agency or transferee body, the exemption applies both to the agency and to 'any member, officer or servant'. It extends to 'anything done or omitted in the discharge or purported discharge of the functions exercisable by the agency by virtue of a delegation order or, as the case may be, by virtue of a transfer order unless the act or omission is shown to have been in bad faith' (s 187(3)).

21.05 The functions to which the exemptions for self-regulating organisations and designated agencies apply also include monitoring functions 'delegated' to them by recognised self-regulating organisations, professional bodies, investment exchanges, designated agencies and by clearing houses (s 187(5)).

21.06 The third exemption applies to 'the competent authority' and 'any member, officer or servant of that authority'. It extends to 'anything done or omitted in the discharge or purported discharge of any functions of the authority under Part IV' of the Act, unless the act or omission is shown to have been in bad faith. Regulation 8(1) of The Stock Exchange (Listing) Regulations 1984 (SI 1984 No 716) is accordingly replaced by a new and more extensive exemption. (The regulations are revoked by Sch 17.)

21.07 There is also a provision dealing with the liability of a recognised professional body. This does not, however, itself provide an exemption. Instead, it authorises the body to make it a condition of the issue of an investment business certificate that neither the body, nor any of its officers or servants or members of its governing body, are to be liable in damages for anything done in the discharge or purported discharge of certain functions, unless the act or omission is shown to have been in bad faith (s 187(6)–(7)). The significance of the different approach is that a condition in a certificate cannot bind members of the public. Express reference in the legislation to such a procedure may be expected, however, to avoid such a condition falling foul of the Unfair Contract Terms Act 1977.

JURISDICTION AS RESPECTS ACTIONS CONCERNING DESIGNATED AGENCY, ETC

21.08   Proceedings arising out of any act or omission (or proposed act or omission) of a designated agency, transferee body or the competent authority in the discharge or purposed discharge of any of its functions under the Act may be brought either in the High Court or in the Court of Session (s 188(1)). The usual provisions for allocation of jurisdiction in civil proceedings within the UK (contained in Sch 4 to the Civil Jurisdiction and Judgements Act 1982), are disapplied (s 188(2)).

RESTRICTION OF REHABILITATION OF OFFENDERS ACT 1974

21.09   The Rehabilitation of Offenders Act 1974 is directed to promoting the rehabilitation of individuals who have been convicted of offences. For this purpose, it provides for convictions to become spent after particular periods of time. A conviction will not become spent, though, where particular kinds of sentence are imposed (including sentences of more than thirty months' imprisonment) either on the conviction itself or on a subsequent conviction during the rehabilitation period (1974 Act, s 1(1)). It should be noted that the 1974 Act only applies to convictions of individuals.

21.10   Once a conviction becomes spent, various benefits are conferred. These are, though, restricted in the financial services sector (s 189 and Sch 14) in order to strike a balance between the aims of rehabilitation and the particular need for honesty and proper conduct in the sector. The restriction on rehabilitation only applies to two particular kinds of offence, which these comments will refer to as 'restricted rehabilitation offences'. The first kind are offences 'involving fraud or other dishonesty'. In this case, the field of activity in which the offence took place is irrelevant. The second kind are offences (whether or not involving fraud or dishonesty) under legislation dealing with particular matters in financial services and related areas (s 189(1)).

21.11   Section 4(1) of the 1974 Act provides for rehabilitated persons, in general, to be treated as not having been convicted of any conviction which has become spent. Evidence about spent convictions is accordingly not to be admitted or required in 'proceedings before a judicial authority'. The effect of the restriction under the Financial Services Act is to exclude from this provision the kinds of proceeding, listed in Pt 1 of the Schedule (s 189(2)). Accordingly, in proceedings of those kinds, it is possible to determine issues, or admit or require evidence, relating to spent convictions for restricted rehabilitation offences or relating to ancillary circumstances. It will be noted that the proceedings are identified by their subject-matter (for example, 'proceedings with respect to ... refusing ... an authorisation') rather than the tribunal or court concerned. The wording is accordingly apt to cover any judicial review proceedings, as well, for example, as proceedings of the Financial Services Tribunal.

21.12 Section 4(2) of the 1974 Act covers questions asked outside judicial proceedings (for example, in a job interview), and enables them in general to be treated as not relating to spent convictions. The effect of the restriction under the Financial Services Act is essentially that a conviction for a restricted rehabilitation offence is not to be regarded as spent for this purpose if two conditions are fulfilled. The first is that the question is put by or on behalf of a person specified in Pt II of Sch 14 and relates to an individual (who may or may not be the person questioned) who is 'specified in relation to the person putting the question' in Sch 14 (ibid). So questioners of each kind specified in the Schedule can ask questions relating only to particular kinds of people. The second condition is that the person questioned is informed when the question is put that, by virtue of this section, spent convictions for such an offence are to be disclosed (s 189(3)).

21.13 Section 4(3)(b) of the 1974 Act provides for spent convictions not to be a proper ground for dismissing or excluding a person from any office, profession, occupation or employment, or for prejudicing him in any way in any occupation or employment. This is qualified under the Financial Services Act so that specified kinds of action can be taken by reason, or partly by reason, of a spent conviction for a restricted rehabilitation offence. This is only the case, though, if the spent conviction is that of an individual who is:

(a) 'the person in respect of whom the action is taken';

(b) 'an associate of that person', in the case of certain action taken by financial services regulators;

(c) the operator or trustee of an authorised unit trust or a recognised collective investment scheme (or an associate of that operator or trustee), in the case of a decision to refuse or revoke authorisation of the unit trust or recognition of the scheme (s 189(4)).

Where this provision enables action to be taken by reason of an individual's spent conviction, that action may also be taken 'by reason of any circumstances ancillary to such a conviction or of failure (whether or not by that individual) to disclose such conviction or any such circumstances' (ibid).

21.14 The expression 'associate' is defined for the purpose of these restrictions of the 1974 Act (s 189(6)). The definition does not extend expressly to employees.

21.15 It may be expected that the relevant exclusions in the Rehabilitation of Offenders Act 1974 (Exceptions) Order 1975 (SI 1975 No 1023) will in due course be revoked.

DATA PROTECTION

21.16   Section 190 extends the effect of s 30 of the Data Protection Act 1984 to certain data held by SROs and RPBs. Section 30 of the 1984 Act allows an order to be made exempting from the subject access provisions of that Act certain data held for the purpose of designated functions conferred by statute, including the regulation of financial services. It was realised that it would be difficult to regard SROs and RPBs as exercising statutory functions for this purpose, and so s 190 allows an order to be made:

(a) regarding any functions of an SRO in connection with the admission, expulsion, or suspension of members, and the supervision or regulation of its members in carrying on an investment business;

(b) regarding any function of an RPB in connection with the issue, withdrawal or suspension of certificates allowing authorisation under Pt I of the Act, and the supervision or regulation of its certified members in carrying on investment business; and

(c) regarding any function of an SRO for friendly societies in connection with the supervision or regulation of its member societies.

In these cases the data is to be deemed to be held for the purpose of a statutory function.

As s 190 is an extension of the existing exclusions for subject access it needs to comply with the Council of Europe Convention for the Protection of Individuals with Regard to Automatic Processing of Personal Data (Strasburg) 1980 which is expected to be ratified in 1987 when the Data Protection Act comes fully into force. Under art 9 of that Convention, exclusions of this type are permitted if they are in the interests of state security, public safety, the monetary interests of the State or the suppression of criminal offences. Assuming s 190 is seen to fall within one of these and so long as the UK notifies the Council, under art 3, of the full scope of the exclusion it should not affect such ratification.

OCCUPATIONAL PENSION SCHEMES

21.17   A person who engages in the activity of 'managing investments' will generally be treated as carrying on investment business where the assets concerned are held for the purposes of an occupational pension scheme, even though he is not managing by way of business (s 191(1)). Those who are not managing by way of business are accordingly 'deemed' to be doing so.

21.18   This will not be the case, though, where all decisions, or all day-to-day decisions, are taken on behalf of the person concerned by:

(a) an authorised person; or

(b) an exempted person acting in the course of the business for which he is exempt; or

(c) an 'overseas person' who does not require authorisation to manage the assets as a result of Pt IV of Sch 1 (s 191(2)).

21.19 Nor will it be the case where an exempting order under s 191(3) applies. Such an order can exempt managers of schemes where it appears 'that management by an authorised or exempted person is unnecessary having regard to the size of the scheme and the control exercisable over its affairs by the members' (s 191(3)). It may therefore be expected to be appropriate for the schemes known as 'small self-administered pension schemes'. The power to make exempting orders of this kind is given to the Secretary of State and is not capable of transfer to a designated agency. Orders under it are 'subject to annulment in pursuance of a resolution of either House of Parliament' (s 191(4)).

21.20 The usual exclusion for trustees (Sch 1, para 22) does not apply for the purpose of the 'deeming' effect of s 191(1) (s 191(5)). Trustees may, of course, be able to avoid the need for authorisation or exemption through s 191(2).

21.21 The purpose of this provision is thus essentially to ensure that there is at least one authorised or exempted person involved in the 'management' of each occupational pension scheme. Since the role for exempted and overseas persons may be expected to be small, this will generally enable rules to be applied to the management of the scheme through the financial services regime.

21.22 For the exclusion of occupational pension schemes from constituting collective investment schemes, see para **6.17**. For the exclusion of rights under such schemes from constituting investments, see that paragraph and para **2.17**.

INTERNATIONAL OBLIGATIONS

21.23 In order to ensure compliance with international obligations, the Act confers a power to give directions, exercisable over a recognised self-regulating organisation, designated agency, transferee body or competent authority. It arises where it appears that:

(a) action proposed would be incompatible with community obligations or any other international obligations of the United Kingdom; or

(b) any action which it has power to take is required for the purpose of implementing any such obligations (s 192(1)).

Where the power arises, it enables directions to be given to the organisation, agency, body or authority not to take, or, as the case may be, to take the action in question. Directions under this power may include supplementary or incidental requirements where thought necessary or expedient (s 192(3)).

21.24   There is no provision for the exercise of the power over a recognised professional body or clearing house. Nor is there provision for its exercise over a recognised investment exchange generally, although it can be exercised over a recognised investment exchange which is an approved exchange within the meaning of Pt V of the Act (s 192(2)). In that case, it can only be used 'in respect of any action which it proposes to take or has power to take in respect of rules applying to a prospectus by virtue of a direction under section 162(3)'.

21.25   The power is exercisable by the Secretary of State and is not capable of transfer to a designated agency. Where the function of making or revoking a recognition order in respect of a self-regulating organisation is exercisable by a designated agency, any direction under this power in respect of that organisation is to be a direction requiring the agency to give the organisation such a direction as is specified in the direction given by the Secretary of State (s 192(5)).

21.26   Directions under this power are enforceable, on the application of the Secretary of State (or, as the case may be, agency), by mandamus or, in Scotland, by an order for specific performance under s 91 of the Court of Session Act 1868 (s 192(5)).

21.27   This provision will be seen to offer considerably greater flexibility than the usual power for implementing community obligations contained in s 2(2) of the European Communities Act 1972. In particular:

(a) it extends to other international obligations;

(b) it can be exercised by administrative direction, rather than needing an Order in Council or regulations;

(c) it is not subject to the restrictions in para 1 of Sch 2 to that Act.

EXEMPTION FROM BANKING ACT 1979

21.28   Section 193 provides an exemption from s 1(1) of the Banking Act 1979, the provision which, subject to certain exceptions, limits the acceptance of a deposit in the course of carrying on a deposit-taking business to the Bank of England, recognised banks and licensed deposit-takers.

21.29   The new exemption is a wide one. It exempts 'the acceptance of a deposit by an authorised or exempted person in the course of, or for the purpose of' engaging in particular activities (s 193(1)). In the case of an exempted person, the activity must be one in respect of which he is exempt (s 193(2)).

21.30   The activities for which the exemption applies are:

(a) 'dealing in investments' with or on behalf of the person by whom or on whose behalf the deposit is made; and

(b) 'arranging deals in investments', 'managing investments', and 'establishing etc, collective investment schemes' on behalf of that person.

In this case, the relevant paragraphs of Sch 1 are to be construed without reference to the exclusions in Pts III and IV.

21.31   For the ability to cover deposits with authorised persons under client money regulations, see para **4.51**.

21.32   Paragraph 9 of Sch 1 to the Banking Act provided an exclusion from the controls on deposit-taking for 'a member of The Stock Exchange in the course of business as a stockbroker or stockjobber'. This is repealed by Sch 17. It may also be possible to revoke or amend the exception for commodity brokers, traded option brokers and clearing houses in reg 14 of the Banking Act 1979 (Exempt Transactions) Regulations 1983 (SI 1983 No 1865). The new exemption is, though, without prejudice to any exemption from the 1979 Act which applies apart from this provision.

21.33   It should be noted that the exemption is only from the provisions of the Banking Act on control of deposit-taking, essentially through the system of recognition and licensing operated by the Bank of England. Other provisions of the 1979 Act continue to apply to deposits of this kind, including, for example, s 39 (fraudulent inducement to make a deposit) which is in similar terms to s 47(1) and 133(1) of the Financial Services Act.

TRANSFER TO AND FROM RECOGNISED CLEARING HOUSES

21.34   Section 194 updates various statutory references to Stock Exchange nominees, such as SEPON (Stock Exchange Pool Nominees Limited, designated by the Stock Exchange (Designation of Nominees) Order 1979 (SI 1979 No 238)), to reflect the new concepts introduced by the Financial Services Act. The essential character of this updating is to substitute, for references to Stock Exchange nominees, references to 'a recognised clearing house or nominee of a recognised clearing or of a recognised investment exchange'. The provisions updated are those which, both in Great Britain and in Northern Ireland, permit trustees to acquire or dispose of securities under a deferred settlement system involving such a nominee and those which provide exemption from the usual duty of a company to issue certificates for shares, debentures or debenture stock.

OFFERS OF SHORT-DATED DEBENTURES

21.35 Section 195 is designed to facilitate a new market in sterling commercial paper. This is a form of short-term negotiable debt which companies can issue as an alternative to bank borrowing. There already is a flourishing market in the USA in the equivalent dollar instruments.

Section 195(a) achieves this by extending the benefits of s 79(2) of the Companies Act 1985 to UK companies. Currently s 79(2) applies only to foreign companies and exempts offers to professionals from the prospectus requirements under the Companies Act. Section 79(2) is now to apply to companies governed by Ch I of Pt III of that Act (ie UK companies) as it applies to companies subject to Ch II (ie foreign companies). Sterling commercial paper will be issued in a minimum denomination of £500,000 and the market will effectively be limited to professionals.

Although Ch I of Pt III of the 1985 Act will be repealed by Pt I of Sch 17 to the 1986 Act this is to be at a time specified by order under s 211(1) of that Act. Section 211(2), however, provides that s 195 came into effect on Royal Assent in order to prevent any delay in establishing the new market. It will therefore ultimately be replaced by rules made in accordance with Pt V of the 1986 Act (see chapter 16, ante), at the time when the Companies Act prospectus provisions are repealed.

Section 195(b) applies to the corresponding provisions in Northern Ireland (ie art 89(2) of the Companies (Northern Ireland) Order 1986).

FINANCIAL ASSISTANCE FOR EMPLOYEE SHARE SCHEMES

21.36 Section 196 amends s 153 of the Companies Act 1985. Section 153(4)(b) of the 1985 Act exempts the funding of an employees' share scheme by a company from the prohibition in s 151 of that Act against companies providing financial assistance for the acquisition of their shares and there is some doubt as to whether this is wide enough to allow companies to provide facilities to allow beneficiaries under the scheme and their dependants to trade in such shares between themselves. The new provisions are intended to allow for this up to the limits, in the case of public companies, contained in s 154 of that Act.

Section 196(2) adds a new para (4)(bb) to s 153 of the Companies Act 1985. It exempts anything done by a company, or its subsidiaries in connection with that company or a company connected with it (see next paragraph) 'for the purpose of enabling or facilitating transactions in shares' in that company, between, and involving the acquisition of beneficial ownership of those shares by, the bona fide employees or former employees of that company (or of another company in the same group) or their dependants. The latter are their spouses, widows or minor children and step-children.

Section 196(3) adds a new sub-s (5) to s 153 of the Companies Act 1985 to define two concepts. First, for the purposes of new sub-s (4)(bb), a company is connected with another company if either it is a member of the same group (see below), or one company together with any other company in the same group controls the majority of the voting right of the share capital exercisable generally at meetings of the company or its holding company. Second, for the purpose of s 153 as a whole, a group is the company concerned, its holding company, its subsidiary companies and any other subsidiaries of that holding company (for the definitions of those terms, see s 736 of the Companies Act 1985). In fact 'group' only occurs in new sub-s (4)(bb) and (5).

Section 196(4)–(6) applies similar changes to the equivalent provision in Northern Ireland (ie art 163 of the Companies (Northern Ireland) Order 1986.

DISCLOSURE OF INTERESTS IN SHARES: INTEREST HELD BY MARKET MAKER

21.37 Section 197 amends s 209 of the Companies Act 1985 to provide for the new concept of a 'market maker' following the 'Big Bang' in the City whereby the distinction between jobbers and brokers has ceased to exist. Section 209 sets out the interests in shares which are to be disregarded in determining whether or not a person has a five per cent interest in the shares of a company notifiable under ss 198 and 199 of that Act. Currently an exempt interest of a recognised jobber is exempt under that section.

Section 197(1)(a) adds to the exemptions an exempt interest of a market maker by amending s 209(1)(f) of the 1985 Act to that effect.

Section 197(1)(b) then adds a new sub-s (4A) to s 209 of the 1985 Act to define both a market maker and an exempt interest for this purpose.

The definition of a market maker is similar to that introduced into the Company Securities (Insider Dealing) Act 1985 by section 174 of this Act (see para **18.04**, ante). He must hold himself out at all normal times in compliance with the rules of a recognised investment exchange, other than an overseas investment exchange, as willing to buy and sell securities at prices specified by him and be recognised by that investment exchange as doing so. Investment exchange and overseas investment exchange are as defined in s 207 of the 1986 Act.

An exempt interest is any interest of such a person if he holds the interest for the purpose of his business as a market maker in the United Kingdom and is subject to rules in the carrying on of that business.

Section 197(2) applies similar provisions to Northern Ireland by amending art 217 of the Companies (Northern Ireland) Order 1986.

POWER TO PETITION FOR A WINDING UP OR ADMINISTRATION ORDER

21.38 Section 198 amends s 440 of the Companies Act 1985 and s 8 of the Companies Directors Disqualification Act 1986. At present s 440 of the 1985 Act allows the Secretary of State to petition the court for the winding up of a company if it appears to him from a report of inspectors appointed under that Act (eg into the affairs of a company) or information obtained under that Act, that this is in the public interest. The Financial Services Act authorises such investigations under ss 94 and 105 into various aspects of an investment business. It is possible that as a result of such an investigation information will be obtained which may require the Secretary of State to bring a winding up petition against a company. To do this at present a second investigation under the Companies Act would have to be instigated.

To avoid this, s 198(1) amends s 440 of the Companies Act to enable such a petition to be brought as the result of information obtained by a report or otherwise under ss 94 or 105 of the 1986 Act.

The amendment in s 198(2) to s 8 of the Company Directors Disqualification Act 1986 similarly allows the Secretary of State to petition for a disqualification order against a director or shadow director if it is expedient in the public interest to do so as the result of an investigation under ss 94 or 105 of the Financial Services Act into an investment business or an investigation under s 177 of that Act into a suspected case of insider dealing.

Section 198(3) applies similar provisions to Northern Ireland by amending art 433 of the Companies (Northern Ireland) Order 1986.

POWERS OF ENTRY

21.39   A justice of the peace may issue an entry warrant under s 199 if satisfied on information on oath laid by or on behalf of the Secretary of State that one of two grounds applies. (For transferability of the Secretary of State's functions, see para **21.49**).

21.40   The first ground on which an entry warrant may be issued is that there are reasonable grounds for believing that an offence has been committed under ss 4, 47, 57, 130, 133 or 171(2) or (3) of the Financial Services Act or ss 1, 2, 4 or 5 of the Company Securities (Insider Dealing) Act 1985 and that there are on any premises documents (see para **21.51**) relevant to the question whether that offence has been committed (s 199(1))

21.41   The second ground on which an entry warrant may be issued is that there are reasonable grounds for believing that there are on any premises owned or occupied by a person whose affairs, or any aspect of whose affairs, are being investigated under s 105 (investigation powers) documents (see para **21.51**) whose production has been required under that section and which have not been produced in compliance with that requirement. This ground only applies, though, if the person is an authorised person, a person whose direct authorisation or authorisation as a Europerson has been suspended, or an appointed representative of an authorised person. It would appear possible that the powers are not therefore exercisable on this ground as opposed to the first ground against the 'appointed representative' of a person whose authorisation is suspended.

21.42   There is also a separate power for a justice to issue an entry warrant in support of the investigation powers applying for collective investment schemes under s 94 (s 199(2)). This enables a justice to issue an entry warrant if satisfied on information on oath laid by an inspector appointed under those powers that there are reasonable grounds for believing that there are on any premises owned or occupied by particular persons any documents whose production has been required under the powers and which have not been produced in compliance with that requirement. The owners and occupiers whose premises are concerned are:

(a) the manager, trustee or operator of any scheme whose affairs are being investigated under the powers; or

(b) a manager, trustee or operator whose own affairs are being investigated.

21.43   The provisions described in the following paragraphs apply to entry warrants granted on information laid by or on behalf of the Secretary of State as well as to those granted on information laid by an inspector under the powers for investigation of collective investment schemes.

21.44   An entry warrant is to authorise a constable, together with any other person named in it and any other constables:

(a) to enter the premises, using such force as is reasonably necessary;

(b) to search the premises and take possession of any such documents or to take any other steps which appear to be necessary for preserving them or preventing interference with them (so long as these are steps 'in relation to' the documents);

(c) to take copies of any such documents; and

(d) to require any person named in the warrant to provide an explanation of them or to state where they may be found (s 199(3)).

21.45   The power of entry conferred is thus a substantial one. It will be noted that it is similar to, but more extensive than, s 448 of the Companies Act 1985, on which it may be taken to be based.

21.46   An entry warrant under these powers continues in force 'until the end of the period of one month beginning with the day on which it is issued' (s 199(4)). Accordingly, a warrant issued at any time during, say, 14 May, may be taken, on normal principles of construction, to expire at midnight on 13 June.

21.47   Any documents of which possession is taken under this power may be retained for a period of three months. If, though, within three months, 'proceedings to which the documents are relevant are commenced against any person for an offence under the Financial Services Act or ss 1, 2, 4 or 5 of the Company Securities (Insider Dealing) Act 1985', the documents may be retained until the conclusion of those proceedings. It will be noted that these proceedings are not limited to proceedings for particular offences under the Financial Services Act (contrast para **21.40**). Similarly, the proceedings may be against 'any person'.

21.48 It is a criminal offence to obstruct the exercise of any rights conferred by an entry warrant under this provision (s 199(6)). It is also an offence to fail without reasonable excuse to comply with a requirement to provide an explanation of documents or to state where they may be found. The penalty on conviction on indictment is an fine. On summary conviction, the penalty is a fine not exceeding the statutory maximum.

21.49 The functions of the Secretary of State under this section are capable of transfer to a designated agency (s 199(7)). Any transfer may be subject to a reservation that the functions transferred are to be exercisable concurrently with the designated agency. Functions exercisable on the basis of reasonable grounds for believing that a particular kind of offence has been committed may be transferred so as to be exercisable subject to such conditions and restrictions as the Secretary of State may from time to time impose.

21.50 Section 199(8) makes the appropriate procedural adaptations in the application of the powers in Scotland and Northern Ireland.

21.51 In these provisions, 'documents' includes 'information recorded in any form' and, where information is recorded 'otherwise than in legible form', references to 'producing' it include producing a copy in legible form (s 199(9)).

FALSE AND MISLEADING STATEMENTS

21.52 Section 200 creates three offences involving false and misleading statements.

21.53 The first offence arises where a person furnishes information:

(a) for the purposes of or in connection with any application under this Act; or

(b) in purported compliance with any requirement imposed on him under this Act,

and the person who furnishes the information knows it to be false or misleading in a material particular or recklessly furnishes information which is false or misleading in a material particular (s 200(1)).

21.54 As far as concerns paragraph (a), it is doubted whether an application for membership of a recognised self-regulating organisation, professional body or investment exchange is an 'application under this

Act'. An application for direct authorisation, or, indeed, for recognition as such an organisation, body, or exchange would certainly be covered.

21.55   As far as concerns paragraph (b), it will be noted that a mere failure to comply with a requirement to supply information is not made an offence.

21.56   The penalty for committing the offence is:

(a) on indictment, imprisonment for not more than two years or a fine or both;

(b) on summary conviction, imprisonment for not more than six months or a fine not exceeding the statutory maximum or both (s 200(5)).

21.57   The second offence is committed, subject to a 'due diligence' defence, where a person who is not an authorised or exempted person:

(a) describes himself as such a person; or

(b) so holds himself out as to indicate or be reasonably understood to indicate that he is such a person (s 200(2)).

21.58   The penalty for committing this offence is, on summary conviction, imprisonment for not more than six months or a fine not exceeding the fifth level on the standard scale or both (s 200(6)). Where the offence involves a display, though, the maximum fine which may be imposed is an amount equal to the fifth level on the standard scale multiplied by the number of days for which the display has continued.

21.59   The third offence protects the status of being a recognised self-regulating organisation, recognised professional body, recognised investment exchange or recognised clearing house. The offence is committed, subject to a 'due diligence' defence, where a person who does not have the status concerned:

(a) describes himself as having that status; or

(b) so holds himself out as to indicate or be reasonably understood to indicate that he has that status (s 200(3)–(4)).

21.60   The penalty for committing this offence is, on summary conviction, imprisonment for not more than six months or a fine not exceeding the fifth level on the standard scale or both (s 200(6)–(7)). Where the offence involves a display, though, the maximum fine which may be imposed is an amount equal to the fifth level on the standard scale multiplied by the number of days for which the display has continued.

21.61   It will be noted that there is no offence applying to the status of designated agency or competent authority. Instances may be expected to be infrequent and capable of abatement without recourse to an expressly provided criminal offence. Since the status of being a recognised investment exchange covers both overseas exchanges and non-overseas exchanges, it would appear that the offence does not apply to one arrogating to itself the status of the other. Examples are again likely to be rare!

PROSECUTIONS

21.62 All the offences under the Act are 'restricted prosecution' offences. By s 201, prosecutions may only be brought 'by or with the consent of' the appropriate authority. It is considered that a restriction on prosecution imposes a duty on the authority concerned to consider the exercise of its powers to prosecute or give consent.

21.63 In all cases (except for contravention of a partial restriction notice relating to banking business see para **20.13**), prosecutions may be undertaken 'by or with the consent of' the Secretary of State. Except in the cases of prosecutions for 'misleading statements as to insurance contracts' (see para **13.09**) the function of initiating proceedings for offences is capable of transfer to a designated agency (s 201(4)). A transfer of the function of initiating proceedings must, though, be subject to a reservation that it is to be exercisable by the Secretary of State concurrently with the designated agency, and so as to be exercisable by the agency 'subject to such conditions or restrictions as the Secretary of State may from time to time impose' (ibid). The function of consenting to the initiation of proceedings is not capable of transfer.

21.64 All prosecutions under the Act may be undertaken by, or with the consent of, the Director of Public Prosecutions or, as appropriate, the Director of Public Prosecutions for Northern Ireland. In addition, prosecutions for the 'misleading statements as to insurance contracts' offence may be undertaken in England and Wales by or with the consent of the Industrial Assurance Commissioner (s 201(2)(a)). Prosecutions for the 'partial restriction' offence may be undertaken in any part of the United Kingdom by or with the consent of the Treasury (s 201(3)(a)).

OFFENCES BY BODIES CORPORATE, PARTNERSHIPS AND UNINCORPORATED ASSOCIATIONS

21.65 Section 202 is a standard form of section which provides for the lifting of the veil of incorporation to allow for the prosecution of the individuals who are responsible for a company's failure to comply with the requirement of the Act. It also applies to the prosecution of individuals involved in offences committed by partnerships and unincorporated associations.

Sections 202(1) and 202(2) apply to companies and extend criminal liability under the Act to any director, secretary or similar person (or a person purporting to act as such) or controller of the company where the offence was committed with his consent or connivance can be attributable to any neglect on the part of such a person. Where the affairs of the company are managed by the members they are to be treated as directors for this purpose.

In most respects s 202(1) and (2) uses the same wording as s 733 of the Companies Act 1985. The only difference is the liability of the controller of a company under s 202 to which there is no reference in s 733. A controller for this purpose is defined in s 207(5) as a person exercising or being able to control the exercise of at least 15 per cent of that company's voting power (or of its holding company). Voting rights of a person's associates are to be included in this calculation, ie his spouse, minor or step-child, employees, partners or any company's subsidiaries, or employees of such subsidiaries. Control is used in a very diffuse sense indeed.

21.66 Section 202(3) applies to partnerships. Its wording, however, leaves much to be desired since it provides that every partner is to be guilty of an offence committed by that partnership (see ss 10 and 11 of the Partnership Act 1890) under the Act 'other than a partner who is proved to have been ignorant of or to have attempted to prevent the commission of the offence.' Whilst the general burden of proof remains with the prosecution (cf the wording of s 202(1), ante, which already requires the prosecution to prove the relevant consent or connivance etc) the wording of this subsection suggests that it is for the partner concerned to prove ignorance of the relevant attempt. Since it is difficult for the prosecution to prove ignorance the court may well require the prosecution only to prove the offence and the partnership's involvement in it.

In another sense this subsection is misleading since the partnership itself cannot commit an offence—only the partners themselves, either vicariously or as immediate offenders. The partnership itself has no legal personality and liability has to be established under ss 10 or 11 of the Partnership Act 1890 if the partner concerned is not the immediate offender.

21.67 Section 202(4) applies to unincorporated associations other than partnerships. Liability extends to any officer of the association whose duty was to fulfil the criteria, breach of which constitutes an offence, or if there is no such officer, any member other than one 'who is proved to have been ignorant of or to have attempted to prevent the commission of the offence' (see the previous paragraph).

JURISDICTION AND PROCEDURE IN RESPECT OF OFFENCES

21.68 Section 203 is another standard section and covers two aspects of criminal procedure relating to offences under the Act.

The first aspect relates to summary proceedings against individuals, companies and unincorporated associations. Section 203(1) provides that such proceedings may be brought against any company or association at any place at which it has a place of business, and against an individual at any place where he is for the time being. Section 731(1) of the Companies Act 1985 is in similar terms in relation to companies under the Act.

The second aspect relates to the procedural rules for offences committed by unincorporated associations. Section 203(2) and (3) allow proceedings to be brought in the name of the association and the procedural rules to operate as if it were a company. Section 203(6) requires any fine imposed to be paid out of the funds of the association. Section 203(4) and (5) applies similar provisions to Scotland and Northern Ireland respectively.

SERVICE OF NOTICES

21.69   Section 204 is a procedural section which provides for the correct service of any notice, direction or other document under the Act on any person other than the Secretary of State, the Chief Registrar of friendly societies or the Registrar of friendly societies for Northern Ireland.

Service can be effected by delivery, leaving it at the 'proper address' or by post to that address (s 204(2)). The 'proper address' for this purpose is a person's last known address (either private or business). In the case of a member of an SRO or a firm certified by a recognised professional body who has no such address in the United Kingdom, the address of that organisation or body will suffice. In the case of a body corporate, its secretary or clerk, the address of its registered office or principal office in the United Kingdom will suffice, and in the case of an unincorporated association (except a partnership) or a member of its governing body, its principal office in the United Kingdom will be sufficient (s 204(4)). Alternatively a person can notify the Secretary of State of an address, or a new address, for notices etc to be served to him. In such a case that address is to be his proper address rather than those specified in sub-s (4) (s 204(5)).

Service by post is governed by s 7 of the Interpretation Act 1978 as to the method and timing of such service (ie posting is sufficient unless the contrary is found).

Section 204(3) applies to service on companies, etc. Service on a body corporate can be effected (in the proper manner and to the correct address) by service on the secretary or clerk concerned; service on a partnership by service on any partners; service on any other unincorporated associations on any member of its governing body; and service on an appointed representative (see s 44, paras **3.128** ff, ante) by service on his principal.

REGULATIONS, RULES AND ORDERS

21.70   Section 205 gives the Secretary of State the requisite general authority to make regulations, etc under the Act. Such regulations, rules and orders may, with certain exceptions, be made by statutory instrument and may make different provisions for different cases. In the case of rules and regulations the statutory instrument is, unless otherwise provided, to be subject to the negative resolution procedure in Parliament (ss 205(2)–(4)).

The exceptions to the statutory instrument procedure are recognition orders (ie of an SRO, professional body, investment exchange or clearing house—s 207(1)), orders declaring a collective investment scheme to be an authorised unit trust scheme or a recognised scheme (under Ch VIII of Pt I of the Act), and orders revoking any such order (s 205(5)).

PUBLICATION OF INFORMATION AND ADVICE

21.71 Section 206(1) confers on the Secretary of State the function of publishing information or giving advice about (a) the operation of the Act and the rules and regulations made under it; (b) matters relating to the function of the Secretary of State under the Act or any such rules and regulations; and (c) any other matter which is desirable for the protection of investors or any class of investors.

This power extends not only to the publishing of information generally but also of giving advice or information privately. The wording of para (a) is very wide and although it is specifically directed to the rights of investors, the duties of authorised persons and enforcement of those rights or duties, it clearly allows for information or advice to be given on virtually anything involved in the Act. Note that neither paras (a) or (b) are limited to information or advice for the protection of investors so that a firm could be advised how to comply with a particular obligation without necessarily having actively to show that it was so intended. This only applies to duties imposed by the Act — it does not apply to obligations undertaken in the rules of an SRO or RPB.

It is clearly intended that these functions of advice and information are to be transferred to a designated agency since s 206(4) provides for this. However, the wording of s 206(1) is not limited to those functions actually carried out by an agency. It could for example apply to insider dealing, offers of shares (listed or unlisted) etc which remain the province of the DTI or Stock Exchange.

Section 206(2) allows any information which is available to the public to be offered for sale at a reasonable price, but s 206(3) restricts the ambit of subs (1) by excluding information restricted under s 179 of the Act (see para **19.02** ff above).

INTERPRETATION

21.72 Section 207 is the general interpretation section for the whole Act. Section 207(1) defines 29 different phrases as used in the Act, some of which apply definitions given in specific sections of the Act to the Act as a whole. The following are those definitions which are not found in any of the other sections:

(i) authorised unit trust—any unit trust scheme declared to be so by an order of the Secretary of State;

(ii) body corporate—includes any such body constituted under a foreign law;

(iii) director—includes anyone occupying such a position whether he is called that, or someone in accordance with whose directives or instructions the directors are accustomed to act (other than professional advice) cf s 741(2) of the Companies Act 1985;

(iv) group—this is any company, its holding company or subsidiary and other subsidiaries or that holding company. Subsidiary and holding companies are defined by reference to s 736 of the Companies Act 1985;

(v) occupational pension scheme—any scheme (however constituted) which is capable of having effect in relation to a category of employment so as to provide benefits payable on the termination of service, or on death or retirement related to qualifying services in that employment;

(vi) partnership—includes overseas partnerships;

(vii) prescribed—means prescribed by regulations made by the Secretary of State;

(viii) private company—a company under s 1(3) of the Companies Act 1985 or the corresponding Northern Ireland provision;

(ix) recognised clearing house—a body declared to be such by the Secretary of State (or agency);

(x) recognised investment exchange—a body declared to be such by the Secretary of State (or agency);

(xi) recognised professional body—a body declared to be such by the Secretary of State (or agency);

(xii) recognised self regulating organisation—a body declared to be such by the Secretary of State (or agency);

(xiii) recognition order—an order declaring a body to be recognised under the Act for a particular purpose;

(xiv) registered friendly society—a body within s 7(1)(a) of the Friendly Societies Act 1974 and registered under that Act (or its Northern Irish equivalent);

(xv) Tribunal - the Financial Services Tribunal.

21.73 Section 207(2) defines an advertisement for the purpose of the Act, ie for the various sections controlling investment advertising. It is defined very widely to include 'every form of advertising' including various forms of display, circulars and catalogues, films, broadcasting, recordings or 'in any other manner'.

Section 207(3) is concerned with the circumstances in which an advertisement or other information issued outside the United Kingdom is nevertheless to be treated as having been issued in the United Kingdom, and so subject to various restrictions in the Act. There are two alternative criteria: (i) if it is directed to persons in the United Kingdom; or (ii) if it is made available to them. However, (ii) does not apply if the advertisement etc appears in a newspaper or periodical publication published and circulating principally outside the United Kingdom or in a broadcast (radio or television) transmitted principally for reception outside the United Kingdom. It may yet prove important for the courts to decide how this definition is to work in practice.

Section 207(4) is an unusual subsection to appear in an interpretation section since it provides that the Independent Broadcasting Authority will not be liable under any provision of the Act if it transmits an advertisement in accordance with the Broadcasting Act 1981.

Section 207(5) defines the controller of a company or unincorporated association. For the former this is control of at least 15 per cent of the general voting rights of the company or its holding company and for the latter it requires either control of the officers or members of the governing body (ie they are accustomed to act on his directions) or the 15 per cent test applied to voting power at any general meeting of the association. For both purposes associated persons are to be included. For an individual these are his spouse, minor child or step-child, employee, partner and any company of which he is a director (not which he controls). For a company the categories are the latter three plus its subsidiaries and employees of those subsidiaries.

Section 207(6) defines a manager for the purposes of a unit trust or registered friendly society. This is an employee who is directly responsible to his employer for the conduct of business or a person directly responsible (or responsible for a manager who is so responsible) who exercises managerial functions or maintains accounts or other records. Where the employer is a company, the directors are deemed to be the employer for this purpose. Similarly the partners stand as such for a partnership and the officers or members of a governing body for any other unincorporated association.

Section 207(7) defines an insurance business, insurance company and contract of insurance by reference to the Insurance Companies Act 1982.

Similarly s 207(8) defines a holding and subsidiary company by reference to s 736 of the Companies Act 1985.

Section 207(9) provides that for Scotland the words 'actionable at the suit of any person' be read as being 'actionable at the instance' of that person.

Section 207(10) discounts any day which is a public holiday in any part of the United Kingdom in calculating the various periods under the Act. (It will be necessary to note holidays in Scotland and Northern Ireland for this purpose—they apply equally to English cases.)

Finally s 207(11) exempts from Pt 1 of the Act any investment business being carried on by an agent or other person acting on behalf of the Crown.

GIBRALTAR

21.74 Section 208 makes provision for investment business in Gibraltar. There are, for example, many insurance companies registered in Gibraltar. The effect of s 208(1) is to treat Gibraltar as if it were a member state of the Community in its own right for the purposes of ss 31 (authorisation in other member state), 58 (investment advertisements issued in the course of a business carried on in a member state) and 130 (exemption from insurance restrictions for member state's companies). Section 208(2) treats citizens of British Dependent Territories or companies incorporated in Gibraltar as nationals of a member state for this purpose.

The necessity to regard Gibraltar as a member state arises because Gibraltar's position under the Treaty of Accession effectively regards Gibraltar as part of the Community in relation to financial services whilst at the same time Gibraltar enacts its own legislation.

However, since Gibraltar has not yet adopted the EEC directives on insurance there is no intention to implement this section until it has done so (HL Vol 479 Official Report (6th series) Col 813). Further, the benefits of s 86 will only be in operation when the UCITS Directive has been implemented in Gibraltar. Section 208(3) makes it clear that it is this directive which is referred to. Section 208(4) gives the Secretary of State power to make regulations covering the notice required of a collective investment scheme under s 86(2) and schemes operating in Gibraltar but operated under the rules of another member state.

NORTHERN IRELAND

21.75 Section 209 extends the Act to Northern Ireland. The regulation of investment businesses, the official listing of securities and offers of unlisted securities are not to be transferred matters under the Northern Ireland Constitution Act 1973, ie they are to be administered from Whitehall, although they may subsequently be transferred by an order under s (1)(a) of the 1973 Act. Section 3(2) of the 1973 Act (references to the role of Northern Ireland Assembly in transferred matters) is effectively excluded from these matters.

EXPENSES AND RECEIPTS

21.76 Section 210 is the standard financial section, allowing any expenses incurred by the Secretary of State to be paid out of public funds and any fees or other sums he receives to be paid into the Consolidated Fund.

There are two additional points, however. Firstly, for the financial position of a designated agency, the reader should refer to Sch 9, paras 10, 11. Secondly, in respect of the financial consequences of his work under this Act, any fees received by the Chief Registrar of friendly societies (including Northern Ireland) are to be paid into the Consolidated Fund and any expenses incurred paid out of public funds.

COMMENCEMENT AND TRANSITIONAL PROVISIONS

21.77 Section 211(1) applies the now familiar commencement provisions allowing the Act to come into force as and when the Secretary of State appoints, with different parts coming into effect at different times. The one exception to this is s 195 (offers of short-term debentures—see para **21.35**, ante) which came into effect on Royal Assent.

Section 211(3) implements Sch 15 as to the transitional provisions. That Schedule provides for : interim authorisation to deal in investment business either by application to the Secretary of State or SRO prior to a specified date; the treatment of fees and deposits paid under ss 3 and 4 of the Prevention of Fraud (Investments) Act 1958; the interim recognition of professional bodies until they comply fully with the new requirements and interim authorisation by such bodies; overseas authorised persons, authorised unit trusts under s 17 of the 1958 Act; recognised collective investment schemes prior to s 86 of the Act coming into force and Northern Ireland.

SHORT TITLE, CONSEQUENTIAL AMENDMENTS AND APPEALS

21.78 Section 212 names the Act and implements the consequential amendments set out in Sch 16 to the Act and the repeals contained in Sch 17.

Appendix

Financial Services Act 1986

(1986 c 60)

Arrangement of Sections

Appendix

CHAPTER IV

EXEMPTED PERSONS

The Bank of England

CHAPTER X

INFORMATION

CHAPTER XI

AUDITORS

CHAPTER XII

FEES

CHAPTER XIII

TRANSFER OF FUNCTIONS TO DESIGNATED AGENCY

CHAPTER XIV

PREVENTION OF RESTRICTIVE PRACTICES

Examination of rules and practices

Consultation with Director General of Fair Trading

Consequential exemptions from competition law

Schedule 12—Takeover offers: provisions substituted for sections 428, 429
           and 430 of Companies Act 1985.
Schedule 13—Disclosure of information.
Schedule 14—Restriction of Rehabilitation of Offenders Act 1974.
Schedule 15—Transitional provisions.
Schedule 16—Consequential amendments.
Schedule 17—Repeals and revocations.

An Act to regulate the carrying on of investment business; to make related provision with respect to insurance business and business carried on by friendly societies; to make new provision with respect to the official listing of securities, offers of unlisted securities, takeover offers and insider dealing; to make provision as to the disclosure of information obtained under enactments relating to fair trading, banking, companies and insurance; to make provision for securing reciprocity with other countries in respect of facilities for the provision of financial services; and for connected purposes. [7 November 1986]

PART I

REGULATION OF INVESTMENT BUSINESS

CHAPTER I

PRELIMINARY

1. Investments and investment business

(1) In this Act, unless the context otherwise requires, 'investment' means any asset, right or interest falling within any paragraph in Part I of Schedule 1 to this Act.

(2) In this Act 'investment business' means the business of engaging in one or more of the activities which fall within the paragraphs in Part II of that Schedule and are not excluded by Part III of that Schedule.

(3) For the purposes of this Act a person carries on investment business in the United Kingdom if he—

(a) carries on investment business from a permanent place of business maintained by him in the United Kingdom; or

(b) engages in the United Kingdom in one or more of the activities which fall within the paragraphs in Part II of that Schedule and are not excluded by Part III or IV of that Schedule and his doing so constitutes the carrying on by him of a business in the United Kingdom.

(4) Parts I to IV of that Schedule shall be construed in accordance with Part V.

2. Power to extend or restrict scope of Act

(1) The Secretary of State may by order amend Schedule 1 to this Act so as—

(a) to extend or restrict the meaning of investment for the purposes of all or any provisions of this Act; or

(b) to extend or restrict for the purposes of all or any of those provisions the activities that are to constitute the carrying on of investment business or the carrying on of such business in the United Kingdom.

237

(2)   The amendments that may be made for the purposes of subsection (1)(b) above include amendments conferring powers on the Secretary of State, whether by extending or modifying any provision of that Schedule which confers such powers or by adding further such provisions.

(3)   An order under this section which extends the meaning of investment or extends the activities that are to constitute the carrying on of investment business or the carrying on of such business in the United Kingdom shall be laid before Parliament after being made and shall cease to have effect at the end of the period of twenty-eight days beginning with the day on which it is made (but without prejudice to anything done under the order or to the making of a new order) unless before the end of that period the order is approved by a resolution of each House of Parliament.

(4)   In reckoning the period mentioned in subsection (3) above no account shall be taken of any time during which Parliament is dissolved or prorogued or during which both Houses are adjourned for more than four days.

(5)   Any order under this section to which subsection (3) above does not apply shall be subject to annulment in pursuance of a resolution of either House of Parliament.

(6)   An order under this section may contain such transitional provisions as the Secretary of State thinks necessary or expedient.

CHAPTER II

RESTRICTION ON CARRYING ON BUSINESS

3.   Persons entitled to carry on investment business
No person shall carry on, or purport to carry on, investment business in the United Kingdom unless he is an authorised person under Chapter III or an exempted person under Chapter IV of this Part of this Act.

4.   Offences
(1)   Any person who carries on, or purports to carry on, investment business in contravention of section 3 above shall be guilty of an offence and liable—

   (a)   on conviction on indictment, to imprisonment for a term not exceeding two years or to a fine or to both;
   (b)   on summary conviction, to imprisonment for a term not exceeding six months or to a fine not exceeding the statutory maximum or to both.

(2)   In proceedings brought against any person for an offence under this section it shall be a defence for him to prove that he took all reasonable precautions and exercised all due diligence to avoid the commission of the offence.

5.   Agreements made by or through unauthorised persons
(1)   Subject to subsection (3) below, any agreement to which this subsection applies—

   (a)   which is entered into by a person in the course of carrying on investment business in contravention of section 3 above; or
   (b)   which is entered into—

(i) by a person who is an authorised person or an exempted person in respect of the investment business in the course of which he enters into the agreement; but

(ii) in consequence of anything said or done by a person in the course of carrying on investment business in contravention of that section,

shall be unenforceable against the other party; and that party shall be entitled to recover any money or other property paid or transferred by him under the agreement, together with compensation for any loss sustained by him as a result of having parted with it.

(2)   The compensation recoverable under subsection (1) above shall be such as the parties may agree or as the court may, on the application of either party, determine.

(3)   A court may allow an agreement to which subsection (1) above applies to be enforced or money and property paid or transferred under it to be retained if it is satisfied—

(a) in a case within paragraph (a) of that subsection, that the person mentioned in that paragraph reasonably believed that his entering into the agreement did not constitute a contravention of section 3 above;

(b) in a case within paragraph (b) of that subsection that the person mentioned in sub-paragraph (i) of that paragraph did not know that the agreement was entered into as mentioned in sub-paragraph (ii) of that paragraph; and

(c) in either case, that it is just and equitable for the agreement to be enforced or, as the case may be, for the money or property paid or transferred under it to be retained.

(4)   Where a person elects not to perform an agreement which by virtue of this section is unenforceable against him or by virtue of this section recovers money paid or other property transferred by him under an agreement he shall repay any money and return any other property received by him under the agreement.

(5)   Where any property transferred under an agreement to which this section applies has passed to a third party the references to that property in subsections (1), (3) and (4) above shall be construed as references to its value at the time of its transfer under the agreement.

(6)   A contravention of section 3 above shall not make an agreement illegal or invalid to any greater extent than is provided in this section.

(7)   Subsection (1) above applies to any agreement the making or performance of which by the person seeking to enforce it or from whom money or other property is recoverable under this section constitutes an activity which falls within any paragraph of Part II of Schedule 1 to this Act is not excluded by Part III or IV of that Schedule.

6.   Injunctions and restitution orders

(1)   If on the application of the Secretary of State, the court is satisfied—

(a) that there is a reasonable likelihood that a person will contravene section 3 above; or

(b) that any person has contravened that section and that there is a reasonable likelihood that the contravention will continue or be repeated,

239

the court may grant an injunction restraining the contravention or, in Scotland, an interdict prohibiting the contravention.

(2)   If, on the application of the Secretary of State, the court is satisfied that a person has entered into any transaction in contravention of section 3 above the court may order that person and any other person who appears to the court to have been knowingly concerned in the contravention to take such steps as the court may direct for restoring the parties to the position in which they were before the transaction was entered into.

(3)   The court may, on the application of the Secretary of State, make an order under subsection (4) below or, in relation to Scotland, under subsection (5) below if satisfied that a person has been carrying on investment business in contravention of section 3 above and—

   (a)   that profits have accrued to that person as a result of carrying on that business; or
   (b)   that one or more investors have suffered loss or been otherwise adversely affected as a result of his contravention of section 47 or 56 below or failure to act substantially in accordance with any of the rules or regulations made under Chapter V of this Part of this Act.

(4)   The court may under this subsection order the person concerned to pay into court, or appoint a receiver to recover from him, such sum as appears to the court to be just having regard—

   (a)   in a case within paragraph (a) of subsection (3) above, to the profits appearing to the court to have accrued;
   (b)   in a case within paragraph (b) of that subsection, to the extent of the loss or other adverse effect; or
   (c)   in a case within both paragraphs (a) and (b) of that subsection, to the profits and to the extent of the loss or other adverse effect.

(5)   The court may under this subsection order the person concerned to pay to the applicant such sum as appears to the court to be just having regard to the considerations mentioned in paragraphs (a) to (c) of subsection (4) above.

(6)   Any amount paid into court by or recovered from a person in pursuance of an order under subsection (4) or (5) above shall be paid out to such person or distributed among such persons as the court may direct, being a person or persons appearing to the court to have entered into transactions with that person as a result of which the profits mentioned in paragraph (a) of subsection (3) above have accrued to him or the loss or other adverse effect mentioned in paragraph (b) of that subsection has been suffered.

(7)   On an application under subsection (3) above the court may require the person concerned to furnish it with such accounts or other information as it may require for establishing whether any and, if so, what profits have accrued to him as mentioned in paragraph (a) of that subsection and for determining how any amounts are to be paid or distributed under subsection (6) above; and the court may require any such accounts or other information to be verified in such manner as it may direct.

(8)   The jurisdiction conferred by this section shall be exercisable by the High Court and the Court of Session.

(9)   Nothing in this section affects the right of any person other than the Secretary of State to bring proceedings in respect of any of the matters to which this section applies.

CHAPTER III

AUTHORISED PERSONS

Members of recognised self-regulating organisations

7.   Authorisation by membership of recognised self-regulating organisation

(1)   Subject to subsection (2) below, a member of a recognised self-regulating organisation is an authorised person by virtue of his membership of that organisation.

(2)   This section does not apply to a member who is an authorised person by virtue of section 22 or 23 below or an insurance comany which is an authorised person by virtue of section 31 below.

8.   Self-regulating organisations

(1)   In this Act a 'self-regulating organisation' means a body (whether a body corporate or an unincorporated association) which regulates the carrying on of investment business of any kind by enforcing rules which are binding on persons carrying on business of that kind either because they are members of that body or because they are otherwise subject to its control.

(2)   In this Act references to the members of a self-regulating organisation are references to the persons who, whether or not members of the organisation, are subject to its rules in carrying on the business in question.

(3)   In this Act references to the rules of a self-regulating organisation are references to the rules (whether or not laid down by the organisation itself) which the organisation has power to enforce in relation to the carrying on of the business in question or which relate to the admission and expulsion of members of the organisation or otherwise to its constitution.

(4)   In this Act references to guidance issued by a self-regulating organisation are references to guidance issued or any recommendation made by it to all or any class of its members or persons seeking to become members which would, if it were a rule, fall within subsection (3) above.

9.   Applications for recognition

(1)   A self-regulating organisation may apply to the Secretary of State for an order declaring it to be a recognised self-regulating organisation for the purposes of this Act.

(2)   Any such application—

  (a)   shall be made in such manner as the Secretary of State may direct; and
  (b)   shall be accompanied by such information as the Secretary of State may reasonably require for the purpose of determining the application.

(3)   At any time after receiving an application and before determining it the

Secretary of State may require the applicant to furnish additional information.

(4)   The directions and requirements given or imposed under subsections (2) and (3) above may differ as between different applications.

(5)   Any information to be furnished to the Secretary of State under this section shall, if he so requires, be in such form or verified in such manner as he may specify.

(6)   Every application shall be accompanied by a copy of the applicant's rules and of any guidance issued by the applicant which is intended to have continuing effect and is issued in writing or other legible form.

10.   Grant and refusal of recognition

(1)   The Secretary of State may, on an application duly made in accordance with section 9 above and after being furnished with all such information as he may require under that section, make or refuse to make an order ('a recognition order') declaring the applicant to be a recognised self-regulating organisation.

(2)   Subject to subsection (4) below and to Chapter XIV of this Part of this Act, the Secretary of State shall make a recognition order if it appears to him from the information furnished by the organisation making the application and having regard to any other information in his possession that the requirements of subsection (3) below and of Schedule 2 to this Act are satisfied as respects that organisation.

(3)   Where there is a kind of investment business with which the organisation is not concerned, its rules must preclude a member from carrying on investment business of that kind unless he is an authorised person otherwise than by virtue of his membership of the organisation or an exempted person in respect of that business.

(4)   The Secretary of State may refuse to make a recognition order in respect of an organisation if he considers that its recognition is unnecessary having regard to the existence of one or more other organisations which are concerned with investment business of a kind with which the applicant is concerned and which have been or are likely to be recognised under this section.

(5)   Where the Secretary of State refuses an application for a recognition order he shall give the applicant a written notice to that effect specifying a requirement which in the opinion of the Secretary of State is not satisfied, stating that the application is refused on the ground mentioned in subsection (4) above or stating that it is refused by virtue of Chapter XIV.

(6)   A recognition order shall state the date on which it takes effect.

11.   Revocation of recognition

(1)   A recognition order may be revoked by a further order made by the Secretary of State if at any time it appears to him—

(a)   that section 10(3) above or any requirement of Schedule 2 to this Act is not satisfied in the case of the organisation to which the recognition order relates ('the recognised organisation');

(b)   that the recognised organisation has failed to comply with any obligation to which it is subject by virtue of this Act; or

(c)   that the continued recognition of the organisation is undesirable having regard to the existence of one or more other organisations which have been or are to be recognised under section 10 above.

(2)   An order revoking a recognition order shall state the date on which it takes effect and that date shall not be earlier than three months after the day on which the revocation order is made.

(3)   Before revoking a recognition order the Secretary of State shall give written notice of his intention to do so to the recognised organisation, take such steps as he considers reasonably practicable for bringing the notice to the attention of members of the organisation and publish it in such manner as he thinks appropriate for bringing it to the attention of any other persons who are in his opinion likely to be affected.

(4)   A notice under subsection (3) above shall state the reasons for which the Secretary of State proposes to act and give particulars of the rights conferred by subsection (5) below.

(5)   An organisation on which a notice is served under subsection (3) above, any member of the organisation and any other person who appears to the Secretary of State to be affected may within three months after the date of service or publication, or within such longer time as the Secretary of State may allow, make written representations to the Secretary of State and, if desired, oral representations to a person appointed for that purpose by the Secretary of State; and the Secretary of State shall have regard to any representations made in accordance with this subsection in determining whether to revoke the recognition order.

(6)   If in any case the Secretary of State considers it essential to do so in the interests of investors he may revoke a recognition order without regard to the restriction imposed by subsection (2) above and notwithstanding that no notice has been given or published under subsection (3) above or that the time for making representations in pursuance of such a notice has not expired.

(7)   An order revoking a recognition order may contain such transitional provisions as the Secretary of State thinks necessary or expedient.

(8)   A recognition order may be revoked at the request or with the consent of the recognised organisation and any such revocation shall not be subject to the restrictions imposed by subsections (1) and (2) or the requirements of subsections (3) to (5) above.

(9)   On making an order revoking a recognition order the Secretary of State shall give the organisation written notice of the making of the order, take such steps as he considers reasonably practicable for bringing the making of the order to the attention of members of the organisation and publish a notice of the making of the order in such manner as he thinks appropriate for bringing it to the attention of any other persons who are in his opinion likely to be affected.

12.   Compliance orders

(1)   If at any time it appears to the Secretary of State—

(a)   that subsection (3) of section 10 above or any requirement of Schedule 2 to this Act is not satisfied in the case of a recognised organisation; or

(b)   that a recognised organisation has failed to comply with any obligation to which it is subject by virtue of this Act, he may, instead of revoking the recognition order under section 11 above, make an application to the court under this section.

(2)   If on any such application the court decides that subsection (3) of section 10 or the requirement in question is not satisfied or, as the case may be, that the organisation has failed to comply with the obligation in question it may order the organisation to take such steps as the court directs for securing that that subsection or requirement is satisfied or that that obligation is complied with.

(3)   The jurisdiction conferred by this section shall be exercisable by the High Court and the Court of Session.

13.   Alteration of rules for protection of investors

(1)   If at any time it appears to the Secretary of State that the rules of a recognised organisation do not satisfy the requirements of paragraph 3(1) of Schedule 2 to this Act he may, instead of revoking the recognition order or making an application under section 12 above, direct the organisation to alter, or himself alter, its rules in such manner as he considers necessary for securing that the rules satisfy those requirements.

(2)   If at any time it appears to the Secretary of State that the rules or practices of a recognised organisation which is concerned with two or more kinds of investment business do not satisfy any requirement of Schedule 2 to this Act in respect of investment business of any of those kinds he may, instead of revoking the recognition order or making an application under section 12 above, direct the organisation to alter, or himself alter, its rules so that they preclude a member from carrying on investment business of that kind unless he is an authorised person otherwise than by virtue of membership of the organisation or an exempted person in respect of that business.

(3)   Any direction given under this section shall, on the application of the Secretary of State, be enforceable by mandamus or, in Scotland, by an order for specific performance under section 91 of the Court of Session Act 1868.

(4)   Before giving a direction or making any alteration under subsection (1) above the Secretary of State shall consult the organisation concerned.

(5)   A recognised organisation whose rules have been altered by or pursuant to a direction given by the Secretary of State under subsection (1) above may apply to the court and if the court is satisfied—

(a)   that the rules without the alteration satisfied the requirements mentioned in that subsection; or

(b)   that other alterations proposed by the organisation would result in the rules satisfying those requirements,

the court may set aside the alteration made by or pursuant to the direction given by the Secretary of State and, in a case within paragraph (b) above, order the organisation to make the alterations proposed by it; but the setting aside of an alteration under this subsection shall not affect its previous operation.

(6)   The jurisdiction conferred by subsection (5) above shall be exercisable by the High Court and the Court of Session.

(7)   Section 11(2) to (7) and (9) above shall, with the necessary modifications, have effect in relation to any direction given or alteration made by the Secretary

of State under subsection (2) above as they have effect in relation to an order revoking a recognition order.

(8) The fact that the rules of a recognised organisation have been altered by or pursuant to a direction given by the Secretary of State or pursuant to an order made by the court under this section shall not preclude their subsequent alteration or revocation by that organisation.

14. Notification requirements

(1) The Secretary of State may make regulations requiring a recognised organisation to give him forthwith notice of the occurrence of such events relating to the organisation or its members as are specified in the regulations and such information in respect of those events as is so specified.

(2) The Secretary of State may make regulations requiring a recognised organisation to furnish him at such times or in respect of such periods as are specified in the regulations with such information relating to the organisation or its members as is so specified.

(3) The notices and information required to be given or furnished under the foregoing provisions of this section shall be such as the Secretary of State may reasonably require for the exercise of his functions under this Act.

(4) Regulations under the foregoing provisions of this section may require information to be given in a specified form and to be verified in a specified manner.

(5) Any notice or information required to be given or furnished under the foregoing provisions of this section shall be given in writing or in such other manner as the Secretary of State may approve.

(6) Where a recognised organisation amends, revokes or adds to its rules or guidance it shall within seven days give the Secretary of State written notice of the amendment, revocation or addition; but notice need not be given of the revocation of guidance other than such as is mentioned in section 9(6) above or of any amendment of or addition to guidance which does not result in or consist of such guidance as is there mentioned.

(7) Contravention of, or of regulations under, this section shall not be an offence.

Persons authorised by recognised professional bodies

15. Authorisation by certification by recognised professional body

(1) A person holding a certificate issued for the purposes of this Part of this Act by a recognised professional body is an authorised person.

(2) Such a certificate may be issued by a recognised professional body to an individual, a body corporate, a partnership or an unincorporated association.

(3) A certificate issued to a partnership—

(a) shall be issued in the partnership name; and
(b) shall authorise the carrying on of investment business in that name by the partnership to which the certificate is issued, by any partnership which succeeds to that business or by any person who succeeds to that business having previously carried it on in partnership;

and, in relation to a certificate issued to a partnership constituted under the law of

England and Wales or Northern Ireland or the law of any other country or territory under which a partnership is not a legal person, references in this Act to the person who holds the certificate or is certified shall be construed as references to the persons or person for the time being authorised by the certificate to carry on investment business as mentioned in paragraph (b) above.

16. Professional bodies

(1)   In this Act a 'professional body' means a body which regulates the practice of a profession and references to the practice of a profession do not include references to carrying on a business consisting wholly or mainly of investment business.

(2)   In this Act references to the members of a professional body are references to the persons who, whether or not members of the body, are entitled to practise the profession in question and, in practising it, are subject to the rules of that body.

(3)   In this Act references to the rules of a professional body are references to the rules (whether or not laid down by the body itself) which the body has power to enforce in relation to the practice of the profession in question and the carrying on of investment business by persons practising that profession or which relate to the grant, suspension or withdrawal of certificates under section 15 above, the admission and expulsion of members or otherwise to the constitution of the body.

(4)   In this Act references to guidance issued by a professional body are references to guidance issued or any recommendation made by it to all or any class of its members or persons seeking to become members, or to persons or any class of persons who are or are seeking to be certified by the body, and which would, if it were a rule, fall within subsection (3) above.

17. Applications for recognition

(1)   A professional body may apply to the Secretary of State for an order declaring it to be a recognised professional body for the purposes of this Act.

(2)   Subsections (2) to (6) of section 9 above shall have effect in relation to an application under subsection (1) above as they have effect in relation to an application under subsection (1) of that section.

18. Grant and refusal of recognition

(1)   The Secretary of State may, on an application duly made in accordance with section 17 above and after being furnished with all such information as he may require under that section, make or refuse to make an order ('a recognition order') declaring the applicant to be a recognised professional body.

(2)   The Secretary of State may make a recognition order if it appears to him from the information furnished by the body making the application and having regard to any other information in his possession that the requirements of subsection (3) below and of Schedule 3 to this Act are satisfied as respects that body.

(3)   The body must have rules which impose acceptable limits on the kinds of investment business which may be carried on by persons certified by it and the circumstances in which they may carry on such business and which preclude a person certified by that body from carrying on any investment business outside those limits unless he is an authorised person otherwise than by virtue of the certification or an exempted person in respect of that business.

(4) Where the Secretary of State refuses an application for a recognition order he shall give the applicant a written notice to that effect, stating the reasons for the refusal.

(5) A recognition order shall state the date on which it takes effect.

19. Revocation of recognition
(1) A recognition order under section 18 above may be revoked by a further order made by the Secretary of State if at any time it appears to him—

(a) that section 18(3) above or any requirement of Schedule 3 to this Act is not satisfied in the case of the body to which the recognition order relates; or
(b) that the body has failed to comply with any obligation to which it is subject by virtue of this Act.

(2) Subsections (2) to (9) of section 11 above shall have effect in relation to the revocation of a recognition order under this section as they have effect in relation to the revocation of a recognition order under subsection (1) of that section.

20. Compliance orders
(1) If at any time it appears to the Secretary of State—

(a) that subsection (3) of section 18 above or any requirement of Schedule 3 to this Act is not satisfied in the case of a recognised professional body; or
(b) that such a body has failed to comply with any obligation to which it is subject by virtue of this Act,

he may, instead of revoking the recognition order under section 19 above, make an application to the court under this section.

(2) If on any such application the court decides that subsection (3) of section 18 above or the requirement in question is not satisfied or, as the case may be, that the body has failed to comply with the obligation in question it may order the body to take such steps as the court directs for securing that that subsection or requirement is satisfied or that that obligation is complied with.

(3) The jurisdiction conferred by this section shall be exercisable by the High Court and the Court of Session.

21. Notification requirements
(1) The Secretary of State may make regulations requiring a recognised professional body to give him forthwith notice of the occurrence of such events relating to the body, its members or persons certified by it as are specified in the regulations and such information in respect of those events as is so specified.

(2) The Secretary of State may make regulations requiring a recognised professional body to furnish him at such times or in respect of such periods as are specified in the regulations with such information relating to the body, its members and persons certified by it as is so specified.

(3) The notices and information required to be given or furnished under the foregoing provisions of this section shall be such as the Secretary of State may reasonably require for the exercise of his functions under this Act.

(4) Regulations under the foregoing provisions of this section may require information to be given in a specified form and to be verified in a specified manner.

(5)   Any notice or information required to be given or furnished under the foregoing provisions of this section shall be given in writing or in such other manner as the Secretary of State may approve.

(6)   Where a recognised professional body amends, revokes or adds to its rules or guidance it shall within seven days give the Secretary of State written notice of the amendment, revocation or addition; but—

- (a)   notice need not be given of the revocation of guidance other than such as is mentioned in section 9(6) above or of any amendment of or addition to guidance which does not result in or consist of such guidance as is there mentioned; and
- (b)   notice need not be given in respect of any rule or guidance, or rules or guidance of any description, in the case of which the Secretary of State has waived compliance with this subsection by notice in writing to the body concerned;

and any such waiver may be varied or revoked by a further notice in writing.

(7)   Contravention of, or of regulations under, this section shall not be an offence.

Insurance companies

22   Authorised insurers

A body which is authorised under section 3 or 4 of the Insurance Companies Act 1982 to carry on insurance business which is investment business and carries on such insurance business in the United Kingdom is an authorised person as respects—

- (a)   any insurance business which is investment business; and
- (b)   any other investment business which that body may carry on without contravening section 16 of that Act.

Friendly societies

23.   Registered friendly societies

(1)   A society which—

- (a)   is a friendly society within the meaning of section 7(1)(a) of the Friendly Societies Act 1974;
- (b)   is registered within the meaning of that Act as a society but not as a branch of a society;
- (c)   under its rules has its registered office at a place situated in Great Britain; and
- (d)   carries on investment business in the United Kingdom,

is an authorised person as respects any investment business which it carries on for or in connection with any of the purposes mentioned in Schedule 1 to that Act.

(2)   A society which—

- (a)   is a friendly society within the meaning of section 1(1)(a) of the Friendly Societies Act (Northern Ireland) 1970;
- (b)   is registered or deemed to be registered as a society but not as a branch of a society under that Act;
- (c)   under its rules has its registered office at a place situated in Northern Ireland; and

(d)   carries on investment business in the United Kingdom,

is an authorised person as respects any investment business which it carries on for or in connection with any of the purposes mentioned in Schedule 1 to that Act.

Collective investment schemes

24.   Operators and trustees of recognised schemes

The operator or trustee of a scheme recognised under section 86 below is an authorised person as respects—

(a)   investment business which consists in operating or acting as trustee in relation to that scheme; and

(b)   any investment business which is carried on by him in connection with or for the purposes of that scheme.

Persons authorised by the Secretary of State

25.   Authorisation by Secretary of State

A person holding an authorisation granted by the Secretary of State under the following provisions of this Chapter is an authorised person.

26.   Applications for authorisation

(1)   An application for authorisation by the Secretary of State may be made by—

(a)   an individual;
(b)   a body corporate;
(c)   a partnership; or
(d)   an unincorporated association.

(2)   Any such application—

(a)   shall be made in such manner as the Secretary of State may direct;
(b)   shall contain or be accompanied by—

(i)   information as to the investment business which the applicant proposes to carry on and the services which he will hold himself out as able to provide in the carrying on of that business; and

(ii)   such other information as the Secretary of State may reasonably require for the purpose of determining the application; and

(c)   shall contain the address of a place in the United Kingdom for the service on the applicant of any notice or other document required or authorised to be served on him under this Act.

(3)   At any time after receiving an application and before determining it the Secretary of State may require the applicant to furnish additional information.

(4)   The directions and requirements given or imposed under subsections (2) and (3) above may differ as between different applications.

(5)   Any information to be furnished to the Secretary of State under this section shall, if he so requires, be in such form or verified in such manner as he may specify.

27.   Grant and refusal of authorisation

(1)   The Secretary of State may, on an application duly made in accordance with

section 26 above and after being furnished with all such information as he may require under that section, grant or refuse the application.

(2)   The Secretary of State shall grant the application if it appears to him from the information furnished by the applicant and having regard to any other information in his possession that the applicant is a fit and proper person to carry on the investment business and provide the services described in the application.

(3)   In determining whether to grant or refuse an application the Secretary of State may take into account any matter relating to any person who is or will be employed by or associated with the applicant for the purposes of the business in question, to any person who is or will be acting as an appointed representative in relation to that business and—

  (a)   if the applicant is a body corporate, to any director or controller of the body, to any other body corporate in the same group or to any director or controller of any such other body corporate;
  (b)   if the applicant is a partnership, to any of the partners;
  (c)   if the applicant is an unincorporated association, to any member of the governing body of the association or any officer or controller of the association.

(4)   In determining whether to grant or refuse an application the Secretary of State may also have regard to any business which the applicant proposes to carry on in connection with his investment business.

(5)   In the case of an applicant who is authorised to carry on investment business in a member State other than the United Kingdom the Secretary of State shall have regard to that authorisation.

(6)   An authorisation granted to a partnership—

  (a)   shall be granted in the partnership name; and
  (b)   shall authorise the carrying on of investment business in that name (or with the Secretary of State's consent in any other name) by the partnership to which the authorisation is granted, by any partnership which succeeds to that business or by any person who succeeds to that business having previously carried it on in partnership;

and, in relation to an authorisation granted to a partnership constituted under the law of England and Wales or Northern Ireland or the law of any other country or territory under which a partnership is not a legal person, references in this Act to the holder of the authorisation or the authorised person shall be construed as references to the persons or person for the time being authorised by the authorisation to carry on investment business as mentioned in paragraph (b) above.

(7)   An authorisation granted to an unincorporated association shall apply to the carrying on of investment business in the name of the association and in such manner as may be specified in the authorisation.

(8)   The Secretary of State shall give an applicant for authorisation written notice of the grant of authorisation specifying the date on which it takes effect.

28.   Withdrawal and suspension of authorisation
(1)   The Secretary of State may at any time withdraw or suspend any authorisation granted by him if it appears to him—

(a) that the holder of the authorisation is not a fit and proper person to carry on the investment business which he is carrying on or proposing to carry on; or

(b) without prejudice to paragraph (a) above, that the holder of the authorisation has contravened any provision of this Act or any rules or regulations made under it or, in purported compliance with any such provision, has furnished the Secretary of State with false, inaccurate or misleading information or has contravened any prohibition or requirement imposed under this Act.

(2) For the purposes of subsection (1)(a) above the Secretary of State may take into account any such matters as are mentioned in section 27 (3) and (4) above.

(3) Where the holder of the authorisation is a member of a recognised self-regulating organisation the rules, prohibitions and requirements referred to in paragraph (b) of subsection (1) above include the rules of that organisation and any prohibition or requirement imposed by virtue of those rules; and where he is a person certified by a recognised professional body the rules, prohibitions and requirements referred to in that paragraph include the rules of that body which regulate the carrying on by him of investment business and any prohibition or requirement imposed by virtue of those rules.

(4) The suspension of an authorisation shall be for a specified period or until the occurrence of a specified event or until specified conditions are complied with; and while an authorisation is suspended the holder shall not be an authorised person.

(5) Any period, event or conditions specified under subsection (3) above in the case of an authorisation may be varied by the Secretary of State on the application of the holder.

29. Notice of proposed refusal, withdrawal or suspension
(1) Where the Secretary of State proposes—

(a) to refuse an application under section 26 or 28(5) above; or
(b) to withdraw or suspend an authorisation,

he shall give the applicant or the authorised person written notice of his intention to do so, stating the reasons for which he proposes to act.

(2) In the case of a proposed withdrawal or suspension the notice shall state the date on which it is proposed that the withdrawal or suspension should take effect and, in the case of a proposed suspension, its proposed duration.

(3) Where the reasons stated in a notice under this section relate specifically to matters which—

(a) refer to a person identified in the notice other than the applicant or the holder of the authorisation; and
(b) are in the opinion of the Secretary of State prejudicial to that person in any office or employment,

the Secretary of State shall, unless he considers it impracticable to do so, serve a copy of the notice on that person.

(4) A notice under this section shall give particulars of the right to require the case to be referred to the Tribunal under Chapter IX of this Part of this Act.

(5)   Where a case is not required to be referred to the Tribunal by a person on whom a notice is served under this section the Secretary of State shall, at the expiration of the period within which such a requirement can be made—

(a)   give that person written notice of the refusal, withdrawal or suspension; or
(b)   give that person written notice of the grant of the application or, as the case may be, written notice that the authorisation is not to be withdrawn or suspended;

and the Secretary of State may give public notice of any decision notified by him under paragraph (a) or (b) above and the reasons for the decision except that he shall not do so in the case of a decision notified under paragraph (b) unless the person concerned consents to his doing so.

30.   Withdrawal of applications and authorisations by consent

(1)   An application under section 26 above may be withdrawn before it is granted or refused; and, subject to subsections (2) and (3) below, an authorisation granted under section 27 above may be withdrawn by the Secretary of State at the request or with the consent of the authorised person.

(2)   The Secretary of State may refuse to withdraw any such authorisation if he considers that the public interest requires any matter affecting the authorised person to be investigated as a preliminary to a decision on the question whether the Secretary of State should in respect of that person exercise his powers under section 28 above or under any other provision of this Part of this Act.

(3)   The Secretary of State may also refuse to withdraw an authorisation where in his opinion it is desirable that a prohibition or restriction should be imposed on the authorised person under Chapter VI of this Part of this Act or that a prohibition or restriction imposed on that person under that Chapter should continue in force.

(4)   The Secretary of State may give public notice of any withdrawal of authorisation under subsection (1) above.

Persons authorised in other member States

31.   Authorisation in other member State

(1)   A person carrying on investment business in the United Kingdom is an authorised person if—

(a)   he is established in a member State other than the United Kingdom;
(b)   the law of that State recognises him as a national of that or another member State; and
(c)   he is for the time being authorised under that law to carry on investment business or investment business of any particular kind.

(2)   For the purposes of this Act a person is established in a member State other than the United Kingdom if his head office is situated in that State and he does not transact investment business from a permanent place of business maintained by him in the United Kingdom.

(3)   This section applies to a person only if the provisions of the law under which he is authorised to carry on the investment business in question—

(a)   afford to investors in the United Kingdom protection, in relation to his carrying on of that business, which is at least equivalent to that provided for them by the provisions of this Chapter relating to members of recognised self-regulating organisations or to persons authorised by the Secretary of State; or

(b) satisfy the conditions laid down by a Community instrument for the co-ordination or approximation of the laws, regulations or administrative provisions of member States relating to the carrying on of investment business or investment business of the relevant kind.

(4) A certificate issued by the Secretary of State and for the time being in force to the effect that the provisions of the law of a member State comply with the requirements of subsection (3)(a) above, either as respects all investment business or as respects investment business of a particular kind, shall be conclusive evidence of that matter but the absence or revocation of such a certificate shall not be regarded as indicating that those requirements are not complied with.

(5) This section shall not apply to a person by virtue of paragraph (b) of subsection (3) above unless the authority by which he is authorised to carry on the investment business in question certifies that he is authorised to do so under a law which complies with the requirements of that paragraph.

32. Notice of commencement of business

(1) A person who is an authorised person by virtue of section 31 above shall be guilty of an offence unless, not less than seven days before beginning to carry on investment business in the United Kingdom, he has given notice of his intention to do so to the Secretary of State either in writing or in such other manner as the Secretary of State may approve.

(2) The notice shall contain—

(a) information as to the investment business which that person proposes to carry on in the United Kingdom and the services which he will hold himself out as able to provide in the carrying on of that business;

(b) information as to the authorisation of that person in the member State in question;

(c) the address of a place (whether in the United Kingdom or elsewhere) for the service on that person of any notice or other document required or authorised to be served on him under this Act;

(d) such other information as may be prescribed;

and the notice shall comply with such requirements as to the form in which any information is to be given and as to its verification as may be prescribed.

(3) A notice by a person claiming to be authorised by virtue of subsection (3)(b) of section 31 above shall be accompanied by a copy of the certificate required by subsection (5) of that section.

(4) A person guilty of an offence under subsection (1) above shall be liable—

(a) on conviction on indictment, to a fine;

(b) on summary conviction, to a fine not exceeding the statutory maximum.

(5) In proceedings brought against any person for an offence under subsection (1) above it shall be a defence for him to prove that he took all reasonable precautions and exercised all due diligence to avoid the commission of the offence.

33. Termination and suspension of authorisation

(1)   If it appears to the Secretary of State that a person who is an authorised person by virtue of section 31 above has contravened any provision of this Act or of any rules or regulations made under it or, in purported compliance with any such provision, has furnished the Secretary of State with false, inaccurate or misleading information or has contravened any prohibition or requirement imposed under this Act the Secretary of State may direct—

(a)   that he shall cease to be an authorised person by virtue of that section; or
(b)   that he shall not be an authorised person by virtue of that section for a specified period or until the occurrence of a specified event or until specified conditions are complied with.

(2)   In the case of a person who is a member of a recognised self-regulating organisation the rules, prohibitions and requirements referred to in subsection (1) above include the rules of the organisation and any prohibition or requirement imposed by virtue of those rules; and in the case of a person who is certified by a recognised professional body the rules, prohibitions and requirements referred to in that subsection include the rules of that body which regulate the carrying on by him of investment business and any prohibition or requirement imposed by virtue of those rules.

(3)   Any period, event or condition specified in a direction under subsection (1)(b) above may be varied by the Secretary of State on the application of the person to whom the direction relates.

(4)   The Secretary of State shall consult the relevant supervisory authority before giving a direction under this section unless he considers it essential in the interests of investors that the direction should be given forthwith but in that case he shall consult the authority immediately after giving the direction and may then revoke or vary it if he considers it appropriate to do so.

(5)   The Secretary of State shall revoke a direction under this section if he is satisfied, after consulting the relevant supervisory authority, that it will secure that the person concerned will comply with the provisions mentioned in subsection (1) above.

(6)   In this section 'the relevant supervisory authority' means the authority of the member State where the person concerned is established which is responsible for supervising the carrying on of investment business of the kind which that person is or was carrying on.

34. Notice of proposed termination or suspension

(1)   Where the Secretary of State proposes—

(a)   to give a direction under section 33 above; or
(b)   to refuse an application under subsection (3) of that section,

he shall give the authorised person written notice of his intention to do so, stating the reasons for which he proposes to act.

(2)   In the case of a proposed direction under section 33 above the notice shall state the date on which it is proposed that the direction should take effect and, in the case of a proposed direction under subsection (1)(b) of that section, its proposed duration.

(3)   Where the reasons stated in a notice under this section relate specifically to matters which—

(a)   refer to a person identified in the notice other than the authorised person; and

(b)   are in the opinion of the Secretary of State prejudicial to that person in any office or employment,

the Secretary of State shall, unless he considers it impracticable to do so, serve a copy of the notice on that other person.

(4)   A notice under this section shall give particulars of the right to require the case to be referred to the Tribunal under Chapter IX of this Part of this Act.

(5)   Where a case is not required to be referred to the Tribunal by a person on whom a notice is served under this section the Secretary of State shall, at the expiration of the period within which such a requirement can be made—

(a)   give that person written notice of the direction or refusal; or

(b)   give that person written notice that the direction is not to be given or, as the case may be, of the grant of the application;

and the Secretary of State may give public notice of any decision notified by him under paragraph (a) or (b) above and the reasons for the decision except that he shall not do so in the case of a decision within paragraph (b) unless the person concerned consents to his doing so.

CHAPTER IV

EXEMPTED PERSONS

The Bank of England

35.   The Bank of England
The Bank of England is an exempted person.

Recognised investment exchanges and clearing houses

36.   Investment exchanges
(1)   A recognised investment exchange is an exempted person as respects anything done in its capacity as such which constitutes investment business.

(2)   In this Act references to the rules of an investment exchange are references to the rules made or conditions imposed by it with respect to the matters dealt with in Schedule 4 to this Act, with respect to the admission of persons to or their exclusion from the use of its facilities or otherwise relating to its constitution.

(3)   In this Act references to guidance issued by an investment exchange are references to guidance issued or any recommendation made by it to all or any class of its members or users or persons seeking to become members of the exchange or to use its facilities and which would, if it were a rule, fall within subsection (2) above.

37. Grant and revocation of recognition

(1)   Any body corporate or unincorporated association may apply to the Secretary of State for an order declaring it to be a recognised investment exchange for the purposes of this Act.

(2)   Subsections (2) to (5) of section 9 above shall have effect in relation to an application under subsection (1) above as they have effect in relation to an application under subsection (1) of that section; and every application under subsection (1) above shall be accompanied by—

    (a)   a copy of the applicant's rules;

    (b)   a copy of any guidance issued by the applicant which is intended to have continuing effect and is issued in writing or other legible form; and

    (c)   particulars of any arrangements which the applicant has made or proposes to make for the provision of clearing services.

(3)   The Secretary of State may, on an application duly made in accordance with subsection (1) above and after being furnished with all such information as he may require in connection with the application, make or refuse to make an order ('a recognition order') declaring the applicant to be a recognised investment exchange for the purposes of this Act.

(4)   Subject to Chapter XIV of this Part of this Act, the Secretary of State may make a recognition order if it appears to him from the information furnished by the exchange making the application and having regard to any other information in his possession that the requirements of Schedule 4 to this Act are satisfied as respects that exchange.

(5)   Where the Secretary of State refuses an application for a recognition order he shall give the applicant a written notice to that effect stating the reasons for the refusal.

(6)   A recognition order shall state the date on which it takes effect.

(7)   A recognition order may be revoked by a further order made by the Secretary of State if at any time it appears to him—

    (a)   that any requirement of Schedule 4 to this Act is not satisfied in the case of the exchange to which the recognition order relates; or

    (b)   that the exchange has failed to comply with any obligation to which it is subject by virtue of this Act;

and subsections (2) to (9) of section 11 above shall have effect in relation to the revocation of a recognition order under this subsection as they have effect in relation to the revocation of such an order under subsection (1) of that section.

(8)   Section 12 above shall have effect in relation to a recognised investment exchange and the requirements and obligations referred to in subsection (7) above as it has effect in relation to the requirements and obligations there mentioned.

38. Clearing houses

(1)   A recognised clearing house is an exempted person as respects anything done by it in its capacity as a person providing clearing services for the transaction of investment business.

(2)   In this Act references to the rules of a clearing house are references to the rules made or conditions imposed by it with respect to the provision by it or its

members of clearing services under clearing arrangements, that is to say, arrangements with a recognised investment exchange for the provision of clearing services in respect of transactions effected on the exchange.

(3)   In this Act references to guidance issued by a clearing house are references to guidance issued or any recommendation made by it to all or any class of its members or persons using or seeking to use its services and which would, if it were a rule, fall within subsection (2) above.

39.   Grant and revocation of recognition

(1)   Any body corporate or unincorporated association may apply to the Secretary of State for an order declaring it to be a recognised clearing house for the purposes of this Act.

(2)   Subsections (2) to (5) of section 9 above shall have effect in relation to an application under subsection (1) above as they have effect in relation to an application under subsection (1) of that section; and any application under subsection (1) above shall be accompanied by—

   (a)   a copy of the applicant's rules;
   (b)   a copy of any guidance issued by the applicant which is intended to have continuing effect and is issued in writing or other legible form; and
   (c)   particulars of any recognised investment exchange with which the applicant proposes to make clearing arrangements and of any other person (whether or not such an exchange) for whom the applicant provides clearing services.

(3)   The Secretary of State may, on an application duly made in accordance with subsection (1) above and after being furnished with all such information as he may require in connection with the application, make or refuse to make an order ('a recognition order') declaring the applicant to be a recognised clearing house for the purposes of this Act.

(4)   Subject to Chapter XIV of this Part of this Act, the Secretary of State may make a recognition order if it appears to him from the information furnished by the clearing house making the application and having regard to any other information in his possession that the clearing house—

   (a)   has financial resources sufficient for the proper performance of its functions; and
   (b)   has adequate arrangements and resources for the effective monitoring and enforcement of compliance with its rules or, as respects monitoring, arrangements providing for that function to be performed on behalf of the clearing house (and without affecting its responsibility) by another body or person who is able and willing to perform it;
   (c)   provides or is able to provide clearing services which would enable a recognised investment exchange to make arrangements with it that satisfy the requirements of Schedule 4 to this Act; and
   (d)   is able and willing to comply with duties corresponding to those imposed in the case of a recognised investment exchange by paragraph 5 of that Schedule.

(5)   Where the Secretary of State refuses an application for a recognition order he shall give the applicant a written notice to that effect stating the reasons for the refusal.

(6) A recognition order shall state the date on which it takes effect.

(7) A recognition order may be revoked by a further order made by the Secretary of State if at any time it appears to him—

(a) that any requirement of subsection (4) above is not satisfied in the case of the clearing house; or

(b) that the clearing house has failed to comply with any obligation to which it is subject by virtue of this Act;

and subsections (2) to (9) of section 11 above shall have effect in relation to the revocation of a recognition order under this subsection as they have effect in relation to the revocation of such an order under subsection (1) of that section.

(8) Section 12 above shall have effect in relation to a recognised clearing house and the requirements and obligations referred to in subsection (7) above as it has effect in relation to the requirements and obligations there mentioned.

40. Overseas investment exchanges and clearing houses

(1) Any application under section 37(1) or 39(1) above by a body or association whose head office is situated in a country outside the United Kingdom shall contain the address of a place in the United Kingdom for the service on that body or association of notices or other documents required or authorised to be served on it under this Act.

(2) In relation to any such body or association sections 37(4) and 39(4) above shall have effect with the substitution for the requirements there mentioned of the following requirements, that is to say—

(a) that the body or association is, in the country which its head office is situated, subject to supervision which, together with the rules and practices of that body or association, is such that investors in the United Kingdom are afforded protection in relation to that body or association at least equivalent to that provided by the provisions of this Act in relation to investment exchanges and clearing houses in respect of which recognition orders are made otherwise than by virtue of this subsection; and

(b) that the body or association is able and willing to co-operate, by the sharing of information and otherwise, with the authorities, bodies and persons responsible in the United Kingdom for the supervision and regulation of investment business or other financial services; and

(c) that adequate arrangements exist for such co-operation between those responsible for the supervision of the body or association in the country mentioned in paragraph (a) above and the authorities, bodies and persons mentioned in paragraph (b) above.

(3) In determining whether to make a recognition order by virtue of subsection (2) above the Secretary of State may have regard to the extent to which persons in the United Kingdom and persons in the country mentioned in that subsection have access to the financial markets in each others' countries.

(4) In relation to a body or association declared to be a recognised investment exchange or recognised clearing house by a recognition order made by virtue of subsection (2) above—

(a) the reference in section 36(2) above to the matters dealt with in Schedule 4 to this Act shall be construed as a reference to corresponding matters:

    (b)   sections 37(7) and (8) and 39(7) and (8) above shall have effect as if the requirements mentioned in section 37(7)(a) and in section 39(7)(a) were those of subsection (2)(a) and (b) above; and

    (c)   the grounds on which the order may be revoked under section 37(7) or 39(7) above shall include the ground that it appears to the Secretary of State that revocation is desirable in the interests of investors and potential investors in the United Kingdom.

(5)   In this section 'country' includes any territory or any part of a country or territory.

(6)   A body or association declared to be a recognised investment exchange or recognised clearing house by a recognition order made by virtue of subsection (2) above is in this Act referred to as an 'overseas investment exchange' or an 'overseas clearing house'.

41. Notification requirements

(1)   The Secretary of State may make regulations requiring a recognised investment exchange or recognised clearing house to give him forthwith notice of the occurrence of such events relating to the exchange or clearing house as are specified in the regulations and such information in respect of those events as is so specified.

(2)   The Secretary of State may make regulations requiring a recognised investment exchange or recognised clearing house to furnish him at such times or in respect of such periods as are specified in the regulations with such information relating to the exchange or clearing house as is so specified.

(3)   The notices and information required to be given or furnished under the foregoing provisions of this section shall be such as the Secretary of State may reasonably require for the exercise of his functions under this Act.

(4)   Regulations under the foregoing provisions of this section may require information to be given in a specified form and to be verified in a specified manner.

(5)   Where a recognised investment exchange—

    (a)   amends, revokes or adds to its rules or guidance; or
    (b)   makes, terminates or varies any clearing arrangements,

it shall within seven days give written notice to the Secretary of State of the amendment, revocation or addition or, as the case may be, of the matters mentioned in paragraph (b) above.

(6)   Where a recognised clearing house—

    (a)   amends, revokes or adds to its rules or guidance; or
    (b)   makes a change in the persons for whom it provides clearing services,

it shall within seven days give written notice to the Secretary of State of the amendment, revocation or addition or, as the case may be, of the change.

(7)   Notice need not be given under subsection (5) or (6) above of the revocation of guidance other than such as is mentioned in section 37(2)(b) or 39(2)(b) above or of any amendment of or addition to guidance which does not result in or consist of such guidance as is there mentioned.

Other exemptions

42.   Lloyd's
The Society of Lloyd's and persons permitted by the Council of Lloyd's to act as underwriting agents at Lloyd's are exempted persons as respects investment business carried on in connection with or for the purpose of insurance business at Lloyd's.

43.   Listed money market institutions
(1)   A person for the time being included in a list maintained by the Bank of England for the purposes of this section ('a listed institution') is an exempted person in respect of, and of anything done for the purposes of, any transaction to which Part I or Part II of Schedule 5 to this Act applies and in respect of any arrangements made by him with a view to other persons entering into a transaction to which Part III of that Schedule applies.

(2)   The conditions imposed by the Bank of England for admission to the list referred to in this section and the arrangements made by it for a person's admission to and removal from the list shall require the approval of the Treasury; and this section shall cease to have effect if that approval is withdrawn but without prejudice to its again having effect if approval is given for fresh conditions or arrangements.

(3)   The Bank of England shall publish the list as for the time being in force and provide a certified copy of it at the request of any person wishing to refer to it in legal proceedings.

(4)   Such a certified copy shall be evidence or, in Scotland, sufficient evidence of the contents of the list; and a copy purporting to be certified by or on behalf of the Bank shall be deemed to have been duly certified unless the contrary is shown.

44.   Appointed representatives
(1)   An appointed representative is an exempted person as respects investment business carried on by him as such a representative.

(2)   For the purposes of this Act an appointed representative is a person—

   (a)   who is employed by an authorised person (his 'principal') under a contract for services which—

      (i)   requires or permits him to carry on investment business to which this section applies; and

      (ii)   complies with subsections (4) and (5) below; and

   (b)   for whose activities in carrying on the whole or part of that investment business his principal has accepted responsibility in writing,

and the investment business carried on by an appointed representative as such is the investment business for which his principal has accepted responsibility.

(3)   This section applies to investment business carried on by an appointed representative which consists of—

   (a)   procuring or endeavouring to procure the persons with whom he deals to enter into investment agreements with his principal or (if not prohibited by his contract) with other persons;

(b) giving advice to the persons with whom he deals about entering into investment agreements with his principal or (if not prohibited by his contract) with other persons; or

(c) giving advice as to the sale of investments issued by his principal or as to the exercise of rights conferred by an investment whether or not issued as aforesaid.

(4) If the contract between an appointed representative and his principal does not prohibit the representative from procuring or endeavouring to procure persons to enter into investment agreements with persons other than his principal it must make provision for enabling the principal either to impose such a prohibition or to restrict the kinds of investment to which those agreements may relate or the other persons with whom they may be entered into.

(5) If the contract between an appointed representative and his principal does not prohibit the representative from giving advice about entering into investment agreements with persons other than his principal it must make provision for enabling the principal either to impose such a prohibition or to restrict the kinds of advice which the representative may give by reference to the kinds of investment in relation to which or the persons with whom the representative may advise that investment agreements should be made.

(6) The principal of an appointed representative shall be responsible, to the same extent as if he had expressly authorised it, for anything said or done or omitted by the representative in carrying on the investment business for which he has accepted responsibility.

(7) In determining whether an authorised person has complied with—

(a) any provision contained in or made under this Act; or

(b) any rules of a recognised self-regulating organisation or recognised professional body,

anything which a person who at the material time is or was an appointed representative of the authorised person has said, done or omitted as respects investment business for which the authorised person has accepted responsibility shall be treated as having been said, done or omitted by the authorised person.

(8) Nothing in subsection (7) above shall cause the knowledge or intentions of an appointed representative to be attributed to his principal for the purpose of determining whether the principal has committed a criminal offence unless in all the circumstances it is reasonable for them to be attributed to him.

(9) In this Act 'investment agreement' means any agreement the making or performance of which by either party constitutes an activity which falls within any paragraph of Part II of Schedule 1 to this Act or would do so apart from Parts III and IV of that Schedule.

45. Miscellaneous exemptions

(1) Each of the following persons is an exempted person to the extent specified in relation to that person—

(a) the President of the Family Division of the High Court when acting in the exercise of his functions under section 9 of the Administration of Estates Act 1925;

(b) the Probate Judge of the High Court of Northern Ireland when acting in the exercise of his functions under section 3 of the Administration of Estates Act (Northern Ireland) 1955;

(c) the Accountant General of the Supreme Court when acting in the exercise of his functions under Part VI of the Administration of Justice Act 1982;

(d) the Accountant of Court when acting in the exercise of his functions in connection with the consignation or deposit of sums of money;

(e) the Public Trustee when acting in the exercise of his functions under the Public Trustee Act 1906;

(f) the Master of the Court of Protection when acting in the exercise of his functions under Part VII of the Mental Health Act 1983;

(g) the Official Solicitor to the Supreme Court when acting as judicial trustee under the Judicial Trustees Act 1896;

(h) a registrar of a county court when managing funds paid into court;

(i) a sheriff clerk when acting in the exercise of his functions in connection with the consignation or deposit of sums of money;

(j) a person acting in his capacity as manager of a fund established under section 22 of the Charities Act 1960, section 25 of the Charities Act (Northern Ireland) 1964, section 11 of the Trustee Investments Act 1961 or section 42 of the Administration of Justice Act 1982;

(k) the Central Board of Finance of the Church of England or a Diocesan Authority within the meaning of the Church Funds Investment Measure 1958 when acting in the exercise of its functions under that Measure;

(l) a person acting in his capacity as an official receiver within the meaning of section 399 of the Insolvency Act 1986 or in that capacity within the meaning of any corresponding provision in force in Northern Ireland.

(2) Where a bankruptcy order is made in respect of an authorised person or of a person whose authorisation is suspended under section 28 above or who is the subject of a direction under section 33(1)(b) above or a winding-up order is made in respect of a partnership which is such a person, the trustee in bankruptcy or liquidator acting in his capacity as such is an exempted person but—

(a) sections 48 to 71 below and, so far as relevant to any of those provisions, Chapter IX of this Part of this Act; and

(b) sections 104, 105 and 106 below,

shall apply to him to the same extent as they applied to the bankrupt or partnership and, if the bankrupt or partnership was subject to the rules of a recognised self-regulating organisation or recognised professional body, he shall himself also be subject to those rules.

(3) In the application of subsection (2) above to Scotland—

(a) for the reference to a bankruptcy order being made in respect of a person there shall be substituted a reference to the estate of that person being sequestrated;

(b) the reference to a winding-up order in respect of a partnership is a reference to such an order made under section 72 below;

(c) for the reference to the trustee in bankruptcy there shall be substituted a reference to the interim trustee or permanent trustee within the meaning of the Bankruptcy (Scotland) Act 1985; and

(d) for the references to the bankrupt there shall be substituted references to the debtor.

(4) In the application of subsection (2) above to Northern Ireland for the reference to a bankruptcy order there shall be substituted a reference to an order of adjudication of bankruptcy and the reference to a trustee in bankruptcy shall include a reference to an assignee in bankruptcy.

Supplemental

46. Power to extend or restrict exemptions

(1) The Secretary of State may by order provide—

(a) for exemptions additional to those specified in the foregoing provisions of this Chapter; or

(b) for removing or restricting any exemption conferred by section 42, 43 or 45 above;

and any such order may contain such transitional provisions as the Secretary of State thinks necessary or expedient.

(2) An order making such provision as is mentioned in paragraph (a) of subsection (1) above shall be subject to annulment in pursuance of a resolution of either House of Parliament; and no order making such provision as is mentioned in paragraph (b) of that subsection shall be made unless a draft of it has been laid before and approved by a resolution of each House of Parliament.

CHAPTER V

CONDUCT OF INVESTMENT BUSINESS

47. Misleading statements and practices

(1) Any person who—

(a) makes a statement, promise or forecast which he knows to be misleading, false or deceptive or dishonestly conceals any material facts; or

(b) recklessly makes (dishonestly or otherwise) a statement, promise or forecast which is misleading, false or deceptive,

is guilty of an offence if he makes the statement, promise or forecast or conceals the facts for the purpose of inducing, or is reckless as to whether it may induce, another person (whether or not the person to whom the statement, promise or forecast is made or from whom the facts are concealed) to enter or offer to enter into, or to refrain from entering or offering to enter into, an investment agreement or to exercise, or refrain from exercising, any rights conferred by an investment.

(2) Any person who does any act or engages in any course of conduct which creates a false or misleading impression as to the market in or the price or value of any investments is guilty of an offence if he does so for the purpose of creating that impression and of thereby inducing another person to acquire, dispose of, subscribe for or underwrite those investments or to refrain from doing so or to exercise, or refrain from exercising, any rights conferred by those investments.

(3) In proceedings brought against any person for an offence under subsection (2) above it shall be a defence for him to prove that he reasonably believed that his act or conduct would not create an impression that was false or misleading as to the matters mentioned in that subsection.

(4)   Subsection (1) above does not apply unless—

  (a)   the statement, promise or forecast is made in or from, or the facts are concealed in or from, the United Kingdom;
  (b)   the person on whom the inducement is intended to or may have effect is in the United Kingdom; or
  (c)   the agreement is or would be entered into or the rights are or would be exercised in the United Kingdom.

(5)   Subsection (2) above does not apply unless—

  (a)   the act is done or the course of conduct is engaged in in the United Kingdom; or
  (b)   the false or misleading impression is created there.

(6)   A person guilty of an offence under this section shall be liable—

  (a)   on conviction on indictment, to imprisonment for a term not exceeding seven years or to a fine or to both;
  (b)   on summary conviction, to imprisonment for a term not exceeding six months or to a fine not exceeding the statutory maximum or to both.

48.   Conduct of business rules

(1)   The Secretary of State may make rules regulating the conduct of investment business by authorised persons but those rules shall not apply to members of a recognised self-regulating organisation or persons certified by a recognised professional body in respect of investment business in the carrying on of which they are subject to the rules of the organisation or body.

(2)   Rules under this section may in particular make provision—

  (a)   prohibiting a person from carrying on, or holding himself out as carrying on—

    (i)   investment business of any kind specified in the rules; or
    (ii)   investment business of a kind or on a scale other than that notified by him to the Secretary of State in connection with an application for authorisation under Chapter III of this Part of this Act, in a notice under section 32 above or in accordance with any provision of the rules or regulations in that behalf;

  (b)   prohibiting a person from carrying on investment business in relation to persons other than those of a specified class or description;
  (c)   regulating the manner in which a person may hold himself out as carrying on investment business;
  (d)   regulating the manner in which a person makes a market in any investments;
  (e)   as to the form and content of advertisements in respect of investment business;
  (f)   requiring the principals of appointed representatives to impose restrictions on the investment business carried on by them;
  (g)   requiring the disclosure of the amount or value, or of arrangements for the payment or provision, of commissions or other inducements in connection with investment business and restricting the matters by reference to which or the manner in which their amount or value may be determined;
  (h)   enabling or requiring information obtained by an authorised person in the

264

course of carrying on one part of his business to be withheld by him from persons with whom he deals in the course of carrying on another part and for that purpose enabling or requiring persons emloyed in one part of that business to withhold information from those employed in another part;

(i) as to the circumstances and manner in which and the time when or the period during which action may be taken for the purpose of stabilising the price of investments of any specified description;

(j) for arrangements for the settlement of disputes;

(k) requiring the keeping of accounts and other records, as to their form and content and for their inspection;

(l) requiring a person to whom the rules apply to make provision for the protection of investors in the event of the cessation of his investment business in consequence of his death, incapacity or otherwise.

(3) Subsection (2) above is without prejudice to the generality of subsection (1) above and accordingly rules under this section may make provision for matters other than those mentioned in subsection (2) or further provision as to any of the matters there mentioned except that they shall not impose limits on the amount or value of commissions or other inducements paid or provided in connection with investment business.

(4) Rules under this section may also regulate or prohibit the carrying on in connection with investment business of any other business or the carrying on of any other business which is held out as being for the purposes of investment.

(5) In paragraph (e) of subsection (2) above 'advertisement' does not include any advertisement which is subject to section 154 below or which is required or permitted to be published by listing rules under Part IV of this Act and relates to securities which have been admitted to listing under that Part; and rules under that paragraph shall have effect subject to the provisions of Part V of this Act.

(6) Nothing done in conformity with rules made under paragraph (h) of subsection (2) above shall be regarded as a contravention of section 47 above.

(7) Section 47(2) above shall not be regarded as contravened by anything done for the purpose of stabilising the price of investments if it is done in conformity with rules made under this section and—

(a) in respect of investments which fall within any of paragraphs 1 to 5 of Schedule 1 to this Act and are specified by the rules; and

(b) during such period before or after the issue of those investments as is specified by the rules.

(8) The Secretary of State may by order amend subsection (7) above—

(a) by restricting or extending the kinds of investment to which it applies;

(b) by restricting it so as to apply only in relation to the issue of investments in specified circumstances or by extending it, in respect of investments of any kind specified in the order, so as to apply to things done during a specified period before or after events other than the issue of those investments.

(9) No order shall be made under subsection (8) above unless a draft of it has been laid before and approved by a resolution of each House of Parliament.

(10) Rules under this section may contain such incidental and transitional provisions as the Secretary of State thinks necessary or expedient.

49. Financial resources rules

(1) The Secretary of State may make rules requiring persons authorised to carry on investment business by virtue of section 25 or 31 above to have and maintain in respect of that business such financial resources as are required by the rules.

(2) Without prejudice to the generality of subsection (1) above, rules under this section may—

(a) impose requirements which are absolute or which are to vary from time to time by reference to such factors as are specified in or determined in accordance with the rules;

(b) impose requirements which take account of any business (whether or not investment business) carried on by the person concerned in conjunction with or in addition to the business mentioned in subsection (1) above;

(c) make provision as to the assets, liabilities and other matters to be taken into account in determining a person's financial resources for the purposes of the rules and the extent to which and the manner in which they are to be taken into account for that purpose.

50. Modification of conduct of business and financial resources rules for particular cases

(1) The Secretary of State may, on the application of any person to whom any rules made under section 48 or 49 above apply, alter the requirements of the rules so as to adapt them to the circumstances of that person or to any particular kind of business carried on or to be carried on by him.

(2) The Secretary of State shall not exercise the powers conferred by subsection (1) above in any case unless it appears to him that—

(a) compliance with the requirements in question would be unduly burdensome for the applicant having regard to the benefit which compliance would confer on investors; and

(b) the exercise of those powers will not result in any undue risk to investors.

(3) The powers conferred by subsection (1) above may be exercised unconditionally or subject to conditions.

51. Cancellation rules

(1) The Secretary of State may make rules for enabling a person who has entered or offered to enter into an investment agreement with an authorised person to rescind the agreement or withdraw the offer within such period and in such manner as may be prescribed.

(2) Without prejudice to the generality of subsection (1) above, rules under this section may make provision—

(a) for requiring the service of notices with respect to the rights exercisable under the rules;

(b) for the restitution of property and the making or recovery of payments where those rights are exercised; and

(c) for such other incidental matters as the Secretary of State thinks necessary or expedient.

52. Notification regulations

(1) The Secretary of State may make regulations requiring authorised persons to give him forthwith notice of the occurrence of such events as are specified in the

regulations and such information in respect of those events as is so specified.

(2)   The Secretary of State may make regulations requiring authorised persons to furnish him at such times or in respect of such periods as are specified in the regulations with such information as is so specified.

(3)   Regulations under this section shall not apply to a member of a recognised self-regulating organisation or a person certified by a recognised professional body unless he carries on investment business in the carrying on of which he is subject to any of the rules made under section 48 above.

(4)   Without prejudice to the generality of subsections (1) and (2) above, regulations under this section may relate to—

(a)   the nature of the investment business being carried on;
(b)   the nature of any other business carried on with or for the purposes of the investment business;
(c)   any proposal of an authorised person to alter the nature or extent of any business carried on by him;
(d)   any person becoming or ceasing to be a person of the kind to whom regard could be had by the Secretary of State under subsection (3) of section 27 above in deciding an application for authorisation under that section;
(e)   the financial position of an authorised person as respects his investment business or any other business carried on by him;
(f)   any property managed, and any property or money held, by an authorised person on behalf of other persons.

(5)   Regulations under this section may require information to be given in a specified form and to be verified in a specified manner.

(6)   Any notice or information required to be given or furnished under this section shall be given in writing or in such other manner as the Secretary of State may approve.

53.   Indemnity rules

(1)   The Secretary of State may make rules concerning indemnity against any claim in respect of any description of civil liability incurred by an authorised person in connection with his investment business.

(2)   Rules under this section shall not apply to a member of a recognised self-regulating organisation or a person certified by a recognised professional body in respect of investment business in the carrying on of which he is subject to the rules of the organisation or body unless that organisation or body has requested that rules under this section should apply to him; and any such request shall not be capable of being withdrawn after rules giving effect to it have been made but without prejudice to the power of the Secretary of State to revoke the rules if he thinks fit.

(3)   For the purpose of providing indemnity the rules—

(a)   may authorise the Secretary of State to establish and maintain a fund or funds;
(b)   may authorise the Secretary of State to take out and maintain insurance with insurers authorised to carry on insurance business under the law of the United Kingdom or any other member State;
(c)   may require any person to whom the rules apply to take out and maintain

insurance with any such insurer.

(4) Without prejudice to the generality of the foregoing provisions, the rules may—

    (a) specify the terms and conditions on which, and the extent to which, indemnity is to be available and any circumstances in which the right to it is to be excluded or modified;

    (b) provide for the management, administration and protection of any fund maintained by virtue of subsection (3)(a) above and require persons to whom the rules apply to make payments to any such fund;

    (c) require persons to whom the rules apply to make payments by way of premium on any insurance policy maintained by the Secretary of State by virtue of subsection (3)(b) above;

    (d) prescribe the conditions which an insurance policy must satisfy for the purposes of subsection (3)(c) above;

    (e) authorise the Secretary of State to determine the amount which the rules require to be paid to him or an insurer, subject to such limits or in accordance with such provisions as may be prescribed by the rules;

    (f) specify circumstances in which, where sums are paid by the Secretary of State or an insurer in satisfaction of claims against a person subject to the rules, proceedings may be taken against that person by the Secretary of State or the insurer;

    (g) specify circumstances in which persons are exempt from the rules;

    (h) empower the Secretary of State to take such steps as he considers necessary or expedient to ascertain whether or not the rules are being complied with; and

    (i) contain incidental or supplementary provisions.

54. Compensation fund

(1) The Secretary of State may by rules establish a scheme for compensating investors in cases where persons who are or have been authorised persons are unable, or likely to be unable, to satisfy claims in respect of any decription of civil liability incurred by them in connection with their investment businesses.

(2) Without prejudice to the generality of subsection (1) above, rules under this section may—

    (a) provide for the administration of the scheme and, subject to the rules, the determination and regulation of any matter relating to its operation by a body appearing to the Secretary of State to be representative of, or of any class of, authorised persons;

    (b) establish a fund out of which compensation is to be paid;

    (c) provide for the levying of contributions from, or from any class of, authorised persons and otherwise for financing the scheme and for the payment of contributions and other money into the fund;

    (d) specify the terms and conditions on which, and the extent to which, compensation is to be payable and any circumstances in which the right to compensation is to be excluded or modified;

    (e) provide for treating compensation payable under the scheme in respect of a claim against any person as extinguishing or reducing the liability of that person in respect of the claim and for conferring on the body administering the scheme a right of recovery against that person, being, in the event of his

insolvency, a right not exceeding such right, if any, as the claimant would
have had in that event; and

(f) contain incidental and supplementary provisions;

(3) A scheme under this section shall not be made so as to apply to persons who
are members of a recognised self-regulating organisation except after consultation
with that organisation or, except at the request of a recognised professional body,
to persons who are certified by it and subject to its rules in carrying on all the
investment business carried on by them; and no scheme applying to such persons
shall be made unless the Secretary of State is satisfied that the rules establishing it
make sufficient provision—

(a) for the administration of the scheme by a body on which the interests of
those persons are adequately represented; and

(b) for securing that the amounts which they are liable to contribute reflect, so
far as practicable, the amount of the claims made or likely to be made in
respect of those persons.

(4) Where a scheme applies to such persons as are mentioned in subsection (3)
above the rules under this section may—

(a) constitute the recognised self-regulating organisation or recognised
professional body in question as the body administering the scheme in
relation to those persons;

(b) provide for the levying of contributions from that organisation or body
instead of from those persons; and

(c) establish a separate fund for the contributions and compensation payable in
respect of those persons, with or without provision for payments and
repayments in specified circumstances between that and any other fund
established by the scheme.

(5) A request by a recognised professional body under subsection (3) above shall
not be capable of being withdrawn after rules giving effect to it have been made
but without prejudice to the power of the Secretary of State to revoke the rules if
he thinks fit.

(6) Rules may be made—

(a) for England and Wales, under sections 411 and 412 of the Insolvency Act
1986;

(b) for Scotland—

(i) under the said section 411; and

(ii) in relation to the application of this section where the persons who
are or have been authorised persons are persons whose estates may be
sequestrated under the Bankruptcy (Scotland) Act 1985, by the
Secretary of State under this section; and

(c) for Northern Ireland, under Article 613 of the Companies (Northern
Ireland) Order 1986 and section 65 of the Judicature (Northern Ireland)
Act 1978,

for the purpose of integrating any procedure for which provision is made by virtue
of subsection (2)(e) above into the general procedure on a winding-up, bankruptcy
or sequestration.

55. Clients' money
(1) The Secretary of State may make regulations with respect to money (in this

section referred to as 'clients' money') which authorised persons, or authorised persons of any description, hold in such circumstances as are specified in the regulations.

(2)   Without prejudice to the generality of subsection (1) above, regulations under this section may—

(a)   provide that clients' money held by an authorised person is held on trust;
(b)   require clients' money to be paid into an account the title of which contains the word 'client' and which is with an institution of a kind specified in the regulations or, in the case of a member of a recognised self-regulating organisation or a person certified by a recognised professional body, by the rules of that organisation or body;
(c)   make provision with respect to the opening and keeping of clients' accounts, including provision as to the circumstances in which money other than clients' money may be paid into such accounts and the circumstances in which and the persons to whom money held in such accounts may be paid out;
(d)   require the keeping of accounts and records in respect of clients' money;
(e)   require any such accounts to be examined by an accountant having such qualifications as are specified in the regulations and require the accountant to report to the Secretary of State or, in the case of a member of a recognised self-regulating organisation or a person certified by a recognised professional body, to that organisation or body, whether in his opinion the provisions of the regulations have been complied with and on such other matters as may be specified in the regulations;
(f)   authorise the retention, to such extent and in such cases as may be specified in regulations, of so much of clients' money as represents interest.

(3)   Where an authorised person is required to have an auditor, whether by virtue of any provision contained in or made under any enactment (including this Act) or of the rules of any such organisation or body as is mentioned in paragraph (b) of subsection (2) above, the regulations may require the examination and report referred to in paragraph (e) of that subsection to be carried out and made by that auditor.

(4)   An institution with which an account is kept in pursuance of regulations made under this section does not incur any liability as constructive trustee where money is wrongfully paid from the account unless the institution permits the payment with knowledge that it is wrongful or having deliberately failed to make enquiries in circumstances in which a reasonable and honest person would have done so.

(5)   In the application of this section to Scotland for the reference to money being held on trust there shall be substituted a reference to its being held as agent for the person who is entitled to call for it to be paid over to him or to be paid on his direction or to have it otherwise credited to him.

56.   Unsolicited calls
(1)   Except so far as permitted by regulations made by the Secretary of State, no person shall in the course of or in consequence of an unsolicited call—

(a)   made on a person in the United Kingdom; or
(b)   made from the United Kingdom on a person elsewhere,

by way of business enter into an investment agreement with the person on whom the call is made or procure or endeavour to procure that person to enter into such an agreement.

(2)   A person shall not be guilty of an offence by reason only of contravening subsection (1) above, but subject to subsection (4) below—

    (a)   any investment agreement which is entered into in the course of or in consequence of the unsolicited call shall not be enforceable against the person on whom the call was made; and

    (b)   that person shall be entitled to recover any money or other property paid or transferred by him under the agreement, together with compensation for any loss sustained by him as a result of having parted with it.

(3)   The compensation recoverable under subsection (2) above shall be such as the parties may agree or as the court may, on the application of either party, determine.

(4)   A court may allow an agreement to which subsection (2) above applies to be enforced or money and property paid or transferred under it to be retained if it is satisfied—

    (a)   that the person on whom the call was made was not influenced, or not influenced to any material extent, by anything said or done in the course of or in consequence of the call;

    (b)   without prejudice to paragraph (a) above, that the person on whom the call was made entered into the agreement—

        (i)   following discussions between the parties of such a nature and over such a period that his entering into the agreement can fairly be regarded as a consequence of those discussions rather than the call; and

        (ii)   was aware of the nature of the agreement and any risks involved in entering into it; or

    (c)   that the call was not made by—

        (i)   the person seeking to enforce the agreement or to retain the money or property or a person acting on his behalf or an appointed representative whose principal he was; or

        (ii)   a person who has received or is to receive, or in the case of an appointed representative whose principal has received or is to receive, any commission or other inducement in respect of the agreement from a person mentioned in sub-paragraph (i) above.

(5)   Where a person elects not to perform an agreement which by virtue of this section is unenforceable against him or by virtue of this section recovers money paid or other property transferred by him under an agreement he shall repay any money and return any other property received by him under the agreement.

(6)   Where any property transferred under an agreement to which this section applies has passed to a third party the references to that property in this section shall be construed as references to its value at the time of its transfer under the agreement.

(7)   In the application of this section to anything done by a member of a recognised self-regulating organisation or a person certified by a recognised

professional body in carrying on investment business in the carrying on of which he is subject to the rules of the organisation or body the reference in subsection (1) above to regulations made by the Secretary of State shall be construed as references to the rules of the organisation or body.

(8)   In this section 'unsolicited call' means a personal visit or oral communication made without express invitation.

57.   Restrictions on advertising

(1)   Subject to section 58 below, no person other than an authorised person shall issue or cause to be issued an investment advertisement in the United Kingdom unless its contents have been approved by an authorised person.

(2)   In this Act 'an investment advertisement' means any advertisement inviting persons to enter or offer to enter into an investment agreement or to exercise any rights conferred by an investment to acquire, dispose of, underwrite or convert an investment or containing information calculated to lead directly or indirectly to persons doing so.

(3)   Subject to subsection (4) below, any person who contravenes this section shall be guilty of an offence and liable—

  (a)   on conviction on indictment, to imprisonment for a term not exceeding two years or to a fine or to both;
  (b)   on summary conviction, to imprisonment for a term not exceeding six months or to a fine not exceeding the statutory maximum or to both.

(4)   A person who in the ordinary course of a business other than investment business issues an advertisement to the order of another person shall not be guilty of an offence under this section if he proves that he believed on reasonable grounds that the person to whose order the advertisement was issued was an authorised person, that the contents of the advertisement were approved by an authorised person or that the advertisement was permitted by or under section 58 below.

(5)   If in contravention of this section a person issues or causes to be issued an advertisement inviting persons to enter or offer to enter into an investment agreement or containing information calculated to lead directly or indirectly to persons doing so, then, subject to subsection (8) below—

  (a)   he shall not be entitled to enforce any agreement to which the advertisement related and which was entered into after the issue of the advertisement; and
  (b)   the other party shall be entitled to recover any money or other property paid or transferred by him under the agreement, together with compensation for any loss sustained by him as a result of having parted with it.

(6)   If in contravention of this section a person issues or causes to be issued an advertisement inviting persons to exercise any rights conferred by an investment or containing information calculated to lead directly or indirectly to persons doing so, then, subject to subsection (8) below—

  (a)   he shall not be entitled to enforce any obligation to which a person is subject as a result of any exercise by him after the issue of the advertisement of any rights to which the advertisement related; and
  (b)   that person shall be entitled to recover any money or other property paid or transferred by him under any such obligation, together with

compensation for any loss sustained by him as a result of having parted with it.

(7)   The compensation recoverable under subsection (5) or (6) above shall be such as the parties may agree or as a court may, on the application of either party, determine.

(8)   A court may allow any such agreement or obligation as is mentioned in subsection (5) or (6) above to be enforced or money or property paid or transferred under it to be retained if it is satisfied—

  (a)   that the person against whom enforcement is sought or who is seeking to recover the money or property was not influenced, or not influenced to any material extent, by the advertisement in making his decision to enter into the agreement or as to the exercise of the rights in question; or

  (b)   that the advertisement was not misleading as to the nature of the investment, the terms of the agreement or, as the case may be, the consequences of exercising the rights in question and fairly stated any risks involved in those matters.

(9)   Where a person elects not to perform an agreement or an obligation which by virtue of subsection (5) or (6) above is unenforceable against him or by virtue of either of those subsections recovers money paid or other property transferred by him under an agreement or obligation he shall repay any money and return any other property received by him under the agreement or, as the case may be, as a result of exercising the rights in question.

(10)   Where any property transferred under an agreement or obligation to which subsection (5) or (6) above applies has passed to a third party the references to that property in this section shall be construed as references to its value at the time of its transfer under the agreement or obligation.

58.   Exceptions from restrictions on advertising
(1)   Section 57 above does not apply to—

  (a)   any advertisement issued or caused to be issued by, and relating only to investments issued by—

    (i)   the government of the United Kingdom, of Northern Ireland or of any country or territory outside the United Kingdom;
    (ii)   a local authority in the United Kingdom or elsewhere;
    (iii)   the Bank of England or the central bank of any country or territory outside the United Kingdom; or
    (iv)   any international organisation the members of which include the United Kingdom or another member State;

  (b)   any advertisement issued or caused to be issued by a person who is exempt under section 36, 38, 42, 43, 44 or 45 above, or by virtue of an order under section 46 above, if the advertisement relates to a matter in respect of which he is exempt;

  (c)   any advertisement which is issued or caused to be issued by a national of a member State other than the United Kingdom in the course of investment business lawfully carried on by him in such a State and which conforms with any rules made under section 48(2)(e) above;

  (d)   any advertisement which—

> (i) is subject to section 154 below; or
> (ii) consists of or any part of listing particulars, supplementary listing particulars or any other document required or permitted to be published by listing rules under Part IV of this Act or by an approved exchange under Part V of this Act.

(2) Section 57 above does not apply to an advertisement inviting persons to subscribe in cash for any investments to which Part V of this Act applies if the advertisement is issued or caused to be issued by the person by whom the investments are to be issued and either the advertisement consists of a prospectus registered in accordance with that Part or the following matters (and no others that would make it an investment advertisement) are contained in the advertisement—

> (a) the name of that person and his address or particulars of other means of communicating with him;
> (b) the nature of the investments, the number offered for subscription and their nominal value and price;
> (c) a statement that a prospectus for the purposes of that Part of this Act is or will be available and, if it is not yet available, when it will be; and
> (d) instructions for obtaining a copy of the prospectus.

(3) Section 57 above does not apply to an advertisement issued in such circumstances as may be specified in an order made by the Secretary of State for the purpose of exempting from that section—

> (a) advertisements appearing to him to have a private character, whether by reason of a connection between the person issuing them and those to whom they are issued or otherwise;
> (b) advertisements appearing to him to deal with investment only incidentally; or
> (c) advertisements issued to persons appearing to him to be sufficiently expert to understand any risks involved; or
> (d) such other classes of advertisement as he thinks fit.

(4) An order under subsection (3) above may require any person who by virtue of the order is authorised to issue an advertisement to comply with such requirements as are specified in the order.

(5) An order made by virtue of paragraph (a), (b) or (c) of subsection (3) above shall be subject to annulment in pursuance of a resolution of either House of Parliament; and no order shall be made by virtue of paragraph (d) of that subsection unless a draft of it has been laid before and approved by a resolution of each House of Parliament.

(6) Subsections (1)(c) and (2) above do not apply to any advertisement relating to an investment falling within paragraph 5 of Schedule 1 to this Act.

59. Employment of prohibited persons

(1) If it appears to the Secretary of State that any individual is not a fit and proper person to be employed in connection with investment business or investment business of a particular kind he may direct that he shall not, without the written consent of the Secretary of State, be employed in connection with investment business or, as the case may be, investment business of that kind—

> (a) by authorised persons or exempted persons; or

(b) by any specified person or persons, or by persons of any specified description, falling within paragraph (a) above.

(2)   A direction under this section ('a disqualification direction') shall specify the date on which it is to take effect and a copy of it shall be served on the person to whom it relates.

(3)   Any consent by the Secretary of State to the employment of a person who is the subject of a disqualification direction may relate to employment generally or to employment of a particular kind, may be given subject to conditions and restrictions and may be varied by him from time to time.

(4)   Where the Secretary of State proposes—

(a) to give a disqualification direction in respect of any person; or
(b) to refuse an application for his consent under this section or for the variation of such consent,

he shall give that person or the applicant written notice of his intention to do so, stating the reasons for which he proposes to act and giving particulars of the right to require the case to be referred to the Tribunal under Chapter IX of this Part of this Act.

(5)   Any person who accepts or continues in any employment in contravention of a disqualification direction shall be guilty of an offence and liable on summary conviction to a fine not exceeding the fifth level on the standard scale.

(6)   It shall be the duty of an authorised person and an appointed representative to take reasonable care not to employ or continue to employ a person in contravention of a disqualification direction.

(7)   The Secretary of State may revoke a disqualification direction.

(8)   In this section references to employment include references to employment otherwise than under a contract of service.

60. Public statement as to person's misconduct

(1)   If it appears to the Secretary of State that a person who is or was an authorised person by virtue of section 22, 24, 25 or 31 above has contravened—

(a) any provision of rules or regulations made under this Chapter or of section 56 to 59 above; or
(b) any condition imposed under section 50 above,

he may publish a statement to that effect.

(2)   Before publishing a statement under subsection (1) above the Secretary of State shall give the person concerned written notice of the proposed statement and of the reasons for which he proposes to act.

(3)   Where the reasons stated in the notice relate specifically to matters which—

(a) refer to a person identified in the notice other than the person who is or was the authorised person; and
(b) are in the opinion of the Secretary of State prejudicial to that person in any office or employment,

the Secretary of State shall, unless he considers it impracticable to do so, serve a copy of the notice on that other person.

(4) A notice under this section shall give particulars of the right to have the case referred to the Tribunal under Chapter IX of this Part of this Act.

(5) Where a case is not required to be referred to the Tribunal by a person on whom a notice is served under this section the Secretary of State shall, at the expiration of the period within which such a requirement can be made, give that person written notice that the statement is or is not to be published; and if it is to be published the Secretary of State shall after publication send a copy of it to that person and to any person on whom a copy of the notice under subsection (2) above was served.

61. Injunctions and restitution orders

(1) If on the application of the Secretary of State the court is satisfied—

   (a) that there is a reasonable likelihood that any person will contravene any provision of—

      (i) rules or regulations made under this Chapter;
      (ii) sections 47, 56, 57 or 59 above;
      (iii) any requirements imposed by an order under section 58(3) above; or
      (iv) the rules of a recognised self-regulating organisation, recognised professional body, recognised investment exchange or recognised clearing house to which that person is subject and which regulate the carrying on by him of investment business,

   or any condition imposed under section 50 above;

   (b) that any person has contravened any such provision
   there is a reasonable likelihood that the contravention will continue or be repeated; or

   (c) that any person has contravened any such provision or condition and that there are steps that could be taken for remedying the contravention,

the court may grant an injunction restraining the contravention or, in Scotland, an interdict prohibiting the contravention or, as the case may be, make an order requiring that person and any other person who appears to the court to have been knowingly concerned in the contravention to take such steps as the court may direct to remedy it.

(2) No application shall be made by the Secretary of State under subsection (1) above in respect of any such rules as are mentioned in subsection (1)(a)(iv) above unless it appears to him that the organisation, body, exchange or clearing house is unable or unwilling to take appropriate steps to restrain the contravention or to require the person concerned to take such steps as are mentioned in subsection (1) above.

(3) The court may, on the application of the Secretary of State, make an order under subsection (4) below or, in relation to Scotland, under subsection (5) below if satisfied—

   (a) that profits have accrued to any person as a result of his contravention of any provision or condition mentioned in subsection (1)(a) above; or
   (b) that one or more investors have suffered loss or been otherwise adversely affected as a result of that contravention.

(4) The court may under this subsection order the person concerned to pay into

court, or appoint a receiver to recover from him, such sum as appears to the court to be just having regard—

(a) in a case within paragraph (a) of subsection (3) above, to the profits appearing to the court to have accrued;

(b) in a case within paragraph (b) of that subsection, to the extent of the loss or other adverse effect; or

(c) in a case within both paragraphs (a) and (b) of that subsection, to the profits and to the extent of the loss or other adverse effect.

(5) The court may under this subsection order the person concerned to pay to the applicant such sum as appears to the court to be just having regard to the considerations mentioned in paragraphs (a) to (c) of subsection (4) above.

(6) Any amount paid into court by or recovered from a person in pursuance of an order under subsection (4) or (5) above shall be paid out to such person or distributed among such persons as the court may direct, being a person or persons appearing to the court to have entered into transactions with that person as a result of which the profits mentioned in paragraph (a) of subsection (3) above have accrued to him or the loss or adverse effect mentioned in paragraph (b) of that subsection has been suffered.

(7) On an application under subsection (3) above the court may require the person concerned to furnish it with such accounts or other information as it may require for establishing whether any and, if so, what profits have accrued to him as mentioned in paragraph (a) of that subsection and for determining how any amounts are to be paid or distributed under subsection (6) above; and the court may require any such accounts or other information to be verified in such manner as it may direct.

(8) The jurisdiction conferred by this section shall be exercisable by the High Court and the Court of Session.

(9) Nothing in this section affects the right of any person other than the Secretary of State to bring proceedings in respect of the matters to which this section applies.

62. Actions for damages

(1) Without prejudice to section 61 above, a contravention of—

(a) any rules or regulations made under this Chapter;
(b) any conditions imposed under section 50 above;
(c) any requirements imposed by an order under section 53(3) above;
(d) the duty imposed by section 59(6) above,

shall be actionable at the suit of a person who suffers loss as a result of the contravention subject to the defences and other incidents applying to actions for breach of statutory duty.

(2) Subsection (1) applies also to a contravention by a member of a recognised self-regulating organisation or a person certified by a recognised professional body of any rules of the organisation or body relating to a matter in respect of which rules or regulations have been or could be made under this Chapter in relation to an authorised person who is not such a member or so certified.

(3) Subsection (1) above does not apply—

(a) to a contravention of rules made under section 49 or conditions imposed under section 50 in connection with an alteration of the requirements of those rules; or

(b) by virtue of subsection (2) above to a contravention of rules relating to a matter in respect of which rules have been or could be made under section 49.

(4) A person shall not be guilty of an offence by reason of any contravention to which this subsection (1) above applies or of a contravention of rules made under section 49 above or such conditions as are mentioned in subsection (3)(a) above and no such contravention shall invalidate any transaction.

63. Gaming contracts

(1) No contract to which this section applies shall be void or unenforceable by reason of—

(a) section 18 of the Gaming Act 1845, section 1 of the Gaming Act 1892 or any corresponding provisions in force in Northern Ireland; or

(b) any rule of the law of Scotland whereby a contract by way of gaming or wagering is not legally enforceable.

(2) This section applies to any contract entered into by either or each party by way of business and the making or performance of which by either party constitutes an activity which falls within paragraph 12 of Schedule 1 to this Act or would do so apart from Parts III and IV of that Schedule.

CHAPTER VI

POWERS OF INTERVENTION

64. Scope of powers

(1) The powers conferred on the Secretary of State by this Chapter shall be exercisable in relation to any authorised person or, except in the case of the power conferred by section 65 below, any appointed representative of his if it appears to the Secretary of State—

(a) that the exercise of the powers is desirable for the protection of investors;

(b) that the authorised person is not fit to carry on investment business of a particular kind or to the extent to which he is carrying it on or proposing to carry it on; or

(c) that the authorised person has contravened any provision of this Act or of any rules or regulations made under it or, in purported compliance with any such provision, has furnished the Secretary of State with false, inaccurate or misleading information or has contravened any prohibition or requirement imposed under this Act.

(2) For the purposes of subsection (1)(b) above the Secretary of State may take into account any matters that could be taken into account in deciding whether to withdraw or suspend an authorisation under Chapter III of this Part of this Act.

(3) The powers conferred by this Chapter may be exercised in relation to a person whose authorisation is suspended under section 28 above or who is the

subject of a direction under section 33(1)(b) above and references in this Chapter to an authorised person shall be construed accordingly.

(4)   The powers conferred by this Chapter shall not be exercisable in relation to—

   (a)   an authorised person who is a member of a recognised self-regulating organisation or a person certified by a recognised professional body and is subject to the rules of such an organisation or body in carrying on all the investment business carried on by him; or

   (b)   an appointed representative whose principal or, in the case of such a representative with more than one principal, each of whose principals is a member of such an organisation or body and is subject to the rules of such an organisation or body in carrying on the investment business in respect of which his principal or each of his principals has accepted responsibility for his activities;

except that the powers conferred by virtue of section 67(1)(b) below may on any of the grounds specified in subsection (1) above be exercised in relation to such a person at the request of any such organisation of which he or, in the case of an appointed representative, any of his principals is a member or any such body by which he or, as the case may be, any of his principals is certified.

65.   Restriction of business

(1)   The Secretary of State may prohibit an authorised person from—

   (a)   entering into transactions of any specified kind or entering into them except in specified circumstances or to a specified extent;

   (b)   soliciting business from persons of a specified kind or otherwise than from such persons or in a specified country or territory outside the United Kingdom;

   (c)   carrying on business in a specified manner or otherwise than in a specified manner.

(2)   A prohibition under this section may relate to transactions entered into in connection with or for the purposes of investment business or to other business which is carried on in connection with or for the purposes of investment business.

66.   Restriction on dealing with assets

(1)   The Secretary of State may prohibit an authorised person or appointed representative from disposing of or otherwise dealing with any assets, or any specified assets, of that person or, as the case may be, representative in any specified manner or otherwise than in a specified manner.

(2)   A prohibition under this section may relate to assets outside the United Kingdom.

67.   Vesting of assets in trustee

(1)   The Secretary of State may impose a requirement that all assets, or all assets of any specified class or description, which at any time while the requirement is in force—

   (a)   belong to an authorised person or appointed representative; or

   (b)   belong to investors and are held by or to the order of an authorised person or appointed representative, shall be transferred to and held by a trustee approved by the Secretary of State.

(2)   Where a requirement is imposed under this section it shall be the duty of the authorised person or, as the case may be, appointed representative to transfer the assets to the trustee and to give him all such other assistance as may be required to enable him to discharge his functions in accordance with the requirement.

(3)   Assets held by a trustee in accordance with a requirement under this section shall not be released or dealt with except in accordance with directions given by the Secretary of State or in such circumstances as may be specified by him.

(4)   A requirement under this section may relate to assets outside the United Kingdom.

68.   Maintenance of assets in United Kingdom

(1)   The Secretary of State may require an authorised person or appointed representative to maintain in the United Kingdom assets of such value as appears to the Secretary of State to be desirable with a view to ensuring that the authorised person or, as the case may be, appointed representative will be able to meet his liabilities in respect of investment business carried on by him in the United Kingdom.

(2)   The Secretary of State may direct that for the purposes of any requirement under this section assets of any specified class or description shall or shall not be taken into account.

69.   Rescission and variation

The Secretary of State may, either of his own motion or on the application of a person on whom a prohibition or requirement has been imposed under this Chapter, rescind or vary the prohibition or requirement if it appears to the Secretary of State that it is no longer necessary for the prohibition or requirement to take effect or continue in force or, as the case may be, that it should take effect or continue in force in a different form.

70.   Notices

(1)   The power to impose, rescind or vary a prohibition or requirement under this Chapter shall be exercisable by written notice served by the Secretary of State on the person concerned; and any such notice shall take effect on such date as is specified in the notice.

(2)   If the Secretary of State refuses to rescind or vary a prohibition or requirement on the application of the person to whom it applies he shall serve that person with a written notice of the refusal.

(3)   A notice imposing a prohibition or requirement, or varying a prohibition or requirement otherwise than on the application of the person to whom it applies, and a notice under subsection (2) above shall state the reasons for which the prohibition or requirement was imposed or varied or, as the case may be, why the application was refused.

(4)   Where the reasons stated in a notice to which subsection (3) above applies relate specifically to matters which—

   (a)   refer to a person identified in the notice other than the person to whom the prohibition or requirement applies; and

(b) are in the opinion of the Secretary of State prejudicial to that person in any office or employment,

the Secretary of State shall, unless he considers it impracticable to do so, serve a copy of the notice on that person.

(5) A notice to which subsection (3) above applies shall give particulars of the right to have the case referred to the Tribunal under Chapter IX of this Part of this Act.

(6) The Secretary of State may give public notice of any prohibition or requirement imposed by him under this Chapter and of the rescission and variation of any such prohibition or requirement; and any such notice may, if the Secretary of State thinks fit, include a statement of the reasons for which the prohibition or requirement was imposed, rescinded or varied.

71. Breach of prohibition or requirement
(1) Sections 60, 61, and 62 above shall have effect in relation to a contravention of a prohibition or requirement imposed under this Chapter as they have effect in relation to any such contravention as is mentioned in those sections.

(2) In its application by virtue of this section, section 62(2) shall have effect with the substitution—

(a) for the reference to the rules of a recognised self-regulating organisation of a reference to any prohibition or requirement imposed by it in the exercise of powers for purposes corresponding to those of this Chapter; and

(b) for the reference to the rules of a recognised professional body of a reference to any prohibition or requirement imposed in the exercise of powers for such purposes by that body or by any other body or person having functions in respect of the enforcement of the recognised professional body's rules relating to the carrying on of investment business.

(3) This section is without prejudice to any equitable remedy available in respect of property which by virtue of a requirement under section 67 above is subject to a trust.

CHAPTER VII

WINDING UP AND ADMINISTRATION ORDERS

72. Winding up orders
(1) On a petition presented by the Secretary of State by virtue of this section, the court having jurisdiction under the Insolvency Act 1986 may wind up an authorised person or appointed representative to whom this subsection applies if—

(a) the person is unable to pay his debts within the meaning of section 123 or, as the case may be , section 221 of that Act; or

(b) the court is of the opinion that it is just and equitable that the person should be wound up.

(2) Subsection (1) above applies to any authorised person, any person whose authorisation is suspended under section 28 above or who is the subject of a

direction under section 33(1)(b) above or any appointed representative who is—

- (a) a company within the meaning of section 735 of the Companies Act 1985;
- (b) an unregistered company within the meaning of section 220 of the Insolvency Act 1986;
- (c) an oversea company within the meaning of section 744 of the Companies Act 1985; or
- (d) a partnership.

(3) For the purposes of a petition under subsection (1) above a person who defaults in an obligation to pay any sum due and payable under any investment agreement shall be deemed to be unable to pay his debts.

(4) Where a petition is presented under subsection (1) above for the winding up of a partnership on the ground mentioned in paragraph (b) of subsection (1) above or, in Scotland, on a ground mentioned in paragraph (a) or (b) of that subsection, the court shall have jurisdiction and the Insolvency Act 1986 shall have effect as if the partnership were an unregistered company within the meaning of section 220 of that Act.

(5) The Secretary of State shall not present a petition under subsection (1) above for the winding up of any person who is an authorised person by virtue of membership of a recognised self-regulating organisation or certification by a recognised professional body and is subject to the rules of the organisation or body in the carrying on of all investment business carried on by him, unless that organisation or body has consented to his doing so.

73. Winding up orders: Northern Ireland

(1) On a petition presented by the Secretary of State by virtue of this section, the High Court in Northern Ireland may wind up an authorised person or appointed representative to whom this subsection applies if—

- (a) the person is unable to pay his debts within the meaning of Article 480 or, as the case may be, Article 616 of the Companies (Northern Ireland) Order 1986; or
- (b) the court is of the opinion that it is just and equitable that the person should be wound up.

(2) Subsection (1) above applies to any authorised person, any person whose authorisation is suspended under section 28 above or who is the subject of a direction under section 33(1)(b) above or any appointed representative who is—

- (a) a company within the meaning of Article 3 of the Companies (Northern Ireland) Order 1986;
- (b) an unregistered company within the meaning of Article 615 of that Order; or
- (c) a Part XXIII company within the meaning of Article 2 of that Order; or
- (d) a partnership.

(3) For the purposes of a petition under subsection (1) above a person who defaults in an obligation to pay any sum due and payable under any investment agreement shall be deemed to be unable to pay his debts.

(4) Where a petition is presented under subsection (1) above for the winding up of a partnership on the ground mentioned in paragraph (b) of subsection (1) above, the High Court in Northern Ireland shall have jurisdiction and the Companies

(Northern Ireland) Order 1986 shall have effect as if the partnership were an unregistered company within the meaning of Article 615 of that Order.

(5)   The Secretary of State shall not present a petition under subsection (1) above for the winding up of any person who is an authorised person by virtue of membership of a recognised self-regulating organisation or certification by a recognised professional body and is subject to the rules of the organisation or body in the carrying on of all investment business carried on by him, unless that organisation or body has consented to his doing so.

74.   Administration orders

A petition may be presented under section 9 of the Insolvency Act 1986 (applications for administration orders) in relation to a company to which section 8 of that Act applies which is an authorised person, a person whose authorisation is suspended under section 28 above or who is the subject of a direction under section 33(1)(b) above or an appointed representative—

(a)   in the case of an authorised person who is an authorised person by virtue of membership of a recognised self-regulating organisation or certification by a recognised professional body, by that organisation or body; and

(b)   in the case of an appointed representative or an authorised person who is not authorised as mentioned in paragraph (a) above or is so authorised but is not subject to the rules of the organisation or body in question in the carrying on of all investment business carried on by him, by the Secretary of State.

CHAPTER VIII

COLLECTIVE INVESTMENT SCHEMES

Preliminary

75.   Interpretation

(1)   In this Act 'a collective investment scheme' means, subject to the provisions of this section, any arrangements with respect to property of any description, including money, the purpose or effect of which is to enable persons taking part in the arrangements (whether by becoming owners of the property or any part of it or otherwise) to participate in or receive profits or income arising from the acquisition, holding, management or disposal of the property or sums paid out of such profits or income.

(2)   The arrangements must be such that the persons who are to participate as mentioned in subsection (1) above (in this Act referred to as 'participants') do not have day to day control over the management of the property in question, whether or not they have the right to be consulted or to give directions; and the arrangements must also have either or both of the characteristics mentioned in subsection (3) below.

(3)   Those characteristics are—

(a)   that the contributions of the participants and the profits or income out of which payments are to be made to them are pooled;

(b)   that the property in question is managed as a whole by or on behalf of the operator of the scheme.

(4)   Where any arrangements provide for such pooling as is mentioned in paragraph (a) of subsection (3) above in relation to separate parts of the property in question, the arrangements shall not be regarded as constituting a single collective investment scheme unless the participants are entitled to exchange rights in one part for rights in another.

(5)   Arrangements are not a collective investment scheme if—

(a)   the property to which the arrangements relate (other than cash awaiting investment) consists of investments falling within any of paragraphs 1 to 5, 6 (so far as relating to units in authorised unit trust schemes and recognised schemes) and 10 of Schedule 1 to this Act;

(b)   each participant is the owner of a part of that property and entitled to withdraw it at any time; and

(c)   the arrangements do not have the characteristics mentioned in paragraph (a) of subsection (3) above and have those mentioned in paragraph (b) of that subsection only because the parts of the property belonging to different participants are not bought and sold separately except where a person becomes or ceases to be a participant.

(6)   The following are not collective investment schemes—

(a)   arrangements operated by a person otherwise than by way of business;

(b)   arrangements where each of the participants carries on a business other than investment business and enters into the arrangements for commercial purposes related to that business;

(c)   arrangements where each of the participants is a body corporate in the same group as the operator;

(d)   arrangements where—

(i)   each of the participants is a bona fide employee or former employee (or the wife, husband, widow, widower, child or step-child under the age of eighteen of such an employee or former employee) of a body corporate in the same group as the operator; and

(ii)   the property to which the arrangements relate consists of shares or debentures (as defined in paragraph 20(4) of Schedule 1 to this Act) in or of a member of that group;

(e)   arrangements where the receipt of the participants' contributions constitutes the acceptance of deposits in the course of a business which is a deposit-taking business for the purposes of the Banking Act 1979 and does not constitute a transaction prescribed for the purposes of section 2 of that Act by regulations made by the Treasury;

(f)   franchise arrangements, that is to say, arrangements under which a person earns profits or income by exploiting a right conferred by the arrangements to use a trade name or design or other intellectual property or the good-will attached to it;

(g)   arrangements the predominant purpose of which is to enable persons participating in them to share in the use or enjoyment of a particular property or to make its use or enjoyment available gratuitously to other persons;

(h)   arrangements under which the rights or interests of the participants are investments falling within paragraph 5 of Schedule 1 to this Act;

(i)   arrangements the purpose of which is the provision of clearing services and which are operated by an authorised person, a recognised clearing house or a recognised investment exchange;

(j)   contracts of insurance;

(h) occupational pension schemes.

(7) No body incorporated under the law of, or of any part of, the United Kingdom relating to building societies or industrial and provident societies or registered under any such law relating to friendly societies, and no other body corporate other than an open-ended investment company, shall be regarded as constituting a collective investment scheme.

(8) In this Act—

'a unit trust scheme' means a collective investment scheme under which the property in question is held on trust for the participants;

'an open-ended investment company' means a collective investment scheme under which—

(a) the property in question belongs beneficially to, and is managed by or on behalf of, a body corporate having as its purpose the investment of its funds with the aim of spreading investment risk and giving its members the benefit of the results of the management of those funds by or on behalf of that body; and

(b) the rights of the participants are represented by shares in or securities of that body which—

    (i) the participants are entitled to have redeemed or repurchased, or which (otherwise than under Chapter VII of Part V of the Companies Act 1985 or the corresponding Northern Ireland provision) are redeemed or repurchased from them by, or out of funds provided by, that body; or

    (ii) the body ensures can be sold by the participants on an investment exchange at a price related to the value of the property to which they relate;

'trustee', in relation to a unit trust scheme, means the person holding the property in question on trust for the participants and, in relation to a collective investment scheme constituted under the law of a country or territory outside the United Kingdom, means any person who (whether or not under a trust) is entrusted with the custody of the property in question;

'units' means the rights or interests (however described) of the participants in a collective investment scheme;

'the operator', in relation to a unit trust scheme with a separate trustee, means the manager and, in relation to an open-ended investment company, means that company.

(9) If an order under section 2 above amends the references to a collective investment scheme in Schedule 1 to this Act it may also amend the provisions of this section.

Promotion of schemes

76. Restrictions on promotion

(1) Subject to subsections (2), (3) and (4) below, an authorised person shall not—

(a) issue or cause to be issued in the United Kingdom any advertisement inviting persons to become or offer to become participants in a collective investment scheme or containing information calculated to lead directly or indirectly to persons becoming or offering to become participants in such a scheme; or

(b) advise or procure any person in the United Kingdom to become or offer to become a participant in such a scheme,

unless the scheme is an authorised unit trust scheme or a recognised scheme under the following provisions of this Chapter.

(2) Subsection (1) above shall not apply if the advertisement is issued to or the person mentioned in paragraph (b) of that subsection is—

(a) an authorised person; or

(b) a person whose ordinary business involves the acquisition and disposal of property of the same kind as the property, or a substantial part of the property, to which the scheme relates.

(3) Subsection (1) above shall not apply to anything done in accordance with regulations made by the Secretary of State for the purpose of exempting from that subsection the promotion otherwise than to the general public of schemes of such descriptions as are specified in the regulations.

(4) The Secretary of State may by regulations make provision for exempting single property schemes from subsection (1) above.

(5) For the purposes of subsection (4) above a single property scheme is a scheme which has the characteristics mentioned in subsection (6) below and satisfies such other requirements as are specified in the regulations conferring the exemption.

(6) The characteristics referred to above are—

(a) that the property subject to the scheme (apart from cash or other assets held for management purposes) consists of—

(i) a single building (or a single building with ancillary buildings) managed by or on behalf of the operator of the scheme; or

(ii) a group of adjacent or contiguous buildings managed by him or on his behalf as a single enterprise,

with or without ancillary land and with or without furniture, fittings or other contents of the building or buildings in question; and

(b) that the units of the participants in the scheme are either dealt in on a recognised investment exchange or offered on terms such that any agreement for their acquisition is conditional on their admission to dealings on such an exchange.

(7) Regulations under subsection (4) above may contain such supplementary and transitional provisions as the Secretary of State thinks necessary and may also contain provisions imposing obligations or liabilities on the operator and trustee (if any) of an exempted scheme, including, to such extent as he thinks appropriate, provisions for purposes corresponding to those for which provision can be made under section 85 below in relation to authorised unit trust schemes.

77. Applications for authorisation

(1)   Any application for an order declaring a unit trust scheme to be an authorised unit trust scheme shall be made by the manager and trustee, or proposed manager and trustee, of the scheme and the manager and trustee shall be different persons.

(2)   Any such application—

(a)   shall be made in such manner as the Secretary of State may direct; and

(b)   shall contain or be accompanied by such information as he may reasonably require for the purpose of determining the application.

(3)   At any time after receiving an application and before determining it the Secretary of State may require the applicant to furnish additional information.

(4)   The directions and requirements given or imposed under subsections (2) and (3) above may differ as between different applications.

(5)   Any information to be furnished to the Secretary of State under this section shall, if he so requires, be in such form or verified in such manner as he may specify.

78. Authorisation orders

(1)   The Secretary of State may, on an application duly made in accordance with section 77 above and after being furnished with all such information as he may require under that section, make an order declaring a unit trust scheme to be an authorised unit trust scheme for the purposes of this Act if—

(a)   it appears to him that the scheme complies with the requirements of the regulations made under section 81 below and that the following provisions of this section are satisfied; and

(b)   he has been furnished with a copy of the trust deed and a certificate signed by a solicitor to the effect that it complies with such of those requirements as relate to its contents.

(2)   The manager and the trustee must be persons who are independent of each other.

(3)   The manager and the trustee must each be a body corporate incorporated in the United Kingdom or another member State, the affairs of each must be administered in the country in which it is incorporated, each must have a place of business in the United Kingdom and, if the manager is incorporated in another member State, the scheme must not be one which satisfies the requirements prescribed for the purposes of section 86 below.

(4)   The manager and the trustee must each be an authorised person and neither must be prohibited from acting as manager or trustee, as the case may be, by or under rules under section 48 above, by or under the rules of any recognised self-regulating organisation of which the manager or trustee is a member or by a prohibition imposed under section 65 above.

(5)   The name of the scheme must not be undesirable or misleading; and the purposes of the scheme must be reasonably capable of being successfully carried into effect.

(6)   The participants must be entitled to have their units redeemed in accordance with the scheme at a price related to the net value of the property to which the

units relate and determined in accordance with the scheme; but a scheme shall be treated as complying with this subsection if it requires the manager to ensure that a participant is able to sell his units on an investment exchange at a price not significantly different from that mentioned in this subsection.

(7)   The Secretary of State shall inform the applicants of his decision on the application not later than six months after the date on which the application was received.

(8)   On making an order under this section the Secretary of State may issue a certificate to the effect that the scheme complies with the conditions necessary for it to enjoy the rights conferred by any relevant Community instrument.

79.   Revocation of authorisation

(1)   The Secretary of State may revoke an order declaring a unit trust scheme to be an authorised unit trust scheme if it appears to him—

   (a)   that any of the requirements for the making of the order are no longer satisfied;

   (b)   that it is undesirable in the interests of the participants or potential participants that the scheme should continue to be authorised; or

   (c)   without prejudice to paragraph (b) above, that the manager or trustee of the scheme has contravened any provision of this Act or any rules or regulations made under it or, in purported compliance with any such provision, has furnished the Secretary of State with false, inaccurate or misleading information or has contravened any prohibition or requirement imposed under this Act.

(2)   For the purposes of subsection (1)(b) above the Secretary of State may take into account any matter relating to the scheme, the manager or trustee, a director or controller of the manager or trustee or any person employed by or associated with the manager or trustee in connection with the scheme.

(3)   In the case of a manager or trustee who is a member of a recognised self-regulating organisation the rules, prohibitions and requirements referred to in subsection (1)(c) above include the rules of that organisation and any prohibition or requirement imposed by virtue of those rules.

(4)   The Secretary of State may revoke an order declaring a unit trust scheme to be an authorised unit trust scheme at the request of the manager or trustee of the scheme; but he may refuse to do so if he considers that any matter concerning the scheme should be investigated as a preliminary to a decision on the question whether the order should be revoked or that revocation would not be in the interests of the participants or would be incompatible with a Community obligation.

80.   Representations against refusal or revocation

(1)   Where the Secretary of State proposes—

   (a)   to refuse an application for an order under section 78 above; or

   (b)   to revoke such an order otherwise than at the request of the manager or trustee of the scheme,

he shall give the applicants or, as the case may be, the manager and trustee of the scheme written notice of his intention to do so, stating the reasons for which he proposes to act and giving particulars of the rights conferred by subsection (2) below.

(2)   A person on whom a notice is served under subsection (1) above may, within twenty-one days of the date of service, make written representations to the Secretary of State and, if desired, oral representations to a person appointed for that purpose by the Secretary of State.

(3)   The Secretary of State shall have regard to any representations made in accordance with subsection (2) above in determining whether to refuse the application or revoke the order, as the case may be.

81.   Constitution and management

(1)   The Secretary of State may make regulations as to the constitution and management of authorised unit trust schemes, the powers and duties of the manager and trustee of any such scheme and the rights and obligations of the participants in any such scheme.

(2)   Without prejudice to the generality of subsection (1) above, regulations under this section may make provision—

(a)   as to the issue and redemption of the units under the scheme;
(b)   as to the expenses of the scheme and the means of meeting them;
(c)   for the appointment, removal, powers and duties of an auditor for the scheme;
(d)   for restricting or regulating the investment and borrowing powers exercisable in relation to the scheme;
(e)   requiring the keeping of records with respect to the transactions and financial position of the scheme and for the inspection of those records;
(f)   requiring the preparation of periodical reports with respect to the scheme and the furnishing of those reports to the participants and to the Secretary of State; and
(g)   with respect to the amendment of the scheme.

(3)   Regulations under this section may make provision as to the contents of the trust deed, including provision requiring any of the matters mentioned in subsection (2) above to be dealt with in the deed; but regulations under this section shall be binding on the manager, trustee and participants independently of the contents of the deed and, in the case of the participants, shall have effect as if contained in it.

(4)   Regulations under this section shall not impose limits on the remuneration payable to the manager of a scheme.

(5)   Regulations under this section may contain such incidental and transitional provisions as the Secretary of State thinks necessary or expedient.

82.   Alteration of schemes and changes of manager or trustee

(1)   The manager of an authorised unit trust scheme shall give written notice to the Secretary of State of—

(a)   any proposed alteration to the scheme; and
(b)   any proposal to replace the trustee of the scheme;

and any notice given in respect of a proposed alteration involving a change in the trust deed shall be accompanied by a certificate signed by a solicitor to the effect that the change will not affect the compliance of the deed with the regulations made under section 81 above.

(2)   The trustee of an authorised unit trust scheme shall give written notice to the Secretary of State of any proposal to replace the manager of the scheme.

(3)   Effect shall not be given to any such proposal unless—

(a)   the Secretary of State has given his approval to the proposal; or
(b)   one month has elapsed since the date on which the notice was given under subsection (1) or (2) above without the Secretary of State having notified the manager or trustee that the proposal is not approved.

(4)   Neither the manager nor the trustee of an authorised unit trust scheme shall be replaced except by persons who satisfy the requirements of section 78(2) to (4) above.

83.   Restrictions on activities of manager

(1)   The manager of an authorised unit trust scheme shall not engage in any activities other than those mentioned in subsection (2) below.

(2)   Those activities are—

(a)   acting as manager of—

(i) a unit trust scheme;
(ii) an open-ended investment company or any other body corporate whose business consists of investing its funds with the aim of spreading investment risk and giving its members the benefit of the results of the management of its funds by or on behalf of that body; or
(iii) any other collective investment scheme under which the contributions of the participants and the profits or income out of which payments are to be made to them are pooled;

(b)   activities for the purposes of or in connection with those mentioned in paragraph (a) above.

(3)   A prohibition under section 65 above may prohibit the manager of an authorised unit trust scheme from inviting persons in any specified country or territory outside the United Kingdom to become participants in the scheme.

84.   Avoidance of exclusion clauses

Any provision of the trust deed of an authorised unit trust scheme shall be void in so far as it would have the effect of exempting the manager or trustee from liability for any failure to exercise due care and diligence in the discharge of his functions in respect of the scheme.

85.   Publication of scheme particulars

(1)   The Secretary of State may make regulations requiring the manager of an authorised unit trust scheme to submit to him and publish or make available to the public on request a document ('scheme particulars') containing information about the scheme and complying with such requirements as are specified in the regulations.

(2)   Regulations under this section may require the manager of an authorised unit trust scheme to submit and publish or make available revised or further scheme particulars if—

(a) there is a significant change affecting any matter contained in such particulars previously published or made available whose inclusion was required by the regulations; or

(b) a significant new matter arises the inclusion of information in respect of which would have been required in previous particulars if it had arisen when those particulars were prepared.

(3) Regulations under this section may provide for the payment, by the person or persons who in accordance with the regulations are treated as responsible for any scheme particulars, of compensation to any person who has become or agreed to become a participant in the scheme and suffered loss as a result of any untrue or misleading statement in the particulars or the omission from them of any matter required by the regulations to be included.

(4) Regulations under this section shall not affect any liability which any person may incur apart from the regulations.

Recognition of overseas schemes

86. Schemes constituted in other member States

(1) Subject to subsection (2) below, a collective investment scheme constituted in a member State other than the United Kingdom is a recognised scheme if it satisfies such requirements as are prescribed for the purposes of this section.

(2) Not less than two months before inviting persons in the United Kingdom to become participants in the scheme the operator of the scheme shall give written notice to the Secretary of State of his intention to do so, specifying the manner in which the invitation is to be made; and the scheme shall not be a recognised scheme by virtue of this section if within two months of receiving the notice the Secretary of State notifies—

(a) the operator of the scheme; and

(b) the authorities of the State in question who are responsible for the authorisation of collective investment schemes,

that the manner in which the invitation is to be made does not comply with the law in force in the United Kingdom.

(3) The notice to be given to the Secretary of State under subsection (2) above—

(a) shall be accompanied by a certificate from the authorities mentioned in subsection (2)(b) above to the effect that the scheme complies with the conditions necessary for it to enjoy the rights conferred by any relevant Community instrument;

(b) shall contain the address of a place in the United Kingdom for the service on the operator of notices or other documents required or authorised to be served on him under this Act; and

(c) shall contain or be accompanied by such other information and documents as may be prescribed.

(4) A notice given by the Secretary of State under subsection (2) above shall give the reasons for which he considers that the law in force in the United Kingdom will not be complied with and give particulars of the rights conferred by subsection (5) below.

(5)   A person on whom a notice is served by the Secretary of State under subsection (2) above may, within twenty-one days of the date of service, make written representations to the Secretary of State and, if desired, oral representations to a person appointed for that purpose by the Secretary of State.

(6)   The Secretary of State may in the light of any representations made in accordance with subsection (5) above withdraw his notice and in that event the scheme shall be a recognised scheme from the date on which the notice is withdrawn.

(7)   Rules under section 48 above shall not apply to investment business in respect of which the operator or trustee of a scheme recognised under this section is an authorised person by virtue of section 24 above except so far as they make provision as respects—

  (a)   procuring persons to become participants in the scheme and advising persons on the scheme and the exercise of the rights conferred by it;
  (b)   matters incidental to those mentioned in paragraph (a) above.

(8)   For the purposes of this section a collective investment scheme is constituted in a member State if—

  (a)   it is constituted under the law of that State by a contract or under a trust and is managed by a body corporate incorporated under that law; or
  (b)   it takes the form of an open-ended investment company incorporated under that law.

(9)   If the operator of a scheme recognised under this section gives written notice to the Secretary of State stating that he desires the scheme no longer to be recognised under this section it shall cease to be so recognised when the notice is given.

87. Schemes authorised in designated countries or territories

(1)   Subject to subsection (3) below, a collective investment scheme which is not a recognised scheme by virtue of section 86 above but is managed in and authorised under the law of a country or territory outside the United Kingdom is a recognised scheme if—

  (a)   that country or territory is designated for the purposes of this section by an order made by the Secretary of State; and
  (b)   the scheme is of a class specified by the order.

(2)   The Secretary of State shall not make an order designating any country or territory for the purposes of this section unless he is satisfied that the law under which collective investment schemes of the class to be specified by the order are authorised and supervised in that country or territory affords to investors in the United Kingdom protection at least equivalent to that provided for them by this Chapter in the case of an authorised unit trust scheme.

(3)   A scheme shall not be recognised by virtue of this section unless the operator of the scheme gives written notice to the Secretary of State that he wishes it to be recognised; and the scheme shall not be recognised if within such period from receiving the notice as may be prescribed the Secretary of State notifies the operator that the scheme is not to be recognised.

(4)   The notice given by the operator under subsection (3) above—

(a) shall contain the address of a place in the United Kingdom for the service on the operator of notices or other documents required or authorised to be served on him under this Act; and

(b) shall contain or be accompanied by such information and documents as may be prescribed.

(5)   Section 85 above shall have effect in relation to a scheme recognised under this section as it has effect in relation to an authorised unit trust scheme, taking references to the manager as references to the operator and, in the case of an operator who is not an authorised person, references to publishing particulars as references to causing them to be published; and regulations made by virtue of this subsection may make provision whereby compliance with any requirements imposed by or under the law of a country or territory designated under this section is treated as compliance with any requirement of the regulations.

(6)   An order under subsection (1) above may contain such transitional provisions as the Secretary of State thinks necessary or expedient and shall be subject to annulment in pursuance of a resolution of either House of Parliament.

88.   Other overseas schemes

(1)   The Secretary of State may, on the application of the operator of a scheme which—

(a) is managed in a country or territory outside the United Kingdom; but

(b) does not satisfy the requirements mentioned in section 86(1) above and in relation to which there is no relevant order under section 87(1) above,

make an order declaring the scheme to be a recognised scheme if it appears to him that it affords adequate protection to the participants, makes adequate provision for the matters dealt with by regulations under section 81 above and satisfies the following provisions of this section.

(2)   The operator must be a body corporate or the scheme must take the form of an open-ended investment company.

(3)   Subject to subsection (4) below, the operator and the trustee, if any, must be fit and proper persons to act as operator or, as the case may be, as trustee; and for that purpose the Secretary of State may take into account any matter relating to—

(a) any person who is or will be employed by or associated with the operator or trustee for the purposes of the scheme;

(b) any director or controller of the operator or trustee;

(c) any other body corporate in the same group as the operator or trustee and any director or controller of any such other body.

(4)   Subsection (3) above does not apply to an operator or trustee who is an authorised person and not prohibited from acting as operator or trustee, as the case may be, by or under rules under section 48 above, by or under the rules of any recognised self-regulating organisation of which he is a member or by any prohibition imposed under section 65 above.

(5)   If the operator is not an authorised person he must have a representative in the United Kingdom who is an authorised person and has power to act generally for the operator and to accept service of notices and other documents on his behalf.

(6)   The name of the scheme must not be undesirable or misleading; and the

purposes of the scheme must be reasonably capable of being successfully carried into effect.

(7)   The participants must be entitled to have their units redeemed in accordance with the scheme at a price related to the net value of the property to which the units relate and determined in accordance with the scheme; but a scheme shall be treated as complying with this subsection if it requires the operator to ensure that a participant is able to sell his units on an investment exchange at a price not significantly different from that mentioned in this subsection.

(8)   Subsections (2) to (5) of section 77 above shall apply also to an application under this section.

(9)   So much of section 82 above as applies to an alteration of the scheme shall apply also to a scheme recognised under this section, taking references to the manager as references to the operator and with the omission of the requirement relating to the solicitor's certificate; and if the operator or trustee of any such scheme is to be replaced the operator or, as the case may be, the trustee, or in either case the person who is to replace him, shall give at least one month's notice to the Secretary of State.

(10)   Section 85 above shall have effect in relation to a scheme recognised under this section as it has effect in relation to an authorised unit trust scheme, taking references to the manager as references to the operator and, in the case of an operator who is not an authorised person, references to publishing particulars as references to causing them to be published.

89.   Refusal and revocation of recognition
(1)   The Secretary of State may at any time direct that a scheme shall cease to be recognised by virtue of section 87 above or revoke an order under section 88 above if it appears to him—

(a)   that it is undesirable in the interests of the participants or potential participants in the United Kingdom that the scheme should continue to be recognised;

(b)   without prejudice to paragraph (a) above, that the operator or trustee of the scheme has contravened any provision of this Act or any rules or regulations made under it or, in purported compliance with any such provision, has furnished the Secretary of State with false, inaccurate or misleading information or has contravened any prohibition or requirement imposed under this Act; or

(c)   in the case of an order under section 88 that any of the requirements for the making of the order are no longer satisfied.

(2)   For the purposes of subsection (1)(a) above the Secretary of State may take into account any matter relating to the scheme the operator or trustee, a director or controller of the operator or trustee or any person employed by or associated with the operator or trustee in connection with the scheme.

(3)   In the case of an operator or trustee who is a member of a recognised self-regulating organisation the rules, prohibitions and requirements referred to in subsection (1)(b) above include the rules of that organisation and any prohibition or requirement imposed by virtue of those rules.

(4)   The Secretary of State may give such a direction or revoke such an order as is mentioned in subsection (1) above at the request of the operator or trustee of the

scheme; but he may refuse to do so if he considers that any matter concerning the scheme should be investigated as a preliminary to a decision on the question whether the direction should be given or the order revoked or that the direction or revocation would not be in the interests of the participants.

(5)   Where the Secretary of State proposes—

   (a)   to notify the operator of a scheme under section 87(3) above; or
   (b)   to give such a direction or to refuse to make or to revoke such an order as is mentioned in subsection (1) above,

he shall give the operator written notice of his intention to do so, stating the reasons for which he proposes to act and giving particulars of the rights conferred by subsection (6) below.

(6)   A person on whom a notice is served under subsection (5) above may, within twenty-one days of the date of service, make written representations to the Secretary of State and, if desired, oral representations to a person appointed for that purpose by the Secretary of State.

(7)   The Secretary of State shall have regard to any representations made in accordance with subsection (6) above in determining whether to notify the operator, give the direction or refuse to make or revoke the order, as the case may be.

90.   Facilities and information in the United Kingdom

(1)   The Secretary of State may make regulations requiring operators of recognised schemes to maintain in the United Kingdom, or in such part or parts of it as may be specified in the regulations, such facilities as he thinks desirable in the interests of participants and as are specified in the regulations.

(2)   The Secretary of State may by notice in writing require the operator of any recognised scheme to include such explanatory information as is specified in the notice in any investment advertisement issued or caused to be issued by him in the United Kingdom in which the scheme is named.

Powers of intervention

91.   Directions

(1)   If it appears to the Secretary of State —

   (a)   that any of the requirements for the making of an order declaring a scheme to be an authorised unit trust scheme are no longer satisfied;
   (b)   that the exercise of the power conferred by this subsection is desirable in the interests of participants or potential participants in the scheme; or
   (c)   without prejudice to paragraph (b) above, that the manager or trustee of such a scheme has contravened any provision of this Act or any rules or regulations made under it or, in purported compliance with any such provision, has furnished the Secretary of State with false, inaccurate or misleading information or has contravened any prohibition or requirement imposed under this Act.

he may give a direction under subsection (2) below.

(2)   A direction under this subsection may—

   (a)   require the manager of the scheme to cease the issue or redemption, or both the issue and redemption, of units under the scheme on a date specified in the direction until such further date as is specified in that or another direction;

(b) require the manager and trustee of the scheme to wind it up by such date as is specified in the direction or, if no date is specified, as soon as practicable.

(3) The revocation of the order declaring an authorised unit trust scheme to be such a scheme shall not affect the operation of any direction under subsection (2) above which is then in force; and a direction may be given under that subsection in relation to a scheme in the case of which the order declaring it to be an authorised unit trust scheme has been revoked if a direction under that subsection was already in force at the time of revocation.

(4) Sections 60, 61 and 62 above shall have effect in relation to a contravention of a direction under subsection (2) above as they have effect in relation to any such contravention as is mentioned in those sections.

(5) If it appears to the Secretary of State—

(a) that the exercise of the power conferred by this subsection is desirable in the interests of participants or potential participants in a scheme recognised under section 87 or 88 above who are in the United Kingdom;

(b) without prejudice to paragraph (a) above, that the operator of such a scheme has contravened any provision of this Act or any rules or regulations made under it or, in purported compliance with any such provision, has furnished the Secretary of State with false, inaccurate or misleading information or has contravened any prohibition or requirement imposed under this Act; or

(c) that any of the requirements for the recognition of a scheme under section 88 above are no longer satisfied,

he may direct that the scheme shall not be a recognised scheme for a specified period or until the occurrence of a specified event or until specified conditions are complied with.

(6) For the purposes of subsections (1)(b) and (5)(a) above the Secretary of State may take into account any matter relating to the scheme, the manager, operator or trustee, a director or controller of the manager, operator or trustee or any person employed by or associated with the manager, operator or trustee in connection with the scheme.

(7) In the case of a manager, operator or trustee who is a member of a recognised self-regulating organisation the rules, prohibitions and requirements referred to in subsections (1)(c) and (5)(b) above include the rules of that organisation and any prohibition or requirement imposed by virtue of those rules.

(8) The Secretary of State may, either of his own motion or on the application of the manager, trustee or operator of the scheme concerned, withdraw or vary a direction given under this section if it appears to the Secretary of State that it is no longer necessary for the direction to take effect or continue in force or, as the case may be, that it should take effect or continue in force in a different form.

92. Notice of directions

(1) The power to give a direction under section 91 above in relation to a scheme shall be exercisable by written notice served by the Secretary of State on the manager and trustee or, as the case may be, on the operator of the scheme and any such notice shall take effect on such date as is specified in the notice.

(2)   If the Secretary of State refuses to withdraw or vary a direction on the application of the manager, trustee or operator of the scheme concerned he shall serve that person with a written notice of refusal.

(3)   A notice giving a direction, or varying it otherwise than on the application of the manager, trustee or operator concerned, or refusing to withdraw or vary a direction on the application of such a person shall state the reasons for which the direction was given or varied or, as the case may be, why the application was refused.

(4)   The Secretary of State may give public notice of a direction given by him under section 91 above and of any withdrawal or variation of such a direction; and any such notice may, if the Secretary of State thinks fit, include a statement of the reasons for which the direction was given, withdrawn or varied.

93.   Applications to the court

(1)   In any case in which the Secretary of State has power to give a direction under section 91(2) above in relation to an authorised unit trust scheme or, by virtue of subsection (3) of that section, in relation to a scheme which has been such a scheme, he may apply to the court—

(a)   for an order removing the manager or trustee, or both the manager and trustee, of the scheme and replacing either or both of them with a person or persons nominated by him and appearing to him to satisfy the requirements of section 78 above; or

(b)   if it appears to the Secretary of State that no, or no suitable, person satisfying those requirements is available, for an order removing the manager or trustee, or both the manager and trustee, and appointing an authorised person to wind the scheme up.

(2)   On an application under this section the court may make such order as it thinks fit; and the court may, on the application of the Secretary of State, rescind any such order as is mentioned in paragraph (b) of subsection (1) above and substitute such an order as is mentioned in paragraph (a) of that subsection.

(3)   The Secretary of State shall give written notice of the making of an application under this section to the manager and trustee of the scheme concerned and take such steps as he considers appropriate for bringing the making of the application to the attention of the participants.

(4)   The jurisdiction conferred by this section shall be exercisable by the High Court and the Court of Session.

(5)   Section 83 above shall not apply to a manager appointed by an order made on an application under subsection (1)(b) above.

Supplemental

94.   Investigations

(1)   The Secretary of State may appoint one or more competent inspectors to investigate and report on—

(a)   the affairs of, or of the manager or trustee of, any authorised unit trust scheme;

(b)   the affairs of, or of the operator or trustee of, any recognised scheme so far as relating to activities carried on in the United Kingdom; or

(c) the affairs of, or of the operator or trustee of, any other collective investment scheme,

if it appears to the Secretary of State that it is in the interests of the participants to do so or that the matter is of public concern.

(2)   An inspector appointed under subsection (1) above to investigate the affairs of, or of the manager, trustee or operator of, any scheme may also, if he thinks it necessary for the purposes of that investigation, investigate the affairs of, or of the manager, trustee or operator of, any other such scheme as is mentioned in that subsection whose manager, trustee or operator is the same person as the manager, trustee or operator of the first-mentioned scheme.

(3)   Sections 434 to 436 of the Companies Act 1985 (production of documents and evidence to inspectors), except section 435(1)(a) and (b) and (2), shall apply in relation to an inspector appointed under this section as they apply to an inspector appointed under section 431 of that Act but with the modifications specified in subsection (4) below.

(4)   In the provisions applied by subsection (3) above for any reference to a company or its affairs there shall be substituted a reference to the scheme under investigation by virtue of this section and the affairs mentioned in subsection (1) or (2) above and any reference to an officer or director of the company shall include a reference to any director of the manager, trustee or operator of the scheme.

(5)   A person shall not under this section be required to disclose any information or produce any document which he would be entitled to refuse to disclose or produce on grounds of legal professional privilege in proceedings in the High Court or on grounds of confidentiality as between client and professional legal adviser in proceedings in the Court of Session except that a lawyer may be required to furnish the name and address of his client.

(6)   Where a person claims a lien on a document its production under this section shall be without prejudice to the lien.

(7)   Nothing in this section shall require a person carrying on the business of banking to disclose any information or produce any document relating to the affairs of a customer unless—

(a)   the customer is a person who the inspector has reason to believe may be able to give information relevant to the investigation; and

(b)   the Secretary of State is satisfied that the disclosure or production is necessary for the purposes of the investigation.

(8)   An inspector appointed under this section may, and if so directed by the Secretary of State shall, make interim reports to the Secretary of State and on the conclusion of his investigation shall make a final report to him.

(9)   Any such report shall be written or printed as the Secretary of State may direct and the Secretary of State may, if he thinks fit—

(a)   furnish a copy, on request and on payment of the prescribed fee, to the manager, trustee or operator or any participant in a scheme under investigation or any other person whose conduct is referred to in the report; and

(b) cause the report to be published.

95. Contraventions

(1) A person who contravenes any provision of this Chapter, a manager or trustee of an authorised unit trust scheme who contravenes any regulations made under section 81 above and a person who contravenes any other regulations made under this Chapter shall be treated as having contravened rules made under Chapter V of this Part of this Act or, in the case of a person who is an authorised person by virtue of his membership of a recognised self-regulating organisation or certification by a recognised professional body, the rules of that organisation or body.

(2) Subsection (1) above applies also to any contravention by the operator of a recognised scheme of a requirement imposed under section 90(2) above.

CHAPTER IX

THE TRIBUNAL

96. The Financial Services Tribunal

(1) For the purposes of this Act there shall be a Tribunal known as the Financial Services Tribunal (in this Act referred to as 'the Tribunal').

(2) There shall be a panel of not less than ten persons to serve as members of the Tribunal when nominated to do so in accordance with subsection (3) below; and that panel shall consist of—

(a) persons with legal qualifications appointed by the Lord Chancellor after consultation with the Lord Advocate, including at least one person qualified in Scots Law; and

(b) persons appointed by the Secretary of State who appear to him to be qualified by experience or otherwise to deal with the cases that may be referred to the Tribunal.

(3) Where a case is referred to the Tribunal the Secretary of State shall nominate three persons from the panel to serve as members of the Tribunal in respect of that case and nominate one of them to be chairman.

(4) The person nominated to be chairman of the Tribunal in respect of any case shall be a person with legal qualifications and, so far as practicable, at least one of the other members shall be a person with recent practical experience in business relevant to the case.

(5) If while a case is being dealt with by the Tribunal one of the three persons serving as members in respect of that case becomes unable to act the case may, with the consent of the Secretary of State and of the person or persons at whose request the case was referred to the Tribunal, be dealt with by the other two members.

(6) Schedule 6 to this Act shall have effect as respects the Tribunal and its proceedings.

97. References to the Tribunal

(1) Any person—

(a) on whom a notice is served under section 29, 34, 59(4), 60(2) or 70 above; or

> (b) on whom a copy of a notice under section 29, 34, 60(2) or 70 above is served or on whom the Secretary of State considers that a copy of such a notice would have been served if it had been practicable to do so,

may within twenty-eight days of the date of service of the notice require the Secretary of State to refer the matter to which the notice relates to the Tribunal and, subject to the provisions of this section, the Secretary of State shall refer that matter accordingly.

(2) The Secretary of State need not refer a matter to the Tribunal at the request of the person on whom a notice was served under section 29, 34, 59(4) or 60(2) above if within the period mentioned in subsection (1) above he—

> (a) decides to grant the application or, as the case may be, decides not to withdraw or suspend the authorisation, give the direction or publish the statement to which the notice relates; and
> (b) gives written notice of his decision to that person.

(3) The Secretary of State need not refer a matter to the Tribunal at the request of the person on whom a notice is served under section 70 above if—

> (a) that matter is the refusal of an application for the rescission or variation of a prohibition or requirement and within the period mentioned in subsection (1) above he—
>> (i) decides to grant the application; and
>> (ii) gives written notice of his decision to that person; or
> (b) that matter is the imposition or variation of a prohibition or requirement, being a prohibition, requirement or variation which has not yet taken effect, and within the period mentioned in subsection (1) above and before the prohibition, requirement or variation takes effect he—
>> (i) decides to rescind the prohibition or requirement or decides not to make the variation; and
>> (ii) gives written notice of his decision to that person.

(4) Where the notice served on a person under section 29 or 34 above—

> (a) proposed the withdrawal of an authorisation or the giving of a direction under section 33(1)(a) above; or
> (b) proposed the suspension of an authorisation or the giving of a direction under section 33(1)(b) above,

and at any time within the period mentioned in subsection (1) above the Secretary of State serves a new notice on that person in substitution for that previously served, then, if the substituted notice complies with subsection (5) below, subsection (1) above shall have effect in relation to the substituted notice instead of the original notice and as if the period there mentioned were twenty-eight days after the date of service of the original notice or fourteen days after the date of service of the substituted notice, whichever ends later.

(5) A notice served in substitution for a notice within subsection (4)(a) above complies with this subsection if it proposes—

> (a) the suspension of an authorisation or the giving of a direction under section 33(1)(b) above; or
> (b) the exercise of the power conferred by section 60 above;

and a notice served in substitution for a notice within subsection (4)(b) above complies with this subsection if it proposes a less severe suspension or direction under section 33(1)(b) or the exercise of the power conferred by section 60 above.

(6)   The reference of the imposition or variation of a prohibition or requirement under Chapter VI of this Part of this Act to the Tribunal shall not affect the date on which it comes into effect.

98.   Decisions on references by applicant or authorised person etc

(1)   Where a case is referred to the Tribunal at the request of a person within section 97(1)(a) above the Tribunal shall—

(a)   investigate the case; and
(b)   make a report to the Secretary of State stating what would in its opinion be the appropriate decision in the matter and the reasons for that opinion;

and it shall be the duty of the Secretary of State to decide the matter forthwith in accordance with the Tribunal's report.

(2)   Where the matter referred to the Tribunal is the refusal of an application the Tribunal may under this section report that the appropriate decision would be to grant or refuse the application or—

(a)   in the case of an application for the variation of a suspension, direction, consent, prohibition or requirement, to vary it in a specified manner;
(b)   in the case of an application for the rescission of a prohibition or requirement, to vary the prohibition or requirement in a specified manner.

(3)   Where the matter referred to the Tribunal is any action of the Secretary of State other than the refusal of an application the Tribunal may report that the appropriate decision would be—

(a)   to take or not to take the action taken or proposed to be taken by the Secretary of State or to take any other action that he could take under the provision in question; or
(b)   to take instead or in addition any action that he could take in the case of the person concerned under any one or more of the provisions mentioned in subsection (4) below other than that under which he was acting or proposing to act.

(4)   Those provisions are sections 28, 33 and 60 above and Chapter VI of this Part of this Act; and sections 29, 34, 60(2) and (3) and 70(2) and (4) above shall not apply to any action taken by the Secretary of State in accordance with the Tribunal's report.

(5)   The Tribunal shall send a copy of its report under this section to the person at whose request the case was referred to it; and the Secretary of State shall serve him with a written notice of the decision made by him in accordance with the report.

99.   Decisions on references by third parties

Where a case is referred to the Tribunal at the request of a person within section 97(1)(b) above the Tribunal shall report to the Secretary of State whether the reasons stated in the notice in question which relate to that person are substantiated; and the Tribunal shall send a copy of the report to that person and to the person on whom the notice was served.

100. Withdrawal of references

(1) A person who has required a case to be referred to the Tribunal may at any time before the conclusion of the proceedings before the Tribunal withdraw the reference.

(2) The Secretary of State may at any such time withdraw any reference made at the request of a person on whom a notice was served under any of the provisions mentioned in subsection (1)(a) of section 97 above if he—

(a) decides as mentioned in subsection (2)(a) or (3)(a)(i) or (b)(i) of that section; and

(b) gives such a notice as is mentioned in subsection (2)(b) or (3)(a)(ii) or (b)(ii) of that section;

but a reference shall not be withdrawn by virtue of such a decision and notice as are mentioned in paragraph (b) of subsection (3) unless the decision is made and the notice is given before the prohibition, requirement or variation has taken effect.

(3) Where a case is withdrawn from the Tribunal under this section the Tribunal shall not further investigate the case or make a report under section 98 or 99 above; but where the reference is withdrawn otherwise than by the Secretary of State he may require the Tribunal to make a report to him on the results of its investigation up to the time when the reference was withdrawn.

(4) Where two or more persons have required a case to be referred to the Tribunal the withdrawal of the reference by one or more of them shall not affect the functions of the Tribunal as respects the case so far as relating to a person who has not withdrawn the reference.

(5) Where a person on whom a notice was served under section 29, 34 or 60 above withdraws a case from the Tribunal subsection (5) of each of those sections shall apply to him as if he had not required the case to be referred.

101. Reports

(1) In preparing its report on any case the Tribunal shall have regard to the need to exclude, so far as practicable, any matter which relates to the affairs of a particular person (not being a person who required or could have required the case to be referred to the Tribunal) where the publication of that matter would or might, in the opinion of the Tribunal, seriously and prejudicially affect the interests of that person.

(2) The Secretary of State may, in such cases as he thinks fit, publish the report of the Tribunal and offer copies of any such report for sale.

(3) The Secretary of State may, on request and on payment of the prescribed fee, supply a copy of a report of the Tribunal to any person whose conduct is referred to in the report or whose interests as a client or creditor are affected by the conduct of a person to whom the proceedings before the Tribunal related.

(4) If the Secretary of State is of opinion that there is good reason for not disclosing any part of a report he may cause that part to be omitted from the report as published under subsection (2) or from the copy of it supplied under subsection (3) above.

(5) A copy of a report of the Tribunal endorsed with a certificate signed by or on behalf of the Secretary of State stating that it is a true copy shall be admissible as evidence of the opinion of the Tribunal as to any matter referred to in the report;

and a certificate purporting to be signed as aforesaid shall be deemed to have been duly signed unless the contrary is shown.

CHAPTER X

INFORMATION

102. Register of authorised persons and recognised organisations etc
(1) The Secretary of State shall keep a register containing an entry in respect of—

(a) each person who is an authorised person by virtue of an authorisation granted by the Secretary of State;
(b) each other person who appears to him to be an authorised person by virtue of any provision of this Part of this Act;
(c) each recognised self-regulating organisation, recognised professional body, recognised investment exchange and recognised clearing house;
(d) each authorised unit trust scheme and recognised scheme;
(e) each person in respect of whom a direction under section 59 above is in force.

(2) The entry in respect of each authorised person shall consist of—

(a) a statement of the provision by virtue of which he is an authorised person;
(b) in the case of a person who is an authorised person by virtue of membership of a recognised self-regulating organisation or certification by a recognised professional body, the name and address of the organisation or body;
(c) in the case of a person who is an authorised person by virtue of section 25 or 31 above, information as to the services which that person holds himself out as able to provide;
(d) in the case of a person who is an authorised person by virtue of section 31 above, the address notified to the Secretary of State under section 32 above;
(e) in the case of a person who is an authorised person by virtue of any provision other than section 31 above, the date on which he became an authorised person by virtue of that provision; and
(f) such other information as the Secretary of State may determine.

(3) The entry in respect of each such organisation, body, exchange or clearing house as is mentioned in subsection (1)(c) above shall consist of its name and address and such other information as the Secretary of State may determine.

(4) The entry in respect of each such scheme as is mentioned in subsection (1)(d) above shall consist of its name and, in the case of an authorised unit trust scheme, the name and address of the manager and trustee and, in the case of a recognised scheme, the name and address of the operator and of any representative of the operator in the United Kingdom and, in either case, such other information as the Secretary of State may determine.

(5) The entry in respect of each such person as is mentioned in subsection (1)(e) above shall include particulars of any consent for that person's employment given by the Secretary of State.

(6) Where it appears to the Secretary of State that any person in respect of whom there is an entry in the register by virtue of subsection (1)(a) or (b) above has

ceased to be an authorised person (whether by death, by withdrawal or other cessation of his authorisation, as a result of his ceasing to be a member of a recognised self-regulating organisation or otherwise) the Secretary of State shall make a note to that effect in the entry together with the reason why the person in question is no longer an authorised person.

(7) Where—

(a) an organisation, body, exchange or clearing house in respect of which there is an entry in the register by virtue of paragraph (c) of subsection (1) above has ceased to be recognised or ceased to exist;

(b) an authorised unit trust scheme or recognised scheme in respect of which there is an entry in the register by virtue of paragraph (d) of that subsection has ceased to be authorised or recognised; or

(c) the direction applying to a person in respect of whom there is an entry in the register by virtue of paragraph (e) of that subsection has ceased to have effect,

the Secretary of State shall make a note to that effect in the entry.

(8) An entry in respect of which a note is made under subsection (6) or (7) above may be removed from the register at the end of such period as the Secretary of State thinks appropriate.

103. Inspection of register

(1) The information contained in the entries included in the register otherwise than by virtue of section 102(1)(e) above shall be open to inspection; and the Secretary of State may publish the information contained in those entries in any form he thinks appropriate and may offer copies of any such information for sale.

(2) A person shall be entitled to ascertain whether there is an entry in the register by virtue of subsection (1)(e) of section 102 above (not being an entry in respect of which there is a note under subsection (7) of that section) in respect of a particular person specified by him and, if there is such an entry, to inspect it.

(3) Except as provided by subsection (2) above the information contained in the register by virtue of section 102(1)(e) above shall not be open to inspection by any person unless he satisfies the Secretary of State that he has a good reason for seeking the information.

(4) A person to whom information is made available by the Secretary of State under subsection (3) above shall not, without the consent of the Secretary of State or of the person to whom the information relates, make use of it except for the purpose for which it was made available.

(5) Information which by virtue of this section is open to inspection shall be open to inspection free of charge but only at such times and places as the Secretary of State may appoint; and a person entitled to inspect any information may obtain a certified copy of it from the Secretary of State on payment of the prescribed fee.

(6) The register may be kept by the Secretary of State in such form as he thinks appropriate with a view to facilitating inspection of the information which it contains.

104. Power to call for information

(1) The Secretary of State may by notice in writing require a person who is

authorised to carry on investment business by virtue of section 22, 24, 25 or 31 above to furnish him with such information as he may reasonably require for the exercise of his functions under this Act.

(2)   The Secretary of State may by notice in writing require a recognised self-regulating organisation, recognised professional body, recognised investment exchange or recognised clearing house to furnish him with such information as he may reasonably require for the exercise of his functions under this Act.

(3)   The Secretary of State may require any information which he requires under this section to be furnished within such reasonable time and verified in such manner as he may specify.

(4)   Sections 60, 61 and 62 above shall have effect in relation to a contravention of a requirement imposed under subsection (1) above as they have effect in relation to a contravention of the provisions to which those sections apply.

105.   Investigation powers

(1)   The powers of the Secretary of State under this section shall be exercisable in any case in which it appears to him that there is good reason to do so for the purpose of investigating the affairs, or any aspect of the affairs, of any person so far as relevant to any investment business which he is or was carrying on or appears to the Secretary of State to be or to have been carrying on.

(2)   Those powers shall not be exercisable for the purpose of investigating the affairs of any exempted person unless he is an appointed representative or the investigation is in respect of investment business in respect of which he is not an exempted person and shall not be exercisable for the purpose of investigating the affairs of a member of a recognised self-regulating organisation or a person certified by a recognised professional body in respect of investment business in the carrying on of which he is subject to its rules unless—

(a)   that organisation or body has requested the Secretary of State to investigate those affairs; or
(b)   it appears to him that the organisation or body is unable or unwilling to investigate them in a satisfactory manner.

(3)   The Secretary of State may require the person whose affairs are to be investigated ('the person under investigation') or any connected person to attend before the Secretary of State at a specified time and place and answer questions or otherwise furnish information with respect to any matter relevant to the investigation.

(4)   The Secretary of State may require the person under investigation or any other person to produce at a specified time and place any specified documents which appear to the Secretary of State to relate to any matter relevant to the investigation; and—

(a)   if any such documents are produced, the Secretary of State may take copies or extracts from them or require the person producing them or any connected person to provide an explanation of any of them;
(b)   if any such documents are not produced, the Secretary of State may require the person who was required to produce them to state, to the best of his knowledge and belief, where they are.

(5)   A statement by a person in compliance with a requirement imposed by virtue

of this section may be used in evidence against him.

(6)   A person shall not under this section be required to disclose any information or produce any document which he would be entitled to refuse to disclose or produce on grounds of legal professional privilege in proceedings in the High Court or on grounds of confidentiality as between client and professional legal adviser in proceedings in the Court of Session except that a lawyer may be required to furnish the name and address of his client.

(7)   The Secretary of State shall not require a recognised bank or licensed institution within the meaning of the Banking Act 1979 to disclose any information or produce any document relating to the affairs of a customer unless the Secretary of State considers it necessary to do so for the purpose of investigating any investment business carried on, or appearing to the Secretary of State to be carried on or to have been carried on, by the bank, institution or customer or, if the customer is a related company of the person under investigation, by that person.

(8)   Where a person claims a lien on a document its production under this section shall be without prejudice to the lien.

(9)   In this section—

'connected person', in relation to any other person means—

(a)   any person who is or was that other person's partner, employee, agent, appointed representative, banker, auditor or solicitor; and

(b)   where the other person is a body corporate, any person who is or was a director, secretary or controller of that body corporate or of another body corporate of which it is or was a subsidiary; and

(c)   where the other person is an unincorporated association, any person who is or was a member of the governing body or an officer or controller of the association; and

(d)   where the other person is an appointed representative, any person who is or was his principal; and

(e)   where the other person is the person under investigation (being a body corporate), any related company of that body corporate and any person who is a connected person in relation to that company;

'documents' includes information recorded in any form and, in relation to information recorded otherwise than in legible form, references to its production include references to producing a copy of the information in legible form;

'related company', in relation to a person under investigation (being a body corporate), means any other body corporate which is or at any material time was—

(a)   a holding company or subsidiary of the person under investigation;

(b)   a subsidiary of a holding company of that person; or

(c)   a holding company of a subsidiary of that person,

and whose affairs it is in the Secretary of State's opinion necessary to investigate for the purpose of investigating the affairs of that person.

(10)   Any person who without reasonable excuse fails to comply with a requirement imposed on him under this section shall be guilty of an offence and liable on summary conviction to imprisonment for a term not exceeding six

months or to a fine not exceeding the fifth level on the standard scale or to both.

106. Exercise of investigation powers by officer etc

(1)   The Secretary of State may authorise any officer of his or any other competent person to exercise on his behalf all or any of the powers conferred by section 105 above but no such authority shall be granted except for the purpose of investigating the affairs, or any aspects of the affairs, of a person specified in the authority.

(2)   No person shall be bound to comply with any requirement imposed by a person exercising powers by virtue of an authority granted under this section unless he has, if required to do so, produced evidence of his authority.

(3)   Where the Secretary of State authorises a person other than one of his officers to exercise any powers by virtue of this section that person shall make a report to the Secretary of State in such manner as he may require on the exercise of those powers and the results of exercising them.

CHAPTER XI

AUDITORS

107. Appointment of auditors

(1)   The Secretary of State may make rules requiring a person who is authorised to carry on investment business by virtue of section 25 or 31 above and who, apart from the rules, is not required by or under any enactment to appoint an auditor to appoint as an auditor a person satisfying such conditions as to qualifications and otherwise as may be specified in or imposed under the rules.

(2)   Rules under this section may make provisions—

  (a)   specifying the manner in which and the time within which an auditor is to be appointed;
  (b)   requiring the Secretary of State to be notified of any such appointment and enabling the Secretary of State to make an appointment if no appointment is made or notified as required by the rules;
  (c)   with respect to the remuneration of an auditor appointed under the rules;
  (d)   with respect to the term of office, removal and resignation of any such auditor;
  (e)   requiring any such auditor who is removed, resigns or not reappointed to notify the Secretary of State whether there are any circumstances connected with his ceasing to hold office which he considers should be brought to the Secretary of State's attention.

(3)   An auditor appointed under the rules shall in accordance with the rules examine and report on the accounts of the authorised person in question and shall for that purpose have such duties and powers as are specified in the rules.

108. Power to require second audit

(1)   If in any case it appears to the Secretary of State that there is good reason to do so he may direct any person who is authorised to carry on investment business by virtue of section 25 or 31 above to submit for further examintion by a person approved by the Secretary of State—

  (a)   any accounts on which that person's auditor has reported or any information given under section 52 or 104 above which has been verified by that auditor; or

(b) such matters contained in any such accounts or information as are specified in the direction;

and the person making the further examination shall report his conclusions to the Secretary of State.

(2) Any further examination and report required by a direction under this section shall be at the expense of the authorised person concerned and shall be carried out and made within such time as is specified in the direction or within such further time as the Secretary of State may allow.

(3) The person carrying out an examination under this section shall have all the powers that were available to the auditor; and it shall be the duty of the auditor to afford him all such assistance as he may require.

(4) Where a report made under this section relates to accounts which under any enactment are required to be sent to or made available for inspection by any person or to be delivered for registration, the report, or any part of it (or a note that such a report has been made) may be similarly sent, made available or delivered by the Secretary of State.

109. Communication by auditor with supervisory authorities

(1) No duty to which an auditor of an authorised person may be subject shall be regarded as contravened by reason of his communicating in good faith to the Secretary of State, whether or not in response to a request from him, any information or opinion on a matter of which the auditor has become aware in his capacity as auditor of that person and which is relevant to any functions of the Secretary of State under this Act.

(2) If it appears to the Secretary of State that any auditor or class of auditor to whom subsection (1) above applies is not subject to satisfactory rules made or guidance issued by a professional body specifying circumstances in which matters are to be communicated to the Secretary of State as mentioned in that subsection the Secretary of State may himself make rules applying to that auditor or that class of auditor and specifying such circumstances; and it shall be the duty of an auditor to whom the rules made by the Secretary of State apply to communicate a matter to the Secretary of State in the circumstances specified by the rules.

(3) The matters to be communicated to the Secretary of State in accordance with any such rules or guidance may include matters relating to persons other than the authorised person.

(4) No such rules as are mentioned in subsection (2) above shall be made by the Secretary of State unless a draft of them has been laid before and approved by a resolution of each House of Parliament.

(5) This section applies to—

(a) the communication by an auditor to a recognised self-regulating organisation or recognised professional body of matters relevant to its function of determining whether a person is a fit and proper person to carry on investment business; and

(b) the communication to such an organisation or body or any other authority or person of matters relevant to its or his function of determining whether a person is complying with the rules applicable to his conduct of investment business,

as it applies to the communication to the Secretary of State of matters relevant to his functions under this Act.

110. Overseas business

(1)   A person incorporated or having his head office outside the United Kingdom who is authorised as mentioned in subsection (1) of section 107 above may, whether or not he is required to appoint an auditor apart from the rules made under that subsection, appoint an auditor in accordance with those rules in respect of the investment business carried on by him in the United Kingdom and in that event that person shall be treated for the purposes of this Chapter as the auditor of that person.

(2)   In the case of a person to be appointed as auditor of a person incorporated or having his head office outside the United Kingdom the conditions as to qualifications imposed by or under the rules made under that section may be regarded as satisfied by qualifications obtained outside the United Kingdom which appear to the Secretary of State to be equivalent.

(3)   A person incorporated or having his head office outside the United Kingdom shall not be regarded for the purposes of section 25 above as a fit and proper person to carry on investment business unless—

 (a)   he has appointed an auditor in accordance with rules made under section 107 above in respect of the investment business carried on by him in the United Kingdom; or

 (b)   he has an auditor having qualifications, powers and duties appearing to the Secretary of State to be equivalent to those applying to an auditor appointed in accordance with those rules,

and, in either case, the auditor is able and willing to communicate with the Secretary of State and other bodies and persons as mentioned in section 109 above.

111. Offences and enforcement

(1)   Any authorised person and any officer, controller or manager of an authorised person, who knowingly or recklessly furnishes an auditor appointed under the rules made under section 107 or a person carrying out an examination under section 108 above with information which the auditor or that person requires or is entitled to require and which is false or misleading in a material particular shall be guilty of an offence and liable—

 (a)   on conviction on indictment, to imprisonment for a term not exceeding two years or to a fine or to both;

 (b)   on summary conviction, to imprisonment for a term not exceeding six months or to a fine not exceeding the statutory maximum or to both.

(2)   The duty of an auditor under section 108(3) above shall be enforceable by mandamus or, in Scotland, by an order for specific performance under section 91 of the Court of Session Act 1868.

(3)   If it appears to the Secretary of State that an auditor has failed to comply with the duty mentioned in section 109(2) above, the Secretary of State may disqualify him from being the auditor of an authorised person or any class of authorised

person; but the Secretary of State may remove any disqualification imposed under this subsection if satisfied that the person in question will in future comply with that duty.

(4)   An authorised person shall not appoint as auditor a person disqualified under subsection (3) above; and a person who is an authorised person by virtue of membership of a recognised self-regulating organisation or certification by a recognised professional body who contravenes this subsection shall be treated as having contravened the rules of the organisation or body.

CHAPTER XII

FEES

112.   Application fees

(1)   An applicant for a recognition order under Chapter III or IV of this Part of this Act shall pay such fees in respect of his application as may be required by a scheme made and published by the Secretary of State; and no application for such an order shall be regarded as duly made unless this subsection is complied with.

(2)   A scheme made for the purposes of subsection (1) above shall specify the time when the fees are to be paid and may—

   (a)   provide for the determination of the fees in accordance with a specified scale or other specified factors;
   (b)   provide for the return or abatement of any fees where an application is refused or withdrawn; and
   (c)   make different provision for different cases.

(3)   Any scheme made for the purposes of subsection (1) above shall come into operation on such date as is specified in the scheme (not being earlier than the day on which it is first published) and shall apply to applications made on or after the date on which it comes into operation.

(4)   The power to make a scheme for the purposes of subsection (1) above includes power to vary or revoke a previous scheme made under those provisions.

(5)   Every application under section 26, 77 or 88 above shall be accompanied by the prescribed fee and every notice given to the Secretary of State under section 32, 86(2) or 87(3) above shall be accompanied by such fee as may be prescribed; and no such application or notice shall be regarded as duly made or given unless this subsection is complied with.

113.   Periodical fees

(1)   Every recognised self-regulating organisation, recognised professional body, recognised investment exchange and recognised clearing house shall pay such periodical fees to the Secretary of State as may be prescribed.

(2)   So long as a body is authorised under section 22 above to carry on insurance business which is investment business it shall pay to the Secretary of State such periodical fees as may be prescribed.

(3)   So long as a society is authorised under section 23 above to carry on investment business it shall—

   (a)   if it is authorised by virtue of subsection (1) of that section, pay to the Chief

Registrar of friendly societies such periodical fees as he may by regulations specify; and

(b) if it is authorised by virtue of subsection (2) of that section, pay to the Registrar of Friendly Societies for Northern Ireland such periodical fees as he may by regulations specify.

(4) A person who is an authorised person by virtue of section 25 or 31 above shall pay such periodical fees to the Secretary of State as may be prescribed.

(5) If a person fails to pay any fee which is payable by him under subsection (4) above the Secretary of State may serve on him a written notice requiring him to pay the fee within twenty-eight days of service of the notice; and if the fee is not paid within that period that person's authorisation shall cease to have effect unless the Secretary of State otherwise directs.

(6) A direction under subsection (5) above may be given so as to have retrospective effect; and the Secretary of State may under that subsection direct that the person in question shall continue to be an authorised person only for such period as is specified in the direction.

(7) Subsection (5) above is without prejudice to the recovery of any fee as a debt due to the Crown.

(8) The manager of each authorised unit trust scheme and the operator of each recognised scheme shall pay such periodical fees to the Secretary of State as may be prescribed.

CHAPTER XIII

TRANSFER OF FUNCTIONS TO DESIGNATED AGENCY

114. Power to transfer functions to designated agency
(1) If it appears to the Secretary of State—

(a) that a body corporate has been established which is able and willing to discharge all or any of the functions to which this section applies; and
(b) that the requirements of Schedule 7 to this Act are satisfied in the case of that body,

he may, subject to the provisions of this section and Chapter XIV of this Part of this Act, make an order transferring all or any of those functions to that body.

(2) The body to which functions are transferred by the first order made under subsection (1) above shall be the body known as The Securities and Investments Board Limited if it appears to the Secretary of State that it is able and willing to discharge them, that the requirements mentioned in paragraph (b) of that subsection are satisfied in the case of that body and that he is not precluded from making the order by the subsequent provisions of this section or Chapter XIV of this Part of this Act.

(3) An order under subsection (1) above is in this Act referred to as 'a delegation order' and a body to which functions are transferred by a delegation order is in this Act referred to as 'a designated agency'.

(4) Subject to subsections (5) and (6) below, this section applies to any functions of the Secretary of State under Chapters II to XII of this Part of this Act and to his

functions under paragraph 23 and 25(2) of Schedule 1 and paragraphs 4, 5 and 15 of Schedule 15 to this Act.

(5) This section does not apply to any functions under—

   (a) section 31(4);
   (b) section 46;
   (c) section 48(8);
   (d) section 58(3);
   (e) section 86(1) or 87(1);
   (f) section 96;
   (g) section 109(2) above.

(6) This section does not apply to the making or revocation of a recognition order in respect of an overseas investment exchange or overseas clearing house or the making of an application to the court under section 12 above in respect of any such exchange or clearing house.

(7) Any function may be transferred by a delegation order either wholly or in part.

(8) In the case of a function under section 6 or 72 or a function under section 61 which is exercisable by virtue of subsection (1)(a)(ii) or (iii) of that section, the transfer may be subject to a reservation that it is to be exercisable by the Secretary of State concurrently with the designated agency and any transfer of a function under section 94, 105 or 106 shall be subject to such a reservation.

(9) The Secretary of State shall not make a delegation order transferring any function of making rules or regulations to a designated agency unless—

   (a) the agency has furnished him with a copy of the rules and regulations which it proposes to make in the exercise of those functions; and
   (b) he is satisfied that those rules and regulations will afford investors an adequate level of protection and, in the case of such rules and regulations as are mentioned in Schedule 8 to this Act, comply with the principles set out in that Schedule.

(10) The Secretary of State shall also before making a delegation order transferring any functions to a designated agency require it to furnish him with a copy of any guidance intended to have continuing effect which it proposes to issue in writing or other legible form and the Secretary of State may take any such guidance into account in determining whether he is satisfied as mentioned in subsection (9)(b) above.

(11) No delegation order shall be made unless a draft of it has been laid before and approved by a resolution of each House of Parliament.

(12) In this Act references to guidance issued by a designated agency are references to guidance issued or any recommendation made by it which is issued or made to persons generally or to any class of persons, being, in either case, persons who are or may be subject to rules or regulations made by it, or who are or may be recognised or authorised by it, in the exercise of its functions under a delegation order.

115. Resumption of transferred functions
(1) The Secretary of State may at the request or with the consent of a designated

agency make an order resuming all or any of the functions transferred to the agency by a delegation order.

(2)   The Secretary of State may, in the circumstances mentioned in subsection (3), (4) or (5) below, make an order resuming—

(a)   all the functions transferred to a designated agency by a delegation order; or
(b)   all, all legislative or all administrative functions transferred to a designated agency by a delegation order so far as relating to investments or investment business of any class.

(3)   An order may be made under subsection (2) above if at any time it appears to the Secretary of State that any of the requirements of Schedule 7 to this Act are not satisfied in the case of the agency.

(4)   An order may be made under subsection (2) above as respects functions relating to any class of investment or investment business if at any time it appears to the Secretary of State that the agency is unable or unwilling to discharge all or any of the transferred functions in respect of all or any investments or investment business falling within that class.

(5)   Where the transferred functions consist of or include any functions of making rules or regulations an order may be made under subsection (2) above if at any time it appears to the Secretary of State that the rules or regulations made by the agency do not satisfy the requirements of section 114(9)(b) above.

(6)   An order under subsection (1) above shall be subject to annulment in pursuance of a resolution of either House of Parliament; and no other order shall be made under this section unless a draft of it has been laid before and approved by a resolution of each House of Parliament.

(7)   In subsection (2)(b) above—

(a)   'legislative functions' means functions of making rules or regulations;
(b)   'administrative functions' means functions other than legislative functions;

but the resumption of legislative functions shall not deprive a designated agency of any function of prescribing fees to be paid or information to be furnished in connection with administrative functions retained by the agency; and the resumption of administrative functions shall extend to the function of prescribing fees to be paid and information to be furnished in connection with those administrative functions.

116.   Status and exercise of transferred functions
Schedule 9 to this Act shall have effect as respects the status of a designated agency and the exercise of the functions transferred to it by a delegation order.

117.   Reports and accounts
(1)   A designated agency shall at least once in each year for which the delegation order is in force make a report to the Secretary of State on the discharge of the functions transferred to it by the order and on such other matters as the order may require.

(2)   The Secretary of State shall lay before Parliament copies of each report received by him under this section.

(3)   The Secretary of State may give directions to a designated agency with respect to its accounts and the audit of its accounts; and it shall be the duty of the agency to comply with the directions.

(4)   Subsection (3) above shall not apply to a designated agency which is a company to which section 227 of the Companies Act 1985 applies; but the Secretary of State may require any designated agency (whether or not such a company) to comply with any provisions of that Act which would not otherwise apply to it or direct that any provision of that Act shall apply to the agency with such modifications as are specified in the direction; and it shall be the duty of the agency to comply with any such requirement or direction.

(5)   In subsection (4) above the references to the Companies Act 1985 and section 227 of that Act include references to the corresponding Northern Ireland provisions.

118.   Transitional and supplementary provisions

(1)   A delegation order shall not affect anything previously done in the exercise of a function which is transferred by the order; and any order resuming a function shall not affect anything previously done by the designated agency in the exercise of a function which is resumed.

(2)   A delegation order and an order resuming any functions transferred by a delegation order may contain, or the Secretary of State may by a separate order under this section make, such transitional and other supplementary provisions as he thinks necessary or expedient in connection with the delegation order or the order resuming the functions in question.

(3)   The provisions that may be made under subsection (2) above in connection with a delegation order include, in particular, provisions—

- (a)   for modifying or excluding any provision of this Act in its application to any function transferred by the order;
- (b)   for applying to a designated agency, in connection with any such function, any provision applying to the Secretary of State which is contained in or made under any other enactment;
- (c)   for the transfer of any property, rights or liabilities from the Secretary of State to a designated agency;
- (d)   for the carrying on and completion by a designated agency of anything in process of being done by the Secretary of State when the order takes effect; and
- (e)   for the substitution of a designated agency for the Secretary of State in any instrument, contract or legal proceedings.

(4)   The provisions that may be made under subsection (2) above in connection with an order resuming any functions include, in particular, provisions—

- (a)   for the transfer of any property, rights or liabilities from the agency to the Secretary of State;
- (b)   for the carrying on and completion by the Secretary of State of anything in process of being done by the agency when the order takes effect;
- (c)   for the substitution of the Secretary of State for the agency in any instrument, contract or legal proceedings; and
- (d)   in a case where some functions remain with the agency, for modifying or excluding any provision of this Act in its application to any such functions.

(5)   In a case where any function of a designated agency is resumed and is to be immediately transferred by a delegation order to another designated agency, the provisions that may be made under subsection (2) above may include provisions for any of the matters mentioned in paragraphs (a) to (c) of subsection (4) above, taking references to the Secretary of State as references to that other agency.

(6)   Any order under this section shall be subject to annulment in pursuance of a resolution of either House of Parliament.

CHAPTER XIV

PREVENTION OF RESTRICTIVE PRACTICES

Examination of rules and practices

119.   Recognised self-regulating organisations, investment exchanges and clearing houses

(1)   The Secretary of State shall not make a recognition order in respect of a self-regulating organisation, investment exchange or clearing house unless he is satisfied that—

  (a)   the rules and any guidance of which copies are furnished with the application for the order; and

  (b)   in the case of an investment exchange, any arrangements of which particulars are furnished with the application,

do not have, and are not intended or likely to have, to any significant extent the effect of restricting, distorting or preventing competition or, if they have or are intended or likely to have that effect to any significant extent, that the effect is not greater than is necessary for the protection of investors.

(2)   The powers conferred by subsection (3) below shall be exercisable by the Secretary of State if at any time it appears to him that—

  (a)   any rules made or guidance issued by a recognised self-regulating organisation, investment exchange or clearing house or any clearing arrangements made by a recognised clearing house;

  (b)   any practices of any such organisation, exchange or clearing house; or

  (c)   any practices of persons who are members of, or otherwise subject to the rules made by, any such organisation, exchange or clearing house,

have, or are intended or likely to have, to a significant extent the effect of restricting, distorting or preventing competition and that that effect is greater than is necessary for the protection of investors.

(3)   The powers exercisable under this sub-section are—

  (a)   to revoke the recognition order of the organisation, exchange or clearing house;

  (b)   to direct it to take specified steps for the purpose of securing that the rules, guidance, arrangements or practices in question do not have the effect mentioned in subsection (2) above;

  (c)   to make alterations in the rules for that purpose;

and subsections (2) to (5), (7) and (9) of section 11 above shall have effect in relation to the revocation of a recognition order under this subsection as they have effect in relation to the revocation of such an order under subsection (1) of that section.

(4) Subsection (3)(c) above does not apply to an overseas investment exchange or overseas clearing house.

(5) The practices referred to in paragraph (b) of subsection (2) above are practices of the organisation, exchange or clearing house in its capacity as such, being, in the case of a clearing house, practices in respect of its clearing arrangements; and the practices referred to in paragraph (c) of that subsection are practices in relation to business in respect of which the persons in question are subject to the rules of the organisation, exchange or clearing house and which are required or contemplated by its rules or guidance or otherwise attributable to its conduct in its capacity as such.

120. Modification of s 119 where recognition function is transferred

(1) This section applies instead of section 119 above where the function of making or revoking a recognition order in respect of a self-regulating organisation, investment exchange or clearing house is exercisable by a designated agency.

(2) The designated agency—

(a) shall send to the Secretary of State a copy of the rules and of any guidance or arrangements of which copies or particulars are furnished with any application made to the agency for a recognition order together with any other information supplied with or in connection with the application; and

(b) shall not make the recognition order without the leave of the Secretary of State;

and he shall not give leave in any case in which he would (apart from the delegation order) have been precluded by section 119(1) above from making the recognition order.

(3) A designated agency shall send the Secretary of State a copy of any notice received by it under section 14(6) or 41(5) or (6) above.

(4) If at any time it appears to the Secretary of State in the case of a recognised self-regulating organisation, recognised investment exchange or recognised clearing house that there are circumstances such that (apart from the delegation order) he would have been able to exercise any of the powers conferred by subsection (3) of section 119 above he may, notwithstanding the delegation order, himself exercise the power conferred by paragraph (a) of that subsection or direct the designated agency to exercise the power conferred by paragraph (b) or (c) of that subsection in such manner as he may specify.

121. Designated agencies

(1) The Secretary of State shall not make a delegation order transferring any function to a designated agency unless he is satisfied that any rules, regulations and guidance of which copies are furnished to him under section 114(9) or (10) above do not have, and are not intended or likely to have, to any significant extent the effect of restricting, distorting or preventing competition or, if they have or are intended or likely to have that effect to any significant extent, that the effect is not greater than is necessary for the protection of investors.

(2) The powers conferred by subsection (3) below shall be exercisable by the

Secretary of State if at any time it appears to him that—

(a) any rules or regulations made by a designated agency in the exercise of functions transferred to it by a delegation order or any guidance issued by a designated agency;

(a) any practices of a designated agency; or

(b) any practices of persons who are subject to rules or regulations made by it in the exercise of those functions,

have, or are intended or are likely to have, to any significant extent the effect of restricting, distorting or preventing competition and that that effect is greater than is necessary for the protection of investors.

(3) The powers exercisable under this subsection are—

(a) to make an order in respect of the agency under section 115(2) above as if the circumstances were such as are there mentioned; or

(b) to direct the agency to take specified steps for the purpose of securing that the rules, regulations, guidance or practices in question do not have the effect mentioned in subsection (2) above.

(4) The practices referred to in paragraph (b) of subsection (2) above are practices of the designated agency in its capacity as such; and the practices referred to in paragraph (c) of that subsection are practices in relation to business in respect of which the persons in question are subject to any such rules or regulations as are mentioned in paragraph (a) of that subsection and which are required or contemplated by those rules or regulations or by any such guidance as is there mentioned or are otherwise attributable to the conduct of the agency in its capacity as such.

Consultation with Director General of Fair Trading

122. Reports by Director General of Fair Trading

(1) The Secretary of State shall before deciding—

(a) whether to refuse to make, or to refuse leave for the making of, a recognition order in pursuance of section 119(1) or 120(2) above; or

(b) whether he is precluded by section 121(1) above from making a delegation order,

send to the Director General of Fair Trading (in this Chapter referred to as 'the Director') a copy of the rules and regulations and of any guidance or arrangements which the Secretary of State is required to consider in making that decision together with such other information as the Secretary of State considers will assist the Director in discharging his functions under subsection (2) below.

(2) The Director shall report to the Secretary of State whether, in his opinion, the rules, regulations, guidance or arrangements of which copies are sent to him under subsection (1) above have, or are intended or likely to have, to any significant extent the effect of restricting, distorting, or preventing competition and, if so, what that effect is likely to be; and in making any such decision as is mentioned in that subsection the Secretary of State shall have regard to the Director's report.

(3) The Secretary of State shall send the Director copies of any notice received by him under section 14(6), 41(5) or (6) or 120(3) above or under paragraph 4 of

Schedule 9 to this Act together with such other information as the Secretary of State considers will assist the Director in discharging his functions under subsections (4) and (5) below.

(4)   The Director shall keep under review—

(a)   the rules, guidance, arrangements and regulations mentioned in section 119(2) and 121(2) above; and

(b)   the matters specified in the notices of which copies are sent to him under subsection (3) above;

and if at any time he is of the opinion that any such rules, guidance, arrangements, regulations or matters, or any such rules, guidance, arrangements or regulations taken together with any such matters, have, or are intended or likely to have, to any significant extent the effect mentioned in subsection (2) above, he shall make a report to the Secretary of State stating his opinion and what that effect is or is likely to be.

(5)   The Director may report to the Secretary of State his opinion that any such matter as is mentioned in subsection (4)(b) above does not in his opinion have, and is not intended or likely to have, to any significant extent the effect mentioned in subsection (2) above.

(6)   The Director may from time to time consider whether any such practices as are mentioned in section 119(2) or 121(2) above have, or are intended or likely to have, to any significant extent the effect mentioned in subsection (2) above and, if so, what that effect is or is likely to be; and if he is of that opinion he shall make a report to the Secretary of State stating his opinion and what the effect is or is likely to be.

(7)   The Secretary of State shall not exercise his powers under section 119(3), 120(4) or 121(3) above except after receiving and considering a report from the Director under subsection (4) or (6) above.

(8)   The Director may, if he thinks fit, publish any report made by him under this section but shall exclude from a published report, so far as practicable, any matter which relates to the affairs of a particular person (other than the self-regulating organisation, investment exchange, clearing house or designated agency concerned) the publication of which would or might in his opinion seriously and prejudicially affect the interests of that person.

123.   Investigations by Director General of Fair Trading

(1)   For the purpose of investigating any matter with a view to its consideration under section 122 above the Director may by a notice in writing—

(a)   require any person to produce, at a time and place specified in the notice, to the Director or to any person appointed by him for the purpose, any documents which are specified or described in the notice and which are documents in his custody or under his control and relating to any matter relevant to the investigation; or

(b)   require any person carrying on any business to furnish to the Director such information as may be specified or described in the notice, and specify the time within which, and the manner and form in which, any such information is to be furnished.

(2)   A person shall not under this section be required to produce any document or

disclose any information which he would be entitled to refuse to produce or disclose on grounds of legal professional privilege in proceedings in the High Court or on grounds of confidentiality as between client and professional legal adviser in proceedings in the Court of Session.

(3)   Subsections (5) to (8) of section 85 of the Fair Trading Act 1973 (enforcement provisions) shall apply in relation to notice under this section as they apply in relation to a notice under subsection (1) of that section.

Consequential exemptions from competition law

124.   The Fair Trading Act 1973

(1)   For the purpose of determining whether a monopoly situation within the meaning of the Fair Trading Act 1973 exists by reason of the circumstances mentioned in section 7(1)(c) of that Act, no account shall be taken of—

(a)   the rules made or guidance issued by a recognised self-regulating organisation, recognised investment exchange or recognised clearing house or any conduct constituting such a practice as is mentioned in section 119(2) above;

(b)   any clearing arrangements or any conduct required or contemplated by any such arrangements; or

(c)   the rules or regulations made or guidance issued by a designated agency in the exercise of functions transferred to it by a delegation order or any conduct constituting such a practice as is mentioned in section 121(2) above.

(2)   Where a recognition order is revoked there shall be disregarded for the purpose mentioned in subsection (1) above any such conduct as is mentioned in that subsection which occurred while the order was in force.

(3)   Where on a monopoly reference under section 50 or 51 of the said Act of 1973 falling with section 49 of that Act the Monopolies and Mergers Commission find that a monopoly situation within the meaning of that Act exists and—

(a)   that the person (or, if more than one, any of the persons) in whose favour it exists is subject to the rules of a recognised self-regulating organisation, recognised investment exchange or recognised clearing house or to the rules or regulations made by a designated agency in the exercise of functions transferred to it by a delegation order; or

(b)   that any such person's conduct in carrying on any business to which those rules or regulations relate is the subject of guidance issued by such an organisation, exchange, clearing house or agency; or

(c)   that any such person is a party to any clearing arrangements; or

(d)   that the person (or, if more than one, any of the persons) in whose favour the monopoly situation exists is such an organisation, exchange or clearing house as is mentioned in paragraph (a) above or a designated agency,

the Commission, in making their report on that reference, shall exclude from their consideration the question whether the rules, regulations, guidance or clearing arrangements or any acts or omissions of such an organisation, exchange, clearing house or agency as is mentioned in paragraph (d) above in its capacity as such operate, or may be expected to operate, against the public interest; and section 54(3) of that Act shall have effect subject to the provisions of this subsection.

125. The Restrictive Trade Practices Act 1976

(1) The Restrictive Trade Practices Act 1976 shall not apply to any agreement for the constitution of a recognised self-regulating organisation, recognised investment exchange or recognised clearing house, including any term deemed to be contained in it by virtue of section 8(2) or 16(3) of that Act.

(2) The said Act of 1976 shall not apply to any agreement the parties to which consist of or include—

(a) any such organisation, exchange or clearing house as is mentioned in subsection (1) above; or

(b) a person who is subject to the rules of any such organisation, exchange or clearing house or to the rules or regulations made by a designated agency in the exercise of functions transferred to it by a delegation order,

by reason of any term the inclusion of which in the agreement is required or contemplated by the rules, regulations or guidance of that organisation, exchange, clearing house or agency.

(3) The said Act of 1976 shall not apply to any clearing arrangements or to any agreement between a recognised investment exchange and a recognised clearing house by reason of any term the inclusion of which in the agreement is required or contemplated by any clearing arrangements.

(4) Where the recognition order in respect of a self-regulating organisation, investment exchange or clearing house is revoked the foregoing provisions shall have effect as if the organisation, exchange or clearing house had continued to be recognised until the end of the period of six months beginning with the day on which the revocation takes effect.

(5) Where an agreement ceases by virtue of this section to be subject to registration—

(a) the Director shall remove from the register maintained by him under the said Act of 1976 any particulars which are entered or filed in that register in respect of the agreement; and

(b) any proceedings in respect of the agreement which are pending before the Restrictive Practices Court shall be discontinued.

(6) Where an agreement which has been exempt from registration by virtue of this section ceases to be exempt in consequence of the revocation of a recognition order, the time within which particulars of the agreement are to be furnished in accordance with section 24 of and Schedule 2 to the said Act of 1976 shall be the period of one month beginning with the day on which the agreement ceased to be exempt from registration.

(7) Where in the case of an agreement registered under the said Act of 1976 a term ceases to fall within subsection (2) or (3) above in consequence of the revocation of a recognition order and particulars of that term have not previously been furnished to the Director under section 24 of that Act, those particulars shall be furnished to him within the period of one month beginning with the day on which the term ceased to fall within that subsection.

(8) The Restrictive Trade Practices (Stock Exchange) Act 1984 shall cease to have effect.

126. The Competition Act 1980

(1)   No course of conduct constituting any such practice as is mentioned in section 119(2) or 121(2) above shall constitute an anti-competitive practice for the purposes of the Competition Act 1980.

(2)   Where a recognition order or delegation order is revoked, there shall not be treated as an anti-competitive practice for the purposes of that Act any such course of conduct as is mentioned in subsection (1) above which occurred while the order was in force.

Recognised professional bodies

127.   Modification of Restrictive Trade Practices Act 1976 in relation to recognised professional bodies

(1)   This section applies to—

(a)   any agreement for the constitution of a recognised professional body, including any term deemed to be contained in it by virtue of section 16(3) of the Restrictive Trade Practices Act 1976; and

(b)   any other agreement—

(i)   the parties to which consist of or include such a body, a person certified by such a body or a member of such a body; and

(ii)   to which that Act applies by virtue of any term the inclusion of which in the agreement is required or contemplated by rules or guidance of that body relating to the carrying on of investment business by persons certified by it.

(2)   If it appears to the Secretary of State that the restrictions in an agreement to which this section applies—

(a)   do not have, and are not intended or likely to have, to any significant extent the effect of restricting, distorting or preventing competition; or

(b)   if all or any of them have, or are intended or likely to have, that effect to any significant extent, that the effect is not greater than is necessary for the protection of investors,

he may give a direction to the Director requiring him not to make an application to the Restrictive Practices Court under Part I of the said Act of 1976 in respect of the agreement.

(3)   If it appears to the Secretary of State that one or more (but not all) of the restrictions in an agreement to which this section applies—

(a)   do not have, and are not intended or likely to have, to any significant extent the effect mentioned in subsection (2) above; or

(b)   if they have, or are intended or likely to have, that effect to any significant extent that the effect is not greater than is necessary for the protection of investors,

he may make a declaration to that effect and give notice of it to the Director and the Restrictive Practices Court.

(4)   The Restrictive Practices Court shall not in any proceedings begun by an application made after notice has been given to it of a declaration under this section make any finding or exercise any power under Part I of the said Act of 1976 in relation to a restriction in respect of which the declaration has effect.

321

(5) The Director shall not make any application to the Restrictive Practices Court under Part I of the said Act of 1976 in respect of any agreement to which this section applies unless—

    (a) he has notified the Secretary of State of his intention to do so; and

    (b) the Secretary of State has either notified him that he does not intend to give a direction or make a declaration under this section or has given him notice of a declaration in respect of it;

and where the Director proposes to make any such application he shall furnish the Secretary of State with particulars of the agreement and the restrictions by virtue of which the said Act of 1976 applies to it and such other information as he considers will assist the Secretary of State in deciding whether to exercise his powers under this section or as the Secretary of State may request.

(6) The Secretary of State may—

    (a) revoke a direction or declaration under this section;

    (b) vary any such declaration; or

    (c) give a direction or make a declaration notwithstanding a previous notification to the Director that he did not intend to give a direction or make a declaration,

if he is satisfied that there has been a material change of circumstances such that the grounds for the direction or declaration have ceased to exist, that there are grounds for a different declaration or that there are grounds for giving a direction or making a declaration, as the case may be.

(7) The Secretary of State shall give notice to the Director of the revocation of a direction and to the Director and the Restrictive Practices Court of the revocation or variation of a declaration; and no such variation shall have effect so as to restrict the powers of the Court in any proceedings begun by an application already made by the Director.

(8) A direction or declaration under this section shall cease to have effect if the agreement in question ceases to be one to which this section applies.

(9) This section applies to information provisions as it applies to restrictions.

Supplemental

128. Supplementary provisions

(1) Before the Secretary of State exercises a power under section 119(3)(b) or (c) above, his power to refuse leave under section 120(2) above or his power to give a direction under section 120(4) above in respect of a self-regulating organisation, investment exchange or clearing house, or his power under section 121(3)(b) above in respect of a designated agency, he shall—

    (a) give written notice of his intention to do so to the organisation, exchange, clearing house or agency and take such steps (whether by publication or otherwise) as he thinks appropriate for bringing the notice to the attention of any other person who in his opinion is likely to be affected by the exercise of the power; and

    (b) have regard to any representation made within such time as he considers reasonable by the organisation, exchange, clearing house or agency or by any such other person.

(2)   A notice under subsection (1) above shall give particulars of the manner in which the Secretary of State proposes to exercise the power in question and state the reasons for which he proposes to act; and the statement of reasons may include matters contained in any report received by him under section 122 above.

(3)   Any direction given under this Chapter shall, on the application of the person by whom it was given, be enforceable by mandamus or, in Scotland, by an order for specific performance under section 91 of the Court of Session Act 1868.

(4)   The fact that any rules or regulations made by a recognised self-regulating organisation, investment exchange or clearing house or by a designated agency have been altered by or pursuant to a direction given by the Secretary of State under this Chapter shall not preclude their subsequent alteration or revocation by that organisation, exchange, clearing house or agency.

(5)   In determining under this Chapter whether any guidance has, or is likely to have, any particular effect the Secretary of State and the Director may assume that the persons to whom it is addressed will act in conformity with it.

PART II

INSURANCE BUSINESS

129.   Application of investment business provisions to regulated insurance companies

Schedule 10 to this Act shall have effect with respect to the application of the foregoing provisions of this Act to regulated insurance companies, that is to say—

(a)   insurance companies to which Part II of the Insurance Companies Act 1982 applies; and

(b)   insurance companies which are authorised persons by virtue of section 31 above.

130.   Restriction on promotion of contracts of insurance

(1)   Subject to subsections (2) and (3) below, no person shall—

(a)   issue or cause to be issued in the United Kingdom an advertisement—

(i)   inviting any person to enter or offer to enter into a contract of insurance rights under which constitute an investment for the purposes of this Act, or

(ii)   containing information calculated to lead directly or indirectly to any person doing so; or

(b) in the course of a business, advise or procure any person in the United Kingdom to enter into such a contract.

(2)   Subsection (1) above does not apply where the contract of insurance referred to in that subsection is to be with—

(a) a body authorised under section 3 or 4 of the Insurance Companies Act 1982 to effect and carry out such contracts of insurance;

(b) a body registered under the enactments relating to friendly societies;

(c) an insurance company the head office of which is in a member State other than the United Kingdom and which is entitled to carry on there insurance business of the relevant class;

(d) an insurance company which has a branch or agency in such a member State and is entitled under the law of that State to carry on there insurance business of the relevant class;

and in this subsection 'the relevant class' means the class of insurance business specified in Schedule 1 or 2 to the Insurance Companies Act 1982 into which the effecting and carrying out of the contract in question falls.

(3)   Subsection (1) above also does not apply where—

(a) the contract of insurance referred to in that subsection is to be with an insurance company authorised to effect or carry out such contracts of insurance in any country or territory which is for the time being designated for the purposes of this section by an order made by the Secretary of State; and

(b) any conditions imposed by the order designating the country or territory have been satisfied.

(4)   The Secretary of State shall not make an order designating any country or territory for the purposes of this section unless he is satisfied that the law under which insurance companies are authorised and supervised in that country or territory affords adequate protection to policy holders and potential policy holders against the risk that the companies may be unable to meet their liabilities; and, if at any time it appears to him that the law of a country or territory which has been designated under this section does not satisfy that requirement, he may by a further order revoke the order designating that country or territory.

(5)   An order under this section shall be subject to annulment in pursuance of a resolution of either House of Parliament.

(6)   Subject to subsections (7) and (8) below, any person who contravenes this section shall be guilty of an offence and liable—

(a) on conviction on indictment, to imprisonment for a term not exceeding two years or to a fine or to both;

(b) on summary conviction, to imprisonment for a term not exceeding six months or to a fine not exceeding the statutory maximum or to both.

(7)   A person who in the ordinary course of a business other than investment business issues an advertisement to the order of another person shall not be guilty of an offence under this section if he proves that the matters contained in the advertisement were not (wholly or in part) devised or selected by him or by any person under his direction or control and that he believed on reasonable grounds after due enquiry that the person to whose order the advertisement was issued was an authorised person.

(8)   A person other than the insurance company with which the contract of insurance is to be made shall not be guilty of an offence under this section if he proves that he believed on reasonable grounds after due enquiry that subsection (2) or (3) above applied in the case of the contravention in question.

131.   Contracts made after contravention of s 130

(1)   Where there has been a contravention of section 130 above, then, subject to subsections (3) and (4) below—

(a) the insurance company shall not be entitled to enforce any contract of insurance with which the advertisement, advice or procurement was concerned and which was entered into after the contravention occurred; and

(b) the other party shall be entitled to recover any money or other property paid or transferred by him under the contract, together with compensation for any loss sustained by him as a result of having parted with it.

(2) The compensation recoverable under subsection (1) above shall be such as the parties may agree or as a court may, on the application of either party, determine.

(3) In a case where the contravention referred to in subsection (1) above was a contravention by the insurance company with which the contract was made, the court may allow the contract to be enforced or money or property paid or transferred under it to be retained if it is satisfied—

(a) that the person against whom enforcement is sought or who is seeking to recover the money or property was not influenced, or not influenced to any material extent, by the advertisement or, as the case may be, the advice in making his decision to enter into the contract; or

(b) that the advertisement or, as the case may be, the advice was not misleading as to the nature of the company with which the contract was to be made or the terms of the contract and fairly stated any risks involved entering into it.

(4) In a case where the contravention of section 130 above referred to in subsection (1) above was a contravention by a person other than the insurance company with which the contract was made the court may allow the contract to be enforced or money or property paid or transferred under it to be retained if it is satisfied that at the time the contract was made the company had no reason to believe that any contravention of section 130 above had taken place in relation to the contract.

(5) Where a person elects not to perform a contract which by virtue of subsection (1) above is unenforceable against him or by virtue of that subsection recovers money paid or other property transferred by him under a contract he shall not be entitled to any benefits under the contract and shall repay any money and return any other property received by him under the contract.

(6) Where any property transferred under a contract to which this section applies has passed to a third party the references to that property in this section shall be construed as references to its value at the time of its transfer under the contract.

(7) A contravention of section 130 above by an authorised person shall be actionable at the suit of any person who suffers loss as a result of the contravention.

(8) Section 61 above shall have effect in relation to a contravention or proposed contravention of section 130 above as it has effect in relation to a contravention or proposed contravention of section 57 above.

132. Insurance contracts effected in contravention of s 2 of Insurance Companies Act 1982

(1) Subject to subsection (3) below, a contract of insurance (not being an agreement to which section 5(1) above applies) which is entered into by a person in the course of carrying on insurance business in contravention of section 2 of the Insurance Companies Act 1982 shall be unenforceable against the other party; and

that party shall be entitled to recover any money or other property paid or transferred by him under the contract, together with compensation for any loss sustained by him as a result of having parted with it.

(2)   The compensation recoverable under subsection (1) above shall be such as the parties may agree or as a court may, on the application of either party, determine.

(3)   A court may allow a contract to which subsection (1) above applies to be enforced or money or property paid or transferred under it to be retained if it is satisfied—

> (a) that the person carrying on insurance business reasonably believed that his entering into the contract did not constitute a contravention of section 2 of the said Act of 1982; and
> (b) that it is just and equitable for the contract to be enforced or, as the case may be, for the money or property paid or transferred under it to be retained.

(4)   Where a person elects not to perform a contract which by virtue of this section is unenforceable against him or by virtue of this section recovers money or property paid or transferred under a contract he shall not be entitled to any benefits under the contract and shall repay any money and return any other property received by him under the contract.

(5)   Where any property transferred under a contract to which this section applies has passed to a third party the references to that property in this section shall be construed as references to its value at the time of its transfer under the contract.

(6)   A contravention of section 2 of the said Act of 1982 shall not make a contract of insurance illegal or invalid to any greater extent than is provided in this section; and a contravention of that section in respect of a contract of insurance shall not affect the validity of any re-insurance contract entered into in respect of that contract.

133.   Misleading statements as to insurance contracts
(1)   Any person who—

> (a) makes a statement, promise or forecast which he knows to be misleading, false or deceptive or dishonestly conceals any material facts; or
> (b) recklessly makes (dishonestly or otherwise) a statement, promise or forecast which is misleading, false or deceptive,

is guilty of an offence if he makes the statement, promise or forecast or conceals the facts for the purpose of inducing, or is reckless as to whether it may induce, another person (whether or not the person to whom the statement, promise or forecast is made or from whom the facts are concealed) to enter into or offer to enter into, or to refrain from entering or offering to enter into, a contract of insurance with an insurance company (not being an investment agreement) or to exercise, or refrain from exercising, any rights conferred by such a contract.

(2)   Subsection (1) above does not apply unless—

> (a) the statement, promise or forecast is made in or from, or the facts are concealed in or from, the United Kingdom;
> (b) the person on whom the inducement is intended to or may have effect is in the United Kingdom; or
> (c) the contract is or would be entered into or the rights are or would be exercisable in the United Kingdom.

(3) A person guilty of an offence under this section shall be liable—

(a) on conviction on indictment, to imprisonment for a term not exceeding seven years or to a fine or to both;

(b) on summary conviction, to imprisonment for a term not exceeding six months or to a fine not exceeding the statutory maximum or to both.

134. Controllers of insurance companies
In section 7(4)(c)(ii) of the Insurance Companies Act 1982 (definition of controller by reference to exercise of not less than one-third of voting power) for the words 'one-third' there shall be substituted the words '15 per cent'.

135. Communication by auditor with Secretary of State
(1) After section 21 of the Insurance Companies Act 1982 there shall be inserted—

'21A. Communication by auditor with Secretary of State
(1) No duty to which an auditor of an insurance company to which this Part of this Act applies may be subject shall be regarded as contravened by reason of his communicating in good faith to the Secretary of State, whether or not in response to a request from him, any information or opinion on a matter of which the auditor has become aware in his capacity as auditor of that company and which is relevant to any functions of the Secretary of State under this Act.

(2) If it appears to the Secretary of State that any auditor or class of auditor to whom subsection (1) above applies is not subject to satisfactory rules made or guidance issued by a professional body specifying circumstances in which matters are to be communicated to the Secretary of State as mentioned in that subsection the Secretary of State may make regulations applying to that auditor or class of auditor and specifying such circumstances; and it shall be the duty of an auditor to whom the regulations made by the Secretary of State apply to communicate a matter to the Secretary of State in the circumstances specified by the regulations.

(3) The matters to be communicated to the Secretary of State in accordance with any such rules or guidance or regulations may include matters relating to persons other than the company.

(4) No regulations shall be made under subsection (2) above unless a draft of them has been laid before and approved by a resolution of each House of Parliament.

(5) If it appears to the Secretary of State that an auditor has failed to comply with the duty mentioned in subsection (2) above, the Secretary of State may disqualify him from being the auditor of an insurance company or any class of insurance company to which Part II of this Act applies; but the Secretary of State may remove any disqualification imposed under this subsection if satisfied that the person in question will in future comply with that duty.

(6) An insurance company to which this Part of this Act applies shall not appoint as auditor a person disqualified under subsection (5) above.'

(2) In section 71(7) of that Act (which lists the provisions of that Act default in complying with which is not an offence) after the words 'section 16' there shall be inserted the word '21A', and in section 97(4) of that Act (which provides that regulations under that Act are to be subject to annulment) after the word 'Act'

there shall be inserted the words ', except regulations under section 21A(3),'.

136. Arrangements to avoid unfairness between separate insurance funds etc

(1) After section 31 of the Insurance Companies Act 1982 there shall be inserted—

'31A. Arrangements to avoid unfairness between separate insurance funds etc

(1) An insurance company to which this Part of this Act applies which carries on long term business in the United Kingdom shall secure that adequate arrangements are in force for securing that transactions affecting assets of the company (other than transactions outside its control) do not operate unfairly between the section 28 fund or funds and the other assets of the company or, in a case where the company has more than one identified fund, between those funds.

(2) In this section—

"the section 28 fund or funds" means the assets representing the fund or funds maintained by the company under section 28(1)(b) above; and
"identified fund", in relation to a company, means assets representing the company's receipts from a particular part of its long term business which can be identified as such by virtue of accounting or other records maintained by the company.'

(2) In section 71(7) of that Act (which lists the provisions of that Act default in complying with which is not an offence) before the word 'or' there shall be inserted the word '31A'.

137. Regulations in respect of linked long term policies

In section 78(2) of the Insurance Companies Act 1982 (regulations in respect of linked long term policies) after paragraph (a) there shall be inserted—

'(aa) restricting the proportion of those benefits which may be determined by reference to property of a specified description or a specified index;'.

138. Insurance brokers

(1) Rules made under section 8 of the Insurance Brokers (Registration) Act 1977 may require an applicant for registration or enrolment to state whether he is an authorised person or exempted person under Part I of this Act and, if so, to give particulars of the authorisation or exemption; and an individual shall be treated as satisfying the requirements of section 3(2)(a) of that Act (applicant for registration to satisfy Council as to his character and suitability) if he is an authorised person or a member of a partnership or unincorporated association which is an authorised person.

(2) In drawing up any statement under section 10 of that Act or making any rules under section 11 or 12 of that Act after the coming into force of this section the Insurance Brokers Registration Council shall take proper account of any provisions applicable to, and powers exercisable in relation to, registered insurance brokers or enrolled bodies corporate under this Act.

(3) In section 12(1) and (2) of that Act (which requires the Council to make professional indemnity rules) for the words 'The Council shall' there shall be

substituted the words 'The Council may'.

(4)   In section 15 of that Act (erasure from register and list for unprofessional conduct etc.) after subsection (2) there shall be inserted—

'(2A)   The Disciplinary Committee may, if they think fit, direct that the name of a registered insurance broker or enrolled body corporate shall be erased from the register or list if it appears to the Committee that any responsible person has concluded that the broker (or a related person) or the body corporate has contravened or failed to comply with—

(a)   any provision of the Financial Services Act 1986 or any rule or regulation made under it to which he or it is or was subject at the time of the contravention or failure; or

(b)   any rule of any recognised self-regulating organisation or recognised professional body (within the meaning of that Act), to which he is or was subject at that time.

(2B)   In subsection (2A) above—

(a)   "responsible person" means a person responsible under the Financial Services Act 1986 or under the rules of any recognised self-regulating organisation or recognised professional body (within the meaning of that Act) for determining whether any contravention of any provision of that Act or rules or regulations made under it or any rules of that organisation or body has occurred; and

(b)   "related person" means a partnership or unincorporated association of which the broker in question is (or was at the time of the failure or contravention in question) a member or a body corporate of which he is (or was at that time) a director.'

(5)   The Insurance Brokers Registration Council shall co-operate, by the sharing of information and otherwise, with the Secretary of State and any other authority, body or person having responsibility for the supervision or regulation of investment business or other financial services.

(6)   For the purposes of the said Act of 1977 'authorised insurers' shall include—

(a) an insurance company the head office of which is in a member State other than the United Kingdom and which is entitled to carry on there insurance business corresponding to that mentioned in the definition of 'authorised insurers' in that Act; and

(b) an insurance company which has a branch or agency in such a member State and is entitled under the law of that State to carry on there insurance business corresponding to that mentioned in that definition.

139.   Industrial assurance

(1)   In section 5 of the Industrial Assurance Act 1923 (prohibition on issue of illegal policies) the references to policies which are illegal or not within the legal powers of a society or company shall not be construed as applying to any policy issued—

(a) in the course of carrying on investment business in contravention of section 3 above; or

(b) in the course of carrying on insurance business in contravention of section 2 of the Insurance Companies Act 1982.

(2)   In section 20(4) of the said Act of 1923 the reference to a person employed by a collecting society or industrial assurance company and in section 34 of that Act the references to a person in the regular employment of such a society or company shall include references to an appointed representative of such a society or company but as respects section 34 only if the contract in question is an investment agreement.

(3)   Where it appears to the Industrial Assurance Commissioner that rules made by virtue of section 48(2)(j) (or corresponding rules made by a recognised self-regulating organisation) make arrangements for the settlement of a dispute referred to him under section 32 of the said Act of 1923 or that such rules relate to some of the matters in dispute he may, if he thinks fit, delegate his functions in respect of the dispute so as to enable it to be settled in accordance with the rules.

(4)   If such rules provide that any dispute may be referred to the Industrial Assurance Commissioner he may deal with any dispute referred to him in pursuance of those rules as if it were a dispute referred under section 77 of the Friendly Societies Act 1974 and may delegate his functions in respect of any such dispute to any other person.

(5)   The foregoing provisions of this section shall apply to Northern Ireland with the substitution for the references to sections 5, 20(4), 32 and 34 of the said Act of 1923 and section 77 of the said Act of 1974 of references to Articles 20, 27(2), 36 and 38 of the Industrial Assurance (Northern Ireland) Order 1979 and section 65 of the Friendly Societies Act (Northern Ireland) 1970 and for the references to the Industrial Assurance Commissioner of references to the Industrial Assurance Commissioner for Northern Ireland.

PART III

FRIENDLY SOCIETIES

140.   Friendly societies
Schedule 11 to this Act shall have effect as respects the regulation of friendly societies.

141.   Indemnity schemes
(1)   Any two or more registered friendly societies may, notwithstanding any provision to the contrary in their rules, enter into arrangements for the purpose of making funds available to meet losses incurred by any society which is a party to the arrangements or by the members of any such society by virtue of their membership of it.

(2)   No such arrangements shall come into force unless they have been approved by the Chief Registrar of Friendly Societies or, as the case may be, the Registrar of Friendly Societies for Northern Ireland.

PART IV

OFFICIAL LISTING OF SECURITIES

142.   Official listing
(1)   No investment to which this section applies shall be admitted to the Official

List of The Stock Exchange except in accordance with the provisions of this Part of this Act.

(2)   Subject to subsections (3) and (4) below, this section applies to any investment falling within paragraph 1, 2, 4 or 5 of Schedule 1 to this Act.

(3)   In the application of those paragraphs for the purposes of subsection (2) above—

  (a) paragraphs 1, 4 and 5 shall have effect as if paragraph 1 did not contain the exclusion relating to building societies, industrial and provident societies or credit unions;
  (b) paragraph 2 shall have effect as if it included any instrument falling within paragraph 3 issued otherwise than by the government of a member State or a local authority in a member State; and
  (c) paragraphs 4 and 5 shall have effect as if they referred only to investments falling within paragraph 1.

(4)   The Secretary of State may by order direct that this section shall apply also to investments falling within paragraph 6 of Schedule 1 to this Act or to such investments of any class or description.

(5)   An order under subsection (4) above shall be subject to annulment in pursuance of a resolution of either House of Parliament.

(6)   In this Part of this Act 'the competent authority' means, subject to section 157 below, the Council of The Stock Exchange; and that authority may make rules (in this Act referred to as 'listing rules') for the purposes of any of the following provisions.

(7)   In this Part of this Act—

'issuer', in relation to any securities, means the person by whom they have been or are to be issued except that in relation to a certificate or other instrument falling within paragraph 5 of Schedule 1 to this Act it means the person who issued or is to issue the securities to which the certificate or instrument relates;

'the Official List' means the Official List of The Stock Exchange;

'securities' means investments to which this section applies;

and references to listing are references to inclusion in the Official List in pursuance of this Part of this Act.

(8)   Any functions of the competent authority under this Part of this Act may be exercised by any committee, sub-committee, officer or servant of the authority except that listing rules—

  (a) shall be made only by the authority itself or by a committee or sub-committee of the authority; and
  (b) if made by a committee or sub-committee, shall cease to have effect at the end of the period of twenty-eight days beginning with the day on which they are made (but without prejudice to anything done under them) unless before the end of that period they are confirmed by the authority.

(9)   Nothing in this Part of this Act affects the powers of the Council of The Stock Exchange in respect of investments to which this section does not apply and such investments may be admitted to the Official List otherwise than in

accordance with this Part of this Act.

143. Applications for listing

(1)   An application for listing shall be made to the competent authority in such manner as the listing rules may require.

(2)   No application for the listing of any securities shall be made except by or with the consent of the issuer of the securities.

(3)   No application for listing shall be made in respect of securities to be issued by a private company or by an old public company within the meaning of section 1 of the Companies Consolidation (Consequential Provisions) Act 1985 or the corresponding Northern Ireland provision.

144. Admission to list

(1)   The competent authority shall not admit any securities to the Official List except on an application duly made in accordance with section 143 above and unless satisfied that—

   (a) the requirements of the listing rules made by the authority for the purposes of this section and in force when the application is made; and
   (b) any other requirements imposed by the authority in relation to that application,

are complied with.

(2)   Without prejudice to the generality of the power of the competent authority to make listing rules for the purposes of this section, such rules may, in particular, require as a condition of the admission of any securities of the Official List—

   (a) the submission to, and approval by, the authority of a document (in this Act referred to as 'listing particulars') in such form and containing such information as may be specified in the rules; and
   (b) the publication of that document;

or, in such cases as may be specified by the rules, the publication of a document other than listing particulars.

(3)   The competent authority may refuse an application—

   (a) if it considers that by reason of any matter relating to the issuer the admission of the securities would be detrimental to the interests of investors; or
   (b) in the case of securities already officially listed in another member State, if the issuer has failed to comply with any obligations to which he is subject by virtue of that listing.

(4)   The competent authority shall notify the applicant of its decision on the application within six months from the date on which the application is received or, if within that period the authority has required the applicant to furnish further information in connection with the application, from the date on which that information is furnished.

(5)   If the competent authority does not notify the applicant of its decision within the time required by subsection (4) above it shall be taken to have refused the application.

(6)   When any securities have been admitted to the Official List their admission shall not be called in question on the ground that any requirement or condition for their admission has not been complied with.

145.   Discontinuance and suspension of listing

(1)   The competent authority may, in accordance with the listing rules, discontinue the listing of any securities if satisfied that there are special circumstances which preclude normal regular dealings in the securities.

(2)   The competent authority may in accordance with the listing rules suspend the listing of any securities.

(3)   Securities the listing of which is suspended under subsection (2) above shall nevertheless be regarded as listed for the purposes of sections 153 and 155 below.

(4)   This section applies to securities included in the Official List at the coming into force of this Part of this Act as it applies to securities included by virtue of this Part.

146.   General duty of disclosure in listing particulars

(1)   In addition to the information specified by listing rules or required by the competent authority as a condition of the admission of any securities to the Official List any listing particulars submitted to the competent authority under section 144 above shall contain all such information as investors and their professional advisers would reasonably require, and reasonably expect to find there, for the purpose of making an informed assessment of—

(a) the assets and liabilities, financial position, profits and losses, and prospects of the issuer of the securities; and
(b) the rights attaching to those securities.

(2)   The information to be included by virtue of this section shall be such information as is mentioned in subsection (1) above which is within the knowledge of any person responsible for the listing particulars or which it would be reasonable for him to obtain by making enquiries.

(3)   In determining what information is required to be included in listing particulars by virtue of this section regard shall be had—

(a) to the nature of the securities and of the issuer of the securities;
(b) to the nature of the persons likely to consider their acquisition; and
(c) to the fact that certain matters may reasonably be expected to be within the knowledge of professional advisers of any kind which those persons may reasonably be expected to consult; and
(d) to any information available to investors or their professional advisers by virtue of requirements imposed under section 153 below or by or under any other enactment or by virtue of requirements imposed by a recognised investment exchange for the purpose of complying with paragraph 2(2)(b) of Schedule 4 to this Act.

147.   Supplementary listing particulars

(1)   If at any time after the preparation of listing particulars for submission to the competent authority under section 144 above and before the commencement of dealings in the securities following their admission to the Official List—

333

(a) there is a significant change affecting any matter contained in those particulars whose inclusion was required by section 146 above or by listing rules or by the competent authority;

(b) a significant new matter arises the inclusion of information in respect of which would have been so required if it had arisen when the particulars were prepared,

the issuer of the securities shall, in accordance with listing rules made for the purposes of this section, submit to the competent authority for its approval and, if approved, publish supplementary listing particulars of the change or new matter.

(2)   In subsection (1) above 'significant' means significant for the purpose of making an informed assessment of the matters mentioned in section 146(1) above.

(3)   Where the issuer of the securities is not aware of the change or new matter in question he shall not be under any duty to comply with subsection (1) above unless he is notified of it by a person responsible for the listing particulars; but it shall be the duty of any person responsible for those particulars who is aware of such a matter to give notice of it to the issuer.

(4)   Subsection (1) above applies also as respects matters contained in any supplementary listing particulars previously published under this section in respect of the securities in question.

148.   Exemptions from disclosure

(1)   The competent authority may authorise the omission from listing particulars or supplementary listing particulars of any information the inclusion of which would otherwise be required by section 146 above—

(a) on the ground that its disclosure would be contrary to the public interest;

(b) subject to subsection (2) below, on the ground that its disclosure would be seriously detrimental to the issuer of the securities; or

(c) in the case of securities which fall within paragraph 2 of Schedule 1 to this Act as modified by section 142(3)(b) above and are of any class specified by listing rules, on the ground that its disclosure is unnecessary for persons of the kind who may be expected normally to buy or deal in the securities.

(2)   No authority shall be granted under subsection (1)(b) above in respect of, and no such authority shall be regarded as extending to, information the non-disclosure of which would be likely to mislead a person considering the acquisition of the secutities as to any facts the knowledge of which it is essential for him to have in order to make an informed assessment.

(3)   The Secretary of State or the Treasury may issue a certificate to the effect that the disclosure of any information (including information that would otherwise have to be included in particulars for which they are themselves responsible) would be contrary to the public interest and the competent authority shall be entitled to act on any such certificate in exercising its powers under subsection (1)(a) above.

(4)   This section is without prejudice to any powers of the competent authority under rules made by virtue of section 156(2) below.

149.   Registration of listing particulars

(1)   On or before the date on which listing particulars or supplementary listing particulars are published as required by listing rules a copy of the particulars shall

be delivered for registration to the registrar of companies and a statement that a copy has been delivered to him shall be included in the particulars.

(2)   In subsection (1) above 'the registrar of companies' means—

(a) if the securities in question are or are to be issued by a company incorporated in Great Britain, the registrar of companies in England and Wales or the registrar of companies in Scotland according to whether the company's registered office is in England and Wales or in Scotland;
(b) if the securities in question are or are to be issued by a company incorporated in Northern Ireland, the registrar of companies for Northern Ireland;
(c) in any other case, any of those registrars.

(3)   If any particulars are published without a copy of them having been delivered as required by this section the issuer of the securities in question and any person who is knowingly a party to the publication shall be guilty of an offence and liable—

(a) on conviction on indictment, to a fine;
(b) on summary conviction, to a fine not exceeding the statutory maximum.

150.   Compensation for false or misleading particulars

(1)   Subject to section 151 below, the person or persons responsible for any listing particulars or supplementary listing particulars shall be liable to pay compensation to any person who has acquired any of the securities in question and suffered loss in respect of them as a result of any untrue or misleading statement in the particulars or the omission from them of any matter required to be included by section 146 or 147 above.

(2)   Where listing rules require listing particulars to include information as to any particular matter on the basis that the particulars must include a statement either as to that matter or, if such is the case, that there is no such matter, the omission from the particulars of the information shall be treated for the purposes of subsection (1) above as a statement that there is no such matter.

(3)   Subject to section 151 below, a person who fails to comply with section 147 above shall be liable to pay compensation to any person who has acquired any of the securities in question and suffered loss in respect of them as a result of the failure.

(4)   This section does not affect any liability which any person may incur apart from this section.

(5)   References in this section to the acquisition by any person of securities include references to his contracting to acquire them or an interest in them.

(6)   No person shall by reason of being a promoter of a company or otherwise incur any liability for failing to disclose any information which he would not be required to disclose in listing particulars in respect of a company's securities if he were responsible for those particulars or, if he is responsible for them, which he is entitled to omit by virtue of section 148 above.

151.   Exemption from liability to pay compensation

(1)   A person shall not incur any liability under section 150(1) above for any loss in respect of securities caused by any such statement or omission as is there mentioned if he satisfies the court that at the time when the particulars were

submitted to the competent authority he reasonably believed, having made such enquiries (if any) as were reasonable, that the statement was true and not misleading or that the matter whose omission caused the loss was properly omitted and—

(a) that he continued in that belief until the time when the securities were acquired; or
(b) that they were acquired before it was reasonably practicable to bring a correction to the attention of persons likely to acquire the securities in question; or
(c) that before the securities were acquired he had taken all such steps as it was reasonable for him to have taken to secure that a correction was brought to the attention of those persons; or
(d) that he continued in that belief until after the commencement of dealings in the securities following their admission to the Official List and that the securities were acquired after such a lapse of time that he ought in the circumstances to be reasonably excused.

(2)   A person shall not incur any liability under section 150(1) above for any loss in respect of securities caused by a statement purporting to be made by or on the authority of another person as an expert which is, and is stated to be, included in the particulars with that other person's consent if he satisfies the court that at the time when the particulars were submitted to the competent authority he believed on reasonable grounds that the other person was competent to make or authorise the statement and had consented to its inclusion in the form and context in which it was included and—

(a) that he continued in that belief until the time when the securities were acquired; or
(b) that they were acquired before it was reasonably practicable to bring the fact that the expert was not competent or had not consented to the attention of persons likely to acquire the securities in question; or
(c) that before the securities were acquired he had taken all such steps as it was reasonable for him to have taken to secure that that fact was brought to the attention of those persons; or
(d) that he continued in that belief until after the commencement of dealings in the securities following their admission to the Official List and that the securities were acquired after such a lapse of time that he ought in the circumstances to be reasonably excused.

(3) Without prejudice to subsections (1) and (2) above, a person shall not incur any liability under section 150(1) above for any loss in respect of any securities caused by any such statement or omission as is there mentioned if he satisfies the court—

(a) that before the securities were acquired a correction, or where the statement was such as is mentioned in subsection (2), the fact that the expert was not competent or had not consented had been published in a manner calculated to bring it to the attention of persons likely to acquire the securities in question; or
(b) that he took all such steps as it was reasonable for him to take to secure such publication and reasonably believed that it had taken place before the securities were acquired.

(4)   A person shall not incur any liability under section 150(1) above for any loss

resulting from a statement made by an offical person or contained in a public official document which is included in the particulars if he satisfies the court that the statement is accurately and fairly reproduced.

(5)   A person shall not incur any liability under section 150(1) or (3) above if he satisfies the court that the person suffering the loss acquired the securities in question with knowledge that the statement was false or misleading, of the omitted matter or of the change or new matter, as the case may be.

(6)   A person shall not incur any liability under section 150(3) above if he satisfies the court that he reasonably believed that the change or new matter in question was not such as to call for supplementary listing particulars.

(7)   In this section 'expert' includes any engineer, valuer, accountant or other person whose profession, qualifications or experience give authority to a statement made by him; and references to the acquisition of securities include references to contracting to acquire them or an interest in them.

152.   Persons responsible for particulars
(1)   For the purposes of this Part of this Act the persons responsible for listing particulars or supplementary listing particulars are—

   (a) the issuer of the securities to which the particulars relate;
   (b) where the issuer is a body corporate, each person who is a director of that body at the time when the particulars are submitted to the competent authority;
   (c) where the issuer is a body corporate, each person who has authorised himself to be named, and is named, in the particulars as a director or as having agreed to become a director of that body either immediately or at a future time;
   (d) each person who accepts, and is stated in the particulars as accepting, responsibility for, or for any part of, the particulars;
   (e) each person not falling within any of the foregoing paragraphs who has authorised the contents of, or any part of, the particulars.

(2)   A person is not responsible for any particulars by virtue of subsection (1)(b) above if they are published without his knowledge or consent and on becoming aware of their publication he forthwith gives reasonable public notice that they were published without his knowledge or consent.

(3)   Where a person has accepted responsibility for, or authorised, only part of the contents of any particulars, he is responsible under subsection (1)(d) or (e) above for only that part and only if it is included in (or substantially in) the form and context to which he has agreed.

(4)   Where the particulars relate to securities which are to be issued in connection with an offer by (or by a wholly-owned subsidiary of), the issuer for, or an agreement for the acquisition by (or by a wholly-owned subsidiary of) the issuer of, securities issued by another person or in connection with any arrangement whereby the whole of the undertaking of another person is to become the undertaking of the issuer (of a wholly-owned subsidiary of the issuer or of a body corporate which will become such a subsidiary by virtue of the arrangement) then if—

   (a) that other person; and

(b) where that other person is a body corporate, each person who is a director of that body at the time when the particulars are submitted to the competent authority and each other person who has authorised himself to be named, and is named, in the particulars as a director of that body,

is responsible by virtue of paragraph (d) of subsection (1) above for any part of the particulars relating to that other person or to the securities or undertaking to which the offer, agreement or arrangement relates, no person shall be responsible for that part under paragraph (a), (b) or (c) of that subsection but without prejudice to his being responsible under paragraph (d).

(5)   Neither paragraph (b) nor paragraph (c) of subsection (1) above applies in the case of an issuer of international securities of a class specified by listing rules for the purposes of section 148(1)(c) above; and neither of those paragraphs nor paragraph (b) of subsection (4) above applies in the case of any director certified by the competent authority as a person to whom that paragraph should not apply by reason of his having an interest, or of any other circumstances, making it inappropriate for him to be responsible by virtue of that paragraph.

(6)   In subsection (5) above 'international securities' means any investment falling within paragraph 2 of Schedule 1 to this Act as modified by section 142(3)(b) above which is of a kind likely to be dealt in by bodies incorporated in or persons resident in a country or territory outside the United Kingdom, is denominated in a currency other than sterling or is otherwise connected with such a country or territory.

(7)   In this section 'wholly-owned subsidiary', in relation to a person other than a body corporate, means any body corporate that would be his wholly-owned subsidiary if he were a body corporate.

(8)   Nothing in this section shall be construed as making a person responsible for any particulars by reason of giving advice as to their contents in a professional capacity.

(9)   Where by virtue of this section the issuer of any shares pays or is liable to pay compensation under section 150 above for loss suffered in respect of shares for which a person has subscribed no account shall be taken of that liability or payment in determining any question as to the amount paid on subscription for those shares or as to the amount paid up or deemed to be paid up on them.

153.   Obligations of issuers of listed securities

(1)   Listing rules may specify requirements to be complied with by issuers of listed securities and make provision with respect to the action that may be taken by the competent authority in the event of non-compliance, including provision—

(a) authorising the authority to publish the fact that an issuer has contravened any provision of the rules; and

(b) if the rules require an issuer to publish any information, authorising the authority to publish it in the event of his failure to do so.

(3)   This section applies to the issuer of securities included in the Official List at the coming into force of this Part of this Act as it applies to the issuer of securities included by virtue of this Part.

154.   Advertisements etc in connection with listing applications

(1)   Where listing particulars are or are to be published in connection with an

application for the listing of any securities no advertisement or other information of a kind specified by listing rules shall be issued in the United Kingdom unless the contents of the advertisement or other information have been submitted to the competent authority and that authority has either—

(a) approved those contents; or

(b) authorised the issue of the advertisement or information without such approval.

(2) An authorised person who contravenes this section shall be treated as having contravened rules made under Chapter V of Part I of this Act or, in the case of a person who is an authorised person by virtue of his membership of a recognised self-regulating organisation or certification by a recognised professional body, the rules of that organisation or body.

(3) Subject to subsection (4) below, a person other than an authorised person, who contravenes this section shall be guilty of an offence and liable—

(a) on conviction on indictment, to imprisonment for a term not exceeding two years or to a fine or to both;

(b) on summary conviction, to a fine not exceeding the statutory maximum.

(4) A person who in the ordinary course of a business other than investment business issues an advertisement or other information to the order of another person shall not be guilty of an offence under this section if he proves that he believed on reasonable grounds that the advertisement or information had been approved or its issue authorised by the competent authority.

(5) Where information has been approved, or its issue has been authorised, under this section neither the person issuing it nor any person responsible for, or for any part of, the listing particulars shall incur any civil liability by reason of any statement in or omission from the information if that information and the listing particulars, taken together, would not be likely to mislead persons of the kind likely to consider the acquisition of the securities in question.

155. Fees
Listing rules may require the payment of fees to the competent authority in respect of applications for listing and the retention of securities in the Official List.

156. Listing rules: general provisions
(1) Listing rules may make different provision for different cases.

(2) Listing rules may authorise the competent authority to dispense with or modify the application of the rules in particular cases and by reference to any circumstances.

(3) Listing rules shall be made by an instrument in writing.

(4) Immediately after an instrument containing listing rules is made it shall be printed and made available to the public with or without payment.

(5) A person shall not be taken to have contravened any listing rule if he shows that at the time of the alleged contravention the instrument containing the rule had not been made available as required by subsection (4) above.

(6) The production of a printed copy of an instrument purporting to be made by the competent authority on which is endorsed a certificate signed by an officer of

the authority authorised by it for that purpose and stating—

    (a) that the instrument was made by the authority;

    (b) that the copy is a true copy of the instrument; and

    (c) that on a specified date the instrument was made available to the public as required by subsection (4) above,

shall be prima facie evidence or, in Scotland, sufficient evidence of the facts stated in the certificate.

(7) Any certificate purporting to be signed as mentioned in subsection (6) above shall be deemed to have been duly signed unless the contrary is shown.

(8) Any person wishing in any legal proceedings to cite an instrument made by the competent authority may require the authority to cause a copy of it to be endorsed with such a certificate as is mentioned in subsection (6) above.

157. Alteration of competent authority

(1) The Secretary of State may by order transfer the functions as competent authority of the Council of The Stock Exchange to another body or other bodies either at the request of the Council or if it appears to him—

    (a) that the Council is exercising those functions in a manner which is unnecessary for the protection of investors and fails to take into account the proper interests of issuers and proposed issuers of securities; or

    (b) that it is necessary to do so for the protection of investors.

(2) The Secretary of State may by order transfer all or any of the functions as competent authority from any body or bodies to which they have been previously transferred under this section to another body or bodies.

(3) Any order made under subsection (1) above at the request of the Council shall be subject to annulment in pursuance of a resolution of either House of Parliament; and no other order shall be made under this section unless a draft of it has been laid before and approved by a resolution of each House of Parliament.

(4) An order under this section shall not affect anything previously done by any body ('the previous authority') in the exercise of functions which are transferred by the order to another body ('the new authority') and may contain such supplementary provisions as the Secretary of State thinks necessary or expedient, including provisions—

    (a) for modifying or excluding any provision of this Part of this Act in its application to any such functions;

    (b) for the transfer of any property, rights or liabilities relating to any such functions from the previous authority to the new authority;

    (c) for the carrying on and completion by the new authority of anything in process of being done by the previous authority when the order takes effect; and

    (d) for the substitution of the new authority for the previous authority in any instrument, contract or legal proceedings.

(5) If by virtue of this section the function of admission to or discontinuance or suspension of listing is exercisable otherwise than by the Council of The Stock Exchange, references in this Part of this Act to the competent authority admitting securities to the Official List or to discontinuing or suspending the listing of any

securities shall be construed as references to the giving of directions to the Council
of The Stock Exchange to admit the securities or to discontinue or suspend their
listing; and it shall be the duty of the Council to comply with any such direction.

PART V

OFFERS OF UNLISTED SECURITIES

158. Preliminary
(1) This Part of this Act applies to any investment—

(a) which is not listed, or the subject of an application for listing, in accordance
with Part IV of this Act; and
(b) falls within paragraph 1, 2, 4 or 5 of Schedule 1 to this Act.

(2) In the application of those paragraphs for the purposes of subsection (1)
above—

(a) paragraphs 4 and 5 shall have effect with the omission of references to
investments falling within paragraph 3; and
(b) paragraph 4 shall have effect as if it referred only to instruments issued by
the person issuing the investment to be subscribed for.

(3) In this Part of this Act—

'issuer', in relation to any securities, means the person by whom they have been
or are to be issued except that in relation to a certificate or other instrument
falling within paragraph 5 of Schedule 1 to this Act it means the person who
issued or is to issue the securities to which the certificate or instrument relates;

'securities' means investments to which this section applies.

(4) For the purposes of this Part of this Act an advertisement offers securities if—

(a) it invites a person to enter into an agreement for or with a view to
subscribing for or otherwise acquiring or underwriting any securities; or
(b) it contains information calculated to lead directly or indirectly to a person
entering into such an agreement.

(5) In this Part of this Act 'the registrar of companies', in relation to any
securities, means—

(a) if the securities are or are to be issued by a company incorporated in Great
Britain, the registrar of companies in England and Wales or the registrar of
companies in Scotland according to whether the company's registered office
is in England and Wales or in Scotland;
(b) if the securities are or are to be issued by a company incorporated in
Northern Ireland, the registrar of companies for Northern Ireland;
(c) in any other case, any of those registrars.

(6) In this Part of this Act 'approved exchange', in relation to dealings in any
securities, means a recognised investment exchange approved by the Secretary of
State for the purposes of this Part of this Act either generally or in relation to such
dealings, and the Secretary of State shall give notice in such manner as he thinks
appropriate of the exchanges which are for the time being approved.

159. Offers of securities on admission to approved exchange
(1) Subject to subsection (2) and section 161 below, no person shall issue or cause
to be issued in the United Kingdom an advertisement offering any securities on the

occasion of their admission to dealings on an approved exchange or on terms that they will be issued if admitted to such dealings unless—

    (a) a document (in this Part of this Act referred to as a 'prospectus') containing information about the securities has been submitted to and approved by the exchange and delivered for registration to the registrar of companies; or

    (b) the advertisement is such that no agreement can be entered into in pursuance of it until such a prospectus has been submitted, approved and delivered as aforesaid.

(2)   Subsection (1) above does not apply if a prospectus relating to the securities has been delivered for registration under this Part of this Act in the previous twelve months and the approved exchange certifies that it is satisfied that persons likely to consider acquiring the securities will have sufficient information to enable them to decide whether to do so from that prospectus and any information published in connection with the admission of the securities.

160.   Other offers of securities

(1)   Subject to subsections (5) and (6) and section 161 below, no person shall issue or cause to be issued in the United Kingdom an advertisement offering any securities which is a primary or secondary offer within the meaning of this section unless—

    (a) he has delivered for registration to the registrar of companies a prospectus relating to the securities and expressed to be in respect of the offer; or

    (b) the advertisement is such that no agreement can be entered into in pursuance of it until such a prospectus has been delivered by him as aforesaid.

(2)   For the purposes of this section a primary offer is an advertisement issued otherwise than as mentioned in section 159(1) above inviting persons to enter into an agreement for or with a view to subscribing (whether or not in cash) for or underwriting the securities to which it relates or containing information calculated to lead directly or indirectly to their doing so.

(3)   For the purposes of this section a secondary offer is any other advertisement issued otherwise than as mentioned in section 159(1) above inviting persons to enter into an agreement for or with a view to acquiring the securities to which it relates or containing information calculated to lead directly or indirectly to their doing so, being an advertisement issued or caused to be issued by—

    (a) a person who has acquired the securities from the issuer with a view to issuing such an advertisement in respect of them;

    (b) a person who, with a view to issuing such an advertisement in respect of them, has acquired the securities otherwise than from the issuer but without their having been admitted to dealings on an approved exchange or held by a person who acquired them as an investment and without any intention that such an advertisement should be issued in respect of them; or

    (c) a person who is a controller of the issuer or has been such a controller in the previous twelve months and who is acting with the consent or participation of the issuer in issuing the advertisement.

(4)   For the purposes of subsection (3)(a) above it shall be presumed in the absence of evidence to the contrary that a person has acquired securities with a view to issuing an advertisement offering the securities if he issues it or causes it to be issued—

(a) within six months after the issue of the securities; or
(b) before the consideration due from him for their acquisition is received by the person from whom he acquired them.

(5)   Subsection (1) above does not apply to a secondary offer if such a prospectus as is mentioned in that subsection has been delivered in accordance with that subsection in respect of an offer of the same securities made in the previous six months by a person making a primary offer or a previous secondary offer.

(6)   Subsection (1) above does not apply to an advertisement issued in such circumstances as may be specified by an order made by the Secretary of State for the purpose of exempting from that subsection—

(a) advertisements appearing to him to have a private character, whether by reason of a connection between the person issuing them and those to whom they are addressed or otherwise;
(b) advertisements appearing to him to deal with investments only incidentally;
(c) advertisements issued to persons appearing to him to be sufficiently expert to understand any risks involved; or
(d) such other classes of advertisement as he thinks fit.

(7)   Without prejudice to subsection (6)(c) above an order made by the Secretary of State may exempt from subsection (1) above an advertisement issued in whatever circumstances if it relates to securities appearing to him to be of a kind that can be expected normally to be bought or dealt in only by persons sufficiently expert to understand any risks involved.

(8)   An order under subsection (6) or (7) above may require any person who by virtue of the order is authorised to issue an advertisement to comply with such requirements as are specified in the order.

(9)   An order made by virtue of subsection (6)(a), (b) or (c) or by virtue of subsection (7) above shall be subject to annulment in pursuance of a resolution of either House of Parliament; and no order shall be made by virtue of subsection (6)(d) above unless a draft of it has been laid before and approved by a resolution of each House of Parliament.

161.   Exceptions

(1)   Sections 159 and 160 above d not apply to any advertisement offering securities if the offer is conditional on their admission to listing in accordance with Part IV of this Act and section 159 above does not apply to any advertisement offering securities if they have been listed in accordance with that Part in the previous twelve months and the approved exchange in question certifies that persons likely to consider acquiring them will have sufficient information to enable them to decide whether to do so.

(2)   Neither of those sections applies to any such advertisement as is mentioned in section 58(2) above.

(3)   Neither of those sections applies if other securities issued by the same person (whether or not securities of the same class as those to which the offer relates) are already dealt in on an approved exchange and the exchange certifies that persons likely to consider acquiring the securities to which the offer relates will have sufficient information to enable them to decide whether to do so having regard to the steps that have been taken to comply in respect of those other securities with

the requirements imposed by the exchange for the purpose of complying with paragraph 2(2)(b) of Schedule 4 to this Act, to the nature of the securities to which the offer relates, to the circumstances of their issue and to the information about the issuer which is available to investors by virtue of any enactment.

(4)   If it appears to the Secretary of State that the law of a country or territory outside the United Kingdom provides investors in the United Kingdom with protection at least equivalent to that provided by Part IV of this Act or this Part of this Act in respect of securities dealt in on an exchange or exchanges in that country or territory he may by order specify circumstances in which those sections are not to apply to advertisments offering those securities.

(5)   An order under subsection (4) above shall be subject to annulment in pursuance of a resolution of either House of Parliament.

162.   Form and content of prospectus

(1)   A prospectus shall contain such information and comply with such other requirements as may be prescribed by rules made by the Secretary of State for the purposes of this section.

(2)   Rules under this section may make provision whereby compliance with any requirements imposed by or under the law of a country or territory outside the United Kingdom is treated as compliance with any requirements of the rules.

(3)   If it appears to the Secretary of State that an approved exchange has rules in respect of prospectuses relating to securities dealt in on the exchange, and practices in exercising any powers conferred by the rules, which provide investors with protection at least equivalent to that provided by rules under this section he may direct that any such prospectus shall be subject to the rules of the exchange instead of the rules made under this section.

163.   General duty of disclosure in prospectus

(1)   In addition to the information required to be included in a prospectus by virtue of rules applying to it by virtue of section 162 above a prospectus shall contain all such information as investors and their professional advisers would reasonably require, and reasonably expect to find there, for the purpose of making an informed assessment of—

  (a) the assets and liabilities, financial position, profits and losses, and prospects of the issuer of the securities; and
  (b) the rights attaching to those securities.

(2)   The information to be included by virtue of this section shall be such information as is mentioned in subsection (1) above which is within the knowledge of any person responsible for the prospectus or which it would be reasonable for him to obtain by making enquiries.

(3)   In determining what information is required to be included in a prospectus by virtue of this section regard shall be had—

  (a) to the nature of the securities and of the issuer of the securities;
  (b) to the nature of the persons likely to consider their acquisition;
  (c) to the fact that certain matters may reasonably be expected to be within the knowledge of professional advisers of any kind which those persons may reasonably be expected to consult; and

(d)   to any information available to investors or their professional advisers by virtue of any enactment or by virtue of requirements imposed by a recognised investment exchange for the purpose of complying with paragraph 2(2)(b) of Schedule 4 to this Act.

164. Supplementary prospectus

(1)   Where a prospectus has been registered under this Part of this Act in respect of an offer of securities and at any time while an agreement in respect of those securities can be entered into in pursuance of that offer—

(a) there is a significant change affecting any matter contained in the prospectus whose inclusion was required by rules applying to it by virtue of section 162 above or by section 163 above; or

(b) a significant new matter arises the inclusion of information in respect of which would have been so required if it had arisen when the propsectus was prepared,

the person who delivered the prospectus for registration to the registrar of companies shall deliver to him for registration a supplementary prospectus containing particulars of the change or new matter.

(2)   In subsection (1) above 'significant' means significant for the purpose of making an informed assessment of the matters mentioned in section 163(1) above.

(3)   Where the person who delivered the prospectus for registration is not aware of the change or new matter in question he shall not be under any duty to comply with subsection (1) above unless he is notified of it by a person responsible for the prospectus; but any person responsible for the prospectus who is aware of such a matter shall be under a duty to give him notice of it.

(4)   Subsection (1) above applies also as respects matters contained in a supplementary prospectus previously registered under this section in respect of the securities in question.

165. Exemptions from disclosure

(1)   If in the case of any approved exchange the Secretary of State so directs, the exchange shall have power to authorise the omission from a prospectus or supplementary prospectus of any information the inclusion of which would otherwise be required by section 163 above—

(a) on the ground that its disclosure would be contrary to the public interest;

(b) subject to subsection (2) below, on the ground that its disclosure would be seriously detrimental to the issuer of the securities; or

(c) in the case of securities which fall within paragraph 2 of Schedule 1 to this Act and are of any class specified by the rules of the exchange, on the ground that its disclosure is unnecessary for persons of the kind who may be expected normally to buy or deal in the securities.

(2)   No authority shall be granted under subsection (1)(b) above in respect of, and no such authority shall be regarded as extending to, information the non-disclosure of which would be likely to mislead a person considering the acquisition of the securities as to any facts the knowledge of which it is essential for him to have in order to make an informed assessment.

(3)   The Secretary of State or the Treasury may issue a certificate to the effect that the disclosure of any information (including information that would otherwise have to be included in a prospectus or supplementary prospectus for which they are themselves responsible) would be contrary to the public interest and the exchange shall be entitled to act on any such certificate in exercising its powers under subsection (1)(a) above.

166.   Compensation for false or misleading prospectus

(1)   Subject to section 167 below, the person or persons responsible for a prospectus or supplementary prospectus shall be liable to pay compensation to any person who has acquired the securities to which the prospectus relates and suffered loss in respect of them as a result of any untrue or misleading statement in the prospectus or the omission from it of any matter required to be included by section 163 or 164 above.

(2)   Where rules applicable to a prospectus by virtue of section 162 above require it to include information as to any particular matter on the basis that the prospectus must include a statement either as to that matter or, if such is the case, that there is no such matter, the omission from the prospectus of the information shall be treated for the purpose of subsection (1) above as a statement that there is no such matter.

(3)   Subject to section 167 below, a person who fails to comply with section 164 above shall be liable to pay compensation to any person who has acquired any of the securities in question and suffered loss in respect of them as a result of the failure.

(4)   This section does not affect any liability which any person may incur apart from this section.

(5)   References in this section to the acquisition by any person of securities include references to his contracting to acquire them or an interest in them.

167.   Exemption from liability to pay compensation

(1)   A person shall not incur any liability under section 166(1) above for any loss in respect of securities caused by any such statement or omission as is there mentioned if he satisfies the court that at the time when the prospectus or supplementary prospectus was delivered for registration he reasonably believed, having made such enquiries (if any) as were reasonable, that the statement was true and not misleading or that the matter whose omission caused the loss was properly omitted and—

(a) that he continued in that belief until the time when the securities were acquired; or
(b) that they were acquired before it was reasonably practicable to bring a correction to the attention of persons likely to acquire the securities in question; or
(c) that before the securities were acquired he had taken all such steps as it was reasonable for him to have taken to secure that a correction was brought to the attention of those persons; or
(d) that the securities were acquired after such a lapse of time that he ought in the circumstances to be reasonably excused;

but paragraph (d) above does not apply where the securities are dealt in on an approved exchange unless he satisfies the court that he continued in that belief until after the commencement of dealings in the securities on that exchange.

(2)   A person shall not incur any liability under section 166(1) above for any loss in respect of securities caused by a statement purporting to be made by or on the authority of another person as an expert which is, and is stated to be, included in the prospectus or supplementary prospectus with that other person's consent if he satisfies the court that at the time when the prospectus or supplementary prospectus was delivered for registration be believed on reasonable grounds that the other person was competent to make or authorise the statement and had consented to its inclusion in the form and context in which it was included and—

(a) that he continued in that belief until the time when the securities were acquired; or
(b) that they were acquired before it was reasonably practicable to bring the fact that the expert was not competent or had not consented to the attention of persons likely to acquire the securities in question; or
(c) that before the securities were acquired he had taken all such steps as it was reasonable for him to have taken to secure that that fact was brought to the attention of those persons; or
(d) that the securities were acquired after such a lapse of time that he ought in the circumstances to be reasonably excused;

but paragraph (d) above does not apply where the securities are dealt in on an approved exchange unless he satisfies the court that he continued in that belief until after the commencement of dealings in the securities on that exchange.

(3)   Without prejudice to subsections (1) and (2) above, a person shall not incur any liability under section 166(1) above for any loss in respect of any securities caused by any such statement or omission as is there mentioned if he satisfies the court—

(a) that before the securities were acquired a correction or, where the statement was such as is mentioned in subsection (2) above, the fact that the expert was not competent or had not consented had been published in a manner calculated to bring it to the attention of persons likely to acquire the securities in question; or
(b) that he took all such steps as it was reasonable for him to take to secure such publication and reasonably believed that it had taken place before the securities were acquired.

(4)   A person shall not incur any liability under section 166(1) above for any loss resulting from a statement made by an official person or contained in a public official document which is included in the prospectus or supplementary prospectus if he satisfies the court that the statement is accurately and fairly reproduced.

(5)   A person shall not incur any liability under section 166(1) or (3) above if he satisfies the court that the person suffering the loss acquired the securities in question with knowledge that the statement was false or misleading, of the omitted matter or of the change or new matter, as the case may be.

(6)   A person shall not incur any liability under section 166(3) above if he satisfies the court that he reasonably believed that the change or new matter in question was not such as to call for a supplementary prospectus.

347

(7)   In this section 'expert' includes any engineer, valuer, accountant or other person whose profession, qualifications or experience give authority to a statement made by him; and references to the acquisition of securities include references to contracting to acquire them or an interest in them.

168.   Persons responsible for prospectus

(1)   For the purposes of this Part of this Act the persons responsible for a prospectus or supplementary prospectus are—

   (a) the issuer of the securities to which the prospectus or supplementary prospectus relates;

   (b) where the issuer is a body corporate, each person who is a director of that body at the time when the prospectus or supplementary prospectus is delivered for registration;

   (c) where the issuer is a body corporate, each person who has authorised himself to be named, and is named, in the prospectus or supplementary prospectus as a director or as having agreed to become a director of that body either immediately or at a future time;

   (d) each person who accepts, and is stated in the prospectus or supplementary prospectus as accepting, responsibility for, or for any part of, the prospectus or supplementary prospectus;

   (e) each person not falling within any of the foregoing paragraphs who has authorised the contents of, or of any part of, the prospectus or supplementary prospectus.

(2)   A person is not responsible under subsection (1)(a), (b) or (c) above unless the issuer has made or authorised the offer in relation to which the prospectus or supplementary prospectus was delivered for registration; and a person is not responsible for a prospectus or supplementary prospectus by virtue of subsection (1)(b) above if it is delivered for registration without his knowledge or consent and on becoming aware of its delivery he forthwith gives reasonable public notice that it was delivered without his knowledge or consent.

(3)   Where a person has accepted responsibility for, or authorised, only part of the contents of any prospectus or supplementary prospectus he is responsible under subsection (1)(d) or (e) above for only that part and only if it is included in (or substantially in) the form and context to which he has agreed.

(4)   Where a prospectus or supplementary prospectus relates to securities which are to be issued in connection with an offer by (or by a wholly-owned subsidiary of) the issuer for, or an agreement for the acquisition by (or by a wholly-owned subsidiary of) the issuer of, securities issued by another person or in connection with any arrangement whereby the whole of the undertaking of another person is to become the undertaking of the issuer (of a wholly-owned subsidiary of the issuer or of a body corporate which will become such a subsidiary by virtue of the arrangement) then if—

   (a) that other person; and

   (b) where that other person is a body corporate, each person who is a director of that body at the time when the prospectus or supplementary prospectus is delivered for registration and each other person who has authorised himself to be named, and is named, in the prospectus or supplementary prospectus as a director of that body,

is responsible by virtue of paragraph (d) of subsection (1) above for any part of the prospectus or supplementary prospectus relating to that other person or to the securities or undertaking to which the offer agreement or arrangement relates, no person shall be responsible for that part under paragraph (a), (b) or (c) of that subsection but without prejudice to his being responsible under paragraph (d).

(5) Neither paragraph (b) nor paragraph (c) of subsection (1) above nor paragraph (b) of subsection (4) above applies in the case of any director if the prospectus or supplementary prospectus is subject to the rules of an approved exchange by virtue of section 162(3) above and he is certified by the exchange as a person to whom that paragraph should not apply by reason of his having an interest, or of any other circumstances, making it inappropriate for him to be responsible by virtue of that paragraph.

(6) In this section 'wholly-owned subsidiary', in relation to a person other than a body corporate, means any body corporate that would be his wholly-owned subsidiary if he were a body corporate.

(7) Nothing in this section shall be construed as making a person responsible for any prospectus or supplementary prospectus by reason only of giving advice as to its contents in a professional capacity.

(8) Where by virtue of this section the issuer of any shares pays or is liable to pay compensation under section 166 above for loss suffered in respect of shares for which a person has subscribed no account shall be taken of that liability or payment in determining any question as to the amount paid on subscription for those shares or as to the amount paid up or deemed to be paid up on them.

169. Terms and implementation of offer

(1) The Secretary of State may make rules—

    (a) regulating the terms on which a person may offer securities by an advertisement to which this Part of this Act applies; and

    (b) otherwise regulating his conduct with a view to ensuring that the persons to whom the offer is addressed are treated equally and fairly.

(2) Rules under this section may, in particular, make provision with respect to the giving of priority as between persons to whom an offer is made and with respect to the payment of commissions.

(3) Section 162(2) above shall apply also to rules made under this section.

170. Advertisements by private companies and old public companies

(1) No private company and no old public company shall issue or cause to be issued in the United Kingdom any advertisement offering securities to be issued by that company.

(2) Subsection (1) above shall not apply to an advertisement issued in such circumstances as may be specified by an order made by the Secretary of State for the purpose of exempting from that subsection such advertisements as are mentioned in section 160(6)(a), (b) or (c) above.

(3)   An order under subsection (2) above may require any person who by virtue of the order is authorised to issue an advertisement to comply with such requirements as are specified in the order.

(4)   An order under subsection (2) above shall be subject to annulment in pursuance of a resolution of either House of Parliament.

(5)   In this section 'old public company' has the meaning given in section 1 of the Companies Consolidation (Consequential Provisions) Act 1985 or the corresponding Northern Ireland provision.

171.   Contraventions

(1)   An authorised person who—

- (a) contravenes section 159 or 160 above or rules made under section 169 above;
- (b) contravenes any requirement imposed by an order under section 160(6) or (7) or 170 above; or
- (c) on behalf of a company issues or causes to be issued an advertisement which that company is prohibited from issuing by section 170 above,

shall be treated as having contravened rules made under Chapter V of Part I of this Act or, in the case of a person who is an authorised person by virtue of his membership of a recognised self-regulating organisation or certification by a recognised professional body, the rules of that organisation or body.

(2)   Section 57 above shall apply to a company which issues or causes to be issued an advertisement in contravention of section 170 above as it applies to a person who issues an advertisement in contravention of that section.

(3)   A person, other than an authorised person, who contravenes section 159 or 160, the rules made under section 169 or any requirement imposed by an order under section 160(6) or (7) or 170 above shall be guilty of an offence and liable—

- (a) on conviction on indictment, to imprisonment for a term not exceeding two years or to a fine or to both;
- (b) on summary conviction, to imprisonment for a term not exceeding six months or to a fine not exceeding the statutory maximum or to both.

(4)   A person who in the ordinary course of a business other than investment business issues an advertisement to the order of another person shall not be guilty of an offence under subsection (3) above in respect of a contravention of section 159 or 160 above if he proves that he believed on reasonable grounds that neither section 159 nor section 160 above applied to the advertisement or that one of those sections had been complied with in respect of the advertisement.

(5)   Without prejudice to any liability under section 166 above, a person shall not be regarded as having contravened section 159 or 160 above by reason only of a prospectus not having fully complied with the requirements of this Part of this Act as to its form and content.

(6)   Any contravention to which this section applies shall be actionable at the suit of a person who suffers loss as a result of the contravention subject to the defences and other incidents applying to actions for breach of statutory duty.

PART VI

TAKEOVER OFFERS

172. Takeover offers
(1) The provisions set out in Schedule 12 to this Act shall be substituted for sections 428, 429 and 430 of the Companies Act 1985.

(2) Subsection (1) above does not affect any case in which the offer in respect of the scheme or contract mentioned in section 428(1) was made before the coming into force of this section.

PART VII

INSIDER DEALING

173. Information obtained in official capacity; public bodies etc
(1) In section 2 of the Company Securities (Insider Dealing) Act 1985 (abuse of information obtained by Crown servants in official capacity) for the word 'Crown' wherever it occurs there shall be substituted the word 'public'.

(2) At the end of that section there shall be added—

'(4) "Public servant" means—

(a) a Crown servant;
(b) a member, officer or servant of a designated agency, competent authority or transferee body (within the meaning of the Financial Services Act 1986);
(c) an officer or servant of a recognised self-regulating organisation, recognised investment exchange or recognised clearing house (within the meaning of that Act);
(d) any person declared by an order for the time being in force under subsection (5) to be a public servant for the purposes of this section.

(5) If it appears to the Secretary of State that the members, officers or employees of or persons otherwise connected with any body appearing to him to exercise public functions may have access to unpublished price sensitive information relating to securities, he may by order declare that those persons are to be public servants for the purposes of this section.

(6) The power to make an order under subsection (5) shall be exercisable by statutory instrument and an instrument containing such an order shall be subject to annulment in pursuance of a resolution of either House of Parliament.'

174. Market makers, off-market dealers etc
(1) In subsection (1) of section 3 of the Company Securities (Insider Dealing) Act 1985 (actions not prohibited by sections 1 and 2 of that Act) at the end of paragraph (c) there shall be inserted the words '; or

(d) doing any particular thing in relation to any particular securities if the information—

(i) was obtained by him in the course of a business of a market maker in those securities in which he was engaged or employed, and

(ii) was of a description which it would be reasonable to expect him to obtain in the ordinary course of that business,

and he does that thing in good faith in the course of that business.".

(2) At the end of that subsection there shall be inserted—

'"Market maker" means a person (whether an individual, partnership or company) who—

(a) holds himself out at all normal times in compliance with the rules of a recognised stock exchange as willing to buy and sell securities at prices specified by him; and
(b) is recognised as doing so by that recognised stock exchange.'.

(3) The existing provisions of section 4 of that Act (off-market deals in advertised securities) shall become subsection (1) of that section and after that subsection there shall be inserted—

'(2) In its application by virtue of this section the definition of "market maker" in section 3(1) shall have effect as if the references to a recognised stock exchange were references to a recognised investment exchange (other than an overseas investment exchange) within the meaning of the Financial Services Act 1986.'.

(4) In section 13 of that Act—

(a) in subsection (1) (which defines dealing in securities and provides that references to dealing on a recognised stock exchange include dealing through an investment exchange) the words from 'and references' onwards shall be omitted; and
(b) for subsection (3) (definition of off-market dealer) there shall be substituted—

'(3) "Off-market dealer" means a person who is an authorised person within the meaning of the Financial Services Act 1986.'.

175. Price stabilisation

For section 6 of the Company Securities (Insider Dealing) Act 1985 (international bonds) there shall be substituted—

'6. Price stabilisation

(1) No provision of section 1, 2, 4 or 5 prohibits an individual from doing anything for the purpose of stabilising the price of securities if it is done in conformity with rules made under section 48 of the Financial Services Act 1986 and—

(a) in respect of securities which fall within any of paragraphs 1 to 5 of Schedule 1 to that Act and are specified by the rules; and
(b) during such period before or after the issue of those securities as is specified by the rules.

(2) Any order under subsection (8) of section 48 of that Act shall apply also in relation to subsection (1) of this section.'.

176. Contracts for differences by reference to securities

After subsection (1) of section 13 of the Company Securities (Insider Dealing) Act

1985 (definition of dealing in securities), there shall be inserted—

'(1A)   For the purposes of this Act a person who (whether as principal or agent) buys or sells or agrees to buy or sell investments within paragraph 9 of Schedule 1 to the Financial Services Act 1986 (contracts for differences etc.) where the purpose or pretended purpose mentioned in that paragraph is to secure a profit or avoid a loss wholly or partly by reference to fluctuations in the value or price of securities shall be treated as if he were dealing in those securites.'

177.   Investigations into insider dealing

(1)   If it appears to the Secretary of State that there are circumstances suggesting that there may have been a contravention of section 1, 2, 4 or 5 of the Company Securities (Insider Dealing) Act 1985, he may appoint one or more competent inspectors to carry out such investigations as are requisite to establish whether or not any such contravention has occurred and to report the results of their investigations to him.

(2)   The appointment under this section of an inspector may limit the period during which he is to continue his investigation or confine it to particular matters.

(3)   If the inspectors consider that any person is or may be able to give information concerning any such contravention they may require that person—

(a) to produce to them any documents in his possession or under his control relating to the company in relation to whose securities the contravention is suspected to have occurred or to its securities;

(b) to attend before them; and

(c) otherwise to give them all assistance in connection with the investigation which he is reasonably able to give;

and it shall be the duty of that person to comply with that requirement.

(4)   An inspector may examine on oath any person who he considers is or may be able to give information concerning any such contravention, and may administer an oath accordingly.

(5)   The inspectors shall make such interim reports to the Secretary of State as they think fit or he may direct and on the conclusion of the investigation they shall make a final report to him.

(6)   A statement made by a person in compliance with a requirement imposed by virtue of this section may be used in evidence against him.

(7)   A person shall not under this section be required to disclose any information or produce any document which he would be entitled to refuse to disclose or produce on grounds of legal professional privilege in proceedings in the High Court or on grounds of confidentiality as between client and professional legal adviser in proceedings in the Court of Session.

(8)   Nothing in this section shall require a person carrying on the business of banking to disclose any information or produce any document relating to the affairs of a customer unless—

(a) the customer is a person who the inspectors have reason to believe may be able to give information concerning a suspected contravention; and

(b) the Secretary of State is satisfied that the disclosure or production is necessary for the purposes of the investigation.

(9) Where a person claims a lien on a document its production under this section shall be without prejudice to his lien.

(10) In this section 'document' includes information recorded in any form; and in relation to information recorded otherwise than in legible form references to its production include references to producing a copy of the information in legible form.

178. Penalties for failure to co-operate with s 177 investigations

(1) If any person—

(a) refuses to comply with any request under subsection (3) of section 177 above; or

(b) refuses to answer any question put to him by the inspectors appointed under that section with respect to any matter relevant for establishing whether or not any suspected contravention has occurred,

the inspectors may certify that fact in writing to the court and the court may inquire into the case.

(2) If, after hearing any witness who may be produced against or on behalf of the alleged offender and any statement which may be offered in defence, the court is satisfied that he did without reasonable excuse refuse to comply with such a request or answer any such question, the court may—

(a) punish him in like manner as if he had been guilty of contempt of the court; or

(b) direct that the Secretary of State may exercise his powers under this section in respect of him;

and the court may give a direction under paragraph (b) above notwithstanding that the offender is not within the jurisdiction of the court if the court is satisfied that he was notified of his right to appear before the court and of the powers available under this section.

(3) Where the court gives a direction under subsection (2)(b) above in respect of an authorised person the Secretary of State may serve a notice on him—

(a) cancelling any authorisation of his to carry on investment business after the expiry of a specified period after the service of the notice;

(b) disqualifying him from becoming authorised to carry on investment business after the expiry of a specified period;

(c) restricting any authorisation of his in respect of investment business during a specified period to the performance of contracts entered into before the notice comes into force;

(d) prohibiting him from entering into transactions of a specified kind or entering into them except in specified circumstances or to a specified extent;

(e) prohibiting him from soliciting business from persons of a specified kind or otherwise than from such persons; or

(f) prohibiting him from carrying on business in a specified manner or otherwise than in a specified manner.

(4)   The period mentioned in paragraphs (a) and (c) of subsection (3) above shall be such period as appears to the Secretary of State reasonable to enable the person on whom the notice is served to complete the performance of any contracts entered into before the notice comes into force and to terminate such of them as are of a continuing nature.

(5)   Where the court gives a direction under subsection (2)(b) above in the case of an unauthorised person the Secretary of State may direct that any authorised person who knowingly transacts investment business of a specified kind, or in specified circumstances or to a specified extent, with or on behalf of that unauthorised person shall be treated as having contravened rules made under Chapter V of Part I of this Act or, in the case of a person who is an authorised person by virtue of his membership of a recognised self-regulating organisation or certification by a recognised professional body, the rules of that organisation or body.

(6)   A person shall not be treated for the purposes of subsection (2) above as having a reasonable excuse for refusing to comply with a request or answer a question in a case where the contravention or suspected contravention being investigated relates to dealing by him on the instructions or for the account of another person, by reason that at the time of the refusal—

(a) he did not know the identity of that other person; or
(b) he was subject to the law of a country or territory outside the United Kingdom which prohibited him from disclosing information relating to the dealing without the consent of that other person, if he might have obtained that consent or obtained exemption from that law.

(7)   A notice served on a person under subsection (3) above may be revoked at any time by the Secretary of State by serving a revocation notice on him; and the Secretary of State shall revoke such a notice if it appears to him that he has agreed to comply with the relevant request or answer the relevant question.

(8)   The revocation of such a notice as is mentioned in subsection (3)(a) above shall not have the effect of reviving the authorisation cancelled by the notice, except where the person would (apart from the notice) at the time of the revocation be an authorised person by virtue of his membership of a recognised self-regulating organisation or certification by a recognised professional body; but nothing in this subsection shall be construed as preventing any person who has been subject to such a notice from again becoming authorised after the revocation of the notice.

(9)   If it appears to the Secretary of State—

(a) that a person on whom he serves a notice under subsection (3) above is an authorised person by virtue of an authorisation granted by a designated agency or by virtue of membership of a recognised self-regulating organisation or certification by a recognised professional body; or
(b) that a person on whom he serves a revocation notice under subsection (7) above was such an authorised person at the time that the notice which is being revoked was served,

he shall serve a copy of the notice on that agency, organisation or body.

(10)   The functions to which section 114 above applies shall include the functions

of the Secretary of State under this section but any transfer of those functions shall be subject to a reservation that they are to be exercisable by him concurrently with the designated agency and so as to be exercisable by the agency subject to such conditions or restrictions as the Secretary of State may from time to time impose.

PART VIII

RESTRICTIONS ON DISCLOSURE OF INFORMATION

179. Restrictions on disclosure of information

(1)   Subject to section 180 below, information which is restricted information for the purposes of this section and relates to the business or other affairs of any person shall not be disclosed by a person mentioned in subsection (3) below ('the primary recipient') or any person obtaining the information directly or indirectly from him without the consent of the person from whom the primary recipient obtained the information and if different, the person to whom it relates.

(2)   Subject to subsection (4) below, information is restricted information for the purposes of this section if it was obtained by the primary recipient for the purposes of, or in the discharge of his functions under, this Act or any rules or regulations made under this Act (whether or not by virtue of any requirement to supply it made under those provisions).

(3)   The persons mentioned in subsection (1) above are—

(a) the Secretary of State;
(b) any designated agency, transferee body or body administering a scheme under section 54 above;
(c) the Director General of Fair Trading;
(d) the Chief Registrar of friendly societies;
(e) the Registrar of Friendly Societies for Northern Ireland;
(f) the Bank of England;
(g) any member of the Tribunal;
(h) any person appointed or authorised to exercise any powers under section 94, 106 or 177 above; and
(i) any officer or servant of any such person.

(4)   Information shall not be treated as restricted information for the purposes of this section if it has been made available to the public by virtue of being disclosed in any circumstances in which or for any purpose for which disclosure is not precluded by this section.

(5)   Subject to section 180 below, information obtained by the competent authority in the exercise of its functions under Part IV of this Act or received by it pursuant to a Community obligation from any authority exercising corresponding functions in another member State shall not be disclosed without the consent of the person from whom the competent authority obtained the information and, if different, the person to whom it relates.

(6)   Any person who contravenes this section shall be guilty of an offence and liable—

(a) on conviction on indictment, to imprisonment for a term not exceeding two years or to a fine or to both;
(b) on summary conviction, to imprisonment for a term not exceeding three months or to a fine not exceeding the statutory maximum or to both.

180. Exceptions from restrictions on disclosure

(1) Section 179 above shall not preclude the disclosure of information—

(a) with a view to the institution of or otherwise for the purposes of criminal proceedings;

(b) with a view to the institution of or otherwise for the purposes of any civil proceedings arising under or by virtue of this Act or proceedings before the Tribunal;

(c) for the purpose of enabling or assisting the Secretary of State to exercise any powers conferred on him by this Act or by the enactments relating to companies, insurance companies or insolvency or for the purpose of enabling or assisting any inspector appointed by him under the enactments relating to companies to discharge his functions;

(d) for the purpose of enabling or assisting the Department of Economic Development for Northern Ireland to exercise any powers conferred on it by the enactments relating to companies or insolvency or for the purpose of enabling or assisting any inspector appointed by it under the enactments relating to companies to discharge his functions;

(e) for the purpose of enabling or assisting a designated agency or transferee body or the competent authority to discharge its functions under this Act or of enabling or assisting the body administering a scheme under section 54 above to discharge its functions under the scheme;

(f) for the purpose of enabling or assisting the Bank of England to discharge its functions under the Banking Act 1979 or any other functions;

(g) for the purpose of enabling or assisting the Deposit Protection Board to discharge its functions under that Act;

(h) for the purpose of enabling or assisting the Chief Registrar of friendly societies or the Registrar of Friendly Societies for Northern Ireland to discharge his functions under this Act or under the enactments relating to friendly societies or building societies;

(i) for the purpose of enabling or assisting the Industrial Assurance Commissioner or the Industrial Assurance Commissioner for Northern Ireland to discharge his functions under the enactments relating to industrial assurance;

(j) for the purpose of enabling or assisting the Insurance Brokers Registration Council to discharge its functions under the Insurance Brokers (Registration) Act 1977;

(k) for the purpose of enabling or assisting an official receiver to discharge his functions under the enactments relating to insolvency or for the purpose of enabling or assisting a body which is for the time being a recognised professional body for the purposes of section 391 of the Insolvency Act 1986 to discharge its functions as such;

(l) for the purpose of enabling or assisting the Building Societies Commission to discharge its functions under the Building Societies Act 1986;

(m)for the purpose of enabling or assisting the Director General of Fair Trading to discharge his functions under this Act;

(n) for the purpose of enabling or assisting a recognised self-regulating organisation, recognised investment exchange, recognised professional body, or recognised clearing house to discharge its functions as such;

(o) with a viw to the institution of, or otherwise for the purposes of, any disciplinary proceedings relating to the exercise by a solicitor, auditor, accountant, valuer or actuary of his professional duties;

(p) for the purpose of enabling or assisting any person appointed or authorised to exercise any powers under section 94, 106 or 177 above to discharge his functions;

(q) for the purpose of enabling or assisting an auditor of an authorised person or a person approved under section 108 above to discharge his functions;

(r) if the information is or has been available to the public from other sources;

(s) in a summary or collection of information framed in such a way as not to enable the identity of any person to whom the information relates to be ascertained; or

(t) in pursuance of any Community obligation.

(2)   Section 179 above shall not preclude the disclosure of information to the Secretary of State or to the Treasury if the disclosure is made in the interests of investors or in the public interest.

(3)   Subject to subsection (4) below, section 179 above shall not preclude the disclosure of information for the purpose of enabling or assisting any public or other authority for the time being designated for the purposes of this section by an order made by the Secretary of State to discharge any functions which are specified in the order.

(4)   An order under subsection (3) above designating an authority for the purposes of that subsection may—

(a) impose conditions subject to which the disclosure of information is permitted by that subsection; and

(b) otherwise restrict the circumstances in which that subsection permits disclosure.

(5)   Section 179 above shall not preclude the disclosure—

(a) of any information contained in an unpublished report of the Tribunal which has been made available to any person under this Act, by the person to whom it was made available or by any person obtaining the information directly or indirectly from him;

(b) of any information contained in any notice or copy of a notice served under this Act, notice of the contents of which has not been given to the public, by the person on whom it was served or any person obtaining the information directly or indirectly from him;

(c) of any information contained in the register kept under section 102 above by virtue of subsection (1)(e) of that section, by a person who has inspected the register under section 103(2) or (3) above or any person obtaining the information directly or indirectly from him.

(6)   Section 179 above shall not preclude the disclosure of information for the purpose of enabling or assisting an authority in a country or territory outside the United Kingdom to exercise functions corresponding to those of the Secretary of State under this Act or the Insurance Companies Act 1982 or to those of the Bank of England under the Banking Act 1979 or to those of the competent authority under this Act or any other functions in connection with rules of law corresponding to the provisions of the Company Securities (Insider Dealing) Act 1985 or Part VII of this Act.

(7)   Section 179 above shall not preclude the disclosure of information by the Director General of Fair Trading or any officer or servant of his or any person

obtaining the information directly or indirectly from the Director or any such officer or servant if the information was obtained by the Director or any such officer or servant for the purposes of or in the discharge of his functions under this Act (whether or not he was the primary recipient of the information within the meaning of section 179 above) and the disclosure is made—

(a) for the purpose of enabling or assisting the Director, the Secretary of State or any other Minister, the Monopolies and Mergers Commission or any Northern Ireland department to discharge any function conferred on him or them by the Fair Trading Act 1973 (other than Part II or III of that Act), the Restrictive Trade Practices Act 1976 or the Competition Act 1980; or
(b) for the purposes of any civil proceedings under any of those provisions;

and information shall not be treated as restricted information for the purposes of section 179 above if it has been made available to the public by virtue of this subsection.

(8) The Secretary of State may by order modify the application of any provision of this section so as—

(a) to prevent the disclosure by virtue of that provision; or
(b) to restrict the extent to which disclosure is permitted by virtue of that provision,

of information received by a person specified in the order pursuant to a Community obligation from a person exercising functions in relation to a collective investment scheme who is also so specified.

(9) An order under subsection (3) or (8) above shall be subject to annulment in pursuance of a resolution of either House of Parliament.

181. Directions restricting disclosure of information overseas

(1) If it appears to the Secretary of State to be in the public interest to do so, he may give a direction prohibiting the disclosure to any person in a country or territory outside the United Kingdom which is specified in the direction, or to such persons in such a country or territory as may be so specified, of such information to which this section applies as may be so specified.

(2) A direction under subsection (1) above—

(a) may prohibit disclosure of the information to which it applies by all persons or only by such persons or classes of person as may be specified in it; and
(b) may prohibit such disclosure absolutely or in such cases or subject to such conditions as to consent or otherwise as may be specified in it;

and a direction prohibiting disclosure by all persons shall be published by the Secretary of State in such manner as appears to him to be appropriate.

(3) This section applies to any information relating to the business or other affairs of any person which was obtained (whether or not by virtue of any requirement to supply it) directly or indirectly—

(a) by a designated agency, a transferee body, the competent authority or any person appointed or authorised to exercise any powers under section 94, 106 or 177 above (or any officer or servant of any such body or person) for the purposes or in the discharge of any functions of that body or person under this Act or any rules or regulations made under this Act or of any monitoring agency functions; or

(b) by a recognised self-regulating organisation, a recognised professional body, a recognised investment exchange or a recognised clearing house other than an overseas investment exchange or clearing house (or any officer or servant of such an organisation, body, investment exchange or clearing house) for the purposes or in the discharge of any of its functions as such or of any monitoring agency functions.

(4)   In subsection (3) above 'monitoring agency functions' means any functions exercisable on behalf of another body by virtue of arrangements made pursuant to paragraph 4(2) of Schedule 2, paragraph 4(6) of Schedule 3, paragraph 3(2) of Schedule 4 or paragraph 3(2) of Schedule 7 to this Act or of such arrangements as are mentioned in section 39(4)(b) above.

(5)   A direction under this section shall not prohibit the disclosure by any person other than a person mentioned in subsection (3) above of—

(a) information relating only to the affairs of that person; or
(b) information obtained by that person otherwise than directly or indirectly from a person mentioned in subsection (3) above.

(6)   A direction under this section shall not prohibit the disclosure of information in pursuance of any Community obligation.

(7)   A person who knowingly discloses information in contravention of a direction under this section shall be guilty of an offence and liable—

(a) on conviction on indictment, to imprisonment for a term not exceeding two years or to a fine or to both;
(b) on summary conviction, to imprisonment for a term not exceeding three months or to a fine not exceeding the statutory maximum or to both.

(8)   A person shall not be guilty of an offence under this section by virtue of anything done or omitted to be done by him outside the United Kingdom unless he is a British citizen, a British Dependent Territories citizen, a British Overseas citizen or a body corporate incorporated in the United Kingdom.

182.   Disclosure of information under enactments relating to fair trading, banking, insurance and companies

The enactments mentioned in Schedule 13 to this Act shall have effect with the amendments there specified (which relate to the circumstances in which information obtained under those enactments may be disclosed).

PART IX

RECIPROCITY

183.   Reciprocal facilities for financial business

(1)   If it appears to the Secretary of State or the Treasury that by reason of—

(a) the law of any country outside the United Kingdom; or
(b) any action taken by or the practices of the government or any other authority or body in that country,

persons connected with the United Kingdom are unable to carry on investment, insurance or banking business in, or in relation to, that country on terms as favourable as those on which persons connected with that country are able to carry on any such business in, or in relation to, the United Kingdom, the Secretary of State or, as the case may be, the Treasury may serve a notice under this subsection on any person connected with that country who is carrying on or appears to them to intend to carry on any such business in, or in relation to, the United Kingdom.

(2)   No notice shall be served under subsection (1) above unless the Secretary of State or, as the case may be, the Treasury consider it in the national interest to serve it; and before doing so the Secretary of State or, as the case may be, the Treasury shall so far as they consider expedient consult such body or bodies as appear to them to represent the interests of persons likely to be affected.

(3)   A notice under subsection (1) above shall state the grounds on which it is given (identifying the country in relation to which those grounds are considered to exist); and any such notice shall come into force on such date as may be specified in it.

(4)   For the purposes of this section a person is connected with a country if it appears to the Secretary of State or, as the case may be, the Treasury—

(a) in the case of an individual, that he is a national of or resident in that country or carries on investment, insurance or banking business from a principal place of business there;
(b) in the case of a body corporate, that it is incorporated or has a principal place of business in that country or is controlled by a person or persons connected with that country;
(c) in the case of a partnership, that it has a principal place of business in that country or that any partner is connected with that country;
(d) in the case of an unincorporated association which is not a partnership, that it is formed under the law of that country, has a principal place of business there or is controlled by a person or persons connected with that country.

(5)   In this section 'country' includes any territory or part of a country or territory; and where it appears to the Secretary of State or, as the case may be, the Treasury that there are such grounds as are mentioned in subsection (1) above in the case of any part of a country or territory their powers under that subsection shall also be exercisable in respect of any person who is connected with that country or territory or any other part or it.

184.   Investment and insurance business

(1)   A notice under section 183 above relating to the carrying on of investment business or insurance business shall be served by the Secretary of State and such a notice may be a disqualification notice, a restriction notice or a partial restriction notice and may relate to the carrying on of business of both kinds.

(2)   A disqualification notice as respects investment business or insurance business shall have the effect of—

(a) cancelling any authorisation of the person concerned to carry on that business after the expiry of such period after the service of the notice as may be specified in it;
(b) disqualifying him from becoming authorised to carry on that business after the expiry of that period; and
(c) restricting any authorisation of the person concerned in respect of that business during that period to the performance of contracts entered into

before the notice comes into force;

and the period specified in such a notice shall be such period as appears to the Secretary of State to be reasonable to enable the person on whom it is served to complete the performance of those contracts and to terminate such of them as are of a continuing nature.

(3)   A restriction notice as respects investment business or insurance business shall have the effect of restricting any authorisation of the person concerned in respect of that business to the performance of contracts entered into before the notice comes into force.

(4)   A partial restriction notice as respects investment business may prohibit the person concerned from—

(a) entering into transactions of any specified kind or entering into them except in specified circumstances or to a specified extent;
(b) soliciting business from persons of a specified kind or otherwise than from such persons;
(c) carrying on business in a specified manner or otherwise than in a specified manner.

(5)   A partial restriction notice as respects insurance business may direct that the person concerned shall cease to be authorised under section 3 or 4 of the Insurance Companies Act 1982 to effect contracts of insurance of any description specified in the notice.

(6)   If it appears to the Secretary of State that a person on whom he serves a notice under section 183 above as respects investment business is an authorised person by virtue of an authorisation granted by a designated agency or by virtue of membership of a recognised self-regulating organisation or certification by a recognised professional body he shall serve a copy of the notice on that agency, organisation or body.

(7)   If it appears to the Secretary of State—

(a) that any person on whom a partial restriction notice has been served by him has contravened any provision of that notice or, in the case of a notice under subsection (5) above, effected a contract of insurance of a description specified in the notice; and
(b) that any such grounds as are mentioned in subsection (1) of section 183 above still exist in the case of the country concerned,

he may serve a disqualification notice or a restriction notice on him under that section.

(8)   Sections 28, 33, 60, 61 and 62 above shall have effect in relation to a contravention of such a notice as is mentioned in subsection (4) above as they have effect in relation to any such contravention as is mentioned in those sections.

185.   Banking business

(1)   A notice under section 183 above relating to the carrying on of a deposit-taking business as a recognised bank or licensed institution within the meaning of the Banking Act 1979 shall be served by the Treasury and may be either a disqualification notice or a partial restriction notice.

(2)   A disqualification notice relating to such business shall have the effect of—

(a) cancelling any recognition or licence granted to the person concerned under the Banking Act 1979; and

(b) disqualifying him from becoming a recognised bank or licensed institution within the meaning of that Act.

(3) A partial restriction notice relating to such business may—

(a) prohibit the person concerned from dealing with or disposing of his assets in any manner specified in the direction;

(b) impose limitations on the acceptance by him of deposits;

(c) prohibit him from soliciting deposits either generally or from persons who are not already depositors;

(d) prohibit him from entering into any other transaction or class of transactions;

(e) require him to take certain steps, to pursue or refrain from pursuing a particular course of activities or to restrict the scope of his business in a particular way.

(4) The Treasury shall serve on the Bank of England a copy of any notice served by them under section 183 above.

(5) Any person who contravenes any provision of a partial restriction notice served on him by the Treasury under this section shall be guilty of an offence and liable—

(a) on conviction on indictment, to a fine;

(b) on summary conviction, to a fine not exceeding the statutory maximum.

(6) Any such contravention shall be actionable at the suit of a person who suffers loss as a result of the contravention subject to the defences and other incidents applying to actions for breach of statutory duty, but no such contravention shall invalidate any transaction.

(7) At the end of subsection (1) of section 8 of the Banking Act 1979 (power to give directions in connection with termination of deposit-taking authority) there shall be inserted—

'(d) at any time after a disqualification notice has been served on the institution by the Treasury under section 183 of the Financial Services Act 1986.'.

186. Variation and revocation of notices

(1) The Secretary of State or the Treasury may vary a partial restriction notice served under section 183 above by a notice in writing served on the person concerned; and any such notice shall come into force on such date as is specified in the notice.

(2) A notice under section 183 above may be revoked at any time by the Secretary of State or, as the case may be, the Treasury by serving a revocation notice on the person concerned; and the Secretary of State or, as the case may be, the Treasury shall revoke a notice if it appears to them that there are no longer any such grounds as are mentioned in subsection (1) of that section in the case of the country concerned.

(3) The revocation of a disqualification notice as respects investment business or insurance business shall not have the effect of reviving the authorisation which was

363

cancelled by the notice except where the notice relates to investment business and the person concerned would (apart from the disqualification notice) at the time of the revocation be an authorised person as respects the investment business in question by virtue of his membership of a recognised self-regulating organisation or certification by a recognised professional body.

(4)   The revocation of a disqualification notice as respects banking business shall not have the effect of reviving the recognition or licence which was cancelled by the notice.

(5)   Nothing in subsection (3) or (4) above shall be construed as preventing any person who has been subject to a disqualification notice as respects any business from again becoming authorised or, as the case may be, becoming a recognised bank or licensed institution within the meaning of the Banking Act 1979 after the revocation of the notice.

(6)   If it appears to the Secretary of State that a person on whom he serves a notice under this section as respects investment business was an authorised person by virtue of an authorisation granted by a designated agency or by virtue of membership of a recognised self-regulating organisation or certification by a recognised professional body at the time that the notice which is being varied or revoked was served, he shall serve a copy of the notice on that agency, organisation or body.

(7)   The Treasury shall serve on the Bank of England a copy of any notice served by them under this section.

PART X

MISCELLANEOUS AND SUPPLEMENTARY

187.   Exemption from liability for damages

(1)   Neither a recognised self-regulating organisation nor any of its officers or servants or members of its governing body shall be liable in damages for anything done or omitted in the discharge or purported discharge of any functions to which this subsection applies unless the act or omission is shown to have been in bad faith.

(2)   The functions to which subsection (1) above applies are the functions of the organisation so far as relating to, or to matters arising out of—

  (a) the rules, practices, powers and arrangements of the organisation to which the requirements in paragraphs 1 to 6 of Schedule 2 to this Act apply;
  (b) the obligations with which paragraph 7 of that Schedule requires the organisation to comply;
  (c) any guidance issued by the organisation;
  (d) the powers of the organisation under section 53(2), 64(4), 72(5), 73(5) or 105(2)(a) above; or
  (e) the obligations to which the organisation is subject by virtue of this Act.

(3)   No designated agency or transferee body nor any member, officer or servant of a designated agency or transferee body shall be liable in damages for anything done or omitted in the discharge or purported discharge of the functions exercisable by the agency by virtue of a delegation order or, as the case may be, the functions exercisable by the body by virtue of a transfer order unless the act or omission is shown to have been in bad faith.

(4)   Neither the competent authority nor any member, officer or servant of that authority shall be liable in damages for anything done or omitted in the discharge or purported discharge of any functions of the authority under Part IV of this Act unless the act or omission is shown to have been in bad faith.

(5)   The functions to which subsections (1) and (3) above apply also include any functions exercisable by a recognised self-regulating organisation, designated agency or transferee body on behalf of another body by virtue of arrangements made pursuant to paragraph 4(2) of Schedule 2, paragraph 4(6) of Schedule 3 and paragraph 3(2) of Schedule 4 or paragraph 3(2) of Schedule 7 to this Act or of such arrangements as are mentioned in section 39(4)(b) above.

(6)   A recognised professional body may make it a condition of a certificate issued by it for the purpose of Part I of this Act that neither the body nor any of its officers or servants or members of its governing body is to be liable in damages for anything done or omitted in the discharge or purported discharge of any functions to which this subsection applies unless the act or omission is shown to have been in bad faith.

(7)   The functions to which subsection (6) above applies are the functions of the body so far as relating to, or to matters arising out of—

(a) the rules, practices and arrangements of the body to which the requirements in paragraphs 2 to 5 of Schedule 3 to this Act apply;
(b) the obligations with which paragraph 6 of that Schedule requires the body to comply;
(c) any guidance issued by the body in respect of any matters dealt with by such rules as are mentioned in paragraph (a) above;
(d) the powers of the body under the provisions mentioned in subsection (2)(d) above or under section 54(3) above; or
(e) the obligations to which the body is subject by virtue of this Act.

188.   Jurisdiction as respects actions concerning designated agency etc
(1)   Proceedings arising out of any act or omission (or proposed act or omission) of a designated agency, transferee body or the competent authority in the discharge or purported discharge of any of its functions under this Act may be brought in the High Court or the Court of Session.

(2)   At the end of Schedule 5 to the Civil Jurisdiction and Judgments Act 1982 (exclusion of certain proceedings from the provisions of Schedule 4 to that Act which determine whether the courts in each part of the United Kingdom have jurisdiction in proceedings) there shall be inserted—

'*Proceedings concerning financial services agencies*

10.   Such proceedings as are mentioned in section 188 of the Financial Services Act 1986.'.

189.   Restriction of Rehabilitation of Offenders Act 1974
(1)   The Rehabilitation of Offenders Act 1974 shall have effect subject to the provisions of this section in cases where the spent conviction is for—

(a) an offence involving fraud or other dishonesty; or
(b) an offence under legislation (whether or not of the United Kingdom) relating to companies (including insider dealing), building societies,

industrial and provident societies, credit unions, friendly societies, insurance, banking or other financial services, insolvency, consumer credit or consumer protection.

(2)   Nothing in section 4(1) (restriction on evidence as to spent convictions in proceedings) shall prevent the determination in any proceedings specified in Part I of Schedule 14 to this Act of any issue, or prevent the admission or requirement in any such proceedings of any evidence, relating to a person's previous convictions for any such offence as is mentioned in subsection (1) above or to circumstances ancillary thereto.

(3)   A conviction for any such offence as is mentioned in subsection (1) above shall not be regarded as spent for the purposes of section 4(2) (questions relating to an individual's previous convictions) if—

(a) the question is put by or on behalf of a person specified in the first column of Part II of that Schedule and relates to an individual (whether or not the person questioned) specified in relation to the person putting the question in the second column of that Part; and
(b) the person questioned is informed when the question is put that by virtue of this section convictions for any such offence are to be disclosed.

(4)   Section 4(3)(b) (spent conviction not to be ground for excluding person from office, occupation etc.) shall not prevent a person specified in the first column of Part III of that Schedule from taking such action as is specified in relation to that person in the second column of that Part by reason, or partly by reason, of a spent conviction for any such offence as is mentioned in subsection (1) above of an individual who is—

(a) the person in respect of whom the action is taken;
(b) as respects action within paragraph 1 or 4 of that Part, an associate of that person; or
(c) as respects action within paragraph 1 of that Part consisting of a decision to refuse or revoke an order declaring a collective investment scheme to be an authorised unit trust scheme or a recognised scheme, the operator or trustee of the scheme or an associate of his,

or of any circumstances ancillary to such a conviction or of a failure (whether or not by that individual) to disclose such a conviction or any such circumstances.

(5)   Parts I, II and III of that Schedule shall have effect subject to Part IV.

(6)   In this section and that Schedule 'associate' means—

(a) in relation to a body corporate, a director, manager or controller;
(b) in relation to a partnership, a partner or manager;
(c) in relation to a registered friendly society, a trustee, manager or member of the committee of the society;
(d) in relation to an unincorporated association, a member of its governing body or an officer, manager or controller;
(e) in relation to an individual, a manager.

(7)   This section and that Schedule shall apply to Northern Ireland with the substitution for the references to the said Act of 1974 and section 4(1), (2) and (3)(b) of that Act of references to the Rehabilitation of Offenders (Northern Ireland) Order 1978 and Article 5(1), (2) and (3)(b) of that Order.

190. Data protection

An order under section 30 of the Data Protection Act 1984 (exemption from subject access provisions of data held for the purpose of discharging designated functions conferred by or under enactments relating to the regulation of financial services etc.) may designate for the purposes of that section as if they were functions conferred by or under such an enactment as is there mentioned—

(a) any functions of a recognised self-regulating organisation in connection with the admission or expulsion of members, the suspension of a person's membership or the supervision or regulation of persons carrying on investment business by virtue of membership of the organisation;

(b) any functions of a recognised professional body in connection with the issue of certificates for the purposes of Part I of this Act, the withdrawal or suspension of such certificates or the supervision or regulation of persons carrying on investment business by virtue of certification by that body;

(c) any functions of a recognised self-regulating organisation for friendly societies in connection with the supervision or regulation of its member societies.

191. Occupational pension schemes

(1) Subject to the provisions of this section, a person who apart from this section would not be regarded as carrying on investment business shall be treated as doing so if he engages in the activity of management falling within paragraph 14 of Schedule 1 to this Act in a case where the assets referred to in that paragraph are held for the purposes of an occupational pension scheme.

(2) Subsection (1) above does not apply where all decisions, or all day to day decisions, in the carrying on of that activity so far as relating to assets which are investments are taken on behalf of the person concerned by—

(a) an authorised person;

(b) an exempted person who in doing so is acting in the course of the business in respect of which he is exempt; or

(c) a person who does not require authorisation to manage the assets by virtue of Part IV of Schedule 1 to this Act.

(3) The Secretary of State may by order direct that a person of such description as is specified in the order shall not by virtue of this section be treated as carrying on investment business where the assets are held for the purposes of an occupational pension scheme of such description as is so specified, being a sheme in the case of which it appears to the Secretary of State that management by an authorised or exempted person is unnecessary having regard to the size of the scheme and the control exercisable over its affairs by the members.

(4) An order under subsection (3) above shall be subject to annulment in pursuance of a resolution of either House of Parliament.

(5) For the purposes of subsection (1) above paragraph 14 of Schedule 1 to this Act shall be construed without reference to paragraph 22 of that Schedule.

192. International obligations

(1) If it appears to the Secretary of State—

(a) that any action proposed to be taken by a recognised self-regulating organisation, designated agency, transferee body or competent authority

367

would be incompatible with Community obligations or any other international obligations of the United Kingdom; or

(b) that any action which that organisation, agency, body or authority has power to take is required for the purpose of implementing any such obligations,

he may direct the organisation, agency, body or authority not to take or, as the case may be, to take the action in question.

(2)   Subsection (1) above applies also to an approved exchange within the meaning of Part V of this Act in respect of any action which it proposes to take or has power to take in respect of rules applying to a prospectus by virtue of a direction under section 162(3) above.

(3)   A direction under this section may include such supplementary or incidental requirements as the Secretary of State thinks necessary or expedient.

(4)   Where the function of making or revoking a recognition order in respect of a self-regulating organisation is exercisable by a designated agency any direction under subsection (1) above in respect of that organisation shall be a direction requiring the agency to give the organisation such a direction as is specified in the direction given by the Secretary of State.

(5)   Any direction under this section shall, on the application of the person by whom it was given, be enforceable by mandamus or, in Scotland, by an order for specific performance under section 91 of the Court of Session Act 1868.

193.   Exemption from Banking Act 1979
(1)   Section 1(1) of the Banking Act 1979 (control of deposit-taking) shall not apply to the acceptance of a deposit by an authorised or exempted person in the course or for the purpose of engaging in any activity falling within paragraph 12 of Schedule 1 to this Act with or on behalf of the person by whom or on whose behalf the deposit is made or any activity falling within paragraph 13, 14 or 16 of that Schedule on behalf of that person.

(2)   Subsection (1) above applies to an exempted person only if the activity is one in respect of which he is exempt; and for the purposes of that subsection the paragraphs of Schedule 1 there mentioned shall be construed without reference to Parts III and IV of that Schedule.

(3)   This section is without prejudice to any exemption from the said Act of 1979 which applies to an authorised or exempted person apart from this section.

194.   Transfers to or from recognised clearing houses
(1)   In section 5 of the Stock Exchange (Completion of Bargains) Act 1976 (protection of trustees etc. in case of transfer of shares etc. to or from a stock exchange nominee)—

(a) for the words 'a stock exchange nominee', in the first place where they occur, there shall be substituted the words 'a recognised clearing house or a nominee of a recognised clearing house or of a recognised investment exchange';
(b) for those words in the second place where they occur there shall be substituted the words 'such a clearing house or nominee';
(c) at the end there shall be added the words '; but no person shall be a nominee

for the purposes of this section unless he is a person designated for the purposes of this section in the rules of the recognised investment exchange in question'.

(2) The provisions of that section as amended by subsection (1) above shall become subsection (1) of that section and after that subsection there shall be inserted—

'(2) In this section "a recognised clearing house" means a recognised clearing house within the meaning of the Financial Services Act 1986 acting in relation to a recognised investment exchange within the meaning of that Act and "a recognised investment exchange" has the same meaning as in that Act.'

(3) In Article 7 of the Stock Exchange (Completion of Bargains) (Northern Ireland) Order 1977 (protection of trustees etc. in case of transfer of shares etc. to or from a stock exchange nominee)—

(a) for the words 'a stock exchange nominee', in the first place where they occur, there shall be substituted the words 'a recognised clearing house or a nominee of a recognised clearing house or of a recognised investment exchange';
(b) for those words in the second place where they occur there shall be substituted the words 'such a clearing house or nominee';
(c) at the end there shall be added the words '; but no person shall be a nominee for the purposes of this Article unless he is a person designated for the purposes of this Article in the rules of the recognised investment exchange in question'.

(4) The provisions of that Article as amended by subsection (3) above shall become paragraph (1) of that Article and after that paragraph there shall be inserted—

'(2) In this Article "a recognised clearing house" means a recognised clearing house within the meaning of the Financial Services Act 1986 acting in relation to a recognised investment exchange within the meaning of that Act and "a recognised investment exchange" has the same meaning as in that Act.'

(5) In subsection (4) of section 185 of the Companies Act 1985 (exemption from duty to issue certificates in respect of shares etc. in cases of allotment or transfer to a stock exchange nominee)—

(a) for the words 'a stock exchange nominee' in the first place where they occur there shall be substituted the words 'a recognised clearing house or a nominee of a recognised clearing house or of a recognised investment exchange';
(b) for those words in the second place where they occur there shall be substituted the words 'such a clearing house or nominee';
(c) at the end of the first paragraph in that subsection there shall be inserted the words '; but no person shall be a nominee for the purposes of this section unless he is a person designated for the purposes of this section in the rules of the recognised investment exchange in question'; and
(d) for the second paragraph in that subsection there shall be substituted—

'"Recognised clearing house" means a recognised clearing house within the meaning of the Financial Services Act 1986 acting in relation to a recognised investment exchange and "recognised investment exchange" has the same meaning as in that Act'.

(6)   In subsection (4) of Article 195 of the Companies (Northern Ireland) Order 1986 (duty to issue certificates in respect of shares etc. in cases of allotment or transfer unless it is to a stock exchange nominee)—

- (a) for the words 'a stock exchange nominee' in the first place where they occur there shall be substituted the words 'a recognised clearing house or a nominee of a recognised clearing house or of a recognised investment exchange';
- (b) for those words in the second place where they occur there shall be substituted the words 'such a clearing house or nominee';
- (c) at the end of the first sub-paragraph in that paragraph there shall be inserted the words '; but no person shall be a nominee for the purposes of this Article unless he is a person designated for the purposes of this Article in the rules of the recognised investment exchange in question'; and
- (d) for the second sub-paragraph in that paragraph there shall be substituted '"recognised clearing house" means a recognised clearing house within the meaning of the Financial Services Act 1986 acting in relation to a recognised investment exchange and "recognised investment exchange" has the same meaning as in that Act.'.

195.   Offers of short-dated debentures
As respects debentures which, under the terms of issue, must be repaid within less than one year of the date of issue—

- (a) section 79(2) of the Companies Act 1985 (offer of debentures of oversea company deemed not to be an offer to the public if made to professional investor) shall apply for the purposes of Chapter I of Part III of that Act as well as for those of Chapter II of that Part; and
- (b) Article 89(2) of the Companies (Northern Ireland) Order 1986 (corresponding provisions for Northern Ireland) shall apply for the purposes of Chapter I of Part IV of that Order as well as for those of Chapter II of that Part.

196.   Financial assistance for employees' share schemes
(1)   Section 153 of the Companies Act 1985 (transactions not prohibited by section 151) shall be amended as follows.

(2)   After subsection (4)(b) there shall be inserted—

'(bb)   without prejudice to paragraph (b), the provision of financial assistance by a company or any of its subsidiaries for the purposes of or in connection with anything done by the company (or a company connected with it) for the purpose of enabling or facilitating transactions in shares in the first-mentioned company between, and involving the acquisition of beneficial ownership of those shares by, any of the following persons—

- (i) the bona fide employees or former employees of that company or of another company in the same group; or
- (ii) the wives, husbands, widows, widowers, children or step-children under the age of eighteen of any such employees or former employees.'.

(3)   After subsection (4) there shall be inserted—

'(5)   For the purposes of subsection (4)(bb) a company is connected with another company if—

   (a) they are in the same group; or
   (b) one is entitled, either alone or with any other company in the same group, to exercise or control the exercise of a majority of the voting rights attributable to the share capital which are exercisable in all circumstances at any general meeting of the other company or of its holding company;

and in this section "group", in relation to a company, means that company, any other company which is its holding company or subsidiary and any other company which is a subsidiary of that holding company.'.

(4) Article 163 of the Companies (Northern Ireland) Order 1986 (transactions not prohibited by Article 161) shall be amended as follows.

(5) After paragraph (4)(b) there shall be inserted—

   '(bb) without prejudice to sub-paragraph (b), the provision of financial assistance by a company or any of its subsidiaries for the purposes of or in connection with anything done by the company (or a company connected with it) for the purpose of enabling or facilitating transactions in shares in the first-mentioned company between, and involving the acquisition of beneficial ownership of those shares by, any of the following persons—

      (i) the bona fide employees or former employees of that company or of another company in the same group; or
      (ii) the wives, husbands, widows, widowers, children, step-children or adopted children under the age of eighteen of such employees or former employees.'

(6) After paragraph (4) there shall be inserted—

   '(5) For the purpose of paragraph (4)(bb) a company is connected with another company if—

   (a) they are in the same group; or
   (b) one is entitled, either alone or with any other company in the same group, to exercise or control the exercise of a majority of the voting rights attributable to the share capital which are exerciseable in all circumstances at any general meeting of the other company or of its holding company;

and in this Article "group", in relation to a company, means that company, any other company which is its holding company or subsidiary and any other company which is a subsidiary of that holding company.'.

197. Disclosure of interests in shares: interest held by market maker
(1) In section 209 of the Companies Act 1985 (interests to be disregarded for purposes of sections 198 to 202)—

   (a) in subsection (1)(f) after the word 'jobber' there shall be inserted the words 'or market maker';
   (b) after subsection (4) there shall be inserted—

      '(4A) A person is a market maker for the purposes of subsection (1)(f) if—

Appendix

(a) he holds himself out at all normal times in compliance with the rules of a recognised investment exchange other than an overseas investment exchange (within the meaning of the Financial Services Act 1986) as willing to buy and sell securities at prices specified by him; and

(b) is recognised as doing so by that investment exchange;

and an interest of such a person in shares is an exempt interest if he carries on business as a market maker in the United Kingdom, is subject to such rules in the carrying on of that business and holds the interest for the purposes of that business.'.

(2) In Article 217 of the Companies (Northern Ireland) Order 1986 (interests to be disregarded for purposes of Articles 206 to 210 (disclosure of interests in shares))—

(a) in paragraph (1)(d) after the word 'jobber' there shall be inserted the words 'or market maker';

(b) after paragraph (4) there shall be inserted—

'(4A)   A person is a market maker for the purposes of paragraph (1)(d) if—

(a) he holds himself out at all normal times in compliance with the rules of a recognised investment exchange other than an overseas investment exchange (within the meaning of the Financial Services Act 1986) as willing to buy and sell securities at a price specified by him; and

(b) is recognised as doing so by that investment exchange,

and an interest of such a person in shares is an exempt interest if he carries on business as a market maker in the United Kingdom, is subject to such rules in the carrying on of that business and holds the interest for the purposes of that business.'.

198. Power to petition for winding up etc on information obtained under Act

(1)   In section 440 of the Companies Act 1985—

(a) after the words 'section 437' there shall be inserted the words 'above or section 94 of the Financial Services Act 1986'; and

(b) after the words '448 below' there shall be inserted the words 'or section 105 of that Act'.

(2)   In section 8 of the Company Directors Disqualification Act 1986—

(a) after the words 'the Companies Act' there shall be inserted the words 'or section 94 or 177 of the Financial Services Act 1986'; and

(b) for the words 'that Act' there shall be substituted the words 'the Companies Act or section 105 of the Financial Services Act 1986'.

(3)   In Article 433 of the Companies (Northern Ireland) Order 1986—

(a) after the words 'Article 430' there shall be inserted the words 'or section 94 of the Financial Services Act 1986'; and

(b) after the word '441' there shall be inserted the words 'or section 105 of that Act'.

199. Powers of entry

(1) A justice of the peace may issue a warrant under this section if satisfied on information on oath laid by or on behalf of the Secretary of State that there are reasonable grounds for believing—

(a) that an offence has been committed under section 4, 47, 57, 130, 133 or 171(2) or (3) above or section 1, 2, 4 or 5 of the Company Securities (Insider Dealing) Act 1985 and that there are on any premises documents relevant to the question whether that offence has been committed; or

(b) that there are on any premises owned or occupied by a person whose affairs, or any aspect of whose affairs, are being investigated under section 105 above documents whose production has been required under that section and which have not been produced in compliance with that requirement;

but paragraph (b) above applies only if the person there mentioned is an authorised person, a person whose authorisation has been suspended or who is the subject of a direction under section 33(1)(b) above or an appointed representative of an authorised person.

(2) A justice of the peace may issue a warrant under this section if satisfied on information on oath laid by an inspector appointed under section 94 above that there are reasonable grounds for believing that there are on any premises owned or occupied by—

(a) the manager, trustee or operator of any scheme the affairs of which are being investigated under subsection (1) of that section; or

(b) a manager, trustee or operator whose affairs are being investigated under that subsection,

any documents whose production has been required under that section and which have not been produced in compliance with that requirement.

(3) A warrant under this section shall authorise a constable, together with any other person named in it and any other constables—

(a) to enter the premises specified in the information, using such force as is reasonably necessary for the purpose;

(b) to search the premises and take possession of any documents appearing to be such documents as are mentioned in subsection (1)(a) or (b) or, as the case may be, in subsection (2) above or to take, in relation to any such documents, any other steps which may appear to be necessary for preserving them or preventing interference with them;

(c) to take copies of any such documents; and

(d) to require any person named in the warrant to provide an explanation of them or to state where they may be found.

(4) A warrant under this section shall continue in force until the end of the period of one month beginning with the day on which it is issued.

(5) Any documents of which possession is taken under this section may be retained—

(a) for a period of three months; or

(b) if within that period proceedings to which the documents are relevant are commenced against any person for an offence under this Act or section 1, 2, 4 or 5 of the said Act of 1985, until the conclusion of those proceedings.

(6)   Any person who obstructs the exercise of any rights conferred by a warrant issued under this section or fails without reasonable excuse to comply with any requirement imposed in accordance with subsection (3)(d) above shall be guilty of an offence and liable—

(a) on conviction on indictment, to a fine;
(b) on summary conviction, to a fine not exceeding the statutory maximum.

(7)   The functions to which section 114 above applies shall include the functions of the Secretary of State under this section; but if any of those functions are transferred under that section the transfer may be subject to a reservation that they are to be exercisable by the Secretary of State concurrently with the designated agency and, in the case of functions exercisable by virtue of subsection (1.)(a) above, so as to be exercisable by the agency subject to such conditions or restrictions as the Secretary of State may from time to time impose.

(8)   In the application of this section to Scotland the references to a justice of the peace shall include references to a sheriff and for references to the laying of information on oath there shall be substituted references to furnishing evidence on oath; and in the application of this section to Northern Ireland for references to the laying of information on oath there shall be substituted references to making a complaint on oath.

(9)   In this section 'documents' includes information recorded in any form and, in relation to information recorded otherwise than in legible form, references to its production include references to producing a copy of the information in legible form.

200.   False and misleading statements
(1)   A person commits an offence if—

(a) for the purposes of or in connection with any application under this Act; or
(b) in purported compliance with any requirement imposed on him by or under this Act,

he furnishes information which he knows to be false or misleading in a material particular or recklessly furnishes information which is false or misleading in a material particular.

(2)   A person commits an offence if, not being an authorised person or exempted person, he—

(a) describes himself as such a person; or
(b) so holds himself out as to indicate or be reasonably understood to indicate that he is such a person.

(3)   A person commits an offence if, not having a status to which this subsection applies, he—

(a) describes himself as having that status, or
(b) so holds himself out as to indicate or be reasonably understood to indicate that he has that status.

(4)   Subsection (3) above applies to the status of recognised self-regulating organisation, recognised professional body, recognised investment exchange or recognised clearing house.

(5)   A person guilty of an offence under subsection (1) above shall be liable—

(a) on conviction on indictment, to imprisonment for a term not exceeding two years or to a fine or to both;
(b) on summary conviction, to imprisonment for a term not exceeding six months or to a fine not exceeding the statutory maximum or to both.

(6)   A person guilty of an offence under subsection (2) or (3) above shall be liable on summary conviction to imprisonment for a term not exceeding six months or to a fine not exceeding the fifth level on the standard scale or to both.

(7)   Where a contravention of subsection (2) or (3) above involves a public display of the offending description or other matter the maximum fine that may be imposed under subsection (6) above shall be an amount equal to the fifth level on the standard scale multiplied by the number of days for which the display has continued.

(8)   In proceedings brought against any person for an offence under subsection (2) or (3) above it shall be a defence for him to prove that he took all reasonable precautions and exercised all due diligence to avoid the commission of the offence.

201.   Prosecutions
(1)   Proceedings in respect of an offence under any provision of this Act other than section 133 or 185 shall not be instituted—

(a) in England and Wales, except by or with the consent of the Secretary of State or the Director of Public Prosecutions; or
(b) in Northern Ireland, except by or with the consent of the Secretary of State or the Director of Public Prosecutions for Northern Ireland.

(2)   Proceedings in respect of an offence under section 133 above shall not be instituted—

(a) in England and Wales, except by or with the consent of the Secretary of State, the Industrial Assurance Commissioner or the Director of Public Prosecutions; or
(b) in Northern Ireland, except by or with the consent of the Secretary of State or the Director of Public Prosecutions for Northern Ireland.

(3)   Proceedings in respect of an offence under section 185 above shall not be instituted—

(a) in England and Wales, except by or with the consent of the Treasury or the Director of Public Prosecutions; or
(b) in Northern Ireland, except by or with the consent of the Treasury or the Director of Public Prosecutions for Northern Ireland.

(4)   The functions to which section 114 above applies shall include the function of the Secretary of State under subsection (1) above to institute proceedings but any transfer of that function shall be subject to a reservation that it is to be exercisable by him concurrently with the designated agency and so as to be exercisable by the agency subject to such conditions or restrictions as the Secretary of State may from time to time impose.

202.   Offences by bodies corporate, partnerships and unincorporated associations
(1)   Where an offence under this Act committed by a body corporate is proved to

have been committed with the consent or connivance of, or to be attributable to any neglect on the part of—

(a) any director, manager, secretary or other similar officer of the body corporate, or any person who was purporting to act in any such capacity; or
(b) a controller of the body corporate,

he, as well as the body corporate, shall be guilty of that offence and liable to be proceeded against and punished accordingly.

(2)   Where the affairs of a body corporate are managed by the members subsection (1) above shall apply in relation to the acts and defaults of a member in connection with his functions of management as if he were a director of the body corporate.

(3)   Where a partnership is guilty of an offence under this Act every partner, other than a partner who is proved to have been ignorant of or to have attempted to prevent the commission of the offence, shall also be guilty of that offence and be liable to be proceeded against and punished accordingly.

(4)   Where an unincorporated association (other than a partnership) is guilty of an offence under this Act—

(a) every officer of the association who is bound to fulfil any duty of which the breach is the offence; or
(b) if there is no such officer, every member of the governing body other than a member who is proved to have been ignorant of or to have attempted to prevent the commission of the offence,

shall also be guilty of the offence and be liable to be proceeded against and punished accordingly.

203.   Jurisdiction and procedure in respect of offences

(1)   Summary proceedings for an offence under this Act may, without prejudice to any jurisdiction exercisable apart from this section, be taken against any body corporate or unincorporated association at any place at which it has a place of business and against an individual at any place where he is for the time being.

(2)   Proceedings for an offence alleged to have been committed under this Act by an unincorporated association shall be brought in the name of the association (and not in that of any of its members) and for the purposes of any such proceedings any rules of court relating to the service of documents shall have effect as if the association were a corporation.

(3)   Section 33 of the Criminal Justice Act 1925 and Schedule 3 to the Magistrates' Courts Act 1980 (procedure on charge of offence against a corporation) shall have effect in a case in which an unincorporated association is charged in England and Wales with an offence under this Act in like manner as they have effect in the case of a corporation.

(4)   In relation to any proceedings on indictment in Scotland for an offence alleged to have been committed under this Act by an unincorporated association, section 74 of the Criminal Procedure (Scotland) Act 1975 (proceedings on indictment against bodies corporate) shall have effect as if the association were a body corporate.

(5)   Section 18 of the Criminal Justice Act (Northern Ireland) 1945 and

Schedule 4 to the Magistrates' Courts (Northern Ireland) Order 1981 (procedure on charge of offence against a corporation) shall have effect in a case in which an unincorporated association is charged in Northern Ireland with an offence under this Act in like manner as they have effect in the case of a corporation.

(6) A fine imposed on an unincorporated association on its conviction of an offence under this Act shall be paid out of the funds of the association.

204. Service of notices

(1) This section has effect in relation to any notice, direction or other document required or authorised by or under this Act to be given to or served on any person other than the Secretary of State, the Chief Registrar of friendly societies or the Registrar of Friendly Societies for Northern Ireland.

(2) Any such document may be given to or served on the person in question—

(a) by delivering it to him;
(b) by leaving it at his proper address; or
(c) by sending it by post to him at that address.

(3) Any such document may—

(a) in the case of a body corporate, be given to or served on the secretary or clerk of that body;
(b) in the case of a partnership, be given to or served on any partner;
(c) in the case of an unincorporated association other than a partnership, be given to or served on any member of the governing body of the association;
(d) in the case of an appointed representative, be given to or served on his principal.

(4) For the purposes of this section and section 7 of the Interpretation Act 1978 (service of documents by post) in its application to this section, the proper address of any person is his last known address (whether of his residence or of a place where he carries on business or is employed) and also any address applicable in his case under the following provisions—

(a) in the case of a member of a recognised self-regulating organisation or a person certified by a recognised professional body who does not have a place of business in the United Kingdom, the address of that organisation or body;
(b) in the case of a body corporate, its secretary or its clerk, the address of its registered or principal office in the United Kingdom;
(c) in the case of an unincorporated association (other than a partnership) or a member of its governing body, its principal office in the United Kingdom.

(5) Where a person has notified the Secretary of State of an address or a new address at which documents may be given to or served on him under this Act that address shall also be his proper address for the purposes mentioned in subsection (4) above or, as the case may be, his proper address for those purposes in substitution for that previously notified.

205. Regulations, rules and orders

(1) The Secretary of State may make regulations prescribing anything which by this Act is authorised or required to be prescribed.

(2) Subject to subsection (5) below, any power of the Secretary of State to make

regulations, rules or orders under this Act shall be exercisable by statutory instrument.

(3)   Subject to subsection (5) below, any regulations, rules or orders made under this Act by the Secretary of State may make different provision for different cases.

(4)   Except as otherwise provided, a statutory instrument containing regulations or rules under this Act shall be subject to annulment in pursuance of a resolution of either House of Parliament.

(5)   Subsections (2) and (3) above do not apply to a recognition order, an order declaring a collective investment scheme to be an authorised unit trust scheme or a recognised scheme or to an order revoking any such order.

206.   Publication of information and advice

(1)   The Secretary of State may publish information or give advice, or arrange for the publication of information or the giving of advice, in such form and manner as he considers appropriate with respect to—

  (a) the operation of this Act and the rules and regulations made under it, including in particular the rights of investors, the duties of authorised persons and the steps to be taken for enforcing those rights or complying with those duties;

  (b) any matters relating to the fu..ctions of the Secretary of State under this Act or any such rules or regulations;

  (c) any other matters about which it appears to him to be desirable to publish information or give advice for the protection of investors or any class of investors.

(2)   The Secretary of State may offer for sale copies of information published under this section and may, if he thinks fit, make a reasonable charge for advice given under this section at any person's request.

(3)   This section shall not be construed as authorising the disclosure of restricted information within the meaning of section 179 above in any case in which it could not be disclosed apart from the provisions of this section.

(4)   The functions to which section 114 above applies shall include the functions of the Secretary of State under this section.

207.   Interpretation

(1)   In this Act, except where the context otherwise requires—

   'appointed representative' has the meaning given in section 44 above;
   'authorised person' means a person authorised under Chapter III of Part I of this Act;
   'authorised unit trust scheme' means a unit trust scheme declared by an order of the Secretary of State for the time being in force to be an authorised unit trust scheme for the purposes of this Act;
   'body corporate' includes a body corporate constituted under the law of a country or territory outside the United Kingdom;
   'certified' and 'certification' mean certified or certification by a recognised professional body for the purposes of Part I of this Act;
   'clearing arrangements' has the meaning given in section 38(2) above;
   'competent authority' means the competent authority for the purposes of Part IV of this Act;

'collective investment scheme' has the meaning given in section 75 above;

'delegation order' and 'designated agency' have the meaning given in section 114(3) above;

'director', in relation to a body corporate, includes a person occupying in relation to it the position of a director (by whatever name called) and any person in accordance with whose directions or instructions (not being advice given in a professional capacity) the directors of that body are accustomed to act;

'exempted person' means a person exempted under Chapter IV of Part I of this Act;

'group', in relation to a body corporate, means that body corporate, any other body corporate which is its holding company or subsidiary and any other body corporate which is a subsidiary of that holding company.

'guidance', in relation to a self-regulating organisation, professional body, investment exchange, clearing house or designated agency, has the meaning given in section 8(4), 16(4), 36(3), 38(3) or 114(12) above;

'investment advertisement' has the meaning given in section 57(2) above;

'investment agreement' has the meaning given in section 44(9) above;

'listing particulars' has the meaning given in section 144(2) above;

'member', in relation to a self-regulating organisation or professional body, has the meaning given in section 8(2) or 16(2) above;

'occupational pension scheme' means any scheme or arrangement which is comprised in one or more instruments or agreements and which has, or is capable of having, effect in relation to one or more descriptions or categories of employment so as to provide benefits, in the form of pensions or otherwise, payable on termination of service, or on death or retirement, to or in respect of earners with qualifying service in an employment of any such description or category;

'operator', in relation to a collective investment scheme, shall be construed in accordance with section 75(8) above;

'open-ended investment company' has the meaning given in section 75(8) above;

'overseas investment exchange' and 'overseas clearing house' mean a recognised investment exchange or recognised clearing house in the case of which the recognition order was made by virtue of section 40 above;

'participant' has the meaning given in section 75(2) above;

'partnership' includes a partnership constituted under the law of a country or territory outside the United Kingdom;

'prescribed' means prescribed by regulations made by the Secretary of State;

'principal', in relation to an appointed representative, has the meaning given in section 44 above;

'private company' has the meaning given in section 1(3) of the Companies Act 1985 or the corresponding Northern Ireland provision;

'recognised clearing house' means a body declared by an order of the Secretary of State for the time being in force to be a recognised clearing house for the purposes of this Act;

'recognised investment exchange' means a body declared by an order of the Secretary of State for the time being in force to be a recognised investment exchange for the purposes of this Act;

'recognised professional body' means a body declared by an order of the Secretary of State for the time being in force to be a recognised professional body for the purposes of this Act;

'recognised scheme' means a scheme recognised under section 86, 87 or 88 above;

'recognised self-regulating organisation' means a body declared by an order of the Secretary of State for the time being in force to be a recognised self-regulating organisation for the purposes of this Act;

'recognised self-regulating organisation for friendly societies' has the meaning given in paragraph 1 of Schedule 11 to this Act;

'recognition order' means an order declaring a body to be a recognised self-regulating organisation, self-regulating organisation for friendly societies, professional body, investment exchange or clearing house;

'registered friendly society' means—

(a) a society which is a friendly society within the meaning of section 7(1)(a) of the Friendly Societies Act 1974 and is registered within the meaning of that Act; or

(b) a society which is a friendly society within the meaning of section 1(1)(a) of the Friendly Societies Act (Northern Ireland) 1970 and is registered or deemed to be registered under that Act;

'rules', in relation to a self-regulating organisation, professional body, investment exchange or clearing house, has the meaning given in section 8(3), 16(3), 36(2) or 38(2) above;

'transfer order' and 'transferee body' have the meaning given in paragraph 28(4) of Schedule 11 to this Act;

'the Tribunal' means the Financial Services Tribunal;

'trustee', in relation to a collective investment scheme, has the meaning given in section 75(8) above;

'unit trust scheme' and 'units' have the meaning given in section 75(8) above.

(2)   In this Act 'advertisement' includes every form of advertising, whether in a publication, by the display of notices, signs, labels or showcards, by means of circulars, catalogues, price lists or other documents, by an exhibition of pictures or photographic or cinematographic films, by way of sound broadcasting or television, by the distribution of recordings, or in any other manner; and references to the issue of an advertisement shall be construed accordingly.

(3)   For the purposes of this Act an advertisement or other information issued outside the United Kingdom shall be treated as issued in the United Kingdom if it is directed to persons in the United Kingdom or is made available to them otherwise than in a newspaper, journal, magazine or other periodical publication published and circulating principally outside the United Kingdom or in a sound or television broadcast transmitted principally for reception outside the United Kingdom.

(4)   The Independent Broadcasting Authority shall not be regarded as contravening any provision of this Act by reason of broadcasting an advertisement in accordance with the provisions of the Broadcasting Act 1981.

(5)   In this Act 'controller' means—

(a) in relation to a body corporate, a person who, either alone or with any associate or associates, is entitled to exercise, or control the exercise of, 15 per cent or more of the voting power at any general meeting of the body corporate or another body corporate of which it is a subsidiary; and

(b) in relation to an unincorporated association—

(i) any person in accordance with whose directions or instructions, either alone or with those of any associate or associates, the officers or members of the governing body of the association are accustomed to act (but disregarding advice given in a professional capacity); and

(ii) any person who, either alone or with any associate or associates, is entitled to exercise, or control the exercise of, 15 per cent or more of the voting power at any general meeting of the association;

and for the purposes of this subsection 'associate', in relation to any person, means that person's wife, husband or minor child or step-child, any body corporate of which that person is a director, any person who is an employee or partner of that person and, if that person is a body corporate, any subsidiary of that body corporate and any employee of any such subsidiary.

(6) In this Act, except in relation to a unit trust scheme or a registered friendly society, 'manager' means an employee who—

(a) under the immediate authority of his employer is responsible, either alone or jointly with one or more other persons, for the conduct of his employer's business; or

(b) under the immediate authority of his employer or of a person who is a manager by virtue of paragraph (a) above exercises managerial functions or is responsible for maintaining accounts or other records of his employer;

and, where the employer is not an individual, references in this subsection to the authority of the employer are references to the authority, in the case of a body corporate, of the directors, in the case of a partnership, of the partners and, in the case of an unincorporated association, of its officers or the members of its governing body.

(7) In this Act 'insurance business', 'insurance company' and 'contract of insurance' have the same meanings as in the Insurance Companies Act 1982.

(8) Section 736 of the Companies Act 1985 (meaning of subsidiary and holding company) shall apply for the purposes of this Act.

(9) In the application of this Act to Scotland, references to a matter being actionable at the suit of a person shall be construed as references to the matter being actionable at the instance of that person.

(10) For the purposes of any provision of this Act authorising or requiring a person to do anything within a specified number of days no account shall be taken of any day which is a public holiday in any part of the United Kingdom.

(11) Nothing in Part I of this Act shall be construed as applying to investment business carried on by any person when acting as agent or otherwise on behalf of the Crown.

208. Gibraltar

(1) Subject to the provisions of this section, section 31, 58(1)(c), 86 and 130(2)(c) and (d) above shall apply as if Gibraltar were a member State.

(2) References in those provisions to a national of a member State shall, in relation to Gibraltar, be construed as references to a British Dependent Territories citizen or a body incorporated in Gibraltar.

(3) In the case of a collective investment scheme constituted in Gibraltar the

reference in subsection (3)(a) of section 86 above to a relevant Community instrument shall be taken as a reference to any Community instrument the object of which is the co-ordination or approximation of the laws, regulations or administrative provisions of member States relating to collective investment schemes of a kind which satisfy the requirements prescribed for the purposes of that section.

(4)   The Secretary of State may by regulations make such provision as appears to him to be necessary or expedient to secure—

(a) that he may give notice under subsection (2) of section 86 above on grounds relating to the law of Gibraltar; and
(b) that this Act applies as if a scheme which is constituted in a member State other than the United Kingdom and recognised in Gibraltar under provisions which appear to the Secretary of State to give effect to the provisions of a relevant Community instrument were a scheme recognised under that section.

209.   Northern Ireland
(1)   This Act extends to Northern Ireland.

(2)   Subject to any Order made after the passing of this Act by virtue of subsection (1)(a) of section 3 of the Northern Ireland Constitution Act 1973 the regulation of investment business, the offical listing of securities and offers of unlisted securities shall not be transferred matters for the purposes of that Act but shall for the purposes of subsection (2) of that section be treated as specified in Schedule 3 to that Act.

210.   Expenses and receipts
(1)   Any expenses incurred by the Secretary of State under this Act shall be defrayed out of moneys provided by Parliament.

(2)   Any fees or other sums received by the Secretary of State under this Act shall be paid into the Consolidated Fund.

(3)   Subsections (1) and (2) above apply also to expenses incurred and fees received under this Act by the Chief Registrar of friendly societies; and any fees received under this Act by the Registrar of Friendly Societies for Northern Ireland shall be paid into the Consolidated Fund of Northern Ireland.

211.   Commencement and transitional provisions
(1)   This Act shall come into force on such day as the Secretary of State may by order appoint and different days may be appointed for different provisions or different purposes.

(2)   Subsection (1) above does not apply to section 195 which shall come into force when this Act is passed.

(3)   Schedule 15 to this Act shall have effect with respect to the transitional matters there mentioned.

212.   Short title, consequential amendments and repeals
(1)   This Act may be cited as the Financial Services Act 1986.

(2)   The enactments and instruments mentioned in Schedule 16 to this Act shall

have effect with the amendments there specified, being amendments consequential on the provisions of this Act.

(3) The enactments mentioned in Part I of Schedule 17 to this Act and the instruments mentioned in Part II of that Schedule are hereby repealed or revoked to the extent specified in the third column of those Parts.

SCHEDULES

SCHEDULE 1 (Sections 1 and 2)

INVESTMENTS AND INVESTMENT BUSINESS

PART I

INVESTMENTS

Shares etc

1. Shares and stock in the share capital of a company.

Note. In this paragraph 'company' includes any body corporate and also any unincorporated body constituted under the law of a country or territory outside the United Kingdom but does not include an open-ended investment company or any body incorporated under the law of, or of any part of, the United Kingdom relating to building societies, industrial and provident societies or credit unions.

Debentures

2. Debentures, including debenture stock, loan stock, bonds, certificates of deposit and other instruments creating or acknowledging indebtedness, not being instruments falling within paragraph 3 below.

Note. This paragraph shall not be construed as applying—

(a) to any instrument acknowledging or creating indebtedness for, or for money borrowed to defray, the consideration payable under a contract for the supply of goods or services;

(b) to a cheque or other bill of exchange, a banker's draft or a letter of credit; or

(c) to a banknote, a statement showing a balance in a current, deposit or savings account or (by reason of any financial obligation contained in it) to a lease or other disposition of property, a heritable security or an insurance policy.

Government and public securities

3. Loan stock, bonds and other instruments creating or acknowledging indebtedness issued by or on behalf of a government, local authority or public authority.

Notes

(1) In this paragraph 'government, local authority or public authority' means—

(a) the government of the United Kingdom, of Northern Ireland, or of any country or territory outside the United Kingdom;

(b) a local authority in the United Kingdom or elsewhere;

(c) any international organisation the members of which include the United Kingdom or another member State.

(2) The Note to paragraph 2 above shall, so far as applicable, apply also to this paragraph.

Instruments entitling to shares or securities

4. Warrants or other instruments entitling the holder to subscribe for investments falling within paragraph 1, 2 or 3 above.

Notes

(1) It is immaterial whether the investments are for the time being in existence or identifiable.

(2) An investment falling within this paragraph shall not be regarded as falling within paragraph 7, 8 or 9 below.

Certificates representing securities

5. Certificates or other instruments which confer—

    (a) property rights in respect of any investment falling within paragraph 1, 2, 3 or 4 above;

    (b) any right to acquire, dispose of, underwrite or convert an investment, being a right to which the holder would be entitled if he held any such investment to which the certificate or instrument relates; or

    (c) a contractual right (other than an option) to acquire any such investment otherwise than by subscription.

Note. This paragraph does not apply to any instrument which confers rights in respect of two or more investments issued by different persons or in respect of two or more different investments falling within paragraph 3 above and issued by the same person.

Units in collective investment scheme

6. Units in a collective investment scheme, including shares in or securities of an open-ended investment company.

Options

7. Options to acquire or dispose of—

    (a) an investment falling within any other paragraph of this Part of this Schedule;

    (b) currency of the United Kingdom or of any other country or territory;

    (c) gold or silver; or

    (d) an option to acquire or dispose of an investment falling within this paragraph by virtue of (a), (b) or (c) above.

Futures

8. Rights under a contract for the sale of a commodity or property of any other description under which delivery is to be made at a future date and at a price agreed upon when the contract is made.

Notes

(1) This paragraph does not apply if the contract is made for commercial and not investment purposes.

(2) A contract shall be regarded as made for investment purposes if it is made or traded on a recognised investment exchange or made otherwise than on a recognised investment exchange but expressed to be as traded on such an exchange or on the same terms as those on which an equivalent contract would be made on such an exchange.

(3) A contract not falling within Note (2) above shall be regarded as made for commercial purposes if under the terms of the contract delivery is to be made within seven days.

(4) The following are indications that any other contract is made for a commercial purpose and the absence of any of them is an indication that it is made for investment purposes—

    (a) either or each of the parties is a producer of the commodity or other property or uses it in his business;

    (b) the seller delivers or intends to deliver the property or the purchaser takes or intends to take delivery of it.

(5) It is an indication that a contract is made for commercial purposes that the price, the lot, the delivery date or the other terms are determined by the parties for the purposes of the particular contract and not by reference to regularly published prices, to standard lots or delivery dates or to standard terms.

(6) The following are also indications that a contract is made for investment purposes—

    (a) it is expressed to be as traded on a market or on an exchange;

    (b) performance of the contract is ensured by an investment exchange or a clearing house;

    (c) there are arrangements for the payment or provision of margin.

(7) A price shall be taken to have been agreed upon when a contract is made—

    (a) notwithstanding that it is left to be determined by reference to the price at which a contract is to be entered into on a market or exchange or could be entered into at a time and place specified in the contract; or

    (b) in a case where the contract is expressed to be by reference to a standard lot and quality, notwithstanding that provision is made for a variation in the price to take account of any variation in quantity or quality on delivery.

Contracts for differences etc

9. Rights under a contract for differences or under any other contract the purpose or pretended purpose of which is to secure a profit or avoid a loss by reference to fluctuations in the value or price of property of any description or in an index or other factor designated for that purpose in the contract.

Note. This paragraph does not apply where the parties intend that the profit is to be obtained or the loss avoided by taking delivery of any property to which the contract relates.

Long term insurance contracts

10. Rights under a contract the effecting and carrying out of which constitutes long term business within the meaning of the Insurance Companies Act 1982.

Notes

(1) This paragraph does not apply to rights under a contract of insurance if—

    (a) the benefits under the contract are payable only on death or in respect of incapacity due to injury, sickness or infirmity;

    (b) no benefits are payable under the contract on a death (other than a death due to accident) unless it occurs within ten years of the date on which the life of the person in question was first insured under the contract or before that person attains a specified age not exceeding seventy years;

    (c) the contract has no surrender value or the consideration consists of a single premium and the surrender value does not exceed that premium; and

    (d) the contract does not make provision for its conversion or extension in a manner that would result in its ceasing to comply with paragraphs (a), (b) and (c) above.

(2) Where the provisions of a contract of insurance are such that the effecting and carrying out of the contract—

    (a) constitutes both long term business within the meaning of the Insurance Companies Act 1982 and general business within the meaning of that Act; or

(b) by virtue of section 1(3) of that Act constitutes long term business notwithstanding the inclusion of subsidiary general business provisions,

references in this paragraph to rights and benefits under the contract are references only to such rights and benefits as are attributable to the provisions of the contract relating to long term business.

(3) This paragraph does not apply to rights under a re-insurance contract.

(4) Rights falling within this paragraph shall not be regarded as falling within paragraph 9 above.

Rights and interests in investments

11. Rights to and interests in anything which is an investment falling within any other paragraph of this Part of this Schedule.

Notes

(1) This paragraph does not apply to interests under the trusts of an occupational pension scheme.

(2) This paragraph does not apply to rights or interests which are investments by virtue of any other paragraph of this Part of this Schedule.

PART II

ACTIVITIES CONSTITUTING INVESTMENT BUSINESS

Dealing in investments

12. Buying, selling, subscribing for or underwriting investments or offering or agreeing to do so, either as principal or as an agent.

Arranging deals in investments

13. Making, or offering or agreeing to make

(a) arrangements with a view to another person buying, selling, subscribing for or underwriting a particular investment; or
(b) arrangements with a view to a person who participates in the arrangements buying, selling, subscribing for or underwriting investments.

Notes

(1) This paragraph does not apply to a person by reason of his making, or offering or agreeing to make, arrangements with a view to a transaction to which he will himself be a party as principal or which will be entered into by him as agent for one of the parties.

(2) The arrangements in (a) above are arrangements which bring about or would bring about the transaction in question.

Managing investments

14. Managing, or offering or agreeing to manage, assets, belonging to another person if—

(a) those assets consist of or include investments; or
(b) the arrangements for their management are such that those assets may consist of or include investments at the discretion of the person managing or offering or agreeing to manage them and either they have at any time since the date of the coming into force of section 3 of this Act done so or the arrangements have at any time (whether before or after that date) been held out as arrangements under which they would do so.

Investment advice

15. Giving, or offering or agreeing to give, to persons in their capacity as investors or potential investors advice on the merits of their purchasing, selling, subscribing for or underwriting an investment, or exercising any right conferred by an investment to acquire, dispose of, underwrite or convert an investment.

Establishing etc collective investment schemes

16. Establishing, operating or winding up a collective investment scheme, including acting as trustee of an authorised unit trust scheme.

PART III

EXCLUDED ACTIVITIES

Dealings as principal

17.—(1) Paragraph 12 above applies to a transaction which is or is to be entered into by a person as principal only if—

  (a) he holds himself out as willing to enter into transactions of that kind at prices determined by him generally and continuously rather than in respect of each particular transaction; or
  (b) he holds himself out as engaging in the business of buying investments with a view to selling them and those investments are or include investments of the kind to which the transaction relates; or
  (c) he regularly solicits members of the public for the purpose of inducing them to enter as principals or agents into transactions to which that paragraph applies and the transaction is or is to be entered into as a result of his having solicited members of the public in that manner.

(2) In sub-paragraph (1) above 'buying' and 'selling' means buying and selling by transactions to which paragraph 12 above applies and 'members of the public', in relation to the person soliciting them ('the relevant person'), means any other persons except—

  (a) authorised persons, exempted persons, or persons holding a permission under paragraph 23 below;
  (b) members of the same group as the relevant person;
  (c) persons who are, or propose to become, participators with the relevant person in a joint enterprise;
  (d) any person who is solicited by the relevant person with a view to—
    (i) the acquisition by the relevant person of 20 per cent or more of the voting shares in a body corporate (that is to say, shares carrying not less than that percentage of the voting rights attributable to share capital which are exercisable in all circumstances at any general meeting of the body); or
    (ii) if the relevant person (either alone or with other members of the same group as himself) holds 20 per cent or more of the voting shares in a body corporate, the acquisition by him of further shares in the body or the disposal by him of shares in that body to the person solicited or to a member of the same group as that person; or
    (iii) if the person solicited (either alone or with other members of the same group as himself) holds 20 per cent or more of the voting shares in a body corporate, the disposal by the relevant person of further shares in that body to the person solicited or to a member of the same group as that person;
  (e) any person whose head office is outside the United Kingdom, who is solicited by an approach made or directed to him at a place outside the United Kingdom and whose ordinary business involves him in engaging in activities which fall within Part II of this Schedule or would do so apart from this Part of Part IV.

(3) Sub-paragraph (1) above applies only if the investment to which the transaction relates or will relate falls within any of paragraphs 1 to 6 above or, so far as relevant to any of those paragraphs, paragraph 11 above.

(4) Paragraph 12 above does not apply to a transaction which relates or is to relate to any other investment and which is or is to be entered into by a person as principal if he is not an authorised person and the transaction is or is to be entered into by him—

    (a) with or through an authorised person, an exempted person or a person holding a permission under paragraph 23 below; or

    (b) through an office outside the United Kingdom, maintained by a party to the transaction, and with or through a person whose head office is situated outside the United Kingdom and whose ordinary business is such as is mentioned in sub-paragraph (2)(e) above.

Groups and joint enterprises

18.—(1) Paragraph 12 above does not apply to any transaction which is or is to be entered into by a person as principal with another person if—

    (a) they are bodies corporate in the same group; or

    (b) they are, or proposed to become, participators in a joint enterprise and the transaction is or is to be entered into for the purposes of, or in connection with, that enterprise.

(2) Paragraph 12 above does not apply to any transaction which is or is to be entered into by any person as agent for another person in the circumstances mentioned in sub-paragraph (1)(a) or (b) above if—

    (a) where the investment falls within any of paragraphs 1 to 6 above or, so far as relevant to any of those paragraphs, paragraph 11 above, the agent does not—

        (i) hold himself out (otherwise than to other bodies corporate in the same group or persons who are or propose to become participators with him in a joint enterprise) as engaging in the business of buying investments with a view to selling them and those investments are or include investments of the kind to which the transaction relates; or

        (ii) regularly solicit members of the public for the purpose of inducing them to enter as principals or agents into transactions to which paragraph 12 above applies; and the transaction is not or is not to be entered into as a result of his having solicited members of the public in that manner;

    (b) where the investment is not as mentioned in paragraph (a) above—

        (i) the agent enters into the transaction with or through an authorised person, an exempted person or a person holding a permission under paragraph 23 below; or

        (ii) the transaction is effected through an office outside the United Kingdom, maintained by a party to the transaction, and with or through a person whose head office is situated outside the United Kingdom and whose ordinary business involves him in engaging in activities which fall within Part II of this Schedule or would do so apart from this Part of Part IV.

(3) Paragraph 13 above does not apply to arrangements which a person makes or offers or agrees to make if—

    (a) that person is a body corporate and the arrangements are with a view to another body corporate in the same group entering into a transaction of the kind mentioned in that paragraph; or

    (b) that person is or proposes to become a participator in a joint enterprise and the arrangements are with a view to another person who is or proposes to become a participator in the enterprise entering into such a transaction for the purposes of or in connection with that enterprise.

(4) Paragraph 14 above does not apply to a person by reason of his managing or offering or agreeing to manage the investments of another person if—

  (a) they are bodies corporate in the same group; or
  (b) they are, or propose to become, participators in a joint enterprise and the investments are or are to be managed for the purposes of, or in conection with, that enterprise.

(5) Paragraph 15 above does not apply to advice given by a person to another person if—

  (a) they are bodies corporate in the same group; or
  (b) they are, or propose to become, participators in a joint enterprise and the advice is given for the purposes of, or in connection with, that enterprise.

(6) The definitions in paragraph 17(2) above shall apply also for the purposes of sub-paragraph (2)(a) above except that the relevant person referred to in paragraph 17(2)(d) shall be the person for whom the agent is acting.

Sale of goods and supply of services

Could be cut down

19.—(1) This paragraph has effect where a person ('the supplier') sells or offers or agrees to sell goods to another person ('the customer') or supplies or offers or agrees to supply him with services and the supplier's main business is to supply goods or services and not to engage in activities falling within Part II of this Schedule.

(2) Paragraph 12 above does not apply to any transaction which is or is to be entered into by the supplier as principal if it is or is to be entered into by him with the customer for the purposes of or in connection with the sale or supply or a related sale or supply (that is to say, a sale or supply to the customer otherwise than by the supplier but for or in connection with the same purpose as the first-mentioned sale or supply).

(3) Paragraph 12 above does not apply to any transaction which is or is to be entered into by the supplier as agent for the customer if it is or is to be entered into for the purposes of or in connection with the sale or supply or a related sale or supply and—

  (a) where the investment falls within any of paragraphs 1 to 6 above or, so far as relevant to any of those paragraphs, paragraph 11 above, the supplier does not—

    (i) hold himself out (otherwise than to the customer) as engaging in the business of buying investments with a view to selling them and those investments are or include investments of the kind to which the transaction relates; or
    (ii) regularly solicit members of the public for the purpose of inducing them to enter as principals or agents into transactions to which paragraph 12 above applies;

  and the transaction is not or is not to be entered into as a result of his having solicited members of the public in that manner;

  (b) where the investment is not as mentioned in paragraph (a) above, the supplier enters into the transaction—

    (i) with or through an authorised person, an exempted person or a person holding a permission under paragraph 23 below; or
    (ii) through an office outside the United Kingdom, maintained by a party to the transaction, and with or through a person whose head office is situated outside the United Kingdom and whose ordinary business involves him in engaging in activities which fall within Part II of this Schedule or would do so apart from this Part or Part IV.

(4) Paragraph 13 above does not apply to arrangements which the supplier makes or offers or agrees to make with a view to the customer entering into a transaction for the purposes of or in connection with the sale or supply or a related sale or supply.

(5) Paragraph 14 above does not apply to the supplier by reason of his managing or offering or agreeing to manage the investments of the customer if they are or are to be managed for the purposes of or in connection with the sale or supply or a related sale or supply.

(6) Paragraph 15 above does not apply to advice given by the supplier to the customer for the purposes of or in connection with the sale or supply or a related sale or supply or to a person with whom the customer proposes to enter into a transaction for the purposes of or in connection with the sale or supply or a related sale or supply.

(7) Where the supplier is a body corporate and a member of a group sub-paragraphs (2) to (6) above shall apply to any other member of the group as they apply to the supplier; and where the customer is a body corporate and a member of a group references in those sub-paragraphs to the customer include references to any other member of the group.

(8) The definitions in paragraph 17(2) above shall apply also for the purposes of sub-paragraph (3)(a) above.

Employees' share schemes

20.—(1) Paragraphs 12 and 13 above do not apply to anything done by a body corporate, a body corporate connected with it or a relevant trustee for the purpose of enabling or facilitating transactions in shares in or debentures of the first-mentioned body between or for the benefit of any of the persons mentioned in sub-paragraph (2) below or the holding of such shares or debentures by or for the benefit of any such persons.

(2) The persons referred to in sub-paragraph (1) above are—

    (a) the bona fide employees or former employees of the body corporate or of another body corporate in the same group; or

    (b) the wives, husbands, widows, widowers, or children or step-children under the age of eighteen of such employees or former employees.

(3) In this paragraph 'a relevant trustee' means a person holding shares in or debentures of a body corporate as trustee in pursuance of arrangements made for the purpose mentioned in sub-paragraph (1) above by, or by a body corporate connected with, that body corporate.

(4) In this paragraph 'shares' and 'debentures' include any investment falling within paragraph 1 or 2 above and also include any investment falling within paragraph 4 or 5 above so far as relating to those paragraphs or any investment falling within paragraph 11 above so far as relating to paragraph 1, 2, 4 or 5.

(5) For the purposes of this paragraph a body corporate is connected with another body corporate if—

    (a) they are in the same group; or

    (b) one is entitled, either alone or with any other body corporate in the same group, to exercise or control the exercise of a majority of the voting rights attributable to the share capital which are exercisable in all circumstances at any general meeting of the other body corporate or of its holding company.

Sale of private company

21.—(1) Paragraphs 12 and 13 above do not apply to the acquisition or disposal of, or to anything done for the purposes of the acquisition or disposal of, shares in a private company, and paragraph 15 above does not apply to advice given in connection with the acquisition or disposal of such shares, if—

    (a) the shares consist of or include shares carrying 75 per cent or more of the voting rights attributable to share capital which are exercisable in all circumstances at any general meeting of the company; or

    (b) the shares, together with any already held by the person acquiring them, carry not less than that percentage of those voting rights; and

(c) in either case, the acquisition and disposal is, or is to be, between parties each of whom is a body corporate, a partnership, a single individual or a group of connected individuals.

(2) For the purposes of subsection (1)(c) above 'a group of connected individuals', in relation to the party disposing of the shares, means persons each of whom is, or is a close relative of, a director or manager of the company and, in relation to the party acquiring the shares, means persons each of whom is, or is a close relative of, a person who is to be a director or manager of the company.

(3) In this paragraph 'private company' means a private company within the meaning of section 1(3) of the Companies Act 1985 or the corresponding Northern Ireland provision and 'close relative' means a person's spouse, his children and step-children, his parents and step-parents, his brothers and sisters and his step-brothers and step-sisters.

Trustees and personal representatives
22.—(1) Paragraph 12 above does not apply to a person by reason of his buying, selling or subscribing for an investment or offering or agreeing to do so if—

    (a) the investment is or, as the case may be, is to be held by him as bare trustee or, in Scotland, as nominee for another person;
    (b) he is acting on that person's instructions; and
    (c) he does not hold himself out as providing a service of buying and selling investments.

(2) Paragraph 13 above does not apply to anything done by a person as trustee or personal representative with a view to—

    (a) a fellow trustee or personal representative and himself engaging in their capacity as such in an activity falling within paragraph 12 above; or
    (b) a beneficiary under the trust, will or intestacy engaging in any such activity,

unless that person is remunerated for what he does in addition to any remuneration he receives for discharging his duties as trustee or personal representative.

(3) Paragraph 14 above does not apply to anything done by a person as trustee or personal representative unless he holds himself out as offering investment management services or is remunerated for providing such services in addition to any remuneration he receives for discharging his duties as trustee or personal representative.

(4) Paragraph 15 above does not apply to advice given by a person as trustee or personal representative to—

    (a) a fellow trustee or personal representative for the purposes of the trust or estate; or
    (b) a beneficiary under the trust, will or intestacy concerning his interest in the trust fund or estate,

unless that person is remunerated for doing so in addition to any remuneration he receives for discharging his duties as trustee or personal representative.

(5) Sub-paragraph (1) above has effect to the exclusion of paragraph 17 above as respects any transaction in respect of which the conditions in sub-paragraph (1)(a) and (b) are satisfied.

Dealings in course of non-investment business
23.—(1) Paragraph 12 above does not apply to anything done by a person—

    (a) as principal;
    (b) if that person is a body corporate in a group, as agent for another member of the group; or
    (c) as agent for a person who is or proposes to become a participator with him in a joint enterprise and for the purposes of or in connection with that enterprise,

if it is done in accordance with the terms and conditions of a permission granted to him by the Secretary of State under this paragraph.

(2) Any application for permission under this paragraph shall be accompanied or supported by such information as the Secretary of State may require and shall not be regarded as duly made unless accompanied by the prescribed fee.

(3) The Secretary of State may grant a permission under this paragraph if it appears to him—

- (a) that the applicant's main business, or if he is a member of a group the main business of the group, does not consist of activities for which a person is required to be authorised under this Act;
- (b) that the applicant's business is likely to involve such activities which fall within paragraph 12 above; and
- (c) that, having regard to the nature of the applicant's main business and, if he is a member of a group, the main business of the group taken as a whole, the manner in which, the persons with whom and the purposes for which the applicant proposes to engage in activities that would require him to be an authorised person and to any other relevant matters, it is inappropriate to require him to be subject to regulation as an authorised person.

(4) Any permission under this paragraph shall be granted by a notice in writing; and the Secretary of State may by a further notice in writing withdraw any such permission if for any reason it appears to him that it is not appropriate for it to continue in force.

(5) The Secretary of State may make regulations requiring persons holding permissions under this paragraph to furnish him with information for the purpose of enabling him to determine whether those permissions should continue in force; and such regulations may, in particular, require such persons—

- (a) to give him notice forthwith of the occurrence of such events as are specified in the regulations and such information in respect of those events as is so specified;
- (b) to furnish him at such times or in respect of such periods as are specified in the regulations with such information as is so specified.

(6) Section 61 of this Act shall have effect in relation to a contravention of any condition imposed by a permission under this paragraph as it has effect in relation to any such contravention as is mentioned in subsection (1)(a) of that section.

(7) Section 104 of this Act shall apply to a person holding a permission under this paragraph as if he were authorised to carry on investment business as there mentioned; and sections 105 and 106 of this Act shall have effect as if anything done by him in accordance with such permission constituted the carrying on of investment business.

Advice given in course of profession or non-investment business

24.—(1) Paragraph 15 above does not apply to advice—

- (a) which is given in the course of the carrying on of any profession or of a business not otherwise constituting investment business; and
- (b) the giving of which is a necessary part of other advice or services given in the course of carrying on that profession or business.

(2) Advice shall not be regarded as falling within sub-paragraph (1)(b) above if it is remunerated separately from the other advice or services.

Newspapers

25.—(1) Paragraph 15 above does not apply to advice given in a newspaper, journal, magazine or other periodical publication if the principal purpose of the publication, taken as a whole and including any advertisements contained in it, is not to lead persons to invest in any particular investment.

(2) The Secretary of State may, on the application of the proprietor of any periodical publication, certify that it is of the nature described in sub-paragraph (1) above and revoke any such certificate if he considers that it is no longer justified.

(3) A certificate given under sub-paragraph (2) above and not revoked shall be conclusive evidence of the matters certified.

PART IV

ADDITIONAL EXCLUSIONS FOR PERSONS WITHOUT PERMANENT PLACE OF BUSINESS IN UNITED KINGDOM

Transactions with or through authorised or exempted persons

26.—(1) Paragraph 12 above does not apply to any transaction by a person not falling within section 1(3)(a) of this Act ('an overseas person') with or through—

   (a) an authorised person; or
   (b) an exempted person acting in the course of business in respect of which he is exempt.

(2) Paragraph 13 above does not apply if—

   (a) the arrangements are made by an overseas person with, or the offer or agreement to make them is made by him to or with, an authorised person or an exempted person and, in the case of an exempted person, the arrangements are with a view to his entering into a transaction in respect of which he is exempt; or
   (b) the transactions with a view to which the arrangements are made are, as respects transactions in the United Kingdom, confined to transactions by authorised persons and transactions by exempted persons in respect of which they are exempt.

Unsolicited or legitimately solicited transactions etc with or for other persons

27.—(1) Paragraph 12 above does not apply to any transaction entered into by an overseas person as principal with, or as agent for, a person in the United Kingdom, paragraphs 13, 14 and 15 above do not apply to any offer made by an overseas person to or agreement made by him with a person in the United Kingdom and paragraph 15 above does not apply to any advice given by an overseas person to a person in the United Kingdom if the transaction, offer, agreement or advice is the result of—

   (a) an approach made to the overseas person by or on behalf of the person in the United Kingdom which either has not been in any way solicited by the overseas person or has been solicited by him in a way which has not contravened section 56 or 57 of this Act; or
   (b) an approach made by the overseas person which has not contravened either of those sections.

(2) Where the transaction is entered into by the overseas person as agent for a person in the United Kingdom, sub-paragraph (1) above applies only if—

   (a) the other party is outside the United Kingdom; or
   (b) the other party is in the United Kingdom and the transaction is the result of such an approach by the other party as is mentioned in sub-paragraph (1)(a) above or of such an approach as is mentioned in sub-paragraph (1)(b) above.

PART V

INTERPRETATION

28.—(1) In this Schedule—

    (a) 'property' includes currency of the United Kingdom or any other country or territory;

    (b) references to an instrument include references to any record whether or not in the form of a document;

    (c) references to an offer include references to an invitation to treat;

    (d) references to buying and selling include references to any acquisition or disposal for valuable consideration.

(2) In sub-paragraph (1)(d) above 'disposal' includes—

    (a) in the case of an investment consisting of rights under a contract or other arrangements, assuming the corresponding liabilities under the contract or arrangements;

    (b) in the case of any other investment, issuing or creating the investment or granting the rights or interests of which it consists;

    (c) in the case of an investment consisting of rights under a contract, surrendering, assigning or converting those rights.

(3) A company shall not by reason of issuing its own shares or share warrants, and a person shall not by reason of issuing his own debentures or debenture warrants, be regarded for the purposes of this Schedule as disposing of them or, by reason of anything done for the purpose of issuing them, be regarded as making arrangements with a view to a person subscribing for or otherwise acquiring them or underwriting them.

(4) In sub-paragraph (3) above 'company' has the same meaning as in paragraph 1 above, 'shares' and 'debentures' include any investments falling within paragraph 1 or 2 above and 'share warrants' and 'debenture warrants' means any investment which falls within paragraph 4 above and relates to shares in the company concerned or, as the case may be, to debentures issued by the person concerned.

29. For the purposes of this Schedule a transaction is entered into through a person if he enters into it as agent or arranges for it to be entered into by another person as principal or agent.

30. For the purposes of this Schedule a group shall be treated as including any body corporate which is a related company within the meaning of paragraph 92 of Schedule 4 to the Companies Act 1985 of any member of the group or would be such a related company if the member of the group were a company within the meaning of that Act.

31. In this Schedule 'a joint enterprise' means an enterprise into which two or more persons ('the participators') enter for commercial reasons related to a business or businesses (other than investment business) carried on by them; and where a participator is a body corporate and a member of a group each other member of the group shall also be regarded as a participator in the enterprise.

32. Where a person is an exempted person as respects only part of the investment business carried on by him anything done by him in carrying on that part shall be disregarded in determining whether any paragraph of Part III or IV of this Schedule applies to anything done by him in the course of business in respect of which he is not exempt.

33. In determining for the purposes of this Schedule whether anything constitutes an investment or the carrying on of investment business section 18 of the Gaming Act 1845, section 1 of the Gaming Act 1892, any corresponding provision in force in Northern Ireland and any rule of the law of Scotland whereby a contract by way of gaming or wagering is not legally enforceable shall be disregarded.

SCHEDULE 2 (Section 10)

REQUIREMENTS FOR RECOGNITION OF SELF-REGULATING ORGANISATION

Members to be fit and proper persons

1.—(1) The rules and practices of the organisation must be such as to secure that its members are fit and proper persons to carry on investment business of the kind with which the organisation is concerned.

(2) Where the organisation is concerned with investment business of different kinds its rules and practices must be such as to secure that a member carrying on investment business of any of those kinds is a fit and proper person to carry on investment business of that kind.

(3) The matters which may be taken into account under the rules in determining whether a person is a fit and proper person must include those that the Secretary of State may take into account under section 27 above.

(4) This paragraph does not apply to a person who is not an authorised person by virtue of being a member of the organisation.

Admission, expulsion and discipline

2. The rules and practices of the organisation relating to—

   (a) the admission and expulsion of members; and
   (b) the discipline it exercises over its members,

must be fair and reasonable and include adequate provision for appeals.

Safeguards for investors

3.—(1) The rules of the organisation governing the carrying on of investment business of any kind by its members must afford investors protection at least equivalent to that afforded in respect of investment business of that kind by the rules and regulations for the time being in force under Chapter V of Part I of this Act.

(2) The rules under that Chapter to be taken into account for the purposes of sub-paragraph (1) above include the rules made under section 49 and under sections 53 and 54 so far as not themselves applying to the members of the organisation.

(3) The organisation must, so far as practicable, have powers for purposes corresponding to those of Chapter VI of Part I of this Act.

(4) The rules of the organisation must enable it to prevent a member resigning from the organisation if the organisation considers that any matter affecting him should be investigated as a preliminary to a decision on the question whether he should be expelled or otherwise disciplined or if it considers that it is desirable that a prohibition or requirement should be imposed on him under the powers mentioned in sub-paragraph (3) above or that any prohibition or requirement imposed on him under those powers should continue in force.

Monitoring and enforcement

4.—(1) The organisation must have adequate arrangements and resources for the effective monitoring and enforcement of compliance with its rules and with any rules or regulations to which its members are subject under Chapter V of Part I of this Act in respect of investment business of a kind regulated by the organisation.

(2) The arrangements for monitoring may make provision for that function to be performed on behalf of the organisation (and without affecting its responsibility) by any other body or person who is able and willing to perform it.

Appendix

The governing body

5.—(1) The arrangements of the organisation with respect to the appointment, removal from office and functions of the persons responsible for making or enforcing the rules of the organisation must be such as to secure a proper balance—

    (a) between the interests of the different members of the organisation; and

    (b) between the interests of the organisation or its members and the interests of the public.

(2) The arrangements shall not be regarded as satisfying the requirements of this paragraph unless the persons responsible for those matters include a number of persons independent of the organisation and its members sufficient to secure the balance referred to in sub-paragraph (1)(b) above.

Investigation of complaints

6.—(1) The organisation must have effective arrangements for the investigation of complaints against the organisation or its members.

(2) The arrangements may make provision for the whole or part of that function to be performed by and to be the responsibility of a body or person independent of the organisation.

Promotion and maintenance of standards

7. The organisation must be able and willing to promote and maintain high standards of integrity and fair dealing in the carrying on of investment business and to co-operate, by the sharing of information and otherwise, with the Secretary of State and any other authority, body or person having responsibility for the supervision or regulation of investment business or other financial services.

SCHEDULE 3 (Section 18)

REQUIREMENTS FOR RECOGNITION OF PROFESSIONAL BODY

Statutory status

1. The body must—

    (a) regulate the practice of a profession in the exercise of statutory powers; or

    (b) be recognised (otherwise than under this Act) for a statutory purpose by a Minister of the Crown or by, or by the head of, a Northern Ireland department; or

    (c) be specified in a provision contained in or made under an enactment as a body whose members are qualified to exercise functions or hold offices specified in that provision.

Certification

2.—(1) The body must have rules, practices and arrangements for securing that no person can be certified by the body for the purposes of Part I of this Act unless the following conditions are satisfied.

(2) The certified person must be either—

    (a) an individual who is a member of the body; or

    (b) a person managed and controlled by one or more individuals each of whom is a member of a recognised professional body and at least one of whom is a member of the certifying body.

(3) Where the certified person is an individual his main business must be the practice of the

396

profession regulated by the certifying body and he must be practising that profession otherwise than in partnership; and where the certified person is not an individual that person's main business must be the practice of the profession or professions regulated by the recognised professional body or bodies of which the individual or individuals mentioned in sub-paragraph (2)(b) above are members.

(4) In the application of sub-paragraphs (2) and (3) above to a certificate which is to be or has been issued to a partnership constituted under the law of England and Wales or Northern Ireland or the law of any other country or territory under which a partnership is not a legal person, references to the certified person shall be construed as references to the partnership.

Safeguards for investors

3.—(1) The body must have rules regulating the carrying on of investment business by persons certified by it; and those rules must in respect of investment business of any kind regulated by them afford to investors protection at least equivalent to that afforded in respect of investment business of that kind by the rules and regulations for the time being in force under Chapter V of Part I of this Act.

(2) The rules under that Chapter to be taken into account for the purposes of this paragraph include the rules made under section 49 and under sections 53 and 54 so far as not themselves applying to persons certified by the body.

Monitoring and enforcement

4.—(1) The body must have adequate arrangements and resources for the effective monitoring of the continued compliance by persons certified by it with the conditions mentioned in paragraph 2 above and rules, practices and arrangements for the withdrawal or suspension of certification (subject to appropriate transitional provisions) in the event of any of those conditions ceasing to be satisfied.

(2) The body must have adequate arrangements and resources for the effective monitoring and enforcement of compliance by persons certified by it with the rules of the body relating to the carrying on of investment business and with any rules or regulations to which those persons are subject under Chapter V of Part I of this Act in respect of business of a kind regulated by the body.

(3) The arrangements for enforcement must include provision for the withdrawal or suspension of certification and may include provision for disciplining members of the body who manage or control a certified person.

(4) The arrangements for enforcement may make provision for the whole or part of that function to be performed by and to be the responsibility of a body or person independent of the professional body.

(5) The arrangements for enforcement must be such as to secure a proper balance between the interests of persons certified by the body and the interests of the public; and the arrangements shall not be regarded as satisfying that requirement unless the persons responsible for enforcement include a sufficient number of persons who are independent of the body and its members and of persons certified by it.

(6) The arrangements for monitoring may make provision for that function to be performed on behalf of the body (and without affecting its responsibility) by any other body or person who is able and willing to perform it.

Investigation of complaints

5.—(1) The body must have effective arrangements for the investigation of complaints relating to—

 (a) the carrying on by persons certified by it of investment business in respect of which they are subject to its rules; and
 (b) its regulation of investment business.

(2) Paragraph 4(4) above applies also to arrangements made pursuant to this paragraph.

Promotion and maintenance of standards

6. The body must be able and willing to promote and maintain high standards of integrity and fair dealing in the carrying on of investment business and to co-operate, by the sharing of information and otherwise, with the Secretary of State and any other authority, body or person having responsibility for the supervision or regulation of investment business or other financial services.

SCHEDULE 4 (Sections 36 and 37)

REQUIREMENTS FOR RECOGNITION OF INVESTMENT EXCHANGE

Financial resources

1. The exchange must have financial resources sufficient for the proper performance of its functions.

Safeguards for investors

2.—(1) The rules and practices of the exchange must ensure that business conducted by means of its facilities is conducted in an orderly manner and so as to afford proper protection to investors.

(2) The exchange must—

 (a) limit dealings on the exchange to investments in which there is a proper market; and
 (b) where relevant, require issuers of investments dealt in on the exchange to comply with such obligations as will, so far as possible, afford to persons dealing in the investments proper information for determining their current value.

(3) In the case of securities to which Part IV of this Act applies compliance by The Stock Exchange with the provisions of that Part shall be treated as compliance by it with sub-paragraph (2) above.

(4) The exchange must either have its own arrangements for ensuring the performance of transactions effected on the exchange or ensure their performance by means of services provided under clearing arrangements made by it with a recognised clearing house.

(5) The exchange must either itself have or secure the provision on its behalf of satisfactory arrangements for recording the transactions effected on the exchange.

(6) Sub-paragraphs (2), (4) and (5) above are without prejudice to the generality of sub-paragraph (1) above.

Monitoring and enforcement

3.—(1) The exchange must have adequate arrangements and resources for the effective monitoring and enforcement of compliance with its rules and any clearing arrangements made by it.

(2) The arrangements for monitoring may make provision for that function to be performed on behalf of the exchange (and without affecting its responsibility) by any other body or person who is able and willing to perform it.

Investigation of complaints

4. The exchange must have effective arrangements for the investigation of complaints in respect of business transacted by means of its facilities.

Promotion and maintenance of standards

5. The exchange must be able and willing to promote and maintain high standards of integrity and fair dealing in the carrying on of investment business and to co-operate, by the sharing of information and otherwise, with the Secretary of State and any other authority, body or person having responsibility for the supervision or regulation of investment business or other financial services.

SCHEDULE 5 (Section 43)

LISTED MONEY MARKET INSTITUTIONS

PART I

TRANSACTIONS NOT SUBJECT TO MONETARY LIMIT

1. This Part of this Schedule applies to any transaction entered into by the listed institution as principal (or as agent for another listed institution) with another listed institution or the Bank of England (whether acting as principal or agent) if the transaction falls within paragraph 2 or 3 below.

2.—(1) A transaction falls within this paragraph if it is in respect of an investment specified in sub-paragraph (2) below and—

  (a) in the case of an investment within any of paragraphs (a) to (d) of that sub-paragraph, the transaction is not regulated by the rules of a recognised investment exchange; and

  (b) in the case of any other investment specified in that sub-paragraph, the transaction is not made on such an exchange or expressed to be as so made.

(2) The investments referred to above are—

  (a) a debenture or other instrument falling within paragraph 2 of Schedule 1 to this Act which is issued—

    (i) by a recognised bank or licensed institution within the meaning of the Banking Act 1979 or a building society incorporated in, or in any part of, the United Kingdom; and

    (ii) on terms requiring repayment not later than five years from the date of issue;

  (b) any other debenture or instrument falling within paragraph 2 of Schedule 1 to this Act which is issued on terms requiring repayment not later than one year from the date of issue;

  (c) loan stock, or any other instrument, falling within paragraph 3 of Schedule 1 to this Act which is issued on terms requiring repayment not later than one year or, if issued by a local authority in the United Kingdom, five years from the date of issue;

  (d) a warrant or other instrument falling within paragraph 4 of Schedule 1 to this Act which entitles the holder to subscribe for an investment within paragraph (a), (b) or (c) above;

  (e) any certificate or other instrument falling within paragraph 5 or 11 of Schedule 1 to this Act and relating to an investment within paragraph (a), (b) or (c) above;

  (f) an option falling within paragraph 7 of Schedule 1 to this Act and relating to—

(i) an investment within paragraph (a), (b) or (c) above;
(ii) currency of the United Kingdom or of any other country or territory; or
(iii) gold or silver;

(g) rights under a contract falling within paragraph 8 of Schedule 1 to this Act for the sale of—

(i) an investment within paragraph (a), (b) or (c) above;
(ii) currency of the United Kingdom or of any other country or territory; or
(iii) gold or silver;

(h) rights under a contract falling within paragraph 9 of Schedule 1 to this Act by reference to fluctuations in—

(i) the value or price of any investment falling within any of the foregoing paragraphs; or
(ii) currency of the United Kingdom or of any other country or territory; or
(iii) the rate of interest on loans in any such currency or any index of such rates;

(i) an option to acquire or dispose of an investment within paragraph (f), (g) or (h) above.

3.—(1) A transaction falls within this paragraph if it is a transaction by which one of the parties agrees to sell or transfer an investment falling within paragraph 2 or 3 of Schedule 1 to this Act and if by the same or a collateral agreement that party agrees, or acquires an option, to buy back or re-acquire that investment or an equivalent amount of a similar investment within twelve months of the sale or transfer.

(2) For the purposes of this paragraph investments shall be regarded as similar if they entitle their holders to the same rights against the same persons as to capital and interest and the same remedies for the enforcement of those rights.

PART II

TRANSACTIONS SUBJECT TO MONETARY LIMIT

4.—(1) This Part of this Schedule applies to any transaction entered into by the listed institution—

(a) as principal (or as agent for another listed institution) with an unlisted person (whether acting as principal or agent);
(b) as agent for an unlisted person with a listed institution or the Bank of England (whether acting as principal or agent); or
(c) as agent for an unlisted person with another unlisted person (whether acting as principal or agent),

if the transaction falls within paragraph 2 or 3 above and the conditions in paragraph 5 or, as the case may be, paragraph 7 below are satisfied.

(2) In this Part of this Schedule and in Part III below 'unlisted person' means a person who is neither a listed institution nor the Bank of England.

5.—(1) In the case of a transaction falling within paragraph 2 above the conditions referred to above are as follows but subject to paragraph 6 below.

(2) The consideration for a transaction in respect of an investment falling within paragraph (2)(a), (b), (c) or (e) above must be not less than £100,000.

(3) The consideration payable on subscription in the case of an investment falling within paragraph 2(2)(d) must not be less than £500,000.

(4) The value or price of the property in respect of which an option within paragraph 2(2)(f) above is granted must not be less than £500,000.

(5) The price payable under a contract within paragraph 2(2)(g) above must be not less than £500,000.

(6) The value or price the fluctuation in which, or the amount the fluctuation in the interest on which, is relevant for the purposes of a contract within paragraph 2(2)(h) above must not be less than £500,000.

(7) In the case of an option falling within paragraph 2(2)(i) above the condition in sub-paragraph (4), (5) or (6) above, as the case may be, must be satisfied in respect of the investment to which the option relates.

6. The conditions in paragraph 5 above do not apply to a transaction entered into by the listed institution as mentioned in paragraph (a), (b) or (c) of paragraph 4(1) above if—

(a) the unlisted person mentioned in paragraph (a) or (b) or, as the case may be, each of the unlisted persons mentioned in paragraph (c) has in the previous eighteen months entered into another transaction in respect of an investment specified in paragraph 2(2) above;

(b) those conditions were satisfied in the case of that other transaction; and

(c) that other transaction was entered into by that person (whether acting as principal or agent) with the listed institution (whether acting as principal or agent) or was entered into by that person through the agency of that institution or was entered into by him (whether acting as principal or agent) as a result of arrangements made by that institution.

7. In the case of a transaction falling within paragraph 3 above the condition referred to in paragraph 4 above is that the consideration for the sale or transfer must be not less than £100,000.

8. The monetary limits mentioned in this Part of this Schedule refer to the time when the transaction is entered into; and where the consideration, value, price or amount referred to above is not in sterling it shall be converted at the rate of exchange prevailing at that time.

PART III

TRANSACTIONS ARRANGED BY LISTED INSTITUTIONS

9. Subject to paragraphs 10 and 11 below, this Part of this Schedule applies to any transaction arranged by the listed institution which—

(a) is entered into by another listed institution as principal (or as agent for another listed institution) with another listed institution or the Bank of England (whether acting as principal or agent);

(b) is entered into by another listed institution (whether acting as principal or agent) with an unlisted person (whether acting as principal or agent); or

(c) is entered into between unlisted persons (whether acting as principal or agent),

if the transaction falls within paragraph 2 or 3 above.

10. In the case of a transaction falling within paragraph 2 above paragraph 9(b) and (c) above do not apply unless either the conditions in paragraph 5 above are satisfied or—

(a) the unlisted person mentioned in paragraph (b) or, as the case may be, each of the unlisted persons mentioned in paragraph (c) has in the previous eighteen months entered into another transaction in respect of an investment specified in paragraph 2(2) above;

(b) those conditions were satisfied in the case of that other transaction; and

(c) that other transaction was entered into by that person (whether acting as principal or agent) with the listed institution making the arrangements (whether acting as principal or agent) or through the agency of that institution or was entered into by that person (whether acting as principal or agent) as a result of arrangements made by that institution.

11. In the case of a transaction falling within paragraph 3 above paragraph 9(b) and (c) above do not apply unless the condition in paragraph 7 above is satisfied.

SCHEDULE 6 (Section 96(6))

THE FINANCIAL SERVICES TRIBUNAL

Term of office of members

1.—(1) A person appointed to the panel mentioned in section 96(2) of this Act shall hold and vacate his office in accordance with the terms of his appointment and on ceasing to hold office shall be eligible for re-appointment.

(2) A member of the panel appointed by the Lord Chancellor may resign his office by notice in writing to the Lord Chancellor; and a member of the panel appointed by the Secretary of State may resign his office by notice in writing to the Secretary of State.

Expenses

2. The Secretary of State shall pay to the persons serving as members of the Tribunal such remuneration and allowances as he may determine and shall defray such other expenses of the Tribunal as he may approve.

Staff

3. The Secretary of State may provide the Tribunal with such officers and servants as he thinks necessary for the proper discharge of its functions.

Procedure

4.—(1) The Secretary of State may make rules for regulating the procedure of the Tribunal, including provision for the holding of any proceedings in private, for the awarding of costs (or, in Scotland, expenses) and for the payment of expenses to persons required to attend before the Tribunal.

(2) The Tribunal may appoint counsel or a solicitor to assist it in proceedings before the Tribunal.

Evidence

5.—(1) The Tribunal may by summons require any person to attend, at such time and place as is specified in the summons, to give evidence or to produce any document in his custody or under his control which the Tribunal considers it necessary to examine.

(2) The Tribunal may take evidence on oath and for that purpose administer oaths or may, instead of administering an oath, require the person examined to make and subscribe a declaration of the truth of the matters in respect of which he is examined.

(3) Any person who without reasonable excuse—

   (a) refuses or fails to attend in obedience to a summons issued by the Tribunal or to give evidence; or

   (b) alters, suppresses, conceals or destroys or refuses to produce a document which he may be required to produce for the purposes of proceedings before the Tribunal,

shall be guilty of an offence.

(4) A person guilty of an offence under paragraph (a) of sub-paragraph (3) above shall be

liable on summary conviction to a fine not exceeding the fifth level on the standard scale; and a person guilty of an offence under paragraph (b) of that sub-paragraph shall be liable—

(a) on conviction on indictment, to imprisonment for a term not exceeding two years or to a fine or to both;

(b) on summary conviction, to a fine not exceeding the statutory maximum.

(5) A person shall not under this paragraph be required to disclose any information or produce any document which he would be entitled to refuse to disclose or produce on grounds of legal professional privilege in proceedings in the High Court or on grounds of confidentiality as between client and professional legal adviser in proceedings in the Court of Session except that a lawyer may be required to furnish the name and address of his client.

(6) Any reference in this paragraph to the production of a document includes a reference to the production of a legible copy of information recorded otherwise than in legible form; and the reference to suppressing a document includes a reference to destroying the means of reproducing information recorded otherwise than in legible form.

Appeals and supervision by Council on Tribunals

6. The Tribunals and Inquiries Act 1971 shall be amended as follows—

(a) in section 8(2) after '6A' there shall be inserted '6B';

(b) in section 13(1) after '6' there shall be inserted '6B';

(c) in Schedule 1, after paragraph 6A there shall be inserted—

'Financial services.   6B. The Financial Services Tribunal established by section 96 of the Financial Services Act 1986.'

Parliamentary disqualification

7.—(1) In Part III of Schedule 1 to the House of Commons Disqualification Act 1975 (disqualifying offices) there shall be inserted at the appropriate place 'Any member of the Financial Services Tribunal in receipt of remuneration'.

(2) A corresponding amendment shall be made in Part III of Schedule 1 to the Northern Ireland Assembly Disqualification Act 1975.

SCHEDULE 7 (Section 114)

QUALIFICATIONS OF DESIGNATED AGENCY

Constitution

1.—(1) The constitution of the agency must provide for it to have—

(a) a chairman; and

(b) a governing body consisting of the chairman and other members;

and the provisions of the constitution relating to the chairman and the other members of the governing body must comply with the following provisions of this paragraph.

(2) The chairman and other members of the governing body must be persons appointed and liable to removal from office by the Secretary of State and the Governor of the Bank of England acting jointly.

(3) The members of the governing body must include—

(a) persons with experience of investment business of a kind relevant to the functions or proposed functions of the agency; and

    (b) other persons, including regular users on their own account or on behalf of others of services provided by persons carrying on investment business of any such kind;

and the composition of that body must be such as to secure a proper balance between the interests of persons carrying on investment business and the interests of the public.

Arrangements for discharge of functions

2.—(1) The agency's arrangements for the discharge of its functions must comply with the following provisions of this paragraph.

(2) Any rules or regulations must be made by the governing body of the agency.

(3) Any decision taken in the exercise of other functions must be taken at a level appropriate to the importance of the decision.

(4) In the case of functions to be discharged by the governing body, the members falling respectively within paragraphs (a) and (b) of paragraph 1(3) above must, so far as practicable, have an opportunity to express their opinions.

(5) Subject to sub-paragraphs (2) to (4) above, the arrangements may enable any functions to be discharged by a committee, sub-committee, officer or servant of the agency.

Monitoring and enforcement

3.—(1) The agency must have a satisfactory system—

    (a) for enabling it to determine whether persons regulated by it are complying with the obligations which it is the responsibility of the agency to enforce; and

    (b) for the discharge of the agency's responsibility for the enforcement of those obligations.

(2) The system may provide for the functions mentioned in sub-paragraph (1)(a) to be performed on its behalf (and without affecting its responsibility) by any other body or person who is able and willing to perform them.

Investigation of complaints

4.—(1) The agency must have effective arrangements for the investigation of complaints arising out of the conduct of investment business by authorised persons or against any recognised self-regulating organisation, professional body, investment exchange or clearing house.

(2) The arrangements must make provision for the investigation of complaints in respect of authorised persons to be carried out in appropriate cases independently of the agency and those persons.

Promotion and maintenance of standards

5. The agency must be able and willing to promote and maintain high standards of integrity and fair dealing in the carrying on of investment business and to co-operate, by the sharing of information and otherwise, with the Secretary of State and any other authority, body or person having responsibility for the supervision or regulation of investment business or other financial services.

Records

6. The agency must have satisfactory arrangements for recording decisions made in the exercise of its functions and for the safekeeping of those records which ought to be preserved.

SCHEDULE 8 (Section 114)

PRINCIPLES APPLICABLE TO DESIGNATED AGENCY'S RULES AND REGULATIONS

Standards

1. The rules made under section 48 of this Act (in this Schedule referred to as 'conduct of business rules') and the other rules and regulations made under Part I of this Act must promote high standards of integrity and fair dealing in the conduct of investment business.

2. The conduct of business rules must make proper provision for requiring an authorised person to act with due skill, care and diligence in providing any service which he provides or holds himself out as willing to provide.

3. The conduct of business rules must make proper provision for requiring an authorised person to subordinate his own interests to those of his clients and to act fairly between his clients.

4. The conduct of business rules must make proper provision for requiring an authorised person to ensure that, in anything done by him for the persons with whom he deals, due regard is had to their circumstances.

Disclosure

5. The conduct of business rules must make proper provision for the disclosure by an authorised person of interests in, and facts material to, transactions which are entered into by him in the course of carrying on investment business or in respect of which he gives advice in the course of carrying on such business, including information as to any commissions or other inducements received or receivable from a third party in connection with any such transaction.

6. The conduct of business rules must make proper provision for the disclosure by an authorised person of the capacity in which and the terms on which he enters into any such transaction.

7. The conduct of business rules, or those rules and rules under section 51 of this Act, must make proper provision for requiring an authorised person who in the course of carrying on investment business enters or offers to enter into a transaction in respect of an investment with any person, or gives any person advice about such a transaction, to give that person such information as to the nature of the investment and the financial implications of the transaction as will enable him to make an informed decision.

8. Rules made under section 48 of this Act regulating action for the purpose of stabilising the price of investments must make proper provision for ensuring that where action is or is to be taken in conformity with the rules adequate arrangements exist for making known that the price of the investments in respect of which the action is or is to be taken (and, where relevant, of any other investments) may be affected by that action and the period during which it may be affected; and where a transaction is or is to be entered into during a period when it is known that the price of the investment to which it relates may be affected by any such action the information referred to in paragraph 7 above includes information to that effect.

Protection

9. The conduct of business rules and any regulations made under section 55 of this Act must make proper provision for the protection of property for which an authorised person is liable to account to another person.

10. Rules made under sections 53 and 54 of this Act must make the best provision that can reasonably be made under those sections.

Records

11. The conduct of business rules must require the keeping of proper records and make provision for their inspection in appropriate cases.

Classes of investors

12. The conduct of business rules and the other rules and regulations made under Chapter V of Part I of this Act must take proper account of the fact that provisions that are appropriate for regulating the conduct of business in relation to some classes of investors may not (by reason of their knowledge, experience or otherwise) be appropriate in relation to others.

SCHEDULE 9 (Section 116)

DESIGNATED AGENCIES: STATUS AND EXERCISE OF TRANSFERRED FUNCTIONS

Status

1.—(1) A designated agency shall not be regarded as acting on behalf of the Crown and its members, officers and servants shall not be regarded as Crown servants.

(2) In Part III of Schedule 1 to the House of Commons Disqualification Act 1975 (disqualifying offices) there shall be inserted at the appropriate place—

'Chairman of a designated agency within the meaning of the Financial Services Act 1986 if he is in receipt of remuneration'.

(3) An amendment corresponding to that in sub-paragraph (2) above shall be made in Part III of Schedule 1 to the Northern Ireland Assembly Disqualification Act 1975.

Exemption from requirement of 'limited' in name of designated agency

2.—(1) A company is exempt from the requirements of the Companies Act 1985 relating to the use of 'limited' as part of the company name if—

(a) it is a designated agency; and
(b) its memorandum or articles comply with the requirements specified in paragraph (b) of subsection (3) of section 30 of that Act.

(2) In subsection (4) of that section (statutory declaration of compliance with requirements entitling company to exemption) the reference to the requirements of subsection (3) of that section shall include a reference to the requirements of sub-paragraph (1) above.

(3) In section 31 of that Act (provisions applicable to exempted companies) the reference to a company which is exempt under section 30 of that Act shall include a reference to a company that is exempt under this paragraph and, in relation to such a company, the power conferred by subsection (2) of that section (direction to include 'limited' in company name) shall be exercisable on the ground that the company has ceased to be a designated agency instead of the ground mentioned in paragraph (a) of that subsection.

(4) In this paragraph references to the said Act of 1985 and sections 30 and 31 of that Act include references to the corresponding provisions in force in Northern Ireland.

The Tribunal

3.—(1) Where a case is referred to the Tribunal by a designated agency the Tribunal shall send the Secretary of State a copy of any report made by it to the agency in respect of that case.

(2) Where the powers which the Tribunal could, apart from any delegation order, require

the Secretary of State to exercise are, by virtue of such an order or of an order resuming any function transferred by it, exercisable partly by the Secretary of State and partly by a designated agency or designated agencies the Tribunal may require any of them to exercise such of those powers as are exercisable by them respectively.

Legislative functions

4.—(1) A designated agency shall send the Secretary of State a copy of any rules or regulations made by it by virtue of functions transferred to it by a delegation order and give him written notice of any amendment or revocation of or addition to any such rules or regulations.

(2) A designated agency shall—

(a) send the Secretary of State a copy of any guidance issued by the agency which is intended to have continuing effect and is issued in writing or other legible form; and

(b) give him written notice of any amendment, revocation of or addition to guidance issued by it;

but notice need not be given of the revocation of guidance other than such as is mentioned in paragraph (a) above or of any amendment or addition which does not result in or consist of such guidance as is there mentioned.

5. Paragraphs 6 to 9 below shall have effect instead of section 205 (2) and (4) of this Act in relation to rules and regulations made by a designated agency in the exercise of functions transferred to it by a delegation order.

6. The rules and regulations shall be made by an instrument in writing.

7. The instrument shall specify the provision of this Act under which it is made.

8.—(1) Immediately after an instrument is made it shall be printed and made available to the public with or without payment.

(2) A person shall not be taken to have contravened any rule or regulation if he shows that at the time of the alleged contravention the instrument containing the rule or regulation had not been made available as required by this paragraph.

9.—(1) The production of a printed copy of an instrument purporting to be made by the agency on which is endorsed a certificate signed by an officer of the agency authorised by it for that purpose and stating—

(a) that the instrument was made by the agency;

(b) that the copy is a true copy of the instrument; and

(c) that on a specified date the instrument was made available to the public as required by paragraph 8 above,

shall be prima facie evidence or, in Scotland, sufficient evidence of the facts stated in the certificate.

(2) Any certificate purporting to be signed as mentioned in sub-paragraph (1) above shall be deemed to have been duly signed unless the contrary is shown.

(3) Any person wishing in any legal proceedings to cite an instrument made by the agency may require the agency to cause a copy of it to be endorsed with such a certificate as is mentioned in this paragraph.

Fees

10.—(1) A designated agency may retain any fees payable to it by virtue of the delegation order.

(2) Any such fees shall be applicable for meeting the expenses of the agency in discharging its functions under the order and for any purposes incidental thereto.

Appendix

(3) Any fees payable to a designated agency by virtue of a delegation order made before the coming into force of section 3 of this Act may also be applied for repaying the principal of, and paying interest on, any money borrowed by the agency (or by any other person whose liabilities in respect of the money are assumed by the agency) which has been used for the purpose of defraying expenses incurred before the making of the order (whether before or after the passing of this Act) in making preparations for the agency becoming a designated agency.

11. If the function of prescribing the amount of any fee, or of making a scheme under section 112 above, is exercisable by a designated agency it may prescribe or make provision for such fees as will enable it to defray any such expenses as are mentioned in paragraph 10 above.

Consultation

12.—(1) Before making any rules or regulations by virtue of functions transferred to it by a delegation order a designated agency shall, subject to sub-paragraphs (2) and (3) below, publish the proposed rules and regulations in such manner as appears to the agency to be best calculated to bring them to the attention of the public, together with a statement that representations in respect of the proposals can be made to the agency within a specified period; and before making the rules or regulations the agency shall have regard to any representations duly made in accordance with that statement.

(2) Sub-paragraph (1) above does not apply in any case in which the agency considers that the delay involved in complying with that sub-paragraph would be prejudicial to the interests of investors.

(3) Sub-paragraph (1) above does not apply to the making of any rule or regulation if it is in the same terms (or substantially the same terms) as a proposed rule or regulation which was furnished by the agency to the Secretary of State for the purposes of section 114(9) of this Act.

Exchange of information

13.—(1) The Secretary of State may communicate to a designated agency any information in his possession of which he could have availed himself for the purpose of exercising any function which by virtue of a delegation order is for the time being exercisable by the agency.

(2) A designated agency may in the exercise of any function which by virtue of a delegation order is for the time being exercisable by it communicate to any other person any information which has been communicated to the agency by the Secretary of State and which the Secretary of State could have communicated to that person in the exercise of that function.

(3) No communication of information under sub-paragraph (1) above shall constitute publication for the purposes of the law of defamation.

SCHEDULE 10 (Section 129)

REGULATED INSURANCE COMPANIES

Preliminary

1. In this Part of this Schedule 'a regulated insurance company' means any such company as is mentioned in section 129 of this Act.

Authorisations for investment business and insurance business

2.—(1) An insurance company to which section 22 of this Act applies shall not be an authorised person except by virtue of that section.

(2) If an insurance company to which Part II of the Insurance Companies Act 1982 applies but to which section 22 of this Act does not apply becomes an authorised person by virtue of any other provision of this Act it shall be an authorised person only as respects the management of the investments of any pension fund which is established solely for the benefit of the officers or employees and their dependents of that company or of any other body corporate in the same group as that company.

(3) An insurance company to which section 31 of this Act applies shall not, so long as it is an authorised person by virtue of that section, be an authorised person by virtue of any other provision of this Act.

(4) None of the provisions of Part I of this Act shall be construed as authorising any person to carry on insurance business in any case in which he could not lawfully do so apart from those provisions.

Recognition of self-regulating organisation with insurance company members

3.—(1) In the case of a self-regulating organisation whose members include or may include regulated insurance companies the requirements of Schedule 2 to this Act shall include a requirement that the rules of the organisation must take proper account of Part II of the Insurance Companies Act 1982 or, as the case may be, of the provisions for corresponding purposes in the law of any member State in which such companies are established.

(2) Where the function of making or revoking a recognition order in respect of such a self-regulating organisation is exercisable by a designated agency it shall not regard that requirement as satisfied unless the Secretary of State has certified that he also regards it as satisfied.

(3) A delegation order—

  (a) may reserve to the Secretary of State the function of revoking a recognition order in respect of such a self-regulating organisation as is mentioned in sub-paragraph (1) above on the ground that the requirement there mentioned is not satisfied; and
  (b) shall not transfer to a designated agency the function of revoking any such recognition order on the ground that the organisation has contravened sub-paragraphs (3) or (4) of paragraph 6 below as applied by sub-paragraph (5) of that paragraph.

(4) In the case of such a self-regulating organisation as is mentioned in sub-paragraph (1) above the requirements of Schedule 2 to this Act referred to in section 187(2)(a) of this Act shall include the requirement mentioned in that sub-paragraph.

Modification of provisions as to conduct of investment business

4.—(1) The rules under section 48 of this Act shall not apply to a regulated insurance company except so far as they make provision as respects the matters mentioned in sub-paragraph (2) below.

(2) The matters referred to in sub-paragraph (1) above are—

  (a) procuring proposals for policies the rights under which constitute an investment for the purposes of this Act and advising persons on such policies and the exercise of the rights conferred by them;
  (b) managing the investments of pension funds, procuring persons to enter into contracts for the management of such investments and advising persons on such contracts and the exercise of the rights conferred by them;
  (c) matters incidental to those mentioned in paragraph (a) and (b) above.

(3) The rules under section 49 of this Act shall not apply to an insurance company which is an authorised person by virtue of section 31 of this Act.

(4) The rules under sections 53 and 54 of this Act shall not apply to loss arising as a result of a regulated insurance company being unable to meet its liabilities under a contract of insurance.

(5) A direction under section 59 of this Act shall not prohibit the employment of a person by a regulated insurance company except in connection with—

    (a) the matters mentioned in sub-paragraph (2) above; or

    (b) investment business carried on in connection with or for the purposes of those matters.

(6) The Secretary of State shall not make a delegation order transferring any functions of making rules or regulations under Chapter V of Part I of this Act in relation to a regulated insurance company unless he is satisfied that those rules and regulations will take proper account of Part II of the Insurance Companies Act 1982 or, as the case may be, of the provisions for corresponding purposes in the law of the member State in which the company is established; and in section 115(5) of this Act the reference to the requirements of section 114(9)(b) shall include a reference to the requirements of this sub-paragraph.

Restriction of provisions as to conduct of insurance business

5.—(1) Regulations under section 72 of the Insurance Companies Act 1982 (insurance advertisements) shall not apply to so much of any advertisement issued by an authorised person as relates to a contract of insurance the rights under which constitute an investment for the purposes of this Act.

(2) No requirement imposed under section 74 of that Act (intermediaries in insurance transactions) shall apply in respect of an invitation issued by, or by an appointed representative of, an authorised person in relation to a contract of insurance the rights under which constitute an investment for the purposes of this Act.

(3) Subject to sub-paragraph (4) below, sections 75 to 77 of that Act (right to withdraw from long-term policies) shall not apply to a regulated insurance company in respect of a contract of insurance the rights under which constitute an investment for the purposes of this Act.

(4) Sub-paragraph (3) above does not affect the operation of the said sections 75 to 77 in a case in which the statutory notice required by those sections has been or ought to have been served before the coming into force of that sub-paragraph.

Exercise of powers of intervention etc

6.—(1) The powers conferred by Chapter VI of Part I of this Act shall not be exercisable in relation to a regulated insurance company on the ground specified in section 64(1)(a) of this Act for reasons relating to the ability of the company to meet its liabilities to policy holders or potential policy holders.

(2) The powers conferred by sections 66 and 68 of this Act, and those conferred by section 67 of this Act so far as applicable to assets belonging to the authorised person, shall not be exercisable in relation to a regulated insurance company.

(3) A designated agency shall not in the case of a regulated insurance company impose any prohibition or requirement under section 65 or 67 of this Act, or vary any such prohibition or requirement, unless it has given reasonable notice of its intention to do so to the Secretary of State and informed him—

    (a) of the manner in which and the date on or after which it intends to exercise that power; and

    (b) in the case of a proposal to impose a prohibition or requirement, on which of the grounds specified in section 64(1) of this Act it proposes to act and its reasons for considering that the ground in question exists and that it is necessary to impose the prohibition or requirement.

(4) A designated agency shall not exercise any power to which sub-paragraph (3) above applies if the Secretary of State has before the date specified in accordance with sub-paragraph (3) above served on it a notice in writing directing it not to do so; and the Secretary of State may serve such a notice if he considers it desirable for protecting policy holders or potential policy holders of the company against the risk that it may be unable to meet its liabilities or to fulfil the reasonable expectations of its policy holders or potential policy holders.

(5) Sub-paragraphs (3) and (4) above shall, with the necessary modifications, apply also where a recognised self-regulating organisation proposes to exercise, in the case of a member who is a regulated insurance company, any powers of the organisation for purposes corresponding to those of Chapter VI of Part I of this Act.

(6) The powers conferred by sections 72 and 73 of this Act shall not be exercisable in relation to a regulated insurance company.

Withdrawal of insurance business authorisation

7.—(1) At the end of section 11(2)(a) of the Insurance Companies Act 1982 (withdrawal of authorisation in respect of new business where insurance company has failed to satisfy an obligation to which it is subject by virtue of that Act) there shall be inserted the words 'or the Financial Services Act 1986 or, if it is a member of a recognised self-regulating organisation within the meaning of that Act, an obligation to which it is subject by virtue of the rules of that organisation'.

(2) After subsection (2) of section 13 of that Act (final withdrawal of authorisation) there shall be inserted—

'(2A) The Secretary of State may direct that an insurance company shall cease to be authorised to carry on business which is insurance business by virtue of section 95(c)(ii) of this Act if it appears to him that the company has failed to satisfy an obligation to which it is subject by virtue of the Financial Services Act 1986 or, if it is a member of a recognised self-regulating organisation within the meaning of that Act, an obligation to which it is subject by virtue of the rules of that organisation.

(2B) Subsections (3), (5) and (6) of section 11 and subsections (1) and (5) to (8) of section 12 above shall apply to a direction under subsection (2A) above as they apply to a direction under section 11.'

Termination of investment business authorisation of insurer established in other member State

8.—(1) Sections 33(1)(b) and 34 of this Act shall not apply to a regulated insurance company.

(2) A direction under section 33(1)(a) of this Act in respect of such an insurance company may provide that the company shall cease to be an authorised person except as respects investment business of a kind specified in the direction and shall not make it unlawful for the company to effect a contract of insurance in pursuance of a subsisting contract of insurance.

(3) Where the Secretary of State proposes to give a direction under section 33(1)(a) of this Act in respect of such an insurance company he shall give it written notice of his intention to do so, giving particulars of the grounds on which he proposes to act and of the rights exercisable under sub-paragraph (4) below.

(4) An insurance company on which a notice is served under sub-paragraph (3) above may within fourteen days after the date of service make written representations to the Secretary of State and, if desired, oral representations to a person appointed for that purpose by the Secretary of State; and the Secretary of State shall have regard to any representations made in accordance with this sub-paragraph in determining whether to give the direction.

(5) After giving a direction under section 33(1)(a) of this Act in respect of a regulated

insurance company the Secretary of State shall inform the company in writing of the reasons for giving the direction.

(6) A delegation order shall not transfer to a designated agency the function of giving a direction under section 33(1)(a) of this Act in respect of a regulated insurance company.

Powers of Tribunal

9. In the case of a regulated insurance company the provisions mentioned in section 98(4) of this Act shall include sections 11 and 13(2A) of the Insurance Companies Act 1982 but where the Tribunal reports that the appropriate decision would be to take action under either of those sections or under section 33(1)(a) of this Act the Secretary of State shall take the report into consideration but shall not be bound to act upon it.

Consultation with designated agencies

10.—(1) Where any functions under this Act are for the time being exercisable by a designated agency in relation to regulated insurance companies the Secretary of State shall, before issuing an authorisation under section 3 of the Insurance Companies Act 1982 to an applicant who proposes to carry on in the United Kingdom insurance business which is investment business—

    (a) seek the advice of the designated agency with respect to any matters which are relevant to those functions of the agency and relate to the applicant, his proposed business or persons who will be associated with him in, or in connection with, that business; and

    (b) take into account any advice on those matters given to him by the agency before the end of the period within which the application is required to be decided.

(2) The Secretary of State may for the purpose of obtaining the advice of a designated agency under sub-paragraph (1) above furnish it with any information obtained by him in connection with the application.

(3) If a designated agency by which any functions under this Act are for the time being exercisable in relation to regulated insurance companies has reasonable grounds for believing that any such insurance company has failed to comply with an obligation to which it is subject by virtue of this Act it shall forthwith give notice of that fact to the Secretary of State so that he can take it into consideration in deciding whether to give a direction in respect of the company under section 11 or 13(2A) of the said Act of 1982 or section 33 of this Act.

(4) A notice under sub-paragraph (3) above shall contain particulars of the obligation in question and of the agency's reasons for considering that the company has failed to satisfy that obligation.

(5) A designated agency need not give a notice under sub-paragraph (3) above in respect of any matter unless it considers that that matter (either alone or in conjunction with other matters) would justify the withdrawal of authorisation under section 28 of this Act in the case of a person to whom that section applies.

SCHEDULE 11 (Section 140)

FRIENDLY SOCIETIES

PART I

PRELIMINARY

1. In this Schedule—

'a regulated friendly society' means a society which is an authorised person by virtue of section 23 of this Act as respects such investment business as is mentioned in that section;

'regulated business', in relation to a regulated friendly society, means investment business as respects which the society is authorised by virtue of that section;

'a self-regulating organisation for friendly societies' means a self-regulating organisation which is permitted under its rules to admit regulated friendly societies as members and to regulate the carrying on by such societies of regulated business;

'a recognised self-regulating organisation for friendly societies' means a body declared by an order of the Registrar for the time being in force to be a recognised self-regulating organisation for friendly societies for the purposes of this Schedule;

'a member society' means a regulated friendly society which is a member of an appropriate recognised self-regulating organisation for friendly societies and is subject to its rules in carrying on all its regulated business and, for the purposes of this definition, 'an appropriate recognised self-regulating organisation for friendly societies' means—

(a) in the case of any such society as is mentioned in section 23(1) of this Act, an organisation declared by an order of the Chief Registrar of friendly societies for the time being in force to be a recognised self-regulating organisation for friendly societies for the purposes of this Schedule; and

(b) in the case of any such society as is mentioned in section 23(2) of this Act, an organisation declared by an order of the Registrar of Friendly Societies for Northern Ireland for the time being in force to be such an organisation;

'the Registrar' means—

(a) in relation to any such society as is mentioned in section 23(1) of this Act, or to any self-regulating organisation for friendly societies which has applied for or been granted a recognition order made by him, the Chief Registrar of friendly societies; and

(b) in relation to any such society as is mentioned in section 23(2) of this Act, or to any self-regulating organisation for friendly societies which has applied for or been granted a recognition order made by him, the Registrar of Friendly Societies for Northern Ireland.

PART II

SELF-REGULATING ORGANISATIONS FOR FRIENDLY SOCIETIES

Recognition

2.—(1) A self-regulating organisaion for friendly societies may apply to the Chief Registrar of friendly societies or the Registrar of Friendly Societies for Northern Ireland for an order declaring it to be a recognised self-regulating organisation for friendly societies for the purposes of this Schedule.

(2) An application under sub-paragraph (1) above—

(a) shall be made in such manner as the Registrar may direct; and
(b) shall be accompanied by such information as the Registrar may reasonably require for the purpose of determining the application.

(3) At any time after receiving an application and before determining it the Registrar may require the applicant to furnish additional information.

(4) The directions and requirements given or imposed under sub-paragraphs (2) and (3) above may differ as between different applications.

(5) Any information to be furnished to the Registrar under this paragraph shall, if he so

requires, be in such form or verified in such manner as he may specify.

(6) Every application shall be accompanied by a copy of the applicant's rules and of any guidance issued by the applicant which is intended to have continuing effect and is issued in writing or other legible form.

3.—(1) If, on an application duly made in accordance with paragraph (2) above and after being furnished with all such information as he may require under that paragraph, it appears to the Registrar from that information and having regard to any other information in his possession that the requirements mentioned in paragraph 4 below are satisfied as respects that organisation, he may, with the consent of the Secretary of State and subject to sub-paragraph (2) below, make an order ('a recognition order') declaring the applicant to be a recognised self-regulating organisation for friendly societies.

(2) Where the Registrar proposes to grant an application for a recognition order he shall send to the Secretary of State a copy of the application together with a copy of the rules and any guidance accompanying the application and the Secretary of State shall not consent to the making of the recognition order unless he is satisfied that the rules and guidance of which copies have been sent to him under this sub-paragraph do not have, and are not intended or likely to have, to any significant extent the effect of restricting, distorting or preventing competition or, if they have or are intended or likely to have that effect to any significant extent, that the effect is not greater than is necessary for the protection of investors.

(3) Section 122 of this Act shall apply in relation to the decision whether to consent to the making of a recognition order under this paragraph as it applies to the decisions mentioned in subsection (1) of that section.

(4) Subsections (1) and (2) of section 128 of this Act shall apply for the purposes of this paragraph as if the powers there mentioned included the power of refusing consent to the making of a recognition order under this paragraph and subsection (5) of that section shall apply for that purpose as if the reference to Chapter XIV of Part I included a reference to this paragraph.

(5) The Registrar may refuse to make a recognition order in respect of an organisation if he considers that its recognition is unnecessary having regard to the existence of one or more other organisations which are concerned with such investment business as is mentioned in section 23 of this Act and which have been or are likely to be recognised under this paragraph.

(6) Where the Registrar refuses an application for a recognition order he shall give the applicant a written notice to that effect specifying a requirement which in the opinion of the Registrar is not satisfied, stating that the application is refused on the ground mentioned in sub-paragraph (5) above or stating that the Secretary of State has refused to consent to the making of the order.

(7) A recognition order shall state the date on which it takes effect.

4.—(1) The requirements referred to in paragraph 3 above are that mentioned in sub-paragraph (2) below and those set out in paragraphs 2 to 7 of Schedule 2 to this Act as modified in sub-paragraphs (3) to (5) below.

(2) The rules of the organisation must take proper account of the Friendly Societies Act 1974, or as the case may be, the Friendly Societies Act (Northern Ireland) 1970.

(3) References in paragraphs 2, 3, 4 and 6 of Schedule 2 to members are to members who are regulated friendly societies.

(4) In paragraph 3 of that Schedule—

   (a) in sub-paragraph (1) for the reference to Chapter V of Part I of this Act there shall be substituted a reference to paragraphs 14 to 22 below; and

(b) in sub-paragraph (2) the reference to section 49 of this Act shall be omitted and for the reference to sections 53 and 54 there shall be substituted a reference to paragraphs 17 and 18 below; and

(c) in sub-paragraph (3) for the reference to Chapter VI of that Part there shall be substituted a reference to the powers exercisable by the Registrar by virtue of paragraph 23 below.

(5) In paragraph 4 of that Schedule for the reference to Chapter V of Part I of this Act there shall be substituted references to paragraphs 14 to 22 below.

Revocation of recognition

5.—(1) A recognition order may be revoked by a further order made by the Registrar if at any time it appears to him—

(a) that any requirement mentioned in paragraph 4(1) above is not satisfied in the case of the organisation to which the recognition order relates ('the recognised organisation');

(b) that the recognised organisation has failed to comply with any obligation to which it is subject by virtue of this Act; or

(c) that the continued recognition of the organisation is undesirable having regard to the existence of one or more other organisations which have been or are to be recognised under paragraph 3 above.

(2) Subsections (2) to (9) of section 11 of this Act shall have effect in relation to the revocation of a recognition order under this paragraph as they have effect in relation to the revocation of a recognition order under subsection (1) of that section but with the substitution—

(a) for references to the Secretary of State of references to the Registrar;

(b) for the reference in subsection (3) to members of a reference to members of the organisation which are member societies in relation to it; and

(c) for the reference in subsection (6) to investors of a reference to members of the societies which are member societies in relation to the organisation.

Compliance orders

6.—(1) If at any time it appears to the Registrar—

(a) that any requirement mentioned in paragraph 3 above is not satisfied in the case of a recognised self-regulating organisation for friendly societies; or

(b) that such an organisation has failed to comply with any obligation to which it is subject by virtue of this Act,

he may, instead of revoking the recognition order under paragraph 5 above, make an application to the court under this paragraph.

(2) If on any such application the court decides that the requirement in question is not satisfied or, as the case may be, that the organisation has failed to comply with the obligation in question it may order the organisation concerned to take such steps as the court directs for securing that that requirement is satisfied or that that obligation is complied with.

(3) The jurisdiction conferred by this paragraph shall be exercisable by the High Court and the Court of Session.

7.—(1) If at any time it appears to the Registrar that the rules of a recognised self-regulating organisation for friendly societies do not satisfy the requirements of paragraph 3(1) of Schedule 2 to this Act as modified by paragraph 4(4) above he may, instead of revoking the recognition order or making an application under paragraph 6 above, direct the organisation to alter, or himself alter, its rules in such manner as he considers necessary for securing that the rules satisfy those requirements.

(2) Before giving a direction or making any alteration under this paragraph the Registrar shall consult the organisation concerned.

(3) Any direction given under sub-paragraph (1) above shall, on the application of the Registrar, be enforceable by mandamus or, in Scotland, by an order for specific performance under section 91 of the Court of Session Act 1868.

(4) A recognised self-regulating organisation for friendly societies whose rules have been altered by or pursuant to a direction given by the Registrar under sub-paragraph (1) above may apply to the court and if the court is satisfied—

(a) that the rules without the alteration satisfied the requirements mentioned in that sub-paragraph; or
(b) that other alterations proposed by the organisation would result in the rules satisfying those requirements,

the court may set aside the alteration made by or pursuant to the direction given by the Registrar and, in a case within paragraph (b) above, order the organisation to make the alterations proposed by it; but the setting aside of an alteration under this sub-paragraph shall not affect its previous operation.

(5) The jurisdiction conferred by sub-paragraph (4) above shall be exercisable by the High Court and the Court of Session.

(6) Subsections (2) to (7) and (9) of section 11 of this Act shall, with the modifications mentioned in paragraph 5(2) above and any other necessary modifications, have effect in relation to any direction given or alteration made by the Registrar under sub-paragraph (1) above as they have effect in relation to an order revoking a recognition order.

(7) The fact that the rules of an organisation have been altered by or pursuant to a direction given by the Registrar, or pursuant to an order made by the court, under this paragraph shall not preclude their subsequent alteration or revocation by that organisation.

8.—(1) The Registrar or the Secretary of State may make regulations requiring a recognised self-regulating organisation for friendly societies to give the Registrar or, as the case may be, the Secretary of State forthwith notice of the occurrence of such events relating to the organisation or its members as are specified in the regulations and such information in respect of those events as is so specified.

(2) The Registrar or the Secretary of State may make regulations requiring a recognised self-regulating organisation for friendly societies to furnish the Registrar or, as the case may be, the Secretary of State at such times or in respect of such periods as are specified in the regulations with such information relating to the organisation or its members as is so specified.

(3) The notices and information required to be given or furnished under the foregoing provisions of this paragraph shall be such as the Registrar or, as the case may be, the Secretary of State may reasonably require for the exercise of his functions under this Act.

(4) Regulations under the foregoing provisions of this paragraph may require information to be given in a specified form and to be verified in a specified manner.

(5) A notice or information required to be given or furnished under the foregoing provisions of this paragraph shall be given in writing or such other manner as the Registrar or, as the case may be, the Secretary of State may approve.

(6) Where a recognised self-regulating organisation for friendly societies amends, revokes or adds to its rules or guidance it shall within seven days give the Registrar written notice of the amendment, revocation or addition; but notice need not be given of the revocation of guidance other than such as is mentioned in paragraph 2(6) above or of any amendment of or

addition to guidance which does not result in or consist of such guidance as is there mentioned.

(7) The Registrar shall send the Secretary of State a copy of any notice given to him under sub-paragraph (6) above.

(8) Contravention of or of regulations under this paragraph shall not be an offence.

9.—(1) A recognised self-regulating organisation for friendly societies shall not exercise any powers for purposes corresponding to those of the powers exercisable by the Registrar by virtue of paragraph 23 below in relation to a regulated friendly society unless it has given reasonable notice of its intention to do so to the Registrar and informed him—

(a) of the manner in which and the date on or after which it intends to exercise the power; and

(b) in the case of a proposal to impose a prohibition or requirement, of the reason why it proposes to act and its reasons for considering that that reason exists and that it is necessary to impose the prohibition or requirement.

(2) A recognised self-regulating organisation for friendly societies shall not exercise any power to which sub-paragraph (1)(a) above applies if before the date given in the notice in pursuance of that sub-paragraph the Registrar has served on it a notice in writing directing it not to do so; and the Registrar may serve such a notice if he considers it is desirable for protecting members or potential members of the society against the risk that it may be unable to meet its liabilities or to fulfil the reasonable expectations of its members or potential members.

Prevention of restrictive practices

10.—(1) The powers conferred by sub-paragraph (2) below shall be exercisable by the Secretary of State if at any time it appears to him that—

(a) any rules made or guidance issued by a recognised self-regulating organisation for friendly societies;

(b) any practices of any such organisation; or

(c) any practices of persons who are members of, or otherwise subject to the rules made by, any such organisation,

have, or are intended or likely to have, to a significant extent the effect of restricting, distorting or preventing competition and that that effect is greater than is necessary for the protection of investors.

(2) The powers exercisable under this sub-paragraph are to direct the Registrar—

(a) to revoke the recognition order of the organisation;

(b) to direct the organisation to take specified steps for the purpose of securing that the rules, guidance or practices in question do not have the effect mentioned in sub-paragraph (1) above;

(c) to make alterations in the rules for that purpose;

and subsections (2) to (5), (7) and (9) of section 11 of this Act, as applied by sub-paragraph (2) of paragraph 5 above, shall have effect in relation to the revocation of a recognition order by virtue of a direction under this sub-paragraph as they have effect in relation to the revocation of such an order under sub-paragraph (1) of that paragraph.

(3) The practices referred to in paragraph (b) of sub-paragraph (1) above are practices of the organisation in its capacity as such; and the practices referred to in paragraph (c) of that sub-paragraph are practices in relation to business in respect of which the persons in question are subject to the rules of the organisation and which are required or contemplated by its rules or guidance or otherwise attributable to its conduct in its capacity as such.

417

Appendix

(4) Subsections (3) to (8) of section 122 of this Act shall apply for the purposes of this paragraph as if—

  (a) the reference to a notice in subsection (3) included a notice received under paragraph 8(7) above or 33(4) below;
  (b) the reference to rules and guidance in subsection (4) included such rules and guidance as are mentioned in sub-paragraph (1) above;
  (c) the reference to practices in subsection (6) included such practices as are mentioned in sub-paragraph (1) above; and
  (d) the reference to the Secretary of State's powers in subsection (7) included his powers under sub-paragraph (2) above.

(5) Section 128 of this Act shall apply for the purposes of this paragraph as if—

  (a) the powers referred to in subsection (1) of that section included the powers conferred by sub-paragraph (2)(b) and (c) above;
  (b) the references to Chapter XIV of Part I included references to this paragraph; and
  (c) the reference to a recognised self-regulating organisation included a reference to a recognised self-regulating organisation for friendly societies.

Fees

11.—(1) An applicant for a recognition order under paragraph 3 above shall pay such fees in respect of his application as may be required by a scheme made and published by the Registrar; and no application for such an order shall be regarded as duly made unless this sub-paragraph is complied with.

(2) Subsections (2) to (4) of section 112 of this Act apply to a scheme under sub-paragraph (1) above as they apply to a scheme under subsection (1) of that section.

(3) Every recognised self-regulating organisation for friendly societies shall pay such periodical fees to the Registrar as he may by regulations prescribe.

Application of provisions of this Act

12.—(1) Subject to the following provisions of this paragraph, sections 44(7), 102(1)(c), 124, 125, 126, 180(1)(n), 181, 187, 192 and 200(4) of this Act shall apply in relation to recognised self-regulating organisations for friendly societies as they apply in relation to recognised self-regulating organisations.

(2) In its application by virtue of sub-paragraph (1) above section 126(1) of this Act shall have effect as if the reference to section 119(2) were a reference to paragraph 10(1) above.

(3) In its application by virtue of sub-paragraph (1) above subsection (2) of section 187 of this Act shall have effect as if—

  (a) the reference in paragraph (a) to paragraphs 1 to 6 of Schedule 2 were to paragraphs 2 to 6 of that Schedule (as they apply by virtue of paragraph 4 above) and to sub-paragraph (2) of paragraph 4 above; and
  (b) paragraph (d) referred to the powers of the organisation under paragraph 23(4) below.

(4) A direction under subsection (1) of section 192 of this Act as it applies by virtue of sub-paragraph (1) above shall direct the Registrar to direct the organisation not to take or, as the case may be, to take the action in question; and where the function of making or revoking a recognition order in respect of a self-regulating organisation for friendly societies is exercisable by a transferee body any direction under that subsection as it applies as aforesaid shall be a direction requiring the Registrar to direct the transferee body to give the organisation such a direction as is specified in the direction given by the Secretary of State.

418

(5) Subsection (5) of that section shall not apply to a direction given to the Registrar by virtue of this paragraph.

PART III

REGISTRAR'S POWERS IN RELATION TO REGULATED FRIENDLY SOCIETIES

Special provisions for regulated friendly societies

13. Paragraphs 14 to 25 below shall have effect in connection with the exercise of powers for the regulation of regulated friendly societies in relation to regulated business, but nothing in this Part of this Schedule shall affect the exercise of any power conferred by this Act in relation to a regulated friendly society which is an authorised person by virtue of section 25 of this Act to the extent that the power relates to other investment business.

Conduct of investment business

14.—(1) The rules under section 48 of this Act shall not apply to a regulated friendly society but the Registrar may, with the consent of the Secretary of State, make such rules as may be made under that section regulating the conduct of any such society other than a member society as respects the matters mentioned in sub-paragraph (2) below.

(2) The matters referred to in sub-paragraph (1) above are—

(a) procuring persons to transact regulated business with it and advising persons as to the exercise of rights conferred by investments acquired from the society in the course of such business;

(b) managing the investments of pension funds, procuring persons to enter into contracts for the management of such investments and advising persons on such contracts and the exercise of the rights conferred by them;

(c) matters incidental to those mentioned in paragraphs (a) and (b) above.

(3) Section 50 of this Act shall apply in relation to rules under this paragraph as it applies in relation to rules under section 48 except that—

(a) for the reference to the Secretary of State there shall be substituted reference to the Registrar; and

(b) the Registrar shall not exercise the power under subsection (1) to alter the requirements of rules made under this paragraph without the consent of the Secretary of State.

15.—(1) The rules under section 51 of this Act shall not apply to any investment agreement which a person has entered or offered to enter into with a regulated friendly society if, as respects the society, entering into the agreement constitutes the carrying on of regulated business but the Registrar may, with the consent of the Secretary of State, make rules for enabling a person who has entered or offered to enter into such an agreement to rescind the agreement or withdraw the offer within such period and in such manner as may be specified in the rules.

(2) Subsection (2) of section 51 of this Act shall apply in relation to rules under this paragraph as it applies in relation to rules under that section but with the substitution for the reference to the Secretary of State of a reference to the Registrar.

16.—(1) Regulations under section 52 of this Act shall not apply to any regulated friendly society but the Registrar may, with the consent of the Secretary of State, make such regulations as may be made under that section imposing requirements on regulated friendly societies other than member societies.

(2) Any notice or information required to be given or furnished under this paragraph shall be given in writing or in such other manner as the Registrar may approve.

17.—(1) Rules under section 53 of this Act shall not apply to any regulated friendly society but the Registrar may, with the consent of the Secretary of State make rules concerning indemnity against any claim in respect of any description of civil liability incurred by a regulated friendly society in connection with any regulated business.

(2) Such rules shall not apply to a member society of a recognised self-regulating organisation for friendly societies unless that organisation has requested that such rules should apply to it; and any such request shall not be capable of being withdrawn after rules giving effect to it have been made but without prejudice to the power of the Registrar to revoke the rules if he and the Secretary of State think fit.

(3) Subsections (3) and (4) of section 53 of this Act shall apply in relation to such rules as they apply to rules under that section but with the substitution for references to the Secretary of State of references to the Registrar.

18.—(1) No scheme established by rules under section 54 shall apply in cases where persons who are or have been regulated friendly societies are unable, or likely to be unable, to satisfy claims in respect of any description of civil liability incurred by them in connection with any regulated business but the Registrar may, with the consent of the Secretary of State, by rules establish a scheme for compensating investors in such cases.

(2) Subject to sub-paragraph (3) below, subsections (2) to (4) and (6) of that section shall apply in relation to such rules as they apply to rules under that section but with the substitution for the references to the Secretary of State, authorised persons, members and a recognised self-regulating organisation of references respectively to the Registrar, regulated friendly societies, member societies and a recognised self-regulating organisation for friendly societies.

(3) Subsection (3) of that section shall have effect with the substitution for the words 'the Secretary of state is satisfied' of the words 'the Registrar and the Secretary of State are satisfied'.

(4) The references in section 179(3)(b) and 180(1)(e) of this Act to the body administering a scheme established under section 54 of this Act shall include the body administering a scheme established under this paragraph.

19.—(1) Regulations under section 55 of this Act shall not apply to money held by regulated friendly societies but the Registrar may, with the consent of the Secretary of State, make regulations with respect to money held by a regulated friendly society in such circumstances as may be specified in the regulations.

(2) Regulations under this paragraph shall not provide that money held by a regulated friendly society shall be held as mentioned in paragraph (a) of subsection (2) of that section but paragraphs (b) to (f) of that subsection and subsections (3) and (4) of that section shall apply in relation to regulations made under this paragraph as they apply in relation to regulations under that section (but with the substitution for the reference in paragraphs (b) and (e) of subsection (2) to a member of a recognised self-regulating organisation of a reference to a member society of a recognised self-regulating organisation for friendly societies and for the reference in paragraph (e) of that subsection to the Secretary of State of a reference to the Registrar).

20. Regulations under section 56(1) of this Act shall not permit anything to be done by a regulated friendly society but that section shall not apply to anything done by such a society in the course of or in consequence of an unsolicited call which, as respects the society constitutes the carrying on of regulated business, if it is permitted to be done by the society in those circumstances—

(a) in the case of a member society, by the rules of the recognised self-regulating organisation for friendly societies of which it is a member; and
(b) in any other case, by regulations made by the Registrar with the consent of the Secretary of State.

21.—(1) If it appears to the Registrar that a regulated friendly society other than a member society has contravened—

- (a) any provision of rules or regulations made under this Schedule or of section 56 or 59 of this Act;
- (b) any condition imposed under section 50 of this Act as it applies by virtue of paragraph 14(3) above;
- (c) any prohibition or requirement imposed under Chapter VI of Part I of this Act as it applies by virtue of paragraph 23 below; or
- (d) any requirement imposed under paragraph 24 below;

he may publish a statement to that effect.

(2) Subsections (2) to (5) of section 60 above shall apply in relation to the power under sub-paragraph (1) above as they apply in relation to the power in subsection (1) of that section but with the substitution for the references to the Secretary of State of references to the Registrar.

22.—(1) If on the application of the Registrar the court is satisfied—

- (a) that there is a reasonable likelihood that any regulated friendly society will contravene any provision of—
  - (i) any prohibition or requirement imposed under Chapter VI of Part I of this Act as it applies by virtue of paragraph 23 below;
  - (ii) the rules or regulations made under this Schedule;
  - (iii) any requirement imposed under paragraph 24 below;
  - (iv) section 47, 56 or 59 of this Act;
  - (v) the rules of a recognised self-regulating organisation for friendly societies in relation to which it is a member society,

or any condition imposed under section 50 of this Act as it applies by virtue of paragraph 14(3) above;

- (b) that any regulated friendly society has contravened any such provision or condition and that there is a reasonable likelihood that the contravention will continue or be repeated; or
- (c) that any person has contravened any such provision or condition and that there are steps that could be taken for remedying the contravention,

the court may grant an injunction restraining the contravention or, in Scotland, an interdict prohibiting the contravention or, as the case may be, make an order requiring the society and any other person who appears to the court to have been knowingly concerned in the contravention to take steps to remedy it.

(2) No application shall be made by the Registrar under sub-paragraph (1) above in respect of any such rules as are mentioned in paragraph (a)(v) of that sub-paragraph unless it appears to him that the organisation is unable or unwilling to take appropriate steps to restrain the contravention or to require the society concerned to take such steps as are mentioned in sub-paragraph (1) above.

(3) Subsections (3) to (9) of section 61 of this Act apply to such a contravention as is mentioned in sub-paragraph (1)(a) above as they apply to such a contravention as is mentioned in subsection (3) of that section, but with the substitution for the references to the Secretary of State of references to the Registrar.

(4) Without prejudice to the preceding provisions of this paragraph—

- (a) a contravention of any rules or regulations made under this Schedule;
- (b) a contravention of any prohibition or requirement imposed under Chapter VI of Part I of this Act as it applies by virtue of paragraph 23 below;
- (c) a contravention of any requirement imposed under paragraph 24 below;

(d) a contravention by a member society of any rules of the recognised self-regulating organisation for friendly societies of which it is a member relating to a matter in respect of which rules or regulations have been or could be made under this Schedule or of any requirement or prohibition imposed by the organisation in the exercise of powers for purposes corresponding to those of the said Chapter VI or paragraph 24;

shall be actionable at the suit of a person who suffers loss as a result of the contravention subject to the defences and other incidents applying to actions for breach of statutory duty, but no person shall be guilty of an offence by reason of any such contravention and no such contravention shall invalidate any transaction.

(5) This paragraph is without prejudice to any equitable remedy available in respect of property which by virtue of a requirement under section 67 of this Act as it applies by virtue of paragraph 23 below is subject to a trust.

Intervention, information and investigations

23.—(1) The powers conferred by Chapter VI of Part I of this Act shall not be exercisable in relation to a regulated friendly society or the appointed representative of such a society by the Secretary of State but instead shall be exercisable by the Registrar; and accordingly references in that Chapter to the Secretary of State shall as respects the exercise of powers in relation to a regulated friendly society or such a representative be taken as references to the Registrar.

(2) Section 64 of this Act shall not apply to the exercise of those powers by virtue of sub-paragraph (1) above but those powers shall only be exercisable by the Registrar if it appears to him—

(a) that the exercise of the powers is desirable in the interests of members or potential members of the regulated friendly society; or
(b) that the society is not a fit person to carry on regulated business of a particular kind or to the extent to which it is carrying it on or proposing to carry it on; or
(c) that the society has contravened any provision of this Act or of any rules or regulations made under it or in purported compliance with any such provision has furnished him with false, inaccurate or misleading information or has contravened any prohibition or requirement imposed under this Act.

(3) For the purposes of sub-paragraph (2)(b) above the Registrar may take into account any matters that could be taken into account in deciding whether to withdraw or suspend an authorisation under Chapter III of Part I of this Act.

(4) The powers conferred by this paragraph shall not be exercisable in relation—

(a) to a member society which is subject to the rules of a recognised self-regulating organisation for friendly societies in carrying on all the investment business carried on by it; or
(b) to an appointed representative of a member society if that member society, and each other member society which is his principal, is subject to the rules of such an organisation in carrying on the investment business in respect of which it has accepted responsibility for his activities;

except that the powers conferred by virtue of section 67(1)(b) of this Act may on any of the grounds mentioned in sub-paragraph (2) above be exercised in relation to a member society or appointed representative at the request of the organisation in relation to which the society or, as the case may be, the society which is the representative's principal is a member society.

24.—(1) The Registrar may by notice in writing require any regulated friendly society (other than a member society) or any self-regulating organisation for friendly societies to furnish him with such information as he may reasonably require for the exercise of his functions under this Act.

(2) The Registrar may require any information which he requires under this paragraph to be furnished within such reasonable time and verified in such manner as he may specify.

25.—(1) Where a notice or copy of a notice is served on any person under section 60 or section 70 of this Act as they apply by virtue of paragraph 21(2) or 23 above, Chapter IX of Part I of this Act (other than section 96) shall, subject to sub-paragraph (2) below, have effect—

(a) with the substitution for the references to the Secretary of State of references to the Registrar; and

(b) as if for the references in section 98(4) to sections 28, 33 and 60 of this Act there were substituted references to paragraphs 21, 23, 24, 26 and 27 of this Schedule.

(2) Where the friendly society in question is an authorised person by virtue of section 25 of this Act the provisions mentioned in sub-paragraph (1) above shall have effect as if the references substituted by that sub-paragraph had effect in addition to rather than in substitution for the references for which they are there substituted.

(3) Where the Tribunal reports that the appropriate decision is to take action under paragraph 26 or 27 of this Schedule the Registrar shall take the report into account but shall not be bound to act on it.

Exercise of powers under enactments relating to friendly societies

26.—(1) If it appears to the Chief Registrar of friendly societies that a regulated friendly society which is an authorised person by virtue of section 23(1) of this Act—

(a) has contravened any provision of—

(i) this Act or any rules or regulations made under it;

(ii) any requirement imposed under paragraph 24 above;

(iii) the rules of a recognised self-regulating organisation for friendly societies in relation to which it is a member society; or

(b) in purported compliance with any such provision has furnished false, inaccurate or misleading information,

he may exercise any of the powers mentioned in sub-paragraph (2) below in relation to that society.

(2) The powers mentioned in sub-paragraph (1) above are those under subsection (1) of section 87 (inspection and winding up of registered friendly societies), subsection (1) of section 88 (suspension of business of registered friendly societies), subsections (1) and (2) of section 89 (production of documents) and subsections (1) and (2) of section 91 (cancellation and suspension of registration) of the Friendly Societies Act 1974; and subject to sub-paragraph (3) below the remaining provisions of those sections shall apply in relation to the exercise of those powers by virtue of this paragraph as they do in relation to their exercise in the circumstances mentioned in those sections.

(3) In its application by virtue of this paragraph—

(a) section 88 of the said Act of 1974 shall have effect with the omission of subsections (3), (5) and (9); and

(b) section 89 of that Act shall have effect with the omission of subsection (7).

27.—(1) If it appears to the Registrar of Friendly Societies for Northern Ireland that a regulated friendly society which is an authorised person by virtue of section 23(2) of this Act—

(a) has contravened any provision of—

(i) this Act or any rules or regulations made under it;

(ii) any requirement imposed under paragraph 24 above;

Appendix

> (iii) the rules of a recognised self-regulating organisation for friendly societies in relation to which it is a member society; or

> (b) in purported compliance with any such provision has furnished false, inaccurate or misleading information,

he may exercise any of the powers mentioned in sub-paragraph (2) below in relation to that society.

(2) The powers mentioned in sub-paragraph (1) above are those under subsection (1) of section 77 (inspection and winding up of registered friendly societies), subsection (1) of section 78 (suspension of business of registered friendly societies), subsections (1) and (2) of section 79 (production of documents) and subsections (1) and (2) of section 80 (cancellation and suspension of registration) of the Friendly Societies Act (Northern Ireland) 1970; and subject to sub-paragraph (3) below the remaining provisions of those sections shall apply in relation to the exercise of those powers by virtue of this paragraph as they do in relation to their exercise in the circumstances mentioned in those sections.

(3) In its application by virtue of this paragraph section 78 of the said Act of 1970 shall have effect with the omission in subsection (2) of the words from 'and such notice' onwards and of subsection (4).

PART IV

TRANSFER OF REGISTRAR'S FUNCTIONS

28.—(1) If it appears to the Registrar—

> (a) that a body corporate has been established which is able and willing to discharge all or any of the functions to which this paragraph applies; and

> (b) that the requirements of Schedule 7 to this Act (as it has effect by virtue of sub-paragraph (3) below) are satisfied in the case of that body,

he may, with the consent of the Secretary of State and subject to the following provisions of this paragraph and paragraphs 29 and 30 below, make an order transferring all or any of those functions to that body.

(2) The body to which functions are transferred by the first order made under sub-paragraph (1) above shall be the body known as The Securities and Investments Board Limited if the Secretary of State consents to the making of the order and it appears to the Registrar that that body is able and willing to discharge those functions, that the requirements mentioned in paragraph (b) of that sub-paragraph are satisfied in the case of that body and that he is not precluded from making the order by the following provisions of this paragraph or paragraph 29 or 30 below.

(3) For the purposes of sub-paragraph (1) above Schedule 7 shall have effect as if—

> (a) for references to a designated agency there were substituted references to a transferee body; and

> (b) for the reference to complaints in paragraph 4 there were substituted a reference to complaints arising out of the conduct by regulated friendly societies of regulated business.

(4) An order under sub-paragraph (1) above is in this Act referred to as a transfer order and a body to which functions are transferred by a transfer order is in this Act referred to as a transferee body.

(5) Subject to sub-paragraphs (6) and (8) below, this paragraph applies to the functions of the Registrar under section 113(3) of this Act and paragraph 38 below and any functions conferred on him by virtue of paragraphs 2 to 25 above other than the powers under sections 66 and 68 of this Act and, so far as applicable to assets belonging to a regulated friendly society, the power under section 67 of this Act.

424

(6) If the Registrar transfers his functions under Chapter VI of Part I of this Act they shall not be exercisable by the transferee body if the only reasons by virtue of which it appears to the body as mentioned in paragraph 23(2) above relate to the sufficiency of the funds of the society to meet existing claims or of the rates of contribution to cover benefits assured.

(7) Any function may be transferred by an order under this paragraph either wholly or in part and a function may be transferred in respect of all societies or only in respect of such societies as are specified in the order.

(8) A transfer order—

(a) may reserve to the Registrar the function of revoking a recognition order in respect of a self-regulating organisation for friendly societies on the ground that the requirement mentioned in paragraph 4(2) above is not satisfied; and

(b) shall not transfer to a transferee body the function of revoking any such recognition order on the ground that the organisation has contravened the provisions of paragraph 9 above.

(9) No transfer order shall be made unless a draft of it has been laid before and approved by a resolution of each House of Parliament.

29. The Registrar shall not make a transfer order transferring any function of making rules or regulations to a transferee body unless—

(a) the body has furnished him and the Secretary of State with a copy of the rules or regulations which it proposes to make in the exercise of those functions; and

(b) they are both satisfied that those rules or regulations will—

(i) afford investors an adequate level of protection,

(ii) in the case of rules and regulations corresponding to those mentioned in Schedule 8 of this Act comply with the principles set out in that Schedule, and

(iii) take proper account of the supervision of the friendly societies by the Registrar under the enactments relating to friendly societies.

30.—(1) The Registrar shall also before making a transfer order transferring any functions to a transferee body require it to furnish him and the Secretary of State with a copy of any guidance intended to have continuing effect which it proposes to issue in writing or other legible form and they may take such guidance into account in determining whether they are satisfied as mentioned in paragraph 29(b) above.

(2) In this Act references to guidance issued by a transferee body are references to guidance issued or any recommendation made by it which is issued or made to regulated friendly societies or self-regulating organisations for friendly societies generally or to any class of regulated friendly societies or self-regulating organisations for friendly societies, being societies which are or may be subject to rules or regulations made by it or organisations which are or may be recognised by it in the exercise of its functions under a transfer order.

31.—(1) Subject to the provisions of this paragraph, sections 115, 116, 117(3) to (5) and 118 of this Act shall apply in relation to the transfer of functions under paragraph 28 above as they apply in relation to the transfer of functions under section 114 of this Act.

(2) Subject to sub-paragraphs (5) and (6)(b) below, for references in those provisions to the Secretary of State, a designated agency and a delegation order there shall be substituted respectively references to the Registrar, a transferee body and a transfer order.

(3) The Registrar may not exercise the powers conferred by subsections (1) and (2) of section 115 except with the consent of the Secretary of State.

(4) In subsection (3) of section 115 for the reference to Schedule 7 to this Act there shall be substituted a reference to that Schedule as it has effect by virtue of paragraph 28(3) above and in subsection (5) of that section for the reference to section 114(9)(b) of this Act there shall be substituted a reference to paragraph 29(b) above.

(5) Section 118(3)(b) shall have effect as if the reference to any provision applying to the Secretary of State were a reference to any provision applying to the Secretary of State or the Registrar.

(6) In Schedule 9 to this Act—

(a) paragraph 1(2) and (3) shall be omitted;
(b) paragraph 4 shall have effect as if the references to the Secretary of State were references to the Secretary of State and the Registrar;
(c) paragraph 5 shall have effect as if the reference to section 205(2) were a reference to paragraph 45(1) below;
(d) paragraph 12(3) shall have effect as if the reference to section 114(9) were a reference to paragraph 29(1) above.

(7) The power mentioned in paragraph 2(3) of Schedule 9 to this Act shall not be exercisable on the ground that the company has ceased to be a designated agency or, as the case may be, a transferee body if the company remains a transferee body or, as the case may be, a designated agency.

32. A transferee body shall at least once in each year for which the transfer order is in force make a report to the Registrar on the discharge of the functions transferred to it by the order and on such other matters as the order may require and the Registrar shall send a copy of each report received by him under this paragraph to the Secretary of State who shall lay copies of the report before Parliament.

33.—(1) This paragraph applies where the function of making or revoking a recognition order in respect of a self-regulating organisation for friendly societies is exercisable by a transferee body.

(2) Paragraph 3(2) above shall have effect as if the first reference to the Secretary of State included a reference to the Registrar.

(3) The transferee body shall not regard the requirement mentioned in paragraph 4(2) as satisfied unless the Registrar has certified that he also regards it as satisfied.

(4) A transferee body shall send the Registrar and the Secretary of State a copy of any notice received by it under paragraph 8(6) above.

(5) Where the Secretary of State exercises any of the powers conferred by paragraph 10(2) above in relation to an organisation the Registrar shall direct the transferee body to take the appropriate action in relation to that organisation and such a direction shall, on the application of the Registrar, be enforceable by mandamus or, in Scotland, by an order for specific performance under section 91 of the Court of Session Act 1868.

34. A transferee body to which the Registrar has transferred any function of making rules or regulations may make those rules or regulations without the consent of the Secretary of State.

35.—(1) A transferee body shall not impose any prohibition or requirement under section 65 or 67 of this Act on a regulated friendly society or vary any such prohibition or requirement unless it has given reasonable notice of its intention to do so to the Registrar and informed him—

(a) of the manner in which and the date on or after which it intends to exercise the power; and
(b) in the case of a proposal to impose a prohibition or requirement, on which of the grounds specified in paragraph 23(2) above it proposes to act and its reasons for considering that the ground in question exists and that it is necessary to impose the prohibition or requirement.

(2) A transferee body shall not exercise any power to which sub-paragraph (1) above applies if before the date given in the notice in pursuance of sub-paragraph (1)(a) above the Registrar has served on it a notice in writing directing it not to do so; and the Registrar may

serve such a notice if he considers it is desirable for protecting members or potential members of the regulated friendly society against the risk that it may be unable to meet its liabilities or to fulfil the reasonable expectations of its members or potential members.

36.—(1) The Secretary of State shall not consent to the making of an order by the Registrar under paragraph 28 above transferring any functions to a transferee body unless he is satisfied that any rules, regulations, guidance and recommendations of which copies are furnished to him under paragraphs 29(a) and 30(1) above do not have, and are not intended or likely to have, to any significant extent the effect of restricting, distorting or preventing competition or, if they have or are intended or likely to have that effect to any significant extent, that the effect is not greater than is necessary for the protection of investors.

(2) Section 121(2) and (4) and sections 122 to 128 above shall have effect in relation to transferee bodies and transfer orders as they have effect in relation to designated agencies and designation orders but subject to the following modifications.

(3) Those provisions shall have effect as if the powers exercisable under section 121(3) were—

   (a) to make an order transferring back to the Registrar all or any of the functions transferred to the transferee body by a transfer order; or
   (b) to direct the Registrar to direct the transferee body to take specified steps for the purpose of securing that the rules, regulations, guidance or practices in question do not have the effect mentioned in sub-paragraph (1) above.

(4) No order shall be made by virtue of sub-paragraph (3) above unless a draft of it has been laid before and approved by a resolution of each House of Parliament.

(5) For the decisions referred to in section 122(1) there shall be substituted a reference to the Secretary of State's decision whether he is precluded by sub-paragraph (1) above from giving his consent to the making of a transfer order.

(6) Section 128 shall apply as if—

   (a) the powers referred to in subsection (1) of that section included the power conferred by sub-paragraph (3)(b) above; and
   (b) the references to Chapter XIV of Part I included references to this paragraph.

37.—(1) If a transferee body has reasonable grounds for believing that any regulated friendly society has failed to comply with an obligation to which it is subject by virtue of this Act it shall forthwith give notice of that fact to the Registrar so that he can take it into consideration in deciding whether to exercise in relation to the society any of the powers conferred on him by sections 87 to 89 and 91 of the Friendly Societies Act 1974 or, as the case may be, sections 77 to 80 of the Friendly Societies Act (Northern Ireland) 1970 (inspection, winding up, suspension of business and cancellation and suspension of registration).

(2) A notice under sub-paragraph (1) above shall contain particulars of the obligation in question and of the transferee body's reasons for considering that the society has failed to satisfy that obligation.

(3) A transferee body need not give a notice under sub-paragraph (1) above in respect of any matter unless it considers that that matter (either alone or in conjunction with other matters) would justify the withdrawal of authorisation under section 28 of this Act in the case of a person to whom that provision applies.

PART V

MISCELLANEOUS AND SUPPLEMENTAL

38.—(1) The Registrar may publish information or give advice, or arrange for the publication of information or the giving of advice, in such form and manner as he considers appropriate with respect to—

    (a) the operation of this Schedule and the rules and regulations made under it in relation to registered friendly societies, including in particular the rights of their members, the duties of such societies and the steps to be taken for enforcing those rights or complying with those duties;

    (b) any matters relating to the functions of the Registrar under this Schedule or any such rules or regulations;

    (c) any other matters about which it appears to him to be desirable to publish information or give advice for the protection of those members or any class of them.

(2) The Registrar may offer for sale copies of information published under this paragraph and may, if he thinks fit, make reasonable charges for advice given under this paragraph at any person's request.

(3) This paragraph shall not be construed as authorising the disclosure of restricted information within the meaning of section 179 of this Act in any case in which it could not be disclosed apart from the provisions of this paragraph.

39. In the case of an application for authorisation under section 26 of this Act made by a society which is registered under the Friendly Societies Act 1974 within the meaning of that Act or is registered or deemed to be registered under the Friendly Societies Act (Northern Ireland) 1970 ('a registered society'), section 27(3)(c) of this Act shall have effect as if it referred only to any person who is a trustee manager or member of the committee of the society.

40. Where the other person mentioned in paragraph (c) of the definition of 'connected person' in section 105(9) of this Act is a registered society that paragraph shall have effect with the substitution for the words from 'member' onwards of the words 'trustee, manager or member of the committee of the society'.

41. In relation to any such document as is mentioned in subsection (1) of section 204 of this Act which is required or authorised to be given to or served on a registered society—

    (a) subsection (3)(c) of that section shall have effect with the substitution for the words from 'member' onwards of the words 'trustee, manager or member of the committee of the society'; and

    (b) subsection (4)(c) of that section shall have effect as if for the words from 'member' onwards there were substituted the words 'trustee, manager or member of the committee of the society, the office which is its registered office in accordance with its rules'.

42. Rules under paragraphs 14, 15, 17 and 18 above and regulations under paragraphs 16, 19 and 20 above shall apply notwithstanding any provision to the contrary in the rules of any regulated friendly society to which they apply.

43.—(1) Where it appears to the Registrar, the assistant registrar for Scotland, the Industrial Assurance Commissioner or the Industrial Assurance Commissioner for Northern Ireland that any such rules as are mentioned in section 48(2)(j) of this Act which are made by virtue of paragraph 14 above (or any corresponding rules made by a self-regulating organisation for friendly societies) make arrangements for the settlement of a dispute referred to him under section 77 of the Friendly Societies Act 1974, section 65 of the Friendly Societies Act (Northern Ireland) 1970, section 32 of the Industrial Assurance Act 1923 or Article 36 of the Industrial Assurance (Northern Ireland Order) 1979 or that such rules relate to some of the matters in dispute he may, if he thinks fit, delegate his functions in respect of the dispute so as to enable it to be settled in accordance with the rules.

(2) If such rules provide that any dispute may be referred to such a person, that person may deal with any dispute referred to him in pursuance of those rules as if it were a dispute referred to him as aforesaid and may delegate his functions in respect of any such dispute to any other person.

44.—(1) In Part III of Schedule 1 to the House of Commons Disqualification Act 1975 (disqualifying offices) there shall be inserted at the appropriate place—

'Chairman of a transferee body within the meaning of Schedule 11 to the Financial Services Act 1986 if he is in receipt of remuneration.'

(2) A corresponding amendment shall be made in Part III of Schedule 1 to the Northern Ireland Assembly Disqualification Act 1975.

45.—(1) Any power of the Chief Registrar of friendly societies to make regulations, rules or orders which is exercisable by virtue of this Act shall be exercisable by statutory instrument and the Statutory Instruments Act 1946 shall apply to any such power as if the Chief Registrar of friendly societies were a Minister of the Crown.

(2) Any such power of the Registrar of Friendly Societies for Northern Ireland shall be exercisable by statutory rule for the purposes of the Statutory Rules (Northern Ireland) Order 1979.

(3) Any regulations, rules or orders made under this Schedule by the Registrar may make different provision for different cases.

SCHEDULE 12 (Section 172)

TAKEOVER OFFERS:

PROVISIONS SUBSTITUTED FOR SECTIONS 428, 429 and 430 OF COMPANIES ACT 1985

PART XIIIA

TAKEOVER OFFERS

428. 'Takeover offers'
(1) In this Part of this Act 'a takeover offer' means an offer to acquire all the shares, or all the shares of any class or classes, in a company (other than shares which at the date of the offer are already held by the offeror), being an offer on terms which are the same in relation to all the shares to which the offer relates or, where those shares include shares of different classes, in relation to all the shares of each class.

(2) In subsection (1) 'shares' means shares which have been allotted on the date of the offer but a takeover offer may include among the shares to which it relates all or any shares that are subsequently allotted before a date specified in or determined in accordance with the terms of the offer.

(3) The terms offered in relation to any shares shall for the purposes of this section be treated as being the same in relation to all the shares or, as the case may be, all the shares of a class to which the offer relates notwithstanding any variation permitted by subsection (4).

(4) A variation is permitted by this subsection where—

   (a) the law of a country or territory outside the United Kingdom precludes an offer of consideration in the form or any of the forms specified in the terms in question or precludes it except after compliance by the offeror with conditions with which he is unable to comply or which he regards as unduly onerous; and
   (b) the variation is such that the persons to whom an offer of consideration in that form is precluded are able to receive consideration otherwise than in that form but of substantially equivalent value.

(5) The reference in subsection (1) to shares already held by the offeror includes a reference to shares which he has contracted to acquire but that shall not be construed as including shares which are the subject of a contract binding the holder to accept the offer when it is made, being a contract entered into by the holder either for no consideration and under seal

or for no consideration other than a promise by the offeror to make the offer.

(6) In the application of subsection (5) to Scotland, the words 'and under seal' shall be omitted.

(7) Where the terms of an offer make provision for their revision and for acceptances on the previous terms to be treated as acceptances on the revised terms, the revision shall not be regarded for the purposes of this Part of this Act as the making of a fresh offer and references in this Part of this Act to the date of the offer shall accordingly be construed as references to the date on which the original offer was made.

(8) In this Part of this Act 'the offeror' means, subject to section 430D, the person making a takeover offer and 'the company' means the company whose shares are the subject of the offer.

429. Right of offeror to buy out minority shareholders

(1) If, in a case in which a takeover offer does not relate to shares of different classes, the offeror has by virtue of acceptances of the offer acquired or contracted to acquire not less than nine-tenths in value of the shares to which the offer relates he may give notice to the holder of any shares to which the offer relates which the offeror has not acquired or contracted to acquire that he desires to acquire those shares.

(2) If, in a case in which a takeover offer relates to shares of different classes, the offeror has by virtue of acceptances of the offer acquired or contracted to acquire not less than nine-tenths in value of the shares of any class to which the offer relates, he may give notice to the holder of any shares of that class which the offeror has not acquired or contracted to acquire that he desires to acquire those shares.

(3) No notice shall be given under subsection (1) or (2) unless the offeror has acquired or contracted to acquire the shares necessary to satisfy the minimum specified in that subsection before the end of the period of four months beginning with the date of the offer; and no such notice shall be given after the end of the period of two months beginning with the date on which he has acquired or contracted to acquire shares which satisfy that minimum.

(4) Any notice under this section shall be given in the prescribed manner; and when the offeror gives the first notice in relation to an offer he shall send a copy of it to the company together with a statutory declaration by him in the prescribed form stating that the conditions for the giving of the notice are satisfied.

(5) Where the offeror is a company (whether or not a company within the meaning of this Act) the statutory declaration shall be signed by a director.

(6) Any person who fails to send a copy of a notice or a statutory declaration as required by subsection (4) or makes such a declaration for the purposes of that subsection knowing it to be false or without having reasonable grounds for believing it to be true shall be liable to imprisonment or a fine, or both, and for continued failure to send the copy or declaration, to a daily default fine.

(7) If any person is charged with an offence for failing to send a copy of a notice as required by subsection (4) it is a defence for him to prove that he took reasonable steps for securing compliance with that subsection.

(8) Where during the period within which a takeover offer can be accepted the offeror acquires or contracts to acquire any of the shares to which the offer relates but otherwise than by virtue of acceptances of the offer, then, if—

    (a) the value of the consideration for which they are acquired or contracted to be acquired ('the acquisition consideration') does not at that time exceed the value of the consideration specified in the terms of the offer; or

    (b) those terms are subsequently revised so that when the revision is announced the value of the acquisition consideration, at the time mentioned in paragraph (a) above, no longer exceeds the value of the consideration specified in those terms,

the offeror shall be treated for the purposes of this section as having acquired or contracted to acquire those shares by virtue of acceptances of the offer; but in any other case those shares shall be treated as excluded from those to which the offer relates.

430. Effect of notice under s 429

(1) The following provisions shall, subject to section 430C, have effect where a notice is given in respect of any shares under section 429.

(2) The offeror shall be entitled and bound to acquire those shares on the terms of the offer.

(3) Where the terms of an offer are such as to give the holder of any shares a choice of consideration the notice shall give particulars of the choice and state—

- (a) that the holder of the shares may within six weeks from the date of the notice indicate his choice by a written communication sent to the offeror at an address specified in the notice; and
- (b) which consideration specified in the offer is to be taken as applying in default of his indicating a choice as aforesaid;

and the terms of the offer mentioned in subsection (2) shall be determined accordingly.

(4) Subsection (3) applies whether or not any time-limit or other conditions applicable to the choice under the terms of the offer can still be complied with; and if the consideration chosen by the holder of the shares—

- (a) is not cash and the offeror is no longer able to provide it; or
- (b) was to have been provided by a third party who is no longer bound or able to provide it,

the consideration shall be taken to consist of an amount of cash payable by the offeror which at the date of the notice is equivalent to the chosen consideration.

(5) At the end of six weeks from the date of the notice the offeror shall forthwith—

- (a) send a copy of the notice to the company; and
- (b) pay or transfer to the company the consideration for the shares to which the notice relates.

(6) If the shares to which the notice relates are registered the copy of the notice sent to the company under subsection (5)(a) shall be accompanied by an instrument of transfer executed on behalf of the shareholder by a person appointed by the offeror; and on receipt of that instrument the company shall register the offeror as the holder of those shares.

(7) If the shares to which the notice relates are transferable by the delivery of warrants or other instruments the copy of the notice sent to the company under subsection (5)(a) shall be accompanied by a statement to that effect; and the company shall on receipt of the statement issue the offeror with warrants or other instruments in respect of the shares and those already in issue in respect of the shares shall become void.

(8) Where the consideration referred to in paragraph (b) of subsection (5) consists of shares or securities to be allotted by the offeror the reference in that paragraph to the transfer of the consideration shall be construed as a reference to the allotment of the shares or securities to the company.

(9) Any sum received by a company under paragraph (b) of subsection (5) and any other consideration received under that paragraph shall be held by the company on trust for the person entitled to the shares in respect of which the sum or other consideration was received.

(10) Any sum received by a company under paragraph (b) of subsection (5), and any dividend or other sum accruing from any other consideration received by a company under that paragraph, shall be paid into a separate bank account, being an account the balance on

which bears interest at an appropriate rate and can be withdrawn by such notice (if any) as is appropriate.

(11) Where after reasonable enquiry made at such intervals as are reasonable the person entitled to any consideration held on trust by virtue of subsection (9) cannot be found and twelve years have elapsed since the consideration was received or the company is wound up the consideration (together with any interest, dividend or other benefit that has accrued from it) shall be paid into court.

(12) In relation to a company registered in Scotland, subsections (13) and (14) shall apply in place of subsection (11).

(13) Where after reasonable enquiry made at such intervals as are reasonable the person entitled to any consideration held on trust by virtue of subsection (9) cannot be found and twelve years have elapsed since the consideration was received or the company is wound up—

- (a) the trust shall terminate;
- (b) the company or, as the case may be, the liquidator shall sell any consideration other than cash and any benefit other than cash that has accrued from the consideration; and
- (c) a sum representing—
  - (i) the consideration so far as it is cash;
  - (ii) the proceeds of any sale under paragraph (b) above; and
  - (iii) any interest, dividend or other benefit that has accrued from the consideration,

  shall be deposited in the name of the Accountant of Court in a bank account such as is referred to in subsection (10) and the receipt for the deposit shall be transmitted to the Accountant of Court.

(14) Section 58 of the Bankruptcy (Scotland) Act 1985 (so far as consistent with this Act) shall apply with any necessary modifications to sums deposited under subsection (13) as that section applies to sums deposited under section 57(1)(a) of that Act.

(15) The expenses of any such enquiry as is mentioned in subsection (11) or (13) may be defrayed out of the money or other property held on trust for the person or persons to whom the enquiry relates.

430A. Right of minority shareholder to be bought out by offeror

(1) If a takeover offer relates to all the shares in a company and at any time before the end of the period within which the offer can be accepted—

- (a) the offeror has by virtue of acceptances of the offer acquired or contracted to acquire some (but not all) of the shares to which the offer relates; and
- (b) those shares, with or without any other shares in the company which he has acquired or contracted to acquire, amount to not less than nine-tenths in value of all the shares in the company,

the holder of any shares to which the offer relates who has not accepted the offer may by a written communication addressed to the offeror require him to acquire those shares.

(2) If a takeover offer relates to shares of any class or classes and at any time before the end of the period within which the offer can be accepted—

- (a) the offeror has by virtue of acceptances of the offer acquired or contracted to acquire some (but not all) of the shares of any class to which the offer relates; and
- (b) those shares, with or without any other shares of that class which he has acquired or contracted to acquire, amount to not less than nine-tenths in value of all the shares of that class,

the holder of any shares of that class who has not accepted the offer may by a written communication addressed to the offeror require him to acquire those shares.

(3) Within one month of the time specified in subsection (1) or, as the case may be, subsection (2) the offeror shall give any shareholder who has not accepted the offer notice in the prescribed manner of the rights that are exercisable by him under that subsection; and if the notice is given before the end of the period mentioned in that subsection it shall state that the offer is still open for acceptance.

(4) A notice under subsection (3) may specify a period for the exercise of the rights conferred by this section and in that event the rights shall not be exercisable after the end of that period; but no such period shall end less than three months after the end of the period within which the offer can be accepted.

(5) Subsection (3) does not apply if the offeror has given the shareholder a notice in respect of the shares in question under section 429.

(6) If the offeror fails to comply with subsection (3) he and, if the offeror is a company, every officer of the company who is in default or to whose neglect the failure is attributable, shall be liable to a fine and, for continued contravention, to a daily default fine.

(7) If an offeror other than a company is charged with an offence for failing to comply with subsection (3) it is a defence for him to prove that he took all reasonable steps for securing compliance with that subsection.

430B. Effect of requirement under s 430A
(1) The following provisions shall, subject to section 430C, have effect where a shareholder exercises his rights in respect of any shares under section 430A.

(2) The offeror shall be entitled and bound to acquire those shares on the terms of the offer or on such other terms as may be agreed.

(3) Where the terms of an offer are such as to give the holder of shares a choice of consideration the holder of the shares may indicate his choice when requiring the offeror to acquire them and the notice given to the holder under section 430A(3)—

(a) shall give particulars of the choice and of the rights conferred by this subsection; and
(b) may state which consideration specified in the offer is to be taken as applying in default of his indicating a choice;

and the terms of the offer mentioned in subsection (2) shall be determined accordingly.

(4) Subsection (3) applies whether or not any time-limit or other conditions applicable to the choice under the terms of the offer can still be complied with; and if the consideration chosen by the holder of the shares—

(a) is not cash and the offeror is no longer able to provide it; or
(b) was to have been provided by a third party who is no longer bound or able to provide it,

the consideration shall be taken to consist of an amount of cash payable by the offeror which at the date when the holder of the shares requires the offeror to acquire them is equivalent to the chosen consideration.

430C. Applications to the court
(1) Where a notice is given under section 429 to the holder of any shares the court may, on an application made by him within six weeks from the date on which the notice was given—

(a) order that the offeror shall not be entitled and bound to acquire the shares; or
(b) specify terms of acquisition different from those of the offer.

(2) If an application to the court under subsection (1) is pending at the end of the period mentioned in subsection (5) of section 430 that subsection shall not have effect until the application has been disposed of.

(3) Where the holder of any shares exercises his rights under section 430A the court may,

on an application made by him or the offeror, order that the terms on which the offeror is entitled and bound to acquire the shares shall be such as the court thinks fit.

(4) No order for costs or expenses shall be made against a shareholder making an application under subsection (1) or (3) unless the court considers—

    (a) that the application was unnecessary, improper or vexatious; or

    (b) that there has been unreasonable delay in making the application or unreasonable conduct on his part in conducting the proceedings on the application.

(5) Where a takeover offer has not been accepted to the extent necessary for entitling the offeror to give notices under subsection (1) or (2) of section 429 the court may, on the application of the offeror, make an order authorising him to give notices under that subsection if satisfied—

    (a) that the offeror has after reasonable enquiry been unable to trace one or more of the persons holding shares to which the offer relates;

    (b) that the shares which the offeror has acquired or contracted to acquire by virtue of acceptances of the offer, together with the shares held by the person or persons mentioned in paragraph (a), amount to not less than the minimum specified in that subsection; and

    (c) that the consideration offered is fair and reasonable;

but the court shall not make an order under this subsection unless it considers that it is just and equitable to do so having regard, in particular, to the number of shareholders who have been traced but who have not accepted the offer.

430D. Joint offers

(1) A takeover offer may be made by two or more persons jointly and in that event this Part of this Act has effect with the following modifications.

(2) The conditions for the exercise of the rights conferred by sections 429 and 430A shall be satisfied by the joint offerors acquiring or contracting to acquire the necessary shares jointly (as respects acquisitions by virtue of acceptances of the offer) and either jointly or separately (in other cases); and, subject to the following provisions, the rights and obligations of the offeror under those sections and sections 430 and 430B shall be respectively joint rights and joint and several obligations of the joint offerors.

(3) It shall be a sufficient compliance with any provision of those sections requiring or authorising a notice or other document to be given or sent by or to the joint offerors that it is given or sent by or to any of them; but the statutory declaration required by section 429(4) shall be made by all of them and, in the case of a joint offeror being a company, signed by a director of that company.

(4) In sections 428, 430(8) and 430E references to the offeror shall be construed as references to the joint offerors or any of them.

(5) In section 430(6) and (7) references to the offeror shall be construed as references to the joint offerors or such of them as they may determine.

(6) In sections 430(4)(a) and 430B(4)(a) references to the offeror being no longer able to provide the relevant consideration shall be construed as references to none of the joint offerors being able to do so.

(7) In section 430C references to the offeror shall be construed as references to the joint offerors except that any application under subsection (3) or (5) may be made by any of them and the reference in subsection (5)(a) to the offeror having been unable to trace one or more of the persons holding shares shall be construed as a reference to none of the offerors having been able to do so.

430E. Associates

(1) The requirement in section 428(1) that a takeover offer must extend to all the shares, or all the shares of any class or classes, in a company shall be regarded as satisfied

notwithstanding that the offer does not extend to shares which associates of the offeror hold or have contracted to acquire; but, subject to subsection (2), shares which any such associate holds or has contracted to acquire, whether at the time when the offer is made or subsequently, shall be disregarded for the purposes of any reference in this Part of this Act to the shares to which a takeover offer relates.

(2) Where during the period within which a takeover offer can be accepted any associate of the offeror acquires or contracts to acquire any of the shares to which the offer relates, then, if the condition specified in subsection (8)(a) or (b) of section 429 is satisfied as respects those shares they shall be treated for the purposes of that section as shares to which the offer relates.

(3) In section 430A(1)(b) and (2)(b) the reference to shares which the offeror has acquired or contracted to acquire shall include a reference to shares which any associate of his has acquired or contracted to acquire.

(4) In this section 'associate', in relation to an offeror means—

   (a) a nominee of the offeror;
   (b) a holding company, subsidiary or fellow subsidiary of the offeror or a nominee of such a holding company, subsidiary or fellow subsidiary;
   (c) a body corporate in which the offeror is substantially interested; or
   (d) any person who is, or is a nominee of, a party to an agreement with the offeror for the acquisition of, or of an interest in, the shares which are the subject of the take-over offer, being an agreement which includes provisions imposing obligations or restrictions such as are mentioned in section 204(2)(a).

(5) For the purposes of subsection (4)(b) a company is a fellow subsidiary of another body corporate if both are subsidiaries of the same body corporate but neither is a subsidiary of the other.

(6) For the purposes of subsection (4)(c) an offeror has a substantial interest in a body corporate if—

   (a) that body or its directors are accustomed to act in accordance with his directions or instructions; or
   (b) he is entitled to exercise or control the exercise of one-third or more of the voting power at general meetings of that body.

(7) Subsections (5) and (6) of section 204 shall apply to subsection (4)(d) above as they apply to that section and subsections (3) and (4) of section 203 shall apply for the purposes of subsection (6) above as they apply for the purposes of subsection (2)(b) of that section.

(8) Where the offeror is an individual his associates shall also include his spouse and any minor child or step-child of his.

430F. Convertible securities
(1) For the purposes of this Part of this Act securities of a company shall be treated as shares in the company if they are convertible into or entitle the holder to subscribe for such shares; and references to the holder of shares or a shareholder shall be construed accordingly.

(2) Subsection (1) shall not be construed as requiring any securities to be treated—

   (a) as shares of the same class as those into which they are convertible or for which the holder is entitled to subscribe; or
   (b) as shares of the same class as other securities by reason only that the shares into which they are convertible or for which the holder is entitled to subscribe are of the same class.

SCHEDULE 13 (Section 182)

DISCLOSURE OF INFORMATION

1. In section 133(2)(a) of the Fair Trading Act 1973 after the words 'the

Telecommunications Act 1984' there shall be inserted the words 'or Chapter XIV of Part I of the Financial Services Act 1986'.

2. In section 41(1)(a) of the Restrictive Trade Practices Act 1976 after the words 'the Telecommunications Act 1984' there shall be inserted the words 'or Chapter XIV of Part I of the Financial Services Act 1986'.

3.—(1) In section 19 of the Banking Act 1979 after subsection (2) there shall be inserted—

'(2A) Nothing in subsection (1) above prohibits the disclosure of information by the Bank to any person specified in the first column of the following Table if the Bank considers—

(a) that the disclosure would enable or assist the Bank to discharge its functions under this Act; or
(b) that it would enable or assist that person to discharge the functions specified in relation to him in the second column of that Table.

TABLE

Person	*Functions*
The Secretary of State.	Functions under the Insurance Companies Act 1982 or the Financial Services Act 1986.
The Chief Registrar of friendly societies or the Registrar of Friendly Societies for Northern Ireland.	Functions under the Financial Services Act 1986 or under the enactments relating to friendly societies.
A designated agency or transferee body or the competent authority (within the meaning of the Financial Services Act 1986).	Functions under the Financial Services Act 1986.
A recognised self-regulating organisation, recognised professional body, recognised investment exchange, recognised clearing house or recognised self-regulating organisation for friendly societies (within the meaning of the Financial Services Act 1986).	Functions in its capacity as an organisation, body, exchange or clearing house recognised under the Financial Services Act 1986.
A person appointed or authorised to exercise any powers under section 94, 106 or 177 of the Financial Services Act 1986.	Functions arising from his appointment or authorisation under that section.
The body administering a scheme under section 54 of or paragraph 18 of Schedule 11 to the Financial Services Act 1986.	Functions under the scheme.

(2B) Nothing in subsection (1) above prohibits the disclosure by a person specified in the first column of the Table in subsection (2A) above of information obtained by him by virtue of a disclosure authorised by that subsection if he makes the disclosure with the consent of the Bank and for the purpose of enabling or assisting himself to discharge any functions specified in relation to him in the second column of that Table; and before deciding whether to give its consent to such a disclosure by any person the Bank shall take account of any representations made by him as to the desirability of or the necessity for the disclosure.'.

(2) For subsection (6) of that section there shall be substituted—

'(6) Nothing in subsection (1) above prohibits the disclosure of information by or with the consent of the Bank for the purpose of enabling or assisting an authority in a country or territory outside the United Kingdom to exercise functions corresponding to those of the Bank under this Act, or to those of the Secretary of State under the Insurance Companies Act 1982 or the Financial Services Act 1986 or to those of the competent authority under the said Act of 1986 or any other functions in connection with rules of law corresponding to the provisions of the Company Securities (Insider Dealing) Act 1985 or Part VII of the said Act of 1986.'.

4. In section 20(4) of that Act—

(a) for the words 'in a country or territory outside the United Kingdom' there shall be substituted the words 'in a members State other than the United Kingdom'; and

(b) in paragraph (b) for the words 'subsections (4) to (6)' there shall be substituted the words 'subsections (2A), (2B) and (4) to (6)'.

5. At the end of section 19(3) of the Competition Act 1980 there shall be inserted—

'(h) Chapter XIV of Part I of the Financial Services Act 1986'.

6. For subsections (1) and (2) of section 47A of the Insurance Companies Act 1982 there shall be substituted—

'(1) Subject to the following provisions of this section, no information relating to the business or other affairs of any person which has been obtained under section 44(2) to (4) above shall be disclosed without the consent of the person from whom the information was obtained and, if different, the person to whom it relates.

(2) Subsection (1) above shall not preclude the disclosure of information to any person who is a competent authority for the purposes of section 449 of the Companies Act 1985.

(2A) Subsection (1) above shall not preclude the disclosure of information as mentioned in any of the paragraphs except (m) of subsection (1) of section 180 of the Financial Services Act 1986 or in subsection (3) or (4) of that section or as mentioned in section 449(1) of the Companies Act 1985.

(2B) Subsection (1) above shall not preclude the disclosure of any such information as is mentioned in section 180(5) of the Financial Services Act 1986 by any person who by virtue of that section is not precluded by section 179 of that Act from disclosing it.'

7. After subsection (1) of section 437 of the Companies Act 1985 there shall be inserted—

'(1A) Any persons who have been appointed under section 431 or 432 may at any time and, if the Secretary of State directs them to do so, shall inform him of any matters coming to their knowledge as a result of their investigations.';

and subsection (2) of section 433 of that Act shall be omitted.

8. In section 446 of that Act—

(a) in subsection (3) for the words 'to 436' there shall be subsituted the words 'to 437'; and

(b) subsection (5) shall be omitted.

9.—(1) In subsection (1) of section 449 of that Act—

(a) for paragraphs (a) and (b) there shall be substituted—
'(a) with a view to the institution of or otherwise for the purposes of criminal proceedings;'.

(b) for paragraph (d) there shall be substituted—
'(d) for the purpose of enabling or assisting the Secretary of State to exercise any of his functions under this Act, the Insider Dealing Act, the Prevention of Fraud (Investments) Act 1958, the Insurance Companies Act 1982, the Insolvency Act 1986, the Company Directors Disqualification Act 1986 or the Financial Services Act 1986.

(dd) for the purpose of enabling or assisting the Department of Economic Development for Northern Ireland to exercise any powers conferred on it by the enactments relating to companies or insolvency or for the purpose of enabling or assisting any inspector appointed by it under the enactments relating to companies to discharge his functions';

Appendix

(c) after paragraph (e) there shall be inserted—

'(f) for the purpose of enabling or assisting the Bank of England to discharge its functions under the Banking Act 1979 or any other functions,

(g) for the purpose of enabling or assisting the Deposit Protection Board to discharge its functions under that Act,

(h) for any purpose mentioned in section 180(1)(b), (e), (h), (n) or (p) of the Financial Services Act 1986,

(i) for the purpose of enabling or assisting the Industrial Assurance Commissioner or the Industrial Assurance Commissioner for Northern Ireland to discharge his functions under the enactments relating to industrial assurance,

(j) for the purpose of enabling or assisting the Insurance Brokers Registration Council to discharge its functions under the Insurance Brokers (Registration) Act 1977,

(k) for the purpose of enabling or assisting an official receiver to discharge his functions under the enactments relating to insolvency or for the purpose of enabling or assisting a body which is for the time being a recognised professional body for the purposes of section 391 of the Insolvency Act 1986 to discharge its functions as such,

(l) with a view to the institution of, or otherwise for the purposes of, any disciplinary proceedings relating to the exercise by a solicitor, auditor, accountant, valuer or actuary of his professional duties,

(m) for the purpose of enabling or assisting an authority in a country or territory outside the United Kingdom to exercise corresponding supervisory functions.'.

(2) After subsection (1) of that section there shall be inserted—

'(1A) In subsection (1) above "corresponding supervisory functions" means functions corresponding to those of the Secretary of State or the competent authority under the Financial Services Act 1986 or to those of the Secretary of State under the Insurance Companies Act 1982 or to those of the Bank of England under the Banking Act 1979 or any other functions in connection with rules of law corresponding to the provisions of the Insider Dealing Act or Part VII of the Financial Services Act 1986.

(1B) Subject to subsection (1C), subsection (1) shall not preclude publication or disclosure for the purpose of enabling or assisting any public or other authority for the time being designated for the purposes of this section by the Secretary of State by an order in a statutory instrument to discharge any functions which are specified in the order.

(1C) An order under subsection (1B) designating an authority for the purpose of that subsection may—

(a) impose conditions subject to which the publication or disclosure of any information or document is permitted by that subsection; and
(b) otherwise restrict the circumstances in which that subsection permits publication or disclosure.

(1D) Subsection (1) shall not preclude the publication or disclosure of any such information as is mentioned in section 180(5) of the Financial Services Act 1986 by any person who by virtue of that section is not precluded by section 179 of that Act from disclosing it.'

(3) For subsection (3) of that section (competent authorities) there shall be substituted—

'(3) For the purposes of this section each of the following is a competent authority—

(a) the Secretary of State,

(b) the Department of Economic Development for Northern Ireland and any officer of that Department,

(c) an inspector appointed under this Part by the Secretary of State,

(d) the Treasury and any officer of the Treasury,

(e) the Bank of England and any officer or servant of the Bank,

(f) the Lord Advocate,

(g) the Director of Public Prosecutions, and the Director of Public Prosecutions for Northern Ireland,

(h) any designated agency or transferee body within the meaning of the Financial Services Act 1986 and any officer or servant of such an agency or body,

(i) any person appointed or authorised to exercise any powers under section 94, 106 or 177 of the Financial Services Act 1986 and any officer or servant of such a person,

(j) the body administering a scheme under section 54 of or paragraph 18 of Schedule 11 to that Act and any officer or servant of such a body,

(k) the Chief Registrar of Friendly Societies and the Registrar of Friendly Societies for Northern Ireland and any officer or servant of either of them,

(l) the Industrial Assurance Commissioner and the Industrial Assurance Commissioner for Northern Ireland and any officer of either of them,

(m) any constable,

(n) any procurator fiscal.

(4) A statutory instrument containing an order under subsection (1B) is subject to annulment in pursuance of a resolution of either House of Parliament.'.

10. After section 451 of that Act there shall be inserted—

'451A. Disclosure of information by Secretary of State
The Secretary of State may, if he thinks fit, disclose any information obtained under this Part of this Act—

(a) to any person who is a competent authority for the purposes of section 449, or

(b) in any circumstances in which or for any purpose for which that section does not preclude the disclosure of the information to which it applies.'

11. After Article 430(1) of the Companies (Northern Ireland) Order 1986 there shall be inserted—

'(1A) Any persons who have been appointed under Article 424 or 425 may at any time and, if the Department directs them to do so shall, inform it of any matters coming to their knowledge as a result of their investigation.';

and Article 426(2) of that Order shall be omitted.

12. In Article 439 of that Order—

(a) in paragraph (3) for the words 'to 429' there shall be substituted the words 'to 430'; and

(b) paragraph (5) shall be omitted.

13.—(1) In paragraph (1) of Article 442 of that Order—

(a) for sub-paragraphs (a) and (b) there shall be substituted—

'(a) with a view to the institution of or otherwise for the purposes of criminal proceedings;';

(b) for sub-paragraph (d) there shall be substituted—

'(d) for the purpose of enabling or assisting the Department to exercise any of its functions under this Order, the Insider Dealing Order or the Prevention of Fraud (Investments) Act (Northern Ireland) 1940;

(dd) for the purpose of enabling or assisting the Secretary of State to exercise any functions conferred on him by the enactments relating to companies or insolvency, the Prevention of Fraud (Investments) Act 1958, the Insurance Companies Act 1982, or the Financial Services Act 1986, or for the purpose of enabling or assisting any inspector appointed by him under the enactments relating to companies to discharge his functions';

(c) after sub-paragraph (e) there shall be inserted—

'(f) for the purposes of enabling or assisting the Bank of England to discharge its functions under the Banking Act 1979 or any other functions;

(g) for the purposes of enabling or assisting the Deposit Protection Board to discharge its functions under that Act;

(h) for any purpose mentioned in section 180(1)(b), (e), (h), (n) or (p) of the Financial Services Act 1986;

(i) for the purpose of enabling or assisting the Industrial Assurance Commissioner for Northern Ireland or the Industrial Assurance Commissioner in Great Britain to discharge his functions under the enactments relating to industrial assurance;

(j) for the purpose of enabling or assisting the Insurance Brokers Registration Council to discharge its functions under the Insurance Brokers (Registration) Act 1977;

(k) for the purpose of enabling or assisting the official assignee to discharge his functions under the enactments relating to companies or bankruptcy;

(l) with a view to the institution of, or otherwise for the purposes of, any disciplinary proceedings relating to the exercise by a solicitor, auditor, accountant, valuer or actuary of his professional duties;

(m) for the purpose of enabling or assisting an authority in a country or territory outside the United Kingdom to exercise corresponding supervisory functions.'.

(2) After paragraph (1) of that Article there shall be inserted—

'(1A) In paragraph (1) "corresponding supervisory functions" means functions corresponding to those of the Secretary of State or the competent authority under the Financial Services Act 1986 or to those of the Secretary of State under the Insurance Companies Act 1982 or to those of the Bank of England under the Banking Act 1979 or any other functions in connection with rules of law corresponding to the provisions of the Insider Dealing Order or Part VII of the Financial Services Act 1986.

(1B) Subject to paragraph (1C), paragraph (1) shall not preclude publication or disclosure for the purpose of enabling or assisting any public or other authority for the time being designated for the purposes of this Article by an order made by the Department to discharge any functions which are specified in the order.

(1C) An order under paragraph (1B) designating an authority for the purpose of that paragraph may—

(a) impose conditions subject to which the publication or disclosure of any information or document is permitted by that paragraph; and

(b) otherwise restrict the circumstances in which that paragraph permits publication or disclosure.

(1D) Paragraph (1) shall not preclude the publication or disclosure of any such information as is mentioned in section 180(5) of the Financial Services Act 1986 by any person who by virtue of that section is not precluded by section 179 of that Act from disclosing it.'.

(3) For paragraph (3) of that Article (competent authorities) there shall be substituted—

'(3) For the purposes of this Article each of the following is a competent authority—

(a) the Department and any officer of the Department,

(b) the Secretary of State,

(c) an inspector appointed under this Part by the Department,

(d) the Department of Finance and Personnel and any officer of that Department;

(e) the Treasury and any officer of the Treasury,

(f) the Bank of England and any officer or servant of the Bank,

(g) the Lord Advocate,

(h) the Director of Public Prosecutions for Northern Ireland and the Director of Public Prosecutions in England and Wales,

(i) any designated agency or transferee body within the meaning of the Financial Services Act 1986 and any officer or servant of such an agency or body,

(j) any person appointed or authorised to exercise any powers under section 94, 106 or 177 of the Financial Services Act 1986 and any officer or servant of such a person,

(k) the body administering a scheme under section 54 of or paragraph 18 of Schedule 11 to that Act and any officer or servant of such a body,

(l) the Registrar of Friendly Societies and the Chief Registrar of friendly societies in Great Britain and any officer or servant of either of them,

(m) the Industrial Assurance Commissioner for Northern Ireland and the Industrial Assurance Commissioner in Great Britain and any officer of either of them,

(n) any constable,

(o) any procurator fiscal.

(4) An order under paragraph (1B) is subject to negative resolution.'

14. After Article 444 of that order there shall be inserted—

'Disclosure of information by Department

444A. The Department may, if it thinks fit, disclose any information obtained under this Part—

(a) to any person who is a competent authority for the purposes of Article 442, or

(b) in any circumstances in which or for any purpose for which that Article does not preclude the disclosure of the information to which it applies.'.

SCHEDULE 14 (Section 189)

RESTRICTION OF REHABILITATION OF OFFENDERS ACT 1974

PART I

EXEMPTED PROCEEDINGS

1. Any proceedings with respect to a decision or proposed decision of the Secretary of State or a designated agency—

(a) refusing, withdrawing or suspending an authorisation;

(b) refusing an application under section 28(5) of this Act;

(c) giving a direction under section 59 of this Act or refusing an application for consent or for the variation of a consent under that section;

(d) exercising a power under Chapter VI of Part I of this Act or refusing an application for the rescission or variation of a prohibition or requirement imposed under that Chapter;

(e) refusing to make or revoking an order declaring a collective investment scheme to be an authorised unit trust scheme or a recognised scheme.

2. Any proceedings with respect to a decision or proposed decision of a recognised self-regulating organisation—

(a) refusing or suspending a person's membership of the organisation;

(b) expelling a member of the organisation;

(c) exercising a power of the organisation for purposes corresponding to those of Chapter VI of Part I of this Act.

3.—(1) Any proceedings with respect to a decision or proposed decision of a recognised professional body—

(a) refusing or suspending a person's membership of the body;

(b) expelling a member of the body.

(2) Any proceedings with respect to a decision or proposed decision of a recognised professional body or of any other body or person having functions in respect of the enforcement of the recognised professional body's rules relating to the carrying on of investment business—

(a) exercising a power for purposes corresponding to those of Chapter VI of Part I of this Act;

(b) refusing, suspending or withdrawing a certificate issued for the purposes of Part I of this Act.

4. Any proceedings with respect to a decision or proposed decision of the competent authority under Part IV of this Act refusing an application for listing or to discontinue or suspend the listing of any securities.

5. Any proceedings with respect to a decision or proposed decision of the Chief Registrar of friendly societies, the Registrar of Friendly Societies for Northern Ireland or a transferee body, exercising a power exercisable by virtue of paragraph 23 of Schedule 11 to this Act or refusing an application for the rescission or variation of a prohibition or requirement imposed in the exercise of such a power.

6. Any proceedings with respect to a decision or proposed decision of a recognised self-regulating organisation for friendly societies—

(a) refusing or suspending a society's membership of the organisation;

(b) expelling a member of the organisation;

(c) exercising a power of the organisation for purposes corresponding to those for which powers are exercisable by the Registrar by virtue of paragraph 23 of Schedule 11 to this Act.

PART II

EXEMPTED QUESTIONS

Person putting question	*Individual to whom question relates*
1. The Secretary of State or a designated agency.	(a) An authorised person.
	(b) An applicant for authorisation under section 26 of this Act.
	(c) A person whose authorisation is suspended.
	(d) The operator or trustee of a recognised scheme or a collective investment scheme in respect of which a notice has been given by the operator under section 87(3) or an application made under section 88 of this Act.

Person putting question	*Individual to whom question relates*
	(e) An individual who is an associate of a person (whether or not an individual) described in paragraph (a), (b), (c) or (d) above.
2. A recognised self-regulating organisation or recognised professional body.	(a) A member of the organisation or body.
	(b) An applicant for membership of the organisation or body.
	(c) A person whose membership of the organisation or body is suspended.
	(d) An individual who is an associate of a person (whether or not an individual) described in paragraph (a), (b) or (c) above.
3. A recognised professional body.	(a) A person certified by the body.
	(b) An applicant for certification by the body.
	(c) A person whose certification by the body is suspended.
	(d) An individual who is an associate of a person (whether or not an individual) described in paragraph (a), (b) or (c) above.
4. A person (whether or not an individual) described in paragraph 1(a), (b), (c) or (d) paragraph 2(a), (b) or (c) or paragraph 3(a), (b) or (c) above.	An individual who is or is seeking to become an associate of the person in column 1.
5. The competent authority or any other person.	An individual from or in respect of whom information is sought in connection with an application for listing under Part IV of this Act.
6. The competent authority.	An individual who is or is seeking to become an associate of the issuer of securities listed under Part IV of this Act and from or in respect of whom information is sought which the issuer of the securities is required to furnish under listing rules.
7. The Chief Registrar of friendly societies, the Registrar of Friendly Societies for Northern Ireland or a transferee body.	An individual who is an associate of a society which is authorised under section 23 of this Act.
8. A recognised self-regulating organisation for friendly societies.	An individual who is an associate of a member or an applicant for membership of the organisation or of a society whose membership of the organisation is suspended.

PART III

EXEMPTED ACTIONS

Person taking action	*Exempted action*
1. The Secretary of State, a designated agency, a recognised self-regulating organisation, a recognised professional body, any other body or person mentioned in paragraph 3(2) of Part I of this Schedule or the competent authority.	Any such decision or proposed decision as is mentioned in Part I of this Schedule.
2. A person (whether or not an individual) described in paragraph 1(a), (b), (c) or (d), paragraph 2(a), (b) or (c) or paragraph 3(a), (b) or (c) of Part II of this Schedule.	Dismissing or excluding an individual from being or becoming an associate of the person in column 1.
3. The issuer of securities listed or subject to an application for listing under Part IV of this Act.	Dismissing or excluding an individual from being or becoming an associate of the issuer.
4. The Chief Registrar of friendly societies, the Registrar of Friendly Societies for Northern Ireland, a transferee body or a recognised self-regulating organisation for friendly societies.	Any such decision or proposed decision as is mentioned in Part I of this Schedule.

PART IV

SUPPLEMENTAL

1. In Part I of this Schedule 'proceedings' includes any proceedings within the meaning of section 4 of the Rehabilitation of Offenders Act 1974.

2. In Parts II and III of this Schedule—

   (a) references to an applicant for authorisation, membership or certification are references to an applicant who has not yet been informed of the decision on his application;
   (b) references to an application for listing under Part IV of this Act are references to an application the decision on which has not yet been communicated to the applicant and which is not taken by virtue of section 144(5) of this Act to have been refused.

3. Paragraph 1(d) of Part II of this Schedule and so much of paragraph 1(e) as relates to it—

   (a) apply only if the question is put to elicit information for the purpose of determining whether the operator or trustee is a fit and proper person to act as operator or trustee of the scheme in question;
   (b) apply in the case of a scheme in respect of which a notice has been given under subsection (3) of section 87 only until the end of the period within which the operator may receive a notification from the Secretary of State under that subsection or, if earlier, the receipt by him of such a notification;
   (c) apply in the case of a scheme in respect of which an application has been made under section 88 only until the applicant has been informed of the decision on the application.

SCHEDULE 15 (Section 211(3))

TRANSITIONAL PROVISIONS

Interim authorisation

1.—(1) If before such day as is appointed for the purposes of this paragraph by an order made by the Secretary of State a person has applied—

(a) for membership of any body which on that day is a recognised self-regulating organisation; or

(b) for authorisation by the Secretary of State,

and the application has not been determined before the day on which section 3 of this Act comes into force, that person shall, subject to sub-paragraphs (2), (3) and (4) below, be treated until the determination of the application as if he had been granted an authorisation by the Secretary of State.

(2) Sub-paragraph (1) above does not apply to a person who immediately before the day on which section 3 of this Act comes into force is prohibited by the Prevention of Fraud (Investments) Act 1958 (in this Schedule referred to as 'the previous Act') from carrying on the business of dealing in securities—

(a) by reason of the refusal or revocation at any time before that day of a licence under that Act; or

(b) by reason of the revocation at any time before that day of an order declaring him to be an exempted dealer.

(3) If a person who has made any such application as is mentioned in sub-paragraph (1) above has before the day on which section 3 of this Act comes into force been served with a notice under section 6 or 16(3) of the previous Act (proposed refusal or revocation of licence or proposed revocation of exemption order) but the refusal or revocation to which the notice relates has not taken place before that day—

(a) the provisions of that Act with respect to the refusal or revocation of a licence or the revocation of an order under section 16 of that Act shall continue to apply to him until the application mentioned in sub-paragraph (1) above is determined; and

(b) that sub-paragraph shall cease to apply to him if before the determination of the application mentioned in that sub-paragraph his application for a licence under that Act is refused, his licence under that Act is revoked or the order declaring him to be an exempted dealer under that Act is revoked.

(4) Notwithstanding sub-paragraph (1) above section 102(1)(a) of this Act shall not apply to a person entitled to carry on investment business by virtue of that sub-paragraph but the Secretary of State may make available for public inspection the information with respect to the holders of principal's licences mentioned in section 9 of the previous Act, any information in his possession by virtue of section 15(3) or (4) of that Act and the information mentioned in section 16(4) of that Act.

(5) Notwithstanding subsection (2) of section 3 of the previous Act a licence granted under that section before the day on which section 3 of this Act comes into force shall, unless revoked under section 6 of that Act, continue in force until that day.

Return of fees on pending applications

2. Any fee paid in respect of an application under section 3 of the previous Act which is pending on the day on which that Act is repealed shall be repaid to the applicant.

Deposits and undertakings

3. The repeal of section 4 of the previous Act shall not affect the operation of that section in a case where—

(a) a sum deposited in accordance with that section has become payable as provided in subsection (2) of that section before the date on which the repeal takes effect; or

(b) a sum has become payable before that date in pursuance of an undertaking given under subsection (4) of that section,

but, subject as aforesaid, any sum deposited under that section may be withdrawn by the depositor on application to the Accountant General of the Supreme Court and any undertaking given under that section shall be discharged.

Interim recognition of professional bodies

4.—(1) If on an application made under section 17 of this Act it appears to the Secretary of State that any of the requirements of section 18(3) of this Act or paragraphs 2 to 6 of Schedule 3 to this Act are not satisfied he may in accordance with this paragraph make a recognition order under section 18 of this Act ('an interim recognition order') notwithstanding that all or any of those requirements are not satisfied.

(2) The Secretary of State may, subject to sub-paragraphs (3) and (4) below, make an interim recognition order if he is satisfied—

(a) that the applicant proposes to adopt rules and practices and to make arrangements which will satisfy such of the requirements mentioned in sub-paragraph (1) above as are not satisfied;

(b) that it is not practicable for those rules, practices and arrangements to be brought into effect before the date on which section 3 of this Act comes into force but that they will be brought into effect within a reasonable time thereafter; and

(c) that in the meantime the applicant will enforce its existing rules in such a way, and issue such guidance, as will in respect of investment business of any kind carried on by persons certified by it (or by virtue of paragraph 5 below treated as certified by it) afford to investors protection as nearly as may be equivalent to that provided as respects investment business of that kind by the rules and regulations under Chapter V of Part I of this Act.

(3) Where the requirements which are not satisfied consist of or include those mentioned in paragraph 2 of Schedule 3 to this Act an application for an interim recognition order shall be accompanied by—

(a) a list of the persons to whom the applicant proposes to issue certificates for the purposes of Part I of this Act; and

(b) particulars of the criteria adopted for determining the persons included in the list;

and the Secretary of State shall not make the order unless it appears to him that those criteria conform as nearly as may be to the conditions mentioned in that paragraph and that the applicant will, until the requirements of that paragraph are satisfied, have arrangements for securing that no person is certified by it (or by virtue of paragraph 5 below treated as certified by it) except in accordance with those criteria and for the effective monitoring of continued compliance by those persons with those criteria.

(4) Where the requirements which are not satisfied consist of or include that mentioned in paragraph 6 of Schedule 3 to this Act, the Secretary of State shall not make an interim recognition order unless it appears to him that the applicant will, until that requirement is satisfied, take such steps for complying with it as are reasonably practicable.

(5) An application for an interim recognition order shall be accompanied by a copy of the rules and by particulars of the practices and arrangements referred to in sub-paragraph (2)(a) above.

(6) An interim recognition order shall not be revocable but shall cease to be in force at the end of such period as is specified in it; and that period shall be such as will in the opinion of

the Secretary of State allow a reasonable time for the rules, practices and arrangements mentioned in sub-paragraph (5) above to be brought into effect.

(7) The Secretary of State may on the application of the body to which an interim recognition order relates extend the period specified in it if that body satisfies him—

(a) that there are sufficient reasons why the rules, practices and arrangements mentioned in sub-paragraph (5) above cannot be brought into effect by the end of that period; and

(b) that those rules, practices and arrangements, or other rules, practices and arrangements which satisfy the requirements mentioned in sub-paragraph (2)(a) above and of which copies or particulars are furnished to the Secretary of State, will be brought into effect within a reasonable time thereafter.

but not more than one application shall be made by a body under this sub-paragraph.

(8) A recognition order under section 18 of this Act shall cease to be an interim recognition order if before it ceases to be in force—

(a) the rules, practices and arrangements of which copies or particulars were furnished to the Secretary of State under sub-paragraph (5) or (7)(b) above are brought into effect; or

(b) the Secretary of State certifies that other rules, practices and arrangements which have been brought into effect comply with the requirements mentioned in sub-paragraph (1) above.

(9) In this paragraph references to the adoption of rules or the making of arrangements include references to taking such other steps as may be necessary for bringing them into effect.

Interim authorisation by recognised professional bodies

5.—(1) If at the time when an interim recognition order is made in respect of a professional body that body is unable to issue certificates for the purposes of this Act, any person who at that time is included in the list furnished by that body to the Secretary of State in accordance with paragraph 4(3)(a) above shall be treated for the purposes of this Act as a person certified by that body.

(2) If at any time while an interim recognition order is in force in respect of a professional body and before the body is able to issue certificates as mentioned in sub-paragraph (1) above the body notifies the Secretary of State that a person not included in that list satisfies the criteria of which particulars were furnished by the body in accordance with paragraph 4(3)(b) above, that person shall, on receipt of the notification by the Secretary of State, be treated for the purposes of this Act as a person certified by that body.

(3) If at any time while an interim recognition order is in force in respect of a professional body it appears to the body—

(a) that a person treated by virtue of sub-paragraph (1) or (2) above as certified by it has ceased (after the expiration of such transitional period, if any, as appears to the body to be appropriate) to satisfy the criteria mentioned in sub-paragraph (2) above; or

(b) that any such person should for any other reason cease to be treated as certified by it,

it shall forthwith give notice of that fact to the Secretary of State and the person in question shall, on receipt of that notification by the Secretary of State, cease to be treated as certified by that body.

(4) Where by virtue of this paragraph a partnership is treated as certified by a recognised professional body section 15(3) of this Act shall apply as it applies where a certificate has in fact been issued to a partnership.

(5) Where by virtue of this paragraph any persons are treated as certified by a recognised

professional body the requirements of paragraph 2 of Schedule 3 of this Act so far as relating to the retention by a person of a certificate issued by that body and the requirements of paragraph 4 of that Schedule shall apply to the body as if the references to persons certified by it included references to persons treated as certified.

Power of recognised professional body to make rules required by this Act

6.—(1) Where a recognised professional body regulates the practice of a profession in the exercise of statutory powers the matters in respect of which rules can be made in the exercise of those powers shall, if they would not otherwise do so, include any matter in respect of which rules are required to be made—

(a) so that the recognition order in respect of that body can cease to be an interim recognition order; or

(b) where the recognition order was not, or has ceased to be, an interim recognition order, so that the body can continue to be a recognised professional body.

(2) Rules made by virtue of this paragraph may in particular make provision for the issue, withdrawal and suspension of certificates for the purposes of this Act and the making of charges in respect of their issue and may accordingly apply to persons who are, or are to be, certified or treated as certified by the body in question whether or not they are persons in relation to whom rules could be made apart from this paragraph.

(3) Rules made by virtue of this paragraph may make different provision for different cases.

(4) The Secretary of State may at the request of a recognised professional body by order extend, modify or exclude any statutory provision relating to the regulation of the conduct, practice, or discipline of members of that body to such extent as he thinks necessary or expedient in consequence of the provisions of this paragraph; and any order made by virtue of this sub-paragraph shall be subject to annulment in pursuance of a resolution of either House of Parliament.

Notice of commencement of business

7. In the case of a person who is carrying on investment business in the United Kingdom on the day on which section 31 of this Act comes into force, section 32 of this Act shall have effect as if it required him to give the notice referred to in that section forthwith.

Advertisements

8.—(1) So long as Part III of the Companies Act 1985 remains in force section 57 of this Act shall not apply—

(a) in relation to any distribution of a prospectus to which section 56 of that Act applies or would apply if not excluded by subsection (5)(b) of that section or to which section 72 of that Act applies or would apply if not excluded by subsection (6)(b) of that section or by section 76 of that Act, or in relation to any distribution of a document relating to securities of a corporation incorporated in Great Britain which is not a registered company, being a document which—

(i) would, if the corporation were a registered company, be a prospectus to which section 56 of that Act applies or would apply if not excluded as aforesaid, and

(ii) contains all the matters and is issued with the consents which, by virtue of sections 72 to 75 of that Act, it would have to contain and be issued with if the corporation were a company incorporated outside Great Britain and the document were a prospectus issued by that company;

(b) in relation to any issue of a form of application for shares in, or debentures of, a corporation, together with—

(i) a prospectus which complies with the requirements of section 56 of that Act or is not required to comply with them because excluded by subsection (5)(b) of that section, or complies with the requirements of Chapter II of Part III of that Act relating to prospectuses and is not issued in contravention of sections 74 and 75 of that Act, or

(ii) in the case of a corporation incorporated in Great Britain which is not a registered company, a document containing all the matters and issued with the consents mentioned in sub-paragraph (a)(ii) of this paragraph, or in connection with a bona fide invitation to a person to enter into an underwriting agreement with respect to the shares or debentures.

(2) The provisions of this paragraph shall apply to Northern Ireland with the substitution for the references to Part III and Chapter II of Part III of the Companies Act 1985 of references to Part IV and Chapter II of Part IV of the Companies (Northern Ireland) Order 1986, for the references to sections 56, 56(5)(b), 72, 72(6)(b), 74, 76 and 72 to 75 of the Companies Act 1985 of references to Articles 66, 66(5)(b), 82, 82(6)(b), 84, 86 and 82 to 85 of the Companies (Northern Ireland) Order 1986, for the references to a corporation incorporated in Great Britain of references to a corporation incorporated in Northern Ireland and for the reference to a company incorporated outside Great Britain of a reference to a company incorporated outside the United Kingdom.

Authorised unit trust schemes

9.—(1) Where an order under section 17 of the previous Act (authorisation of unit trust schemes) is in force in respect of a unit trust scheme immediately before the coming into force of Chapter VIII of Part I of this Act the scheme shall be treated as an authorised unit trust scheme under that Part and the order as an order under section 78 of this Act.

(2) In relation to any such authorised unit trust scheme the reference in section 79(1)(a) of this Act to the requirements for the making of the order shall be construed as a reference to the requirements for the making of an order under section 78, but the scheme shall not be regarded as failing to comply with those requirements by reason of the manager or trustee not being an authorised person if he is treated as such a person by virtue of paragraph 1 above.

(3) If before the day on which Chapter VIII of Part I comes into force a notice in respect of a scheme has been served under subsection (2) of section 17 of the previous Act (proposed revocation of authorisation of unit trust scheme) but the revocation has not taken place before that day, the provisions of that subsection shall continue to apply in relation to the scheme and sub-paragraph (1) above shall cease to apply to it if the authorisation is revoked under that subsection.

Recognised collective investment schemes

10.—(1) If at any time before the coming into force of section 86 of this Act it appears to the Secretary of State that the law of a member State other than the United Kingdom confers rights on the managers and trustees of authorised unit trust schemes entitling them to carry on in that State on terms equivalent to those of that section—

(a) investment business which consists in operating or acting as trustee in relation to such schemes; and

(b) any investment business which is carried on by them in connection with or for the purposes of such schemes,

he may by order direct that schemes constituted in that State which satisfy such requirements as are specified in the order shall be recognised schemes for the purposes of this Act.

(2) Subsections (2) to (9) of section 86 of this Act shall have effect in relation to any scheme recognised by virtue of this paragraph; and the references in sections 24 and 207(1) of this Act to a scheme recognised under section 86, and in section 76(1) of this Act to a scheme recognised under Chapter VIII of Part I of this Act, shall include references to any scheme

Appendix

recognised by virtue of this paragraph.

(3) In section 86(3)(a) as applied by sub-paragraph (2) above the reference to the rights conferred by any relevant Community instrument shall be construed as a reference to the rights conferred by virtue of an order made under this paragraph.

11.—(1) Subsection (7) of section 88 of this Act shall not apply to a scheme which is in existence on the date on which this Act is passed if—

  (a) the units under the scheme are included in the Official List of The Stock Exchange and have been so included throughout the period of five years ending on the date on which this paragraph comes into force;
  (b) the law of the country or territory in which the scheme is established precludes the participants being entitled or the operator being required as mentioned in that subsection; and
  (c) throughout the period of five years ending on the date on which the application is made under that section, units under the scheme have in fact been regularly redeemed as mentioned in that subsection or the operator has in fact regularly ensured that participants were able to sell their units as there mentioned.

(2) The grounds for revoking an order made under section 88 of this Act by virtue of this paragraph shall include the ground that it appears to the Secretary of State that since the making of the order units under the scheme have ceased to be regularly redeemed or the operator has ceased regularly to ensure their sale as mentioned in sub-paragraph (1)(c) above.

Delegation orders

12.—(1) A delegation order may transfer a function notwithstanding that the provision conferring it has not yet come into force but no such function shall be exercisable by virtue of the order until the coming into force of that provision.

(2) Sub-paragraph (1) above applies also to a transfer order under paragraph 28(1) of Schedule 11 to this Act.

Disclosure of information

13. In determining for the purposes of section 180(6) of this Act and the enactments amended by paragraphs 3(2), 9(2) and 13(2) of Schedule 13 to this Act whether the functions of an authority in a country or territory outside the United Kingdom correspond to functions conferred by any of the provisions of this Act regard shall be had to those provisions whether or not they have already come into force.

Temporary exemptions for friendly societies

14.—(1) A registered friendly society which transacts no investment business after the date on which section 3 of this Act comes into force except for the purpose of making or carrying out relevant existing members' contracts shall be treated for the purposes of that section as if it were an exempted person under Chapter IV of Part I of this Act.

(2) Subject to sub-paragraph (3) below, for the purposes of this paragraph 'relevant existing members' contracts', in relation to any society, means—

  (a) contracts made by the society before that date; and
  (b) in the case of a small income society—

      (i) during the period of three years beginning with that date, tax exempt investment agreements made by it with persons who were members of the society before that date; and
      (ii) after the expiry of that period, tax exempt investment agreements made by it with such persons before the expiry of that period.

(3) Paragraph (b) of sub-paragraph (2) above shall not apply to a registered friendly society

after the expiry of the period of two years beginning with that date unless before the expiry of that period it has by special resolution (within the meaning of the Friendly Societies Act 1974 or, as the case may be, the Friendly Societies Act (Northern Ireland) 1970) determined—

(a) to transact no further investment business except for the purpose of carrying out contracts entered into before the expiry of the said period of three years; or

(b) to take such action as is necessary to procure the transfer of its engagements to another such society or a company or the amalgamation of the society with another such society under section 82 of the said Act of 1974 or, as the case may be, section 70 of the said Act of 1970,

and a copy of that resolution has been registered in accordance with section 86 of the said Act of 1974 or, as the case may be, section 75 of the said Act of 1970.

(4) For the purpose of sub-paragraph (2) above a society is a small income society if its income in 1985 from members' contributions did not exceed £50,000.

(5) For the purposes of sub-paragraph (2) above an investment agreement is a tax exempt investment agreement if the society by which it is made may obtain exemption from income and corporation tax on the profits from it under section 332 of the Income and Corporation Taxes Act 1970.

(6) A society to which sub-paragraph (1) or (2) above applies shall not be an authorised person for the purposes of this Act nor a regulated friendly society for the purposes of the provisions of Schedule 11 to this Act.

Dealings in course of non-investment business

15. If before the day on which section 3 of this Act comes into force a person has applied for permission under paragraph 23 of Schedule 1 to this Act and the application has not been determined before that day, that person shall, until the determination of the application and subject to his complying with such requirements as the Secretary of State may impose, be treated as if he had been granted a permission under that paragraph.

Northern Ireland

16. The foregoing provisions shall apply to Northern Ireland with the substitution for references to the previous Act or any provision of that Act of references to the Prevention of Fraud (Investments) Act (Northern Ireland) 1940 and the corresponding provision of that Act.

SCHEDULE 16 (Section 212(2))

CONSEQUENTIAL AMENDMENTS

1. In section 22 of the Charities Act 1960—

(a) subsection (10) shall be omitted; and
(b) in subsection (11) for the words 'Subsections (9) and (10)' there shall be substituted the words 'Subsection (9)'.

2. In the Trustee Investments Act 1961—

(a) in section 11(3) for the words 'the Prevention of Fraud (Investments) Act 1958 or the Prevention of Fraud (Investments) Act (Northern Ireland) 1940' there shall be substituted the words 'the Financial Services Act 1986';
(b) for paragraph 3 of Part III of Schedule 1 there shall be substituted—

'3. In any units of an authorised unit trust scheme within the meaning of the Financial Services Act 1986';

(c) in paragraph 2(a) of Part IV of Schedule 1 for the words from 'a recognised stock exchange' onwards there shall be substituted the words 'a recognised investment exchange within the meaning of the Financial Services Act 1986';

(d) in the definition of 'securities' in paragraph 4 of Part IV of that Schedule after the word 'debentures' there shall be inserted the words 'units within paragraph 3 of Part III of this Schedule'.

3. In section 32 of the Clergy Pensions Measure 1961 No. 3—

(a) for paragraph (t) of subsection (1) there shall be substituted—

'(t) in any units in any authorised unit trust scheme or a recognised scheme within the meaning of the Financial Services Act 1986'; and

(b) in subsection (5)(a) for the words from 'a recognised stock exchange' onwards there shall be substituted the words 'a recognised investment exchange within the meaning of the Financial Services Act 1986.'.

4. In the Stock Transfer Act 1963—

(a) for paragraph (e) of section 1(4) there shall be substituted—

'(e) units of an authorised unit trust scheme or a recognised scheme within the meaning of the Financial Services Act 1986'; and

(b) in the definition of 'securities' in section 4(1) for the words from 'unit trust scheme' to 'scheme' there shall be substituted the words 'collective investment scheme within the meaning of the Financial Services Act 1986'.

5. In the Stock Transfer Act (Northern Ireland) 1963—

(a) for paragraph (e) of section 1(4) there shall be substituted—

'(e) units of an authorised unit trust scheme or a recognised scheme within the meaning of the Financial Services Act 1986'; and

(b) in the definition of 'securities' in section 4(1) for the words from 'unit trust scheme' to 'scheme' there shall be substituted the words 'collective investment scheme within the meaning of the Financial Services Act 1986'.

6. In section 25 of the Charities Act (Northern Ireland) 1964—

(a) subsection (16) shall be omitted; and
(b) in subsection (17) for the words 'Subsections (15) and (16)' there shall be substituted the words 'Subsection (15)'.

7. In the Local Authorities' Mutual Investment Trust Act 1968—

(a) in section 1(2) for the words 'recognised stock exchange within the meaning of the Prevention of Fraud (Investments) Act 1958' there shall be substituted the words 'recognised investment exchange within the meaning of the Financial Services Act 1986'; and
(b) in the definition of 'unit trust scheme' in section 2 for the words 'Prevention of Fraud (Investments) Act 1958' there shall be substituted the words 'Financial Services Act 1986'.

8. In the Local Government Act 1972—

(a) in section 98(1) for the words from 'and' onwards there shall be substituted the words 'means—

(a) investments falling within any of paragraphs 1 to 6 of Schedule 1 to the Financial Services Act 1986 or, so far as relevant to any of those paragraphs, paragraph 11 of that Schedule; or
(b) rights (whether actual or contingent) in respect of money lent to, or deposited with, any society registered under the Industrial and Provident Societies Act 1965 or any building society within the meaning of the Building

Societies Act 1986.'; and

(b) for the definition of 'securities' in section 146(2) there shall be substituted—
"'securities" has the meaning given in section 98(1) above'.

9. For subsection (1) of section 42 of the Local Government (Scotland) Act 1973 there shall be substituted—

'(1) In sections 39 and 41 of this Act "securities" means—

(a) investments falling within any of paragraphs 1 to 6 of Schedule 1 to the Financial Services Act 1986 or, so far as relevant to any of those paragraphs, paragraph 11 of that Schedule; or
(b) rights (whether actual or contingent) in respect of money lent to, or deposited with, any society registered under the Industrial and Provident Societies Act 1965 or any building society within the meaning of the Building Societies Act 1986.'

10. For paragraph 20 of Schedule 1 to the Industry Act 1975 there shall be substituted—

'20. Section 57 of the Financial Services Act 1986 (restrictions on advertising) shall not apply to any investment advertisement within the meaning of that section which the Board issue or cause to be issued in the discharge of their functions.'

11. For paragraph 20 of Schedule 1 to the Scottish Development Agency Act 1975 there shall be substituted—

'20. Section 57 of the Financial Services Act 1986 (restrictions on advertising) shall not apply to any investment advertisement within the meaning of that section which the Agency issue or cause to be issued in the discharge of their functions.'

12. For paragraphs 21 of Schedule 1 to the Welsh Development Agency Act 1975 there shall be substituted—

'21. Section 57 of the Financial Services Act 1986 (restrictions on advertising) shall not apply to any investment advertisement within the meaning of that section which the Agency issue or cause to be issued in the discharge of their functions.'.

13. In section 3(5) of the Aircraft and Shipbuilding Industries Act 1977 the words 'Sections 428 to 430 of the Companies Act 1985 and' shall be omitted and for the words 'those sections' there shall be substituted the words 'that section'.

14. In paragraph 10(1)(c) of Part II of Schedule 10 to the Finance Act 1980 for the words 'sections 428 to 430' there shall be substituted the words 'sections 428 to 430F'.

15. For the definition of 'securities' in section 3(6) of the Licensing (Alcohol Education and Research) Act 1981 there shall be substituted—

"'securities" means any investments falling within any of paragraphs 1 to 6 of Schedule 1 to the Financial Services Act 1986 or, so far as relevant to any of those paragraphs, paragraph 11 of that Schedule'.

16. In section 97 of the Companies Act 1985—

(a) in subsection (1) after the word 'conditions' there shall be inserted the words 'and any conditions which apply in respect of any such payment by virtue of rules made under section 169(2) of the Financial Services Act 1986'; and
(b) in subsection (2)(a) for the words from '10 per cent.' onwards there shall be substituted the words—

'(i) any limit imposed on it by those rules or, if none is so imposed, 10 per cent, of the price at which the shares are issued; or
(ii) the amount or rate authorised by the articles, whichever is the less'.

17. In section 163 of the Companies Act 1985—

(a) for the words 'a recognised stock exchange' in each place where they occur there shall be substituted the words 'a recognised investment exchange';

(b) for the words 'that stock exchange' in subsection (1) there shall be substituted the words 'that investment exchange';

(c) in subsection (2) in paragraph (a) for the words 'on that stock exchange' there shall be substituted the words 'under Part IV of the Financial Services Act 1986' and in paragraph (b) for the words 'that stock exchange' in both places where they occur there shall be substituted the words 'that investment exchange';

(d) after subsection (3) of that section there shall be inserted—

'(4) In this section "recognised investment exchange" means a recognised investment exchange other than an overseas investment exchange within the meaning of the Financial Services Act 1986.'

18. In section 209(1)(c) of the Companies Act 1985 for the words 'the Prevention of Fraud (Investments) Act 1958' there shall be substituted the words 'the Financial Services Act 1986'.

19. In section 265(4)(a) of the Companies Act 1985 for the words 'recognised stock exchange' there shall be substituted the words 'recognised investment exchange other than an overseas investment exchange within the meaning of the Financial Services Act 1986'.

20. In section 329(1) of the Companies Act 1985 for the words 'recognised stock exchange', 'that stock exchange' and 'the stock exchange' there shall be substituted respectively the words 'recognised investment exchange other than an overseas investment exchange within the meaning of the Financial Services Act 1986', 'that investment exchange' and 'the investment exchange'.

21. For paragraphs (a) to (c) of section 446(4) of the Companies Act 1985 there shall be substituted—

'(a) to any individual who is an authorised person within the meaning of the Financial Services Act 1986;

(b) to any individual who holds a permission granted under paragraph 23 of Schedule 1 to that Act;

(c) to any officer (whether past or present) of a body corporate which is such an authorised person or holds such a permission;

(d) to any partner (whether past or present) in a partnership which is such an authorised person or holds such a permission;

(e) to any member of the governing body or officer (in either case whether past or present) of an unincorporated association which is such an authorised person or holds such a permission'.

22. At the end of sections 716(2) and 717(1) of the Companies Act 1985 there shall be inserted the words—

'and in this subsection "recognised stock exchange" means The Stock Exchange and any other stock exchange which is declared to be a recognised stock exchange for the purposes of this section by an order in a statutory instrument made by the Secretary of State which is for the time being in force;'.

23. In Schedule 4 to the Companies Act 1985—

(a) in paragraph 45 for the words 'recognised stock exchange' there shall be substituted the words 'recognised investment exchange other than an overseas investment exchange within the meaning of the Financial Services Act 1986'; and

(b) in paragraph 84 for the words from 'on a recognised stock exchange' onwards there shall be substituted the words 'on a recognised investment exchange other than an overseas investment exchange within the meaning of the Financial Services Act 1986 or on any stock exchange of repute outside Great Britain'.

24. In Schedule 9 to the Companies Act 1985 in paragraphs 10(3) and 33 for the words 'recognised stock exchange' there shall be substituted the words 'recognised investment

exchange other than an overseas investment exchange within the meaning of the Financial Services Act 1986'.

25. In paragraph 11 of Schedule 13 to the Companies Act 1985 for paragraph (a) there shall be substituted—

(a) any unit trust scheme which is an authorised unit trust scheme within the meaning of the Financial Services Act 1986'.

26. In Schedule 22 to the Companies Act 1985, in the second column of the entry relating to section 185(4) for the words 'stock exchange' there shall be substituted the words 'clearing house or'.

27. In Schedule 24 to the Companies Act 1985—

(a) in the second column of the entry relating to section 329(3) for the words 'stock exchange' there shall be substituted the words 'investment exchange'; and
(b) after the entry relating to section 427(5) there shall be inserted—

'429(6)	Offeror failing to send copy of notice or making statutory declaration knowing it to be false, etc.	1. On indictment.	2 years or a fine; or both.	
		2. Summary.	6 months or the statutory maximum; or both.	One-fiftieth of the statutory maximum.
430A(6)	Offeror failing to give notice of rights to minority shareholders.	1. On indictment.	A fine.	One-fiftieth of the statutory maximum.
		2. Summary.	The statutory maximum.	'

28. In section 16 of the Company Securities (Insider Dealing) Act 1985—

(a) in subsection (1) for the definition of 'recognised stock exchange' there shall be substituted—

'"recognised stock exchange" means The Stock Exchange and any other investment exchange which is declared by an order of the Secretary of State for the time being in force to be a recognised stock exchange for the purposes of this Act;'; and

(b) after that subsection there shall be inserted—

'(1A) The power to make an order under subsection (1) above shall be exercisable by statutory instrument.';

(c) in subsection (2) for the word '15' there shall be substituted the word '14'.

29. For paragraph (c) of section 10(1) of the Bankruptcy (Scotland) Act 1985 there shall be substituted—

'(c) a petition is before a court for the winding up of the debtor under Part IV or V of the Insolvency Act 1986 or section 72 of the Financial Services Act 1986;'.

30. In section 101 of the Building Societies Act 1986—

(a) for paragraph (1)(a) there shall be substituted—

'(a) offer for sale or invite subscription for any shares in or debentures of the company or allot or agree to allot any such shares or debentures with a view to their being offered for sale;';
(b) in subsection (1) after the words 'the effect of the offer' there shall be inserted the words 'the invitation'; and
(c) in subsection (2) for the words 'the public' there shall be substituted the words ', invite subscription for,'.

31. In Article 107 of the Companies (Northern Ireland) Order 1986—

(a) in paragraph (1) after the word 'conditions' there shall be inserted the words 'and any conditions which apply in respect of any such payment by virtue of rules made under section 169(2) of the Financial Services Act 1986',

(b) in sub-paragraph (2)(a) for the words from '10 per cent.' onwards there shall be substituted the words—

'(i) any limit imposed on it by those rules or, if none is so imposed, 10 per cent. of the price at which the shares are issued; or

(ii) the amount or rate authorised by the articles, whichever is the less'.

32. In Article 173 of the Companies (Northern Ireland) Order 1986—

(a) for the words 'a recognised stock exchange', in each place where they occur, there shall be substituted the words 'a recognised investment exchange';

(b) for the words 'that stock exchange' in paragraph (1) there shall be substituted the words 'that investment exchange';

(c) in paragraph (2), in sub-paragraph (a) for the words 'on that stock exchange' there shall be substituted the words 'under Part IV of the Financial Services Act 1986' and in sub-paragraph (b) for the words 'that stock exchange' in both places where they occur there shall be substituted the words 'that investment exchange';

(d) after paragraph (3) there shall be inserted—

'(4) In this Article "recognised investment exchange" means a recognised investment exchange other than an overseas investment exchange within the meaning of the Financial Services Act 1986.'

33. In Article 217(1)(b) of the Companies (Northern Ireland) Order 1986 for the words 'the Prevention of Fraud (Investments) Act (Northern Ireland) 1940 or of the Prevention of Fraud (Investments) Act 1958' there shall be substituted the words 'the Financial Services Act 1986'.

34. In Article 273(4)(a) of the Companies (Northern Ireland) Order 1986 for the words 'recognised stock exchange' there shall be substituted the words 'recognised investment exchange other than an overseas investment exchange within the meaning of the Financial Services Act 1986'.

35. In Article 337(1) of the Companies (Northern Ireland) Order 1986 for the words 'recognised stock exchange', 'that stock exchange' and 'the stock exchange' there shall be substituted respectively the words 'recognised investment exchange', 'that investment exchange' and 'the investment exchange'.

36. For sub-paragraphs (a) to (c) of Article 439(4) of the Companies (Northern Ireland) Order 1986 there shall be substituted—

'(a) to any individual who is an authorised person within the meaning of the Financial Services Act 1986;

(b) to any individual who holds a permission granted under paragraph 23 of Schedule 1 to that Act;

(c) to an officer (whether past or present) of a body corporate which is such an authorised person or holds such a permission;

(d) to any partner (whether past or present) in a partnership which is such an authorised person or holds such a permission;

(e) to any member of the governing body or officer (in either case whether past or present) of an unincorporated association which is such an authorised person or holds such a permission'.

37. At the end of Article 665(2) and 666(1) of the Companies (Northern Ireland) Order 1986 there shall be inserted the words—

'and in this paragraph "recognised stock exchange" means The Stock Exchange and any other stock exchange which is declared by an order of the Department for the time being in force to be a recognised stock exchange for the purposes of this Article;'.

38. In Schedule 4 to the Companies (Northern Ireland) Order 1986—

(a) in paragraph 45 for the words 'recognised stock exchange' there shall be substituted the words 'recognised investment exchange other than an overseas investment exchange within the meaning of the Financial Services Act 1986'

(b) in paragraph 83 for the words from 'on a recognised stock exchange' onwards there shall be substituted the words 'on a recognised investment exchange other than an overseas investment exchange within the meaning of the Financial Services Act 1986 or on any stock exchange of repute outside Northern Ireland'.

39. In Schedule 9 to the Companies (Northern Ireland) Order 1986, in paragraph 10(3) and 33 for the words 'recognised stock exchange' there shall be substituted the words 'recognised investment exchange other than an overseas investment exchange within the meaning of the Financial Services Act 1986.'

40. In paragraph 11 of Schedule 132 to the Companies (Northern Ireland) Order 1986 for paragraph (a) there shall be substituted—

'(a) any unit trust scheme which is an authorised unit trust scheme within the meaning of the Financial Services Act 1986'.

41. In Schedule 21 to the Companies (Northern Ireland) Order 1986 in the second colum of the entry relating to Article 195(4) for the words 'stock exchange' there shall be substituted the words 'clearing house or'.

42. In Schedule 23 to the Companies (Northern Ireland) Order 1986 in the second column of the entry relating to Article 337(3) for the words 'stock exchange' there shall be substituted the words 'investment exchange'.

43. In Article 2(1) of the Companies Securities (Insider Dealing) (Northern Ireland) Order 1986, for the definition of 'recognised stock exchange' there shall be substituted—

'"recognised stock exchange" means The Stock Exchange and any other investment exchange which is declared by an order of the Department for the time being in force to be a recognised stock exchange for the purposes of this Order;'.

SCHEDULE 17 (Section 212(3))

REPEALS AND REVOCATIONS

PART I

ENACTMENTS

Chapter	Short title	Extent of repeal
4 & 5 Geo 6 c 9 (NI).	The Prevention of Fraud (Investments) Act (Northern Ireland) 1940.	The whole Act.
6 & 7 Eliz 2 c 45.	The Prevention of Fraud (Investments) Act 1958.	The whole Act.
8 & 9 Eliz 2 c 58	The Charities Act 1960	Section 22(10).
10 & 11 Eliz 2 c 23.	The South Africa Act 1962.	In Schedule 4, the entry relating to the Prevention of Fraud (Investments) Act 1958.
1964 c 33 (NI).	The Charities Act (Northern Ireland) 1964.	Section 25(16).
1965 c 2.	The Administration of Justice Act 1965.	Section 14(1)(e) and (5)(e). In Schedule 1, the entry relating to the Prevention of Fraud (Investments) Act 1958.

Chapter	Short title	Extent of repeal
1971 c 62.	The Tribunals and Inquiries Act 1971.	In Part I of Schedule 1, the entry relating to the tribunal constituted under section 6 of the Prevention of Fraud (Investments) Act 1958.
1972 c 71.	The Criminal Justice Act 1972.	In Schedule 5, the entry relating to the Prevention of Fraud (Investments) Act 1958.
1975 c 24.	The House of Commons Disqualification Act 1975.	In Part II of Schedule 1 the words 'The Tribunal established under the Prevention of Fraud (Investments) Act 1958'.
1975 c 68.	The Industry Act 1975.	In Schedule 1, paragraph 19.
1975 c 69.	The Scottish Development Agency Act 1975.	In Schedule 1, paragraph 19.
1975 c 70.	The Welsh Development Agency Act 1975.	In Schedule 1, paragraph 22.
1976 c 47.	The Stock Exchange (Completion of Bargains) Act 1976.	Section 7(2).
1977 c 3.	The Aircraft and Shipbuilding Industries Act 1977.	In section 3(5), the words 'Sections 428 to 430 of the Companies Act 1985 and'.
1978 c 23.	The Judicature (Northern Ireland) Act 1978.	Section 84(3)(c).
1979 c 37.	The Banking Act 1979.	Section 20(1) to (3). In Schedule 1, paragraph 9. In Schedule 6, paragraphs 4 and 5.
1982 c 50.	The Insurance Companies Act 1982.	Section 73. Section 79.
1982 c 53.	The Administration of Justice Act 1982.	Section 42(8).
1984 c 2.	The Restrictive Trade Practices (Stock Exchange) Act 1984.	The whole Act.
1985 c 6.	The Companies Act 1985.	Part III. Sections 81 to 83. In section 84(1) the words from 'This' onwards. In section 85(1) the words '83 or'. Sections 86 and 87. In section 97, subsection (2)(b) together with the word 'and' immediately preceding it and subsections (3) and (4). Section 433(2). Section 446(5) and (6). In section 449(1)(d), the words 'the Prevention of Fraud (Investments) Act 1958'. In section 693, paragraph (a) and

Chapter	Short title	Extent of repeal
		in paragraph (d) the words 'in every such prospectus as abovementioned and'. Section 709(2) and (3). In section 744, the definitions of 'recognised stock exchange' and 'prospectus issued generally'. Schedule 3. In Schedule 22, the entries relating to Parts III and IV. In Schedule 24, the entries relating to sections 56(4), 61, 64(5), 70(1), 78(1), 81(2), 82(5), 86(6), 87(4) and 97(4).
1985 c 8.	The Company Securities (Insider Dealing) Act 1985.	In section 3(1), the word 'or' immediately preceding paragraph (c). In section 13, in subsection (1), the words from 'and references' onwards and subsection (2). Section 15.
1985 c 9.	The Companies Consolidation (Consequential Provisions) Act 1985.	Section 7. In Schedule 2, the entries relating to the Prevention of Fraud (Investments) Act 1958, paragraph 19 of Schedule 1 to the Scottish Development Agency Act 1975, paragraph 22 of Schedule 1 to the Welsh Development Agency Act 1975, the Stock Exchange (Completion of Bargains) Act 1976, section 3(5) of the Aircraft and Shipbuilding Industries Act 1977 and section 20 of the Banking Act 1979.
1986 c 31.	The Airport Act 1986.	Section 10.
1986 c 44.	The Gas Act 1986.	Section 58.
1986 c 60.	The Financial Services Act 1986.	Section 195.

PART II

INSTRUMENTS

Number	Short title	Extent of revocation
SI 1977/1254 (NI 21).	The Stock Exchange (Completion of Bargains) (Northern Ireland) Order 1977.	Article 2(2).
SI 1986/1032 (NI 6).	The Companies (Northern Ireland) Order 1986.	In Article 2(1), the definitions of 'prospectus issued generally' and 'recognised stock exchange'.

Number	Short title	Extent of revocation
		Part IV. Articles 91 to 93. In Article 94(1) the words from 'This' onwards. In Article 95(1) the words '93 or'. Articles 96 and 97. In Article 107, paragraph (2)(b) together with the word 'and' immediately preceding it and paragraphs (3) and (4). Article 426(2). Article 439(5) and (6). In Article 442(1)(d), the words 'the Prevention of Fraud (Investments) Act (Northern Ireland) 1940'. In Article 643(1), sub-paragraph (a) and in sub-paragraph (d) the words 'in every such prospectus as is mentioned in sub-paragraph (a) and'. Article 658(2) and (3). Schedule 3. In Schedule 21, the entries relating to Parts IV and V. In Schedule 23, the entries relating to Articles 66(4), 71, 74(5), 80(1), 88(1), 91(2), 92(5), 96(6), 97(4) and 107(4).
SI 1986/1035 (NI 9).	The Companies (Consequential Provisions) (Northern Ireland) Order 1986.	In Schedule 2, the entries relating to the Prevention of Fraud (Investments) Act (Northern Ireland) 1940 and section 20 of the Banking Act 1979.
SI 1984/716	The Stock Exchange (Listing) Regulations 1984.	The whole Regulations.

Index

461